ABOUT OUR COVER

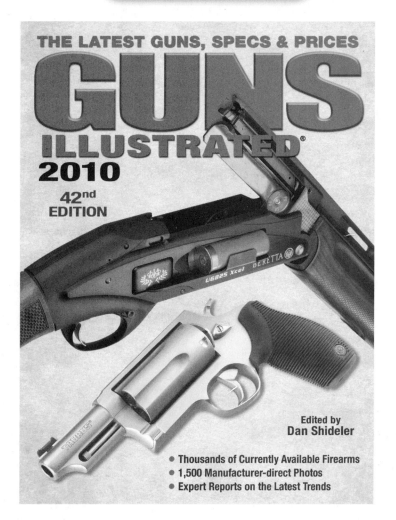

THE LATEST GUNS, SPECS & PRICES

GUNS ILLUSTRATED® 2010

42nd EDITION

UGB25 Xcel BERETTA

TAURUS

Edited by
Dan Shideler

- Thousands of Currently Available Firearms
- 1,500 Manufacturer-direct Photos
- Expert Reports on the Latest Trends

The **Beretta UGB25 Xcel** semiautomatic gun features an innovative locking system with break-open barrel that allows operation in complete safety during competitions. Unlike conventional fixed-barrel semiautomatic shotguns, this new type of locking system enables the shooter to move from one firing station to another without having to extract the chambered cartridge, simply by levering the barrel downwards. The single barrel offers the advantage of maintaining the point of impact of the second shot exactly in line with that of the first shot, thus ensuring excellent performance. It's exactly the kind of innovation we've come to expect from Beretta.

To many shooters, the **Taurus Judge** .45/.410 is the last word in personal protection revolvers. Capable of chambering both .410 Ga. shotgun shells and .45 Colt ammunition, this amazing five-shot combo gun is ideal for short distances – where most altercations occur – or longer distances with the .45 LC ammunition. The Judge is available in several models and variations including either blue or stainless steel. All models are available in 3-inch or 6-1/2-inch barrel lengths. The newest members of the Judge family are the Ultra-Lite titanium model and a new blue steel 3-inch Magnum variation. All Taurus Judge models include fixed rear sights and fiber optic front sights as well as Taurus' ergonomic Ribber Grips®. Additionally, like all Taurus handguns, the unique Taurus Security System® allows users to securely lock the gun using an inconspicuous key-lock system.

THE LATEST GUNS, SPECS & PRICES

GUNS ILLUSTRATED®
2010

42nd Edition

EDITED BY
Dan Shideler

©2009 Krause Publications, Inc.,
a subsidiary of F+W Media, Inc.

Published by

Gun Digest® Books

An imprint of F+W Media, Inc.
700 East State Street • Iola, WI 54990-0001
715-445-2214 • 888-457-2873
www.gundigestbooks.com

Our toll-free number to place an order or obtain
a free catalog is (800) 258-0929.

Manuscripts, contributions and inquiries, including first class return postage, should be sent to the GUN DIGEST Editorial Offices, Gun Digest Books, 700 East State Street, Iola, WI 54990-0001. All materials received will receive reasonable care, but we will not be responsible for their safe return. Materials accepted is subject to our requirements for editing and revisions. Author payment covers all rights and title to the accepted material, including photos, drawings and other illustrations. Payment is at our current rates.

CAUTION: Technical data presented here, particularly technical data on handloading and on firearms adjustment and altera-tion, inevitably reflects individual experience with particular equipment and components under specific circumstances the reader cannot duplicate exactly. Such data presentations therefore should be used for guidance only and with caution. Gun Digest Books accepts no responsibility for results obtained using these data.

ISSN 0072-9078

ISBN 13: 978-0-89689-838-7
ISBN 10: 0-89689-838-5

Designed by Dave Hauser and Patsy Howell

Edited by Dan Shideler

Printed in the United States of America

CATALOG OF ARMS AND ACCESSORIES

1983 · MODEL 83 · 454 CASULL · 2008

Freedom Arms
25th Anniversary Revolver.

HAND GUNS TODAY:
Sixguns and Others

BY JEFF QUINN

hose of you who are long-time readers will recognize this section as having been written by my good friend John Taffin in years past. Mr. Taffin is alive, well, and still writing, but with his books, magazines, and other commitments, has passed the writing of this section on to me, and I am honored that both he and the editor of this legendary gun annual have bestowed upon me the privilege to try to adequately fill those big boots. I, as much as any of you, will miss Mr. Taffin's writing, as many, including myself, consider him to be the best gunwriter of our time. Anyway, here we are, and it is at an historic time in our nation. Civilian gun sales in the U.S. are at an all-time high since anyone started keeping records on such things.

As I type this, there are five different bills submitted in Congress aimed at curtailing the ownership of firearms, and totally eliminating some types of firearms from production. It is indeed interesting times for gun owners. Still, 2009 has some exciting firearms reaching production, and in this brief review, I will try to touch on some of the most interesting sixguns on the market today, along with a couple of other interesting handguns, including one newly-designed single shot and a lever action handgun that has historical roots and nostalgic memories for fans of old Western TV shows. Let's get started!

AWA (American Western Arms)

AWA, as always, has some high quality 1873 Colt replicas, from their basic Classic series (which is a fine example of what a single action sixgun should be) to their Ultimate, which has a coil mainspring and can be upgraded with better stocks and finishes in addition to engraving. AWA also offers an octagon-barrel model, which is something that really sets it apart from the other Single Action Army replicas on the market, with a distinctive, classic look. Of particular interest is the Lightningbolt, a short, pump-action *handgun* version of the old medium-frame Colt Lightning Magazine Rifle. Offered in three different models (blued, case-hardened, and the White Lightning hard chrome finish) the Lightningbolt pistol is in production right now and should prove to be popular with shooters who want something a bit different but with an Old West flavor. It holds five rounds in a tubular magazine under its 12" barrel and is chambered for the .45 Colt cartridge. AWA also has a neat holster rig custom built to carry this one-of-a-kind handgun.

Beretta

Beretta entered the world of revolvers, and particularly Single Action Army Colt replicas, a couple of years ago with their purchase of Uberti. Uberti has been a well-known maker of fine quality replica firearms for decades, and with that acquisition, Beretta introduced their Stampede line of high

Smith & Wesson makes several variations of their Model 500 Magnum. This one wears a 6.5" ported barrel.

Ruger .44 Special Blackhawk Flattop with Simply Rugged Western Rig.

Freedom Arms Model 83 .500 Wyoming Express is the Perfect Packin' Pistol for use against teeth and claws.

Editor Quinn shooting the Freedom Arms
.500 Wyoming Express.

quality, well-finished replica sixguns. Beretta offers the Stampede with blued, nickel, or deluxe blued finishes.

The blued models have case-colored frames and a standard blue-black finish, while the deluxe has a bright charcoal blue finish to the grip frame, trigger guard, and barrel. The stocks are either walnut or black plastic, while the Bisley models have black plastic stocks only. In addition to the standard barrel lengths, the Stampede Marshall has a shorter 3.5" barrel, a birds-head grip frame and walnut stocks. Also, the Stampede and Stampede Marshall are offered with an Old West finish that resembles an original aged and worn Colt. The Stampede series is offered in a choice of .357 Magnum or .45 Colt chamberings.

Bond Arms

Bond Arms is a Texas outfit that manufacturers what is probably the finest example of the Remington pattern derringers ever built. It is certainly the strongest. The Bond is a stack-barrel derringer that swings open at the hinge pin for loading and unloading, just as the original Remington Double Derringer .41 rimfire did. The barrels are fired one

at a time, and interchangeable barrels are available to allow for changing the caliber quickly and easily. The most popular seems to be their .45 Colt/.410 shotshell version, but other caliber choices include the .22 Long Rifle, .32 H&R, 9x19mm, .38 Special/.357 Magnum, .357 Maximum, .40 S&W, 10mm, .44 Special, .44 WCF, .45 GAP, .45 ACP, and .45 Colt. There should be enough choices there for everyone, but being a fan of the .22 Magnum cartridge, I would like to see that versatile little chambering offered as well.

The Bond Arms derringer is not in the same class as the cheap zinc-frame derringers that we have seen offered during the last half of the past century. The Bond is made from quality materials, and built to last. While offering only two shots before reloading is required, these handguns are very compact and very flat, making it easy and comfortable to carry in a back pocket or in a lightweight hip holster while working around the homestead, or out for a walk in snake country. The .410 shotshell does a real number on poisonous snakes and can also serve very well as gun to repel carjackers. At arms-length, a faceful of .410 shot will change the mind of any carjacker, and the payload is easy to deliver from the barrels of the Bond derringer.

Charter Arms

Charter Arms has been producing reliable, affordable revolvers for decades now. I have owned Charters chambered for the .22 Magnum, .32 H&R, .38 Special, .357 Magnum, .44 Special, and that most-useful of cartridges, the .22 Long Rifle. Charters have always seemed to me no-frills, solid little handguns, and they have never let me down.

Back in my younger days while working undercover for a State Attorney General's Office, I was associating with some of the coarser types of our society. They are by nature a suspicious lot, and the slightest hint that something was out of place could result in a distasteful outcome, to me at least. In those days, I relied upon a Charter .38 tucked into the top of my boot. I had slicked the action, removed the front sight, and bobbed the hammer spur. It was there to resolve up-close and personal social conflicts, and was very comforting to have along. I still have that little five-shot revolver, and it is as useful and reliable as ever. It has never let me down.

Charter Arms makes a variety of small and medium-sized revolvers. One of their latest is chambered for the relatively new .327 Federal cartridge. The .327 Federal is what the .32 H&R Magnum should have been. The .327 Federal launches a .312" diameter bullet at true magnum velocities, and Charter was one of the first to chamber for the cartridge after its initial introduction. Of course, Charter still makes their .44 Bulldog, which is the flagship of the Charter line, having developed a cult-like following over the past few decades. As I type this, Charter is also working on a new revolver that will handle rimless cartridges such as the 9mm Luger and .40 S&W cartridges. I have not yet handled one, but it looks to be promising, and should be in production by the time that you read this.

This recent Single Action Army is as good as any ever produced by Colt.

Cimarron

Cimarron Firearms of Fredericksburg, Texas, has long been a supplier of quality replicas of classic firearms, and they continue that tradition today. Cimarron offers several varieties of 1873 Colt Single Action Army replicas, but they also supply shooters with replicas of some of the lesser-known sixguns of the Old West. Cimarron offers some unique and interesting replicas of the old conversion revolvers that bridged the gap from percussion cap-and-ball guns to modern cartridge revolvers.

I especially like the Smith & Wesson replicas offered by Cimarron, such as the Schofield and Russian models. Many shooters today are not aware of the fact that had it not been for the Russian purchase of a large quantity of S&W sixguns, the company might have folded in the nineteenth century, and the modern double-action revolver that we know today might have never been. Anyway, Cimarron markets replicas of the S&W Number 3 Russian, which is both historical and fun to shoot. These Cimarron Smith & Wesson replicas are offered in .38

Charter Arms Target Bulldog .44 Special.

Thompson-Center G2 Contender single shot pistol.

USFA 12-22 "Twelve Shot Sixgun" holds a handful of .22 Long Rifle cartridges.

Ruger celebrates the 50th anniversary of their Super Blackhawk .44 Magnum with this limited edition sixgun.

Colt

Colt is one of the most recognized names in the world of firearms, steeped in tradition and history. There has probably never been a Western movie made that did not have a Colt or copy thereof on the set somewhere. Colt is what we picture when we think Western sixgun. Most of the shapes, the feel, and the lines of today's single action revolvers can be traced back to the Colt Single Action Army and to the Colt revolvers which preceded it. Today, Colt is still producing the Single Action Army revolver. While quality has varied over the past few decades, the examples of the SAA that I have examined and fired over the past three years show that the Colts now leaving the factory are as good as any that have been produced. The Single Action Army is offered in either blue/casehardened or nickel finishes, in several caliber choices.

EAA (European American Armory)

EAA Corp in Rockledge, Florida, has a couple of revolver lines. Their Bounty Hunter is a Colt SAA replica, which is offered in .22 LR/Magnum, .38/.357 Magnum, .44 Magnum, and .45 Colt in a choice of blued, nickel, or blued/casehardened finishes. The Bounty Hunter uses a transfer bar safety system, but retains the traditional feel to the action and loads/unloads in the half-cock hammer position. The .22 LR/Magnum version has an alloy frame, but the centerfire guns are made of steel. The .22 is also

Special, .44 WCF, .44 Russian, and .45 Colt chamberings. Of course, Cimarron still has many varieties of their Model P SAA replicas, offered in a wide choice of calibers, barrel lengths, and finishes. Their Thunderer revolvers are not really a copy of any old gun, but are a dandy example of what a Single Action Army can be with a modified bird's head grip. Very handy and easy to shoot, the Thunderer – and its little brother, the Lightning – offer the grip frame of the double action Colt Thunderer with the reliability of the Single Action Army.

The latest sixgun on the market from Cimarron is their .22 Long Rifle Plinkerton. *["Plinkerton"? Yes, Plinkerton. – DMS]* This is a no-frills revolver patterned after the Colt SAA, but it's made of a non-ferrous alloy with steel chamber liners and a steel inner barrel. The two that I have fired performed pretty well. There is also a version with an extra cylinder for the .22 Magnum cartridge. Best of all, this revolver is selling for under 200 bucks in most places. It is a really good buy, and a dandy sixgun to start a youngster out shooting.

Ruger 4" Redhawk .45 Colt makes for a powerful, compact outdoorsman's gun.

Smith & Wesson 632 Pro Comp chambered for the .327 Federal Magnum.

offered in a choice of six or eight-shot models.

EAA's double-action revolver is called the Windicator. This small-framed revolver is offered as a steel-framed .357 Magnum or as an alloy-framed .38 Special. It has synthetic rubber grips, a matte blued finish, and a choice of either a 2" or 4" barrel. They are good, basic, reliable revolvers at an affordable price.

Freedom Arms

Freedom Arms is an All-American success story. Mr. Wayne Baker started the company back about 25 years ago, having already been successful in the construction and mining businesses. Starting with a philosophy dedicated to building the finest revolvers every made, they achieved that goal and continue to hold to that standard today.

I am often asked why I like firearms so much, and the answer is a complex one. However, a large part of my love of guns is my appreciation for well-crafted machines. Firearms are still some of the best-built machines in the world. Many still exhibit a great deal of craftsmanship in their design and execution. While many things that we use everyday are made to be disposable, from appliances to electronics, guns are still built to last, and many are built to a higher standard than most everything else that we use.

That having been said, there is no finer example of skilled craftsmanship in the world than a Freedom Arms revolver. Built at first to harness the power of the .454 Casull cartridge, FA revolvers now are offered chambered for the .17 HMR, .22 LR/Magnum, .32 H&R, .327 Federal, .32 WCF, .357 Magnum, .41 Magnum, .44 Magnum, 45 Colt, .454 Casull, and .500 Wyoming Express cartridges. They are also introducing their own .224-32 FA cartridge, firing a .22-caliber bullet from a necked-down .327

Taurus makes dozens of compact revolvers, including this Model 85.

Federal case. Two different frame sizes are currently offered: the original Model 83 and the more compact Model 97.

I have fired many different Freedom Arms revolvers, and have found each one to be an amazing piece of workmanship. Holding a Freedom Arms revolver is like holding a work of art, but a working work of art! I have never fired one that wasn't accurate. Freedom takes care in the way that they align the chambers with the barrel, and it pays off in accuracy. Capable of taking the largest game on earth – and they have done so many times – Freedom Arms revolvers are built for those who appreciate fine workmanship and want to buy the very best.

News flash: Freedom Arms has been working for a couple of years on a new single-shot pistol. I have had the pleasure of shooting the prototype gun at ranges out to 600 yards, and find it to be worthy of the Freedom Arms name. It has interchangeable barrels and extractors to easily switch calibers, and the one that I spent the most trigger-time with was chambered for the 6.5mm JDJ cartridge. I found it to be very accurate, and easy to shoot well.

Taurus Model 941 .22 Magnum.

Cimarron's New Plinkerton .22 Long Rifle sixgun.

Legacy Sports

Legacy Sports has been the distributor for the Puma rifles for several years now, and for 2009, the manufacture of these has been moved from Brazil to Italy. Along with this move, Legacy has a new Puma handgun called the Bounty Hunter, modeled after the "Mare's Laig," a cut-down '92 Winchester carried by Steve McQueen in the old *Wanted, Dead or Alive* TV series. McQueen's character, Josh Randall, a bounty hunter by trade, carried .45-70 cartridges in his belt for effect, but the '92 Winchester was of course built to handle much shorter cartridges. The Bounty Hunter from Legacy is chambered for either the .44 Magnum, .44 WCF, or .45 Colt cartridges, has a 12" barrel and a six-shot magazine. It wears a large loop lever and an abbreviated buttstock, and it just drips with nostalgia.

Legacy Sports also has a new line of 1873 Colt replicas, made in Italy and called the Puma Westerner. They are traditionally styled and offered with a blued/case-hardened finish, nickel plated, or in stainless steel. Grips are one-piece walnut or imitation ivory, with a smooth or checkered option with the walnut.

Magnum Research

Magnum Research is still making the BFR ("Biggest, Finest Revolver," or so it's said) revolver. Made almost entirely of stainless steel, the BFR is a large single action revolver made in two different frame lengths. The shorter frame size still handles some very powerful revolver cartridges such as the .50 Action Express, .454 Casull, and the .475 Linebaugh/.480 Ruger, in addition to the little .22 Hornet. The long frame handles some truly powerful revolver cartridges like the .460 and .500 S&W Magnums, and also rifle cartridges like the .30-30 Winchester, .450 Marlin, and .45/70 Government. The BFRs are well made, built in the USA, and in my limited experience with them, they shoot very well.

North American Arms

NAA has been producing fine little miniature revolvers for many years now, and most shooters are familiar with them. Built mainly with short barrels and chambered for either the .22 Short, .22 Long Rifle or .22 Magnum cartridges, these are handy little five-shot pocket guns that serve as snake repellant in areas where poisonous snakes are a problem, but are mainly carried for protection when nothing larger can be easily or comfortably concealed. While it is hard to hit a target at long range with these short-barreled revolvers, up close and personal, they can be very effective.

The newest offering from NAA is a .22 Magnum five-shot revolver dubbed "The Earl." This one has a 4" barrel, and the retainer for the cylinder pin gives it the look of an old percussion Remington style sixgun. It can be had with just the magnum cylinder, or with a .22 Long Rifle conversion cylinder as

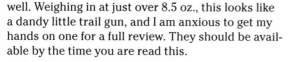

well. Weighing in at just over 8.5 oz., this looks like a dandy little trail gun, and I am anxious to get my hands on one for a full review. They should be available by the time you are read this.

Rossi

Rossi is better known for their handy and affordable rifles and shotguns, but they still produce a limited line of double action revolvers as well. Chambered in either .38 Special or .357 Magnum, you have a choice of blued steel or stainless, and either a 2", 4" or 6" barrel. The two-inch guns have fixed sights, but the longer barreled guns have adjustable sights. They are well-built and affordable revolvers, with a nice exterior finish. Rossi revolvers are a lot of gun for the money.

Ruger

Sturm, Ruger, & Company has been in the revolver business since 1953 and was largely responsible for the comeback of the single-action sixgun. When Western TV shows and movies were creating a demand for the old-style sixguns, Ruger filled the need by creating the Single-Six, a rimfire revolver that is still in production today. The ones built 56 years ago are still in use today, and will shoot right along side the newer versions. The little sixguns just do not wear out. I own several Single-Sixes myself, and would not choose to be without at least one.

Ruger sixguns have proven themselves in the field for many years, whether chambered for the rimfires or the larger, more powerful centerfire magnums. This year, Ruger celebrates the

fiftieth anniversary of their flagship single-action sixgun, the Super Blackhawk. The Super was introduced to the world the same year that I was: 1959. While my design is showing its age, the Super Blackhawk is as relevant and useful today as it was way back then. The Anniversary Super Blackhawk is certainly worthy to wear the name, with a rich, deep blue finish that is reminiscent of the early Supers. The Anniversary Super comes in a special white cardboard box, with a pistol rug to protect the beautiful finish and gold trim.

Also new this year from Ruger is a gun that is dear to the hearts of single-action sixgunners, and Ruger fans in particular. Back in 1956, Ruger had the very successful .357 Blackhawk in production, and had a .44 Special version of that gun in the works. As fate would have it, Bill Ruger found out about the .44 Magnum cartridge that was in development by Remington and Smith & Wesson. Bill Ruger immediately scrapped the .44 Special project and began working on the .44 Magnum Blackhawk instead, actually beating Smith & Wesson in getting the .44 Magnum into production by a few weeks. Anyway, while .44 Special fans could always shoot the shorter cartridge in their .44 Magnum Blackhawks, the .44 Magnums were built on a slightly larger frame than the pre-1973 .357 Magnum Blackhawks, and shooters still longed for the production of a Ruger Blackhawk .44 Special built upon the old .357-sized frame.

Custom gunsmiths have made out pretty well over the past few

Freedom Arms
New single-shot pistol.

AWA Lightningbolt slide action handgun.

USFA Omni Target
Flattop Target sixgun.

decades converting small-frame .357 Flattops and Three-Screws into .44 Special Blackhawks. Skeeter Skelton lobbied Ruger for many years to build a .44 Special on the early small Blackhawk frame, to no avail. After his passing, John Taffin has been carrying the flag for those of us who still wanted a .44 Special Blackhawk that was built on the older, handier original-sized Blackhawk frame. Finally, Ruger is producing such a sixgun, and it was worth the wait. The New Model .44 Special Blackhawk is built on a frame the size of the original Blackhawk, and it even has a Flattop frame with Micro rear sight. Mine is very, very accurate, has tight tolerances, and shoots well. It wears the XR-3 grip frame, which is a very close copy of the profile of the the grip of the old Colt Single Action Army and 1851 Navy revolvers. The grips are well-textured black plastic, and the sixgun itself is a delight to handle. The .44 Flattop balances well, handles quickly, and points like the finger of God. It is only available from dealers who buy through Lipsey's, a wholesaler in Baton Rouge, Louisiana. Ruger is also bringing back their Bisley Vaquero sixgun, now built upon the slightly smaller New Vaquero frame, as the Bisley New Vaquero.

Of course, Ruger has also built a name for itself producing rugged, reliable, and accurate double-action revolvers, and they are still in production. The Redhawk and Super Redhawk sixguns are well-suited to outdoorsmen and hunters, with many of them available with scope rings included to mount optics. For many years, Ruger produced the Redhawk with a choice of 7.5" or 5.5" barrel, but they now offer the Redhawk with a 4" barrel, which makes it much better suited as an everyday packing gun. It still wears good adjustable sights, and serves well as a primary hunting arm, but the shorter barrel makes it much easier to carry around while doing other chores or just bumming around the woods.

Another very handy but powerful Ruger double action is their Super Redhawk Alaskan, which is a version of their Super Redhawk with an abbreviated barrel, cut off right at the front of the cylinder frame extension. These sixguns are very handy to carry on the belt, and are available chambered for the .44 Magnum or .454 Casull/.45 Colt. In the past, the Alaskan was also offered chambered for the .480 Ruger cartridge, and hopefully, it will be again despite the fact that it appears to have been discontinued. A very few were produced last year chambered in .480 Ruger with a five-shot cylinder. I have one of these, and it is a very handy and powerful revolver.

The talk of the SHOT show this past January at the 2009 SHOT Show in Orlando, Florida, was Ruger's entry into the pocket revolver market with their new LCR. The LCR is like nothing else, with a unique polymer grip frame/trigger guard unit that houses all of the fire control parts, such as the trigger and hammer. It is a double-action only design with a concealed hammer, five shot steel cylinder, and an aluminum cylinder frame. I had the pleasure of firing the LCR at the New Hampshire Ruger factory back in December of 2008, and the little revolver is a lightweight, easy-to-shoot firearm. The trigger pull is wonderful, at least on that test gun, and was plenty accurate for social work as well. Chambered for the .38 Special, and Plus P rated, I believe that it will be very popular, and anxiously await the arrival of a production gun for a full review. As you read this, they should already be available on gun dealer's shelves.

Smith & Wesson

The name Smith & Wesson to me has always meant revolvers. That is just the first thing that pops into my mind: revolvers. Smith & Wesson makes some excellent auto pistols, and has done so for decades. They also makes rifles and shotguns, but to me, and many others, S&W means revolvers. That is quite understandable, for Smith & Wesson has been making revolvers for almost 160 years. Some of my all-time favorite sixguns, like the Models 34, 43, 51, 63, and 651 rimfire kit guns bear the S&W logo. Same with the K-frame twenty-twos. I love .22-caliber sixguns, and Smith & Wesson always has a few in the lineup.

As the older models fade from production, new ones are added, like the reintroduction for 2009 of the Model 18. The Model 18 is a K-frame .22 Long Rifle sixgun that is well-balanced and easy to carry, but still has enough heft in its blued-steel frame to make it easy to shoot well. As a kid, I often read the

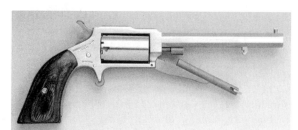

North American Arms "The Earl," shown here with "loading lever" opened.

words of one of my favorite gun writers, Bob Milek, and his adventures with his Model 18 Smith. After being dropped from the catalog a few years ago, I am glad to see that it is back in production.

On the other end of the power scale, Smith & Wesson has an ever-expanding lineup of variations of their huge X-Frame chambered for the .460 XVR and the .500 S&W Magnums. The big X-Frame guns are widely popular. The .460 XVR is a very versatile handgun cartridge, and the revolvers that are chambered for it can also fire the .454 Casull, .45 Colt, and .45 S&W cartridges. The .500 S&W Magnum has been on the market for a few years now, and is a popular choice for not only big game hunters, but for those who just want to own and shoot the most powerful double-action production revolver that they can find. The Big 500 throws a heavy chunk of lead at magnum velocities, and some of the shorter-barreled 500s carry on the hip pretty well.

Between these two extremes, S&W offers a wide variety of chamberings and frame sizes. One of the newest is the Model 632 Carry Comp Pro that is chambered for the hot little .327 Federal cartridge. With a 3" ported barrel and adjustable sights, the 632 is both a good little defensive revolver, as well as a handy little six-shot trail gun. It can shoot the .32 S&W, .32 S&W Long, .32 H&R Magnum, and .327 Federal cartridges, making it a versatile little package. The .327 Federal throws bullets as light as 60 grains and as heavy as at least 135 grains, all at magnum velocities. My favorite factory load is the 100-gr. American Eagle, which throws that jacketed softpoint bullet out at almost 1400 fps from the Smith's 3" barrel.

There is still a huge selection of S&W .357 and .44 Magnum revolvers from which to choose, along with the .41 Magnum and .45 Colt in a couple of models. In the extremely popular J-frame size, S&W rules the market with the top sellers in the five-shot pocket revolver class of .38 Special and .357 Magnum firearms. There is a huge variety of both lightweight and all-steel revolvers in that section of their catalog, and they also offer one snub-nosed .22 Magnum as well. While Smith & Wesson is now a full-line manufacturer of many classes of firearms, they are still very much involved in supplying fine quality revolvers to the world.

Taurus

Taurus has so many revolvers on the market that I cannot keep up with them. In the world of revolvers, there is nothing hotter on the market now than the Taurus Judge. This .45 Colt/.410 shotshell revolver has proved to be very popular, and production still has not caught up with demand after about two years on the market already.

The Judge is, to me, primarily a .410 shotshell revolver with the .45 Colt being secondary. Properly loaded with .410 birdshot or buckshot, it would be ideal to repel attackers at close range, and it is a natural for those who walk in the woods or desert where poisonous snakes are a problem. Right now, Taurus has about a dozen different variations of the Judge, in a variety of finishes, all-steel or lightweight, two barrel lengths, and with either a 2.5" or 3" chamber. Just introduced is an even more compact version of the Judge, based upon the small Model 85 frame size, called the Public Defender. It should prove to be wildly popular as well.

While still on the Taurus website, their Colt SAA replica called the Gaucho seems to be out of production. That is a shame. Mine is a very accurate, good-looking and easy-handling sixgun. Hopefully, it is just not in the production cycle for now, and will come back soon.

Of course, Taurus still makes many double-action revolvers, from compact pocket models to those capable of taking large game, and their Models 94 and 941 are some great little rimfire trail guns. In the defensive gun market, small pocket revolvers are very popular, and Taurus is well represented in that field. They offer both lightweight and all-steel versions of their basic Model 85. Right now, Taurus USA catalogs almost four dozen different small-frame revolvers built for concealed carry. They also manufacture a large variety of double-action revolvers that are suitable for hunting small and large game, as well as for target competition and casual plinking.

Bond Arms compact .410/.45 Colt Snake Slayer offers compact protection from both critters and thugs alike.

Thompson-Center

Thompson-Center has been the leader in single shot handguns for decades now. In the past few years, T-C has entered the muzzleloading and centerfire rifle markets in a big way, but they certainly have not neglected their single-shot handgun line. Introducing their Encore pistol several years ago as a big brother to their popular Contender pistol, the Encore line has expanded with many caliber offerings, making the Encore a very powerful and versatile pistol. Offered in 17 different calibers, with a choice of walnut or synthetic rubber stock material and blued steel or stainless, the Encore is a simple yet thoroughly modern hunting pistol capable of cleanly harvesting small game and vermin, then switching barrels and taking the largest game on earth.

While building the Encore line of single shot pistols, T-C did not ignore their original Contender pistol. Upgrading the design to the new G2 Contender, they offer this pistol in 13 different chamberings. While smaller than the Encore, the G2 can still handle the big .45-70 Government cartridge. The Contender is, and always has been, a handy, versatile break-open single shot, and is still the leader in this type of hunting handguns.

Uberti

Aldo Uberti began in 1959 the company that would become a leader in the world of replica firearms, starting with cap-and-ball replicas, then moving on to other replica firearms from the history of the American West. Today, Uberti is a premier producer of replica firearms, many of which we would not be able to enjoy and shoot, were it not for replicas. Original examples of some of our beloved sixguns are either too rare or expensive for most of us to enjoy.

Uberti recreates these fine sixguns using modern steel and technology, producing firearms that are in many ways superior to the originals. While almost everyone in the replica business replicates the Colt Single Action Army, Uberti doesn't stop there. One of my favorite sixguns is the 1875 Remington. Uberti makes very good replicas of both the 1875 and 1890 Remington revolvers.

Other makers have attempted in recent years to build quality replicas of the Remingtons, but I have yet to see a production gun. Uberti seems to have no problem in producing these in quantity, and they are well-made and accurate sixguns.

The 1875 Remington Outlaw and Frontier are available in blued/color case-hardened or nickel finishes, and the 1890 Police is available in blued/color case-hardened only. The 1875 is chambered for the .45 Colt cartridge, and the 1890 Police also adds the option of the .357 Magnum chambering. The Cattleman is the bread and butter of the Uberti sixgun line, and it is a 1873 Colt Single Action Army replica of very good quality. Offered in a variety of finishes from matte blue to nickel to the highly polished and charcoal blued Frisco with imitation mother of pearl grips. The Cattleman is available withf 4-3/4", 5.5", and 7.5" barrels, in addition to the shorter-barreled Cattleman Bird's Head, which can be had with a 3.5", 4" or 4-3/4" barrel. Chamberings include the .357 Magnum, .44 WCF, and .45 Colt.

Uberti's Stallion is a slightly smaller SAA replica chambered in .22 Long Rifle or .38 Special. It's offered with either fixed or adjustable sights, with the .22 Long Rifle version having the option of a brass grip frame and trigger guard. The Bisley replica is offered in blued/ case-hardened only, in either .357 Magnum or .45 Colt. The top of the line Cattleman is called the "El Patron." It is a special revolver in a choice of stainless steel or blued/case-colored finish, complete with Wolff springs and tuned for a better, smoother action. The El Patron wears one-piece checkered walnut grips and is available in .357 Magnum or .45 Colt chamberings.

Uberti offers an impressive line of quality cap-and-ball replica sixguns, but I still prefer their cartridge guns, and one of my favorite Uberti sixguns is their top-break Smith & Wesson replica. Offered in blued or nickeled steel, these are excellent quality replicas of the Number 3 Schofield and Russian sixguns. The Schofield wears your choice of a 5" or 7" barrel and is chambered in .45 Colt, .38 Special, or .44 WCF. The Russian is offered in .44 Russian or .45 Colt, and there is even a hand-engraved version of the 7" Schofield offered as well.

USFA (United States Fire Arms)

USFA is celebrating 15 years of producing some of the best-built Colt SAA replicas ever produced. Their quality is comparable to any Colt ever built, and in addition to the SAA replica, they also offer some unique firearms of their own, such as the Omni-Potent Six-Shooter, which is kind of a single-action version of the old double-action Colt Model 1878. This fine sixgun is like no other, and is offered as either a fixed-sight or a Flattop Target version. The Omni-Potent Six-Shooter has a unique grip that is reminiscent of the old double-action Colt Thunderer, but in a single-action sixgun. They are beautifully finished and wear checkered walnut stocks. Like most of the USFA lineup, the caliber choices are .32 WCF, .38 Special, .38 WCF, .44 Special, .44 WCF, and .45 Colt. They also offer a short-barreled version of the Omni-Potent, called (appropriately enough) the Snubnose. The Snubnose is available with a choice of a 2", 3" or 4" barrel. This is the definitive single-action belly gun. It has a lanyard ring on the butt and wears two-piece walnut stocks.

Another unique revolver from USFA is the new 12/22. This is a .22 Long Rifle "twelve gun" that of-

The Uberti New Model Russian is a faithful replica of the Smith & Wesson Russian revolver.

The USFA Snubnose is the ultimate single-action belly gun.

Uberti Stallion Rimfire Target sixgun.

Compact .357 Magnum double action sixgun from Rossi.

...fers a lot of firepower for a revolver. Offered in high polish blued or nickeled finishes with a choice of 4-3/4", 5.5", or 7.5" inch barrel, it wears white plastic stocks and looks like a genuine Single Action Army sixgun, but cranks out 12 shots before reloading, just like the sixguns in an old Western movie. The latest from USFA is their Shooting Master Magnum series sixguns. These look like nothing else to ever come out of Hartford. First offered in .357 magnum, with .41 and .44 magnums slated for later, the Shooting Master has an adjustable rear sight and fiber optic front. The most unusual feature of these new sixguns is the finish of the frame. Offered in a choice of black, gray, brown, tan, or two shades of green, this ain't your traditional single action revolver! The Shooting Master is built as a hunting gun, and it should serve in that role very well. The non-glare finish will certainly not endear itself to single-action purists, but it should prove to be very practical in the field.

This about wraps up my attempt to cover the revolver scene for 2009, and is by no means a comprehensive list of everything available to revolver fans. While it looks like the semi-auto pistols are here to stay, there is still a large selection of fine firearms available to us who love the simplicity, accuracy, and convenience of the grand old sixgun, along with the precision and rifle-like accuracy of a good single shot pistol. In this section, I have just hit the high spots, and am sure that in the months ahead, that more new firearms will be introduced that will pique the interest of sixgun shooters. The design of a firearm that holds a half dozen cartridges in a revolving cylinder has been declared obsolete by many for about the last 100 years, but the sixgun is far from dead, and is still by far the best design found to date to easily handle the best and most powerful of the world's handgun cartridges.

BY JOHN MALLOY

HANDGUNS TODAY:
Semi-Autos

Malloy tries out a Beretta PX4 Storm Sub-Compact. The short pistol is now available in 40 S&W caliber.

At the time of this writing in 2009, our country is experiencing an economic downturn. Among the things that are still selling well are firearms and ammunition. Some makers of autoloading handguns report that they are making all they can and selling all they make. Not only autoloading handguns, but AR- and AK-type rifles, and revolvers, and some types of shotguns, appear to be selling in record quantities.

Ordinarily, this would be a happy state of affairs for the firearms industry. However, the conditions are special.

In the previous edition of this publication, I noted that two important things pertinent to the future of autoloading handguns had not occurred by that earlier press time. The US Supreme Court had not yet rendered a decision related to the right to keep and bear arms. The November 2008 elections, which included the presidential election, had not yet taken place.

Now, those events are well in the past, and our questions relating to our autoloading handguns (and firearms in general) have been answered — or have they? Time will tell, as the saying goes.

Apart from — or at least only peripherally related to — the political situation, new things are happening in the world of autoloading handguns.

Perhaps the most interesting is the recent rise in popularity of the downsized .380-caliber autoloading pistol. A decade or so ago, the little ".25-sized .32" pistols chambered for the .32 ACP cartridge appeared on the scene. They filled a niche for the growing number of people who held concealed firearms licenses, which are now offered in most of our states. For those unable to conceal a larger handgun, the new little .32s provided something potentially more effective than most .22- and .25-caliber "vest-pocket-size" pistols.

Now, the new small .380s, only a little bit larger in gun size, but with a cartridge offering more bullet weight and frontal area, seem to provide more effectiveness with just a bit more size and weight. They might be considered "hip-pocket-size" pistols. At least six companies have brought out new scaled-down .380 pistols.

The Colt/Browning 1911 design — fast approaching its 100th birthday also — is still king of the hill in the world of autoloading handguns. By my informal count, at least 28 companies offer pistols of 1911 type. This year, several companies are introducing new 1911s. At least a few more new 1911s that were previously introduced are now in production.

Striker-fired full-size polymer-frame service-type pistols have carved out a niche in the past few years, and you will see new offerings this year.

Other countries have a stake in the firearms industry, and we have, introduced here, self-loading handguns from Turkey, Germany, Israel, Italy, Brazil,

Argentina, and other sources. The Philippines firearms industry continues to grow. Here in the United States, the "traditional" gun-making areas of the country have been joined by unlikely locations in Ohio and Tennessee. New handguns are even being designed and produced in California, a state that seems to do everything possible to discourage the firearms industry.

Frame-mounted rails have taken the place of hooked trigger guards as the current fad of choice. Hardly anyone uses the rails, but anyone who has a pistol with a rail might use the rail, so they are gaining in popularity.

What handgun caliber actually fires the most shots each year? I can't point to any definite research, but my suspicion is that the .22 Long Rifle would be the winner. .22-caliber pistols are popular for target shooting, plinking, small-game hunting, training and recreational shooting. A number of new .22-caliber pistols are being announced, and .22 conversion kits for centerfire autoloaders remain popular.

There are a number of new ideas that have been developed into new pistols, and I think you will be interested in reading about them. Also, I'll continue to include pistol-caliber autoloading carbines and unconventional pistols, because they use pistol-caliber ammunition. Also related are "short barrel rifles" that use autoloading handgun cartridges, and long-range semi-automatic pistols that use rifle cartridges. It all makes for a fascinating group of guns showing amazing creativity.

With all this information in mind, let's take a look at the new guns themselves:

Akdal

The Akdal Ghost pistols were introduced at the January 2009 SHOT Show, are of a "Glock-type" design, and are chambered for the 9 x 19mm cartridge. With a barrel length of 4-¼" inches, the length is 7-3/8". The grip has a flared shape unlike that of the

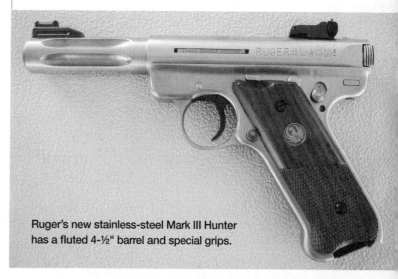

Ruger's new stainless-steel Mark III Hunter has a fluted 4-½" barrel and special grips.

Glock, and there are other differences. The Ghost TR01 has fixed sights, and the Ghost TR02 has adjustable sights on a different slide.

Akdal pistols are made in Turkey. A representative expected sales to begin in the United States during 2009, perhaps under a different brand name.

American Classic

Recall that, with the demise of the Spanish Llama pistols a few years ago, we lost a source of affordable 1911-type .45-caliber handguns. Last year, S&B Distributors introduced the American Classic line, new 1911-style pistols made by a new source in the Philippines. The company believes the new American Classic pistols will fill the niche vacated by Llama.

The pistols are now in production, and S&B is shipping two different models (let's consider them "mil-spec" and "enhanced") at a rate of about 200 a month.

Armalite

For the second year in a row, the Armalite AR-26, a new .45-caliber pistol, was a no-show at the annual SHOT Show. Armalite representatives report that the prototype works fine. However, the AR-26 project has been put on the back burner, as the volume of production of their AR-15 and AR-10 rifle lines is taking most of the company's attention.

ATI

American Tactical Imports has a number of pistols of interest to us here, imported from Turkey and Germany.

The American Tactical C-45 and CS-9 are ported pistols in, respectively, .45 ACP and 9mm calibers. They are conventional double-action (DA) pistols made by the Tisas firm in Turkey. The .45 has a 4.7"

barrel, while the 9 has a 4" barrel. Both variants are available in black, two-tone, or chrome. The ATI catalog also introduced some other Tisas-made pistols.

From Germany comes the GSG-5PK. (The GSG stands for "German Sport Guns.") It is a .22-caliber semi-automatic of unconventional appearance for a pistol. Well, not too unconventional if you expect it to look like a .22-caliber pistol version of an MP5 submachinegun. With its 4.7" barrel, it is no lightweight, cataloged at about 5 lbs. with its 10-round magazine.

Beretta

A few recently-introduced variants have sneaked quietly into Beretta's pistol line.

The PX4 Storm SD is one. This "Special Duty" pistol was designed to meet U.S. SOCOM military specifications. With its standard Picatinny rail and 4.6" barrel, it runs about 29 oz. and measures 8.2" x 5.7". The SD's polymer frame is a dark earth color and features modular backstraps to fit different hands.

The PX4 Storm Sub-Compact, previously offered as a 9mm, is also available now in .40 S&W chambering. Same 3" barrel and same 26-oz. weight. However, the staggered-column magazine holds 10 rounds compared to the 13-round capacity of the 9mm.

Beretta is proud of winning a U.S. military contract for up to 450,000 pistols, calling it the largest U.S. handgun contract since World War II. The Beretta Model 92 FS has been used by the U.S. military since 1985, so Beretta thinks it has stood the test of time.

Bersa

The Argentine-made Bersa line has some new variants. The Thunder 9 and Thunder 40 Pro Series pistols now have frame rails, loaded chamber indicators, polygonal-rifling barrels and special sights. Each pistol comes with two magazines — 17 rounds in 9mm and 13 in .40 S&W.

In progress are special variants, the BP 9 and BP 40, which will be Bersa's first polymer-frame pistols. Tentative plans were to introduce the new pistols late in 2009.

In this recent period of interest in the .380 cartridge, Bersa continues its long-time line of double-action .380 pistols. New is the Thunder 380 Concealed Carry, a "slimline" eight-shot pistol with bobbed hammer and short tang.

Bersa handguns are imported by Eagle Imports.

Colt now offers a 1911 with an integral accessory rail. What to call it? How about "Colt Rail Gun?" Malloy tries one out and finds it to be a good shooter.

The Akdal Ghost TR01 is a new 9mm "Glock-type" pistol from Turkey.

Browning

Is there space in Browning's .22-caliber Buck Mark line to squeeze in another variant? Apparently so, for displayed at the 2009 SHOT Show was the Buck Mark Practical URX. The pistol has a 5-½" tapered bull barrel, and has the ambidextrous "ultragrip." The front sight is from Truglo/Marbles. The new .22 was too new to appear in the 2009 Browning catalog.

Another uncataloged offering was the Hi Power Mark III with a new digital green camo finish. Other visual features, such as black grips, remain the same.

Century

The Arcus 9mm pistols announced by Century International Arms last year are in good supply now. The Arcus is based generally on the Browning Hi Power design, with the addition of a conventional double-action trigger mechanism and other modifications. Century points out that the Arcus pistols are manufactured in Eastern Europe, "in a picturesque town near the Black Sea." They are being used by Iraqi police and military forces now.

The Arcus Model 98 DA is a full-size pistol with a 4.7" barrel and a 15-round magazine. It weighs about 34 oz. The compact version, Model 98 DAC, had a 4" barrel and weighs a couple of ounces less. Magazine capacity is 13 rounds, the same capacity as the original Hi Power. Two magazines come with each Arcus pistol.

Charles Daly

Several new introductions in the Charles Daly line this year.

A prototype of a new steel-frame 1911-style pistol was displayed at the 2009 SHOT Show. Dubbed the Charles Daly G4 1911, the gun will be made by Bul, Ltd. in Israel. Several versions—Standard, Target, Tactical—will be offered, all with 5" barrels and 7-round magazines. A .22-caliber conversion kit will also be offered.

Striker-fired polymer-frame service pistols are popular now, and Charles Daly is also entering that niche. The new pistol, named the CD 9, is made in Turkey. It comes with a 4-½" barrel and 15-round magazine. A 10-round magazine will be available for areas in which the local government doesn't trust its citizens. Looking into the future, a tactical model is planned for later availability. Also, CD 40 and CD 45 variants are in the plans for later introduction.

Longtime readers of this publication may remember the excellent Jericho Model 941 pistol, originally made in Israeli, in 9mm and .41 Action Express. The .41 AE faded away, but the Jericho pistol became the Baby Eagle, the Uzi Eagle, and then the Baby Eagle again. Now it is the Jericho once more, and Charles Daly is offering it in 9, .40 and .45 chamberings in full-size, mid-size and compact versions. Barrel lengths run from 3.5" to 4.4", and magazine capacities are between 10 and 15 rounds, depending on model.

The prototype of the Chiappa 1911-22, a new .22-caliber pistol styled after the 1911 design. The new .22 will be made in America and marketed by MKS Supply.

CZ's new 2075 RAMI BD is a new variant with a decocking lever and a lighter recessed slide.

Here is a sneak preview of the prototype of the new Detonics DTX pistol. The DAO handgun is a departure for Detonics, with polymer frame and striker-fire mechanism.

Guncrafter Industries' two calibers — the .45 ACP and their special .50 GI. The big .50 has a rim rebated to the same diameter as the .45.

The frame and slide are made of Chiappalloy, an alloy that will take conventional cold blue. The pistol's takedown is like that of a 1911, and 1911 grips and sights will interchange.

The new Chiappa pistols will be distributed by MKS Supply, the distributors of Hi-Point autoloaders and Charter Arms revolvers.

Colt

Frame rails for autoloading pistols have been gaining popularity for some years. For 2009, Colt has offered a new Colt with an accessory rail, suitable for attaching a tactical light or a laser. What to call it? Simple. The new "Colt Rail Gun" has a forged stainless-steel frame and slide. The rail is machined into the forward reach of the frame. The Colt Rail Gun is loaded with niceties such as a palm-swell upswept beavertail tang, extended safety lever, Novak rear sight, ventilated burr hammer and eight-round magazine. .45 ACP, of course. I have had a chance to shoot one, and it shot very well indeed. It is just possible that the extra weight of the rail on the forward portion of the frame may provide a little bit of extra steadiness.

Colt's Combat Elite has many of the same features as the Rail Gun. The major visual differences are that it has no frame rail, and it is a two-tone pistol. The frame is stainless steel, and the slide is forged blued carbon steel. Grips are special half-checkered, half-smooth rosewood, with the word "Colt" at the midpoint. .45 ACP, of course.

The return of the 10mm Delta Elite was announced last year, and it is back in production now. The all stainless-steel pistol is enhanced with features similar to those of the previous two pistols.

The World War I replica was introduced last year. This year, the Colt Custom Shop is offering a Presentation Grade of the original pistol with engraving, smooth ivory grips and royal-blue finish. It comes in a walnut presentation case.

With the new interest in pistols for the .380 cartridge, it would seem an opportune time for the reintroduction of Colt's nice little Mustang and Pony .380 pistols. The Colt representatives with whom I spoke were mum on that possibility.

Teresa Starnes, president of Double Star, is the only woman in charge of a company that makes 1911-type pistols. Here, she proudly displays the new Double Star .45.

Chiappa

Those with an interest in firearms might be familiar with the Chiappa name in the context of nice Italian-made replicas of historical firearms, and of blank pistols styled after firearms.

A departure was introduced at the 2009 SHOT Show, at which the prototype of a new .22-caliber 1911-style pistol was displayed. The new Chiappa Model 1911 – 22 will be made of U.S. and Italian parts, and will be built right here in the USA, in Dayton, Ohio. The introduction, scheduled for Spring 2009, will consist of a Standard variant with fixed sights, and a Target version with adjustable sights and adjustable trigger. The Target model is envisioned as suitable for entry-level bullseye shooting—a complete pistol at a price competitive with 1911 .22-caliber conversion kits.

FNH's exotic-looking PS 90 carbine is now available in a version with a C-More Red Dot sight.

This specimen is in Olive Drab green color.

CZ

Regular readers of this publication may recall that last year, the semi-automatic pistol version of the little European "Skorpion" submachinegun was introduced by TG International.

Well, who better to handle the Czech-designed gun than the modern Czech company of CZ? CZ-USA has taken over, and now offers the intriguing Skorpion pistol as the CZ VZ 61, commemorating the 1961 adoption of the original submachinegun by special Czech forces. Caliber is the original .32 ACP. Frames are new, and allow semi-automatic fire only. Barrel is 4-½" and overall length is 10-½". Weight with a 20-round magazine is only 2-½ lbs. (Remember that 2-½ lbs. is 40 oz., about the weight of a Colt 1917 revolver.) The Skorpion is perhaps not for everyone, but it is an interesting little pistol.

Also new for 2009 from CZ is the SP-01 Phantom. The full-size 9mm pistol, built on the CZ 75 design, has a polymer frame—with integral rail—and has a relieved slide that also reduced weight. At 28 oz., the Phantom is 33 percent lighter.

The P-07 Duty pistol has the simplified Omega trigger system, reportedly an improvement on the original CZ 75's trigger design. The decocker mechanism can be changed to a manual safety by simply changing parts, which are included. The new P-07 Duty has a slide with a new profile, covering a 3.8" barrel. Overall length is 7.2", and the pistol weighs 27 oz.

A new variant of the compact CZ Rami pistol, the CZ 2075 Rami BD, has been introduced. It has a decocking lever, lighter recessed slide and 3-dot sights. Caliber is 9mm, barrel length is 3 inches, and weight is 23.5 oz.

CZ markets the Dan Wesson 1911 pistol line. Several new variants of Dan Wesson pistols (*q.v.*) were also introduced.

Dan Wesson

Several new models from Dan Wesson.

A new variant of the Dan Wesson line, the CCO (Concealed Carry Officer) is offered. It has a steel "Commander" slide with an aluminum "Officer" frame, which has a slightly-bobbed heel of the grip frame. The new .45 has a 4-¼" barrel and weighs 27 oz.

The PM 9 is the only 9mm pistol carried in the Dan

The Glock 29 is the "sub-compact" 10mm pistol that is now offered with "short frame" treatment.

Wesson line. Some people just have to have a 9mm 1911, and Dan Wesson wants to accommodate them. The PM 9 has a Clark rib-style slide and a fiber-optic front sight.

The new Marksman pistol is essentially their flagship full-size Pointman Seven with a more classic appearance. Slide retraction grooves are only at the traditional rear position, and the trigger is flat and solid.

The Sportsman, Model RZ-10, is similar to the Marksman, but is chambered for the zippy 10mm Auto cartridge. Full-size, with 5" barrel and 8.75" in overall length.

Detonics

Detonics, recently relocated to Millstadt, IL, offers a growing line of 1911-type pistols of different sizes and styles.

The big eye-catcher at the 2009 SHOT Show, however, was a prototype of their new DTX pistol. This pistol is a real departure for Detonics. It has a polymer frame, and is striker fired, with no manual safety. It is true double-action-only (DAO), with restrike capability. The trigger requires only .55" of travel, and has a 5-½-lb. pull.

At first glance, the most noticeable feature of the Detonics DTX is the increased angle of the grip frame. Various studies, dating back from the WWII techniques of Col. Rex Applegate, to those of the present leadership team of Detonics, were used to

Here, in prototype, is the Hi-Point carbine wearing its new stock. The new variant will be phased in as an in-line change.

Kimber's Celia Crane is happy to display the company's new Crimson Carry II, a .45 that is factory-equipped with Crimson Trace Lasergrips.

design a pistol that could be used for stressful situations in which point shooting is the best response. The slantier grip, lack of manual controls and short, relatively light double-action trigger give a pistol very suitable for such fast shooting. Good square sights and the controllable trigger also allow precise shots.

When will it be available? Because of the early stage of development, company officials could not give an estimate of an actual production date.

Double Star

The Double Star .45 pistol exists! Introduced as a prototype last year, the new Double Star 45 was in inventory in early 2009, and was ready for shipping. Recall that Double Star began making forged 1911 frames with an integral rail about five years ago. Eventually, the company decided to offer a complete pistol.

The firm's primary business is AR-15 type rifles. The recent surge of demand for such arms made company officers reconsider the idea of going ahead with pistol production. A new manufacturing facility was recently constructed, and the decision was made to expand rifle production and also begin pistol production.

The new 1911 has a number of niceties today's shooters seem to like. Beside the rail, the pistol has a ventilated trigger and burr hammer, and a beavertail tang. A stainless-steel 5" match barrel resides in a slide topped by Novak sights.

I had a chance to fire one of the new .45s. Although a two-handed hold is the most practical hold for most pistol shooting, I think the one-handed "Bullseye" hold allows better evaluation of a trigger. The Double Star 45 had an excellent trigger, and I enjoyed making pivoted steel targets swing side to side at 25 yards.

EAA

European American Armory is aware that rails are

"in." Both the Tanfoglio-designed Witness full- and compact-size steel pistols are available now with accessory rails. The polymer-frame Witness pistols also have rails, moulded into the forward part of the frame. Full-size, compact and "carry" polymer Witness pistols have this treatment.

Some have wondered about the status of the unique "tube chamber" Witness that was beautifully introduced in prototype on these pages two years ago. Apparently, development has stopped on that project.

Ed Brown

Ed Brown offers its Special Forces 1911 in desert tan color this year. These 5" single-column pistols come with an eight-round "8-Pack" magazine.

A limited run of engraved Classic Custom pistols will be made. This variant, a high-quality 5" full-size pistol is Ed Brown's top-of-the-line handgun.

EMF

Over many years, EMF has created a tradition of replicas of single-action revolvers and other historical firearms. A company slogan, "The Best in Cowboy Guns Since 1956" reinforces this idea of early-American firearms.

Few remember that EMF originally stood for "Early and Modern Firearms." Now, EMF has revitalized the "modern" portion of the name. Two new series of autoloading handguns have been introduced.

The EMF Model 1911 line is made 100% in the United States (in Tennessee, of all places). The basic variant is the 1911-A1, an essentially "mil-spec" 5" .45 with parkerized finish. The gun can come with either a flat or arched mainspring housing, and choice of grips. Commemorative military models with some tasteful engraving will be offered. They will have "ultra ivory" grips with insignia of either the Army, Navy, Air Force or Marines, and come with the appropriate service medallion and a presentation case. The 1911 Combat Model is an enhanced variant with lightened burr hammer and upswept beavertail tang, and choices of sights, grips and finishes. Scheduled for availability during 2009 was the 1911 CCC (Concealed Carry Compact) Model. These 4-¼" variants will have eight-round magazines and choices of sights and finishes.

Interesting as the EMF 1911 line is, the other pistol offering was the center of attention at the EMF booth at the 2009 SHOT Show.

The new pistol is called the FMK Model 9C1. Chambered for the 9mm cartridge, the polymer-frame pistol has a 4" barrel, is under 7" long and weighs about 23 oz. The sights are "fixed," but, interestingly, each pistol comes with interchangeable front and rear sights to adjust for elevation and windage. So, a shooter can adjust for load and range, and still have the ruggedness of fixed sights. Capacity of the 9C1 is

10 + 1. Trigger action is true DAO, with second-strike capability. Surprisingly, the pistol is made in California, the only gun to be recently approved.

Perhaps the most striking feature of the FMK 9C1 is its lettering. Patriotic Americans may enjoy reading the pistol when not shooting it. In small letters, abbreviated wording of the U.S. Constitution's Bill of Rights appears on the slide. Other patriotic (and possibly politically-incorrect) phrases such as "In God We Trust," "Thank You, U.S. Soldiers" and "Proudly American" also appear in different places on the pistol. I think it is safe to say that there is nothing similar in this niche.

FNH

Selected models of FNH USA pistols are now available with a new FNP Shooters Pack. In a lockable hard case with the pistol are a polymer belt holster, adjustable paddle assembly and a double magazine pouch. Both holster and magazine pouches are tension-adjustable for retention. Also included is a yellow polymer dummy barrel that can be installed in the pistol — simply replacing the original barrel — for training purposes. Special models of the FNP-45, FNP-40 and FNP-9 are offered in this Shooters Pack.

The interesting-looking PS 90 carbine is now available with a special C-More "red dot" sight installed. The little 5.7x28mm rifle is offered in black or olive drab color stocks, and with 10- or 30-round magazines.

Girsan

The Turkish Girsan company has been in business since 1994, making 9mm Yavuz pistols, based on the Beretta 92 action design. At the January 2009 SHOT Show, Girsan displayed a number of new offerings. A Beretta-styled Yavuz pistol, the T40 is now available in .40 S&W chambering. Magazine capacity for the new .40 is 10 rounds.

Also introduced is a new .45-caliber pistol. Using a similar DA trigger mechanism, the pistol has been expanded to .45 ACP caliber, and has been given a tilting-barrel locking system. With a 4" barrel, the pistol measures 7-¾" long, and weighs about 32 oz. (without magazine). The magazine, incidentally, holds 9 rounds, giving the pistol 9 + 1 capacity.

If you are keeping count, chalk up another new .380 for 2009. The Girsan MC 14 is a new introduction in that caliber. However, it is not one of the "down-sized" .380s, but is built in the style of pocket pistols of the last century. With a barrel length of just under 4 inches, it is 6-¾" long and weighs about 22 oz. It is conventional double action. A similar pistol, the MC 13, is also available in .32 ACP caliber.

Glock

Glock has introduced three different variants for 2009.

The new Kahr P380 is Kahr's smallest handgun. Weighing in at about 11 oz. (with magazine), the little pistol has 6+1 capacity.

The Kriss .45 was introduced last year in carbine form, and is offered this year as a "short barrel rifle." Requiring extra federal paperwork and money, the new variant can be said to have an exotic appearance.

One of the new pistols offered by Legacy Sports International is the BUL Cherokee, a 9mm polymer-frame pistol made in Israel. This version is the Cherokee Compact.

The exotic-looking .380-caliber Magnum Research Micro Desert Eagle uses a unique blowback system. The Micro Eagle's trigger is double-action-only, and the barrel length is 2.2 inches.

The unique new Volquartsen V-10X is an interesting new .22-caliber aluminum-frame pistol with unusual features. It is available in hard anodized black, and a number of other colors. Here is a prototype in red.

Two years ago, Glock brought out an "SF" (Short Frame) version of the .45-caliber Model 21. Subtle changes in the frame reduced the distance from backstrap to trigger, and many shooters liked the new feel. Now, Glock has given the "SF" treatment to its powerful 10mm Auto lineup.

The full-size 15 +1 Glock Model 20 10mm is now available with the SF frame. With its 4.6" barrel, it is eight inches long and weighs only about 28 oz.

The "sub-compact" Glock 29 in the 10mm chambering is also available as an SF variant. With a 3.8" barrel, it is 6.8 inches long and weighs 25 oz.

The Glock 22, a .40 S&W pistol, changes the feel of the grip in a different way. The shape and surface of Glock grip frames has changed over the years. The original "pebble" finish gave way to checkering on the front and back straps, and finger grooves on the front. Now, the Glock 22 RTF2 gives us a new variant. The grip frame has a pattern of tiny pyramids to provide better purchase for the shooting hand. Thus it is termed a "rough textured frame" or RTF. If this were not enough to set it apart, the 22 RTF2 also has distinctive arcuate grasping grooves on the slide.

GSG

GSG (German Sport Guns) makes a nifty autoloading carbine styled a bit like the German HK MP-5 submachinegun. The GSG carbine was cleverly named the GSG-5.

Now, a pistol version has been introduced, which is of interest to us here. With no stock and a 4.7" barrel, the big new 22 pistol is about 15 inches long, and weighs about 5 lbs. It has the letter-filled name of GSG-5PK. It is available with 10, 15 or 22-round magazines.

The GSG-5PK is being imported and distributed by American Tactical Imports. (See ATI)

Guncrafter

Regular readers of this report will remember that in the 2004 edition of this publication, a new company, Guncrafter Industries, introduced a new 1911 pistol. The unique aspect of this pistol was that it was redesigned and enlarged to handle a powerful new cartridge with a half-inch bullet diameter—the .50 GI.

The original pistol is now called the Model 1, and there is now a second version. The Model 2 is distinguished by its full-profile (no scallops) slide, and an accessory rail on the frame. Caliber is .50 GI, of course.

However, the Guncrafter firm will make either model of the big pistol in .45 ACP caliber if a shooter wants one. Then, a conversion kit can be acquired to later make it into a .50 GI.

In addition, the company offers "The American," an enhanced regular-size .45-caliber 1911, under the Guncrafter Industries name. Chalk up one more 1911, if you are keeping score.

A new product introduced at the 2009 SHOT Show was a .50-caliber conversion kit for the Glock 21. The kit consists of a magazine and a complete top end (slide, barrel and all associated parts). This is a "drop-in" installation for those who feel they don't have enough caliber options with Glock's standard offerings, or just want a bigger caliber. The .50-caliber Glock conversion kit can be acquired from Guncrafter or from American Tactical Imports.

HK

Heckler & Koch's P 30 pistol was recently designed as a modern 9mm police and security arm. It is conventional double action, but can use other trigger modes such as DAO or HK's Law Enforcement Modification (LEM). A Picatinny rail is moulded into the front of the polymer frame. Capacity is 15 + 1, and it has ambidextrous controls.

The original 3.85" barrel was felt by some to be a bit short, so now there is the P 30 L. The "L" stands for "Long Slide." We must remember that in terminology, things can be relative. The P 30 L has about a half-inch longer barrel, slide and sight radius. With its lengthened 4.45" barrel, the slightly larger pistol's weight goes up from 26 to 27.5 oz.

High Standard

High Standard had added a new .45 to its 1911 pistol line. The new Compact Elite has a 3-5/8" barrel. The parkerized small .45 has niceties such as a beavertail tang, skeletonized hammer and trigger and checkered wood grips. Capacity is 6 + 1.

High Standard also offers the Sentinel Model. (Like S&W and Colt, High Standard apparently felt they might as well recycle some early company names.) Small .45s with no sights have been recently offered by Colt and Kimber, and the new Sentinel also comes without sights. Some pocket pistols of the early 20th century were made without sights, and it is interesting to see this trend come back now.

High Standard's line of .223-caliber AR-type rifles has a new addition, of interest to us here as a pistol-caliber carbine. The new 9mm carbine uses Colt 9mm magazines and can come with the carry handle upper, or as a flat-top. The lower receiver uses a removable magazine block. This gives the owner the option of later converting the 9mm carbine to a .223, if that change is desired.

Since this seems to be the year of the .380, it is worth noting that the DAO stainless-steel AMT .380 BackUp pistol, an early compact .380, is offered by High Standard.

Hi-Point

Green- and tan-colored service autoloaders are offered by other companies, so Hi-Point has gone so far as to offer its first green-colored .40 and .45-caliber pistols. Mechanically identical to current Hi-Point pistols, the new 40G and 45G models were scheduled for availability in early 2009.

The economical Hi-Point carbine, available in 9mm and .40 S&W chamberings, will be wearing a new stock before too long. The new stock, displayed in prototype at the 2009 SHOT Show, is a ventilated unit with a cushioned butt pad. It incorporates rails for mounting lights or lasers or other accessories. Like most of Hi-Point's changes, it will probably sneak in, with little fanfare, as an in-line change.

For those who like the little carbine, good news! The long-awaited .45-caliber variant of the Hi-Point carbine was scheduled to enter production in the last half of 2009.

Hogue

The Hogue Avenger is now a reality for American shooters. Initial production was scheduled to go to Europe, but now the new gun is available in the United States, at least in conversion-kit form.

Recall that the Avenger system will work on a standard 1911 frame. It replaces the 1911 slide but makes it a very different gun. The barrel is fixed, and the sights are always in alignment with the barrel. The unique mechanism unlocks after the bullet has left the barrel, and movement is in a straight line. Putting an Avenger upper unit on a 1911 frame can convert the pistol into a match-ready race gun, says Peter Spielberger, the designer of the Hogue Avenger.

At the present, the Avenger is supplied as a kit with all the instructions and tools included. Someone with a sense of humor named the tools the APT (Avenger Pin Tool) and VST (Very Special Tool).

The Avenger conversion kit is not a firearm by itself, so can be shipped and sold freely. The conversion units are being produced at the rate of 700 per year, of which 300 will go to Europe. Eventually, complete pistols will be marketed, but no time frame has been planned.

The S&W Model SW1911ES ("extended slide") .45 has a short grip frame and longer 4-½" barrel and slide.

ISSC

A .22-caliber Glock? The ISSC M22 pistol certainly looks like one. The Austrian pistol is shaped like a Glock, and until the eye catches the external hammer peeking out at the rear of the slide, it is easy to mistake it for one. The familiar Glock-style trigger safety is part of the design, but because it is hammer-fired, a manual safety on the slide is included.

Designed as a training pistol for those armed with a Glock, the new .22 can, of course, be used for plinking, target shooting, and other recreational shooting. The blowback pistol has a 4-lb. trigger. With its 4" match barrel, the M22 has an overall length of 7". Weight with a magazine is about 24 oz. A version with a longer barrel and slide is also in the works.

The new .22 Long Rifle pistol is imported by Austrian Sporting Arms.

Iver Johnson

The Iver Johnson 1911-style pistols are finally a production reality. Planned in .45 and .22 LR variants, the .45 was in stock by early 2009, and plans were to begin shipping during the spring. The .22 version will come later.

Many companies are offering non-traditional finishes now, and Iver Johson plans to offer a Dura-Coat "Snakeskin" pattern finish as an option with their .45-caliber 1911. The prototype of the new finish was displayed at the 2009 SHOT Show.

Even though the IJ 22 was not yet ready for shipping at the time of this writing, the company offers .22-caliber conversion kits which work on any .45-caliber 1911.

Kahr

Kahr started out years ago with a small DAO 9mm pistol. Over the years they have enlarged the basic design to include .40- and .45-caliber handguns. Now, things are going the other way, and Kahr offers the new, much smaller model P380, chambered for the .380 ACP cartridge.

Like the latest larger Kahr variants, the P380 has a polymer frame, a DAO trigger mechanism, a tilting-barrel locking system and a matte stainless-steel slide. The pistol is scaled down to match the .380

cartridge. The barrel length is 2.5 inches. Overall size is 4.9" long by 3.9" high; the little .380 can easily hide beneath a 4x6 index card. It thus falls into what I consider the "subcompact" class. (Kahr, however, calls it a "micro-compact").

Advertised weight is just under 10 oz. — 9.97 oz., to be exact. They are cheating a little, though, as this figure is without a magazine. With the magazine, the weight goes up to a bit over 11 oz. (As this is two ounces lighter than the 13-oz. weight of the old Colt .25 Auto of 1908, I still am impressed with how light the P380 is.) Capacity of the Kahr P380 is 6 + 1.

Kahr is proud of the fact that the little .380 has "real" sights, with both front and rear sights dovetailed into the slide. Night sights are available.

Kahr also produces Thompson long guns and pistols (q.v.).

Kimber

Kimber's 1911 line has some new models. All the new guns are in .45 ACP.

Last year the stainless-steel Raptor II was introduced with a 5" barrel as a "Custom" pistol. New this year are the Pro Raptor II with a 4" bull barrel and full-length frame, and the Ultra Raptor II with a 3" barrel and short aluminum frame. Raptor pistols have special scaled gripping surfaces on the metal, and logo grip panels carry out the "Raptor" theme. To refresh your memory, here are Kimber's model codes: Custom guns have 5" barrels, Pro series guns are 4-inchers and Ultra pistols have 3" barrels.

Crimson Carry II pistols are equipped with Crimson Trace Lasergrips. Grip-mounted lasers are becoming ever more popular, and these are nicely done. The grips have a rosewood finish and double-diamond checkering. The pistols are two-tone, with bright aluminum frames and blued slides. They are available in Custom, Pro and Ultra variants, and are very attractive pistols.

Two new items have been added to the Tactical pistol line. The Tactical Custom HD II has a new stainless-steel frame. The Tactical Entry II has an elongated forward frame with an integral rail that allows attaching a light or laser or other accessory. The Tactical series guns have ambidextrous safeties, beavertail tangs, night sights, extensive checkering, and other embellishments.

Kriss

Produced by TDI (Transformational Defense Industries), the Kriss .45 ACP carbine was introduced last year. Of unconventional appearance, the Kriss design was originally developed as a submachinegun, with a polymer frame and a unique recoil-reducing mechanism. The action was redesigned for semi-automatic fire, and a longer 16" barrel was used to produce the carbine.

Some people just have to have a gun that looks like a submachinegun, even if it isn't one. So, for 2009, the Kriss is also offered with the short submachinegun barrel. Yes, it is considered a "short barrel rifle" so it takes BATF paperwork and extra money to own one, but if someone wants one, it is available.

Also announced was another caliber option. A 16" carbine in .40 S&W chambering will be offered. The new .40 carbine will use a 30-round .40-caliber Glock-type magazine. Scheduled availability was set for the second half of 2009.

Legacy

Legacy Sports International is known as a provider of rifles and shotguns. Now, the company offers two new autoloading pistols.

The ever-popular 1911 design is offered by Legacy as the "Citadel." Made in the Philippines, the Citadel is an enhanced 1911 offered in two sizes. The Full Size variant has a 5" barrel, beavertail tang, lightened hammer and trigger, Novak-style sights, and ambidextrous manual safety. Each pistol comes with two eight-round magazines.

The Compact (Concealed Carry) version is a smaller pistol with a 3.5" barrel and shorter grip frame. It does not have the ambidextrous safety, but has a bushingless barrel and full-length guide rod. The Compact pistol comes with two six-round magazines.

Citadel 1911 pistols were first displayed at the January 2009 SHOT Show. Pistols were in stock, ready for shipping, at that time.

For those wanting a 9mm pistol of a different design, Legacy offers polymer BUL 9mm pistols. Israeli BUL pistols have a good reputation, and have been offered by other companies under other names. Legacy is offering the polymer-frame, conventional double-action 9mm pistols under the BUL name.

The BUL Cherokee (full size) is based on the CZ 75 trigger mechanism in a polymer frame, locked by a tilting-barrel system. Barrel length is about 4-3/8", with an overall length of close to 8-½". A Cherokee Compact is also offered, with a shorter 3-9/16" barrel. Frames for both variants are the same, with barrel and slide length differentiating the guns. Each BUL pistol comes in a lockable hard case with two 17-round magazines and a nifty little cleaning kit.

Les Baer

The Les Baer H.C. 40, introduced last year, is in the catalog now as a production item. We'll assume that H.C. stands for "high capacity," as the double-column magazine holds 18 rounds. With one in the chamber, that means 19 rounds of .40 S&W ammunition. The pistol is built on a double-stack Caspian frame and has an accuracy guarantee of 2-½" at 50 yards.

Magnum Research

Using a different operating concept from any of the

other new .380-caliber pistols, Magnum Research has introduced its new small-size DAO 380. The "Micro Desert Eagle" has a 2.2" barrel. It measures 4.5" x 3.7"; it could hide under a 3x5 index card if the butt didn't stick out. Weight is a hair under 14 oz.

The pistol is described as "gas assisted blowback system." What on earth does that mean? A Magnum Research representative was kind enough to give me an examination of the inner workings of the pistol, which shows some interesting ideas. The frame is light aluminum (a new 6066 alloy), but to counter recoil, the slide is steel, with dual recoil springs. The fixed barrel is very subtly ported, and the porting assists in recoil control. The 2.2" barrel is very subtly octagon-shaped to allow slide clearance for free operation.

The little Micro Desert Eagle was the star of Magnum Research's new offerings. However, the big Desert Eagle pistol reached its 25th anniversary in 2009. The first version, in .357 Magnum, was introduced in 1984. Later chamberings were .44 Magnum and then .50 Action Express (.50 AE), the big boomer of conventional autoloading handguns. The pistol today is offered in these three calibers. From 2009 on, all Desert Eagle pistols will be manufactured in a new facility in Minnesota.

To celebrate the 25th year of the Desert Eagle, Magnum Research panned to offer 250 commemorative pistols. The pistols will have silver titanium finish with gold-plated triggers, hammers and levers. Each one will come with a walnut display case and a medallion. Caliber? .50 AE, of course.

Nighthawk

Nighthawk Custom's new 1911 9mm Lady Hawk was sized with slim frame and grips to fit women's smaller hands. Introduced last year too late to make the catalog, the pistol sold well — to men! A company representative told me that 80 percent of sales were to men. Now, they will not put "Lady Hawk" on the slide unless requested by the customer.

The T3 pistol, originally designed as a compact 1911-style .45, uses a "Commander" 4-½" slide on a short "Officer" frame. This size proved to be popular, and new Nighthawk T3 variants are now available in 9mm and .40 S&W.

Para

Para's big news is that the company has changed location. The new headquarters is in Charlotte, NC. The first product made at and shipped from the Charlotte plant was their new GI Expert pistol, in early 2009. After that, the schedule called for production of the company's rifle line. By mid-2009, all manufacture, assembly and distribution was scheduled to be from North Carolina.

That said, the big news in Para's firearms line is indeed their GI Expert pistol, the first item to come

from North Carolina. There has been a tendency in the past few decades to enhance the basic 1911 design. Components have been added or modified to suit the gun to special purposes. Lately, though, it seems that a lot of people just want a basic 1911 without a lot of bells and whistles. Para has given substantial thought to a basic .45, and the GI Expert at first glance looks very much like a WWII-era 1911A1. However, some subtle additions have been made. The crisp trigger mechanism uses a trigger of medium length, which should be satisfactory to those who can't decide between a short trigger and a long one. The tang has been slightly lengthened and reshaped to prevent hammer bite by the skeletonized burr hammer. The sights are higher, and both rear and front sights are dovetailed into the slide. The magazine holds eight rounds instead of seven, and the barrel is stainless steel. All in all, the GI Expert seems a basic .45 that even a purist could love.

Robar

After the polymer-frame Glock pistol became popular, some shooters were impressed by the design but didn't really like the polymer frame. Eventually, replacement frames made of aluminum became available. Now Robar of Phoenix, AZ, has introduced a line of complete pistols using the basic Glock mechanism in either aluminum or stainless-steel frames.

Robar believes the metal frame offers positive advantages. The "Alloy Xtreme" frames do not flex, and features such as a "beavertail" tang and better access to the magazine release are possible. Also, interchangeable grip inserts can be added to the lower rear portion of the grip. Stainless-steel frames have the same features, and add additional weight which helps to control recoil.

Robar also has a "Robar Revive!" program to upgrade existing Glock pistols with metal frames and other features.

Rock River

Rock River Arms makes a number of items of interest to us here, including 1911-style pistols, .223-caliber long-range pistols and 9mm AR-style carbines.

For 2009, a .40 S&W caliber carbine was added to the line, but was not available for display at the January SHOT Show because the .40-caliber magazines were not ready.

Rohrbaugh

Last year, I reported that the new Rohrbaugh .380 pistol was "almost in production," but it turned out the introduction was held up by the magazines not being ready. Now, the .380 is in full production, just in time to catch the wave of renewed interest in that caliber.

The new Vltor Standard Model Fortis will be available in the Bren Ten's original 10mm Auto chambering, and in .45 ACP. (right view).

The Rohrbaugh .380 has basically the same specifications as the original all-metal 9mm, weighing 12.8 oz. With its 2.9" barrel, it measures 5.2" x 3.7". The magazine holds six rounds, giving 6 + 1 capacity. Variants with and without sights are available.

Ruger

New variants of the products of Sturm, Ruger & Co. tend to slip in and out of the Ruger lineup with little fanfare. So, let's take a look at the new pistol variants.

The original .22-caliber Mark III Hunter pistol was introduced a few years ago in a long-barrel version. In 2009, a new Mark III Hunter was introduced. The stainless-steel pistol is very distinctive with its 4-½" fluted barrel. For those of us whose first .22 autoloader was the old Ruger Standard model, the new Ruger Mark III pistols are loaded with features. The takedown is still the same, and the manual safety button is still the same. Slowly introduced over the intervening years are a last-shot holdopen (I used an extended plastic follower in my old Mark I to trap the bolt), a loaded chamber indicator and a magazine disconnect. The basic Ruger design has lasted from 1949 into 2009: 60 years and still going strong.

The .22-caliber Charger pistol, a 10"-barrel silhouette and hunting pistol based on the 10/22 rifle action, was introduced last year. New for 2009, the original model with the laminated wood stock is joined by a variant with a black "Axiom" synthetic stock.

Also introduced last year were two new polymer-frame pistols: the SR 9 9mm service-style pistol and the little LCP .380 carry pistol. Since their introduction, some potential problems developed, and Ruger has resolved the situation. For people who purchased SR 9 or LCP pistols in the early days of 2008, Ruger has issued a recall notice. SR 9 pistols with serial number prefix "330" and LCP pistols with serial number prefix "370" are involved. If you have such a pistol, contact Ruger at 1-800-784-3701 or e-mail SR9recall@ruger.com or LCPrecall@ruger.com. They will send a shipping box so you can return the pistol free of charge for a no-cost upgrade. A free extra magazine will be included when the refitted pistol is returned to you. Ruger reports that turnaround is about one week.

Sarsilmaz

Last year, the Turkish Sarsilmaz K2 was introduced. It is a 15 + 1 9mm based on the CZ 75 mechanism. Announced at that time, but not present for display, was the K2C, a compact with a shorter barrel, but using the full-size frame. The 9mm K2C is now in production, and is a catalog item.

The K2 has also been expanded into a .45 ACP version. The new K2-45 has 14 + 1 capacity. With a barrel about 4-½" long, the overall length is 8 inches. The big staggered-column .45 weighs about 40 oz. Finishes are black or white chrome.

Sarsilmaz makes pistols for other companies under other names also.

SIG Sauer

SIG Sauer introduced a new .380 pistol for 2009. The new SIG is different than most of other companies' new .380 introductions, though. It is a single-action, aluminum-frame pistol with the appearance of a 1911 that has been reduced in every dimension. Its black aluminum frame carries a stainless-steel slide which can be left natural or covered with black Nitron. Grips are available in black or natural aluminum. The grooved aluminum grips give the little pistol a distinctive look. With its 2.7" barrel, the pistol measures 5.5" x 3.9", thus falling into my subcompact class (able to hide under a 4x6 index card). The new .380 weighs 15 oz. and has 6 + 1 capacity.

The larger double-action .380 P232 is now available with a new slide design and new sights. Finishes are natural stainless or black Nitron.

A new concept in SIG Sauer products is a long-range pistol. It is a modification of the company's P556 (5.56mm NATO/.223 Remington) semi-automatic rifle. The new P556 pistol has no provision for a stock, and has a 10" barrel. It is available with a polymer forearms or an "alloy quad rail" SWAT version. Weight is about 6.5 lbs. Overall length is 20.5 inches. Such pistols are catching on for recreational shooting as well as for law-enforcement applications. I had a chance to shoot the new P556 pistol, and it is fun to shoot. Interestingly, the guns are marked "PISTOL USE ONLY." You can't put a stock on one.

Smith & Wesson

S&W's two most recent pistol lines—the SW1911 and the polymer-frame M&P series—now dominate the firm's autoloading pistol offerings. A number of new variants appeared for 2009.

In the 1911 line, new is a full-size 9mm, a departure from the traditional .45 ACP chambering. Added to the full-size 5" version (which appeared first), and the "Commander" sized 4-¼" variant, a new 3" compact version has been added.

S&W has also come to the conclusion that the butt of an autoloading handgun is the hardest part to conceal. Using the shortened six-round frame, they have mated the 4-¼" barrel and slide to it, rather than the shorter 3" components. The compact "extended slide" pistol is cataloged as the SW1911ES.

Smith & Wesson is proud of specialty metals in some of the company's guns. In the 1911 line, a new full-size variant in black melonite finish has a titanium firing pin. The model designation? SW1911TFP.

In the M&P polymer-frame pistol line, the full- and compact-size M&Ps have a new optional feature. An ambidextrous thumb safety is now offered for the M&P line. Although the catalog shows it only on the M&P9, it will be available also on the .40 S&W and .357 SIG variants.

Although the catalog shows availability only on the full-size frame, the M&P Compact guns will be available with Crimson Trace Lasergrips.

Springfield

Springfield continues its extensive line of 1911-type handguns, but its new introductions are in the polymer-frame XD line.

The new XD(M) has a number of new features. Either by coincidence (unlikely) or by design (probably), all the new features start with the letter "M." They include a Multi-use carry case, Main-focus sights (low and holster-friendly), Mould-tru backstraps (interchangeable), Multi-adjust rail system (longer rail), Maximum reach magazine release (works from either side), Minimal error disassembly (easier), Mega-capacity magazine (16 in .40, 19 in 9mm), Melonite (black oxide), Minimal reset trigger (short travel reset), Model contour frame (better grip), Mega-lock texture (better purchase on grip), Major grasp slide serrations (deeper) and Match-grade barrel.

Just in case these items don't give you the picture

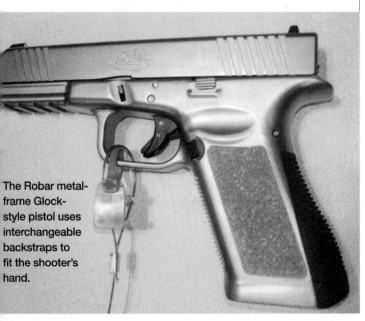

The Robar metal-frame Glock-style pistol uses interchangeable backstraps to fit the shooter's hand.

of the new XD(M), it also has a different contour slide, with beveled sides. Barrel length is 4-½", and the gun is available in black, olive-drab green, or two-tone finishes. It comes in a case with two magazines, a holster, a double magazine pouch, cable lock and cleaning brush. Cataloged now in .40 and 9mm, a .45 ACP version is in the works.

STI

STI International, maker of 1911-type autoloading pistols, introduced a revolver (of all things) last year. This year, the firm offers another departure. The 9mm STI GP6 pistol has a polymer grip over a steel frame, and a polymer accessory rail is included. It is conventional double action, but has ambidextrous thumb safeties. Other ambidextrous controls are the magazine release and the slide stop. The barrel is 4-¼" long, and the overall length is 8". Weight is 26 oz.

STI also displayed a very interesting experimental pistol, a joint venture between STI in America and the QS firm in Italy. The pistol is roughly of 1911 shape, but has a fixed barrel and is described as a delayed blowback. (I do not know the exact mechanical aspects). The pistol has the SFS (Safe Fast Shooting) system described on these pages in past years. The cocked hammer can be pushed forward, which motion automatically applies the thumb safety to its upward position. When the safety is depressed, the hammer automatically recocks.

Still, perhaps the most interesting aspect is the ammunition. The cartridge is named the 7mm Penna, or 7x23mm. The case is the same length as the Super .38 or .45 ACP (.898"), but is only .311" in diameter (about the diameter of a .32 Auto bullet, not cartridge). The nominal 7mm bullet measures .277". The cartridge comes in two loadings.

A very light (aluminum) bullet weighs 15 grains and reaches the zippy speed of 2800 feet per second (fps) from the muzzle. Needless to say, it loses velocity very rapidly and probably loses stability in short order. The concept is that it could be a useful close-range defense load – it could be very effective at close range, yet quickly slow down without endangering other people. A more conventional load is also in progress. A 70-gr. bullet still comes out at 1400 fps. Components are being made in Italy by Fiocchi. This is an interesting development.

Taurus

Lots of new pistols from Taurus, a company that calls itself the "World's Foremost Pistol Maker." Let's start with the PT 738, Taurus' entry into the small .380 market.

Taurus, in their catalog, calls the model 738 the "TCP" pistol. I neglected to ask what the significance of "TCP" was, and can only guess. Tiny Compact Pistol? At any rate, the DAO model PT 738 has a polymer frame and holds 6 + 1 rounds of .380

ammunition. The barrel is a relatively long 3.3", for an overall length of 5". Three variants are offered: the 738B has a blued slide and weighs 10.2 oz; the 738SS has a stainless-steel slide and weighs 10.2 oz; the 738 TI has a titanium slide and weighs just 9 oz. An extension magazine is available that increases capacity to 8 + 1.

The slim look is in for small carry pistols, and Taurus' PT709SLIM pistol has trimmed down. A 9mm, the 709 is a conventional double action. It has a "trigger safety" and a manual thumb safety. Barrel length is 3.2 inches, and overall length is 6.2 inches. Several variants of the SLIM pistol are offered in black, stainless, and titanium. All weigh 19 oz. except the titanium version, which goes 17 oz. Capacity is 7 + 1 or 9 + 1.

Taurus' little .22 and .25 conventional double action pistols are now available with polymer frames. The 22PLY and 25 PLY (I can break this code) have 8 + 1 and 9 + 1 capacity, respectively. Barrels are 2.3", and they each weigh 10.8 oz.

The PT 2045 is a new polymer-frame .45. The pistol is conventional double action, with "Strike Two" capability. The staggered-column magazine gives 12 + 1 capacity. With a 4.2" barrel, it weighs 31.5 oz. The 2045 is available with either a blue or stainless slide.

The 1911 line has several new variants. The PT 1911 has, logically, been a .45, but now both 9mm and .38 Super choices are available, either in blue or stainless. Both calibers are 5" pistols with 9 + 1 capacity. Another new Taurus .45 is the 1911 HC, a wide-frame full-size pistol with 12 + 1 capacity. (I feel certain that HC stands for "high capacity").

The Polymer-frame 24/7, Taurus' original entry into the polymer-frame service pistol niche, is now available in a high-capacity variant, the 24/7 PLS. This variant of the pistol has grown — the barrel is a full five inches, and the grip is longer. Weight, however, is a moderate 31.5 oz. The new 24/7 is available in 9mm and .38 Super with 18 + 1 capacity, and in .40 S&W with 16 + 1 capacity.

Thompson

The line of Thompson "Tommy Gun" long guns and pistols is produced by Kahr Arms. Introduced last year were a "Short Barrel Rifle" variant of the 1927A1 semi-automatic carbine, and a 1927A1 semi-automatic pistol. These variants are in production and are now catalog items.

The 45-caliber 1927A1 Thompson pistol (aka TA5) is available in three configurations: the pistol with a 50-round drum, the pistol with a 100-round drum (Wow!), and the pistol with a special 10-round drum, for those states that do not trust their citizens with more than 10 rounds at a time.

Tisas

A new double-action full-size pistol was introduced by the Turkish Tisas firm two years ago, and was given the name Zigana last year. For 2009, a whole family of Zigana pistols is now offered. Calibers are 9mm and .45 ACP, with differences in grips and finishes. Rails and porting are available on some models.

Some variants of Tisas pistols are now being imported by American Tactical imports. (See ATI)

The experimental STI-QS 7mm pistol looks a bit like a 1911, but uses a special delayed blowback action and fixed barrel.

SIG Sauer's new .380, the P238, is a little pistol based in general design on the 1911. Grip panels on this two-tone specimen are of aluminum.

A new offering from Wilson Combat is the Sentinel pistol, a compact 9mm variant in the company's 1911 line.

Walther's new .380-caliber pistol, the PK380, has a polymer frame and is hammer-fired. This is the "bicolor" version.

Vltor

In the last edition of this publication, Vltor's Fortis pistol was a concept. Vltor Weapon Systems planned to reincarnate the Bren Ten of the early 1980s, a design approved by the late Jeff Cooper. The Bren Ten failed through no fault of the design — the company producing it ran into financial problems.

The Fortis project moved very quickly, and the design became reality. A year later, Vltor displayed a number of working models of the Fortis at the January 2009 SHOT Show. Plans were to be at full production before the end of 2009.

The Fortis can be thought of as an "improved" Bren Ten. Although the Fortis looks, feels and operates like the original design, there is no parts interchangeability. This extends to the magazines, which were a problem with the original Bren Ten. The magazine problem was solved by using magazines designed for EAA's Witness pistols, which have the advantage of proven reliability. A different floorplate is used, however.

The Fortis guns were planned to be offered in a standard 5" two-tone model, and a 4" Special Forces variant. Calibers will be the original 10mm Auto (14 + 1), and .45 ACP (10 + 1).

A lot of people have been hoping for the revival of the Bren Ten design. Want more information? Try www.fortispistol.com.

Volquartsen

Is there room for a new design of precision .22 pistol? Volquartsen thinks so. Their recently-introduced V-10X pistol is CNC-machined from aluminum billet material. The finished pistol can be hard anodized to almost any color the shooter desires. Displayed at the 2009 SHOT Show were prototypes in red and blue.

The grip frame has front finger grooves, matching the contours of the grips. The pistol comes with adjustable sights, and is drilled and tapped for top and bottom rails. A compensator and balance weights will also be available. The pistol uses a 6" barrel internal in the frame, a cylindrical bolt and an adjustable trigger mechanism. It is designed to use Ruger .22 pistol magazines.

The new V-10X was scheduled for Spring 2009 availability.

Walther

Walther already had their splendid PPK pistols in .380 caliber. With all the current interest in that caliber, how would they go about adding a new .380? Why not take the polymer-frame P22 and turn it into a .380?

It wasn't that simple, of course, but the new Walther PK380 is about the same size, and looks much like the earlier .22 pistol. The new .380, like the .22, is hammer-fired. The trigger mechanism is conventional double-action. The pistol has ambidextrous manual safeties on the slide, and ambidextrous magazine releases. Several different variants were offered, with black or nickel slides, and with lasers to fit the integral frame rails.

The new Walther PK380 has a 3.7" barrel, measures 6.2"x5.2", and weighs 19.4 oz. Capacity is 8 + 1.

Wilson

New from Wilson Combat is the Bill Wilson Carry Pistol. The compact 1911-style .45 is patterned after the pistol Wilson himself actually carries. It has a 4" barrel and weighs 35 oz. A noticeable feature is the gently-rounded butt, which gives it a graceful look reminiscent of the nice old Colt pocket automatics of a century ago.

The Sentinel pistol is a 1911 in 9mm chambering, with a 3.6" barrel and short grip. With a lightweight frame, it weighs 27 oz.

Wilson Combat has been fitting some models with their special grooved "G10" grips. The grips have a "sticky" feel that allows the shooter better purchase on the pistol.

Postscript

The year 2010 gives the firearms community a unique opportunity. The Boy Scouts of America (BSA), founded in February 1910, reaches its 100th birthday this year. Shooting has been part of the Boy Scout program ever since BSA's formation. The 2010 National Jamboree will feature 21 different shooting ranges. During 2010, the BSA Centennial, consider supporting their shooting programs. The Jamboree could use Instructors and donations. Local area programs throughout the year can use similar assistance, too. Contact your nearest Boy Scout council office for information.

Author shooting the 7.62
NATO Panther REPR from DPMS.

RIFLES TODAY

BY **JACOB EDSON**

*Jake Edson is Managing Editor of Deer &
Deer Hunting Magazine.*

It's pretty clear which way the rifle market is trending these days. AR-style rifles continue to pour into gun shops, but stores big and small are unable to keep them in stock. This isn't surprising news for many shooters, and yet AR-style rifles weren't immediately accepted by the industry as a whole. For many years, the assault rifle stereotypes lingered — possibly because the gun is still used by so many branches of military, and a large portion of the general public viewed the entire AR-line as synonymous with the M16/M4.

Perhaps now, though, these perceptions are finally changing. Today, the AR is embraced in almost every corner of the shooting industry. Even big game hunters are now reaching for this platform as more and more of us are introduced to it.

If you don't understand the appeal of AR-style rifles you probably have never shot one. Simply put, these guns are a blast to shoot. Plus, the modular design allows endless modification and customization. And now, with even America's largest gunmaker, Remington, offering multiple AR models, the gun seems to have settled firmly into a respected sector of the shooting industry. In fact, the AR really has come full circle, because today's latest trend is to build derivatives of not the AR-15 — which is a .223/5.56 caliber weapon — but its predecessor, the larger-framed AR-10.

Up and down the product lines of most AR manufacturers (and there are now more than 60 manufacturers of AR-style rifles and parts) you can now find an assortment of calibers, from the miniscule 9mm Luger, up to big game hunting calibers such as .243 Win., 7mm-08 Rem., and the original AR-10, the .308 Win.

Larger calibers have even been designed specifically for the platform, including the .450 Bushmaster, .458 SOCOM and .50 Beowulf.

That's not to say all other rifle designs are obsolete. In fact, bolt actions continue to be the favorite among the majority of shooters. In large part, our fascination in turnbolts stems from our love for long-range shooting. And that is precisely where the bolt-action market continues to advance. Tactical and varmint rifles are the fastest growing categories. And surprise, the AR-style guns have influenced this market as well — contributing to current trends toward modular stock designs in many of the newest tactical bolt actions. The other major movement is toward consumer-adjustable triggers. Almost every major bolt-action manufacturer has added a newly revamped trigger to their turnbolt lines.

With that, here's a look at the latest rifles.

If there's a finer production bolt gun made than the Kimber 84M, we're not sure what it might be.

ArmaLite

The AR designation got its start with Eugene Stoner and the Fairchild ArmaLite Corporation more than 50 years ago with the AR-10 .308 rifle. ArmaLite sold its rights to the "AR-10" and "AR-15" names to Colt in 1959, but the "original" AR-10 continues to flourish with its creator. The AR-10T features a free-floated, triple-lapped, stainless steel, match grade barrel. And now, the "T" is also cham-

The Panther
Sportical
by DPMS.

bered in 7mm-08 Rem., .260 Rem., .338 Federal and .243 Win. The rifle is equipped with new lightweight, freefloat handguards and a Picatinny railed upper. Plus, like all of ArmaLite's AR-10 flattop uppers, it is equipped with forward assist.

Barrett

Barrett's new M98B bolt-action rifle is chambered in .338 LM for military and law enforcement applications where a 7.62 NATO or even .300 Win. Mag. might not provide the long range punch necessary for every situation. This long-range tactical rifle features a short-throw bolt design and skeletonized aluminum stock with adjustable comb height and elevation. The modular design allows the user to adapt the rifle to fit their exact needs. The trigger is set at 2.5 lbs. and is shaped for a straight rearward pull. Two nuts prevent the adjustment screws from changing weight with repeated use and can be easily accessed from the top with the receiver broken down. A muzzle brake reduces rise and recoil, which Barrett says is similar to a 20-gauge shotgun. I can believe that, because the rifle weighs 13.5 lbs.!

Benelli

While Benelli's big introduction of 2009 is a shotgun, the company has added to its R1 line of semi-automatic rifles with the R1 Limited Edition. This premium grade R1 rifle is chambered in .30-06. It displays all of the style, balance and attention to detail expected in a fine European hunting rifle — including a highly figured AAA-Grade satin walnut stock and fore-end with 28 line-per-inch, fine-line checkering. The receiver features detailed engraving, gold inlay and highly polished bluing. On the inside, the gun features the R1's clean, efficient A.R.G.O. operating system. However, the Limited is just that, and is only available through Benelli USA World Class Dealers.

Browning

Much like Benelli, Browning's big news for 2009 is an all-new semi-auto shotgun. Yet Browning has added to both its X-Bolt and A-Bolt rifle lines. For a lighter X-Bolt, try the new Micro Hunter with a satin, walnut stock sized for smaller shooters and shorter 20- and 22-inch barrels. The Micro Hunter is available in .22-50 Rem., .243 Win., 7mm-08 Rem., .308 Win., 270 WSM, 7mm WSM, 300 WSM and 325 WSM. It weighs in at 5 lbs., 6 oz., with the Super Short Action receiver and 6 lbs., 7 oz. in Short Action models. The X-Bolt Varmint Stalker goes the other way. It is features a medium-heavy barrel in four classic varmint calibers — .223 Rem., .22-250 Rem., 243 Win., and .308 Win. — with 24" or 26" barrels. The Varmint Stalker weighs about 8 lbs. All the X-Bolt models have a glass bedded and free-floating barrel. They feature the four-screw-per-base X-Lock scope mounting system, Inflex recoil pad and a bolt unlock button to allow the chamber to be opened

Browning's X-Bolt Micro is a trim, snappy little rifle.

with the safety in the on position. This year also finds Super-Short Actions available on the standard X-Bolt models chambered in .223 Rem., and .22-250 Rem.

The already-expansive A-Bolt line gets two additions, the A-Bolt Target and Target Stainless. Both feature a new target-style stock with adjustable comb and a wide, flat fore-end. Both Target models are available in .223 Rem., .308 Win., and 300 WSM.

The BAR line gets a makeover, too, with a handsome new satin nickel finish and Grade II walnut stocks. These new BARs offer a near custom shop look with the same BAR action shooters have come to expect. In addition, 7mm-08 Rem., and .325 WSM have been added to the BAR caliber options.

Finally, the T-Bolt line of rimfire rifles gets the addition of left-hand models across the board. Improvements in materials and design have Browning promising greater accuracy and smoother operation, while the rifles still feature the popular rotary 10-round Double Helix magazine and an adjustable trigger. Lots of fun on the range.

Bushmaster

Bushmaster features a dizzying array of AR-15 rifles, each model with slightly different components. However, two new models are quite noteworthy. The first is the Bushmaster .450. This rifle is chambered for the new Bushmaster .450 round, developed in affiliation with Hornady. The big bore load is tamed by a tweaked AR-type gas impingement operating system and Izzy muzzle brake. The cartridge is adapted from a 6.5mm case with the necking cut off to accommodate a 250-grain Hornady SST FlexTip .450 caliber bullet. The five-round AR-style magazine is fitted with a single stack follower to allow for the diameter of the cartridge. Bullet velocity is reported at 2,200 fps. The chromoly steel barrels are rifled with a 1:24 twist to get the heavy bullet spinning.

The Bushmaster O.R.C. (Optics Ready Carbine) was developed because most sporting AR shooters will want to stick a scope on their pet rifles. Of course, add-on iron sights can be attached to the upper and milled gas block, but the flattop is optics ready right out of the box. Meanwhile, the 16" barrel is chrome-lined in both the bore and chamber to provide accuracy, durability and maintenance ease. The six-position telescoping stock reduces overall length by 4 inches when compressed.

The Bushmaster BA50 rifle is designed for military, law enforcement and recreational shooters who asked Bushmaster for a highly-accurate, low-recoil .50 BMG rifle. The bolt-action gun is designed to remain familiar to AR fans. It features lower and upper receivers machined from aluminum and a manganese phosphate finish. The Bushmaster barrel is free floated within a vented forend. The high-efficiency recoil-reducing brake limits felt recoil.

Finally comes Bushmaster's exclusive license deal with Magpul Industries for the production, future development and sales of Magpul's Masada weapon system. Renamed the Bushmaster ACR (Adaptive Combat Rifle), this weapon is one of the most anticipated releases of the year. At press time only a handful of ACRs were available for viewing, but the product is slowly coming online for military, law enforcement and civilian shooters. It will initially be offered in 5.56 NATO, but the key feature of this weapon system is its tool-less adaptability to a variety of calibers.

Basically, the Bushmaster ACR keeps the fundamentals of the Masada concept, such as the gas piston operating system, tool-less, quick change barrel and relocated charging handle and adds features such as a firing pin block and true ambidextrous controls. For those unfamiliar with the Masada prototypes, the weapon system is a combination of many rifle designs, incorporating a short-stroke gas system similar to the AR-18, the upper receiver charging handle location of the FN SCAR and the liberal use of polymer components popularized by Heckler & Koch. It maintains the M16 or AR15 trigger pack and barrel, while the quick-change barrel, adjustable gas regulator and charging handle, integral flip-up front sight, and storage compartments located in the stock are Magpul innovations. The first ACRs will be offered with 12.5", 16" and 18" barrels and three stock configurations. The 7.62×39mm conversion kits are promised but not yet in production.

Chapparal

Chapparal Arms Co. is already known for its high quality reproductions, including a beautiful Winchester Model 1873. But now the company is reproducing possibly the most popular rifle of all time, the venerable Winchester 1894. These high-quality '94s are available in .44 Rem. Mag, 44/40 WCF, .45 Colt, .30/30 WCF and .410 ga. The accurate reproductions feature high-grade wood and rich bluing. Each rifle is sold in a carefully designed nylon carry-case.

Charles Daly

To complement its line of 1892 lever action standard and take down models, Charles Daly has added the 1892 Lever Action Large Loop carbine in .45 Colt. The rifle features a 20" barrel, walnut stock and saddle ring. Although this gun is a reproduction of the 1892 factory rifle, it features modern CNC machining and a carefully designed over-sized lever loop.

CZ USA

Brno Rifles is the newest brand in the CZ-USA family. It brings a high-end line of fixed-breech firearms from a well-known plant in Brno, Czech Republic, to the growing CZ family of firearms. The Brno Stopper is an over/under double rifle chambered in .458 Win. Mag. It features a select-grade walnut stock, elegant checkering and a semi-Schnabel fore-end. It offers a single mechanical trigger, short radius iron sights for fast shooting, and a barrel mounted sling attachment point.

The Brno Effect single-shot rifle weighs only 6 lbs. and features select walnut, a single set trigger, automatic safety, iron sights and includes scope bases. It is chambered in .30-06.

The Brno Combo gun is a great companion for predator calling or mixed bag hunts. The gun features 23-1/2" barrels: A 12-gauge, 3" magnum with Improved Modified choke sits over your choice of .243 Win., .308 Win., or .30-06. Features include an automatic safety, extractors, barrel mounted sling attachment and quarter rib iron sights. The shotgun barrel is fired with the rear trigger, while the front trigger includes a set function for precision shooting with the rifle barrel.

DPMS

DPMS Panther Arms follows the trend of offering multiple AR platforms in a variety of calibers. The Panther REPR comes with an 18" fluted, chrome-moly steel REPR contour barrel with 1:10 twist. The gun is chambered in 7.62 NATO and comes with a phosphated steel bolt and carrier that is heat-treated. The flattop receiver is thick walled and hard coated, with dust cover, shell deflector and forward assist machined as one unit. It comes with a Magpul Precision Rifle Stock in Coyote Brown and a Micro Gas Block. The rifle weighs 9.5 lbs. empty.

The popular Panther Sportical is also now offered in a 7.62 NATO configuration with 16" chrome-moly steel heavy barrel and A2 flash hider. The upper features a snag-free design and smooth-side look with no dust cover, shell deflector or forward assist. The raised Picatinny rail makes for easy optics mounting. It weighs 8.3 lbs.

FNH USA

FNH USA is now offering a full line of SPR bolt-action tactical precision rifles. The A3 G is chambered in .308 Winchester and offers controlled round feed, blade ejection, a two-lever trigger and a three-position safety. The 24" cold hammer-forged barrel is fluted, with a hard-chromed bore and is held to +/- .001" headspace to produce sub-1/2-MOA accuracy.

The FN A1 and A2 rifles are based on the Winchester Model 70 action. They offer massive external claw extractors for reliable ejection. A variety of barrel lengths and designs are available. The one-piece steel MIL-STD 1913 optical rail with an additional 20 MOA of elevation is factory-installed.

The PSR I rifle features the same rail, but also comes with a three-lever trigger that works on the simple principle of a pivoting lever. The trigger has a pull weight range from 3 to 5 lbs. and is factory set to 3-3/4 lbs.

The FNAR Standard and Heavy are based on the legendary BAR. The Standard is chambered in .308 Win., and offers an ambidextrous magazine release with a 20" cold hammer-forged fluted barrel. The gun features a one-piece, receiver-mounted MIL-STD 1913 optical rail. The pistol grip tactical stock is adjustable for comb height, cast on or cast off and length of pull.

Civilian shooters can now experience the versatility of FN's SCAR with the civilian-legal semi-auto versions of the U.S. Special Operations Command's newest service rifles. The SCAR 16S is chambered in 5.56 NATO, while the SCAR 17S fires the 7.62 NATO cartridge. Both feature the gas-operated, short stroke piston system for reduced fouling and user-interchangeable, free floating barrels. Fully–ambidextrous operating controls are intuitively placed and three accessory rails enable mounting of a wide variety of tactical lights and lasers. The side-folding polymer stock is fully adjustable for comb height and length of pull.

Harrington & Richardson

H&R Handi-Rifles offers accurate, affordable, single-shot rifles in a range of calibers all the way up to .500 S&W. The smaller-framed Compact Handi-Rifle is available in .223 Rem., .243 Win., and 7mm-08 Rem. Plus, the new Handi-Rifles in .44 and .357 Mag. are also available in versatile combo gun packages. Choose from a .44 Magnum/12-gauge slug gun combo or a .357 Mag/20-gauge slug gun combo. Each of these single-shot break-action combo rifles comes with two barrels that can be interchanged on the fly.

Heckler & Koch

The MR556 rifle is a descendent of the HK416 in a semi-automatic civilian version. It fires 5.56 NATO cartridges using the same HK gas piston system found on the HK416. The rifle is being produced at HK's brand new manufacturing facility in Newington, New Hampshire. It features a free-floating four-quadrant rail system/handguard, adjustable buttstock and 10-round magazine. The rifle weighs 8.6 pounds empty and offers a high-quality HK cold hammer forged barrel with a 1:7 twist.

Kimber

The Model 84M is known for its light weight and accuracy. Now, the 84M Classic Stainless is available in .243 Win., 7mm-08 Rem. And .308 Win. Each rifle features a stainless barreled action in a classic walnut stock. In addition, the Model 84M Montana is now available in .204 Ruger and .223 Rem.

The Benelli RI Limited semi-auto is almost too pretty to take out in the field.

Today's classy Browning BAR LongTrac Grade II is a far cry from the original BAR.

Browning X-Bolt Varmint.

Southpaws who are interested in a straight-pull rimfire bolt rifle should take a look at Browning's T-Bolt Left Hand Varmint.

For those who think the M1892 was the sweetest, best-designed pistol-caliber lever carbine ever designed (and many do), the Charles Daly Large Loop in .45 Colt has a lot going for it.

Remington's ultra-funky, all-business Model 700 Target Tactical.

One of the most powerful lever-actions ever produced: the Marlin 1895 MXLR in .338 Marlin Express.

The short-action Marlin XS7 bolt gun.

Mossberg's wood-stocked 4x4 now has the LBA trigger. So does the synthetic version, by the way.

Mossberg's Model 817 Varmint in .17 HMR is a serious, purpose-built small game and varmint rifle.

The new Model 8400 Police Tactical is chambered in .300 Win. Mag., and Kimber is adding several new chamberings to its lines, including .280 Ackley Improved in the Model 8400 Classic Select and Montana models; 7mm Rem. Mag., in the 8400 Classic and Sonora; and .270 Win., and .30-06 Sprg., in the 8400 SuperAmerica.

Legacy Sports International

Legacy Sports is the importer of several new hunting and target rifles. First, the Howa line expands with the Ranchland Full Camo Combo. This package starts with a Howa M-1500 rifle and a Nikko Stirling 3-10x42mm riflescope and a high-quality one-piece base. All of this wears the same King's Desert Shadow camo pattern. The M-1500 features a Hogue OverMolded stock, and shooters can choose from six calibers from .223 Rem. to .308 Win.

The Puma line is new to many U.S. shooters but offers great shootability and good value. The Puma .22 LR is only 33.5" long and features a 16" barrel. It is available with wood or synthetic stock and comes with a 50-round drum magazine for extended shooting sessions. Of course, a 10-round stick magazine is available for use in areas with magazine capacity restrictions. This rimfire is a blast to shoot and is made in by Pietta of Italy. *[Editor's Note: It's nice to see this PPSh-styled fun-gun back in production after several years' absence. Originals have become quite collectible in some circles. – DMS]*

The Puma line also includes a variety of lever-action centerfires made by Chiappa Firearms. The M-92 is offered with 20" or 24-1/4" octagonal barrels and 16" or 20" round barrels. Available calibers include .357 Mag., .44 Mag., .44/40 and .45 Colt. The M-86 is available in .45-70 Gov't and is available in 26" rifle and 22" carbine versions.

Marlin

The Marlin XL7 series of bolt-action rifles has received plenty of acclaim, and now Marlin announces the XS7 short action series of bolt-action rifles. The XS7 series is offered in three classic short action hunting calibers: .243 Win., 7mm-08 Rem., and .308 Win. The rifle comes in composite stock versions in standard black, compact black (with a shorter length of pull) and Realtree APG HD. The XS7 series exhibits all the proven features of the XL7, including are an accuracy enhancing Pro–Fire trigger system; Soft–Tech recoil pad; raised cheek piece; precision button rifled barrel with target-style recessed muzzle crown; fluted bolt; pillar bedded stock; and barrel nut construction to ensure proper headspace for improved accuracy.

The original XL7 also gets a bit of a makeover with more options, including attractive American walnut and brown laminated hardwood stock versions.

This year, Marlin is taking the guide rifle to the extreme with the introduction of the Model 1895SBL. The new 1895SBL is chambered for the legendary .45-70 Govt., and is built to handle the worst weather with a stainless steel barrel, receiver, trigger guard plate, loading gate and enlarged loop lever. Other distinguishing features include a weather-impervious laminated stock, heavy 18-1/2" barrel and six-shot tubular magazine. The 1895SBL features the XS Ghost Ring Sight System. It also comes standard with a XS lever rail that provides a rock-solid mounting platform for a variety of optics.

The popular Marlin Model 925 rimfire expands to include a .22 Win. Mag. It features a 22" Micro-Groove rifled barrel and a black synthetic stock with molded-in checkering and swivel studs. The T-900 Fire Control System, standard on most Marlin bolt-action rimfire rifles, enhances accuracy for target shooting or small game hunting.

Finally, Marlin announces two new lever action rifles chambered for the new .338 Marlin Express. This round is the latest offering in the Marlin Express family of cartridges and drives a 200-gr. bullet at 2,565 fps from a 24" barrel. The 338MXLR features a 24" stainless steel barrel, full pistol grip and black/grey, two-tone laminated stock. The 338MX version is designed for hunters who prefer traditional blued rifles. It features a 22" barrel and walnut stock.

Mossberg

Mossberg's big news is the new Lightning Bolt Action Trigger System for its centerfire bolt-action rifles. The LBA gives the shooter the flexibility to adjust the trigger pull without taking the rifle to a gunsmith. A simple twist of a standard screwdriver can adjust the trigger from 2 to 7 lbs. The design of the LBA trigger's sear engagement offers a crisp, creep-free trigger pull, while the trigger blade blocks the sear from releasing the striker unless the blade is fully depressed. The trigger is available on the full line of 4x4 and 100ATR bolt-action rifles.

The 4x4 line receives an additional upgrade with the availability of a "classic" stock. New 4X4 Classic models feature walnut, laminate and synthetic polymer stocks, each featuring Monte Carlo-style cheek pieces, slim-line grips, and soft, recoil absorbing buttpads. A detachable box magazine, smooth, quick-handling bolt, free-floating, 22" button-rifled barrel, and factory-installed Weaver-style scope bases round out the features.

The 100ATR line's newest member is the Night Train II. The model features the LBA trigger, a free-floating 22" button-rifled barrel, plus a factory-mounted Barska 6-24x60mm scope, muzzlebrake, Harris bipod and neoprene comb raising kit with foam cheek pad inserts. The integral top-load magazine offers a 4+1 capacity in .308 Win.

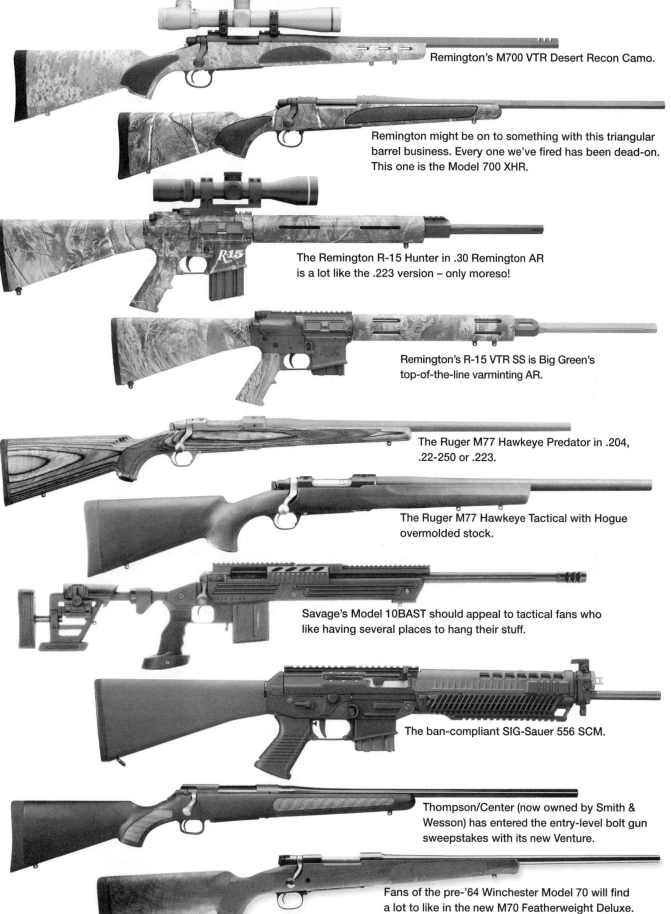

Remington's M700 VTR Desert Recon Camo.

Remington might be on to something with this triangular barrel business. Every one we've fired has been dead-on. This one is the Model 700 XHR.

The Remington R-15 Hunter in .30 Remington AR is a lot like the .223 version – only moreso!

Remington's R-15 VTR SS is Big Green's top-of-the-line varminting AR.

The Ruger M77 Hawkeye Predator in .204, .22-250 or .223.

The Ruger M77 Hawkeye Tactical with Hogue overmolded stock.

Savage's Model 10BAST should appeal to tactical fans who like having several places to hang their stuff.

The ban-compliant SIG-Sauer 556 SCM.

Thompson/Center (now owned by Smith & Wesson) has entered the entry-level bolt gun sweepstakes with its new Venture.

Fans of the pre-'64 Winchester Model 70 will find a lot to like in the new M70 Featherweight Deluxe.

Mossberg also expands its line of 464 lever-action rifles with a 464 Pistol Grip model in .30-30 Win. The design centers on improved accuracy, performance and value. The new pistol-gripped 464 lever-action features diamond patterned cut checkering on the pistol grip and forearm for a stylish look and an easy grip in the field.

For rimfire fans, the all-new 817 Varmint combines the sleek style and handling of the standard 817 bolt-action with a bull barrel. Chambered in .17 HMR caliber, the action rests in a tough black synthetic stock and features a 21" free-floating barrel, recessed muzzle crown and factory-installed Weaver-style scope bases.

Another rimfire is aimed specifically at young shooters. The 801 Half Pint from Mossberg International is small, affordable and a perfect starter gun. This .22 LR has a 12-1/4" length of pull and 16" barrel. It weighs only 4 lbs. As the young shooter becomes more familiar with the gun, and more experienced, the removable single-shot magazine plug can be replaced with an optional 10-shot magazine.

Remington

Big Green made a huge splash last year with its entry into AR market. This year, the company continues to follow the market trend with the release of its own larger-caliber AR, the R-25. This rifle features a flattop upper, Picatinny gas block and fluted barrel with recessed hunting crown. The traditional two-stage trigger found on most AR rifles has been exchanged for a crisp, single-stage version that comes factory set at about 5 lbs. The rifle is available in .243 Win., 7mm-08 Rem., and .308 Win. It is compatible with all DPMS .308 Win.-type magazines. If this rifle doesn't legitimize the AR platform as a real big game hunting option, I don't know what will.

Of course, with the ease in adaptability of the AR platform, Remington fans also shouldn't be surprised that the company has added a few new models to the R-15 line. Most notable is the R-15 Hunter chambered for the brand new .30 Remington AR round. The rifle is similar to past R-15s but is chambered for the first .30 caliber round specifically produced to fit in an AR-15-sized upper. Remington reports big game hunting ballistics out past 200 yards, and the rifle I was able to test fire had little more kick than a standard .223 Rem.

The R-15 VTR SS Varmint features a 24" stainless barrel with the patent-pending Remington triangular barrel contour. The innovative barrel is meant to deliver repeat-shot accuracy of traditional heavy barrels without the weight. The R-15VTR Thumbhole features the maneuverability and rock-solid stability of a Bell & Carlson thumbhole stock. It has a 24" olive drab barrel that is fluted and features a recessed hunting crown.

Of course, the expansive 700 line also gets some new additions. First off, every rifle in the line gets the new X-Mark Pro adjustable trigger. This crisp, clean trigger comes factory set at 3.5 lbs. but is user adjustable with a 2-lb. range.

The Model 700 XHR brings the revolutionary triangular barrel contour from the varmint/target field to the big game realm. The barrel design shaves weight while maintaining the rigidity of a traditional heavy barrel. Plus the surface area facilitates rapid cooling for more accurate follow-up shots. The XHR is available in nine calibers from .243 Win. to 300 Rem. Ultra Mag.

The same barrel and trigger also find their way onto the new Model 700 Target Tactical. This rifle comes in .308 Win., and features a Bell & Carlson Medalist stock with adjustable comb and length of pull. The 5-R hammer-forged tactical target rifling is based on M-24 rifling for extreme accuracy.

Two new Remington varmint rifles are available. The Model 700 VTR Desert Recon offers the same features as the 700 VTR with the addition of Digital Desert camo. Meanwhile, the 700 Varmint SF comes with a 26" heavy-contour barrel that is fluted for weight reduction and rapid cooling. The concave dish crown protects the rifling and promotes the best possible bullet flight.

Lefties get another option with the Model 700 SPS Synthetic in .270 Win., .30-06, 7mm Rem. Mag., and 300 Win. Mag.

Rock River Arms

Rock River Arms is also producing a wide range of AR-style rifles in multiple calibers. Its standard LAR 15 rifles are chambered in the .223 Wylde chamber, which was designed as a match chambering for semi-automatic rifles. It will accommodate both .223 Rem. and 5.56mm NATO ammunition. It is relieved in the case body to aid in extraction and features a shorter throat for improved accuracy. Other available chamberings are the LAR-458 in .458 SOCOM, the LAR-6.8 in 6.8 SPC, the LAR-8 in .308/7.62 and the LAR-9 in 9mm Luger. I expect the LAR-8 Varmint A4 to be a hot-seller among sportsmen. It features a 26" stainless bull barrel with 1:10 twist and weighs in at 11.6 lbs. The rifle promises 1 MOA accuracy at 100 yards.

Rossi

Rossi Firearms introduces its newest version of the Trifecta youth gun system. The system originally included easily interchangeable .243 Win. .22 LR and 20-gauge barrels. Now, Rossi offers more versatility and knock-down power with the option of choosing either a .243 Win., or .44 Magnum barrel. The Trifecta system features a removable cheek piece to gain the proper fit with each barrel option. Remove the cheek piece when using the 20-gauge shotgun barrel for proper alignment of the front-bead sight. With the cheek pad in place, the stock is perfect for using the .22 LR or either of the centerfire barrels with a scope. Both centerfire rifle barrels include a scope mount base that accepts any standard Weaver-style rings. The set also includes a hammer extension, custom carrying case and all-purpose strap. This year, the Trifecta is available in three laminate stock colors: green/brown, pink/black and gray/black.

Ruger

Sturm, Ruger has added several models to two of its most popular lines. Perhaps the most striking are three M77 Hawkeye Predator rifles in .223 Rem., .22-250 Rem. and .204 Ruger calibers. They feature green and brown laminate stocks and matte stainless barrels and receivers. The .223 Rem. features a 26" barrel, while the .22-250 Rem. and .204 Ruger rifles come with 24" barrels. The Ruger two-stage target trigger, designed for precise shot placement, and the full-length medium weight barrels deliver long-range accuracy.

Ruger also announces the introduction of an M77 Hawkeye Tactical rifle. These bolt-action rifles, available in .223 Rem., .243 Win., and .308 Win., feature Hogue OverMolded synthetic stocks, alloy steel barrels, and receivers in the Hawkeye Matte Blue finish. They feature the Ruger two-stage target trigger and 20" heavy barrels. The rifles weigh 8.75 lbs. and are shipped with a Harris bipod.

The third addition to the line is the M77 Hawkeye Compact rifle. These 16-1/2"-barreled rifles have an overall length of 35-1/2 inches, and are ideal for heavy brush. The Hawkeye Compact rifles are available in a Hawkeye Matte Blued with an America walnut stock or the Hawkeye Matte Stainless model with a black laminate stock. The rifles are offered in eight short action calibers, including .300 RCM, 7.62x39 and 6.8SPC. The walnut and blued models weigh approximately 5.75 lbs., while their laminate and stainless counterparts average 6.25 lbs. each. They feature the smooth and crisp Ruger LC6 trigger, Mauser-type controlled feeding and a powerful claw extractor.

Ruger has also added models of the Mini-14 Ranch Rifle and Mini-14 Tactical Rifle. The blued 16-1/8"-barreled ATI Mini-14 comes equipped with a six-position collapsible/side folding buttstock. The stock features an adjustable cheekrest, a rubber buttpad, four picatinny rails, storage for batteries inside the stock tube, and six sling swivel stud mounting locations. The stock folds to the left side of receiver and the rifle can be fired from the folded position. The ATI Mini-14 weighs about 8 lbs. and has an overall length of 37-3/4" with the stock extended.

The Mini-14 Tactical Rifle features a 16-1/8" blued

alloy steel barrel with flash suppressor, black synthetic stock, and is shipped with one 20-round magazine. It weighs approximately 6.75 lbs.

Sako

The new A7 from Sako boasts a bolt body machined from a solid piece of forged steel for superior strength and a smooth throw. The A7 features a lightweight composite stock with unique textured wave patterns for a sure grip in any weather. The barrel is cold-hammer forged with a hand-cut crown. The single-stage trigger system is crisp and precise, adjustable from 2 to 4 lbs. The A7 is available in 12 calibers and features a two-position safety with bolt-lock release. It comes with scope mount bases and features a detachable synthetic magazine with steel feed lips. It's a sharp-looking rifle.

Savage

Savage is rolling out several new tactical-style bolt-action rifles, headlined by the new modular sniper system in the Model 10 BAS. These rifles are based on the long-established 110 action but are built on a modular aluminum chassis that features the same three-dimensional bedding system included in the company's new Accu-Stock. But unlike the standard AccuStock, this system accepts most AR-style buttstocks and pistol grips, allowing the user to customize his bolt rifle – a tasty touch that will appeal to those accustomed to the feel of black guns. The 10 BAS will come in two configurations, the BAS with a M4-style buttstock and the BAS/T with a target-style, multi-adjustable buttstock that borrows from Savage's Model 12 Palma target rifle. Other features include the Savage AccuTrigger, a 10-round detachable magazine, a 24" free-floating, fluted heavy barrel, a proprietary Savage muzzle brake, and an oversized bolt handle.

Savage also announces two new Model 10 precision law enforcement rifles with the standard AccuStock. This stock uses an aluminum spine and 3D bedding cradle molded into polymer composite, giving it many of the same properties of high-end aftermarket stocks. The Model 10 FCP features a 24" heavy, fluted barrel, matte finish and is available in .308 Win. and .223 Rem. Calibers. The Model 10 Precision Carbine comes in Digital Green camo and features a 20-inch medium-contour barrel.

Savage is also expanding its successful line of camouflage package guns with the addition of snow camo. The rifles will include full-coverage Realtree Hardwoods Snow camo on the stock, barrel, action, bases, rings and scope. The new additions include the Model 93 R17 XP Camo in .17 HMR and Model XP Predator Package in all current calibers, plus the addition of .243 Win.

SIG Sauer

SIG Sauer introduces the new SIG556 Classic semi-automatic rifle (chambered in – you guessed it! – 5.56) with an adjustable stock that snaps into a folded position and features an adjustable length of pull. The redesigned trigger housing improves access to the controls. The Classic is also available with a new diopter sighting system. The rear rotary diopter sight utilizes aperture calibrations from close-quarter ranges out to 100, 200 and 300 meters. Another new option is the SIG SCM. It features a fixed A2-style stock, 16" barrel with crowned muzzle, and it ships with a "pre-1994 ban" 10-round magazine.

Smith & Wesson

Smith & Wesson jumped into the long-gun market with both feet with its I-bolt. The gun features a T/C Precision barrel, three-position linear safety and X-bed stock and comes with a Weaver-style scope mount Posi-Lug system that locks the mount to the receiver for a stable optics platform. The I-bolt also features the Tru-Set trigger, which is adjustable from 3 to 6 lbs. I-bolts are available in .25-06 Rem., .270 Win., and .30-06 in black synthetic or Realtree AP HD. They also feature the advanced Weather Shield corrosion protection system.

New this year, Smith & Wesson also adapted its M&P15 to the Soviet 5.45x39 cartridge. The rifle looks the same as a standard M&P15, but internally, it's a new rifle with a new bolt to accept the differing rim diameter of the 5.45 cartridge. The barrel is also customized to .221" with a 1:8-1/2 turn. It is clearly marked "5.45x39mm" to avoid any confusion with standard 5.56 NATO barrels. The magazine is also 5.45 specific. So what's the point of all this, considering the 5.45 isn't all that much different, ballistically speaking, from the 5.56 NATO round? In one word: economy. Surplus 5.45 ammunition can be had at almost half the price of 5.56 NATO rounds and even the high-end stuff is substantially less expensive, if you know where to shop.

Stag Arms

Stag Arms' follows the trend of offering a larger bore AR style rifle with its Stag 7 in 6.8 SPC. This rifle features a 20.77" stainless steel barrel, A3-style flattop upper, two-stage trigger and Hogue grip. Designed for sporting use, it comes with a five-round magazine. Like the rest of the Stag Arms line, it is available in a true left-hand model.

Steyr Arms

The STEYR SSG 08 is designed for sport shooting and tactical defense. It features an aluminum folding, adjustable cheek piece and butt plate with height marking, and an ergonomical, exchangeable pistol grip. Additional features include a Versa-Pod, muzzle brake, a Picatinny rail, UIT rail on the stock and various picatinny rails on the forend.

Thompson/Center

Thompson/Center has introduced a new bolt gun called the Venture. Whereas the company's Icon is what we might call a top-shelf gun, the Venture is designed to deliver top-end accuracy at an entry-level price. It offers a 5R rifled match-grade barrel and match grade crown, adjustable precision trigger and a classic style composite stock. The rifle is guaranteed to deliver minute of angle accuracy at a reasonable price point. The venture is available in .270 Win., 7mm Rem. Mag., .30-06, and 300 Win. Mag.

Weatherby

The biggest news from Weatherby is in the rimfire market. The Mark XXII is now available in .22LR and .17 HMR. It features an eight-groove, target grade, button-rifled barrel, built to exact Olympic competition specifications. The fully adjustable single stage trigger allows for precise adjustment from 2 to 4.4 lbs. A raised comb Monte Carlo walnut stock is precision cut checkered, and the gun features a quick release magazine.

Meanwhile, the new Mark XXII SA was created in cooperation with Magnum Research to offer a semi-automatic rimfire that can boast the accuracy of a bolt-action. This rifle is also available in both .22 LR and .17 HMR. It features a newly designed bolt for more accurate firing pin placement, a quick-release rotary magazine, a hand-tuned trigger and a

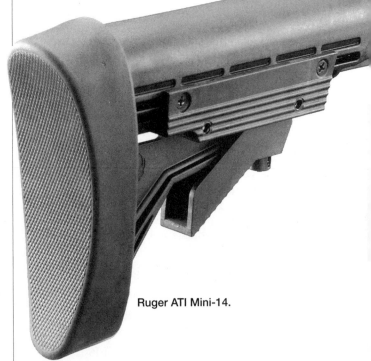

Ruger ATI Mini-14.

20" contoured button-rifled barrel. The chamber is tighter and has a shorter tapered throat to perfectly center the bullet in the rifling prior to firing for enhanced accuracy. Another innovation is the rear cleaning port, which allows easy cleaning of the chamber and barrel.

The Vanguard line gets two new models with the Vanguard Predator and Vanguard Carbine. The Predator features a factory-tuned, fully adjustable trigger, injection molded composite stock, low density recoil pad and a complete Natural Gear camo finish. It is available in .223 Rem., .22-250 Rem., and .308 Win. The Vanguard Carbine weighs just 6.75 lbs. and features a 20" barrel. It is available in .223 Rem., .22-250 Rem., .243 Win., 7mm-08 Rem., and .308 Win.

Winchester

The Model 70 is back — and in a big way. Winchester Repeating Arms is offering the famous M70 in six new configurations.

Each Model 70 features the M.O.A. Trigger System, operating on a simple pivoting lever principle. This trigger mechanism has been completely redesigned to exhibit zero take up, zero creep and zero overtravel. The pull weight ranges from 3 to 5 lbs. and is factory-set at 3-34. Of course the Model 70 still features an improved three-position safety, hammer-forged barrels and the classic blade-type ejector.

The Super Grade is available in five calibers and features a fancy grade walnut stock, one-piece bottom trigger guard and flush-mount hinged floorplate. The Extreme Weather SS features a Bell and Carlson composite stock, free-floating fluted stainless barrel and is available in 11 calibers. The Coyote Light features a medium-heavy fluted stainless barrel that is mounted in a skeletonized aluminum bedding block set in a lightweight carbon fiber composite stock. It is available in six short action and WSM calibers. The Model 70 Featherweight and Sporter models both feature satin finished walnut stocks, controlled round feeding, bedded actions and free-floating barrels along with Pachmayer Decelerator recoil pads. The Featherweight has a schnabel fore-end, and is available in 14 calibers from .22-250 Win. to .338 Win. Mag. The Sporter offers a sculpted cheeckpiece and comes in 10 calibers. Finally, the Ultimate Shadow comes with a lightweight rubberized composite stock. It features WinSorb recoil pad and weighs just 6.5 lbs. It's available in nine popular calibers.

Hunters and collectors will also be interested in Winchester Theodore Roosevelt Safari Centennial Model 1895 lever rifles. Both a Custom Grade and High Grade model feature intricate engraving and are chambered in .405 Win. This is a limited run with only 1,000 Custom Grade rifles and 1,500 High Grades available.

The caliber- convertible Bushmaster ACR (Adaptive Combat Rifle).

SHOTGUNS TODAY

Gail Haviland is posing with her Remington 11-87 Sportsman Turkey with the ShurShot stock she used to take her spring gobbler.

BY JOHN HAVILAND

The nearly incalculable number of shotgun brands and models makes a person wonder who shoots all these guns and where. But it comes into focus when you consider all the target games and bird and big game hunting done with shotguns. During the last year I used shotguns to shoot sporting clays and trap and hunt southern bobwhite quail, grouse on mountain ridges, pheasants on the plains and waterfowl in the muck and mud. Let's see what new guns are out there for all that shooting and more.

Benelli

Benelli is making a 12- and 20-gauge set of limited edition guns based on its Legacy autoloader. The World Class Curator 12- and 20-gauges are limited to 250 specially numbered sets. The guns have AAA-grade walnut stocks and forearms with a satin finish and checkering of 28 lines per inch. A sterling silver medallion that can be custom engraved is set into the grip cap. Matched walnut butt plates are standard and rubber recoil pads are included.

The left side of the Curator's lower receiver is engraved with scrollwork and a medallion portraying a pair of chukar partridges set against a gold-overlaid mountain landscape. Below, floral engraving and cinquefoils frame an engraving of a bounding hare. On the right hand face, the gold details a rising ring-necked pheasant and a landing mallard duck.

The 12- and 20-gauge guns have 26" barrels and identical stock dimensions, but the 12 weighs 7.3 lbs. and the 20 six lbs.

Benelli is celebrating the sale of its two millionth shotgun with 200 World Class BiMIllionaire shotguns each in 12 and 20 gauge. Each gun in this limited release is specially numbered on the bottom of the receiver. The BiMillionaire is stocked in AAA-Grade walnut with a satin finish and the grip and forearm checkered 28 lines per inch. The BiMillionaire comes with a sterling silver medallion that can be custom engraved and set into the grip cap.

The gun's two-tone receiver is covered with floral scrollwork engraving that surrounds gold-accented game scenes. The left face of the receiver features a duck in flight and the right side displays the Spinone Italiano, northern Italy's classic gun dog. A half rosette with entwined gold overlay and shaded background accents both sides of the BiMillionaire's receiver base. The 12- and 20-gauge guns have 26" barrels and identical stock dimensions, but the 12 weighs 7.3 lbs. and the 20 six lbs.

Browning

The Maxus has replaced Browning's Gold autoloading shotgun. The Maxus has several new features and a gas system that fouls less to keep the gun shooting longer before cleaning.

The Power Drive Gas System on the Maxus features a gas piston with large exhaust ports to quickly bleed powder gases from heavy loads to soften recoil. The piston has a 20 percent longer stroke than other systems to reliably cycle light loads down to 1-1/8 oz. target shells. A rubber seal inside the gas piston keeps powder residue out of the action for cleaner operation. Recoil is further dampened with an Inflex Technology recoil pad. The pad is designed with materials with "directional deflection" to pull the comb down and away from the shooter's face.

The Lightning Trigger System on the Maxus produces a trigger with a light pull and a minimum of travel. Locktime averages .0052 seconds. The trigger assembly is also easily removed for cleaning. The safety button is set for right-handed shooters, but it is simple to reverse for left-hand use.

The Speed Lock Forearm uses a lever to lock and remove the forearm, eliminating the traditional screw-on cap. With the forearm removed, the plug in the tube magazine can be removed in a few seconds by using the Turnkey Magazine Plug that works with any vehicle or house key. The Speed Load Plus system takes the first shell fed into the magazine and runs it into the chamber. The Maxus also has a magazine cut-off that allows you to remove the duck shell in the chamber and replace it with a goose load when a goose is flying into range. *[Editor's note: It's nice to see that these features, once standard on the old Browning Auto-5, have found a home in the new Maxus. – DMS]* The magazine cutoff's best benefit is that the chamber can quickly be unloaded to safely cross the untold numbers of fences and ditches a hunter meets during a day afield. Pushing a latch quickly unloads all the shells

Browning Maxus Stalker

in the magazine.

For now, Browning offers its Maxus in 12-gauge in 3" and 3-1/2" inch models. The receiver is aluminum and the barrel has a lightweight profile with flat ventilated rib. The composite stock has a close radius pistol grip with molded textured gripping and Browning's Dura-Touch Armor Coating for a sure grip in all weather conditions. All that adds up to a weight of 6-7/8 pounds.

Surely we will soon see walnut stocked upland, target and deer models.

The Browning Citori 625 over/under line has been expanded to include the 20- and 28-gauge and .410 in Field and Sporting models. The Citori 625 Feather Field has an aluminum receiver that reduces the weight of the 12-gauge Field by ¾ of a pound, to just under seven lbs. The Feather Field in 20-gauge weighs 5-1/2 lbs. All Feather Fields feature an engraved receiver. Forearms wear a Schnabel tip and stocks have a tight radius grip.

The Silver Sporting autoloading has a stock that can easily be adjusted up to 3/4" longer with three 1/4" spacers that fit between the stock and the Decelerator recoil pad.

I hunted with a similar Silver Hunter 20-gauge last fall to shoot mountain grouse and ducks. At 6 lbs., 5 oz., the Hunter was a light carry after blue grouse on the high ridges of grass and sparse stands of Douglas firs. The gun traced the steep downward pitch of the grouse when they flushed and an ounce of 6s tumbled them. In December's sleet and snow, the Hunter and I lay in a mud swamp beneath the whistling wings of greenhead mallards. When the ducks started to set in, tipping side to side to spill air from their wings, I wiped the muck from the gun and sat up. The ducks backpedaled, but it was too late.

Ithaca

David Dlubak and crew and crew in Upper Sandusky, Ohio, have been working for several years to resurrect the Ithaca Model 37 pump shotgun. All that work has paid off and Ithaca is up and running with five Model 37s and a special order 28-gauge pump.

The Ithaca Featherlight 12- and 20-gauge upland gun is made with a steel receiver while the Ultralight has an aluminum receiver and weighs about a pound less. Both models feature a ventilated rib, lengthened forcing cone, engraving on the receiver flats, three Briley choke tubes in 26, 28 or 30 inch barrels and a TRUGLO fiber optic red bead. The black walnut stocks and forearms have point pattern laser cut checkering. The ventilated rib on the barrels is held in place with a single screw.

The Deerslayer III is built on the Model 37 action with a fluted heavy walled rifled barrel with a 1:28 inch twist in 12 gauge and 1:24 inch twist for 20-gauge. Ithaca claims it shoots 4" groups at 200 yards because of the heavy barrel and because the barrel mates in the receiver with threads for a tight lockup. A Weaver optic base on the top of the receiver is included. A Pachmayr 750 Decelerator pad helps soak up recoil from slug loads. The gun is shipped with a hard case.

The Model 37 Defense 12-gauge has an 18-1/2" inch barrel with a cylinder bore and parkerized finish on the metal. The walnut stock wears a Pachmayr Decelerator pad and the "corncob" forearm has ring tail grooves like Model 37s of yesteryear. The gun holds four rounds in the magazine.

The Featherlight 28-gauge is a special order gun with a three inch chamber and a ventilated rib 26 or 28 inch barrel and black walnut stock and forearm. The "A" Grade has some engraving, the" AA" full cover engraving on the receiver. The "AAA" Grade has engraving and gold inlays of three flushing

NEF Pardner Pump Cantilever Slug.

game birds and a pointing dog.

John Browning would be pleased the Model 37 he designed is back in production.

Legacy Sports

After a brief hiatus, Verona shotguns are back.

Legacy Sports is importing the Verona line of side-by-side, over/under and autoloading guns.

The over/unders are made with nickel-plated steel receivers scaled to the12-, 20- and 28-gauges and the .410-bore on a 28-gauge receiver. The chrome-lined 28 inch barrels come with full, improved modified, modified, improved cylinder and skeet choke tubes. The Hunting Combo is a two

Amy Brown is hammering away at sporting clays. Amy, and millions of other shooters, keep dozens of shotgun companies in business.

Erik Smith used a Browning Silver 20-gauge shooting steel shot to take this wood duck.

barrel set for the 20- and 28-gauge.

The Verona box lock side-by-side is made by Fausti in Italy. The receiver is color case hardened with laser engraved long sideplates. The straight grip stock has extended panels of point pattern checkering and the forearm is semi-beavertail. The 12- and 20-gauge models are on the same size receiver while the 28-gauge is made on a reduced size frame. All the guns have automatic ejectors and safeties and full, improved modified, modified, improved cylinder and skeet choke tubes.

The Verona autoloading guns feature an inertia driven pivoting bolt head that locks into an extension of the barrel that reached back into the receiver. This is the same type of operating system used on Benelli and Franchi shotguns, and in fact the Verona guns look suspiciously similar to Franchi guns.

The Verona 12- and 20-gauge guns with 3" chambers have an aluminum receiver that is blued, nickel or grey and with a walnut or black synthetic stock and forearm. Twelve-gauge guns with 3-1/2" chamber have a black synthetic stock and forearm.

Slug guns have been added to the Escort line of 12- and 20-gauge pumps and autoloaders. Badger Barrels makes the 22" barrels with cut rifling and a 1:26 twist to shoot sabot slugs. A cantilever optic

sight base is attached to the barrels and extends back over the receiver.

Merkel

The German Merkel company is so immersed in tradition that it has never offered screw-in choke tubes on its over/under or side-by-side shotguns. That has kept companies such as Briley installing choke tubes on Merkel guns. But Merkel will break with convention this year by offering Briley screw-in chokes on a couple of its over/under guns. Merkel will find great acceptance of these guns because choke tubes make shotguns useful over a wider range of shooting and hunting.

I had the chance to shoot a Merkel Model 1620 EL side-by-side 20 gauge on a pleasant afternoon hunting Alabama bobwhite quail last January. We walked the edges of green grass fields behind a pointing dog. The quail flew in an arc across the open or in a beeline through the timber. The 20 came up in the cups of my hands and the little birds tumbled. After several months of northern winter, the sun felt warm and good on my shoulders.

New England Firearms

New England Firearms has introduced the Pardner Pump Cantilever Slug Gun 12-gauge with a fully rifled 22" barrel. The gun uses Ultragon rifling. The six oval-shaped lands and grooves impart bullet spin without leaving cuts on sabot jackets or lead slugs. The result is a better gas seal and less loss of pressure, which equals higher velocity and better accuracy. To round out this serious slug hunting combination, the Pardner Pump Slug Gun features a strong steel receiver, double action bars and a Monte Carlo-style stock in American Walnut or Black Synthetic, all at an attractive price.

Remington

The 887 Nitro Mag pump is Remington's new shotgun. The 887's barrel and receiver are sealed with a polymer ArmorLokt coating that protects all external metal from rust. The overmolding on the barrel also forms the sighting rib and front sight base. The trigger plate is also formed from polymer and holds a trigger assembly and shell carrier similar to the 870's. The carrier incorporates a "Flexi-Tab" that allows easy removal of shotshells from the magazine. The 887's bolt has dual locking lugs that fasten into the barrel tang. Right and left extractors made of steel ensure that fired shells fly out of the chamber.

The 887's 28" barrel is chambered in 3-1/2" 12-gauge. The Synthetic model weighs 7-3/8 lbs. and has a black synthetic forearm and a SuperCell recoil pad on its stock, modified screw in choke tube and a Hi-Viz fiber optic front bead with interchangeable light pipes. The Waterfowl weighs 7-1/2 lbs. and is

These bobwhite quail were taken with a Merkel 2000 over/under.

covered with Realtree Advantage Max-4 camouflage and has an Extended Over Decoys Rem Choke for nontoxic waterfowl loads.

The 12-ga. Model 870 SPS Super Slug's ShurShot synthetic stock has a large opening that allows a quick grasp of a near vertical grip that right- and left-handed hunters can use and an extended forend for a secure grip. A SuperCell recoil pad soaks up the cruel recoil from slug loads. The ShurShot stock also has molded-in swivel studs. A cantilever Weaver-style optical sight base is mounted on its rifled barrel.

The 870 Express Compact and Compact ShurShot are a bit shorter in the barrel and stock for smaller stature shooters. The Compact has a black synthetic stock with rough texture grip panels. A pink stock and forearm with an overlay camo pattern is also available to match feminine fashion wear.

The 870 Express Tactical line has been expanded to include the Express Tactical with a gray powder coat finish and an 870 Tactical with XS Ghost Ring Sights. The XS Ghost Ring Sights have a front XS blade and an XS Ghost Ring rear sight mounted on the receiver, adjustable for windage and elevation. The guns handle both 2-3/4" and 3" loads. A two-round magazine extension holds seven rounds under an 18-1/2" barrel with an Extended Tactical RemChoke tube.

Anymore, with hard hitting 20-ga. slugs and shotshell loads like Federal's new 1-1/2 oz. of HEAVYWEIGHT, the only thing a 20-gauge gun gives up to the 12 is a couple of pounds of weight. Remington has a couple of new 20-gauge guns:

The Model 870 Express ShurShot Fully Rifled – Cantilever (FR-CL) has a .8" diameter 18-1/2" barrel with a 1:24 twist for 20-ga. sabot slugs. The barrel and receiver are finished in a black-oxide coating to match the synthetic fore-end and ShurShot stock. The gun's Weaver-style optic base is fixed to the barrel and extends back over the receiver. It weighs 6-3/8 lbs.

Four Model 870 Express Compact 20-ga. pump shotguns feature synthetic forearms and stocks with a shorter length of pull than standard 870s and an Adjustable Length of Pull System that adjusts

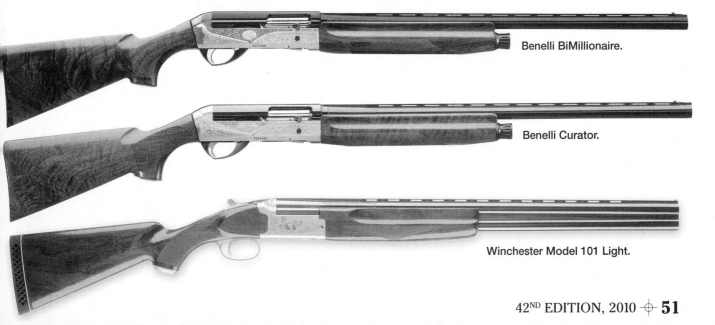

Benelli BiMillionaire.

Benelli Curator.

Winchester Model 101 Light.

LOP incrementally up to 1" with two 1/4" and one .5" spacers on the butt. A SuperCell recoil pad caps it off. The Express Compact weighs 6 lbs. with a 21" barrel and is offered with Black Synthetic, Realtree Hardwoods, Mossy Oak and pink camo stocks. The Express Compact Jr. has an 18-1/4" barrel and weighs 5-3/4 lbs.

The Model 11-87 Compact Sportsman also has the Adjustable Length of Pull System, a 21" barrel with a modified screw-in choke tube and synthetic stock and forearm. It weighs 6-1/2 lbs.

TriStar

A 4" barrel extension is an innovative feature on TriStar's new Viper Turkey/Waterfowl 12- and 20-ga. pumps. The Viper's barrel is 24 inches long and is threaded to accept screw-in choke tubes for turkey hunting. With the choke tube removed, a 4" barrel extension screws in to lengthen the barrel to 28 inches for a smooth swing on waterfowl or upland birds. The seam is nearly unnoticeable between the barrel and extension. The muzzle of the barrel extension is threaded to accept choke tubes.

Weatherby

Weatherby has extended its line of SA-08 autoloading shotguns with synthetic stocked 12- and 20-ga. models. The Black Synthetic reduces weight a few ounces and sells for about $50 less than walnut stocked models.

All SA-08 models now have a dual valve system to help the guns cycle all 2-3/4" and 3" loads. The dual valve system has two valves that adjust gas bleed-off to compensate for different loads. The Light

A 4" barrel extension is an innovative feature on TriStar's new Viper Turkey/Waterfowl 12- and 20-ga. pumps.

The Browning Silver Sporting autoloader has a stock that can easily be adjusted up to 3/4" longer with three 1/4" spacers that fit between the stock and the Decelerator recoil pad.

Weatherby has extended its line of SA-08 autoloading shotguns with synthetic stocked 12- and 20-ga. models.

Load valve cycles 12-ga. loads from 7/8 oz. through 1-1/8 oz. and 20-ga. from 3/4 oz. to 7/8 oz. loads. The Heavy Load valve cycles everything from 2-3/4" to 3" magnum 2-oz. loads in the 12 gauge and 7/8 oz.

Merkel's Einar Hoff is shooting a Merkel Model 1620 EL side-by-side 20 gauge at Alabama quail on a pleasant afternoon.

loads to Federal's new turkey load of 1-1/2 oz. of HEAVYWEIGHT shot.

Winchester

The Winchester Speed Pump has been given some style refinements and renamed the Super X Pump. The Super X Shadow Field comes in 12 gauge with 3" chambers and 26" or 28" barrels. The synthetic stock and forearm have grip panels and some stylish triangles and lines. The Shadow Field comes with full, modified and improved cylinder choke tubes.

The Super X Defender has an 18 " barrel with a cylinder bore. It has a ringtail forearm for a sure grip and control while firing its five-round magazine dry.

The external metal and synthetic stock and forearm of the autoloading Super X3 Gray Shadow are covered with a gunmetal gray Perma-Cote Ultra Tough finish. The Gray Shadow has an Active Valve gas system and Inflex recoil pad to soak up the recoil of 12-gauge 3-1/2" shells.

The Winchester Model 101 Light over/under 12-gauge weighs a pound less than other Model 101s. The Light weighs 6 lbs. with a 26" barrel and 6 lbs., 5 oz. with a 28" barrel. The Light's aluminum receiver is decorated with a quail on the right side and flushing pheasants on the left. The bottom is engraved with a springer spaniel holding a bird. The walnut stock wears a ventilated Pachmayr Decelerator pad. Full, modified and improved cylinder choke tubes are included.

TACTICAL GEAR TODAY

BY KEVIN MICHALOWSKI

Les Baer's AR-based Police Special, possibly the finest civvie M4 available.

an anyone remember a time when there wasn't a Law Enforcement section at the SHOT Show? For a fairly new addition to the program, the LE section has really taken off. I can't remember the exact year, but it must have been two or three years after the creation of the section, when it became clear that such an area would be amazingly popular. As the shuttle bus I was riding pulled up to the convention center, an older gentleman turned to his partner in the seat next to him and said, "Well there certainly seems to be plenty of black pants and brown shirts again this year."

For once in my life I decided to bite my tongue and allow these two members of the braided leather suspender crowd to waddle on to whatever booth they would be manning. I was off in search of black nylon and Velcro and didn't need anyone getting in my way.

Cut to 2009 and the opening bell of the SHOT Show at Orlando's Orange County Convention Center. Once again I was thinking about people getting in my way. Only this time it was people wearing "black pants and brown shirts" blocking the aisles in the Law Enforcement section. Regardless of what people say about overall attendance of the 2009 SHOT show, things in the Law Enforcement section were hopping right from the start. Special thanks for the level of activity in the section can largely be attributed to the Obama Gun Sales Team, which was, at the time of the SHOT show, preparing for an historic Presidential inauguration ceremony. Call it *Fear and Loathing in Orlando.*

Tactical Guns

The big news was, of course the torrid pace of black gun sales. To spend too much time talking about wholesale and retail sales of the AR-15s and their clones would be to overstate the obvious. Suffice to say that everything with detachable magazine, pistol grip and bayonet lug was in high demand. But it wasn't just the black guns flying off the shelves. It was accessories as well. Everything from picatinny rails to collapsible stocks became hot commodities following the 2008 presidential election and the pace did not slow down as the inauguration approached. Demand was so strong that many manufacturers complained of an inability to get part parts.

Early in 2009 some makers were telling tales of woe about receiver shortages. Apparently manufacturers with the ability to machine AR components were not keeping pace with demand and backorders measured in months were common. All this led to some spillover sales for other models. Buyers were placing orders on everything from Springfield Armory's M-1A to the PTR-91 (a G-3 clone) to AK variants. It seemed that dealers just wanted to have some type of black rifle in stock for the coming spring.

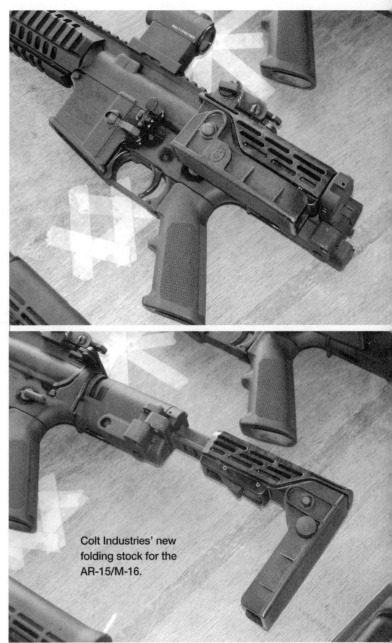

Colt Industries' new folding stock for the AR-15/M-16.

But the truth is a black rifle is a black rifle. One AR clone works pretty much like another and the proliferation of black gun makers didn't really have anything new. A couple different variations on the gas-piston AR upper are now on the market, but they really didn't offer anything new and radical. All the hoopla and buying frenzy was based more on fear upcoming legislation than on anything new in the design arena. Still, as far as I'm concerned, any guns sales are good gun sales. And more buyers of black rifles mean more voters when the issue finally comes to the fore.

Well, there was one AR variant that really caught my eye. The AT-14 marketed by **American Tactical**

Mossberg's new Night Train II .308 ooks good in digital camo.

Imports brings a whole new dimension to the AR platform. Now you can have an AR that fires .410 shotgun shells. Imagine the possibilities. If you thought the lever-action .410 shotguns that hit the market a few years back were fun, the AT-14 should put those to shame. This, of course, is not the first military style rifle to be chambered for the .410. There are still some of the old SMLE conversions floating around out there and the Saiga AK-styled shotguns. But the AT-14 looks to be infinitely more enjoyable.

The AT-14 is currently offered in two styles: the Classic and the Compact, both with five-round magazines, but a 15-round magazine will be available soon. The gun is a smooth bore, open-choke .410 shotgun. Both models have barrels at just over 20", and an overall length of 37.8". The Compact version of the AT-14 differs from the Classic version in its weight, with the Compact weighing in at just 5.73 lbs., while the Classic version tips the scales at 6.28 lbs.

Other big news in area of long guns is the release of the SCAR 16C, the civilian version of **FN**'s popular Special Combat Automatic Rifle, the MK 16. Chosen by the U.S. Special Operations Command as its next generation modular assault rifle, the MK 16 is a selective-fire 5.56x45mm NATO rifle with both full and semi-automatic capability using a short-stroke gas-piston system. The system offers three interchangeable barrels that can, if required, be switched by the individual operator in just minutes. The weapon is completely ambidextrous with a fully free-floating barrel, multiple integral MIL-STD 1913 mounting rails and a telescoping, folding stock with adjustable cheekpiece. Having gotten my hands on the SCAR MK-16 I can tell you from personal experience it to completely controllable in both semi- and full-auto fire and just about perfect in the area of ergonomics. Like all FN products I've carried and tested, the MK-16 was totally reliable under a variety of conditions, but don't take my word for it. I think the USSOCOM trials were a bit tougher than my tests.

As is true with most military firearms, the public started clamoring for a civilian-legal version of the SCAR almost before USSOCOM got their first deliveries. Well, the folks in Belgium followed through with a semi-auto version that should keep shooters happy for years to come.

Another well know name in the firearms industry: **Mossberg** unveiled a couple very nice additions to their product line at the 2009 SHOT show. One is an old favorite that is now available to the general public; the other is a nice addition to the precision rifle community that gives shooters and even smaller agencies a suitable price point to get started.

The first is the venerable Mossberg Model 590A1 combat shotgun. This is the military version of the well-known Model 500. But for those who don't know the subtle differences, the Model 590A1 is beefed up for the rigors of military and police use. This is the only 12-gauge pump shotgun ever to pass the stringent U.S. Military Mil-Spec 3443 standard.

All models will come standard with heavy-walled barrels, metal trigger guards and safety buttons in a durable Parkerized finish. A full range of sighting options are also available in front bead, ghost ring rear or 3-dot configurations. Several variations of stocks will also be available with wood, synthetic, speed feed and adjustable aluminum. All 590A1 models come drilled and tapped from the factory making it easy to mount a picatinny rail, scope base or other optic options. Other accessories available for the 590A1 include heat shields, picatinny rails as well as orange buttstocks and forearms for training purposes.

And there's even an optional bayonet. I haven't yet come up with a practical application for the bayonet, but it sure looks good. And that's good

Les Baer's new double-stack .40 S&W.

enough for me.

Mossberg has also moved up a notch in the tactical rifle market with its new 100ATR Night Train II bolt-action rifle. The Night Train II is a .308 Winchester bolt-gun equipped with the new adjustable LBA™ (Lightning Bolt Action) Trigger System and free-floating 22" button-rifled barrel. While I haven't fired the Night Train II, my initial observations and my first hands-on experience tell me this is nicely balanced and mobile tactical rifle. What

Ruger's new LCR polymer-framed revolver and cylinder frame.

FN's SCAR 16C, the civilian version of FN's popular Special Combat Automatic Rifle/MK 16.

I really like about the unit is that the Night Train II comes complete with a factory-mounted Barska 6-24 x 60mm variable scope; muzzlebrake; Harris Bipod; and neoprene comb raising kit with foam cheek pad inserts — all factory installed and ready to roll and all for one money as the auctioneers like to say. MSRP is just under $1,000, meaning you might be able to find it for about $800 some places. Now this is not a high-dollar package and it is not meant to be. Instead, it should prove to be a good, serviceable rifle with a few nice bells and whistles. It should be a solid improvement over the original Night Train, which got a bad rap in some internet forums largely because people were comparing that gun to rifles costing six times more.

Personally, I want to shoot it. Look over that new trigger system and take a good hard look through the Barska glass. Right now, I see no reason it will not live up to its billing and do what it is reasonably expected to do.

On the handgun side, the big news for 2009 revolved around small guns, with **Ruger**'s new LCR (light compact revolver) being the talk of the show floor. This polymer-framed revolver might not qualify as a true tactical arm, but you can be the little 12-oz. powerhouse will certainly end up as a back-up gun with some police officers on the street.

I say powerhouse because the LCR is designed to digest a steady diet of +P loads. Ruger, in creating the little five-shot revolver, uses a radical mix of design elements and the latest, greatest materials to ensure that the gun remains tough as nails while shaving every ounce. The coating used on the aluminum frame is not new, but it is the first time anyone ever thought to put it on a firearm offered to the commercial market. Another trademark look of the LCR is the radically fluted (almost reverse rebated) cylinder. There certainly is no extra metal left on that thing. Early reports are that the little gun has a bit of bark, as one would expect with a 12-oz. revolver and +P loads, but is certainly controllable and well up to its task as a close-range

defense gun.

This is the second year in a row that Ruger has kept the lid on a "secret" project in order to make a big splash at the SHOT show. The 2008 introduction of the LCP, Ruger's first entry into the pocket pistol market, came with equal fanfare and market interest. When these little revolvers get into gun shops they likely will not stay on the shelves long.

Saying that someone has come out with another 1911 typically gets only a raised eyebrow and perhaps a monosyllabic "hmm" as a response. After 98 years, what more can you do with that classic design? The answer to that rhetorical question came from a rather unlikely source. The folks at **Doublestar** down in Tennessee are well known for making fine AR-15 rifles and carbines. Well, soon they will be well known for making a top-notch 1911 pistol. It seems what you can do with the 1911 is invest in high quality machinery and parts and make sure they're assembled with the utmost diligence and care. That's what they are doing over at Doublestar and their 1911 should give anyone who loves that grand old sidearm the chance to say, "Now that's a nice pistol."

The same is true for **Les Baer**. The company that carries his name has been making top-grade guns for a long time now by doing just what I described above: Taking top-quality parts and putting them together better than anyone else. But this year Les has a new twist as he's building up a double-stack .40 S&W on the 1911 platform. You might say, "It's been done before."

To which I would say, "Not the way Les does it."

And the same would hold true for his Police Special AR-variant. People are calling this thing the best-shooting M-4 clone they have ever seen. In one package you are getting patrol carbine size and precision accuracy, with 100-yard groups coming in at about a half an inch. Which means that rifle can shoot better than most of us can. That's just the

way Les makes his stuff.

That about does it for the gun portion of my SHOT show Tactical Gear round-up. But I should let it be known that I only put the gun stuff on top of this article because this is *GUN Digest*. From my perspective most of the coolest innovations and biggest changes announced at the 2009 SHOT show came on the gear side of the equation. And they came mostly from folks who don't make guns.

There is one notable exception. **Colt** had something really cool. The folks in Hartford, who spent lots of time making M-4s for the soldiers in the sandbox have developed the slickest folding stock for that rifle I have ever seen. Now I don't know about you, but I always thought the original collapsible stock on the AR-15/M-16, making it the CAR-15, was a bit of an afterthought. It appears to me it was whipped up without any real engineering and designed simply to fit over the buffer tube there in the stock.

After 30-some years of that traditional system, Colt put some thinking into a new folding stock and came up with a dual-fold mechanism that actually gets the butt out of the way and still allows shooter to fire the gun while the stock is folded. I'm told it was designed with motorcycle officers in mind, but a quick look says it will be a huge asset for paratroopers and vehicle operators. Now the folded version can be fired without any part of the stock banging into or hanging up on your forearm. Very nice.

Emergency Stuff

Here's a smooth segue. Let's go from guns to getting shot. We want one, but not the other. But the truth of the matter is that if bad guys are trying to get the upper hand, you might just end up with someone getting shot or cut. Then what do you do?

Well, SHOT 2009 brought us two great answers. The first is QuikClot, offered exclusively in the U.S. by **Adventure Medical Kits**. Their Field Trauma Kit retails for about $40 and has everything you need to deal with something like a gunshot wound or other severe injury. QuikClot, when applied to a GSW or severe cut works chemically fill to stop the bleeding in just minutes. You can apply your bandage over the top and alert the doctors at the emergency room that you have used the product. They will know what to do.

It is my opinion that every shooting range (public and private) and every police vehicle and ambulance in the country should have at least one of these kits readily available at all times. There's no telling when you'll need it and you likely won't need it often, but when you need it the QuikClot should be handy.

But, just for the sake of argument, let's say you don't have space in your kit for the Field Trauma bag from Adventure Medical Kits. Well, if that's the case, you should have the SWAT tourniquet from Remote Medical International. In this case SWAT stands for Stretch, Wrap and Tuck. It is just that easy to apply this flexible tourniquet. And, cooler still, the directions are printed right on the tourniquet in such a manner that you will get the proper tension and pressure on the wound when you stretch the material until the visual indicators are correct. I know that was a long sentence, but it just sounds better than, "Pull on the rubber band until the pattern looks like a checkerboard." On second thought, that last sentence is a pretty fair indication of how to use the SWAT tourniquet. At about $10 each, buy one and slip it in the pocket of your cargo pants. Just take it out and transfer it to your other pants before you do the laundry.

A Good Belt

Speaking of an easy way to move things around your duty belt, a new attachment system by **Uncle Mike's Law Enforcement** takes all the headaches out of trying to rearrange your duty belt. No longer do you need to take everything thing off and reweave the whole belt if you want to change flashlight holsters or swap out a handcuff case. The new system lets you flip tabs, open snaps and go. I know what you're thinking. "How tough can it be?" Well, my driver's license says I weigh 225 pounds and I was having a tug-o-war using a duty belt and a double magazine pouch with a guy who went at least 180. The attachment points didn't budge and the newly designed seams take up less space on the belt. It's as if every item is a quarter inch

Mossberg's new 590A1SPX with optional bayonet.

narrower thanks to the way Uncle Mikes is sewing its pouches and other belt accessories. If you don't believe me, get to a retailer and check it out. This is a cool belt.

Light 'Em Up

And if you get a belt you need to get a flashlight to hang on it. I like flashlights because, well, I'm afraid of the dark. Don't ask. There was an incident. This may be hard to believe, but flashlight technology is advancing like Rosie O'Donnell at a buffet line. I still remember when a flashlight was simply a metal tube designed to hold dead batteries.

Today, flashlights are amazing tools that provide illumination and, in some cases, an alternative to force. And the coolest one in the new Light for Life, by **5.11 Tactical**. Thanks to the perfection of new technology the Light For Life offers 90 minutes of run time at 90 lumens with a 90-second recharge time...all without using batteries. On the high setting, you can blast 270 lumen, but that shortens the run time.

My first look at the Light for Life gave me mixed feelings. The technology of the quick-recharge capacitors is awesome, but the light was larger than I expected. Probably because I'm used to a Streamlight or Blackhawk Gladius. While the Light for Life was large, it was incredibly light. In my opinion, I'd like to see the same technology in a light that's smaller and tough enough to break a car window. I think those days are coming.

Bushnell introduced another ultra-cool light. The HD™ Torch takes flashlight technology in a new direction. While conventional flashlight produce circular patterns of light that are uneven and irregular, the new HD Torch projects a perfectly square and uniform beam of light. The benefit is that the light beam is consistent from center to edge without dim areas or doughnuts of light.

Without the shadows that are typical with traditional flashlights, the HD Torch makes objects stand out from their background for better definition and clarity. It is a great tool when searching for lost objects because the square beam lets the user search by quadrant or zone for more precision and efficiency. The HD torch can easily light up an entire wall without moving from side to side.

In the toughness department, the HD Torch is constructed of aircraft-grade aluminum and

PTR-91 (a nice G-3 clone) by – who else – PTR-91 Inc.

ATN PS22-3 Day/Night Tactical Kit with Trijicon 4x32 ACOG 1 QRM.

produces 165 Lumens of light with its powerful LED. Run time is 1.5 hours. It is powered by two 3-volt lithium batteries. There are two operating modes: high and safety-strobe for emergency use.

Another thing on the cool scale is the "Find Me" feature, a glowing "B" rear button that allows serves as a battery life indicator. The flashlight comes with two batteries and a lanyard all for just $80.

Night Vision

The **ATN** PS22-3 Day/Night Tactical Kit with Trijicon 4x32 ACOG 1 QRM is the ultimate operators sighting system by combining the ATN PS22-3 front sight with one of the best names in the daytime optical area – **Trijicon**. The PS22-3 uses ATN's standard third-generation image intensifier tubes (IIT). They have a micro channel plate, GAAs photocathode, and a completely self-contained integral high-voltage power supply. These tubes provide a combined increase in resolution, signal to noise and photosensitivity over tubes with a multi-alkali photocathode. Generation 3 is the standard for the USA military. Highlights of the Gen 3 specifications are the typical SNR of 22 and resolution of 64 lp/mm.

This thermal imaging unit is so good, you won't believe the things you can see.

The PS22-3 is packaged with a Trijicon 4x32 ACOG 1 QRM riflescope. Trijicon 4x32 ACOG scope TA01NSN with Amber Center Illumination for M4A1 fits the AR15/M16 flat-top rifles and includes the TA51 mount. Modifications to this

Trijicon Special Forces TA01 NSN model include an integral rear ghost ring aperture and a tritium glow-in-the-dark front sight (yellow center illumination) for close-quarter-combat/back-up sighting, and includes a flat-top adapter, back-up iron sights and dust cover.

Yes. It is about $5500, but if you need to see in the dark and stop bad guys before they stop you, spend the money.

And Finally, The Big News

It seems everyone had a press conference of some sort at the SHOT show – which, of course, means a reporter can get kind of jaded. One announcement, however, really made an impression. BAE Systems is now under the one banner that is easily recognizable to cops around the world: **Safariland**. I guess if you are going to capitalize on brand identity in the LE community, Safariland is the one to go with. BAE Systems is a multi-billion-dollar company with their fingers in all sorts of things. But when it came to LE gear they were the umbrella for everything from Hatch gloves to Monadnock batons, Hiatt handcuffs

American Tactical Imports AT-14 .410 AR lookalike.

and, of course Safariland holsters and gear. In total, BAE is bringing 19 companies and product lines under one banner; everything from duty gear to forensics equipment. This will be the 800-lb. gorilla in the marketplace and I fully expect they will continue to offer the best products, but now in one easy-to-find location. This might be the wave of the future, a few big players like Safariland, Blackhawk and 5.11 Tactical. We'll keep watching.

Until next time; stay safe.

MUZZLE LOADERS

TODAY

BY WM. HOVEY SMITH

he once old is now new, and the new will once more become old again.

This proverbial statement typifies the present state of the muzzleloading gun industry. There are new replica version of historic firearms, guns that are truer in spirit than in form to the originals, those that are adaptive variants of cartridge guns and new designs.

In the present American market, a competitive inline muzzleloader would appear to need to incorporate all, or most, of the following features:

- Fiber optic sights with the option of mounting a scope or other optical sight.
- Chambering that accommodates elongated .50-caliber bullets.
- Easy to operation function.
- Action, or barrel, parts that move, and remove, to provide easy loading and cleaning.
- Removable breech plug allowing 209 ignition and also be adaptable for musket and #11 percussion caps.
- Stainless-steel barrel option.
- Camo-clad stocks.
- Aluminum ramrod that can take a variety of fittings.
- Availability in several price ranges to appeal to larger market segments.
- Capability of digesting a 150-grain load of pellets or loose powder.
- Overbored or chamfered muzzle for easy bullet seating.
- Recoil pad or other recoil-reduction system.

Once an innovative feature has been pioneered by one company on its inline guns, it does not take long for it to be established as "the new industry standard" and for other companies to produce guns incorporating the new development. The result is that each year brings better muzzleloaders; older patterns are retired; and we who shoot these front-loading guns are the beneficiaries.

Some companies, such as Remington, have

The Ruger Old Army also perfromed well against Georgia gators.

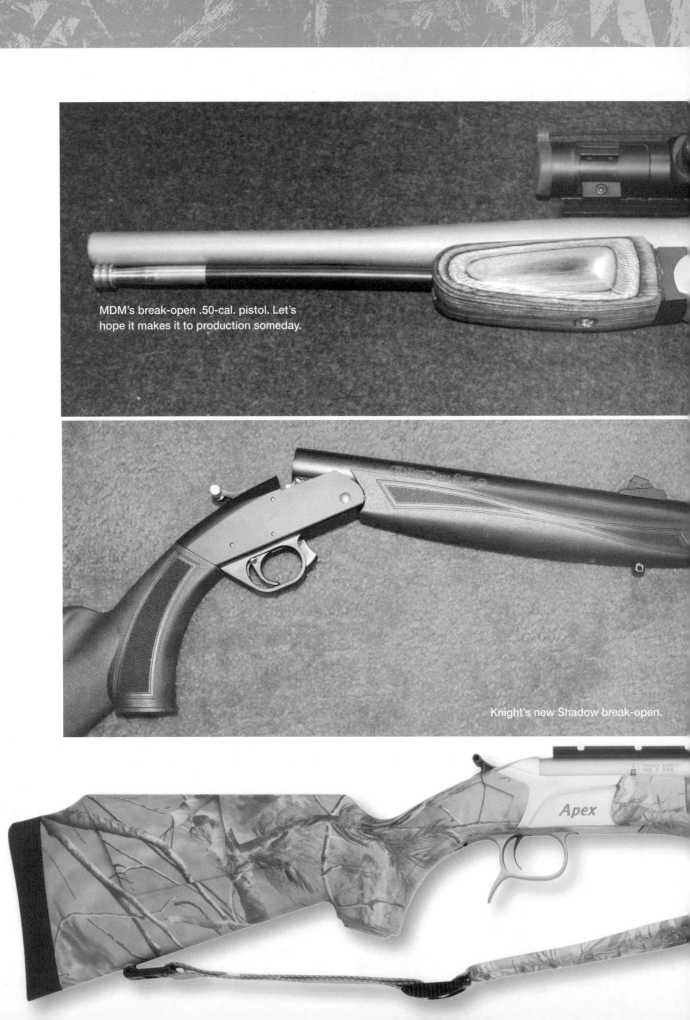

MDM's break-open .50-cal. pistol. Let's hope it makes it to production someday.

Knight's new Shadow break-open.

Apex

withdrawn from the muzzleloading market; CVA and Thompson/Center have stopped, or almost stopped, making side-lock muzzleloaders while more companies are producing substitute powders and accessories.

The Traditions Continue

"Just you wait a gall-darn minute!" I can hear some crusty buckskin-clad character shouting. While sales of inline guns dominate the American muzzleloading market, new replicas of flint and percussion guns are being produced and are enormous fun to use.

A case in point is Davide Pedersoli's Howdah Hunter double-barreled pistol. Of several options available in .50 caliber, 20-gauge and this year in .58-caliber, I used the double .50-caliber version to hunt hogs from a tower stand in Texas. It takes skill to use primitive guns effectively, but they can be mastered.

This triumph over the adverse aspects of shooting traditional matchlock, flint or percussion guns has enduring appeal as does recapturing something of the feel of holding history in your hands.

Hunting Handguns

Black-powder hunters are a subset of hunters and those who prefer the short guns are a tiny fraction of that group. To be a successful handgun hunter, the first step is to learn how to shoot pistol. I did bullseye shooting with cartridge guns for years before I hunted with muzzleloading pistols. The second task is developing effective loads. Mine have ranged from 4 grains of FFFFg for a .22 revolver to 100 grains of Triple Seven pellets for a .50-caliber Encore combined with bullets weighing bullets from 30 to 370 grains.

The penultimate event in handgun hunting is to apply the same sighting and trigger pull discipline that was learned on the target range when a 300-lb. hog is in front of you snapping its teeth.

This is not the jab-the-gun-at-the-target-and-yank-the-trigger shooting style so often shown on TV. Such shots will likely result in a missed animal at 20 yards, or, worse yet, a bad hit. My

CVA's Apex is a nicely-styled contemporary inline.

own standard is if I can shoot squirrels with the pistol and load with a degree of consistency, then I am ready to hunt big game with that gun. It is also helpful to employ a rest, one that taken with you or improvised, as often as possible.

Muzzleloading handguns for small game include any that are .36-caliber and smaller and all percussion revolvers, including the .44s. Standouts in this group include the Traditions Crockett Pistol, a .32-caliber single shot, and the .44-caliber target-sighted Remington-pattern revolvers. Squirrels, rabbits, raccoons, armadillos and the like are suitable targets. I particularly like the now-discontinued Ruger Old Army revolver's adjustable sights that allowed it to be precisely sighted for a given load. Replica Colt and Remington revolvers without adjustable sights often shoot high, making them difficult to hit with. However, some Remington replicas with adjustable sights are available in stainless steel, which partly makes up for the Old Army's regrettable demise.

Loaded with 40-grains of FFg Triple Seven and using a CCI Magnum #11 cap, the Old Army will develop 458 ft/lbs of muzzle energy. Will it kill deer? The answer is yes, but only when bullets are precisely delivered at ranges of less than 20 yards. If a hunter has the fortitude to pass on every deer beyond that range and the ability to put that ball into the heart or spine, this load will take deer. The heart-shot deer will run and there will be no exit wound to give a good blood trail. It is unwise to hunt with such a gun unless you have a dog to help recover your animals. I use the Old Army to finish off game that is down and dying and to kill alligators with brain shots delivered at ranges of a few inches.

The most common big-game-capable muzzleloading pistols that are likely to be encountered are Traditions' Buckhunter and Buckhunter Pro. These .50-caliber single shots have adjustable rear sights, but are best used with pistol scopes. My load for an early Buckhunter with a #11 nipple and a 12-1/2" barrel was 80 grains of FFg black powder and a 275-gr. Silver Lightning .44-caliber lead boattail in a sabot.

Because of its 15" barrel and ability to burn a larger powder charge, I purchased a 209X50 Thompson/Center Arms Encore pistol. This gun has an excellent set of adjustable sights, and I use them because it makes for a convenient holster carry. This is, by far, the most capable muzzleloading handgun that was once generally available. (Barrels can still be purchased through T-C's custom shop.) With a load of two 50-gr. Pyrodex or Triple Seven pellets, an over-powder Wonder Wad and a 370-grain T/C MaxiBall, I have taken several deer, hogs weighing over 300 lbs., and warthog. I've also used it to finish off a blue wildebeest. This load can be depended on to penetrate about 27" of tough game

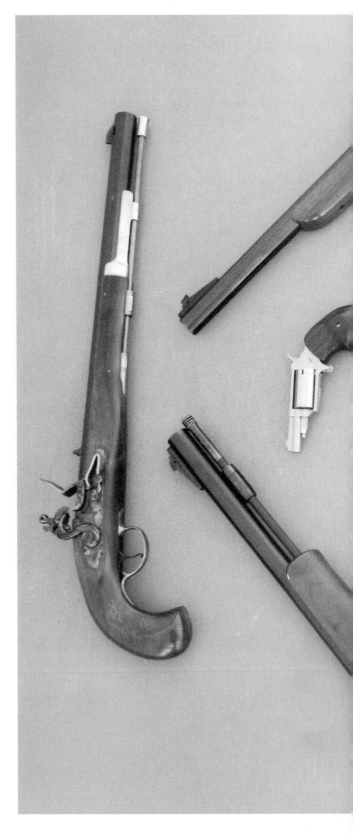

A variety of pistols suitable for handgun hunting. How many can you name?

Pedersoli's double-barreled Howdah Hunter (here broken down) is a replica of the mid-Victorian Howdah pistol. Should be just the thing if a tiger leaps up on your elephant! Note the skull-popper grip cap.

animal and plow through bone to do it.

For those who must shoot flint, there is one traditionally-styled gun that will get the job done. This is the Davide Pedersoli Bounty, which has a 14" .50-caliber barrel. I load this gun with 85 gr. of FFg GOEX black powder and a 295-gr. PowerBelt bullet. The problem is that I had to hang two pounds of lead shot onto the end of the barrel so that I could hold onto the gun. I slowly worked up to this load watching pressure signs along the way (i.e., by how easily the vent plug removed).

A recent addition to the Pedersoli line is the Howdah Hunter. Since it was said to be "a hunter," I was audacious enough to hunt with the double-barreled .50-caliber pistol even though it had no rear sight. Because of the gun's relatively short 10-1/4" barrels, I installed musket cap nipples and worked up a load of 65 gr. of FFg Triple Seven, Wonder Wad and 370-gr. MaxiBall for the right barrel and the same powder charge and a 270-gr. Buffalo Bullet Maxi Ball-et for the left. Two loads were used so that the barrels would shoot to about the same point of aim.

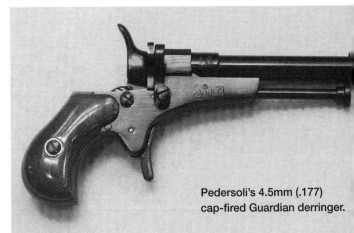

Pedersoli's 4.5mm (.177) cap-fired Guardian derringer.

I took a 200-lb. Texas boar hog with this gun at a range of 20 yards. The first shot was a spine shot to down the animal and the second barrel was used to finish it. The Howdah Hunter will hunt, but is for the close-range work, like shooting tigers off elephants' backs from the howdah.

These pistols and loads shown in the table to the right illustrate a variety of capabilities. The North American Arms Companion as a .22-caliber muzzle-loader is not well sighted and develops even less power than a high speed .22 short. It is not a toy and can penetrate ½ of pine or 40 sheets of typing paper. I mostly use it for finishing off crippled squirrels. I was not impressed with the performance of the 12-gauge round ball fired from the smooth bore 2" turkey barrel fitted to the Encore pistol frame. I did kill deer with this load, but the animal indicated no signs of being hit. The .690" round ball passed through it, cutting like an arrow rather than expanding.

Of the guns that I have used, the Encore 209X50 muzzleloading pistol is my preferred gun for hunting deer-sized game, with the longer-barreled Traditions Buckhunter Pros offering good performance in a less-expensive package.

Because of the small market for big-game-capable muzzleloading handguns, they are often only offered by companies for a year or two and then discontinued. In short, if a potential user sees one that he ikes, it is best to buy it. Traditions has their Buckhunter Pro in redesign and have not set a date for its reintroduction. Similarly, MDM has shown a break-barrel muzzleloading pistol at previous SHOT Shows and plans to introduce it within the next few years.

CVA

CVA's Apex is a new, good-looking, break-open muzzleloading rifle that offers advanced features such as a pull-out trigger group, externally adjustable trigger, redesigned stock and premium-quality interchangeable rimfire and centerfire blued or stainless barrels.

The company went through a learning curve to produce this gun. It took features like the excellent trigger and Bergara Barrels from their Accura and the concept of interchangeable barrels from their Optima Elite and combined them to make the Apex, although barrels will not interchange between the two models. The Apex is available in .45 and .50 calibers as a muzzleloader and presently with .45-70, .300 Win. Mag., .30-06, .270, 7mm-08, .243, .223, .222, .22-250 and .22 Rim-Fire barrels with more to come. As a muzzleloader, it retails for between $575-$650.

For approximately the same price, the older Optima Elite is offered in a break-action combo with both muzzleloading and centerfire barrels in .30-06, .270 and .243. For states that require muzzleloaders with open ignition, the bolt-action Elkhorn Pro offer that option at prices of about $300 for the Elkhorn and $150 for the striker-fired .50-caliber Buckhorn. The Buckhorn and falling-barrel Wolf are CVA's entry priced models with the last being sold for about $200, depending on options. The weights of these guns increase from 6.3 lbs. for the Buckhorn to 8 lbs. for the muzzleloading version of the Apex. This added weight makes the heavier guns more comfortable to shoot with 150-gr. loads and increases the likelihood of making accurate off-hand shots.

In a class by itself the CVA Electra, which employs a battery, circuit boards and electric ignition, is reputed to be enjoying robust sales for those who want to move beyond impact ignition in muzzleloading guns for easier shooting and accurate shot placement.

Knight Rifles

Knight was in somewhat of a holding pattern this

The Author's Hunting Loads

Name	Caliber	Powder	Bullet	Velocity (fps)	Energy (fpe)
North American Arms	.22	4 gr. FFFFg	30 gr. HB	344	7.88
Traditions Crockett	.32	20 gr.FFFg	44 gr.Round ball	1250	153
Ruger Old Army	.45	45 gr.Triple Seven*	143 gr.Round ball	1201	458
CVA Hawken	.50	65 gr. FFg	245 gr. Ball-et	902	443
Traditions Buckhunter Pro	.50/.44	80 gr. FFg	300 gr.**** Sabot	930	576
T/C Scout	.50	85 gr. FFg*	370 gr. MaxiBall	867	618
Pedersoli Bounty	.50	85 gr. FFg***	295 gr. PowerBelt	1060	736
Pedersoli Howdah L. Barrel	.50	60 gr. Triple Seven*	370 gr. MaxiBall	1022	853
Pedersoli Howdah R. Barrel	.50	60 gr. Triple Seven	270 gr. Maxi Ball-et	1088	710
T/C Encore	.50	100 gr. Pyrodex*	370 gr. MaxiBall	1024	858
Pedersoli H.F. 1807	.58/.45*	85 gr.FFg.	250 gr. Sabot	704	275
T/C Encore Turkey Barrel	12-gauge	110 gr. FFg**	.690" Round Ball	731	481

Notes: All powder measurements by volume.
*Loads used a lubricated Wonder Wad between the powder and bullet.
**Ball contained in a Winchester Red AA wad for 1-¼ oz. shot.

***Required the addition of a counterweight taped on the end of the barrel to prevent the pistol from flying from the hand with the shot.
**** Not original bullet used on hunt.

Thompson Center Bone Collector.

year with the principal change being the discontinuance of the Revolution rifle although its Rolling Block muzzleloader (about $400) uses the same frame and much resembles it. Also absent from its current catalogue is the TK-2000 muzzleloading shotgun. Its place is apparently taken by the 12-ga. cartridge barrel offered in the Wurfflein (muzzleloader with rifle or shotgun barrel combo $700-$850). *[Editor's note: It's good to see the grand old name of Wurfflein resurrected after a century or so! – DMS]* There are also new chambering for .444 Marlin and 12-ga. slug barrel in the drop-barreled Wurfflein and some new camo patterns for the Rolling Block and Shadow (about $350). One aspect of the Wurfflein's barrels that improves their accuracy is that the forends are free-floated by being attached to a hanger, rather than being screwed onto the barrel, thus removing one source of shot-to-shot variation.

Davide Pedersoli

Davide Pedersoli is noted for its extensive line of replica firearms and has added some variants to its line. The Gibbs Rifle, which has been available in .45 caliber and 12-ga. shotgun, will also be offered with a .72-caliber rifled barrel for about $1400. This derivation was produced by the expedient of rifling the existing cylinder-bored shotgun and putting sights on it. The result is a single-barreled large-bore gun that could be used on deer, hogs and black bear if employed with patched hardened lead balls and charges of 100-150 grains of FFg black powder. Stiff charges will be uncomfortable to shoot in the 7-¾-lb. gun. The concept is good, but the gun needs a heavier, longer barrel in this caliber.

On the tiny end of the scale, Pedersoli has also introduced a small 4.5mm (.177) Guardian derringer ($236) that uses a 209 primer to fire lead BBs – just the thing for dispatching a trapped mouse in the hunt cabin. New cartridge variants include a handsome Sharps Old West (about $1900) in either maple or walnut stocks, brass name plate and stock keys, that is chambered in .45-70. This 1874-style Sharps accepts the company's extensive line of sights

and accessories. Also new is an aluminum-framed model of the rolling block Mississippi Hunter in .45-70, .38-55, .45 L.C. and .357 Magnum. This rifle is drilled and tapped for users who opt for modern optical sights.

Thompson-Center Arms

I first ran into Michael Waddell nearly a decade ago at Realtree's factory in Columbus, Georgia. He was then a champion turkey caller who had started a few weeks before at Realtree. Nowadays he is a family man with young children and his own "Bone Collector" TV show. Thompson/Center credits him with designing their Bone Collector (about $650) that is based on the aluminum Triumph falling-barrel action, a recoil-absorbing stock and hand-detachable breechplug with, what else, a Realtree AP camo finish.

This gun combined with the company's extensive Encore muzzleloading and cartridge gun line, the newer Endeavor (around $800) frame, the falling-breach Omega ($350-$700) and that old standby, the T/C Hawken ($750) rifle in percussion ignition offer a variety of capable guns for the muzzleloading hunter. My current choice would be between the Omega, which is a simple design that functions very well, and the Hawken percussion rifle in long guns. I consider the highest evolution of the Encore design to be 209X50 muzzleloading pistol.

Traditions

Unlike its competitors, Traditions has expanded its line of side-lock muzzleloading guns and even included a new flintlock Pirate Pistol. The company has also improved the PA Pellet Flintlock by adding a larger specially-hardened frizzen. Also uncommon is that this flintlock is offered in right and left-handed versions. The PA Pellet weighs in at 7 lbs. and retails for about $400, depending on options. The heavyweight in the line is the Rex Over/Under .50-caliber muzzleloading rifle. This gun weighs 12 lbs. and costs about $1,700. I used a 150-grain load of Hodgdon's new IMR Red Hot pellets and a 338-gr. PowerBelt bullet to drop a doe in its tracks this year, and I have an African trip planned for next year for Cape Buffalo. I am also undergoing weight training in preparation for carrying this gun all day and still have enough arm strength to use it when the Cape buffalo appears.

In inline persuasion, Traditions' new gun for 2009 is the Vortek, which has an aluminum action featuring the front-of-trigger-guard opening mechanism used in the company's drop-barreled muzzleloaders. This gun also has a drop-down trigger group and a new accelerator breech plug to allow for easier cleaning. The gun weighs 7-½ lbs., and not the 12-½ as stated in the catalog.

Variants on the company's Pursuit drop barreled rifles include the Tip-up in .45-70 for Mississippi and Louisiana hunters and the Outfitter with interchangeable muzzleloading and centerfire rifle barrels in .243, 270, .308 and .30-06. These sell for about $500 with American-made Wilson barrels. Remaining in the line are the Pursuit muzzleloading rifles, the Yukon drop breech, Tracker 209 striker-fired inline and Evolution bolt action. The Northwest edition of the Pursuit has exposed ignition in the drop-barreled gun for the states that require it. Traditions' bottom-dollar inline is the Tracker, a 6-½-lb. gun that generally retails for less than $200 and will accept scope mounts. This lightweight gun is best used with loads of about 100 grains of powder and bullets not weighing over 300 grains.

For the first time Traditions is offering its miniature shooting cannon in kit form. These have .50-.69 caliber barrels in both land and naval patterns at prices of between about $200-$250.

Other Makers

Still in the muzzleloading business, but with not much happening in regards to new guns, MDM is still producing its distinctive line of drop-barrel muzzleloaders, and Rossi continues to offer very attractive packages with muzzleloading, centerfire

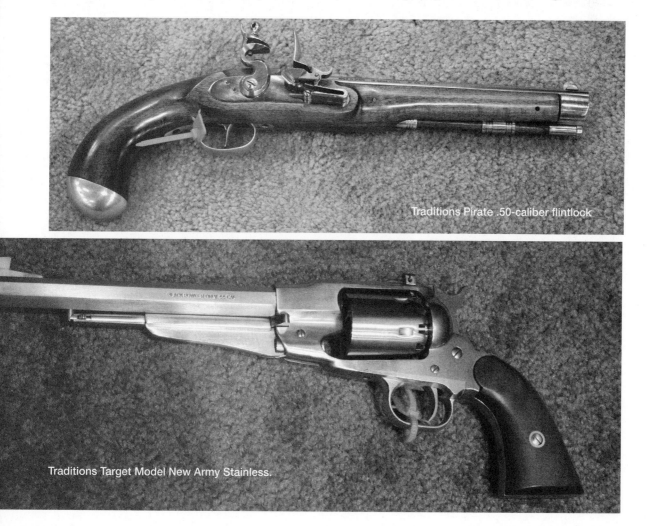

Traditions Pirate .50-caliber flintlock

Traditions Target Model New Army Stainless.

rifle, shotgun and/or rimfire barrels in various combinations. Dixie Gun Works and Navy Arms still offer their lines of imported muzzleloading firearms. No changes were made this year in Savage's model 10ML-II, which is the only muzzleloader designed to use some smokeless powders.

Accessories

Although I shoot a variety of bullets, I have followed the evolution of PowerBelt bullets from the start of the company, when they were called BlackBelts, to the present. Michael McMichael, who started the company, conceived of the notion of loading a plastic-skirted projectile made of soft lead that was sufficiently under-bore-size to be easily loaded and slug-up to groove diameter when it was fired. Over the years I have shot PowerBelts in .45 caliber in Africa and the USA. and in .50 caliber from a number of pistols and rifles on deer and hogs. I have been pleased with their performance.

A few years ago I did a factory visit and Idaho

bear hunt with Dan Hall using prototype Platinum PowerBelts. The silver-colored bullets are still soft lead coated with copper, but with a new molecular arrangement to make the metal slicker in the bore. One shot at 30 yards fatally wounded the bear, although another was used to kill it. These bullets expand well with either hollow or protected points and only the 444-gr. version is now offered in a flat-point version. The steel-pointed Dangerous Game Bullet has now been discontinued. McMichael said that he cannot recommend the 444-gr. bullets for Cape Buffalo because he fears that the soft lead will expand prematurely on the mud-caked hide and ribs and not penetrate sufficiently to take out both lungs on broadside shots. On soft-skinned animals, he says, the bullet works fine.

Modern manufacturing methods in their plant in Nampa, Idaho, ensures top-notch quality for these bullets. I have used them to make kills on deer out to about 135 yards and on kudu and zebra and they have performed very well. Besides their killing capabilities, the best thing about them is the ease with which they can be reloaded for a second shot.

Two knives attracted my attention last year. One is the Texas Buck Buster made by Rodney Parish. This is a one-stop cleaning tool that can skin, gut and quarter whitetail deer very well. Better practiced than I, Parish can skin and quarter a deer in about five minutes using his tool. This product was once licensed to Do All and produced under that brand. That arrangement was dissolved, and Parish offers his original version which he heartily endorses.

The other notable knife is produced by Silver Stag knife company in Blaine, Washington. This, and all the company's knives, are handled in deer or elk antler. The company offers the unique service of putting your antler materials on your special-order knife, which can be as small as a patch knife to as large as a sword. These handles can be installed with or without scrimshaw engraving. I cannot think of a better way to preserve the memory of a youngster's first black-powder buck than having a knife made using the animal's antlers.

In the powder arena, Hodgdon has purchased GOEX and will continue that firm's black powder production at the Louisiana plant. They also announced a new line of IMR White Hot pelletized black power substitute powder. This is available in 50-grain FFg-equivalent pellets. This product joins their existing line of substitute products including loose and pelletized Pyrodex and Triple Seven. Next year I will have more to say about these and other black powder substitutes, including some that are citric-acid based and another made in South Africa.

All told, muzzleloading in 2009 exhibited a vitality that is nothing short of amazing for a technology that only 50 years ago was considered to have reached its highest stage of development in the early 1870s. What's possibly left to do? How about a three-shot .50-caliber muzzleloading revolver with a 15" barrel? Revolvers in .45-70 are already being made. The muzzleloading version's frame would be about as deep and would require some new innards, but it could contain sufficient powder to make hunters out of front-stuffing revolvers. Put adjustable sights on it and the result would be a very heavy, but effective, gun. Projected sales would be very small indeed.

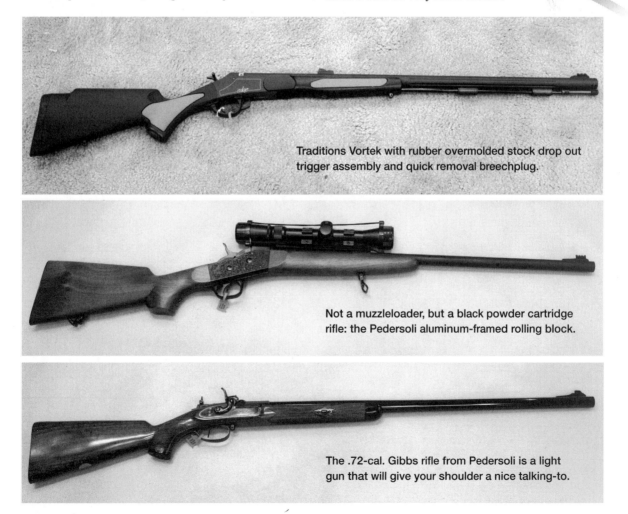

Traditions Vortek with rubber overmolded stock drop out trigger assembly and quick removal breechplug.

Not a muzzleloader, but a black powder cartridge rifle: the Pedersoli aluminum-framed rolling block.

The .72-cal. Gibbs rifle from Pedersoli is a light gun that will give your shoulder a nice talking-to.

AIRGUNS TODAY

BY **MICHAEL SCHOBY**

A majority of hunters and shooters still regard airguns with the nostalgic nod to their days as a youth, rambling around their backyard plinking cans and maybe even occasionally attempting to wing an intruding starling or ground squirrel. But the fact is today's airguns are a far cry from the prized Red Ryder of *Christmas Story* lore. In reality, modern air rifles and air pistols possess what could be considered very adult attitudes, boasting all the engineering and technology of more powerful centerfire arms (including price).

While models designed for the beginning shooter are certainly still available, take a deeper look on the store shelves and you'll spy numerous airguns that can deliver tack-driving performance and enough down-range energy to take down varmints, predators and even large game.

One of the latest trends driving both accuracy and power in the airgun world is the increased interest in PCP models or precharged pneumatics, guns that use a reservoir of compressed air to launch the projectile, be it a pellet or BB. These guns boast virtually no recoil and some models can push a pellet at more than 1,100 fps, a fact that will astound most gunpowder purists. The trend toward PCPs grew into fashion in

Gamo's Hunter Extreme is a .177- or .22-cal. scorcher that shoots pellets at an advertised 1,300 and 1600 fps, respectively.

Europe, but has made its way to our shores in the past few years as noted by many of today's top offerings by manufacturers doing business in the states.

Whether you're curious about the latest PCP model or high-performing traditional powered airguns, following are some of today's guns to consider.

Air Force Air Guns Edge

The Edge is one serious competition-grade airgun and, though it boasts many precision-class features, is approved by the Civilian Marksmanship Program (CMP) for Sporter-class competition. It features an ambidextrous cocking knob, adjustable length of pull and an adjustable forend for a perfect fit to the shooter. The Edge boasts Air Force Air

Guns' TS1 precision target sight along with a hooded front site to reduce glare and enhance sighting, and you can get it in any color you want as long as it's red or blue.

The .177-caliber air rifle has a max fill pressure of 3000 psi or 200 bar of pneumatic pressure, which delivers pellets at 500 to 550 fps. It can handle up to 100 shots on a single tankful of compressed air for lots of shooting before needing to refill. The length of pull is adjustable between 10-1/2 and 15-1/2 inches, the trigger pull is set at 1-1/2 lbs. and the entire gun weighs in at a solid 6-3/4 lbs. Overall length is between 34-1/4 inches and 39-1/4 inches, depending on how a shooter adjusts it to fit. ($600; airforceairguns.com)

Beeman Falcon R

The Falcon R will garner the most high-end gun enthusiast's appreciation with its attention to detail and respect for classic firearm styling. Just some of the luxury features of this PCP tack-driver include custom designed, fine grain wood stocks in either beech or walnut. The Breech Block receiver is manufactured from aircraft-grade #7075 aluminum alloy for reduced weight without sacrificing steel-hard strength. The Lothar Walther barrels come in match grade or 12-groove versions.

The bolt-action Falcon R has an eight-pellet

The top-quality Beeman Falcon R has a free-flating barrel for extreme accuracy.

The AirForce Edge has plenty of serious target features, and it's available in red or blue finish to boot!

magazine and the two-stage, multi-adjustable trigger is factory set at 2 lbs. A single attachment point between the stock and barrel creates a free-floating action for optimal accuracy; this is a feature you don't often find on an airgun. The Falcon R is available in .177, .22, and .25 calibers and delivers a velocity of 970, 860 and 710 fps respectively. Regardless of caliber, each variation has a total length of 43-1/2 inches and tips the scales at just over 7-1/3 lbs. This is one sweet shooter, but it comes at a sweet-shooter's price. Expect to pay more than a grand for this high-end air rifle. ($1,185 for .177 and .22 models, $1,200 for the .25; beeman.com)

Crosman Benjamin Marauder PCP

Through its Benjamin brand Marauder PCP, Crosman has found a way to get 3,000-psi performance (the industry norm) out of a 2,000-psi delivery system. Available in both .177- and .22-caliber multi-shot, bolt-action versions, each caliber delivers pellets at 1,100 fps and 1,000 fps respectively.

The Marauder features a dark, finished hardwood stock with an ambidextrous raised comb and custom checkering. The choked and internal shrouded barrel works to both limit the audible report and enhance accuracy. Other features include a two-stage, adjustable match-grade trigger, machined aluminum breech with a groove designed to accept 11 mm scope mounts, an auto-indexing 10-round clip and a built-in pressure gauge to display the gun's current air charge. The Marauder can operate off compressed air, supplied by Benjamin's patented hand pump, or the gun can be powered from CO_2. A single tank will deliver a minimum of 35 to 45 shots. (crosman.com)

Crosman Recruit

Throughout its history, Crosman has been responsible to introducing the joy of shooting to young participants and it continues this effort with

The Winchester/Daisy 850XS22 .22.

the Recruit, a .177-caliber BB/pellet combo rifle powered by a multi-pump pneumatic charging system. The butt stock is fully adjustable to accommodate shooters of various sizes and is built on Crosman's pneumatic frame. It is finished in an all-black synthetic stock, and the receiver is grooved to accept optics.

The reservoir holds up to 200 BBs and the manual clip holds 5 pellets. The multi-pump pneumatic can deliver velocities of up to 680 fps with BBs and 645 fps with pellets. (crosman.com)

Gamo Hunter Extreme

Designed for serious airgun hunters, Gamo's Hunter Extreme sends PBA Raptor .177-caliber pellets downrange at a blistering 1,600 fps and .22-caliber pellets at an equally impressive 1,300 fps. It is a spring-piston, break-barrel air rifle with a rifled, bull barrel for superior accuracy.

The classic spring piston air rifle: the Daisy Red Ryder.

AIR POWER PLANTS

A quick look at today's airguns reveal countless configurations that run the gamut from traditional hunting rifle designs to target models that look like something out of a science-fiction movie. Despite the variety, all airguns are powered in three basic ways.

Spring Piston

When most people think airguns, they're probably thinking of a spring-piston powered gun, thanks to the classic Daisy Red Ryder BB Gun. Spring-piston airguns are probably the easiest and most affordable to shoot and maintain. And while the Red Ryder works off a cocking lever, most models actually are powered through a break barrel design whereby the gun is cocked by holding the stock in one hand and the barrel in the other and then breaking the airgun in half at the breech.

By breaking the airgun in half, a piston inside the receiver compresses a strong spring, which is locked into place by a trigger sear. Pull the trigger and the spring expands rapidly forward, pushing and compressing a column of air that launches the pellet or BB through the barrel. Besides the under-lever of the Red Ryder and the simple break barrel design, other designs include a side-lever and even an over-lever.

The strength of springs and size of the pistons allow for a wide variance of power delivered by various spring-piston models, and it is this power plant that typically delivers the most recoil because of the action of the spring's release with each shot.

CO_2

These guns are powered by carbon dioxide, either in a small cartridge inserted in the gun or loaded from a bulk tank in the airgun's reservoir. It's a fairly common power plant design and can deliver blistering power, particularly when a cartridge is new or the gun is newly charged.

One challenge that faces shooters of CO_2, however, is the effect temperature can play on the pressure of the gas. At room temperature, a typical CO_2 cylinder produces about 1,000 psi of pressure. But change the temperature up or down just a few degrees and the pressure changes with it. This can really affect

The hardwood stock is checkered and boasts a raised cheekpiece for right-handed shooters. The stock is also fitted with a rubber recoil pad. It also features an automatic cocking safety along with a two-stage adjustable trigger.

Trigger pull is set at 3-3/4 lbs., while the unscoped gun stretches 48-1/2 inches and weighs a hefty 9 lbs. It is set for 58 lbs. cocking effort, so the Hunter Extreme certainly doesn't fall under the "Toy" category. The receiver is topped with a grooved rail for the company's 3x9-50 illuminated center glass-etched reticle. The Hunter Extreme is a great option for small- and medium-sized game. ($530; gamousa.com)

Ruger Airhawk

If you're looking for a gun that truly combines quality with value, the Ruger Airhawk delivers. At a price point below $200, the Airhawk is as stylish as it is functional. The break-barrel rifle is powered by a spring piston and boasts a beautifully shaped ambidextrous thumbhole stock with raised cheek pieces on both sides and a checkered forearm for a sure grip. A fine-looking rifle that bears a passing resemblance to the RWS Diana Model 34, the Airhawk isn't actually manufactured by Ruger and has offshore roots. As of this writing, the Airhawk isn't being promoted on Ruger's website, but it is well-represented on several retailers' webpages including Cabela's and Pyramyd Air.

The blued, rifled barrel features a muzzlebrake for reduced recoil (though there is little anyway), which is also softened by the ventilated rubber recoil pad. The brake also serves as a convenient handhold when cocking the rifle. The gun weighs in at a hefty 9 lbs. and has an overall length of just over 44-3/4 inches. The mainspring tube offers 11

the point of impact of a CO_2 gun. Serious shooters, whether on the range or heading into the woods, will want to allow their gun to sit awhile in the ambient temperature and then sight it in before shooting targets or game. These guns are good for allowing quick second shots and recoil is less than in a spring-piston model.

A frequently-heard complaint about CO_2 guns is that once pressure begins to fall off, it does so noticeably and rapidly. Offsetting this disadvantge, however, is the relatively high rate of fire (for an airgun, anyway) of which most CO_2 guns are capable.

Pneumatic

Pneumatic airguns use compressed air stored in a reservoir to power their shots. The way the air is compressed in the gun varies. The most common type is the multi-stroke or pump-up type of pneumatic airgun. To compress the air, the gun is pumped usually between two and 10 times, typically using a forend pump lever. Multi-stroke pneumatics are moderate in power, but usually compact, lightweight and delivers relatively little, if any, recoil. Because of the time and effort needed to pump them, however, quick second shots are virtually impossible at game or birds. They typically get harder to pump as the air compresses, making them difficult options for young or physically weaker shooters.

Single-stroke pneumatics are available and for close range shooting, these guns remain tack drivers. However, because they are powered by a single stroke or pump, these guns lack in power and aren't great choices for the hunter or longer distance shooter.

PCP (Pre-Charged Pneumatic)

First finding popularity among European hunters where strict gun laws often meant it was the only type of gun allowed for the field, pre-charged pneumatics (PCPs) are growing in popularity among American shooters. Compressed air can either be obtained from a larger bottle (such as a scuba bottle) or it can be manually pumped into the reservoir of the gun with a high-pressure hand pump. Since the reservoir holds multiple shots often one charge will last a single outing, making this a great design for hunters and serious shooters. The guns are super accurate, powerful and generate little recoil. The downside is a higher starting cost as new PCP owners not only need to buy a gun, but also the accessories needed to load the gun with the compressed air.

PCP airguns have been used to take varmints, feral hogs and – believe it or not – small deer. Doing so requires close range and ideal conditions. It's ironic that while PCP airguns represent the cutting edge of modern airgun technology, Meriwether Lewis took an early PCP air rifle on his famous expedition with William Clark – way back in 1803!

mm dovetails for easy mounting of the 3x9-40 mm scope that comes with the gun, but some airgun purists balk at the effectiveness of how well the scope will remain in place given the extreme vibration from a spring-powered gun that delivers pellets at a solid 1,000 fps. ($180)

Smith & Wesson M&P40 CO2

Because you love to shoot airguns doesn't mean you're limited to long arms. There are a number of air pistol offerings as well for the avid target shooter and a fun model under the Smith & Wesson brand (as licensed to Soft Air USA) is a replica model of S&W's M&P 40 semi-auto. The air version

The Airhawk is licensed by Ruger and is a serviceable entry-level air rifle with enough power to get most jobs done.

is powered by CO_2 for a maximum shooting distance of 131 feet, delivered at 380 fps.

The Winchester/Daisy 1100XSU .177.

The Crosman Benjamin Marauder is a PCP gun that can be charged through the use of the patented Benjamin hand pump; it also functions as a CO_2 gun.

The Crosman Recruit has a buttstock that's widely adjustable for length of pull.

It is a semi-auto, non-blowback model, which means the slide doesn't come back when fired. It holds 15 BBs in the magazine. It will fire 250 BBs on a single CO_2 cartridge. The gun features the BAXS Accuracy System to maximize the power delivered by the pressurized carbon dioxide gas. The plastic-bodied gun has a textured grip, a variety of realistic finishes and, as mandated by federal law, an orange tip so it can't be confused for a real 40 cal. semi-auto. The M&P 40 is 7-1/2 inches long and weighs 1-1/2 lbs. ($60, smith-wesson.com)

Licensed by S&W, the M&P40 CO_2 pistol looks just like the real thing.

Winchester 1100XSU and 850XS22

Winchester air rifles, made by Daisy, are attracting attention with a couple of top-performing models in 2009. The Winchester 1100XSU is a .177-caliber pellet rifle that shoots a maximum velocity of 1,100 fps. The 1100XSU features a single pump under-lever action that is more simple than it may sound, but you merely open the bolt, release the cocking lever lock, extend a cocking lever, release the lever latch and return the cocking lever under the forearm. Load a pellet into the action and the gun is ready to shoot.

inches long and weighs 8-3/4 lbs. This is another super small game option. The Winchester Air Rifle 1100SXU Under-Barrel Lever Cocking pellet rifle has an MSRP of $439.99. (daisy.com)

For those who prefer the extra smackdown of a .22-caliber pellet, there's the Winchester 850XS22. It launches ammo at 850 fps for a reported shooting distance of 305 yards. Like the 1100SXU, the single-pump, break-barrel action rifle boasts a solid walnut stock, Tru-Glo fiber-optic

The 1100SXU features a rifled steel barrel, rear button safety and a solid walnut stock with a checkered forearm and grip. It is topped with Tru-Glo fiber-optic front and rear sights for fast and clear target acquisition even in low light. The rifle also comes with a 4x32 Winchester Air Rifle scope if you prefer optics to open sights. The gun has a maximum shooting distance of 335 yards, is 46-1/2

front and rear sights (with the rear sight fully adjustable) and comes with the 4x32 scope.

The 850XS22 utilizes a rear button safety and weighs in at just over 7-1/2 lbs. It is 45 inches long. This is a shooter for a hunter with confidence in his abilities to take game with a single shot. The 850XS22 (850 FPS velocity/.22 cal.) has an MSRP of $319.99. (daisy.com)

GUNSMITHING TODAY

BY KEVIN MURAMATSU

As a gunsmith it's always fun to discover what the multitude of intellects called the American public will come up with. I've found that the tools of the trade that are the most helpful to the gunsmith or home hobbyist are often those that substitute for a third arm. In a similar fashion, those add-ons to our guns, the accessories for men, usually fill a similar role, like a more ergonomically shaped stock or sights that are easier for aging or faulty eyes to see. So it is kind of fun, in a geeky way, to flip through a Brownells catalog. I think every time I've done so, I've noticed something new. Whoever came up with that screw-driven sight pusher concept should be raised to sainthood. And whenever someone comes up with a new gun or somesuch, all sorts of minor tools – and occasionally major ones – for fixing, stripping, or doing whatever it inevitably appear. Examples would be things like the hex-shaped Glock front sight installation tool or the rebound spring installation tool for Smith & Wesson revolvers, the clamshell vice block for AR receivers, and the aforementioned sight pushers.

In light of this, it's rather sad when a political climate discourages innovation and excellence. As I write, the fear of multiple firearm prohibitions and bans looms over the firearm industry like the sword of Damocles. Some companies continue to produce new products; after all, if you don't go forward, you fall behind. One axiom (a rather important one) in business is if a venture is unlikely to make a profit, then it is probably wise not to explore that venture. Some of the most well-known companies in the firearms industry are currently expanding to meet the demand for new guns and gear. Others, fearing harmful legislation, resist that otherwise profitable expansion, since to invest in new tooling, production space or employees could sink the company should some ludicrous anti-gun law be passed. The result is long, long, backlogs for production, with the supply, in my opinion, unlikely to catch up to the demand for some time, if ever.

Likewise, it's my belief that the pace of newly-introduced products for the care, maintenance, and enhancement of firearms has slowed perceptibly. Even at the most recent SHOT show, I expected a glut of new and neat gadgets or parts to slap onto the average Joe's gun – but a glut was not what I found. Sure, there was some pretty cool stuff, but not in the amounts I expected. I mean, who wants to develop a new widget, or the gun that the widget goes onto, if that widget may well be banned in the foreseeable future?

Fortunately, there are still some innovators out there who are flipping the proverbial bird to the haters in the ether. As will be detailed below, even now, there are still new tools and chemicals, accessories, parts, sights, and workable gimmicks this year designed to make your shooting and gunsmithing more exciting, easier, or both. (I'm still waiting for the all-in-one super tool, though.)

Keep It Clean, Guys

Much of the new items for gunsmithing use come in the arena of cleaning and maintenance. An oft-neglected component of firearms ownership, this field is a great one for experimentation in the industry. See, lots of guys who own guns never clean them until they don't work anymore. This means baked-on, caked-on crud, rust and such that needs to be removed. So new cleaners, cleaning tools, and whatzits are discovered in a fairly regular fashion.

For example, **G96 Products**, maker of lubricants, solvents and such, has a new formula which was submitted to Big Brother to meet a new Mil-Spec, 63460E, whatever that stands for. *[Editor's Note: It's the U.S. DoD military procurement specification for "Lubricant, Cleaner and Preservative for Weapons and Weapons Systems." – DMS]* According to Alan Goldman, the owner of the company, one of the criteria in the specifications was dropped after testing in order for more of the competition to pass the bar in a subsequent retesting. Having used the G96 Gun Treatment aerosol extensively and having found it to be an excellent product, I may not need to take that claim with a grain of salt. Living in Minnesota, I'm always interested in a lube that claims works to well below and well above 0˚ F!

G96 Gun Treatment by G96 Products

Perma-Fin spray-on protectant
by Birchwood Casey

Birchwood Casey, maker of many fine finishing products, has come up with a new way to rust-proof your gun. It's called called Perma-Fin. This material is a liquid spray-on protectant that is applied with an airbrush. They supply a kit with two bottles of fluid and the airbrush to hose the gun down with, and when you run out of the stuff, you can buy the bottles separately. It is not a binary compound and it does not require baking. You will need an air compressor for the airbrush. If all you have is the 1200 psi squeezer in your garage, go to the wife's craft store, or Walmart, and get a small one. You don't need a manly compressor to Perma-Fin your rifle.

Tetra Gun is selling a new wipey thingy called a Lead Removal Cloth. Similar to the lubricated gun cloths and silicone impregnated cloths already on the market, this product combines the cleaning and protective properties of the latter while also removing lead residue. I've got three small children at home and I am crazy paranoid about keeping lead contamination away from my kids, so this is going to be one of the first things I buy this year. As my kids grow older and I start taking them shooting, sanitation will be a priority, so this is a welcome addition to the shop and the home.

Tetra GunLead Removal Cloth

OTIS has expanded their lineup of compact flexible cable cleaning systems. I'm a big fan of these kits, having had to use an AR-15 pistol grip kit to do a quick cleanout of my bore once, after falling into the creek. A combination bore brush and mop in all the fun calibers is now available for quickie cleans. Of course, the familiar soft packs are there for more detailed cleaning.

Combination bore
brush and mop from OTIS

What really caught my eye, however, is that OTIS is now marketing a three-part kit that is designed to refurbish your worn bore. They claim an accuracy enhancement of up to 35% in used barrels, a little less in new barrels. This system serves to first clean, lap, and then deposit

Otis Lifeliner
bore treatment

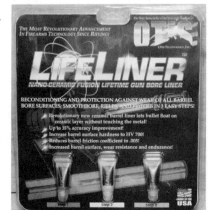

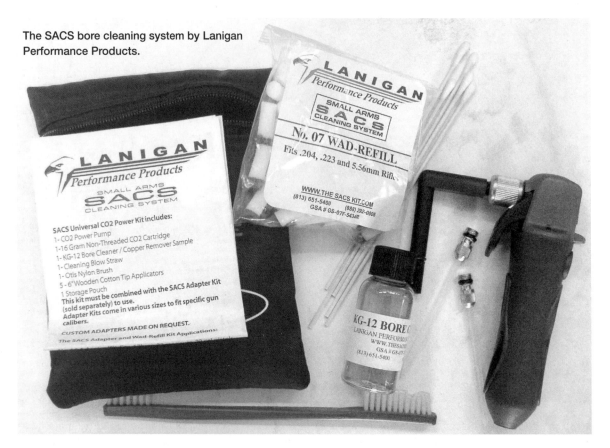

The SACS bore cleaning system by Lanigan Performance Products.

an ultrathin ceramic coating in the bore that also fills the pores in the metal and thus reduces the friction coefficient of the bore. This makes the gun more accurate, allows higher velocity, increases the wear resistance and endurance of the barrel, and makes the firearm much easier to clean. Just the thing to try on your old shooter-grade carbine's worn barrel.

A fun addition to your range bag is a CO_2-powered cleaner called SACS, from **Lanigan Performace Products**. Using a cartridge, it shoots bore-specific wads from bore to muzzle, pick ing up crud and fouling on the way. A universal device, it only requires adaptors to fit any caliber of rifle or pistol, and it is small enough to fit in a small pouch in a pocket of your bag. Such a bag is included with the

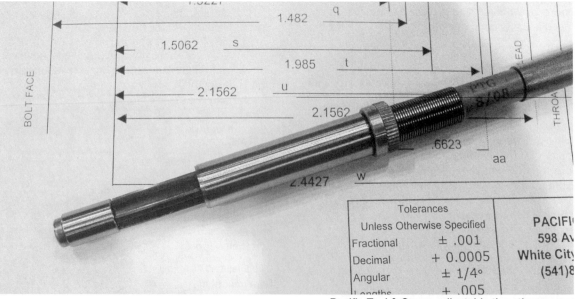

Pacific Tool & Gauge adjustable throating reamer

Reamer and gauge set by Clymer Precision Tools

kit, along with several wads, a bottle of CLP, and some other run-of-the-mill, yet handy, cleaning stuff.

Cool Tools

In the tools category are a couple of new things and a couple of things we should have thought of before.

Pacific Tool & Gauge has developed an adjustable throating reamer for chambering match-grade target guns. If a fellow wants to use a super-heavy bullet in a chamber that may not have a long enough freebore to chamber that bullet, he can now use this reamer to easily determine how much longer the freebore needs to be, and then cut it custom, whip-bam-boom. This will make doing such a task much easier and quicker and should be a welcome addition to the custom gunsmith's tool box. They will be available in multiple calibers and are piloted to the particular bore sizes. I want one. One of each.

Clymer Precision Tools has begun marketing their reamers and gauges together in one package with a slight discount on the set. I can't recall anyone else using this simple concept before, but I may be mistaken. Since we need a reamer and the accompanying go and no-go gauges anyway, why not get them all together at the same time, from the same source? Duh.

While **Wheeler Engineering** has for some time marketed their F.A.T. Wrench torqueing tools, and they are now providing them in a handy Professional Scope Mounting Kit with all the tools a fellow may need to professionally mount a riflescope, such as the wrench, driver bits, levels, and ring lapping tool. Available for 30mm tubes and 1" tubes, the kit can also be purchased as a combo set with tooling for both sizes of scope tubes.

One of the neatest little instruments I've seen in

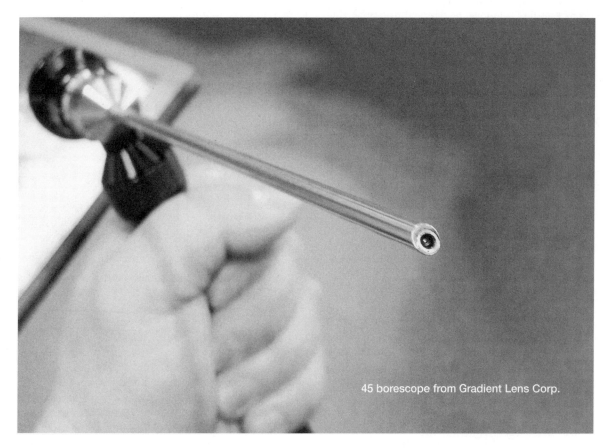

45 borescope from Gradient Lens Corp.

this field is the borescope. **Gradient Lens Corporation**, the makers of the Hawkeye Borescope, have introduced a new version that gives a 45° view of the bore. This can give you a more three-dimensional perspective as you view the rifling; and that perspective, I think, will come in very handy for those who do a lot of barrel inspections. Of course the traditional 90° viewers are still available, and newly appearing is a unit using an LED light source, a setup demanded by the company's customers.

Omega X handguard by Daniel Defense

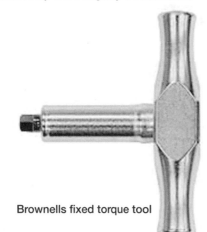

Brownells fixed torque tool

Brownells' torque wrench line has expanded. Already available is their Magna-Tip adjustable torque handle. Coming soon are a series of fixed break handles available in several different settings. This way you can get dedicated wrenches for action screws and scope mount and ring installation. I can't tell you how many times I've snapped the heads off of screws in the shop using my incredible physical prowess. Using a torque wrench should help to prevent that by enabling the gunsmith or hobbyist to consistently tighten any screw to its ideal tightness, exactly.

Sights and Such

Limbsaver has expanded with a new concept in the fiber optic realm. Fiber optic sights have been very helpful for the aged or colorblind eyes among the many shooters and hunters in America, as well as making the sights much more visible and easy to use in low lighting. Last year they combined, in yet another simple yet brilliant concept, fiber optic light tubes of two different colors, one inside the other (red inside of green, for example) to enhance the contrast perceived by the shooter. This year this line of sights has expanded to include the Dual Color Micro Sight for installation on shotgun ribs. Not only does it have those two contrast-

ing colors, it is also very low profile and will fit the ribs of most of the shotguns out in the market.

Another company on the cutting edge of fiber optic innovation is the **Williams Gun Sight Company**. They already have a vast assortment of sights for our projectile projectors, and now more are available for handguns such as the H&K USP, Kimber fixed-sight models, assorted Kahr pistols, Taurus 1911, and the new Ruger SR9. The beautiful thing about these sights is that if you don't like the color, you can change it. I can't see the red light tubes on anyone's FO sights. So I replace them with yellow or green. Much better.

AR-15 Goodies

In the black rifle arena, the sky's the limit. Everyone and their brother seems to be coming out with something new in this very large niche. One of the most interesting is the Omega X handguard from **Daniel Defense**.

Rib-mounted Dual Color Micro Sight by Limbsaver

It is a rifle-length sight pocket handguard for use on carbines. "Uh...what's that?" you say. This handguard is designed to give more forend space for accessories to hang onto, and to give more room for guys who like to hold the handguard as far out toward the muzzle as possible – and it fits on guns with the short carbine gas system. It clamshells on in two pieces, the top fitting around the fixed front sight assembly. These pieces clamp to a proprietary barrel nut, so the gun will have to be partially disassembled for installation. It is rock solid, and best of all, is less than two inches wide and lightweight.

Even with full size rail covers, it feels slimmer than standard plastic handguard pieces. Much nicer for those of us with small hands but who like to hold the handguard with our weak arm extended.

The flavor of the moment in the AR realm is the retrofit piston operating system. Several companies are now offering some incarnation of this ultimate update, some of which are end user-installable, while others require a trip to the factory or a visit to a certified installer. Look for more entries in this niche to add to those available from **Patriot Ordnance Factory**, **Adams Arms**, **Primary Weapons Systems**, **Bushmaster**, **CMMG**, **Colt**, **HK**, and probably a couple others.

Target Stuff

More and more shooters are exploring the long range target disciplines and so need a very accurate rifle. In addition tow good optics and mounts, a quality barrel, top-notch ammunition and and good technique, an accuracy-enhancing stock is a necessity. A new entry into this market is the **JP Enterprises** MOR-07 chassis system. It is built in three sections (action block, stock, and handguard) with the handguard and action block made of big chunks of hard coat anodized aluminum. The company plans on additional models of action block and handguard beyond the original Remington 700 style short action set. Simply switching out the short action for a long action receiver block, or for a block made to any particular spec, allows the MOR to potentially fit onto any bolt action rifle in existence while using the same stock and handguard. The stock is adjustable for length and cheek weld and folds to the left side for more compact storage in a smaller case. According to the company, it should also fit most factory and aftermarket triggers available for the Remington 700. It will be available alone or with JP's proprietary barreled action as a complete rifle.

Whether you are a professional gunsmith or shooter, or just a home hobbyist there are plenty of ways to improve and enhance our everyday firearms. Just exploring a **MidwayUSA** or **Brownells** catalog will overload your mind with potential projects. From building a 1000-meter gun to swapping sights on your XD, whatever you need is available.

And if something just isn't available, then design and market it yourself. The gunsmithing field, like any other, is driven greatly by innovation. While new stuff appears on a regular basis, truly new ideas are rare. Even the relatively simple task that requires the third hand can benefit from an intelligently designed assistant in the form of a fixture, jig, or manipulator extraordinaire. Man, if I had come up with the idea a few years back for those sight installation fixtures, I could buy my own island. That may be a little bit of dreamweaving, but I still want the ultimate gunsmithing tool in my toolbox.

The question is: who's gonna build it?

MOR07 chassis system for Remington M700 by JP Enterprises

OPTICS TODAY

BY WAYNE VAN ZWOLL

Wayne fires a McMillan rifle with a 2-1/2x Sightron.
Small, lightweight scopes are often best!

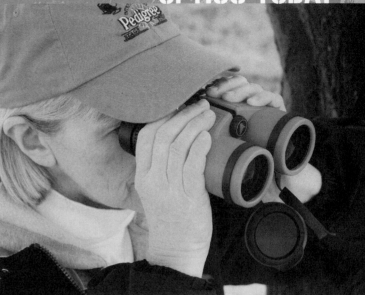

Not everyone on your block will have Alpen's pink binocular; but this is, optically, a real bargain, and a portion of sales go to breast cancer research.

You know, of course, that if you hunted with a Remington 721 shipped in the 1950s and equipped with a Weaver K4 scope, you'd kill as many deer as with a modern rifle and the most sophisticated optics – that if you entered long-range competition with a Lyman Super Targetspot sold then, you'd score as high as with the latest high-power glass.

OK. These days some deer are killed at extremely long range. Some would probably still be afoot if every hunter held his shots to 400 yards – a reasonable limit for the K4. But by and large, modern scopes pose no greater threat to game than did those of my youth. Shooters skilled enough to clean targets with a vintage Lyman would gain few if any Xs with a modern Leupold.

Still, riflemen dote on perfection. And they're much more apt demand it of their hardware than of themselves. With brighter, sharper sight pictures, they want bigger tubes and wider power ranges. They also crave options: rangefinding and illuminated reticles, re-settable windage and elevation dials, turret-mounted parallax dials, quick-focus eyepieces, water-repellent lens coatings. Throw in long eye relief that doesn't change as you crank up the magnification, plus cap-less, waterproof, low-profile knobs that spin with the crisp clickety-snick of target dials. And, now, built-in laser rangefinders.

The basic components and properties that defined worthy rifle-scopes a half-century ago remain. Strip the gingerbread, and a good sight still comprises high-quality lenses and precisely machined, carefully fitted parts – all secured against the recoil of cartridges that release bullets with bomb-blast violence.

Here's a rundown of rifle-scopes new for 2009, with notes on the most intriguing binoculars and spotting scopes. You'll find traditional glass here too – optics so good they don't need changing. Perhaps if they appear often enough in print, makers will keep them around. Not all that's new is better than all that's old.

A final note: Lately I've chosen to hunt without a rifle-scope – not every time, but often. I like it. The most memorable part of any hunt is the approach. Irons force you to get close. The approach is commonly long and difficult; but the last yards are more exciting, the shot more intimate than if you fired from afar. While iron sights no longer come as standard equipment on many rifles, you can get excellent irons from Lyman (lymanproducts.com), Williams (williamsgunsight.com) and XS (XSsights.com). They give lever rifles and short bolt guns an agility you won't sense with a scope. And there's something just plain right about clenching that receiver in your fist as you head for the horizon, the way hunters did long before glass sights blocked their grip and made the hunt an exercise in long shooting.

Aimpoint

In 1975 Swedish inventor Gunnar Sandberg came up with what he called a single-point sight. You couldn't look through this sight; you looked into the tube with one eye while your other registered a dot superimposed on the target. Sandberg refined the device and founded a company. Aimpoint came to define a new type of optical sight, with an illuminated dot suspended in a field you can see from almost anyplace behind the sight. And you needn't worry about parallax. The front lens of an Aimpoint is a compound glass that corrects for parallax – unlike red dot sights whose reflective paths shift with eye position.

Aimpoint's doublet lens brings the dot to your eye in a line parallel with the sight's optical axis, so you'll hit where you see the dot, even when your eye is off-axis. A 1x Aimpoint gives you unlimited eye relief, and it's easy to use with both eyes open. Current Aimpoints (some with magnification) boast what the firm calls Advanced Circuit Efficiency Technology. It reduces power demand; batteries last up to 50,000 hours with a brightness setting of 7 (on a scale of 1 to 11). These sights are lightweight and compact, too. The lightest of the 9000 series weighs just 6.5 oz. Positive windage and elevation clicks each move point of impact 13mm at 100 meters. Sturdy enough for military use, Aimpoint sights have been adopted by armed forces in the U.S. and France, and they serve sportsmen in 40 countries. One of every 10 moose hunters using optical sights in Sweden carries an Aimpoint.

A few years ago, on the receiving end of a game

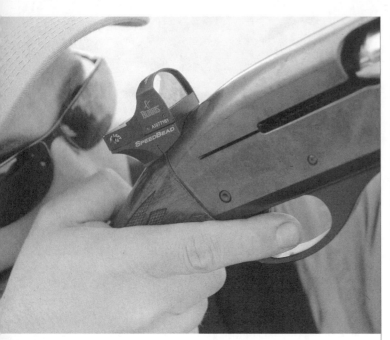

drive in a Swedish forest dark under a dripping fog, I spied a pair of moose hoofing through the trees at a brisk pace. The red dot in my Aimpoint cut through the gloom and glued itself to a shoulder. Bang! The moose stumbled, recovered. I found it dead a short distance farther into the woods. Two other moose, both shot on the go in heavy cover, have convinced me that nothing beats an Aimpoint for fast shots in dim conditions. At the range, I've fired minute-of-angle groups with the same sight. 'Nuf said! (Aimpoint.com)

Alpen

Building a new optics company takes patience and tenacity. The Alpen people have shown a lot of both over the last decade. And their recipe for success is paying off. "Value. We focus on value." Vickie Gardner insists on it from the manufacturers. Rifle-scopes, spotting scopes and binoculars with Alpen's label have been winning industry "best buy" awards like Michael Phelps collected Olympic gold. The list of new items this year is short, but the catalog is still chock-full of bargains.

Top-end Rainier binoculars now come in 8x32 and 10x32 versions that are 20 percent lighter than the 42mm originals but still wear BAK4 lenses, phase-corrected coatings, a locking diopter dial and twist-out eyecups. The AlpenPro Porro series includes an 8x30 that's ideal for the woods. For 2009 the company has announced an 8-16x42 zoom binocular. You may prefer the more traditional roof-prism Wings, of open-frame design. Choose 8x42 or 10x42, ED or standard lenses. You'll get the features of Alpen's best glasses. The new 8.5x50 delivers a very bright image at modest cost. While

pink binoculars might not top your shopping list, Alpen carries a pair (8x25 and 10x42) to draw attention to breast cancer research – where the firm has pledged a portion of pink sales. The Rainier 20-60x80 spotting scope accommodates a camera adapter, for photography at long range. Straight and angled eyepieces index easily. AR rifle-scopes for air guns were developed to endure double-shuffle recoil. Alpen has a new pocket monocular that really does fit in a shirt pocket. The 8x25 (or 10x25) glass is great for a peek into timber when you're traveling light. (Alpenoutdoors.com)

ATK

Last year the Nitrex label, once put on Speer ammunition, was adopted by ATK for a new line of rifle-scopes. ATK (which, incidentally, also owns Speer) just added several scopes to this series. The 1.5-5x32, 3-9x42, 3-10x50 and 6-20x50 AO now wear the "TR-one" label, while five new sights make up the "TR-two" group. All these 1" scopes feature five times magnification – top-end power is five times the lowest setting. All deliver 4" eye relief and a choice of TrexPlex or EBX reticle. There's a 2-10x42, a 2-10x50, a 3-15x42, a 3-15x50, and a 4-20x50. You can specify an illuminated reticle in the 3-15x50, a fine crosswire in the 4-20. Choose matte or silver finish. While the TR-one 6-20x50 AO has a front-end parallax ring, the 3-15x and 4-20x TR-two scopes have turret-mounted focus/parallax dials. These scopes weigh from 23 to 28 ounces. The 4-20x50 has 1/8-minute windage and elevation clicks; the others change in 1/4-minute increments. All Nitrex scopes have fast-focus eyepieces.

As is customary in the American market, ATK kept reticles in the second focal plane. They don't change dimensions as you turn the power dial. I like the generous tube sections on these scopes, for easy mounting on a variety of rifles and the almost-constant eye relief across the power range. Checking windage and elevation movements on a 3-9x42 TR-one (with the rifle snug in a Caldwell Steady Rest), I found the dials gave a reliable return to zero. Bright, sharp images, a flat field and minimal color fringing belie the modest price of the TR-one scopes. While the new TR-two models cost a bit more, they're still bargains in my view. The 42mm front lens carries as much glass as can be clamped in low rings. So my choice would be the 3-15x42. ATK has also slapped the Nitrex brand on 25-ounce roof-prism binoculars, 8x42 and 10x42. Phase-corrected lens coatings enhance images; the click-detent diopter dial won't creep off your preferred setting. Eleven-ounce compact versions, 8x25 and 10x25, are available too. (Nitrexoptics.com)

Barrett

The Barrett Optical Ranging System – BORS – is not a sight. It's a sight attachment, a 13-oz. device you pair with a scope. It includes a small ranging computer powered by a CR-123 lithium battery and featuring a 12x2-character liquid crystal display with a four-button keypad. Factory-installed cartridge tables tailored to your loads enable the computer to give you precise holds for long-distance shooting. The BORS also comprises an elevation knob, a knob adapter and a set of rings that affix the computer to your sight. The rings mount to any M1913 rail and are secured with hex nuts that endure the beating of Barrett rifles in .50 BMG. After you press the 6-o'clock power button on the BORS unit, you're ready to engineer a shot. The screen shows zero range and indicates any cant (tipping of the rifle off vertical), which at long range can cause you to miss. The BORS unit automatically compensates for vertical shot angles. You can adjust the scope for up to 90 degrees of inclination and declination, in increments of 2 degrees! At extreme range, temperature and barometric pressure matter, too. Both come on-screen when you press the 9-o'clock button. To determine range, you specify target size, then move the horizontal wire of your reticle from top to bottom of the target, or vice versa. The range appears in yards or meters. Now you can use the elevation knob to dial the range. The BORS unit must know your load, of course. You provided that data earlier; the unit stores it as a ballistics table. It can hold up to 100 tables for instant access. At the end of this process – which takes longer to explain than to do – you can hold dead-on even at extended range. If the battery dies, you can use the scope as if the electronics were not there. I've attached a BORS unit to a Barrett rifle with Leupold Mark 4 LR/Tactical 4.5-14x50 scope. Recoil and blast from this .50 haven't fazed the instrument. (Barrettrifles.com)

Brunton

Since its start in the 1890s, Brunton has served people who live in the outdoors. Field geologists were the first customers. The product line has grown to include all manner of camping gear, from transits and compasses and GPS units to cookwear and stoves. Binoculars have lately brought Brunton to hunters. Topping that line is the Epoch, a full-size roof-prism glass with 43mm objectives. Choose from 7.5x, 8.5x and 10.5x magnification. At $1,639, the 8-15x35 zoom costs about $340 more. Like its fixed-power stable-mates, it has lockable, twist-out eyecups and accepts a doubler to increase magnification. Less expensive Eterna and Echo binoculars still boast fully multi-coated lenses. Eterna 8x45 and 11x45 versions earned a "Best Buy" rating from

Consumer's Digest. The 8x32 and 10x32 are more portable; the 15x51 with tripod adapter can serve as a spotting scope. But Brunton also makes traditional spotting scopes, from the compact 12-36x50 Echo and 18-38x50 Eterna to full-size 20-60x80 spotting scopes with ED (extra-low dispersion) fluorite glass. Brunton imports rifle-scopes to sell under the NRA banner. At $109 and $119, fixed-power 4x32 and 6x42 scopes offer good value. A 6-24x50 AO target scope lists for just $149 with mil-dot reticle. Variables, from 1.5-6x40 to 6-24x50, start around $100. Word on the street is that Brunton will focus more and more on camping and orienteering hardware. (Brunton.com and nrasportsoptics.com)

Burris

Two new rifle-scopes join the extensive Burris line in 2009. The Six Series comprises a 2-12x40 and a 2-12x50, both with 30mm tubes and up to 4-1/2" of eye relief. The "Six", of course, refers to a six-times power range. Decades ago, when variables started to gain traction with hunters, the 3-9x led the pack. For years, three-times power range seemed sufficient. Then, as shooters demanded more power, came a four-times option. It appeared most notably in 3-12x and 4-16x scopes. Last season I hunted with a scope featuring six-times magnification – more range, I must say, than I needed. But there's no question a 2-12x scope is versatile! I'm pleased Burris has kept the 40mm objective for hunters like me who favor low scope mounting and a relatively compact sight.

On another front, Burris has improved its 1.6-oz. reflex-style red dot sight. FastFire II is now waterproof (fully submersible!). Made to fit Picatinny rails, it's ideal not only for rifles but for handguns and shotguns. A battery-saver mode extends the life of the lithium CR2032 battery to five years. Burris has also announced FastFire mounts for popular lever rifles, and a mounting plate you can sandwich

The Leica Ultravid, now with ED glass, ranks among the very best binoculars in the world.

Leupold's 4.5-14x50 Tactical scope helps this Surgeon rifle in .338 Lapua shoot into one hole.

between receiver and buttstock on repeating shotguns. Called SpeedBead, the red dot sight on the shotgun mount should excel on slug guns. I tried this sight recently, on an 1100 Remington at a clay-target range. The first bird escaped, but after that, the red dot found the target as quickly as would a front bead, and there was no barrel to obscure rising birds. Hitting became easy quickly!

Burris hasn't forgotten the long-range shooter. Its Ballisic Plex and Ballistic Mil-Dot reticles are available in 30mm Euro Diamond and Black Diamond series, and the 1-inch Signature Select and Fullfield II lines. Illuminated reticles define the Fullfield II LRS scopes, which employ flat battery housings on the turret. Fullfield 30s (3-9x40 and 3.5-10x50) feature 30mm tubes at affordable prices. A 1" Timberline series, from 4x20 to 4.5-14x32 AO, fills the "compact" slot. The company also lists a red dot sight: the 1x, 5-oz. tube-style 135. Like many optics firms, Burris is expanding its tactical line. Fullfield II Tactical scopes and Fullfield TAC30 variables (3-9x40, 3.5-10x50 and 4.5-14x42, new last year) have been joined by a 3x AR-332 prism sight, and an AR-Tripler, which you position on a pivot mount behind a 1x red dot sight for extra magnification. Burris catalogs an XTS-135 SpeedDot tube sight, and 1-4x24 and 1.5-6x40 XTRs (Xtreme Tactical Riflescopes). FastFire II complements AR-style battle rifles. The Burris catalog also lists spotting scopes, binoculars and the 4-12x42 Laserscope, a laser-ranging sight. (Burrisoptics.com)

Bushnell

Still new on the Bushnell website is the company's Elite 6500-series rifle-scopes: 2.5-16x42, 2.5-16x50 and 4.5-30x50. The nearly-seven-times magnification range is the broadest in the industry. Bushnell 4200 2.5-10x50 and 6-24x40 scopes are new, and there's now a 3200-series 3-9x40 with Ballistic Reticle. The affordable Trophy series has grown by two: 1x28 red dot and 1x32 red/green dot sights. New 36mm and 42mm Excursion EX binoculars (8x and 10x) sell for $230 to $320 – reasonable prices, given their fully multi-coated optics with PC-3 phase correction. An Excursion spotting scope, with folded light path, comes in 15-45x60 and 20-60x80 versions. Bushnell's most field-worthy laser range-finders may well be the Scout 1000 with ARC, technology that takes shot angle into account so you get a corrected range for accurate shooting at steep vertical angles. The 6.6-oz. instrument fits in a pocket; single-button control makes it easy to use with one hand. In bow mode, it delivers accurate reads between 5 and 100 yards. Rifle mode sets it for reads from 100 to 800 yards. The 5x24 Scout 1000 can range reflective objects to 1,000 yards. If you're GPS-literate, you no doubt have a GPS unit. If not, you may want to dip a toe in the water with Bushnell's Backtrack, a straightforward instrument that stores up to three locations and can bring you back to them. Promoted as an aid to finding your car in a parking lot, it can also help you locate downed game in the hills. (Bushnell.com)

Cabela's

Obviously, Cabela's does not manufacture rifle-scopes. It markets them. The Cabela's brand goes on optics made by and imported from established optics firms that also build rifle-scopes, binoculars and spotting scopes for companies many people think make their own products. These manufacturers have the advantage of what you'll remember from Econ 101 as economies of scale. They own the best of machines and technology and enjoy modest labor costs. So it should come as no surprise if you find Cabela's optics good bargains. The Alaska Guide series of rifle-scopes includes fixed-powers as well as 11 variables. Most useful for big game and varmint hunters: 3-9x, 4-12x AO and 6.5-20x AO scopes, with 40mm objectives and 1" tubes. All list for less than $400. I've relied on a $200 4x Cabela's scope on remote hunts and found it both bright and durable. If the times are really pinching you, consider the Pine Ridge line – it's less expensive still. There's also a series of Cabela's tactical scopes with interchangeable turrets and left-side parallax knobs. The 2-7x32, 3-9x40, 3-12x40 and 6-18x40 start at less than $100, with fully multi-coated lenses and fast-focus eyepieces and adjustable objectives. The company also imports spotting scopes, laser range-finders and roof-prism binoculars. Its catalog includes optics from Nikon, Leupold, Swarovski, Zeiss and other well-known optics makers. (Cabelas.com)

Docter

The Carl Zeiss Jena factory in Thuringia, Germany, began producing Docter optics in 1991. Late in 2006 Merkel USA became the U.S. importer. While it has yet to launch a major marketing campaign here, Docter Optic has wooed hunters Stateside with a series of rifle-scopes featuring 1" tubes and rear-plane reticles. The 3-9x40, 3-10x40, 4.5-14x40 AO and 8-25x50 AO Docter Sport scopes boast qualities of more costly scopes . Docter's line also includes 1" 6x42 and 8x56 fixed-power Classic models, plas 30mm variables: 1-4x24, 1.5-6x42, 2.5-8x48 and 3-12x5 with fast-focus eyepieces, resettable windage/elevation dials and lighted reticles. The electronically controlled Unipoint dot is of constant size, while the first-plane main reticle varies with magnification (and stays in constant relationship with the target). Doctor catalogs three binoculars: 8x42, 10x42 and a bright 8x58. They're of roof-prism design with center focus and four-layer achromatic front lenses. A central diopter dial with vernier scale ensures precise focus down to just 3 feet! All Docter binoculars have aluminum/magnesium bodies and twist-up eyecups. (Merkel-usa.com and docter-germany.com)

Elcan

A subsidiary of Raytheon, Elcan is an optics firm and an acronym: Ernst Leitz, Canada – the Leitz optical company dating to 1849 in Germany. Elcan has been building infrared-sensitive scopes for military units since the 1980s, but it's now pursuing civilian sales with DigitalHunter, a truly innovative rifle-scope. DH1 has an alloy tube and multi-coated optics. It mounts on a Picatinny rail or Weaver bases – but not in scope rings because the body is not round. There's no turret either. A flat panel serves as a control center. You make every adjustment by pressing buttons. Turn the sight on with a button. Pick magnification, from 2.5x to 13.5x, with buttons. Choose one of four downloaded reticles – or design your own – with buttons. As this scope lacks a power ring and windage/elevation dials, it lacks a clear optical path. You cannot see through this scope. The image comes from a digital display triggered by light hitting a sensor. Because target image and reticle share a common plane, you can forget about parallax. DigitalHunter also has long, non-critical eye relief, though in bright light you must press your brow against the flexible eye-shade to get an acceptable image.

Alas, image is the scope's singular weakness. It cannot match what you're used to seeing through high-quality optics. It is, to date, dim and grainy. To be fair, so was early television. Surely technology will come to the rescue. Already it has given DH1 superior windage and elevation adjustments. Each push of a button moves point of impact exactly .2". There's no backlash, and you won't lose track of where you are on the adjustment range because each move stays in an electronic memory bank. No need to hold high at long range. The scope self-adjusts after you install ballistic data specific to your load. For each shot after zeroing, you need only enter the range on the control panel and aim in the middle!

I tested this feature with a .30-06 to ranges beyond 400 yards. Groups were perfectly centered with dead-on holds! Of course there's a battery, and the DH1 will run out of juice after 5 hours of use (sooner in cold weather). You can get more field time by switching the scope to sleep mode; it comes

A quick-focus eyepiece and generous eye relief complement excellent optics in this Meostar R1.

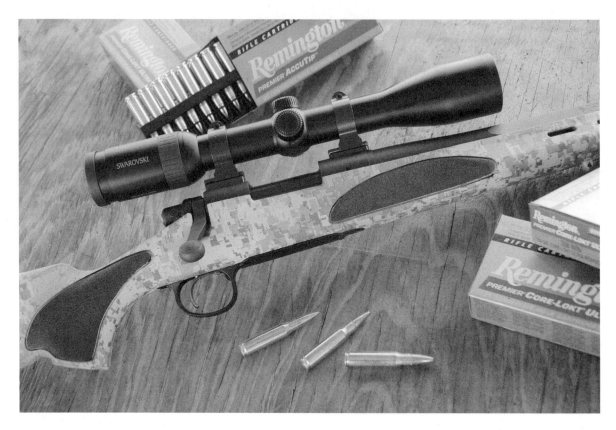

to life almost instantly at your command. Turn it off, and you'll wait about 3 seconds to reboot. At 28 oz., the scope is not light. Neither is it cheap. But the price has dropped substantially in the last two years. Figure about $1200 for the DH1. A new model has a removable tinted cap instead of a tinted front lens, so it can read infrared (you'll need an infrared flashlight) and give you a bright target at night! DH1s can be converted to IR. (Elcansportingoptics.com)

Kahles

A subsidiary of Swarovski, Kahles operates independently. This year, there's not much new from the Austrian firm. But there's plenty of high-quality glass already in the line. Helia C sights include 1" fixed-power and 30mm variable and fixed scopes, with front-plane reticles. Helia CT scopes were designed for the U.S. market. The 2-7x36, 3-9x42 and 3-10x50 have compact 1" tubes and second-plane reticles that do not appear to change size during magnification changes. Kahles catalogs four 30mm CBX models, 1.1-4x24 to 12x56, with lighted rear-plane reticles. CS (30mm) and CL (1") variables, also designed for American tastes, have a Multizero turret (optional) that allows you to preset zeros for as many as five loads or distances. Color-coded dials give you instant access to each zero in the field, and accurate returns. The company's newest rifle-scope series, the KX, is also the most afford-able. It comprises 3-9x42, 3.5-10x50 and 4-12x50 models with 1" tubes. Kahles has pushed many

Remington's new Desert Recon VTR rifle here wears a Swarovski Z6 1.7-10x42.

new products to market recently, including several fine binoculars. But its history is one of more conservative growth. In 1898 in Vienna, Karl Robert Kahles combined the Opto-Mechanical Workshop of Karl Fritsch with the Simon Plossl Company to form the Kahles Company. Two years later it was selling Telorar rifle-scopes. The Helia scope series came along in 1926. Bombing during World War II all but ruined the Kahles factory; however, Freidrich Kahles III had it rebuilt and introduced some of the first variable-power rifle-scopes. Later Kahles pioneered multi-coating of lenses, now standard on most scopes. (Kahlesoptik.com)

Leica

Geovid laser-ranging binoculars now boast the HD fluorite glass of Leica's Ultravid HD binocular series. Fluorite lenses enhance brightness and resolution, and can reduce overall weight slightly. All four Geovids (8x42, 10x42, 8x56 and 12x56) have alloy frames and deliver accurate range reads as far as 1,200 yards. The Ultravid line, which has replaced the time-honored Trinovid, includes 8x20 and 10x25 compact models, and full-size roof-prism glasses from 8x32 to 12x50. HD models feature fluorite in every lens, plus proprietary AquaDura lens coating on exposed glass. This hydrophobic compound beads water and makes lens cleaning easier. Duovid 8 + 12x42 and 10 + 15x50 binoculars offer an instant choice of magnification. Leica Televid 62 and 77 spotting scopes have been joined this year by an 82mm Televid HD. The German company's biggest news, though, is a pair of new rifle-scopes, a 2.5-10x42 and a 3.5-14x42. Specs aren't available at this writing, but you should see these scopes by mid-summer.

A few years ago Leica marketed a series of scopes manufactured by Leupold. The relationship wasn't publicized and soon dissolved. These new Leicas are the first rifle-sights produced in-house in the firm's 100-year history! (Leica-camera.com)

Leupold

Two years ago, Leupold introduced its VX-7 scopes, with a range of features and refinements that defined the best the company could bring to market. The low-profile VX-7L, with a concave belly up front, came along last spring (3.5-14x56 and 4.5-18x56, complementing the VX-7 in 1.5-6x24, 2.5-10x45 and 3.5-14x50). These sights have European-style eyepieces and "lift and lock" SpeedDial W&E dials. Xtended Twilight glass features scratch-resistant DiamondCoat 2 lens coating. The power selector ring is matched to a "Ballistic Aiming System" so you can tailor magnification and reticle to the target and distance. Nitrogen was replaced by Argon/Krypton gas to better prevent fogging. The VX-7 is still top-of-the-line. But in 2009 a new VX-3 series replaces the flagship Vari-X III. Nearly 40 models are listed, all with VX-7's Xtended Twilight lenses and DiamondCoat 2. Cryogenically treated stainless adjustments move 1/4, 1/8 and 1/10 m.o.a. per click in standard, competition and target/varmint versions. An improved spring system ensures precise, positive erector movement. The fast-focus eyepiece has a removable rubber ring. These features appear as well on the new FX-3 6x42, 6x42 AO, 12x40 AO and two scopes designed for metallic silhouette shooting: 25x40 AO and 30x40 AO. You'll find 18 reticle options for the VX-3 and FX-3 series, and five finishes for the 1-inch and 30mm 6061-T6 aircraft alloy tubes.

For black powder rifles and shotguns firing slugs, Leupold now markets two UltimateSlam scopes. The 2-7x33 and 3-9x40 incorporate what the firm calls a Load Selector Ring. After zeroing, you choose a load designation that matches your ammo, then dial that number on the ring every time you shoot The SA. B.R. (for Sabot Ballistics Reticle) reticle comprises two dots and a tight center circle, stacked vertically on a heavy Duplex wire. It all means faster aim at normal hunting ranges (to 300 yards). In the Mark 4 tactical line, there's a new ER/T M1 4.5-14x50 sight with a front-plane reticle. As in European scopes, this reticle stays in constant relationship to the target throughout the magnification span, so you can range a target at any power.

As for oldies, Leupold's FX II 2.5x20 Ultralight scope remains one of my favorites for lever-action carbines. It sits tight to the receiver in extra-low rings, slides easily into scabbards, adds just 7-1/2 oz. to the rifle's weight and has all the magnification you need for big game to 200 yards. For bolt rifles with longer reach, I still prefer the lightweight 4x33 and 6x36 scopes in Leupold's FX II line. My friend Pat Mundy hints of a return of the 3x. "But no promises." The M8 3x ranks among my first picks for hunting elk. I've used that magnification on bulls from 30 to 300 yards. (Leupold.com)

Meopta

European optics are renowned for quality. Meopta's Czech-made R1 4-16x44 Long Range Target Scope boasts low-profile target knobs and an adjustable objective up front, with a 30mm tube and a rear-plane plex or mil dot reticle. Meostar hunting scopes – eight variables and two fixed-powers – also have the second-plane reticle Americans prefer (except the 3-12x56). I've used the 30mm Artemis 3000 3-9x42, a superb sight! The 2000 and illuminated 2100 series are similar, but with steel 30mm tubes. Choose one of four variables: 1.5-6x42, 2-8x42, 3-9x42, 3-12x50. Or a 4x32, 6x42 or 7x50 fixed-power. A pair of range-finding reticles completes Meopta's list of eight. The illuminated versions offer seven levels of brightness, with an "off" detent between each for one-stop control. Meopta W/E adjustments move independently no matter how how close to their limits. The company offers a Meostar S1 spotting scope (75mm objective) with standard or APO glass, straight or angled heel and 30x wide-angle or 20-60 zoom eyepiece. There's a collapsible 75mm scope too. A 12x50 binocular accepts a 2x doubler. Roof-prism binoculars include 7x, 8x and 10x models with 42mm objectives, plus a 7x50, a 10x50 and an 8x56. (Meopta.com)

Millet

Starting out as a supplier of scope mounts, iron sights and related items, Millet soon joined myriad other firms importing rifle-scopes from the Orient. In 2006 Millet introduced target and varmint scopes – a 4-16x and a 6-25x with turret parallax/focus dials, target knobs and the option of illuminated reticles. Buck Gold hunting scopes, 1.5-6x44 to 6-25x56, cover a range of applications. Windage and elevation dials have coil-spring returns and finger-friendly rims. Lighted reticles are available on the high-power models; so too turret-mounted focus. Fast-focus eyepieces come on all. The Buck Silver series comprises 3-9x, 4-12x and 6-18x variables, plus a 2x LEE scope, all with 1" tubes. The 30mm Tactical series, including a 10x and 1-4x and 4-16x

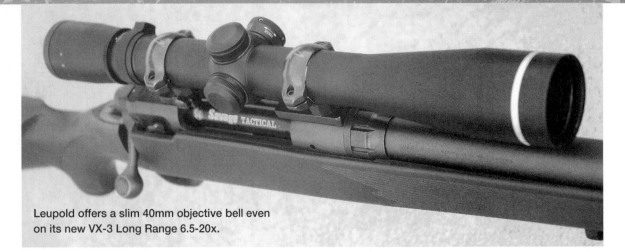

Leupold offers a slim 40mm objective bell even on its new VX-3 Long Range 6.5-20x.

variables, catalogs a lighted Donut-Dot reticle option. Millet's Zoom Dot red dot sight fits rails on handguns and tactical carbines. You'll find Millet rails for popular sporting rifles too. The firm still sells a variety of handgun sights, plus an extensive selection of mount bases and rings. (Millettsights.com)

Nightforce

Made in Idaho. *Idaho?* Yep. Nightforce proudly puts its scopes up against all comers. Four-times magnification gives you great versatility from this 30mm line, from the 3.5-15x50 and 3.5-15x56 NSX to the 5.5-22x50 and 5.5-22x56, the 8-32x56 and 12-42x56. Compact scopes for hunting (a 1-4x24 and a 2.5-10x24) have been joined this year by a 2.5-10x32. Like all but two benchrest models, the new 2.5-10x has a turret-mounted focus/parallax dial. (The 8-32x56 and 12-42x56 bench scopes wear front-sleeve parallax rings, plus resettable 1/8-minute windage and elevation dials.) Also new: the 3.5-15x50 F1, with first-plane reticle. The reticle stays in constant relationship to the target throughout the power range. All Nightforce scopes feature main tubes of lightweight bronze alloy. Dissimilar alloys in the erector assembly guarantee repeatable movement. The illuminated reticles (up to 10 choices per scope model) are distinctive in form and appealing because they cover so little of the field.

Nightforce also markets accessories for competitive and tactical shooters. Mil radian knobs click in mils (.1 per click). Or choose quarter-minute graduations – or a turret with 1-minute elevation and half-minute windage clicks (for big changes in yardage with short dial movement). A "zero-stop" turret has an elevation dial that can be set to return to any of 400 detents in its adjustment range. One-piece steel scope bases have a recoil lug to better secure the mount. Choose from five heights of steel rings. Unimount, machined from 7075-T6 alloy, features titanium crossbolts and a 20-minute taper for long shooting. It stays with the scope, for fast sight changes on Picatinny rails. Nightforce NXS rifle-scopes may well endure the toughest tests in the industry. Each sight must remain leak- and fog-proof after submersion in 100 feet of water for 24 hours, freezing in a box cooled to a minus 80 degrees F, then heating within an hour to 250 degrees F. Every scope gets hammered in a device that delivers 1,250 Gs – backward and forward! Lens coatings must pass mil-spec abrasion tests. Starting at over $1,200, NXS scopes aren't cheap. But then, they're not cheap. To help with those long shots, get the Nightforce Ballistic Program for Windows, or the abbreviated version for Pocket PCs. (Nightforceoptics.com)

Nikon

A new Monarch "African" rifle-scope series tops Nikon's list of new products. The 1-4x20 has a 1" tube; the 1.1-4x24, available also with an illuminated reticle, is a 30mm sight. Both scopes provide 4 inches of eye relief for fast aim and plenty of recoil space. They feature German #4 reticles and 1/2-minute click adjustments. The African rifle-scopes round out a line tilted to high-power optics by the 2008 debut of a 8-32x50ED SF with 1/8-minute adjustments and a turret dial to refine focus and

Sightron has an extensive optics line. This 10x42 binocular is new, excellent, reasonably priced.

zero-out parallax. The 4-16x50SF and 2-8x32, recent additions, are more versatile. For 2009 Nikon has trotted out a pair of "Coyote Special" rifle-scopes – a 3-9x40 and a 4.5-14x40. Both feature BDC (Bullet Drop Compensating) reticles and camouflage finish. A reflection-fighting screen is included for the front lens. A new Omega 1.65-5x36 scope for muzzleloaders has a practical power range and trim front end. So does the suspiciously similar 1.65-5x36 SlugHunter. Both have BDC reticles, though these are slightly different, to fit trajectories of the most common bullets. Omega's parallax setting is 100 yards, that of the SlugHunter 75. Their best feature: 5 inches of eye relief! Both scopes (and a 3-9x40 SlugHunter) have 1" tubes and quarter-minute clicks.

Nikon's EDG binocular series (7x4, 8x42, 10x42, 8x32 and 10x32) appeared a year ago. ED glass, open-bridge design and a locking diopter have boosted sales. Now the company lists an EDG Fieldscope, also with ED glass. Pick the 85mm or 65mm version. Zoom eyepieces (16-48x and 20-60x) interchange with Nikon fixed-power eyepieces. On the binocular front, Nikon has once again bolstered its mid-priced lines. The All Terrain group now includes 8.5x45 and 10.5x45 Monarch X binoculars. You might recognize that moniker – the same as on a Nikon rifle-scope series with 30mm tubes and turret-mounted focus dials. The 2.5-10x and 4-16x feature Nikoplex and mil dot reticles, both etched. The 2.5-10x is available with an illuminated mil dot. Still new at market: Nikon's IRT 4-12x42 laser rangefinding scope that reads reflective objects to 800 yards and delivers 1-yard accuracy out to 400. A BDC reticle helps with holdover. The sight can also give you continuous reads on moving game. (Nikonsportoptics.com)

Pentax

The 2009 binocular line-up at Pentax includes a new 7x50 Marine binocular with built-in compass on a liquid bearing (for quick dampening). It has an LED illuminator. Waterproof, with twist-up eye-cups and a click-stop diopter ring, the rubber-armored 7x50 has all the best features of its roof-prism kindred from the Denver-based firm. DCF roof prism binoculars come in 8x, 10x and 12.5x, with 32mm to 50mm objectives. DCFs feature phase-corrected prisms in aluminum and polycarbonate shells. A Porro prism PCF line includes 8x40, 10x50, 12x50 and 20x60 glasses. Less costly XCF Porros in 8x40, 10x50, 12x50 and 16x50 are great values. Last year I tried a new 9x28 BCF LV roof-prism binocular and found it one of the best lightweights (13 oz.!) I'd ever used. The 3mm exit pupil is adequate for all but the dimmest light. I like the twist-out eyecups and click-stop diopter. The surface is easy to grip. This spring 8x36 and 10x36 DCF NV roof-prism glasses join the 9x28. Their bigger exit pupils but compact size promise good hunting!

Pentax has added a 3-15x50 Gameseeker to its premier rifle-scope line. Five-times magnification offers more versatility than you'll likely need. Like the SL 3-9x32 I carried on a moose hunt last year, it is optically excellent. (That 12-ounce 3-9x32, incidentally, was perfect for my Ruger carbine in .300 RCM. It had the resolution to pick out a sliver

Trijicon's ACOG (Advanced Combat Optical Gunsight) has a big following among AR shooters.

of moose antler 107 yards away in timber! Neither my guide nor my hunting partner saw that moose until it fell.) The Gameseeker stable includes eight 1" variable models and 4x32 and 6x42 fixed-powers. The 30mm Lightseeker 30 series comprises 3-10x40, 4-16x50, 6-24x50 and 8.5-32x50 scopes. A new pair of Pioneer II scopes has just appeared, in 3-9x40 and 4.5-14x42 versions that feature 1-inch tubes with fully multi-coated glass. The Whitetails Unlimited rifle-scope series has been dropped; reflex-style red dot sights remain. Among Pentax spotting scopes, the compact PF-63 Zoom with fixed 20-50x eyepiece is a bargain. It and the top-quality PF-65ED "make weight" for mountain hunting, while

PF-80ED and PF-100ED scopes excel when weight isn't an issue. Interchangeable eyepieces include 32x, 46x and 20-60x for the 37-oz. PF-65ED, which also accepts a Pentax PF-CA35 camera adapter for 35mm SLRs. (Pentaxsportoptics.com)

Schmidt & Bender

Recent changes in the administration of this venerable German firm have not shifted its primary focus. Neither did the celebration, last year, of its first half-century in business. A small company by most standards, S&B caters to people who want the very best in optical sights. Its roots lie in the hunting field, but lately it has brought innovation to the tactical table. Two years ago a S&B 3-12x was adopted by the U.S. Marine Corps for its .30- and .50-caliber sniper rifles. The 34mm Police/Marksman scopes have boldly raised the bar as regards not only tube diameter but sophistication. Lighted mil dot reticles, as on S&B's 4-16x42 P/M II, come with an 11-setting turret-mounted rheostat. An automatic shutoff saves battery – but the previous setting is automatically engaged when you hit the illumination switch again. A side-mounted focus/parallax adjustment shares the left-side turret spot, and cleverly covers the illumination battery cage. Visible "gauges" on the windage and elevation knobs show you where the reticle is in its adjustment range. Flash-dot reticles incorporate a beam-splitter to illuminate a dead-center dot – which vanishes at a touch if you want to use a standard black reticle. For 2009, S&B has announced its first 1" variable rifle-scope, a 2.5-10x40 with second-plane reticle to satisfy U.S. hunters. Called the Summit, this 16-oz. scope has a pleasing profile and, praise be, a relatively short eyepiece. There's tube enough for easy mounting on most rifles. (Schmidt-bender.de or email scopes@cyberportal.net)

Shepherd

The problem with any front-plane reticle is that it grows in apparent size as you dial up the power. So at long range, where targets appear small and you want precise aim, the reticle can obscure the aiming point. Up close, when you power down for quick shots in thickets, the reticle shrinks, becoming hard to see quickly. A second-plane reticle stays the same apparent size throughout the power range. The advantage of a front-plane reticle is that it remains the same size relative to the target throughout the power range. It can be used quickly as a range-finding device at any magnification because the reticle subtends the same area regardless of power.

Shepherd scopes offer both reticles. You get an aiming reticle that doesn't change size and a range-finding reticle that varies in dimension with power changes. Superimposed, they appear as one. The range-finding reticle comprises a series of circles of decreasing diameter, top to bottom. To determine yardage, match a deer-size (18") target with one of the circles, located in the front focal plane. Correct holdover is factored in because the circles are placed to compensate for bullet drop. A trio of range-finding reticles suit the trajectories of popular cartridges. Vertical and horizontal scales are marked in minutes of angle so you can compensate for wind. The newest Shepherd scope, a 6-18x M556 is specially designed for AR-style rifles. (Shepherdscopes.com)

Sightron

It was a start-up company just a few years ago, a new player in the already-competitive arena of sports optics. But Sightron delivered an imported rifle-scope line of impressive quality at modest prices. It grew. The 2009 catalog lists more than 50 scopes in SI, SII and SIII series. New SIII Long Range models feature 30mm tubes, turret-mounted focus/parallax dials and reticles that include mil dot and an illuminated German #4A. Target knobs are tall enough for easy access but not ungainly. From the 3.5-10x44 to the 8-32x56, these scopes feature fully multi-coated optics in one-piece tubes, with resettable ExacTrack windage and elevation adjustments and a fast-focus eyepiece. External lenses wear "Zact-7," a seven-layer coating to transmit the most light possible. A hydrophobic wash disperses raindrops. Eye relief: 3.8 inches.

The SII series comprises a broad range of scopes with 1" tubes and most of the features of the SIIIs. A 1.25-5x20 Dangerous Game sight with over 6 inches of clear tube for mounting has replaced the 2.5x20 that has served me very well on hard-kicking rifles. Big field! Bright images! The SII series now has 4.5-14x40 and 6.5-20x50 scopes with side-focus dials. Sightron has also brought back its 12x42 fixed-power – Hooray! It and the 6x42 hunting scope make long shots easy. High-power variables and the 36x benchrest sights have front-ring parallax adjustments. I like the dot reticle. It's also available in the 5-20x42. Silver finish remains an option on selected models, so too Sightron's Hunter Holdover reticle with a couple of simple hash marks on the lower wire. Specify it on 3-9x42, 3-12x42 and 45.5-14x42 SIIs, and on the 3-9x40 SI.

The SI series for 2009 includes five scopes "back by popular demand." Sightron catalogs two ESDs (Electronic Sighting Devices) masquerading as red dot sights. They feature 33mm tubes, 11-stop rheostats and four reticles you can change with the twist of a dial. New on the binocular front are SIII 8x42 and 10x42 binoculars. I have a 10x42 at hand now. It's optically excellent, a solid value! Also listed: new SIIs and SI roof-prism 8x32 and 10x32 binoculars. (Sightron.com)

Steiner

Had you kept track over the last decade, you'd have noticed Steiner making a purposeful departure from the military profiles that for years defined the brand. Sleek roof-prims binoculars have dominated the news at this European firm. But for 2009 the Predator Pro line has two new Porro prism IF binoculars, and there's a 21-oz. Wildlife Pro 8x30 Porro glass with center focus, the first of its type in Steiner's stable in 20 years! Still the flagship of Steiner's line is the Peregrine XP. This center-focus, open-bridge binocular focuses down to 6-1/2 feet. Large (30mm) eyepieces have twist-up eyecups and flexible wings that can be folded back to ensure against fogging from face moisture. Exterior lens surfaces have hydrophobic "NANO Protection." It beads rainwater so you can see clearly even in a storm. Peregrine XP (8x44 and 10x44) is waterproof and lightweight, with a rugged magnesium frame. It comes with a neoprene hood and a clever Click-Loc strap. The NRA has awarded Peregrine XP its coveted Golden Bullseye Award for excellence, a feather in Steiner's cap! (Steiner-binoculars.com)

Swarovski

There's little new at Swarovski this year – which is hardly an indictment. The Austrian optics (and crystal) maker has introduced a steady stream of new products over the last decade, each an improvement on products many shooters thought were beyond improvement. The SLC binoculars I'd used for years were eclipsed by the EL series. The PH rifle-scopes gave way to the Z6, with six-times magnification. Swarovski borrowed from subsidiary Kahles to produce a Ballistic Turret capable of storing several zero settings. You determine those zeroes with ballistics tables or by live firing, then set a color-coded elevation dial. Change the load and zero; then return to your original in a wink. Ballistic Turret is an option on 1" 4-12x50 and 6-18x50 AV scopes. An even simpler way to engage long-range

Fiber-optic coils help tritium illuminate Trijicon reticles. A movable shield controls light.

targets is the BR reticle. Its ladder-type bottom wire has 10 hash-marks. BR is available in three AV scopes, plus 1.7-10x42 and 2-12x50 Z6 sights. By the way, there is a new Z6: a 2.5-15x56. Like the other three 30mm Z6s, you can specify an illuminated reticle. The switch, atop the eyepiece, has an automatic shutoff and a blinking battery warning. It has two memory locations, one for daytime and one for night use. Turn the switch, and the reticle gets the default illumination for prevailing conditions. These Z6s are very fine scopes; they deliver brilliant, razor-edged images. The 1-6x24 boasts the broadest power range of any "dangerous game" sight. At a generous 4-3/4", its eye relief is longer than even that of its stable-mates. (Swarovskioptik.com)

Trijicon

"We just sold our 500,000th ACOG," said Tom Munson. The ACOG (Advanced Combat Optical Gunsight) vaulted Trijicon into the limelight as an optics maker. Tough and ideally suited for fast shooting with AR-type rifles, the ACOG has endeared itself to military units. But Trijicon didn't stop there. It now offers hunters traditional scopes, and early this spring announced a new reflex-style red dot sight. Labeled RMR (for Ruggedized Miniature Reflex), it can be ordered with an LED (light-emitting diode) that adjusts automatically for changing light conditions; or you can specify a dual-illuminated, battery-free RMR with Trijicon fiber optics and tritium. Both versions have windage and elevation screws – as does the company's RedDot sight. Like the LED RMR, it is powerd by a 17,000-hour lithium battery. The RMR has an alloy housing, the RedDot sight a nylon-polymer frame. Either can be paired with the ACOG.

The newest Trijicon AccuPoint scope is a 5-20x50. It features target knobs and a turret-mounted focus/parallax dial. Like the 1-4x24, 1.25-4x24, 3-9x40 and 2.5-10x56, the 5-20x50 employs both tritium and fiber optics to illuminate the reticle without a battery. An adjustable cover lets you trim light from the fiber optic coil. Last year AccuPoint came with plex and crosswire-and-dot reticles, as alternatives to its original super-fast delta. To acquaint hunters with the famous ACOG, Trijicon now markets a 4x32 version to civilians. It includes an adjustable rail mount and a bullet drop compensator useful to 800 meters. The Michigan-based company continues to produce iron sights with tritium inserts (green, orange and yellow) for handguns and carbines. "We're busy," smiles Tom. (Trijicon.com)

TruGlo

Its luminescent shotgun beads and rifle-sight inserts, with tritium and fiber-optic elements, served shooters well. Now TruGlo offers red dot sights and rifle-scopes too. Waterproof and compatible with any Weaver-style mount, the red dot sights come in tube or reflex (open) styles. Choose 1x or 2x, 1-inch, 30mm or 40mm tubes. An 11-stop rheostat controls reticle brightness. Dual-Color (red and green) Multi-Reticles (pick instantly from four, including the special turkey circle) come standard in some models. All versions of the tube sight have unlimited eye relief, multi-coated lenses, click-stop windage/elevation adjustments. Reflex red dot sights weigh as little as 2 oz. This lightweight model boasts a 4-minute dot with manual and light-sensitive automatic brightness modes. Multi-Reticle, Dual-Color reflex sights offer four reticles in red or green. They're parallax-free beyond 30 yards. Like many optics firms now, TruGlo markets several series of rifle-scopes, topped by the Maxus XLE in 1.5-6x44, 3-9x44 and 3.5-10x50 (also with BDC). The Infinity label goes on 4-16x44 and 6-24x44 scopes with adjustable objectives. To make long-distance hits easier across a variety of loads, each comes with three replaceable BDC elevation knobs. Tru-Brite Xtreme Illuminated rifle-scopes feature dual-color plex and range-finding reticles. Choose a 3-9x44, 3-12x44 or 4-16x50. Muzzleloader versions are available. The 4x32 Compact scope for rimfires and shotguns, a 4x32 for crossbows and a 1.5-5x32 illuminated crossbow model round out the TruGlo line of 1" scopes. New for 2009: a fiber optic AR-15 gas block front sight with protected green bead (it will also mount on Picatinny and Weaver rails). TruGlo offers an expanded line of illuminated iron sights and beads. (Truglo.com)

Vortex

Two lines of rifle-scopes from Vortex differ primarily in front-lens glass and W&E dials. Viper sights comprise six models, from the 1" 2-7x32 to the 30mm 6.5-20x50 AO. Front lenses are of what the company calls XD or extra-low dispersion glass. Dials reset to zero. There's a fast-focus eyepiece. Eye relief ranges from 3.1 to 4.0 inches. Diamond-back rifle-scopes share the aircraft-alloy tubes, argon-gas fog-proofing and fully multi-coated optics of the Viper series; but they lack the resettable dials and XD glass, so they don't cost as much. Choose a 1.75-5x32 or one of six other models in versatile power ranges (2-7x to 4-12x) with BDC (bullet drop compensating) reticles – but not BDC mechanisms.

The widest selection in the Vortex family comes under the Crossfire banner, a line of affordable rifle-scopes from 1.5-4x32 to 8-32x50. It includes 2-7x32 and 4x32 sights for rimfires, a 2x20 handgun scope and a 3x32 for crossbows. As with the Vipers, you get tall target knobs (and 30mm tubes) on the most powerful scopes, low-profile dials on others. Nitrogen gas prevents fogging. Specify a mil dot or illuminated mil dot reticle on the 6-24x50 AO. Vortex also offers a red dot sight, the Strikefire, with fully multi-coated lenses. Choose red or green dots at any time. The sight has a 30mm tube 6 inches long and weighs 7.2 oz. The 2x optical doubler is a useful feature. There's unlimited eye relief, and the Strikefire is parallax-free beyond 50 yards.

Vortex spotting scopes include two new models. The 20-60x80 Nomad complements the budget-priced 20-60x60 Nomad (specify straight or angled eyepiece for both). Adapters allow you to mount most pocket-size digital cameras so you can photograph through your Nomad. At the top end, there's the new Razor HD, with apochromatic lenses and an 85mm objective. The 15" scope weighs 66 ounces with an angled 20-60x eyepiece and rotating body. It has coarse and fine focusing wheels in front of the eyepiece. The die-cast magnesium alloy body is argon-gas purged. (800-426-0048)

Weaver

It was inevitable, I suppose, that after the Grand Slam would come the Super Slam. Weaver's most recent scope line includes 2-10x42, 2-10x50, 3-15x42, 3-15x50 and 4-20x50 models. The scopes are quite similar to the ATK line (Weaver is owned by ATK), from the five-times magnification range to the 1" tubes to the turret-mounted focus/parallax dials. They're not identical, though. Weaver has endowed these sights with pull-up windage and elevation knobs (no caps to lose). A three-point erector design, argon gas purging and scratch-resistant lens coating make them field worthy. Euro-style versions with 30mm tubes

The Zeiss Victory Varipoint 1.1-4x24 now features front-plane reticle with rear-plane lighted dot.

With an 85mm
objective and a 20-60x
eyepiece, the Vortex
Razor weighs 66 oz.

and front-plane reticles are available.

Weaver's Classic Extreme scopes, new last year, remain in the stable with the Grand Slam and Classic V-Series – both of which offer Ballisitc-X reticles this year. Fixed 4x38 and 6x38 K-Series scopes survive. I'm delighted. They're among the best buys in the industry! No frills, just fine optics in a lightweight, foolproof package that looks good on any rifle. New in 2009 is a 4-20x50 Tactical scope with 30mm tube, front-plane mil dot reticle and side-focus parallax dial. For long shooting at small targets, Weaver T-series sights excel. I like the T-24s announced a couple of years ago. Choose a 1/2-minute or 1/8-minute dot reticle. Target adjustments on dual-spring supports ensure quick, repeatable changes. (Weaveroptics.com)

Zeiss

No question, Zeiss is out for more U.S. market share. The highly rated Conquest rifle-scope series was followed last year by 8x45 and 10x45 T* RF binoculars, which feature a laser range-finding unit that requires no "third eye" emitter but delivers 1,300-yard range on reflective targets. This unit is fast – you get a read in about a second – and the LED self-compensates for brightness. The binocular itself is top-drawer, and wears rain-repellent LotuTec coating. You can program the RF with computer data to get holdover for six standard bullet trajectories. This year, the Zeiss news is mostly about scopes. The Victory Varipoint 1.1-4x24 T* and 1.5-6x42 T* are getting a #60 reticle, with a cross-wire in the front focal plane and a lighted dot in the rear. So the main reticle stays in constant relation-ship to the target (for easy ranging), while the dot subtends a tiny area even at high power. A left-side turret knob controls dot brightness on the 1.1-4x24; three other Varipoints (2.5-10x42T*, 2.5-10x50T*, 3-12x56T*) have automatic brightness control. Another headline for 2009: second-plane reticles in 2.5-10x50T* and 3-12x56T* Diavari scopes. Hewing to tastes of U.S. hunters, these reticles stay the same apparent size throughout the power range, so do not block out targets at high magnification. Reticle choices include the #60, Z-Plex and Rapid-Z 800.

Big news for pistol shooters is the first Zeiss handgun scope. This 2-7x has more power than most of us need. But it's a trim, well-shaped sight, with non-critical eye relief and plenty of tube for rings. It is optically superb. So is the Victory PhotoScope, 85T* FL, also new this spring. This 85mm spotting scope with fluorite lens and 45-degree 15-45x eyepiece has at its midpoint a square compartment – not too bulky or obtrusive – housing a 7-megapixel camera, so you can shoot photos through that powerful lens (35mm equivalent: 600mm f2.4 to 1800mm f3.3). The camera uses a 7.4-volt lithium ion battery and SD card to deliver images in standard file formats. PhotoScope 85T* FL weighs 6-1/2 lbs.

Not to be outdone in the range-finder market, Zeiss has introduced the Victory 8x26T* PRF, a "one-touch" device that gives you an LED read to 1,300 yards. In scan mode, it updates distance every 1.5 seconds. Its most distinctive feature may be a Ballistic Information System (BIS) that can be programmed to give you proper holdover for your rifle's load – instantly. (Zeiss.com)

WOMEN'S PERSPECTIVE

BY GILA HAYES

Ruger's reinvention of the snub-nosed
revolver has cutting-edge good looks.

We are happy to include in this edition a notable first: a column written from a woman's perspective. That woman, Gila Hayes, is 10-year veteran of Washington State police departments, where she served as Department Firearms Instructor. In addition, Ms. Hayes has a long career writing for publications including Woman's Outlook, American Guardian, SWAT Magazine, Women & Guns, *and* GUNS Magazine. *With her husband Marty, she operates The Firearms Academy of Seattle, Inc., a practical firearms training school. In addition, Gila has recently started a second business, the Armed Citizens Legal Defense Network* (http://www.armed citizensnetwork.org/).

As women's participation in the world of guns becomes increasingly ordinary, the variety of firearms that work really well for women is greater than ever before. Remember when an anemic .25 ACP with pearly pink grips was the pistol most gun store clerks trotted out for women? Fortunately, that doesn't happen too often anymore, due in part to the increasing variety of very serviceable handguns, shotguns and rifles that fit women's needs. Still, I marvel at the shooting industry's proclivity for coloring a product pink and dubbing it a "ladies' gun."

That kind of marketing is straight out of the mid to late 1950s. If in doubt, consider the amusing history of the ill-fated Dodge La Femme and similarly patronizing General Motors attempts at "women's cars"! When the color concept petered out with merciful rapidity, Detroit's marketing geniuses came to their senses and began promoting creature comforts like heated seats, adjustable pedals and steering wheels, and child-friendly seating.

In the gun industry of 2009, countless variations on ergonomic firearms offer women guns that fit and function properly with quite a reasonable selection from which to choose — no matter the color!

Handgun Choices

On handguns, proper fit is largely determined by the measurement between the backstrap and the face of the trigger. On revolvers, shooters have traditionally custom fit the gun to their hand size with replacement grips. The latest trend in semi-auto pistols is the small-to-large interchangeable back

Short hands just fit well around a 1911, as the author shows here with Para Ordnance's new 9mm LTC.

strap insert, as found on Smith & Wesson's M&P, Walther's PPS, several models of Heckler & Koch handguns, the Beretta Storm, FNH's FNP handguns, Springfield's XD(M), and the Ruger SR9, to list only what comes quickly to mind. SIG Sauer achieves a similar end result with the modular SIG Sauer 250.

The classic 1911 design has long been an ergonomic favorite among female .45 shooters, with the thin grips around the single column magazine and the short trigger reach accommodating a strong grip. Think about this: how powerfully can you hold an object around which your fingers only reach halfway, compared to gripping something your fingers nearly encircle? Thus the thin-gripped 1911 is a natural choice for the smaller-handed shooter.

Does recoil matter? Of course it does, but in shooters of either gender, tolerance to recoil is an individual matter. It is not unusual to see a woman operating a .45 ACP pistol with the same skill as her male counterpart. With good training and well-practiced trigger control, the larger handgun calibers are certainly controllable. Only when tactical engagements require intensely brief shot-to-shot times, do we begin to see the generally smaller and more lightly muscled female shooter better served by lighter recoil.

Because there are plenty of highly ranked men shooting 9mm 1911s in competition, I hesitate to identify models like Kimber's Aegis as "women's guns." Not everyone wants to put up with the hard bump of .45 caliber recoil and its muzzle rise. Para Ordnance, Springfield Armory and Kimber, as well as exclusive shops like STI, Wilson Combat and Cylinder and Slide, all stock a variety of excellent 1911 choices in alternative calibers.

Several years ago, Springfield Armory and Para Ordnance both brought out 9mm 1911 pattern pistols on what was essentially shrunken frames. Para's Carry 9 is a slim, 9mm micro version of Para's popular light double-action pistol. Eight round magazines, plus one in the chamber, make it a nine-shooter.

An exciting new development is chambering the originally 9mm Springfield Enhanced Micro Pistol (EMP) to fire the effective .40 caliber ammunition. The ingenious EMP design remains a favorite with women who love the 1911 single-action operation, but want a smaller grip than the traditional officers model. Now we even have a caliber choice!

The original 9mm EMP is built around a nine-round magazine so it's about a 1/4" longer through the grip than the Para Carry 9. The new .40 caliber EMP has an eight-round magazine.

I would be remiss if mention of the Glock 19 was lost in all the "new-and-improved" chatter! If there is one semi-automatic pistol which shooters, new and old, male and female, find adaptable to their training, practice, and defense needs, it is

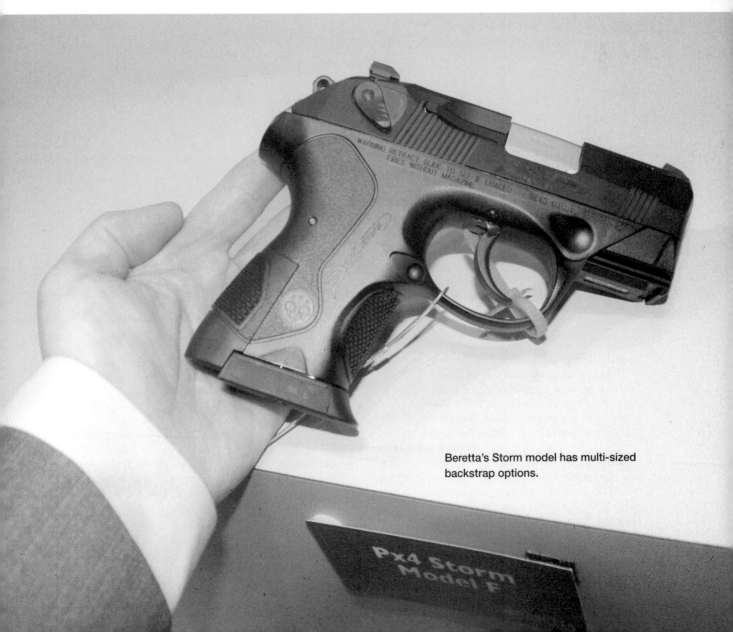

the Glock 19. The Glock Safe Action eliminates the need to accustom the shooter to a thumb safety or decocker, and that mid-sized frame sure soaks up recoil. Though less suitable for beginners, the smaller Glock 26 may well have eclipsed J-frame revolvers as women's single most popular personal protection choice.

Both the Glock 19 and 26 cannot be beat for reliable operation; the array of holsters and carry options made for Glocks cannot be surpassed; and there are hundreds of aftermarket products such as grip reductions, laser sights, night sights, and other replacement parts of all kinds made for Glocks.

Mossberg's Super Bantam Model 500's stock is adjustable between 12" and 13" LOP, plus one of the color options is the distinctive Pink Marble.

How Small Is Too Small?

Too often, people erroneously recommend extremely small, light guns to first-time women gun buyers. At the Firearms Academy of Seattle, which my husband and I operate, we see with heartbreaking regularity novice female shooters who come to class with ultra-light snubby revolvers, or tiny, 8-oz. .380s. Not only are the abbreviated frames often too small for these new shooters to attain a

Beretta's Storm model has multi-sized backstrap options.

With their latest innovation, the LaserGuard, Crimson Trace returns to its roots – a laser sight positioned on the front of the trigger guard.

serviceable shooting grip, the recoil in such a light gun is jarring.

Having acknowledged the extreme disadvantage of training with miniaturized pistols, it is hard to ignore the attraction they pose for the well-trained concealed carry practitioner. Women licensed to carry a concealed handgun face additional concealment challenges, owing to the skimpiness of women's fashions coupled with ladies' generally smaller physiques. Today, our concealed carry gun choices are many and varied.

Kel-Tec and North American Arms enjoy continued loyalty to their respective P-3AT and Guardian semi-autos in .380 ACP, though in 2008, Ruger enchanted many with their LCP. In 2009, SIG Sauer

and Kahr Arms entered the mini-380 market with models that also deserve serious consideration.

Kahr Arms' P380 is a miniaturized version of their already miniscule PM9 pistol. Thus, like the – dare we say larger? – PM9, the P380 is an elegantly simple double-action-only pistol with a stainless steel slide atop a polymer frame. With no external safety, the striker-fired design uses a double action only trigger with a light, but long, pull. Kahr pistols position the barrel very low in the gripping hand, which tames the .380 muzzle rise in this small, 10-oz. frame.

Beyond the smaller dimensions, the new Kahr .380 features rounded edges appropriate to a deep concealment pistol, and honest-to-goodness sights,

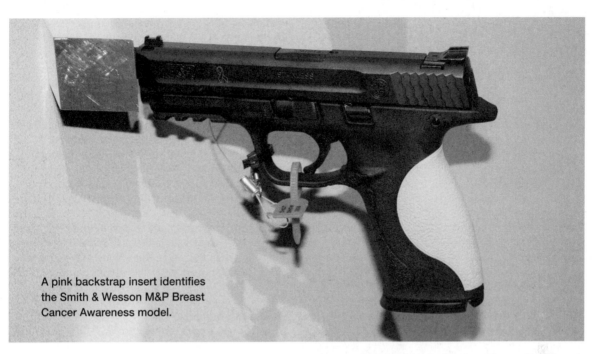

A pink backstrap insert identifies the Smith & Wesson M&P Breast Cancer Awareness model.

something sorely lacking on most miniaturized .380s. Dimensionally, the P380 is slightly shorter from slide to mag base plate than a Kel-Tec, though both use six-round magazines. The Kahr is heavier, and its price about double. Like other Kahr pistols, its locked breech design operates on the short recoil principle, unlike the blowback operation of NAA's Guardian.

Though Colt's Manufacturing hasn't made the Colt Government Pocketlite for over a decade, SIG Sauer's new single-action semi-auto P238 is so reminiscent of that early pocket pistol that I thought I was suffering a flashback when first I saw it. Closer inspection showed that the little single action was identical in height and length to the old Colt .380, though its blocky slide profile is pure SIG.

Both the SIG P238 and Kahr P380 herald good things for the concealed carry practitioner. The Kahr is a little smaller and considerably thinner, while the SIG P238 has the single action operation to which some experienced shooters are so partial.

Revolver Innovations

But not all the innovation focuses on semi-automatic pistols! It is entirely possible that the new product generating the greatest interest at the 2009 Shooting, Hunting and Outdoor Trade Show (SHOT Show) was Ruger's completely redesigned, ultra-lightweight five-shot .38 Special revolver. Recently, Ruger has made a concerted play for the hearts of serious self-defense shooters, in 2008 with their pocket-sized .380 and now with their all-new Lightweight Compact Revolver (LCR).

The LCR is an intriguing re-invention of the double-action revolver: an all-new wheel gun

comprising an aluminum frame, polymer housing around the firing mechanism, and a fluted steel cylinder. Sized like all five-shot snubbies, the LCR weighs between 13 and 13.5 oz., depending on grip option selected.

The innovative LCR has a large, curving trigger guard that should accommodate chubby or gloved trigger fingers, a black pinned front sight blade, and the modular design that accept a variety of replacement grips, including an OEM LaserGrip option.

1911 and .45 ACP are no longer synonymous. Major manufacturers like Kimber have 9mms on the 1911 pattern.

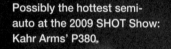

Possibly the hottest semi-
auto at the 2009 SHOT Show:
Kahr Arms' P380.

Angela Harrell w/HK P30
Heckler & Koch's Angela Harrell
shows off features of their P30,
which also includes grip backstrap
inserts in varied sizes.

Ruger's new revolver promises to address one challenge that wheel guns pose for some women: their stiff trigger pull. According to Ruger, "The LCR's trigger pull force builds more gradually, and peaks later in the trigger stroke, resulting in a trigger pull that feels much lighter than it actually is...This results in more controllable shooting, even among those with smaller, weaker hands who find traditional DAO triggers difficult to operate."

A ridiculously over-booked SHOT Show schedule cost me the chance to test fire the all-new revolver, but no less an authority than Massad Ayoob enthusiastically told me that the recoil was quite manageable.

Another innovation making ever-widening ripples in the revolver market is the .327 Federal cartridge. I couldn't help but notice that Smith & Wesson now joins Ruger in producing a revolver chambered for the smaller .327. Now both the Ruger SP101 and S&W's J-framed Model 632 fire six rounds of high pressure, magnumized .32-caliber ammo. The jury is still out on cartridge effectiveness as it has only been with us since November of 2007, but Smith & Wesson's presence brings additional prestige to the new cartridge, giving it "legs," so to speak. I am told that other manufacturers, including Charter Arms and Taurus, have also embraced the new caliber.

Sighting Improvements

Small, hard-to-use sights are the single most troubling characteristic shared by most ultra-small handguns, and they pose problems not only for men but for women, too. The solution? Crimson Trace's LaserGrip and now the new LaserGuard. The LaserGuard is a sleek half-sleeve attaching to Glock, Kahr Arms, Kel-Tec, and Ruger LCP trigger guards to position an aiming laser to the front of the trigger guard.

The design is reminiscent of Crimson Trace's first laser sight, introduced some 15 years ago. It was a complex aftermarket assembly that they painstakingly installed on Glock pistols. Since then, the Crimson Trace laser aiming products have grown increasingly innovative, while continuing to augment traditional sights without compromising conventional sighting and without replacing any of the handgun's operating parts.

Crimson Trace even has several laser sighting options for AR-15 rifles. Not being a big fan of vertical foregrips, I am partial to the slightly more complex LG-525, which I have installed on my AR. I am comforted by the increased low light functionality it adds to the .223 rifle.

Beyond Handguns

If there is one gun that exemplifies this decade's gun industry growth, it must surely be the AR-15 rifle. It seems that companies manufacturing "black rifles" have doubled, if not tripled. Even mainline Smith & Wesson has their famous logo on an AR-15! The good news for women is the light recoil of the .223 cartridge, as well as a plethora of aftermarket accessories to custom fit the rifle to their needs. An AR-15 promises hours of shooting fun, plus a serious tactical rifle for defense emergencies.

With long guns, police raid vests and bulky body armor interfere with stock fit. While most women shooters won't be kitted out that way, the short stocks manufactured to accommodate SWAT and military operators also fit short-statured shooters! While some do fine with collapsible stocks, I prefer the cheek weld of a fixed A-1 stock, which is 5/8" shorter than the common A2 version.

Cavalry Arms injection-molds AR furniture in a variety of colors and has the A1-length butt stock in their product line up. Although not every woman shooter will go all googly-eyed over colored AR furniture, this manufacturer stocks green and brown butt stocks and handgrips, and in the past has run pink, red, yellow and purple choices.

Hunting rifles to fit women seem fewer and farther between, owing to long 14" length of pull (LOP) stocks on most of the bolt-action rifles. Youth models, with a 13" LOP, generally find their way into women's hands, and for my money, Remington's compact Model Seven Youth rifle combines quality construction with caliber choices, ranging from .223 to 7mm-08 Rem., suitable for a variety of hunts. The Model Sevens are slightly more compact and half a pound lighter than Remington's ubiquitous Model 700.

The Remington Model 700, however, has a left-handed youth model. That's important to women, because ladies exhibit eye cross dominance at a higher rate than men. Right-handers with left eye dominance usually simply shoot a rifle or shotgun from the left shoulder, so that left-handed action could make a big difference, even though caliber choices are limited to .243 and 7mm-08.

The ever-popular shotgun is the other long gun on which certain models and modifications make considerable difference for female shooters. Length of pull is again the critical factor, and once more, youth models reduce stock length by about an inch. Often these shorter shotguns are 20-gauges. As with handguns, ability with a 12- or 20-gauge shotgun is an extremely individual attribute. Plenty of women can keep up with or even outshoot the gents at the gun club with a 12-gauge shotgun – if it fits her properly.

Hogue's famous soft rubbery overmolded short butt stocks are a great help when adjusting a 12-gauge for shorter shooters. A really short woman, or one who simply likes a short stock, will be delighted, as was I, with the fit of Hogue's 12" LOP stock for Remington 870s and Mossberg 500s.

Peggy Tartaro, editor of *Women & Guns*, deserves recognition for putting out a magazine exclusively for women who shoot.

KNOWLEDGE IS POWER

Women shooters are also serious about knowing how to shoot their guns well. Twenty years ago, *Women & Guns* magazine started a gun publication solely for women. Editor Peggy Tartaro recently told me that she is inspired by Virginia Woolfe's famous title, "A Room of One's Own," and her goal has been to provide female shooters with a magazine of their own, and thus their own voice. She is proud to note that, "unlike virtually any other women's magazine, *Women & Guns* has, with rare exceptions, used actual women gun owners on our covers and pages throughout its history."

Tartaro believes that the gun industry has "failed itself by not working harder with minorities, women and the urban population in general." Her magazine is not heavily focused on gun rights issues, though its publisher, the Second Amendment Foundation, is a leader in that effort.

Live-fire educational initiatives that women truly appreciate include programs like Women on Target or the Ladies Action Shooting Camp, a competition training program taught by top female shooters, including Kay Clark-Miculek, Lisa Munson, Sheila Bray, and Julie Goloski, just to name a few. Sponsorship by Smith & Wesson and USPSA keeps tuition reasonable.

For more information, visit www.womenshooters.com.

Crimson Trace teams with Smith & Wesson to offer an OEM LaserGrip option that puts a laser in the M&P backstrap insert.

The latest in laser aiming devices, Crimson Trace's LaserGuard, shown on Kahr Arms' CW9.

Walther's 9mm PPS is ultra-slim, but the backstrap insert gives some grip size adjustment.

Mossberg has what is in my opinion the most tastefully done pink gun ever! They've dressed up a Model 500 Super Bantam 20-gauge shotgun in a stock pattern dubbed "Pink Marble." Veins of a dark, contrasting hue run through the pink of the stock and forend. The darker colors tie in the pink to the blued steel of the shotgun's action and barrel. Of course, Super Bantams also come in several camo patterns, black synthetic or the more traditional wooden stock.

The 20-gauge Super Bantam has the added benefit of 12" to 13" LOP adjustability that can be a make-or-break feature for short shooters. If a 13" stock fits, the shooter can choose between 12- and 20-gauge in the Bantam line. The Mossberg tang-mounted safety makes it almost ambidextrous, and it is certainly the most ergonomic place to put a shotgun's safety.

The pink marble Mossberg stock is genuinely attractive. In other instances, I've seen pink accessories that looked as if they were simply slapped onto a black gun with little aesthetic consideration. These make me think of wearing boots with a chiffon ball gown. Bold design contrast can look great, but some mind must be paid to design principles to carry it off!

What Women Want

The prevalence of pink at the 2009 SHOT Show convinced me that the gun industry continues to court the female market, but I wonder if color-coding is intelligent marketing. I looked to women from various walks of life for perspective.

Suzi Huntington, retired San Diego police officer, now managing editor of *American Cop* magazine, dislikes pink guns, feeling they trivialize women. "A gun should not be viewed as a fashion accessory, but as a deadly weapon. It's got one job to do and it's pretty damn hard to get anybody to believe you mean business when the darn thing is pink," she commented, adding, "I think the pink goodies marketed for breast cancer awareness are wonderful. That's a legitimate and noble cause and that's about where this pink thing should end!"

On the other hand, *Concealed Carry Magazine* editor Kathy Jackson, also the woman behind www.corneredcat.com, is annoyed by implications that shooting and self defense are masculine activities. She sees no reason for women to want to be treated like one of the guys. "We can be as absolutely feminine as we want to be, as long as we're competent and capable. People will take the competence and visible capability seriously, whether it's pink and frilly or not," she told me.

Theresa Dec is an avid competition shooter who opines, "I am not a man. I will not do things like a man. I will, however, shoot quickly, accurately and safely. It's great to tease the guys I shoot with, that

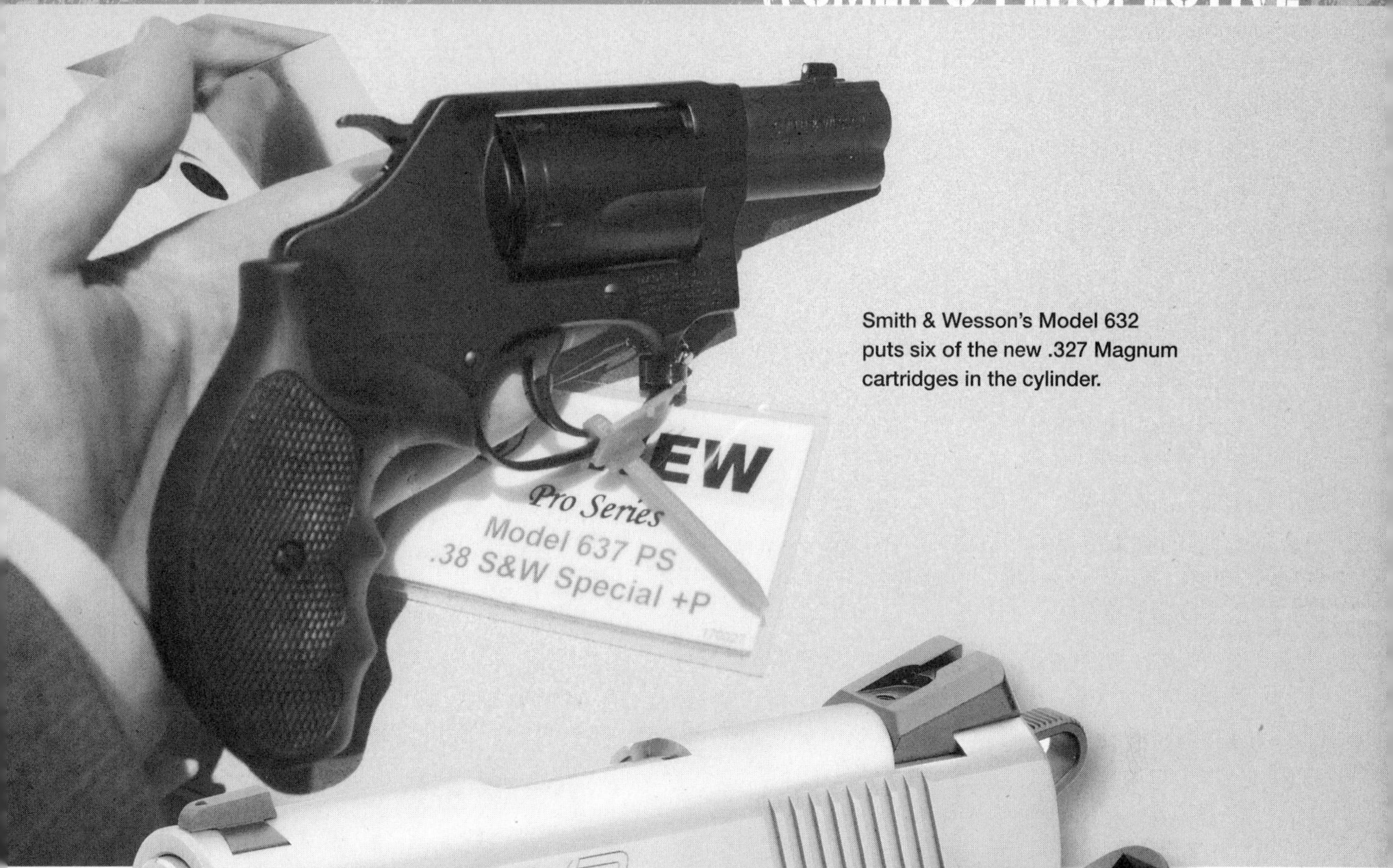

Smith & Wesson's Model 632 puts six of the new .327 Magnum cartridges in the cylinder.

NEW
Pro Series
Model 637 PS
.38 S&W Special +P

not only are they being beat by agirl, they are being beat by a girl with a pink gun."

Most women queried found the idea of pink accents on a wholly sporting firearm acceptable and often appealing, while attempting to feminize purely defensive guns raised some hackles. Not once in my inquiries did a woman complain that she couldn't find firearms that fit her needs.

Viewed that way, it seems that women shooters have a reasonable variety of equipment choices, both colored and plain. The ergonomic challenges of all smaller shooters are fewer than in earlier years, though shooters always welcome innovations that fit guns and equipment to individual needs, especially with shotguns and rifles.

Pink doesn't necessarily make a gun "perfect for women," but the ability to fit a firearm to "her" size, conceal it if appropriate, and trust it to function reliably, may well make a gun a woman's favorite!

Springfield Armory's beautiful new .40 caliber EMP.

EDITOR'S PICKS

BY **DAN SHIDELER**

Superior Concepts Laser Stock (laser visible at end of forend) and barrel-band accessory Mount.

he able Contributing Editors of *Gun Digest* will perhaps forgive me if I take a moment and comment on just a few guns and gadgets that tripped my personal trigger during the past year. Some of these are doubtless discussed elsewhere in this volume, but what can I say? I was here first.

Lord Tennyson wrote, *"In the spring a young man's fancy lightly turns to thoughts of love."* Well, it's spring, and although I can't rightly be termed a young man anymore, I'm in love – with **Ithaca's new 28-gauge Model 37 pump shotgun**. My first shotgun, nearly 35 years ago, was a new Ithaca 20-ga. Deluxe Featherweight, and it pained me when Ithaca fell on tough times a few years ago. Now, however, Ithaca is back is competent hands in their new headquarters in Upper Sandusky, Ohio, and although the company's production is limited to around 3500 guns per year, the guns it does produce are gems. The new 28-ga. M37 is available in three grades, A to AAA, with prices starting around a cool grand. I handled an AAA Grade at the 2009 SHOT Show and, brother, that was it for me. Ithaca's new 28-ga. is available on special order only, and I fully intend to order one as soon as I've bailed out the banks, the Big Three, Moe's Pizza, and apparently everybody else.

It's a shame that many younger shooters are unaware of the Ithaca Model 37. Based on the sainted John Browning's patents for a bottom-ejecting shotgun, the M37 always struck me as the quintessential upland pump. It is so refined, so exquisitely styled, so just plain pretty, that even today I have a hard time passing one up on the used-gun rack. What really hurt the M37, in my opinion, was the fact that it wasn't offered with a 3" chamber until it was rechristened the Model 87 some 20 years ago, and by that time the brand's prestige had already dimmed. In 2005, however, Dave Dlubak acquired the company, and he's really turned it around. I've spoken to Dave and to Ithaca's management team, and I'm glad to report that they are True Believers in the grand old name of Ithaca.

But even bigger news may be in the offing for Ithaca. They've got an all-new, *100% American-made* 12-ga. over/under prototyped, and I hope like hell it makes it all the way to production. Until then, the 28-ga. M37 will do quite nicely for me. Ithaca's back, folks. (See www.ithacagun.com.)

Ithaca's 28-ga. M37. This one's a Grade AA.

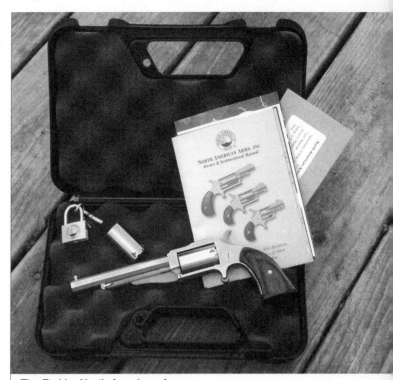
The Earl by North American Arms.

Then there's **The Earl by North American Arms**. For those of you who came in late, NAA is the pre-eminent manufacturer of .22 mini-revolvers (and they field a pretty good team of centerfire pocket pistols, too). The Earl is the latest of NAA's mini-guns, and it's a pip: a five-shot .22 Magnum that looks for all the world like an 1858-pattern Remington percussion revolver. It's made entirely of stainless steel (except the grips, of course) and even includes a faux "loading lever" that serves as a cylinder pin release. It even has a 4" octagonal barrel with a barleycorn front sight.

Initially available in only .22 Magnum rimfire, a .22 Mag/.22LR conversion cylinder is expected to be offered soon, perhaps by the time you read this. At a suggested retail of $289 for the .22 Mag version, I'd have an awfully tough time passing up The Earl. Some shooters condemn all .22 mini-guns as "mouse guns" or worse, but I beg to differ. A .22 in my shirt pocket beats beats a .45 left at home. Besides, The Earl really isn't meant as a self defense gun; NAA's affable president Sandy Chisholm says "it might become your favorite plinker." I can see that. (See naaminis.com.)

I'm happy to report that it seems that **Charter Arms** has really gotten its act together. A few months ago I had the chance to spend some time with their **.357 Target Bulldog Stainless** and was impressed. While its double-action trigger pull was a bit stagy until a few hours of shooting smoothed it

This Charter Arms .357 Target Bulldog did pretty well at 25 yards offhand.

out, its single-action pull was one of the nicest I've ever seen. Its 4" barrel and neoprene grips made it quite comfortable to shoot even with fast-steppin' 125-grainers, and it shot right on the money. With a suggested retail of $449 and a street price a bit less, the five-shot .357 Target Bulldog strikes me as a good buy for the woods bum who wants something small but substantial on his belt. It should serve well as a home defense revolver, too. Those who remember the quality of Charter Arms' first Bulldogs back in the mid-'70s will find a lot to like in the .357 Target Bulldog. Welcome home, Charter Arms! (See www. charterfirerams.com.)

By now you've read all the compliments for **Mossberg's 464 .30-30 lever-action**, and I'll throw a few more on the pile. We wrung one out pretty thoroughly last year and it performed just as advertised: short lever throw, positive ejection, easy loading, etc. Externally it resembles a hybrid between a Marlin 336 and a late-model Winchester 94, but there's an impressive amount of steel in its upper receiver. With a street price hovering around $400, the 464 should find friends among those who believe that a .30-30 is all you really need for woods-range deer hunting. For beginning hunters, it should be an absolute peach. Now: where's that 464 in .22LR? (See www.mossberg. com.)

With a street price of around $1200 as of this writing, Remington's R-15 VTR is a superbly accurate AR.

I have to admit, with all due embarrassment, that until recently I had never owned an AR. I've had plenty of M1 Carbines and AKs and SKSs in addition to the usual complement of Krags and Trapdoors and '03s and Mausers, but somehow the planets never lined up sufficiently for me to buy an AR. That oversight has been corrected in the form of a **Remington R-15 VTR** in .223. As a life-long fan of Remington autoloaders (from the Model 8 of 1906 on up to today's Model 750 Woodsmaster), I'm kind of glad that my first AR had the Remington name on it. A camo-dipped version of a Bushmaster Predator, my R-15 shoots consistent .75" groups at 100 yards if I hold my mouth right. Frankly, I remain amazed by its performance. To anyone who ever questioned whether an AR is a legitimate sporting arm, the R-15 definitely answers in the affirmative. I can't wait to introduce it to some Indiana woodchucks. (See www.remington.com.)

Younger hunters – and some not-so-young – will find plenty of value in the Mossberg 464 .30-30.

Speaking of Remington, I like the looks of Remington's new **.30 Remington AR** cartridge. I have a soft spot for the old .30 Remington Autoloading cartridge (sort of a rimless .30-30 Winchester),

The new 30 Remington AR.

and the new Remington .30 is a worthy successor. Based on a cut-down, necked 450 Bushmaster case, the stubby new .30 provides low-end .308 Winchester ballistics with a 125-gr. spitzer. Make no mistake: the short .30 Remington AR case can't accommodate the longer 150- to 165-gr. bullets like a .308 bolt rifle can, but for someone who wants a real deer-level cartridge in an AR platform, it should prove decisive. I'm not going out on too much of a limb when I predict that this is one case that will be extensively wildcatted.

It seems like I spend at least 25% of my life tying things to the back of trucks: boats, canoes, coolers, unruly children, etc. Since my half-hitches usually come out looking like granny knots, I'm happy to have found the **No-Knot Ropelok by Grabber**

Outdoors. The Ropelok is heavy-duty 8' or 15' poly rope combined with a lever-activated cinching device that's superior to plain knots and ratcheting straps, at least for my needs. Just slip the rope through the Ropelok, draw up the slack, and press the lever. That's it. It's like an automatic knot. Since the Ropelok is made out of polymer, it can't scratch or mar automotive or boat surfaces. (See www.warmers.com.)

I belong to the school that holds that you can't have too many gadgets. And a couple of the more enticing gadgets I've seen lately are the **Superior Concepts 10/22 Laser Stock** and **Accessory Band**. The Laser Stock first: This is a nifty aftermarket stock for the Ruger .22 autoloader that incorporates an easily-adjustable laser sight. The switch for the sight is inset into the left side of the stock's forend, where it falls naturally under the thumb. A little pressure on the switch and *zing!* a brilliant laser dot is projected as far out as you're likely to use one. It's available in a wide variety of stockl styles, from tactical to plain-jane.

The Accessory Band is one of those slap-my-fore-head-why-didn't-I-think-of-that things: an accessory mount that replaces the barrel band of the 10/22. For those such as I who possess only limited gun-smithing skills (okay, very limited), it's a no-brainer. (See www.laserstock.com.)

Rounding out this brief review is the **BreakOut Safety Tool** by **World Class Safety Products**. The BreakOut is a combination window-breaker, seatbelt-cutter and LED signal light that should be standard equipment in your car. Available in a variety of configurations, the BreakOut is a well-thought-out auto accessory that seems superior (to me, anyway) to many hammer-style emergency tools. For one thing, it clips onto your car's sun visor, where it's always within easy reach. I've never forgotten what my Driver's Ed instructor told me: "The next poor SOB upside-down in that water-filled ditch could be you!" If so, I'd rather be there with a BreakOut on my sunvisor than without one. (See www.breakout safetytools.com.)

The BreakOut Safety Tool. A good idea in a handy package.

The Ropelok is as simple as it looks and makes life a lot easier.

EUROPEAN GUNS TODAY

BY **M. RAYMOND CARANTA**
Aix-en-Provence, France

Highlights of IWA 2009

The 36th IWA and outdoor classic gun show was held in Nurnberg this year – as it is every year – from March 13 to 16th, 2009.

The IWA (the German acronym for the International Trade Fair for Hunting and Sporting Arms and Accessories – Europe's counterpart to our own SHOT Show) gathered 1132 exhibitors from 53 nations, including the United States, as compared to 1046 last year, for an 8 percent increase and acknowledged 32,000 professional visitors, a slight increase over last year's attendance.

As all the great international companies are present both at the American SHOT Show held in February and at the European IWA, this report will mainly cover the new or most original products displayed by the more typical exhibitors and those of particular interest for our national shooters and hunters. Therefore, the new products of major companies such as

Beretta, Browning FN, BSA, Franchi, Glock, Heckler und Koch, Merkel, Pedersoli, Perazzi, Sako, Steyr, Tanfoglio, Tikka, Umarex and Walther, for instance, are not mentioned hereunder.

Concerning our selection, the American reader should understand that, in regard to handguns, for instance, in Europe, target shooting is performed according to the ISU (International Shooting Union) rules, with the exception of IPSC. Therefore, our most popular calibers are the .22 Long Rifle, 9mm Luger and .38 Special.

The .22 W. Magnum RF, .32 ACP, .357 Magnum, .44 Magnum and .45 ACP are also available in large shops, but much less common. Other calibers such as the .380 ACP (stupidly classified as "war material" since 1939), .38 Super Auto, .40 SW and .41 Magnum, are quite rare and expensive when available, restricting their use mostly to handloaders.

Here is our selection:

ANICS
(ANICS GROUP, 7 Vorontsovo Pole St. MOSCOU 105062, Russie. www.anics.com)

ANICS is a Russian company specializing in the manufacture of CO_2 pellets guns of .177 caliber.

The ANICS "Berkut" A-2002 pistol features a revolutionary conveyer type 22-shot magazine for .177 pellets; CO_2 cartridge capacity is 75 shots.

Anschutz
(Anschutz J.G. GmbH, Daimlerstrasse 12, D-89079 ULM – Donautal. www.anschutz-sport.com)

Anschutz is a name well-respected throughout the world for accuracy and fine workmanship.

In the "hunting rifles line," the Anschutz Model 1770 bolt action rifle chambered in .223 Remington with a three-shot magazine capacity is 42" long and weighs 7.5 lbs. Barrel length is 22", and trigger pull is factory-adjusted to 2.5 lbs.

Baikal

(Izhevsky Mekhanichesky Zavod, 8, Promyshlennaya Str. Izhevsk 426063, Russie www.baïkalinc.ru)

The most famous Russian gunmaker, Baikal has introduced a full line of sporting guns in all the international calibers and systems. This year, we have noted for you a nice self-loading .22 LR rifle, a Biathlon repeating air rifle and a fancy CO_2 machine pistol for .177 BBs.

The Baïkal "MP-661 K Drozd" CO_2 fancy machine pistol in .177 BB caliber, has a 400-round magazine capacity with an adjustable firing rate of 300 rpm, 450 rpm and 600 rpm (muzzle velocity = 393 fps). It operates with 6 AA-type batteries. Overall length is 27.6"; weight is 4.9 bbs.

The Baïkal "MP-161 K" self-loading .22 LR rifle, featuring a nine-round magazine capacity and a highly modern ergonomic polymer stock, is 39" long with a 20" barrel. It weighs 6.4 lbs.

The Baïkal "M-571 K PCP" compressed air five-shot international competition ISU rifle is 43.3" long with a 15.75" barrel and weighs 9-7 lbs. Operating pressure is the standard 200 bar value.

Blaser

(Blaser Jagdwaffen GmbH, Ziegelstadel, 1, D-88316Isny im Allgau. www.blaser.de)

This year, the general trend, as far as bolt rifles were concerned, was toward "modular systems." In this connection, we have noticed at the German Blaser booth, the "R93" modular system, enabling the fast and easy conversion of any "R93" center fire rifle into a convenient .22 LR five-shot bolt action.

Several right or left hand versions are available with semi-weight, stützen and varmint or match barrels, and special forearms matching Safari or match barrels.

For 2009, Benelli displayed at IWA its 2009 "Concept gun" – a veritable celebration of energy, relentlessly flowing fluidity, and undeniable grace.

Benelli
(Benelli Armi SPA, Via della Stazione, 50. I-61029 URBINO www.benelli.it)

For 2009, Benelli has introduced a new .223 hunting rifle and a striking new "concept gun" shotgun.

The Benelli "MR1" self loading .223 Rem hunting five-shot rifle featuring a delayed blowback action is available with 12.5", 16" or 20" barrels. With the short barrel and flash-hider, it weighs 7 lbs. Features include a rotating bolt head with three lugs and techno-polymer stock.

Being the discoverer of the original pre-production CZ 75 pistol at the Madrid 1975 Gun Show, this writer could not resist mentioning the new CZ 75 P-07 with its so attractive look, regardless of whether it will be imported in the United States.

Ceska Zbrojovk
(Ceska Zbrojowka, Svatopluka Cecha, 1283, 68827 Uhersky Brod, République Tchèque. www.czub.cz)

Among the new items shown at IWA, we have noted the CZ 550 "Exclusive" bolt action rifle chambered in .30-06, the Brno "Stopper" over-under chambered in .458 Win Mag, and the beautiful CZ 75 P-07 16-shot 9 mm Luger pistol with polymer receiver. Empty weight is 27.5 oz.; loaded, it weighs 34 oz. Of course, all of them will be imported in the United States.

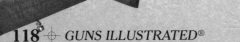

The Brno "Stopper" over-under rifle, chambered in .458 Win. Mag, features independent 23.6" barrels and weighs 9 lbs.

Academia "Il Bulino"
(Il Bulino srl, Via Repubblica 197,
I-25068 Sarezzo (Brescia). www.ilbulinosrl.com)

Il Bulino, Italian for "The Chisel," is is a fascinating
Italian school of engraving, teaching young people this
perrenial art which took its early origin in the prehis-
toric times. These young masters have already being
able to create absolutely outstanding masterpieces of
classic art and remarkable modern designs. Some of
their best work is shown.

An advance view of what the Italian FABARM "Iris" bolt action rifle will be.

FABARM (FABARM, Via Averolda, 31, Zona Industriale, I-25039 Travagliato (BS). www.fabarm.com)
This year, this well-known Italian shotgun maker has displayed at IWA eight new versions of its Axis, Elos and Waterfowl over-under shotguns, a Classic Grade IV side-by-side, a Martial Ultrashort 18" pump shotgun and, in preview, the Iris bolt action rifle.

Renato Gamba's Daytona K2 over-under featuring his patented interchangeable and detachable trigger group.

Renato Gamba
(SAB [SOCIETA ARMI BRESCIANE]
Renato Gamba, Via Artigiani, 93,
I-25063 Gardone Val Trompia (BS)
www.renatogamba.it)

Renato Gamba was, when John T. Amber was the Gun Digest's chief editor in the1970s, the flamboyant gun-maker of the "Italian Miracle" years... and a jolly good fellow! Since then, he is still at work, making on request outstanding Daytona, Prince, London Gold, Ambassador and Mustang double over-under and side-by-side shotguns. Gamba's "Daytona K2" has won, in 2008, at Beijing, a bronze Olympic medal at the Skeet Event, in the capable hands of Antony Terras.

Peter Hambrusch Peter Hambrusch is an Austrian ferlacher who has designed a top precision side–by-side double outside hammer rifle chambered in .450/.400 caliber, featuring quite a sophisticated action. As a matter of fact, it consists of a self-cocking mechanism, the two hammers of which can also be individually cocked when breaking the barrel. Moreover, this gun is also fitted with a conventional safety at the rear of the tang, and a patented Hambrusch Safety Sidelock System.

The outstanding new Hambrusch side-by-side .450/400 caliber rifle (copyright DWJ Special Edition and Roland Zeitler).

Historical Weaponry (www.piecesof history.co.uk)

This is a British company publishing a nice 114-page fullsize catalog of historical Japanese, Chinese and European swords and fractional-scale models of suits of armour.

The Black Knight is a suit of armour 2/3 size model 26-3/4" high.

The Peter Hofer gold inlaid small caliber side-by-side.

Peter Hofer
(Peter Hofer, Kirchgasse 24, A-9170 Ferlach, Autriche www.hoferwaffen.com)

Peter Hofer is a famous Ferlach gunmaker displaying a wonderful small gold inlaid side-by-side with two braces of barrels, one rifled in .22 caliber, and the other one, smoothbore in .410 Magnum.

The colorful Feinwerkbau 700 Evolution match air rifle as per ISU regulations. Overall length is 39 to 41 inches; weight is approximately 8 lbs. Muzzle velocity is 560 fps.

Feinwerkbau
(Feinwerkbau, Westiger & Altenburger, Neckarstrasse, 43, D-78727 Oberndorf/Neckar. www.feinwerkbau.de)

At Feinwerkbau, we have been able to see a new version of their famous Model 700 .177-caliber competition air rifle, the 700 Evolution, with an universal stock designed both for right-hand and left-hand shooters.

Grunig and Elmiger
(Grunig & Elmiger AG, Industriestrasse 22, CH-6102 Malters (LU). www.gruenel.ch)

This is a famous Swiss company making top-class ISU long range competition custom rifles, mostly for the 300-meter programs.

Grunig and Elmiger's FT 300 free rifle is currently available in 10 international competition calibers, from the 6 mm PPC to the .308 Win. Single shot; available in right hand only. Trigger pull adjustable from 4 to 9 oz. Weight is approximately 13 lbs.

KBP

**(KBP, 17 Krasnoarmeysky Prospekt
300041 Tula Russie. www.tulatskib.ru)**

   This is a new and impressive Russian company, holder of four gold medals in its country, who first offers six hunting rifles including the bolt action MTs-19 in .308 Win and 9X64 calibers and five different self-loading models available in .22 LR, .308 Win, 9X64 and 7.62 mm Mossin-Nagant. In addition, KBP lists also four over-unders, two custom grade richly engraved, side-by-side, a conventional automatic gas-operated 12-gauge MTs-22 shotgun and an original pump repeater Rys (Lynx) chambered in the same caliber, but weighing only 6 Ibs., with a seven-shot capacity. However, their most interesting achievement is the MTs-255 revolving shotgun available in 12, 20, 32 and .410 Magnum chamberings, with a five-shot cylinder capacity!

Match Guns

**(Matchguns Srl, Via Cartiera 6/d,
I-43010 Vigatto (Parma)
www.matchguns.com)**

This year, this leading Italian specialist of top grade ISU competition handguns has released the new .22 LR MG free pistol for 50-meter slow fire shooting.

The Match Gun MG5 pistol is a dropping-bolt single-shot design fitted with four adjustable stabilizers. Barrel length is 11.4 inches; weight is 39.8 oz. plain.

Pardini K10 air pistol.

Pardini (Pardini Armi, Via Italica, 154-A,
I-55043 Lido di Camaiore (Lucca). www.pardini.it)

Giampiero Pardini has been a noted Italian pistol champion who created, in the eighties, his own target pistol manufacturing company specialized in ISU competition models. Since then, his guns have won several major international events, namely at the Olympic Games of Atlanta, Sidney, Athens and, last year, Beijing (silver and bronze, in "Rapid fire"). For 2009, Pardini has designed a new "K10" target air pistol in .177 caliber.

Voere
(Voere, Untere Sparchen 56, A-6330 Kufstein/Tirol www.voere.de)

This reputable Austrian company has introduced this year at IWA the new modular LBW Luxus 20-03' bolt action hunting rifle available in four caliber groups and 22 basic calibers, plus custom options. Thanks to Voere's "Variosystem," the bolt travel is short for small calibers and long for others. The bolt features three solid locking lugs with a small opening angle, and the magazine is single row with three- (standard) or five-round (magnum) capacity. Average weight is around 6.6 Ibs., depending on caliber.

The LBW Luxus 20-03 rifle is fitted with modular barrels and stocks, enabling its owner to easily change caliber at will.

Krieghoff
Krieghoff GmbH, Boschstr. 22, Postfach 2610, D-89016 Ulm/Donau www.krieghoff.de)

This famous German company displayed at IWA a beautiful "Trumpf Drilling" available in 12 or 20-gauge for the two side-by-side smooth-bore upper barrels and in 11 different calibers, from 6X70R to 9,3X74R, for the lower rifled barrel. Available barrel lengths are 22" and 24". Weight varies from 6.8 to 8 Ibs.

The new Krieghoff "Trumpf Drilling."

SIG Sauer
(JP Sauer & Sohn GmbH, Sauerstrasse 2-6, D-24340 Eckernforde. www.sauer-waffen.de)

The latest Sig-Sauer handgun creation on the European IPSC market is their P220 X-Six .45 ACP eight-shot pistol. It has a six-inch barrel and weighs 44 oz. unloaded.

Sig-Sauer P220 X-Six pistol.

HANDLOADING TODAY

BY LARRY STERETT

oday's factory ammunition is probably the best it has ever been in the history of factory ammunition. However, handloading permits the use of bullet weights not available in factory loads, and it is often the only way to obtain ammunition for obsolete cartridges and wildcats. Plus, it's fun and the best – and sometimes only – way to tailor loads to improve accuracy. Also, given the impending legislative climate, this might be a good time to consider "rolling your own."

To produce quality handloads you need equipment and components. What follows is a look at the newest available to handloaders.

Bullet pullers are necessary to remove a bullet from a cartridge when it's the wrong bullet for the powder charge, or to salvage the powder and primed case. Sometimes a handloader will decide to replace the bullet with a different bullet design of the same weight. It's a simple process with the correct equipment, but a time-consuming task.

Forster Products has a new Universal Bullet Puller designed for use with the Forster Co-Ax Press, as well as any standard loading press using 7/8" x 14 thread dies. The die is capable of pulling bullets from .17 caliber to .458 caliber using one of the 21 hardened steel collets available separately. In addition to the die, and a proper size collet, a 9/16" wrench is needed to tighten and loosen the collet screw.

RCBS (www.rcbs.com) has a new Bullet Puller designed to pull .416 or .50 BMG bullets using the correct collet. (The collets are sold separately.) Designed for use on the Ammo-Master .50 BMG or AmmoMaster 2 RCBS presses, this puller has 1-1/2" x 12 threads and can be used with any press capable of accepting dies of this size.

RCBS had one of the first

presses available to load the .50 BMG cartridge, and for 2009 the firm expanded the line of accessories for "Big Fifty" reloading. In addition to the Bullet Puller, there's a new Military Crimp Remover, Carbide Primer Pocket Uniformer, Priming System, and Case Trimer Kit. The Case Trimmer will handle, with the correct collet and pilot, all the big cases from the .338 Lapua to the .50 BMG, including most of the Sharps and English Nitro cases, such as the .500 Nitro Express.

The Crimp Remover is designed to be used with the RCBS Trim Prep Center or the RCBS Accessory Handle. It cuts away the primer pocket crimp found on most military .50 BMG brass, permitting easier repriming. The Uniformer utilizes a carbide cutter

Some of the .50 caliber cartridges which handloaders can reload. Left to right: .502 Sabre, .50 ACP, .50 Spotter, .510 DTC Europa, .50 BMG, .500 Phantom, .500 Cyrus, .500 Jeffery, .500 Smith & Wesson.

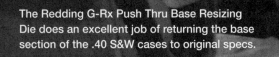

The Redding G-Rx Push Thru Base Resizing Die does an excellent job of returning the base section of the .40 S&W cases to original specs.

to square the bottom of the primer pocket and uniform the depth to permit easier primer seating to a consistent depth.

The new .50 BMG Priming System consists of a bench-mounted, lever-operated device with Safety Shield 20-primer capacity tube. A primer pick-up tube and flat and oval primer seating plugs are a part of the system.

Handloaders who have an RCBS Progressive Press set to load handgun cartridges will appreciate the new Bullet Feeder for such presses. Designed for use with jacketed bullets only—no cast lead bullets—the Feeder is 110-115 VAC operated. It mounts next to the Press, and has a hopper capacity of approximately 200 bullets. The collator unit orients the bullets to drop into the feed mechanism and is said to increase the loading rate by as much as 50 percent. Adapters allow the loading of 9mm/.38 Spl/.357 Magnum, 10mm/.40 S&W, and .45 ACP FMJ or jacketed bullets.

New RCBS reloading dies include those for the .300 and .338 RCM and .50-95 Winchester Express cartridges, plus seven of the big English calibers from the .404 Jeffery to the .505 Gibbs. (The other five are the .450/.400 (.400 Jeffery), .450 Rigby Rimless, .470 Nitro Express, .500 Jeffery, and the .500 Nitro Express. The .500 Jeffery and .505 Gibbs dies have 1" die bodies and require a press adapter bushing to fit loading presses designed for use with 1-1/2" x 123 thread dies.)

RCBS now has loading dies for the .460 Steyr cartridge, but again these dies have 1-1/2" x 12 threads, and can only be used with loading presses such as the AmmoMaster Single Stage with the .50 BMG Conversion Kit installed, or the AmmoMaster 2.

RCBS has reloading dies for untold different cartridges, not counting wildcats, from the .17 Remington Fireball to the .505 Gibbs. In addition, the firm can produce "special order" die sets. based on the dimensioned drawings, or three cases fired in the chamber of the rifle or handgun for which the loading dies are desired. Such dies are expensive, and orders must be prepaid, and are not subject to cancellation or return for credit.

Loading data from RCBS is among the best, and currently the firm has a handbook titled *Shotshell Reloading*, plus the new *Speer Reloading Manual No. 14* covering the metallics. The new shotshell book is one of the most up-to-date on the market today, and features over 2,000 loads for the various gauges. The *Speer* manual continues the tradition started years ago. It has hundred of loads, plus technical data to assist handloaders in the production of accurate reloads. (RCBS also has a software program(RCBS.LOAD) and a 30-minute DVD on handloading that can even benefit "old pros."

If you handload for any cartridge not currently being produced by one of the major ammunition manufacturers you may have difficulty locating a supply of suitable brass. If you have a rifle, or handgun, for which you already have loading dies, great. If you do not have the dies, **Huntington Die Specialities** (www.huntingtons.com) may already have the proper dies in stock, or they can make them for you from a chamber cast, or three empty cases fired in that chamber. Huntington may also have the brass you need for a foreign, wildcat, or obsolete cartridge.

Two other sources for suitable brass include **Quality Cartridge** (www.qual-cart.com) and **Jamison International V LLC** (jamisoninstl@rushmore.com). Both companies can also provide components and custom-loaded ammunition. (These companies do not sell less-than-full box quantities of the bras or loaded ammunition, and the smallest quantity available is usually 20 rounds.)

Quality Cartridge currently lists over 300 dif-

Excellent loading data is available in the complimentary loading guide published by the various powder companies, such as these for Acccurate, VihtaVuori, and Ramshot powders.

ferent calibers, and has the capability to supply custom cases for nearly any wildcat cartridge you can think of, from 5mm to over .550" in size. This firm can also convert your 5mm Remington M591 or M592 bolt action rifle to fire a 5mm centerfire cartridge, without permanently altering the rimfire capability. *[Editor's Note: Aguila is now making loaded 5mm Remington ammunition if you'd prefer not to alter your Remington. It's unknown how long this production will continue, however. – DMS]*

Jamison currently has brass for at least a dozen of the big-bore English cartridges, from the .416 Rigby to the .577 Snider, plus cases for several of the old Sharps. Need cases for the Snider or the .577/.450 Martini-Henry? Jamison produces them.

This handloader firmly believes you can never have too much information on a subject, especially handloading. **Blue Book Publications** has a new 792-page *Ammo Encyclopedia* by Michael Bussard that every handloader needs on their reference shelf. It contains 60 chapters, and while it does not actually contain loading data, it has about everything else, history, photographs, drawings, and more. Beginning with Chapter 38 it covers many of the centerfire — current, obsolete, sporting, military, proprietary and wildcat — cartridges. Dimensional drawings are provided for most of the cartridges, and while the quality of the drawings is

The new RCBS Case Trimmer Kit, with the correct collets and pilots, will handle all the big cases, from the .338 Lapua to the .50 BMG shown here.

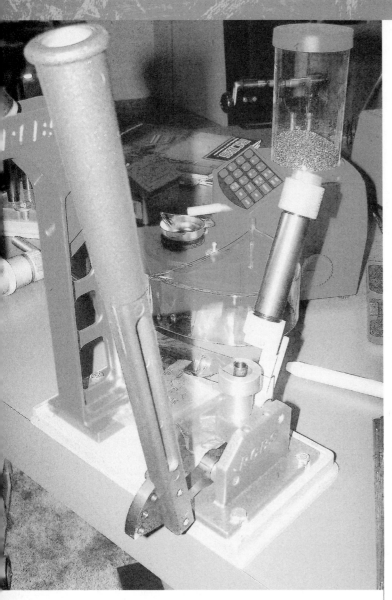

The RCBS .50 BMG Priming System is lever operated, has a 20-primer capacity tube with Safety Shield, and comes with flat and oval primer seating plugs.

guides for the **Accurate** and **Ramshot** powders, respectively. The Accurate guide has new loads for eight additional cartridges, from the 5.7x28mm FN to the .338 Federal, plus a good number of 12 gauge shotshell loads. The handgun loads range from the 5.7x288mm FN to the .500 Smith & Wesson, while the rifle loads cover cartridges from the .17 Remington to the .458 Lott. Ramshot has data for the same eight new metallics as Accurate, but since it's a different powder the loads are different, as they are for the centerfire handgun cartridges. Rifle cartridges for which Ramshot loads are provided are not exactly the same as those for the Accurate powder data, plus Ramshot loads data is provided for five of the most popular handgun cartridges used in Cowboy Action Shooting. Load data for 12 gauge shotshells is also listed in the Ramshot Guide.

Redding Reloading Equipment (www.redding-reloading.com) has new dies for the .30 Remington AR, .338 Marlin Express, .416 Ruger, and a Comp Seater die for the .357 SIG cartridge. Another great die from Redding is the G-Rx Push Thru Base Sizing Die for .40 S&W brass. When the .40 S&W cartridge is fired in most autoloading pistols, it develops a slight bulge near the base. Using the new die irons out or swages this bulge, returning the case to original dimensions in this location. (Conventional full length resizing dies often do not size this area of the fired cases due to the shell holder and die junction.) An optional bottle adapter and HDPE collection bottle are also available to save having to pick up each sized case as it exits the die.

Other new items from Redding include a Case Neck Gauge, Flash Hole Deburring Tools, Primer Pocket Uniformers, and a dip-in dry Imperial Application Media consisting of high density ceramic spheres pre-charged with Imperial Dry Neck Lube. This new Media will handle all case necks from .17 caliber upward.

Redding hasn't added any new bullet moulds to the SAECO line, but current sizes range from .22 to .45. The available moulds include bullet designs suitable for smokeless or black powder use. Depending on the caliber and bullet weight, the moulds can be had in a choice of 1, 2, 3, or 4-cavity sizes.

Shiloh Sharps (www.shilohrifle.com) is known for their excellent line of single shot percussion and cartridge rifles based on the original M1863 and M1874 Sharps designs. Today's Sharps rifles may not have the history of an original, but the new Sharps will be of better materials and have a better finish in most instances. The firm also has some

not equal, nor drawn to the same scale for all, the information is still valuable. Not every wildcat cartridge ever designed or developed is featured, but that would be an impossibility. What is presented covers a wide field, and there are no SAAMI specs or standardized drawings for most wildcats. (The .257 Roberts Improved exists in a dozen or more versions, differing in neck length, shoulder angle, overall case length, case taper, etc., for example. Shortening the case, necking it down, expanding the neck, and other modifications add more wildcats to the same basic case, and the .257 Roberts was itself a wildcat in the beginning.)

Chapters 53 and 54 are devoted to formulas and useful reference data, including chamber pressures, barrel lengths, sectional densities, ballistic coefficients, loading densities, burning propellants emissions, etc. It's handy to have it all in one volume, and there's even a glossary and a pair of indices.

Dealers handling **Western Powders** (www.accuratepowder.com and www.ramshot.com) should have available copies of the latest load reloading equipment designed for use with the rimmed Sharps cases or similar cartridges. A hand-operated depriming tool can deprime those big cases in a hurry. Slip the case over the de-priming rod, slip the case rim into the notch and squeeze the lever. Quick and easy! The end of the lever features a primer pocket cleaning tool, and the handle is threaded to hold a case neck cleaning brush.

Shiloh carries reloading equipment of RCBS and Redding, plus a few others not always easy to locate, such as the MVA Visible Power Measure with non-sparking brass hopper and micrometer adjustable scale. A Case Annealer for those work-hardened case necks, a drop tube for those large capacity cases, and a good 50-hole loading block are other handy Shiloh items. Constructed of solid wood with brass tube and funnel, the drop tube can be used for single cases, or with a loading block, and the 50-hole Shiloh Loading Block is thick enough the tall "fifties" will not tip over. Another handy item is the "paper cartridge kit" for those shooters of muzzleloading black powder rifles. It's complete with cartridge paper, two dowels, glue stick, funnel for filling, and complete directions for use.

Not handloading equipment, but a handy reference is the Sharps Company Cartridge Poster designed by artist Robert Auth. It features a buffalo hunter scene with Sharps rifle and shooting sticks, and thirty Sharps cartridges, from the .36 caliber paper to the .50-140-700 3-1/4".

Brooks' Moulds (www.brooksmoulds.com) will produce custom bullet moulds to a customer's specifications for any design up to 1.55" in length. Precision machined using case iron blocks to fit SAECO handles, and lathe bored, the moulds may be built with nearly any nose shape, groove diameter and number, desired.

Barnes Bullets (www.barnesbullets.com) has a host of new products for handloaders, from new bullets to the copper Club, which (for a nominal fee) permits immediate access to load data for new Barnes bullets as such becomes available from the Barnes ballistics lab. The new bullets range from a 30-gr. .22 Hornet Varmit Grenade design to the 480-gr. .450/400 Banded Solid, plus there's a new line of Barnes Buster heavy-for-caliber handgun/rifle bullets slated for availability about the time you read this. The *Barnes Reloading Manual No. 4* lists data for all Barnes bullets up to the time of publication, but you may not find the mid-2009 designs featured.

Handloaders for the British big-bore cartridges will find Barnes has suitable designs available for most of them, .416, .404, .470, .500, .505, .577, and .600 Nitro Express. (Yes, if you handload for the .600 Nitro, Barnes has a 900-gr. Banded Solid bullet available.)

Barnes Reloading Manual No. 4 features loading data, using Barnes bullets, for many of the newer cartridges, including Winchester's Short and Super Shot Magnums, 6.8mm SPC, .338 Federal, and .375 Ruger. (Owners of a rifle chambered for the .375 Whelen cartridge might want to check out the loading data for the .375 Scovill in the Barnes manual.) In addition, those handloaders set up for the big bores will appreciate the data for the .470 and .577 Nitro Express, .505 Gibbs, and the .50 BMG cartridges.

Handgun cartridges for which loading data is provided range from the .221 Remington Fireball to the .500 Smith & Wesson, include in the .45 GAP. No data for cartridges such as the .25 ACP or .256

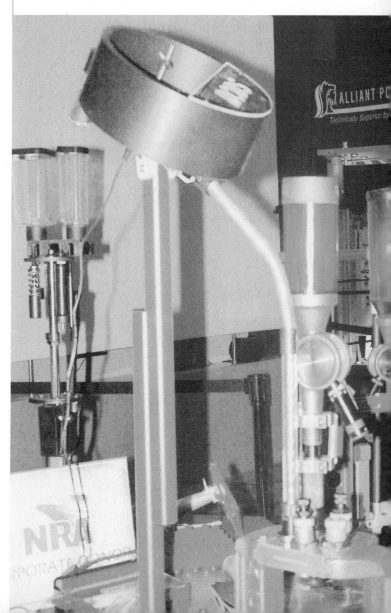

Owners of a RCBS Progressive Press set up for handgun loads will appreciate this new Bullet Feeder. The Feeder mounts next to the press, and is 110-115 VAC operated, with a hopper capacity of approximately 200 bullets. It's said to increase the loading rate by up to 50 percent, and adapters are available to load most handgun cartridges from 9mm to .45 ACP.

Magnum are featured, nor does the rifle section feature any .17 caliber loads. Other features of this 696-page manual include five interesting articles, trajectory tables — short, medium, and long range — energy tables, an excellent glossary, a history of the company, and much more. There's even a section of muzzleloading data for smokepole users, plus dozens of color photographs throughout of successful hunters, all users of Barnes bullets.

VihtaVuori's *Reloading Guide, Edition 7*, has data for more than 50 centerfire rifle cartridges, and two dozen handgun cartridges. This includes revised data for 15 cartridges, from the .204 Ruger to the .45-70 Gov't., including the 6.5x47 Lapua, .260 Remington, and .338 Lapua, using N100 and N500 Series powders. Cowboy Action Shooting loads are provided for five of the most popular cartridges. (This guide has a great "Powder Burning Rate Chart" just inside the front cover that lists the burning rates from fast to slow for 11 brands of smokeless powders that most U. S. handloaders will encounter. It also has a chart inside the back cover for listing favorite personal loads.)

Reliable ballistic data is now available for most **Lapua** bullets through the Lapua website (www.lapua.com) and Quick Target Unlimited ballistic software. Check it out. The data was assembled using continuous Doppler radar measurements, and is stated to be more accurate than using the single number ballistic coefficient method.

Speer's new *Reloading Manual No. 14* is the largest the firm has ever produced. Naturally, it's geared to the use of Speer-manufactured bullets, such as the 115-gr. Gold Dot Hollow Point in the .327 Federal cartridge, but not exclusively.

A couple of sources for reloading data for wildcat and older cartridges are *Wildcat Cartridges, Combo Edition*, and *Pet Loads, Complete Volume*, both published by the **Wolfe Publishing Company** (www.riflemagazine.com). The wildcat tome contains all the articles, with loading data, featured in volumes I and II, covering cartridges from the .14/221 to the .460 Van Horn. The articles are interesting and the loading data may be the only source available, since wildcat loading data is relatively scarce. The *Pet Loads* volume, by Ken Waters, features loads for all the cartridges originally featured in supplements 1 through 24, and again the articles are not only interesting but informative.

Hodgdon has a new Reloading Data Center that handloaders with access to the web can use. Just click on any of the three available web sites—www.hodgdon.com, www.imrpowder.com, or www.wwpowder.com. The first page you see on one of these sites will allow you access. Click on the designated area marked Reloading Data Center, read the warnings and click on I agree. One the next page, pick your reloading preference, and click on either "cartridge" or "shotshell."

The Hodgdon Reloading Data Center shows 52 different powders, including IMR 4007 SSC, and Winchester AA Lite and Super Handicap powders. Loading data is available for 84 handgun cartridges from the .17 Bumble Bee to the .500 Smith & Wesson, and 144 rifle cartridges from the .17 Ackley Hornet to the .50 BMG. (Starting and maximum loads, pressures, and velocities are provided for each cartridge.)

Shotshell handloaders can select from literally thousands of 10, 12, 16, 20 and 28 gauge, plus .410-bore loads. Bismuth, steel, Hevi-Shot, and lead shot, including buckshot, plus slug loads are presented. The RDC data is continually updated with the latest cartridges and components. It provides handloaders using Hodgdon, IMR, and Winchester powders with over 20,000 recipes for handgun, rifle, and shotshell cartridge loads. It's easy to navigate and sort by cartridge, bullet weight, shell size, shotgun loads, powder type, and manufacturer brand, and it's available 24 hours a day, seven days a week.

In addition to lots of new cartridges, unprimed cases, bullets, and loading data for the cartridges, the Really Big News at **Hornady Manufacturing** (www.hornady.com) are the Lock-N-Load Case Preparation Center, the L-N-L Ammo Concentricity Gauge, and the 1500 GS Electronic Scale. The L-N-L Power Case Prep Center literally provides in one

Left to right: .223 Remington, .30-06 Springfield, .50 BMG case, .338 Xtreme, and .308 Winchester. The .338 Xtreme is another cartridge which can be handloaded to achieve different results.

location everything necessary to prepare an empty cartridge case for reloading. It features a power trimmer, chamfer/deburring tool, primer pocket cleaner, and five neck brushes. Primer pocket reamers, uniformer, and flash hole deburring tools can be purchased separately. The Center can be mounted on the bench with four lag screws or bolts. The vertically mounted L-N-L case trimmer is crank adjustable, with the other features mounted on the face of the base portion of the Center.

The new L-N-L Ammo Concentricity Tool allows a shooter to measure bullet run-out and to true-up his handloads, or even factory ammunition. Place the cartridge on the included 60° universal centers in the tool, roll it, and read the dial indicator, accurate to 0.001". If the reading is unsatisfactory, use the threaded pressure-point adjuster to adjust the run-out to zero. Simple, and quick.

The new Hornady Lock'N Load AP EZ-Ject Press will be a big hit with handloaders tired of manually removing each loaded cartridge from the final station. The loaded cartridge, from .25 ACP to .45-70 Gov't., is automatically ejected into a trap suspended on the left of the press. The system is standard on all new L-N-L AP presses, and older models can be upgraded.

Hornady has also introduced loaded ammunition for two new cartridges, .338 Marlin Express and .416 Ruger, in addition to a load for the .300 H & H Magnum, and loads for four of the English big bores, .404 Jeffery, .450, .470 and .500 Nitro Express. There's also a new load for the .50 BMG cartridge, featuring the 750-grain A-MAX bullet. Naturally, the firm now has loading dies for these cartridges, plus shell holds, and unprimed brass. (Hornady introduced unprimed cases for a number of other cartridges also, including the 6.8mm SPC, .30 TC, .32 Winchester Special, and .450 Bushmaster.)

Hornady has more than 20 new bullets available for handloaders, including GMX and FTX designs, plus DGX (Dangerous Game) models for the .404 Jeffery, .470 and .500 Nitro Express cartridges. By the time you read this there may be others.

Anyone handloading for one of the service rifle cartridges of the World War II era knows the surplus ammunition was usually Berdan primed, provided you could find such ammunition in the correct caliber. A source of Boxer-primed new case for nine such cartridges is **Graf & Sons** (www.grafs.com). Graf has loaded ammunition, primed and unprimed cases for cartridges from the 6.5x50mm Japanese to the 8x56R Hungarian Mannlicher, including the 7.5x54mm French, 7.5x55mm Swiss, and the 7.92x33mm Kurz. The firm also handles a wide assortment of reloading equipment and components.

Handloaders who cast their own bullets may have a bit of trouble find a source for lead, etc. They

The new Hornady L-N-L Case Preparation Center features a powder trimmer, chamfer/deburring tool, primer pocket cleaner, and five neck brushes. Accessory tools to fit are also available.

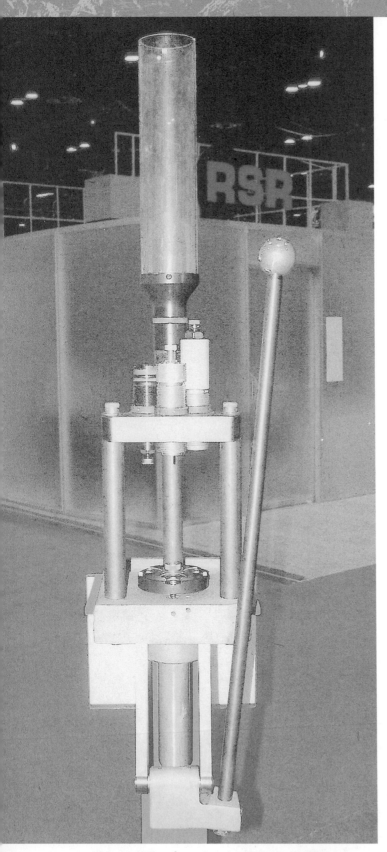

The new Dillon press for reloading the .50 BMG cartridge is massive, with three 1" diameter steel posts supporting the die head. The leverage available for resizing the .50 BMG case is tremendous, and the access space to the shell holder area is ample.

should check out the **Bulletman** (www.bulletmetals.net). Pure lead and several alloys, including linotype metal, are available.

Battenfeld Technologies (www.battenfeldtechnologies.com), known for their Caldwell Lead Sled, now has a Lead Sled Plus, allowing the handloader to test out new loads with comfort. Designed to handle two 25-lb. barbell weights, or up to 100 lbs. of lead shot or sand bags, the LSP is similar to the original Lead Sled in size, and smaller than the Lead Sled PFT. The LSP can reduce recoil up to approximately 95 percent. (There's also a new "large" weight bag available which will hold approximately 20 pounds of sand for use on the Lead Sleds.)

Handloaders needing a shooting rest, but not the recoil reduction feature, should check out the new Caldwell 7 Rest Shooting Rest. Designed high enough, and offset to accommodate the extended magazine of AR-15 rifles and clones, the 7 Rest folds to accommodate left or right-handed shooters. (The 7 Rest folds nearly flat for storage or transportation.) The forearm and buttstock supports are overmolded and screw-adjustable for height.

From the **Frankford Arsenal** division of Battenfeld there's a new DS-750 Digital Electronic Scale with a 750-grain capacity. Powered by two AAA batteries, and complete with integrated protective cover, the DS-750 resembles one of the TI-83 Graphing Calculators, but smaller; it's ideal for use in the field at the shooting bench. Accurate to 0.1-grain, the DS-750 has overload protection, and auto shutoff after 60 seconds to conserve the batteries. Auto calibrated, with tare and counting functions, the DS-750 measures in grains, grams, carats, and ounces, with a blue backlit LCD display. Complete with carry pouch, pan, and calibration weights, the scale is only slightly larger than the Micro Reloading Scale and is suitable for use on the regular reloading bench or at the range for load development.

Not new, but always needed at the reloading bench are the Frankford Arsenal Powder Funnel Kit and the Perfect-Fit Reoading Tray. The Funnel Kit features a large funnel, extension tube, and 16 quick-change specific nozzles to accommodate case necks from .17 to .45 caliber. The Kit is packed in a plastic case with marked cavities. The Trays are available in a dozen sizes to accommodate cases from the .25 ACP to the .500 Nitro Express. Except for tray No. 9, which holds only 45 cases, the other 11 trays have a 50-case capacity. Each tray will accommodate cases whose base or rim diameter is approximately the same. Tray No. 1, for example, will host .22 Hornet, .25 ACP, 5.7x28mm FN, and similar cases, while No. 9 will accommodate .470 N.E., .50-70 Gov't., .500 N.E., etc. cases.

Handloaders loading for only a couple of calibers, or using their own fired brass may not have the

The RCBS Bullet Puller is massive, but it pulls .50 BMG or .416 Barrett bullets with ease.

problem, but sorting range brass can be a headache. **Lamb Labs** (www.lamblabs.com) can help, at least for pistol range brass, with their Shell Sorter. Consisting of an arrangement of screened trays, the Shell Sorter can separate .45 ACP, .40 S&W, and 9mm/.380 fired cases by caliber in seconds. Just dump in the mixed cases and shake. Simple and quick.

Most handloaders who load many cartridges have a tumbler or vibratory-type case cleaner/polisher. You fill it with fired cases and media, close it, turn it on and let it run. But how long, or when is it time to check it?

UniqueTek Inc. (www.uniquetek.com) has a Time-Out Case Cleaner Timer that will ease the situation a bit. It operates on a regular 115 VAC circuit, features an easy-to-read LCD display with a NiNH battery for memory backup, and has dual outlets. It permits operation of the cleaner, thumbler or vibratory, (15 amp/1 hp/1875 watt), from one minute to 10 hours.

Sinclair International (www.sinclairintl.com) always hs some new products for handloaders. There are a couple of new Powder Drop Tubes to fit most Sinclair, Redding and RCBS powder measures, and the Neil Jones measures without an adapter. Four lengths (4", 6", 8", and 10") are available in two sizes, .22 caliber and up, and 6.5mm and up. Bushings may be required. A special 4" drop tube is available for the .27 and .20 caliber cartridges, and custom lengths are possible for the others, if required. (Sinclair drop tubes are now available with bushings to fit Lyman, Dodd, Bruno, and older Sinclair/Culver powder measures, and have the same features as those for the Redding, RCBS measures.)

Other new Sinclair handloading products include a Case Neck Brush Power Screwdriver Adapter, a 17/20 Caliber Piloted Flash Hole Tool, a Case Neck Sorting Tool, and the R.F.D. Culver Style Powder Measure. The Screwdriver Adapter permits case neck brushes to be used in any power screwdriver, hand-held drill, etc., and speeds up the cleaning process. The new .17 and .20 caliber Piloted Flash Hole Tool utilizes stainless steel pilots which index from the case mouth to ensure case-to-case chamfer depth. (Sinclair has a .50 BMG Flash Hole Deburring Tool and Primer Pocket Uniformer that handloaders of the Big Fifty should find handy.)

The new R.F.D. Culver Style Powder Measure is produced on CNC machinery and features an aluminum body with brass metering insert that throws from 0 to 85 grains with four "clicks" between each number on the insert. It will fit onto the Sinclair 11-1100 Measure Stand and comes with a 16-oz. powder hopper and two drop tubes.

Case neck wall thickness is important to accurate handloads and the new Case Neck Sorting Tool works for cartridges from .22 through .45 caliber with the Sinclair Stainless Steel Neck Pilots. (It works with .17 and .20 caliber cases with the use of an optional carbide alignment rod and matching pilots.) The new tool can be used by both left and right-handed reloaders, and its low profile and low center of gravity provide the user with a more

Left to right: .223 Remington, .30-06 Springfield, .416 Ruger, .338 Marlin Express, .404 Jeffery, and .470 Nitro Express Cartridges. The last four are new Hornady loads, and loading dies are available. New Hornady loads not shown include the .450 Nitro Express, .500 Nitro Express, and the .50 BMG cartridges.

Lyman's 49th *Reloading Handbook* covers about everything a handloader needs to know, with plenty of data on both metallics and shotshells.

stable working platform. Currently Sinclair neck pilots are available in 17 popular sizes, including 10mm/.40 and .41/.416 caliber. (A dial or electronic indicator is necessary for use with this tool, and Sinclair currently has five different models from which to choose, if needed, including those produced in the U. S. by the **L. S. Starrett** firm.)

The balance-type powder scale used to be standard, and many handloaders still use them to produce thousands of accurate handloaded cartridges. Today, electronic scales are becoming popular and **Denver Instrument** (www.DenverInstrumentUSA. com) has such a scale with a capability of 1,851 grains and a 0.02-grain readability. It weighs less than 2.5 lbs., stabilizes in three seconds, and has a pan nearly four inches in diameter.

Ammunition testing and adjustment is possible with the German-manufactured **Bersin device**. Distributed in the U. S. by **Century International**

Hornady's new L-N-L Ammo Concentricity Tool allows a shooter to measure bullet run-out to 0.001" and adjust it. Center the cartridge, roll it, read, and adjust. Simple and quick!

Arms, Inc. (www.centuryarms.com) the Bersin is available in four sizes, S (small) M (medium), L (large), and Ultra L, with the last for cases such as the Remington Ultra Magnum and Winchester Short Magnum, etc. It measures and adjusts concentricity to 0.0001" and helps to sort out cartridges with irregular case surfaces and lengths. Said to be capable of improving group sizes by as much as 50 percent, the Bersin can be used on commercial ammunition, or handloads.

MTM Molded Products Co. (www.mtmcase-gard. com) has new 10-round Case-Gard Ammo Boxes to house .50 BMG and .416 Barrett cartridges. The cartons or boxes in which commercial .50 BMG cartridges are packaged are flimsy and if you handload the .50 BMG using surplus brass, you probably purchased the fired brass loose or in bulk. The new MTM boxes cradle the rounds at the shoulder, not the tip, and are built to last. Each box will hold ten .50 BMG, .50 DTC, .460 Steyr, HS .460, .416 Barrett, or .338 Xtreme cartridges.

MTM has many other cartridge cases, loading trays, die storage boxes, self-adhesive loading labels, and while not new, there is a great three-ring binder for recording handloading data. This Handloaders Log provides an excellent way to store personal loads and information in a looseleaf fashion.

More and more serious handloaders are paying attention to the small details, checking individual bullets for weight variations and diameters, case neck thickness, etc. **Rampro Corporation** (www. ramproco.com) has a new Universal Reloaders Gauge capable of measuring more than seven different variation of bullets and/or cartridges from .22 to .470 Nitro Express. User friendly and precision machined, the Gauge includes a digital LCD indicator with 0.0005"

One of the best reference volume for handloaders needing case dimensions is the *Ammo Encyclopedia* by Michael Bussard. Published by Blue Book Publications, it does not feature loading data, but it contains considerable other information pertinent to handloading.

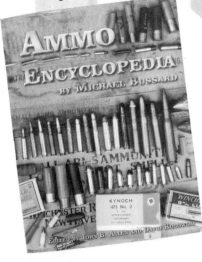

Barnes *Reloading Manual No. 4* not only has loading data for rifle and handgun cartridges, but plenty of other useful information. Trajectory tables—short, medium, and long range—energy tables, and interesting articles are all contained between the covers of this 696-page volume.

The lastest Norma Precision AB reloading manual provides handloading data for all but the latest cartridges. Naturally, Norma components, cases, powders, and bullets, are emphasized. (Norma produces cases and loaded ammunition for a dozen big bore cartridges from the .375 H & H to the .505 Gibbs, plus more than two dozen hunting and target cartridges. Additional new scheduled cartridges include three new Norma Magnums, the .300, .338, and .375 to join the .308 and .358 Norma Magnums.

resolution. The complete kit includes the stand, LCD indicator, indicator tips, cartridge measuring fixture, .22 caliber holder, .220 and .300 caliber pilots (other calibers optional), cartridge centering locators, mounting hardware and instructions. Thus case trimmed length, seated bullet concentricity, cartridge ovality and distortion, bullet diameter and length, bullet seated overall length, and more can be checked all on the same tool. Now, all that's needed is such a tool for use with the .50 BMG cartridge to shrink those 1,000-yard groups.

Shooters who handload dangerous game cartridges are, or should be, cognizant of **Woodleigh** bullets manufactured in Australia (www.woodleigh-bullets.com.au). The firm produces more than 130 different bullet types in calibers from 6.5mm to .700 Nitro. The majority of the bullets are roundnose softpoints, with a few flat nose and protected point. Three dozen of the bullets are full metal jacket designs intended for maximum penetration. The lightest weight bullets are the 130 grain .277" for the .270 Winchester, and the heaviest are the 1,000-gr. .700" projectiles. (Woodleigh bullets are used by several U. S. ammunition manufacturers in their "big bore" loads. **Huntington Die Specialities**

stocks the Woodleigh bullets as components for handloaders.)

Woodleigh may soon be distributing the new "Hydrostatic Stabilization" bullets on which patents are pending. Constructed of a specially formulated copper alloy, the new HS bullets produce breech pressures similar to gilding metal jacketed softpoint bullets of the same weight. Featuring a depressed nose, shallow driving bands and full bore body, the HS is designed to cut a clean hole to promote profuse bleeding, and to travel in a straight line following impact. Following the principle used in the brass extrusion industry to produce hollow bars, the HS bullet produces a pressure ring following impact, and travels onward in a low pressure cavitation bubble. The result is massive hydraulic shock transfer, increased penetration and stabilization. (HS bullets striking bone are said to have a better orientation to the original line of travel than conventional round, flat, or pointed nose bullets.) As components, the new HS bullet will not be inexpensive, but none of the big bore bullets is cheap, and what's the price of a bullet compared to the cost of the hunt, anyway?

Ballistic Products' new "ITX" shot sports a sharp
cutting band around the circumference.

AMMUNITION TODAY: Ammunition, ballistics and components

BY HOLT BODINSON

In terms of the quality of our ammunition and the selection of handloading components, these are the best days of our lives. Just consider for a moment that this year has brought us three new rifle cartridges – the .30 Remington AR, .338 Marlin Express and the .416 Ruger – five new reloading powders and counting – a variety of new bullets – lead-free, rimfire ammunition – and even a steel shot load for the tiny .410.

Recession? Nothing is slowing down or holding back the constant innovation and flow of new products from the ammunition industry.

A-Square

After relocating its ammunition manufacturing plant to Chamberlain, South Dakota, A-Square is fully up to production this year with calibers ranging from the 6.5-06 A-Square to the .700 Nitro Express. For big game hunting, especially in Africa, no ammunition approaches the versatility of A-Square's unique Triad loads. For each major caliber, A-Square loads three bullets with the same weight, same profile and same trajectory. One is a mono-lithic solid; one is a bonded core, controlled expansion soft point; and the third is a thin jacketed soft point designed for rapid, maximum expansion. In short, Triad ammunition provides the hunter with the opportunity to match the bullet to the game at a moment's notice with the assurance that all three loads will shoot to the same point of impact. The Triad is a revolutionary development in the design of big game ammunition. See the Triad and the whole A-Square line at www.asquarecompany.com.

Alliant Powder

A member of the ATK group, Alliant is introducing five new spherical handloading powders this year under the "Power Pro" label. They're designed specifically for magnum pistol, varmint rifle, medium rifle, large rifle and magnum rifle. Handloading data is available at www.alliantpowder.com. The big surprise though is a new powder under the "Reloader" series, Reloader 17.

Reloader 17 snuck into the line without a lot of fanfare. It's a very special powder with a unique chemistry. Made in Switzerland by Nitro Chemie, Reloader 17 is formulated for the short magnum cases and has a burn speed similar to IMR-4350.

Alliant is introducing five, spherical powders under the "Power Pro" label.

Its advantage is that the chemicals that determine the burn rate are saturated into the powder grains rather than being applied to the exterior surface of the grain. The result is a smoother, longer release of energy, producing sensational velocities in the short magnums at normal working pressures. For example, loaded with Reloader 17, the 7mm WSM produces 3,356 fps with a 130-gr. BTSP; the 300 WSM, 3,343 fps with a 150-gr. BTSP. If you shoot a short magnum, you must try Alliant's RE-17. (www.alliantpowder.com.)

Ballistic Products

Ballistic Products offers the most diverse and innovative selection of shotshell reloading components and manuals available. They've just introduced a new, soft, non-toxic shot composed of iron, tungsten and a polymer binder. Going under the "ITX" label, the pellets are perfectly spherical with a broad cutting band around the circumference. Ballistic Products emphasizes that ITX is much softer than other tungsten blends and is similar in density to Bismuth. See their store at www.ballisticproducts.com.

Baschieri & Pellagri (B&P)

Long known for their premium quality shotshells, B&P builds their ammunition using hulls made under the Gordon System patent that features an active, cushioning base wad that reduces felt recoil. This year B&P has used the Gordon hull to develop 12-gauge steel, target loads featuring 7/8 - 1 oz. of #7 and #8.5 shot driven at lead shot velocities for ideal target performance out to 35 meters. Look for them under the F2 Mach and F2 Legend Professional Steel labels. (www.baschieri-pellagri.com and www.kaltronoutdoors.com)

Barnes' new manual is highly focused on the modern "Triple Shock" lines.

The tungsten core of Barnes' new MRX bullet ensures deep penetration and high retained energy at long range.

Barnes "Buster" bullet for handguns and .45-70s is a non-expanding, deep penetrating big game bullet.

Barnes Bullets

Building on the success of their "Tipped Triple-Shock X Bullet" that combines the accuracy and controlled expansion of the conventional Triple-Shock X Bullet with a higher ballistic coefficient offered by the addition of a pointed polymer tip, Barnes is introducing five new Tipped TSX boattail bullets ranging from a .243 (80-gr.) to a 7mm (150-gr.). The conventional Triple-Shock lineup continues to expand as well with a new 6.8 mm (85-gr.) and a .308 (110-gr.).

One of the nightmares of the muzzleloading crowd is a potential ban on lead hunting bullets. Barnes has an answer: the .50-caliber, solid copper, sabot Spit-Fire line. Now offered with a streamlined polymer tip, the Spit-Fire has also been wrapped in a new, easy-loading sabot that's just the answer to tight or fouled bores. For the handgun hunting enthusiast, there is the new "Barnes Buster." Designed for the .44, .45 and .500 magnums and the .45-70 rifle, the Buster is a non-expanding, deep penetrating bullet intended for wild boar, bear,

and even dangerous game like Cape buffalo. Buster bullet weights have yet to be announced. New, too, is an expanded line of lead-free, rifle and handgun bullets for the military and law enforcement communities, offering every quality from precision long range accuracy (TAC-LR) to barrier defeating designs (TAC-XP and TAC-X). For updated bullet specifications go to www.barnesbullets.com and www. barnesbullets.com/mle.

Berger Bullets

With the increasing popularity of the .204 Ruger cartridge for varmint hunting, Berger will offer a long, 55-gr. bullet for the .20-calibers. It should prove ideal for the windy plains of the prairie dog towns. New, too, later in the year, are a number of VLD and conventional bullet designs being developed for the .338 calibers in bullet weights of 200-300 grains. (www.bergerbullets.com)

Barnes' older Triple Shock design has been upgraded with a polymer tip.

Black Hills Ammunition is famous for their rigorous quality control and accuracy standards.

Berry's Manufacturing

Berry's offers an extensive line of copper plated lead handgun bullets at very attractive prices. A new design that is proving to be exceptionally accurate is their hollow base handgun bullet that is offered in 9mm (124-gr.), .40 (155-gr.) and .45 (185-gr.). The .40 and .45 caliber hollow base bullets are premium target bullets that are "double struck," or sized, after being plated to insure they are 100% symmetrical. See Berry's full line of plated, non-plated and "cowboy" bullets at www.berrysmfg.com.

Black Hills Ammunition

Consistently providing some of the most accurate ammunition on the market, Black Hills is offering a variety of new loadings based on Barnes bullet designs that include the TAC-XP bullet in 9mm, .40 S&W and .45 ACP; the 55-gr. TSX and 55-gr. highly frangible MPG bullet in the .223, and a 85-gr. TSX bullet in the .243 Win. (www.blackhills.com.)

Brenneke USA

Long known for their advanced shotgun slug designs, Brenneke is marketing a unique lead-free, .30-caliber (155-gr.) bullet named the Brenneke "Quik-Shok Copper." Similar in concept to Polywad's Quik-Shok rimfire ammunition and shotgun slugs, the Brenneke bullet features a deep, hollow cavity

Brenneke's "Quik-Shok Copper" bullet fragments on impact to create four, large, secondary missiles.

CCI has upgraded the quality and performance of the classic musket cap.

capped with a polymer tip. Upon impact, the front portion of the new bullet fragments into four copper petals, creating four additional wound channels, while the solid rear section assures deep penetration. The new bullet will be offered in loaded ammunition for the .308 and .30-06 with velocities of 2,953 fps and 2,789 fps respectively. See the complete Brenneke line at www. brennekeusa.com.

CCI

Something old and something new. CCI is introducing a new and improved, four wing musket cap for traditional muzzleloaders this year and a 30-gr., lead-free .22 WMR cartridge under CCI's "TNT Green" label. See the details at www.cci-ammunition.com

Century International Arms

As the major USA importer and manufacturer of surplus military firearm models, Century is in unique position to ferret out great ammunition deals from across the globe.

Under their "Hotshot" brand of commercial sporting ammunition, Century offers Boxer primed, noncorrosive, soft point loads in a variety of popular calibers ranging from the 7.62 Nagant to the .30-06. Selling for $12.87/box, Hotshot rifle ammo is the buy of the century. (www.centuryarms.com)

Extreme Shock

With its successful line of frangible rifle and handgun ammunition based on bullets featuring powdered tungsten cores, Extreme Shock is bringing its proprietary technology to bear on the shotgun shell market. Their new .50-caliber, BD-50J slug weighing 325 grains is a copper-jacketed, compressed tung-sten core, 12 ga. sabot round with a muzzle velocity of 1,800 fps. It's designed for rifled shotgun bores and offers maximum expansion on soft tissue. A bit more on the radical side is Shock Shot, compressed cylinders of tungsten powder, equating roughly to #4 and #6 round shot and #00 buckshot. The tactical cylindrical shot delivers extremely wide and open patterns at close range and more ragged and lethal wound channels. Extreme Shock ammunition is wild stuff. See it all at www.extremeshockusa.net.

Federal Premium

Introduced several years ago, Federal's proprietary 12-gauge "FLITECONTROL" wad has a proven track record of delivering exceptionally uniform and dense shot patterns. This year the FLITECONTROL wad technology is being introduced in both the 10-gauge and 20-gauge turkey and waterfowl lines. The new 10- and 20-gauge waterfowl lines now include the loading of Federal's devastating Black Cloud shot.

Even the diminutive .410 is getting some attention due to the popularity of the .410/45LC "Judge" revolver by Taurus. Federal has developed two specialized loadings for the Judge based on 000 buckshot and #4 lead shot. Interesting!

If steel shot is your only option in the field or at the range, there are new steel target and game loads for the 20- and 12-gauge. For the varmint hunter, there's a new V-Shok coyote loading for the 3-inch 12-gauge delivering 1-1/2 oz. of HEAVY-WEIGHT BB's in a FLITECONTROL wad at 1,350 fps. With the increasing popularity of lightweight .38 Special snubbies for personal protection, Federal is bringing back the non-fouling 125-gr. NyClad, hollowpoint load featuring a nylon-coated soft lead HP bullet at an ideal snubby velocity of 830 fps.

Federal has designed two specialty loads for the popular Taurus .410 "Judge" revolver.

Garand and M1A target shooters will be delighted with two new match loads being offered under the American Eagle brand that feature pressure curves to match the semi-automatic gas systems and a harder, staked-in primer to reduce the possibility of slamfires. The .30-06 Garand load sports a 150-gr. FMJ at 2,740 fps and the 7.62x51mm M1A load, a 168-gr. HP match bullet at 2,650 fps.

There is a wide range of new centerfire rifle loadings this year based on Federal's Trophy Bonded Tip, Speer, Barnes, and Sierra bullets. In the big game category, Federal is loading a 286-gr. Barnes Banded Solid at 2,550 fps in the .370 Sako and 500-gr. Barnes Triple-Shock X-Bullet at 2,280 in the .458 Lott. The .338 Federal round will be chambered in an AR-10 platform this year, and Federal is making sure it will be economical to shoot by introducing a 200-gr. soft point load in the popular Power-Shok line. Finally, in the rimfire category, Federal is reintroducing its Olympic winning Ultramatch load consisting of a 40-gr. solid at 1,080 fps. See it all at www.federalpremium.com.

Fiocchi

One of the most common questions raised by our handgun ballistics tables is the inclusion of a listing for the .450 Short Colt cartridge, also known as the .450 Adams. Believe it or not, the 150-year-old cartridge is still loaded – and by a major manufacturer, too.

Yes, the .450 Short Colt is available, and it's loaded under Fiocchi's "Historic Cartridge for Collector's Firearms" category. In that category, under their current handgun cartridge listings, Fiocchi also offers the 7.5 Swiss Ordnance, 7.62 Nagant, 7.63 Mauser, .30 Luger, 8mm Gasser, 8mm Lebel, 8mm Steyr, 9mm Steyr, .38 S&W Short, .380 Long, .44 S&W Russian and .455 Webley. This year Fiocchi is highly focused on their new non-toxic lines that include rifle, pistol and shotgun ammunition. Fiocchi's answer is a proprietary Tundra Tungsten Composite. Fiocchi claims that their Tundra Tungsten shot is safe for all chokes and older pre-steel barrels and performs and deforms like lead shot.

See their latest loads at www.fiocchiusa.com.

Hodgdon

After buying the IMR Powder Company in 2003 and licensing the Winchester branded powders in 2006, Hodgdon has emerged as the largest handloading powder company in the world. Not standing on their laurels for one moment, this year Hodgdon acquired the only black powder manufacturer in the United States, GOEX Powder, Inc., with a history going back to 1802 when it was founded originally

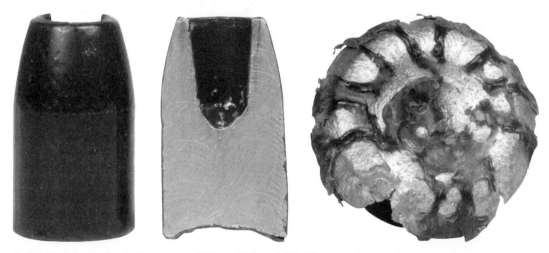

Federal is bringing back the popular 125-gr. .38 Special NyClad round for snubnose revolvers.

as a DuPont company. The only easy way to keep track of Hodgdon and its three powder subsidiaries is through the web at www.hodgdon.com, www.goexpowder.com, www.imrpowder.com, and www.wwpowder.com.

Hodgdon has just released its new 5000+ loads reloading manual that does a good job of covering the latest cartridges like the .300 and .338 Ruger Compact Magnums,. 30 T/C and .327 Federal. Hodgdon also offers an annual muzzleloading manual and basic reloading manual. (www.hodgdon.com)

Hornday

Hornady has developed a new non-toxic, monolithic game bullet made from gilding metal rather than a softer copper alloy. Called the "GMX," it sports a hollow nose cavity capped with a polymer tip, a 10-degree boattail base and has a ballistic coefficient that equals its streamlined SST and InterBond counterparts. Performance specifications call for the GMX to expand 1.5 times its original diameter, retain 95 percent of its original weight and perform across a wide range of velocities from 2,000 fps to 3,400 fps. Initially, it will be available in .270-, 7mm-, .30-, and .338-calibers.

There are two brand new cartridges this year: the .416 Ruger Compact Magnum and the .338 Marlin Express. Loaded with either Hornady's 400-gr. steel jacketed soft point (DGX) or their steel jacketed solid (DGS) at 2,400 fps, the .416 Ruger should be a fantastic complement to Ruger's short, handy Hawkeye Alaskan rifle. The .338 Marlin Express puts some power and range in Marlin's lever action line with a 200-gr. FTX Flextip bullet at 2,565 fps.

Hornady now offers classic ammunition for the .404 Jeffery, .416 Rigby, .470 Nitro Express and .500 Nitro Express.

With a ballistic coefficient of .430, the .338 FTX bullet matches the ballistics of the 180-gr. .30-06 bullet out to 400 yards.

Speaking of big game cartridges, Hornady will be offering classic loads for the .404 Jeffery, .470 Nitro Express and the .500 Nitro Express this year, so stock up.

Finally, there's a new "Critical Defense" line of handgun ammunition for the .380 Auto, 9mm Luger, .38 Special and .38 Special +P. The Critical Defense bullet incorporates a soft polymer insert in its hollow point that insures 100% percent reliable expansion when fired through the toughest of clothing. (www.hornady.com)

Lapua

Is the .222 Remington due for a comeback? Maybe so; it's still a popular light game cartridge in Europe. This year Lapua is producing a true match grade .222 case with extremely tight tolerances in wall thickness and neck concentricity. The .222 has always been an inherently accurate cartridge. Lapua's new brass might make it even better.

Promoting their .338 Lapua Magnum for long range target shooting, Lapua is introducing a heavy 300-gr., extra low drag, Scenar hollowpoint match bullet for the .338. Other precision brass case offerings of interest include the .220 Russian, 6.5x47 Lapua, 6.5 Grendel and the 6.5-284. The full Lapua story is at www.lapua.com.

Hornady's new DGX bullet is a steel jacketed soft point designed for game like the Cape buffalo.

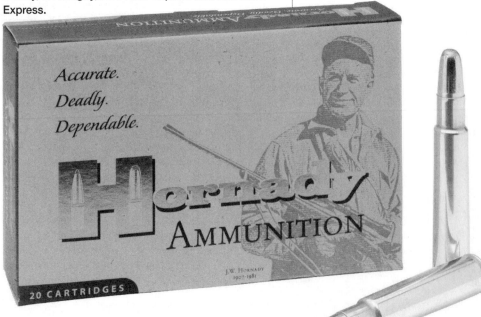

Hornady's Critical Defense handgun ammunition utilizes a polymer tip to ensure the hollow point expands after passing through clothing layers.

Norma

Although it receives little press, Norma's extensive line of match ammunition has been at the forefront of international competition for years. Recently, USA's David Tubb, 11-time NRA High Power Champion and five-time NRA Long Range Champion, developed a new match cartridge in cooperation with Norma. Named the 6XC, the short, compact cartridge features a moly-coated 105-gr. 6mm open point match bullet at 3,018 fps. Zeroed at 300 yards, it is 3.5 inches high at 100 and only 9.8 inches low at 400. It's short enough to fit in an AR platform, giving us the ultimate across-the-board rifle. Norma reports that the accuracy of the 6XC exceeds that of their legendary 6mm Norma Benchrest cartridge, and that's saying a lot. See Norma's extensive lines of hunting and match ammunition at www.norma.cc.

Nosler

Introducing the largest Partition bullet ever offered, Nosler is fielding a .458-caliber, 500-gr. Partition that is ideally matched to large and dangerous game in the .458 Win., .458 Lott and .460 Weatherby. Nosler's AccuBond line has developed a well-deserved reputation for outstanding accuracy and structural integrity. The line is being expanded this year with the introduction of a highly desirable and long awaited 6.5mm 140-gr. AccuBond. The .30-caliber 168-gr. bullet has been an outstanding match bullet for decades, so Nosler is introducing a 168-gr. Ballistic Tip hunting bullet that combines accuracy with excellent terminal performance on soft skinned game. See their complete catalog and the company store at www.nosler.com.

Pinnacle Ammunition

Bismuth is back on the market under the auspices of a new company, Pinnacle Ammunition. The shell is still being loaded by Eley but is now being imported and sold under the Bis-Maxx brand. It's still a bit pricey, but it is a safe waterfowling load for all those classic shotguns with pre-steel era barrels. Pinnacle is also introducing a new steel pellet de-

Polywad's "GreenLite" shotshells leave nothing in the field but steel shot, Kraft paper and fine polymer dust.

signed by Polywad. Polywad called it a "Squound" because it was neither square nor round. Pinnacle calls it "Aerosteel." The pellet looks ever so much like a miniature Foster slug. It flies nose first and is far less wind sensitive than normal shot. It's an exciting development. Read all about it at www.pinnacleammo.com.

Polywad

Polywad's highly creative R&D program is continually spinning off new product designs for a number of commercial ammunition companies as well as offering a substantial line of shotshells themselves. Recently their focus has been on the development of a totally green shotshell payload. They've got it. Going under their "GreenLite" shotshell label, the new shell is designed for small upland bird shooting out to 35 yards and clay targets out to 40 yards+. The 20- and 28-gauge shells feature a soft steel payload of roughly #7.5 shot enclosed in a heavy Kraft paper shot cup. Between the shot cup and the powder is a column of polymer powder. There is no over-powder wad.

When a GreenLite shell is fired, the only residues left in the field are steel shot, a bit of Kraft paper and a puff of polymer powder – all of which are bio- and photodegradable.

The company's full line of innovative products is at www.polywad.com.

Nosler is introducing the largest Partition bullet they've ever made: the 500-gr. .458.

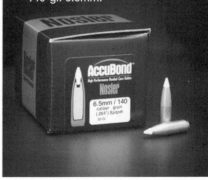

A long awaited addition to the Nosler Partition line is the new 140-gr. 6.5mm.

Precision Ammunition

One of the leaders in the non-toxic industry, Precision Ammunition offers an extensive line of handgun, rifle and shotgun ammunition using projectiles formed from a matrix of copper. Precision calls it their Copper-Matrix NTF Non-Toxic Frangible Ammunition line, and it is torched off using RUAG's GreenFire lead-free primers! It doesn't get much greener! (www.precisionammo.com)

Prvi Partisan

This notable Serbian ammunition company not only offers an extensive selection of affordable rifle and handgun ammunition and components but has earned a reputation for loading many of the harder-to-get military cartridges. Among its latest catalogued offerings of loaded ammunition and components are the 6.5x52 Carcano, 7.5x54 French, 7.5x55 Swiss, 7.65x53 Argentine, 7.62x33 Kurz, 8x56 RS Mannlicher and possibly my favorite, the 8x50R Lebel. See their complete catalog at www.prvipartisan.com.

Remington's compact .30 AR cartridge is designed to bring deer hunting capability to the AR rifle.

Remington

Big Green has a new short proprietary cartridge that revs up the power factor of their lightweight R-15 AR platform rifle. Wouldn't you know it, it's called the .30 Remington AR, and it should prove to be a great deer load. Remington sums it up by stating "It hits like a .308 and carries like a .223." Initially, there are three loadings for the new AR cartridge: a 125-gr. Core-Lokt, a 125-gr. AccuTip and a 123-gr. FMJ, all at 2,800 fps. Given the popularity of the AR today, I expect we will see a number of other makers chambering the new round.

In the varmint field, Remington is introducing two frangible, iron-tin core, lead-free loads for the .223 (45 grains at 3,550 fps) and the .22-250 (45 grains at 4,000 fps). They should prove to be destructive and ricochet free. Sharing a berth now with Bushmaster, Remington is offering a load for the .450 Bushmaster featuring a 250-gr. soft point at 2,200 fps. Their excellent and high-tech AccuTip Bonded Sabot Slug line has been expanded to include a 260-gr. 20-gauge loadings in the 2-3/4" and 3" shells at 1,850 fps and 1,900 fps respectively. Finally, like most ammunition companies, Remington is fielding 12- and 20-gauge steel game and target loads this year. See this great company at www.remington.com.

Winchester's .410 steel load features 3/8 oz. of #6 shot at 1,400 fps.

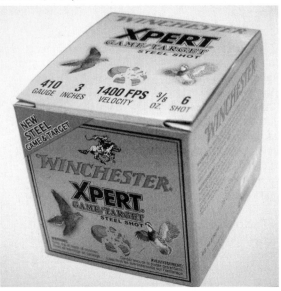

Sierra

Sierra reports they've had a hard time just keeping up with demand this year, much less introducing a number of new products. It's been a common observation in the ammunition and components industry. Nevertheless, Sierra does have a new bullet – the 155-gr. .30 caliber HPBT Palma MatchKing – which should keep your .308 match rifle supersonic out to 1,000 yards. See the bullet smiths at www.sierrabullets.com.

Speer

Responding to the increasing popularity of the 327 Federal, Speer is making its 115-gr. Gold Dot bullet loaded last year in Federal Premium ammunition available as a handloading component. Similarly, their TNT Green bullets, formerly available only in Federal Premium and CCI loaded ammunition, will be available as components for the first time. Much to Speer's credit, the company continues to offer some of the most difficult-to-find bullets to the handloading clan, including a 75-gr. SPFN for the .25-20 Win. and a 130-gr. SPFN for the 7-30 Waters. See their whole component list at www. speer-bullets. com.

Remington's Disintegrator Varmint ammunition in the .223 and .22-250 sports lead-free, frangible bullets.

Winchester Ammunition

At the 2009 Shot Show, I watched a Winchester engineer conduct the complete FBI handgun amunition protocol with Winchester's new Bonded PDX1 ammunition. The results were impressive. The new bullet, which is a bonded core hollowpoint, consistently expanded to 1.5X its diameter and punched through glass, clothing and other media without deviating from its

Winchester's Bonded PDX1 provides FBI protocol assurance for self-defense.

track. Available in the 38 Special (130 grains), 9mm Luger (124 and 147 grains), 40 S&W (165 and 180 grains) and 45 Auto (230 grains), the PDX1 bullet may be the ultimate self-defense pill.

Winchester is carrying their bonded technology over to rifle ammunition with the introduction of the Super-X Power Max Bonded line featuring a bonded core, protected hollowpoint bullet designed specifically for deer hunting. It's available in .270 Win. (130 grains), .270 WSM (130 grains), .30-30 (150 grains), .30-06 (150 grains), .300 WSM (150 grain), .300 Win. Mag. (150 grains) and .308 Win. (150 grains).

What about handgun hunting ammunition and shotgun slugs? Winchester is introducing a third new projectile design called the Supreme Elite Dual

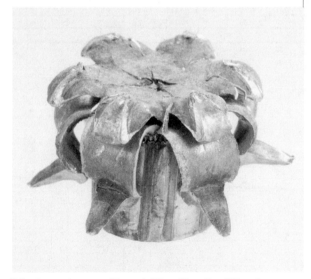

Winchester's new .45- and .50-caliber Dual Bond handgun bullets are designed for the largest game.

Remington's missile-like AccuTip slug has been added to the 20-gauge line.

Winchester has led the pack with the release of its lead-free, tin bullet in the .22 LR.

Bond. The Dual Bond handgun bullet and shotgun slug feature both a bonded core and two bonded jackets, one inside the other. Winchester calls it "the bullet within a bullet," and it's designed for big game up to and including brown bears. Upon impact, a massive hollowpoint initiates expansion up to 2X original bullet diameter, the jackets roll back into a classic talon profile, and due to complete bonding of the jackets and core, the bullet retains nearly 100 percent of its original weight. This year, Dual Bonds will be loaded in the .454 Casull (260 grains), .460 S&W (260 grains), and .500 S&W (375 grains) and as 2-3/4" and 3" shotgun sabot rounds in the 20- and 12-gauges.

Winchester's rimfire line receives quite a facelift with the addition of a 32-gr. Expediter LRHP delivering a muzzle velocity of 1,640 fps and tin base, lead-free bullets in both the .22 LR and .22 Win. Mag. Expanding their lead-free offerings, Winchester is also loading a 55-gr., tin core bullet in the .223 Super-X line and steel shot loads for the .410 and 28 gauge under the Xpert Game and Target line. Our ammunition has never been better! (www.winchester.com)

Many manufacturers do not supply suggested retail prices. Others did not get their pricing to us before press time. All pricing can vary dependent on the exact brand and style of ammo selected and/or the retail outlet from which you make your purchase. Pricing has been rounded to the nearest dollar and represents our best estimate of average pricing. An * after the cartridge means these loads are available with Nosler Partition or Swift A-Frame bullets. Listed pricing may or may not reflect this bullet type.
** = these are packed 50 to box, all others are 20 to box. Wea. Mag.= Weatherby Magnum. Spfd. = Springfield. A-Sq. = A-Square. N.E.=Nitro Express.

Cartridge	Bullet Wgt. Grs.	VELOCITY (fps)					ENERGY (ft. lbs.)					TRAJ. (in.)				Est. Price/ box
		Muzzle	100 yds.	200 yds.	300 yds.	400 yds.	Muzzle	100 yds.	200 yds.	300 yds.	400 yds.	100 yds.	200 yds.	300 yds.	400 yds.	
17, 22																
17 Remington Fireball	20	4000	3380	2840	2360	1930	710	507	358	247	165	1.6	1.5	-2.8	-13.5	NA
17 Remington Fireball	25	3850	3280	2780	2330	1925	823	597	429	301	206	0.9	0.0	-5.4	NA	NA
17 Remington	25	4040	3284	2644	2086	1606	906	599	388	242	143	+2.0	+1.7	-4.0	-17.0	$17
204 Ruger	32	4225	3632	3114	2652	2234	1268	937	689	500	355	.6	0.0	-4.2	-13.4	NA
204 Ruger	40	3900	3451	3046	2677	2336	1351	1058	824	636	485	.7	0.0	-4.5	-13.9	NA
204 Ruger	45	3625	3188	2792	2428	2093	1313	1015	778	589	438	1.00	0.0	-5.5	-16.9	NA
221 Fireball	50	2800	2137	1580	1180	988	870	507	277	155	109	+0.0	-7.0	-28.0	0.0	$14
22 Hornet	34	3050	2132	1415	1017	852	700	343	151	78	55	+0.0	-6.6	-15.5	-29.9	NA
22 Hornet	35	3100	2278	1601	1135	929	747	403	199	100	67	+2.75	0.0	-16.9	-60.4	NA
22 Hornet	45	2690	2042	1502	1128	948	723	417	225	127	90	+0.0	-7.7	-31.0	0.0	$27**
218 Bee	46	2760	2102	1550	1155	961	788	451	245	136	94	+0.0	-7.2	-29.0	0.0	$46**
222 Remington	40	3600	3117	2673	2269	1911	1151	863	634	457	324	+1.07	0.0	-6.13	-18.9	NA
222 Remington	50	3140	2602	2123	1700	1350	1094	752	500	321	202	+2.0	-0.4	-11.0	-33.0	$11
222 Remington	55	3020	2562	2147	1773	1451	1114	801	563	384	257	+2.0	-0.4	-11.0	-33.0	$12
22 PPC	52	3400	2930	2510	2130	NA	1335	990	730	525	NA	+2.0	1.4	-5.0	0.0	NA
223 Remington	40	3650	3010	2450	1950	1530	1185	805	535	340	265	+2.0	+1.0	-6.0	-22.0	$14
223 Remington	40	3800	3305	2845	2424	2044	1282	970	719	522	371	0.84	0.0	-5.34	-16.6	NA
223 Remington	50	3300	2874	2484	2130	1809	1209	917	685	504	363	1.37	0.0	-7.05	-21.8	NA
223 Remington	52/53	3330	2882	2477	2106	1770	1305	978	722	522	369	+2.0	+0.6	-6.5	-21.5	$14
223 Remington	55	3240	2748	2305	1906	1556	1282	922	649	444	296	+2.0	-0.2	-9.0	-27.0	$12
223 Remington	60	3100	2712	2355	2026	1726	1280	979	739	547	397	+2.0	+0.2	-8.0	-24.7	$16
223 Remington	64	3020	2621	2256	1920	1619	1296	977	723	524	373	+2.0	-0.2	-9.3	-23.0	$14
223 Remington	69	3000	2720	2460	2210	1980	1380	1135	925	750	600	+2.0	+0.8	-5.8	-17.5	$15
223 Remington	75	2790	2554	2330	2119	1926	1296	1086	904	747	617	2.37	0.0	-8.75	-25.1	NA
223 Remington	77	2750	2584	2354	2169	1992	1293	1110	948	804	679	1.93	0.0	-8.2	-23.8	NA
223 WSSM	55	3850	3438	3064	2721	2402	1444	1147	1147	904	704	0.7	0.0	-4.4	-13.6	NA
223 WSSM	64	3600	3144	2732	2356	2011	1841	1404	1061	789	574	1.0	0.0	-5.7	-17.7	NA
222 Rem. Mag.	55	3240	2748	2305	1906	1556	1282	922	649	444	296	+2.0	-0.2	-9.0	-27.0	$14
225 Winchester	55	3570	3066	2616	2208	1838	1556	1148	836	595	412	+2.0	+1.0	-5.0	-20.0	$19
224 Wea. Mag.	55	3650	3192	2780	2403	2057	1627	1244	943	705	516	+2.0	+1.2	-4.0	-17.0	$32
22-250 Rem.	40	4000	3320	2720	2200	1740	1420	980	660	430	265	+2.0	+1.8	-3.0	-16.0	$14
22-250 Rem.	50	3725	3264	2641	2455	2103	1540	1183	896	669	491	0.89	0.0	-5.23	-16.3	NA
22-250 Rem.	52/55	3680	3137	2656	2222	1832	1654	1201	861	603	410	+2.0	+1.3	-4.0	-17.0	$13
22-250 Rem.	60	3600	3195	2826	2485	2169	1727	1360	1064	823	627	+2.0	+2.0	-2.4	-12.3	$19
220 Swift	40	4200	3678	3190	2739	2329	1566	1201	904	666	482	+0.51	0.0	-4.0	-12.9	NA
220 Swift	50	3780	3158	2617	2135	1710	1586	1107	760	506	325	+2.0	+1.4	-4.4	-17.9	$20
220 Swift	50	3850	3396	2970	2576	2215	1645	1280	979	736	545	0.74	0.0	-4.84	-15.1	NA
220 Swift	55	3800	3370	2990	2630	2310	1765	1390	1090	850	650	0.8	0.0	-4.7	-14.4	NA
220 Swift	55	3650	3194	2772	2384	2035	1627	1246	939	694	506	+2.0	+2.0	-2.6	-13.4	$19
220 Swift	60	3600	3199	2824	2475	2156	1727	1364	1063	816	619	+2.0	+1.6	-4.1	-13.1	$19
22 Savage H.P.	71	2790	2340	1930	1570	1280	1225	860	585	390	190	+2.0	-1.0	-10.4	-35.7	NA
6mm (24)																
6mm BR Rem.	100	2550	2310	2083	1870	1671	1444	1185	963	776	620	+2.5	-0.6	-11.8	0.0	$22
6mm Norma BR	107	2822	2667	2517	2372	2229	1893	1690	1506	1337	1181	+1.73	0.0	-7.24	-20.6	NA
6mm PPC	70	3140	2750	2400	2070	NA	1535	1175	895	665	NA	+2.0	+1.4	-5.0	0.0	NA
243 Winchester	55	4025	3597	3209	2853	2525	1978	1579	1257	994	779	+0.6	0.0	-4.0	-12.2	NA
243 Winchester	60	3600	3110	2660	2260	1890	1725	1285	945	680	475	+2.0	+1.8	-3.3	-15.5	$17
243 Winchester	70	3400	3040	2700	2390	2100	1795	1435	1135	890	685	1.1	0.0	-5.9	-18.0	NA
243 Winchester	75/80	3350	2955	2593	2259	1951	1993	1551	1194	906	676	+2.0	+0.9	-5.0	-19.0	$16
243 Winchester	85	3320	3070	2830	2600	2380	2080	1770	1510	1280	1070	+2.0	+1.2	-4.0	-14.0	$18
243 Winchester	90	3120	2871	2635	2411	2199	1946	1647	1388	1162	966	1.4	0.0	-6.4	-18.8	NA
243 Winchester*	100	2960	2697	2449	2215	1993	1945	1615	1332	1089	882	+2.5	+1.2	-6.0	-20.0	$16
243 Winchester	105	2920	2689	2470	2261	2062	1988	1686	1422	1192	992	+2.5	+1.6	-5.0	-18.4	$21
243 Light Mag.	100	3100	2839	2592	2358	2138	2133	1790	1491	1235	1014	+1.5	0.0	-6.8	-19.8	NA
243 WSSM	55	4060	3628	3237	2880	2550	2013	1607	1280	1013	794	0.6	0.0	-3.9	-12.0	NA
243 WSSM	95	3250	3000	2763	2538	2325	2258	1898	1610	1359	1140	1.2	0.0	-5.7	-16.9	NA
243 WSSM	100	3110	2838	2583	2341	2112	2147	1789	1481	1217	991	1.4	0.0	-6.6	-19.7	NA
6mm Remington	80	3470	3064	2694	2352	2036	2139	1667	1289	982	736	+2.0	+1.1	-5.0	-17.0	$16
6mm Remington	100	3100	2829	2573	2332	2104	2133	1777	1470	1207	983	+2.5	+1.6	-5.0	-17.0	$16
6mm Remington	105	3060	2822	2596	2381	2177	2105	1788	1512	1270	1059	+2.5	+1.1	-3.3	-15.0	$21
6mm Rem. Light Mag.	100	3250	2997	2756	2528	2311	2345	1995	1687	1418	1186	1.59	0.0	-6.33	-18.3	NA
6.17(.243) Spitfire	100	3350	3122	2905	2698	2501	2493	2164	1874	1617	1389	2.4	3.20	0.0	-8.0	NA
240 Wea. Mag.	87	3500	3202	2924	2663	2416	2366	1980	1651	1370	1127	+2.0	+2.0	-2.0	-12.0	$32

Many manufacturers do not supply suggested retail prices. Others did not get their pricing to us before press time. All pricing can vary dependent on the exact brand and style of ammo selected and/or the retail outlet from which you make your purchase. Pricing has been rounded to the nearest dollar and represents our best estimate of average pricing.
An * after the cartridge means these loads are available with Nosler Partition or Swift A-Frame bullets. Listed pricing may or may not reflect this bullet type.
** = these are packed 50 to box, all others are 20 to box. Wea. Mag.= Weatherby Magnum. Spfd. = Springfield. A-Sq. = A-Square. N.E.=Nitro Express.

Cartridge	Bullet Wgt. Grs.	VELOCITY (fps)					ENERGY (ft. lbs.)					TRAJ. (in.)				Est. Price/ box
		Muzzle	100 yds.	200 yds.	300 yds.	400 yds.	Muzzle	100 yds.	200 yds.	300 yds.	400 yds.	100 yds.	200 yds.	300 yds.	400 yds.	
240 Wea. Mag.	100	3395	3106	2835	2581	2339	2559	2142	1785	1478	1215	+2.5	+2.8	-2.0	-11.0	$43
25																
25-20 Win.	86	1460	1194	1030	931	858	407	272	203	165	141	0.0	-23.5	0.0	0.0	$32**
25-35 Win.	117	2230	1866	1545	1282	1097	1292	904	620	427	313	+2.5	-4.2	-26.0	0.0	$24
250 Savage	100	2820	2504	2210	1936	1684	1765	1392	1084	832	630	+2.5	+0.4	-9.0	-28.0	$17
257 Roberts	100	2980	2661	2363	2085	1827	1972	1572	1240	965	741	+2.5	-0.8	-5.2	-21.6	$20
257 Roberts+P	117	2780	2411	2071	1761	1488	2009	1511	1115	806	576	+2.5	-0.2	-10.2	-32.6	$18
257 Roberts+P	120	2780	2560	2360	2160	1970	2060	1750	1480	1240	1030	+2.5	+1.2	-6.4	-23.6	$22
257 Roberts	122	2600	2331	2078	1842	1625	1831	1472	1169	919	715	+2.5	0.0	-10.6	-31.4	$21
257 Light Mag.	117	2940	2694	2460	2240	2031	2245	1885	1572	1303	1071	+1.7	0.0	-7.6	-21.8	NA
25-06 Rem.	87	3440	2995	2591	2222	1884	2286	1733	1297	954	686	+2.0	+1.1	-2.5	-14.4	$17
25-06 Rem.	90	3440	3043	2680	2344	2034	2364	1850	1435	1098	827	+2.0	+1.8	-3.3	-15.6	$17
25-06 Rem.	100	3230	2893	2580	2287	2014	2316	1858	1478	1161	901	+2.0	+0.8	-5.7	-18.9	$17
25-06 Rem.	117	2990	2770	2570	2370	2190	2320	2000	1715	1465	1246	+2.5	+1.0	-7.9	-26.6	$19
25-06 Rem.*	120	2990	2730	2484	2252	2032	2382	1985	1644	1351	1100	+2.5	+1.2	-5.3	-19.6	$17
25-06 Rem.	122	2930	2706	2492	2289	2095	2325	1983	1683	1419	1189	+2.5	+1.8	-4.5	-17.5	$23
25 WSSM	85	3470	3156	2863	2589	2331	2273	1880	1548	1266	1026	1.0	0.0	-5.2	-15.7	NA
25 WSSM	115	3060	284	2639	2442	2254	2392	2066	1778	1523	1398	1.4	0.0	-6.4	-18.6	NA
25 WSSM	120	2990	2717	2459	2216	1987	2383	1967	1612	1309	1053	1.6	0.0	-7.4	-21.8	NA
257 Wea. Mag.	87	3825	3456	3118	2805	2513	2826	2308	1870	1520	1220	+2.0	+2.7	-0.3	-7.6	$32
257 Wea. Mag.	100	3555	3237	2941	2665	2404	2806	2326	1920	1576	1283	+2.5	+3.2	0.0	-8.0	$32
257 Scramjet	100	3745	3450	3173	2912	2666	3114	2643	2235	1883	1578	+2.1	+2.77	0.0	-6.93	NA
6.5																
6.5x47 Lapua	123	2887	NA	2554	NA	2244	2285	NA	1788	NA	1380	NA	4.53	0.00	-10.7	NA
6.5x50mm Jap.	139	2360	2160	1970	1790	1620	1720	1440	1195	985	810	+2.5	-1.0	-13.5	0.0	NA
6.5x50mm Jap.	156	2070	1830	1610	1430	1260	1475	1155	900	695	550	+2.5	-4.0	-23.8	0.0	NA
6.5x52mm Car.	139	2580	2360	2160	1970	1790	2045	1725	1440	1195	985	+2.5	0.0	-9.9	-29.0	NA
6.5x52mm Car.	156	2430	2170	1930	1700	1500	2045	1630	1285	1005	780	+2.5	-1.0	-13.9	0.0	NA
6.5x52mm Carcano	160	2250	1963	1700	1467	1271	1798	1369	1027	764	574	+3.8	0.0	-15.9	-48.1	NA
6.5x55mm Light Mag.	129	2750	2549	2355	2171	1994	2166	1860	1589	1350	1139	+2.0	0.0	-8.2	-23.9	NA
6.5x55mm Swe.	140	2550	NA	NA	NA	NA	2020	NA	NA	NA	NA	0.0	0.0	0.0	0.0	$18
6.5x55mm Swe.*	139/140	2850	2640	2440	2250	2070	2525	2170	1855	1575	1330	+2.5	+1.6	-5.4	-18.9	$18
6.5x55mm Swe.	156	2650	2370	2110	1870	1650	2425	1950	1550	1215	945	+2.5	0.0	-10.3	-30.6	NA
260 Remington	125	2875	2669	2473	2285	2105	2294	1977	1697	1449	1230	1.71	0.0	-7.4	-21.4	NA
260 Remington	140	2750	2544	2347	2158	1979	2351	2011	1712	1448	1217	+2.2	0.0	-8.6	-24.6	NA
6.5 Creedmoor	120	3020	2815	2619	2430	2251	2430	2111	1827	1574	1350	1.4	0.0	-6.5	-18.9	NA
6.5 Creedmoor	140	2820	2654	2494	2339	2190	2472	2179	1915	1679	1467	1.7	0.0	-7.2	-20.6	NA
6.5-284 Norma	142	3025	2890	2758	2631	2507	2886	2634	2400	2183	1982	1.13	0.0	-5.7	-16.4	NA
6.71 (264) Phantom	120	3150	2929	2718	2517	2325	2645	2286	1969	1698	1440	+1.3	0.0	-6.0	-17.5	NA
6.5 Rem. Mag.	120	3210	2905	2621	2353	2102	2745	2248	1830	1475	1177	+2.5	+1.7	-4.1	-16.3	Disc.
264 Win. Mag.	140	3030	2782	2548	2326	2114	2854	2406	2018	1682	1389	+2.5	+1.4	-5.1	-18.0	$24
6.71 (264) Blackbird	140	3480	3261	3053	2855	2665	3766	3307	2899	2534	2208	+2.4	+3.1	0.0	-7.4	NA
6.8mm Rem.	115	2775	2472	2190	1926	1683	1966	1561	1224	947	723	+2.1	0.0	-3.7	-9.4	NA
27																
270 Winchester	100	3430	3021	2649	2305	1988	2612	2027	1557	1179	877	+2.0	+1.0	-4.9	-17.5	$17
270 Win. (Rem.)	115	2710	2482	2265	2059	NA	1875	1485	1161	896	NA	0.0	4.8	-17.3	0.0	NA
270 Winchester	130	3060	2776	2510	2259	2022	2702	2225	1818	1472	1180	+2.5	+1.4	-5.3	-18.2	$17
270 Win. Supreme	130	3150	2881	2628	2388	2161	2865	2396	1993	1646	1348	1.3	0.0	-6.4	-18.9	NA
270 Winchester	135	3000	2780	2570	2369	2178	2697	2315	1979	1682	1421	+2.5	+1.4	-6.0	-17.6	$23
270 Winchester*	140	2940	2700	2480	2260	2060	2685	2270	1905	1590	1315	+2.5	+1.8	-4.6	-17.9	$20
270 Win. Light Magnum	130	3215	2998	2790	2590	2400	2983	2594	2246	1936	1662	1.21	0.0	-5.83	-17.0	NA
270 Winchester*	150	2850	2585	2336	2100	1879	2705	2226	1817	1468	1175	+2.5	+1.2	-6.5	-22.0	$17
270 Win. Supreme	150	2930	2693	2468	2254	2051	2860	2416	2030	1693	1402	1.7	0.0	-7.4	-21.6	NA
270 WSM	130	3275	3041	2820	2609	2408	3096	2669	2295	1564	1673	1.1	0.0	-5.5	-16.1	NA
270 WSM	140	3125	2865	2619	2386	2165	3035	2559	2132	1769	1457	1.4	0.0	-6.5	-19.0	NA
270 WSM	150	3120	2923	2734	2554	2380	3242	2845	2490	2172	1886	1.3	0.0	-5.9	-17.2	NA
270 Wea. Mag.	100	3760	3380	3033	2712	2412	3139	2537	2042	1633	1292	+2.0	+2.4	-1.2	-10.1	$32
270 Wea. Mag.	130	3375	3119	2878	2649	2432	3287	2808	2390	2026	1707	+2.5	-2.9	-0.9	-9.9	$32
270 Wea. Mag.*	150	3245	3036	2837	2647	2465	3507	3070	2681	2334	2023	+2.5	+2.6	-1.8	-11.4	$47
7mm																
7mm BR	140	2216	2012	1821	1643	1481	1525	1259	1031	839	681	+2.0	-3.7	-20.0	0.0	$23
7mm Mauser*	139/140	2660	2435	2221	2018	1827	2199	1843	1533	1266	1037	+2.5	0.0	-9.6	-27.7	$17
7mm Mauser	145	2690	2442	2206	1985	1777	2334	1920	1568	1268	1017	+2.5	+0.1	-9.6	-28.3	$18
7mm Mauser	154	2690	2490	2300	2120	1940	2475	2120	1810	1530	1285	+2.5	+0.8	-7.5	-23.5	$17

Many manufacturers do not supply suggested retail prices. Others did not get their pricing to us before press time. All pricing can vary dependent on the exact brand and style of ammo selected and/or the retail outlet from which you make your purchase. Pricing has been rounded to the nearest dollar and represents our best estimate of average pricing. An * after the cartridge means these loads are available with Nosler Partition or Swift A-Frame bullets. Listed pricing may or may not reflect this bullet type. ** = these are packed 50 to box, all others are 20 to box. Wea. Mag.= Weatherby Magnum. Spfd. = Springfield. A-Sq. = A-Square. N.E.=Nitro Express.

Cartridge	Bullet Wgt. Grs.	VELOCITY (fps)					ENERGY (ft. lbs.)					TRAJ. (in.)				Est. Price/ box
		Muzzle	100 yds.	200 yds.	300 yds.	400 yds.	Muzzle	100 yds.	200 yds.	300 yds.	400 yds.	100 yds.	200 yds.	300 yds.	400 yds.	
7mm Mauser	175	2440	2137	1857	1603	1382	2313	1774	1340	998	742	+2.5	-1.7	-16.1	0.0	$17
7x57 Light Mag.	139	2970	2730	2503	2287	2082	2722	2301	1933	1614	1337	+1.6	0.0	-7.2	-21.0	NA
7x30 Waters	120	2700	2300	1930	1600	1330	1940	1405	990	685	470	+2.5	-0.2	-12.3	0.0	$18
7mm-08 Rem.	120	3000	2725	2467	2223	1992	2398	1979	1621	1316	1058	+2.0	0.0	-7.6	-22.3	$18
7mm-08 Rem.*	140	2860	2625	2402	2189	1988	2542	2142	1793	1490	1228	+2.5	+0.8	-6.9	-21.9	$18
7mm-08 Rem.	154	2715	2510	2315	2128	1950	2520	2155	1832	1548	1300	+2.5	+1.0	-7.0	-22.7	$23
7mm-08 Light Mag.	139	3000	2790	2590	2399	2216	2777	2403	2071	1776	1515	+1.5	0.0	-6.7	-19.4	NA
7x64mm Bren.	140					Not Yet Announced										$17
7x64mm Bren.	154	2820	2610	2420	2230	2050	2720	2335	1995	1695	1430	+2.5	+1.4	-5.7	-19.9	NA
7x64mm Bren.*	160	2850	2669	2495	2327	2166	2885	2530	2211	1924	1667	+2.5	+1.6	-4.8	-17.8	$24
7x64mm Bren.	175					Not Yet Announced										$17
284 Winchester	150	2860	2595	2344	2108	1886	2724	2243	1830	1480	1185	+2.5	+0.8	-7.3	-23.2	$24
280 Remington	120	3150	2866	2599	2348	2110	2643	2188	1800	1468	1186	+2.0	+0.6	-6.0	-17.9	$17
280 Remington	140	3000	2758	2528	2309	2102	2797	2363	1986	1657	1373	+2.5	+1.4	-5.2	-18.3	$17
280 Remington*	150	2890	2624	2373	2135	1912	2781	2293	1875	1518	1217	+2.5	+0.8	-7.1	-22.6	$17
280 Remington	160	2840	2637	2442	2556	2078	2866	2471	2120	1809	1535	+2.5	+0.8	-6.7	-21.0	$20
280 Remington	165	2820	2510	2220	1950	1701	2913	2308	1805	1393	1060	+2.5	+0.4	-8.8	-26.5	$17
7x61mm S&H Sup.	154	3060	2720	2400	2100	1820	3200	2520	1965	1505	1135	+2.5	+1.8	-5.0	-19.8	NA
7mm Dakota	160	3200	3001	2811	2630	2455	3637	3200	2808	2456	2140	+2.1	+1.9	-2.8	-12.5	NA
7mm Rem. Mag. (Rem.)	140	2710	2482	2265	2059	NA	2283	1915	1595	1318	NA	0.0	-4.5	-1.57	0.0	NA
7mm Rem. Mag.*	139/140	3150	2930	2710	2510	2320	3085	2660	2290	1960	1670	+2.5	+2.4	-2.4	-12.7	$21
7mm Rem. Hvy Mag	139	3250	3044	2847	2657	2475	3259	2860	2501	2178	1890	1.1	0.0	-5.5	-16.2	NA
7mm Rem. Mag.	150/154	3110	2830	2568	2320	2085	3221	2667	2196	1792	1448	+2.5	+1.6	-4.6	-16.5	$21
7mm Rem. Mag.*	160/162	2950	2730	2520	2320	2120	3090	2650	2250	1910	1600	+2.5	+1.8	-4.4	-17.8	$34
7mm Rem. Mag.	165	2900	2699	2507	2324	2147	3081	2669	2303	1978	1689	+2.5	+1.2	-5.9	-19.0	$28
7mm Rem Mag.	175	2860	2645	2440	2244	2057	3178	2718	2313	1956	1644	+2.5	+1.0	-6.5	-20.7	$21
7mm Rem. SA ULTRA MAG	140	3175	2934	2707	2490	2283	3033	2676	2277	1927	1620	1.3	0.0	-6	-17.7	NA
7mm Rem. SA ULTRA MAG	150	3110	2828	2563	2313	2077	3221	2663	2188	1782	1437	2.5	2.1	-3.6	-15.8	NA
7mm Rem. SA ULTRA MAG	160	2960	2762	2572	2390	2215	3112	2709	2350	2029	1743	2.6	2.2	-3.6	-15.4	NA
7mm Rem. WSM	140	3225	3008	2801	2603	2414	3233	2812	2438	2106	1812	1.2	0.0	-5.6	-16.4	NA
7mm Rem. WSM	160	2990	2744	2512	2081	1883	3176	2675	2241	1864	1538	1.6	0.0	-7.1	-20.8	NA
7mm Wea. Mag.	140	3225	2970	2729	2501	2283	3233	2741	2315	1943	1621	+2.5	+2.0	-3.2	-14.0	$35
7mm Wea. Mag.	154	3260	3023	2799	2586	2382	3539	3044	2609	2227	1890	+2.5	+2.8	-1.5	-10.8	$32
7mm Wea. Mag.*	160	3200	3004	2816	2637	2464	3637	3205	2817	2469	2156	+2.5	+2.7	-1.5	-10.6	$47
7mm Wea. Mag.	165	2950	2747	2553	2367	2189	3188	2765	2388	2053	1756	+2.5	+1.8	-4.2	-16.4	$43
7mm Wea. Mag.	175	2910	2693	2486	2288	2098	3293	2818	2401	2033	1711	+2.5	+1.2	-5.9	-19.4	$35
7.21(.284) Tomahawk	140	3300	3118	2943	2774	2612	3386	3022	2693	2393	2122	2.3	3.20	0.0	-7.7	NA
7mm STW	140	3325	3064	2818	2585	2364	3436	2918	2468	2077	1737	+2.3	+1.8	-3.0	-13.1	NA
7mm STW Supreme	160	3150	2894	2652	2422	2204	3526	2976	2499	2085	1727	1.3	0.0	-6.3	-18.5	NA
7mm Rem. Ultra Mag.	140	3425	3184	2956	2740	2534	3646	3151	2715	2333	1995	1.7	1.60	-2.6	-11.4	NA
7mm Firehawk	140	3625	3373	3135	2909	2695	4084	3536	3054	2631	2258	+2.2	+2.9	0.0	-7.03	NA
30																
7.21 (.284) Firebird	140	3750	3522	3306	3101	2905	4372	3857	3399	2990	2625	1.6	2.4	0.0	-6.0	NA
30 Carbine	110	1990	1567	1236	1035	923	977	600	373	262	208	0.0	-13.5	0.0	0.0	$28**
303 Savage	190	1890	1612	1327	1183	1055	1507	1096	794	591	469	+2.5	-7.6	0.0	0.0	$24
30 Remington	170	2120	1822	1555	1328	1153	1696	1253	913	666	502	+2.5	-4.7	-26.3	0.0	$20
7.62x39mm Rus.	123/125	2300	2030	1780	1550	1350	1445	1125	860	655	500	+2.5	-2.0	-17.5	0.0	$13
30-30 Win.	55	3400	2693	2085	1570	1187	1412	886	521	301	172	+2.0	0.0	-10.2	-35.0	$18
30-30 Win.	125	2570	2090	1660	1320	1080	1830	1210	770	480	320	-2.0	-2.6	-19.9	0.0	$13
30-30 Win.	150	2390	2040	1723	1447	1225	1902	1386	989	697	499	0.0	-7.5	-27.0	-63.0	NA
30-30 Win. Supreme	150	2480	2095	1747	1446	1209	2049	1462	1017	697	487	0.0	-6.5	-24.5	0.0	NA
30-30 Win.	160	2300	1997	1719	1473	1268	1879	1416	1050	771	571	+2.5	-2.9	-20.2	0.0	$18
30-30 Win. Lever Evolution	160	2400	2150	1916	1699	NA	2046	1643	1304	1025	NA	3.00	0.20	-12.1	NA	NA
30-30 PMC Cowboy	170	1300	1198	1121			638	474				0.0	-27.0	0.0	0.0	NA
30-30 Win.*	170	2200	1895	1619	1381	1191	1827	1355	989	720	535	+2.5	-5.8	-23.6	0.0	$13
300 Savage	150	2630	2354	2094	1853	1631	2303	1845	1462	1143	886	+2.5	-0.4	-10.1	-30.7	$17
300 Savage	180	2350	2137	1935	1754	1570	2207	1825	1496	1217	985	+2.5	-1.6	-15.2	0.0	$17
30-40 Krag	180	2430	2213	2007	1813	1632	2360	1957	1610	1314	1064	+2.5	-1.4	-13.8	0.0	$18
7.65x53mm Arg.	180	2590	2390	2200	2010	1830	2685	2280	1925	1615	1345	+2.5	0.0	-27.6	0.0	NA
7.5x53mm Argentine	150	2785	2519	2269	2032	1814	2583	2113	1714	1376	1096	+2.0	0.0	-8.8	-25.5	NA
308 Marlin Express	160	2660	2430	2226	2026	1836	2513	2111	1761	1457	1197	3.0	1.7	-6.7	-23.5	NA
307 Winchester	150	2760	2321	1924	1575	1289	2530	1795	1233	826	554	+2.5	-1.5	-13.6	0.0	Disc.
307 Winchester	180	2510	2179	1874	1599	1362	2519	1898	1404	1022	742	+2.5	-1.6	-15.6	0.0	$20
7.5x55 Swiss	180	2650	2450	2250	2060	1880	2805	2390	2020	1700	1415	+2.5	+0.6	-8.1	-24.9	NA
7.5x55mm Swiss	165	2720	2515	2319	2132	1954	2710	2317	1970	1665	1398	+2.0	0.0	-8.5	-24.6	NA
30 Remington AR	123/125	2800	2465	2154	1867	1606	2176	1686	1288	967	716	2.10	0.00	-9.7	-29.4	NA

Many manufacturers do not supply suggested retail prices. Others did not get their pricing to us before press time. All pricing can vary dependent on the exact brand and style of ammo selected and/or the retail outlet from which you make your purchase. Pricing has been rounded to the nearest dollar and represents our best estimate of average pricing. An * after the cartridge means these loads are available with Nosler Partition or Swift A-Frame bullets. Listed pricing may or may not reflect this bullet type. ** = these are packed 50 to box, all others are 20 to box. Wea. Mag.= Weatherby Magnum. Spfd. = Springfield. A-Sq. = A-Square. N.E.=Nitro Express.

Cartridge	Bullet Wgt. Grs.	VELOCITY (fps)					ENERGY (ft. lbs.)					TRAJ. (in.)				Est. Price/ box
		Muzzle	100 yds.	200 yds.	300 yds.	400 yds.	Muzzle	100 yds.	200 yds.	300 yds.	400 yds.	100 yds.	200 yds.	300 yds.	400 yds.	
308 Winchester	55	3770	3215	2726	2286	1888	1735	1262	907	638	435	-2.0	+1.4	-3.8	-15.8	$22
308 Winchester	150	2820	2533	2263	2009	1774	2648	2137	1705	1344	1048	+2.5	+0.4	-8.5	-26.1	$17
308 Winchester	165	2700	2440	2194	1963	1748	2670	2180	1763	1411	1199	+2.5	0.0	-9.7	-28.5	$20
308 Winchester	168	2680	2493	2314	2143	1979	2678	2318	1998	1713	1460	+2.5	0.0	-8.9	-25.3	$18
308 Win. (Fed.)	170	2000	1740	1510	NA	NA	1510	1145	860	NA	NA	0.0	0.0	0.0	0.0	NA
308 Winchester	178	2620	2415	2220	2034	1857	2713	2306	1948	1635	1363	+2.5	0.0	-9.6	-27.6	$23
308 Winchester*	180	2620	2393	2178	1974	1782	2743	2288	1896	1557	1269	+2.5	-0.2	-10.2	-28.5	$17
308 Light Mag.*	150	2980	2703	2442	2195	1964	2959	2433	1986	1606	1285	+1.6	0.0	-7.5	-22.2	NA
308 Light Mag.	165	2870	2658	2456	2263	2078	3019	2589	2211	1877	1583	+1.7	0.0	-7.5	-21.8	NA
308 High Energy	165	2870	2600	2350	2120	1890	3020	2485	2030	1640	1310	+1.8	0.0	-8.2	-24.0	NA
308 Light Mag.	168	2870	2658	2456	2263	2078	3019	2589	2211	1877	1583	+1.7	0.0	-7.5	-21.8	NA
308 High Energy	180	2740	2550	2370	2200	2030	3000	2600	2245	1925	1645	+1.9	0.0	-8.2	-23.5	NA
30-06 Spfd.	55	4080	3485	2965	2502	2083	2033	1483	1074	764	530	+2.0	+1.9	-2.1	-11.7	$22
30-06 Spfd. (Rem.)	125	2660	2335	2034	1757	NA	1964	1513	1148	856	NA	0.0	-5.2	-18.9	0.0	NA
30-06 Spfd.	125	3140	2780	2447	2138	1853	2736	2145	1662	1279	953	+2.0	+1.0	-6.2	-21.0	$17
30-06 Spfd.	150	2910	2617	2342	2083	1853	2820	2281	1827	1445	1135	+2.5	+0.8	-7.2	-23.4	$17
30-06 Spfd.	152	2910	2654	2413	2184	1968	2858	2378	1965	1610	1307	+2.5	+1.0	-6.6	-21.3	$23
30-06 Spfd.*	165	2800	2534	2283	2047	1825	2872	2352	1909	1534	1220	+2.5	+0.4	-8.4	-25.5	$17
30-06 Spfd.	168	2710	2522	2346	2169	2003	2739	2372	2045	1754	1497	+2.5	+0.4	-8.0	-23.5	$18
30-06 Spfd. (Fed.)	170	2000	1740	1510	NA	NA	1510	1145	860	NA	NA	0.0	0.0	0.0	0.0	NA
30-06 Spfd.	178	2720	2511	2311	2121	1939	2924	2491	2111	1777	1486	+2.5	+0.4	-8.2	-24.6	$23
30-06 Spfd.*	180	2700	2469	2250	2042	1846	2913	2436	2023	1666	1362	-2.5	0.0	-9.3	-27.0	$17
30-06 Spfd.	220	2410	2130	1870	1632	1422	2837	2216	1708	1301	988	+2.5	-1.7	-18.0	0.0	$17

30 Mag.

Cartridge	Bullet Wgt. Grs.	Muzzle	100 yds.	200 yds.	300 yds.	400 yds.	Muzzle	100 yds.	200 yds.	300 yds.	400 yds.	100 yds.	200 yds.	300 yds.	400 yds.	Est. Price/ box
30-06 Light Mag.	150	3100	2815	2548	2295	2058	3200	2639	2161	1755	1410	+1.4	0.0	-6.8	-20.3	NA
30-06 Light Mag.	180	2880	2676	2480	2293	2114	3316	2862	2459	2102	1786	+1.7	0.0	-7.3	-21.3	NA
30-06 High Energy	180	2880	2690	2500	2320	2150	3315	2880	2495	2150	1845	+1.7	0.0	-7.2	-21.0	NA
30 T/C	150	3000	2772	2555	2348	2151	2997	2558	2173	1836	1540	1.5	0.0	-6.9	-20.0	NA
30 T/C	165	2850	2644	2447	2258	2078	2975	2560	2193	1868	1582	1.7	0.0	-7.6	-22.0	NA
300 REM SA ULTRA MAG	150	3200	2901	2622	2359	2112	3410	2803	2290	1854	1485	1.3	0.0	-6.4	-19.1	NA
300 REM SA ULTRA MAG	165	3075	2792	2527	2276	2040	3464	2856	2339	1898	1525	1.5	0.0	-7	-20.7	NA
300 REM SA ULTRA MAG	180	2960	2761	2571	2389	2214	3501	3047	2642	2280	1959	2.6	2.2	-3.6	-15.4	NA
7.82 (308) Patriot	150	3250	2999	2762	2537	2323	3519	2997	2542	2145	1798	+1.2	0.0	-5.8	-16.9	NA
300 RCM	150	3300	3056	2825	2606	2397	3627	3110	2658	2262	1914	1.1	0.0	-5.4	-16.0	NA
300 RCM	165	3140	2921	2713	2514	2324	3612	3126	2697	2316	1979	1.3	0.0	-6.0	-17.5	NA
300 RDM	180	3000	2802	2613	2432	2258	3597	3139	2729	2363	2037	1.5	0.0	-6.5	-18.9	NA
300 WSM	150	3300	3061	2834	2619	2414	3628	3121	2676	2285	1941	1.1	0.0	-5.4	-15.9	NA
300 WSM	180	2970	2741	2524	2317	2120	3526	3005	2547	2147	1797	1.6	0.0	-7.0	-20.5	NA
300 WSM	180	3010	2923	2734	2554	2380	3242	2845	2490	2172	1886	1.3	0	-5.9	-17.2	NA
308 Norma Mag.	180	3020	2820	2630	2440	2270	3645	3175	2755	2385	2050	+2.5	+2.0	-3.5	-14.8	NA
300 Dakota	200	3000	2824	2656	2493	2336	3996	3542	3131	2760	2423	+2.2	+1.5	-4.0	-15.2	NA
300 H&H Magnum*	180	2880	2640	2412	2196	1990	3315	2785	2325	1927	1583	+2.5	+0.8	-6.8	-21.7	$24
300 H&H Magnum	220	2550	2267	2002	1757	NA	3167	2510	1958	1508	NA	-2.5	-0.4	-12.0	0.0	NA
300 Win. Mag.	150	3290	2951	2636	2342	2068	3605	2900	2314	1827	1424	+2.5	+1.9	-3.8	-15.8	$22
300 Win. Mag.	165	3100	2877	2665	2462	2269	3522	3033	2603	2221	1897	+2.5	+2.4	-3.0	-16.9	$24
300 Win. Mag.	178	2900	2760	2568	2375	2191	3509	3030	2606	2230	1897	+2.5	+1.4	-5.0	-17.6	$29
300 Win. Mag.*	180	2960	2745	2540	2344	2157	3501	3011	2578	2196	1859	+2.5	+1.2	-5.5	-18.5	$22
300 W.M. High Energy	180	3100	2830	2580	2340	2110	3840	3205	2660	2190	1790	+1.4	0.0	-6.6	-19.7	NA
300 W.M. Light Mag.	180	3100	2879	2668	2467	2275	3840	3313	2845	2431	2068	+1.39	0.0	-6.45	-18.7	NA
300 Win. Mag.	190	2885	1691	2506	2327	2156	3511	3055	2648	2285	1961	+2.5	+1.2	-5.7	-19.0	$26
300 W.M. High Energy	200	2930	2740	2550	2370	2200	3810	3325	2885	2495	2145	+1.6	0.0	-6.9	-20.1	NA
300 Win. Mag.*	200	2825	2595	2376	2167	1970	3545	2991	2508	2086	1742	-2.5	+1.6	-4.7	-17.2	$36
300 Win. Mag.	220	2680	2448	2228	2020	1823	3508	2927	2424	1993	1623	+2.5	0.0	-9.5	-27.5	$23
300 Rem. Ultra Mag.	150	3450	3208	2980	2762	2556	3964	3427	2956	2541	2175	1.7	1.5	-2.6	-11.2	NA
300 Rem. Ultra Mag.	150	2910	2686	2473	2279	2077	2820	2403	2037	1716	1436	1.7	0.0	-7.4	-21.5	NA
300 Rem. Ultra Mag.	180	3250	3037	2834	2640	2454	4221	3686	3201	2786	2407	2.4	0.0	-3.0	-12.7	NA
300 Rem. Ultra Mag.	180	2960	2774	2505	2294	2093	3501	2971	2508	2103	1751	2.7	2.2	-3.8	-16.4	NA
300 Rem. Ultra Mag.	200	3032	2791	2562	2345	2138	4083	3459	2916	2442	2030	1.5	0.0	-6.8	-19.9	NA
300 Wea. Mag.	100	3900	3441	3038	2652	2305	3714	2891	2239	1717	1297	+2.0	+2.6	-0.6	-8.7	$32
300 Wea. Mag.	150	3600	3307	3033	2776	2533	4316	3642	3064	2566	2137	+2.5	+3.2	0.0	-8.1	$32
300 Wea. Mag.	165	3450	3210	3000	2792	2593	4360	3796	3297	2855	2464	+2.5	+3.2	0.0	-7.8	NA
300 Wea. Mag.	178	3120	2902	2695	2497	2308	3847	3329	2870	2464	2104	+2.5	-1.7	-3.6	-14.7	$43
300 Wea. Mag.	180	3330	3110	2910	2710	2520	4430	3875	3375	2935	2540	+1.0	0.0	-5.2	-15.1	NA
300 Wea. Mag.	190	3030	2830	2638	2455	2279	3873	3378	2936	2542	2190	+2.5	+1.6	-4.3	-16.0	$38
300 Wea. Mag.	220	2850	2541	2283	1964	1736	3967	3155	2480	1922	1471	+2.5	+0.4	-8.5	-26.4	$35
300 Warbird	180	3400	3180	2971	2772	2582	4620	4042	3528	3071	2664	+2.59	+3.25	0.0	-7.95	NA

Many manufacturers do not supply suggested retail prices. Others did not get their pricing to us before press time. All pricing can vary dependent on the exact brand and style of ammo selected and/or the retail outlet from which you make your purchase. Pricing has been rounded to the nearest dollar and represents our best estimate of average pricing. An * after the cartridge means these loads are available with Nosler Partition or Swift A-Frame bullets. Listed pricing may or may not reflect this bullet type. ** = these are packed 50 to box, all others are 20 to box. Wea. Mag.= Weatherby Magnum. Spfd. = Springfield. A-Sq. = A-Square. N.E.=Nitro Express.

Cartridge	Bullet Wgt. Grs.	VELOCITY (fps)					ENERGY (ft. lbs.)					TRAJ. (in.)				Est. Price/ box
		Muzzle	100 yds.	200 yds.	300 yds.	400 yds.	Muzzle	100 yds.	200 yds.	300 yds.	400 yds.	100 yds.	200 yds.	300 yds.	400 yds.	
300 Pegasus	180	3500	3319	3145	2978	2817	4896	4401	3953	3544	3172	+2.28	+2.89	0.0	-6.79	NA
31																
32-20 Win.	100	1210	1021	913	834	769	325	231	185	154	131	0.0	-32.3	0.0	0.0	$23**
303 British	150	2685	2441	2210	1992	1787	2401	1984	1627	1321	1064	+2.5	+0.6	-8.4	-26.2	$18
303 British	180	2460	2124	1817	1542	1311	2418	1803	1319	950	687	+2.5	-1.8	-16.8	0.0	$18
303 Light Mag.	150	2830	2570	2325	2094	1884	2667	2199	1800	1461	1185	+2.0	0.0	-8.4	-24.6	NA
7.62x54mm Rus.	146	2950	2730	2520	2320	NA	2820	2415	2055	1740	NA	+2.5	+2.0	-4.4	-17.7	NA
7.62x54mm Rus.	180	2580	2370	2180	2000	1820	2650	2250	1900	1590	1100	+2.5	0.0	-9.8	-28.5	NA
7.7x58mm Jap.	150	2640	2399	2170	1954	1752	2321	1916	1568	1271	1022	+2.3	0.0	-9.7	-28.5	NA
7.7x58mm Jap.	180	2500	2300	2100	1920	1750	2490	2105	1770	1475	1225	+2.5	0.0	-10.4	-30.2	NA
8x56 R	205	2400	2188	1987	1797	1621	2621	2178	1796	1470	1196	+2.9	0.0	-11.7	-34.3	NA
8mm																
8x57mm JS Mau.	165	2850	2520	2210	1930	1670	2965	2330	1795	1360	1015	+2.5	+1.0	-7.7	0.0	NA
32 Win. Special	165	2410	2145	1897	1669	NA	2128	1685	1318	1020	NA	2.0	0.0	- 13.0	-19.9	NA
32 Win. Special	170	2250	1921	1626	1372	1175	1911	1393	998	710	521	+2.5	-3.5	-22.9	0.0	$14
8mm Mauser	170	2360	1969	1622	1333	1123	2102	1464	993	671	476	+2.5	-3.1	-22.2	0.0	$18
325 WSM	180	3060	2841	2632	2432	2242	3743	3226	2769	2365	2009	+1.4	0.0	-6.4	-18.7	NA
325 WSM	200	2950	2753	2565	2384	2210	3866	3367	2922	2524	2170	+1.5	0.0	-6.8	-19.8	NA
325 WSM	220	2840	2605	2382	2169	1968	3941	3316	2772	2300	1893	+1.8	0.0	-8.0	-23.3	NA
8mm Rem. Mag.	185	3080	2761	2464	2186	1927	3896	3131	2494	1963	1525	+2.5	+1.4	-5.5	-19.7	$30
8mm Rem. Mag.	220	2830	2581	2346	2123	1913	3912	3254	2688	2201	1787	+2.5	+0.6	-7.6	-23.5	Disc.
33																
338 Federal	180	2830	2590	2350	2130	1930	3200	2670	2215	1820	1480	1.80	0.00	-8.2	-23.9	NA
338 Marlin Express	200	2565	2365	2174	1992	1820	2922	2484	2099	1762	1471	3.00	1.20	-7.9	-25.9	NA
338 Federal	185	2750	2550	2350	2160	1980	3105	2660	2265	1920	1615	1.90	0.00	-8.3	-24.1	NA
338 Federal	210	2630	2410	2200	2010	1820	3225	2710	2265	1880	1545	2.30	0.00	-9.4	-27.3	NA
338-06	200	2750	2553	2364	2184	2011	3358	2894	2482	2118	1796	+1.9	0.0	-8.22	-23.6	NA
330 Dakota	250	2900	2719	2545	2378	2217	4668	4103	3595	3138	2727	+2.3	+1.3	-5.0	-17.5	NA
338 Lapua	250	2963	2795	2640	2493	NA	4842	4341	3881	3458	NA	+1.9	0.0	-7.9	0.0	NA
338 RCM	200	2950	2744	2547	2359	2179	3865	3344	2881	2471	2108	1.6	0.0	-6.9	-20.0	NA
338 RCM	225	2775	2598	2427	2264	2106	3847	3372	2944	2560	2216	1.8	0.0	-7.7	-22.2	NA
338 Win. Mag.	200	2960	2658	2375	2110	1862	3890	3137	2505	1977	1539	+2.5	+1.0	-6.7	-22.3	$27
338 Win. Mag.*	210	2830	2590	2370	2150	1940	3735	3130	2610	2155	1760	+2.5	+1.4	-6.0	-20.9	$33
338 Win. Mag.*	225	2785	2517	2266	2029	1808	3871	3165	2565	2057	1633	+2.5	+0.4	-8.5	-25.9	$27
338 W.M. Heavy Mag.	225	2920	2678	2449	2232	2027	4259	3583	2996	2489	2053	+1.75	0.0	-7.65	-22.0	NA
338 W.M. High Energy	225	2940	2690	2450	2230	2010	4320	3610	3000	2475	2025	+1.7	0.0	-7.5	-22.0	NA
338 Win. Mag.	230	2780	2573	2375	2186	2005	3948	3382	2881	2441	2054	+2.5	+1.2	-6.3	-21.0	$40
338 Win. Mag.*	250	2660	2456	2261	2075	1898	3927	3348	2837	2389	1999	+2.5	+0.2	-9.0	-26.2	$27
338 W.M. High Energy	250	2800	2610	2420	2250	2080	4350	3775	3260	2805	2395	+1.8	0.0	-7.8	-22.5	NA
338 Ultra Mag.	250	2860	2645	2440	2244	2057	4540	3882	3303	2794	2347	1.7	0.0	-7.6	-22.1	NA
8.59(.338) Galaxy	200	3100	2899	2707	2524	2347	4269	3734	3256	2829	2446	3	3.80	0.0	-9.3	NA
340 Wea. Mag.*	210	3250	2991	2746	2515	2295	4924	4170	3516	2948	2455	+2.5	+1.9	-1.8	-11.8	$56
340 Wea. Mag.*	250	3000	2806	2621	2443	2272	4995	4371	3812	3311	2864	+2.5	+2.0	-3.5	-14.8	$56
338 A-Square	250	3120	2799	2500	2220	1958	5403	4348	3469	2736	2128	+2.5	+2.7	-1.5	-10.5	NA
338-378 Wea. Mag.	225	3180	2974	2778	2591	2410	5052	4420	3856	3353	2902	3.1	3.80	0.0	-8.9	NA
338 Titan	225	3230	3010	2800	2600	2409	5211	4524	3916	3377	2898	+3.07	+3.80	0.0	-8.95	NA
338 Excalibur	200	3600	3361	3134	2920	2715	5755	5015	4363	3785	3274	+2.23	+2.87	0.0	-6.99	NA
338 Excalibur	250	3250	2922	2618	2333	2066	5863	4740	3804	3021	2370	+1.3	0.0	-6.35	-19.2	NA
34, 35																
348 Winchester	200	2520	2215	1931	1672	1443	2820	2178	1656	1241	925	+2.5	-1.4	-14.7	0.0	$42
357 Magnum	158	1830	1427	1138	980	883	1175	715	454	337	274	0.0	-16.2	-33.1	0.0	$25**
35 Remington	150	2300	1874	1506	1218	1039	1762	1169	755	494	359	+2.5	-4.1	-26.3	0.0	$16
35 Remington	200	2080	1698	1376	1140	1001	1921	1280	841	577	445	+2.5	-6.3	-17.1	-33.6	$16
35 Rem. Lever Evolution	200	2225	1963	1721	1503	NA	2198	1711	1315	1003	NA	3.00	-1.30	-17.5	NA	NA
356 Winchester	200	2460	2114	1797	1517	1284	2688	1985	1434	1022	732	+2.5	-1.8	-15.1	0.0	$31
356 Winchester	250	2160	1911	1682	1476	1299	2591	2028	1571	1210	937	+2.5	-3.7	-22.2	0.0	$31
358 Winchester	200	2490	2171	1876	1619	1379	2753	2093	1563	1151	844	+2.5	-1.6	-15.6	0.0	$31
358 STA	275	2850	2562	2292	2039	NA	4958	4009	3208	2539	NA	+1.9	0.0	-8.6	0.0	NA
350 Rem. Mag.	200	2710	2410	2130	1870	1631	3261	2579	2014	1553	1181	+2.5	-0.2	-10.0	-30.1	$33
35 Whelen	200	2675	2378	2100	1842	1606	3177	2510	1958	1506	1145	+2.5	-0.2	-10.3	-31.1	$20
35 Whelen	225	2500	2300	2110	1930	1770	3120	2650	2235	1870	1560	+2.6	0.0	-10.2	-29.9	NA
35 Whelen	250	2400	2197	2005	1823	1652	3197	2680	2230	1844	1515	+2.5	-1.2	-13.7	0.0	$20
358 Norma Mag.	250	2800	2510	2230	1970	1730	4350	3480	2750	2145	1655	+2.5	+1.0	-7.6	-25.2	NA
358 STA	275	2850	2562	229*2	2039	1764	4959	4009	3208	2539	1899	+1.9	0.0	-8.58	-26.1	NA

Many manufacturers do not supply suggested retail prices. Others did not get their pricing to us before press time. All pricing can vary dependent on the exact brand and style of ammo selected and/or the retail outlet from which you make your purchase. Pricing has been rounded to the nearest dollar and represents our best estimate of average pricing.
An * after the cartridge means these loads are available with Nosler Partition or Swift A-Frame bullets. Listed pricing may or may not reflect this bullet type.
** = these are packed 50 to box, all others are 20 to box. Wea. Mag.= Weatherby Magnum. Spfd. = Springfield. A-Sq. = A-Square. N.E.=Nitro Express.

Cartridge	Bullet Wgt. Grs.	VELOCITY (fps)					ENERGY (ft. lbs.)					TRAJ. (in.)				Est. Price/ box
		Muzzle	100 yds.	200 yds.	300 yds.	400 yds.	Muzzle	100 yds.	200 yds.	300 yds.	400 yds.	100 yds.	200 yds.	300 yds.	400 yds.	
9.3mm																
9.3x57mm Mau.	286	2070	1810	1590	1390	1110	2710	2090	1600	1220	955	+2.5	-2.6	-22.5	0.0	NA
9.3x62mm Mau.	286	2360	2089	1844	1623	NA	3538	2771	2157	1670	1260	+2.5	-1.6	-21.0	0.0	NA
370 Sako Mag.	286	3550	2370	2200	2040	2880	4130	3570	3075	2630	2240	2.4	0.0	-9.5	-27.2	NA
9.3x64mm	286	2700	2505	2318	2139	1968	4629	3984	3411	2906	2460	+2.5	+2.7	-4.5	-19.2	NA
9.3x74Rmm	286	2360	2136	1924	1727	1545	3536	2896	2351	1893	1516	0.0	-6.1	-21.7	-49.0	NA
375																
38-55 Win.	255	1320	1190	1091	1018	963	987	802	674	587	525	0.0	-23.4	0.0	0.0	$25
375 Winchester	200	2200	1841	1526	1268	1089	2150	1506	1034	714	527	+2.5	-4.0	-26.2	0.0	$27
375 Winchester	250	1900	1647	1424	1239	1103	2005	1506	1126	852	676	+2.5	-6.9	-33.3	0.0	$27
376 Steyr	225	2600	2331	2078	1842	1625	3377	2714	2157	1694	1319	2.5	0.0	-10.6	-31.4	NA
376 Steyr	270	2600	2372	2156	1951	1759	4052	3373	2787	2283	1855	2.3	0.0	-9.9	-28.9	NA
375 Dakota	300	2600	2316	2051	1804	1579	4502	3573	2800	2167	1661	+2.4	0.0	-11.0	-32.7	NA
375 N.E. 2-1/2"	270	2000	1740	1507	1310	NA	2398	1815	1362	1026	NA	+2.5	-6.0	-30.0	0.0	NA
375 Flanged	300	2450	2150	1886	1640	NA	3998	3102	2369	1790	NA	+2.5	-2.4	-17.0	0.0	NA
375 Ruger	270	2840	2600	2372	2156	1951	4835	4052	3373	2786	2283	1.8	0.0	-8.0	-23.6	NA
375 Ruger	300	2660	2344	2050	1780	1536	4713	3660	2800	2110	1572	2.4	0.0	-10.8	-32.6	NA
375 H&H Magnum	250	2670	2450	2240	2040	1850	3955	3335	2790	2315	1905	+2.5	-0.4	-10.2	-28.4	NA
375 H&H Magnum	270	2690	2420	2166	1928	1707	4337	3510	2812	2228	1747	+2.5	0.0	-10.0	-29.4	$28
375 H&H Magnum*	300	2530	2245	1979	1733	1512	4263	3357	2608	2001	1523	+2.5	-1.0	-10.5	-33.6	$28
375 H&H Hvy. Mag.	270	2870	2628	2399	2182	1976	4937	4141	3451	2150	1845	+1.7	0.0	-7.2	-21.0	NA
375 H&H Hvy. Mag.	300	2705	2386	2090	1816	1568	4873	3793	2908	2195	1637	+2.3	0.0	-10.4	-31.4	NA
375 Rem. Ultra Mag.	270	2900	2558	2241	1947	1678	5041	3922	3010	2272	1689	1.9	2.7	-8.9	-27.0	NA
375 Rem. Ultra Mag.	300	2760	2505	2263	2035	1822	5073	4178	3412	2759	2210	2.0	0.0	-8.8	-26.1	NA
375 Wea. Mag.	300	2700	2420	2157	1911	1685	4856	3901	3100	2432	1891	+2.5	-.04	-10.7	0.0	NA
378 Wea. Mag.	270	3180	2976	2781	2594	2415	6062	5308	4635	4034	3495	+2.5	+2.6	-1.8	-11.3	$71
378 Wea. Mag.	300	2929	2576	2252	1952	1680	5698	4419	3379	2538	1881	+2.5	+1.2	-7.0	-24.5	$77
375 A-Square	300	2920	2626	2351	2093	1850	5679	4594	3681	2917	2281	+2.5	+1.4	-6.0	-21.0	NA
38-40 Win.	180	1160	999	901	827	764	538	399	324	273	233	0.0	-33.9	0.0	0.0	$42**
40, 41																
400 A-Square DPM	400	2400	2146	1909	1689	NA	5116	2092	3236	2533	NA	2.98	0.00	-10.0	NA	NA
400 A-Square DPM	170	2980	2463	2001	1598	NA	3352	2289	1512	964	NA	2.16	0.00	-11.1	NA	NA
408 CheyTac	419	2850	2752	2657	2562	2470	7551	7048	6565	6108	5675	-1.02	0.00	1.9	4.2	NA
405 Win.	300	2200	1851	1545	1296		3224	2282	1589	1119		4.6	0.0	-19.5	0.0	NA
450/400-3"	400	2050	1815	1595	1402	NA	3732	2924	2259	1746	NA	0.0	NA	-33.4	NA	NA
416 Ruger	400	2400	2151	1917	1700	NA	5116	4109	3264	2568	NA	0.00	-6.00	-21.6	0.00	NA
416 Dakota	400	2450	2294	2143	1998	1859	5330	4671	4077	3544	3068	+2.5	-0.2	-10.5	-29.4	NA
416 Taylor	400	2350	2117	1896	1693	NA	4905	3980	3194	2547	NA	+2.5	-1.2	15.0	0.0	NA
416 Hoffman	400	2380	2145	1923	1718	1529	5031	4087	3285	2620	2077	+2.5	-1.0	-14.1	0.0	NA
416 Rigby	350	2600	2449	2303	2162	2026	5253	4661	4122	3632	3189	+2.5	-1.8	-10.2	-26.0	NA
416 Rigby	400	2370	2210	2050	1900	NA	4990	4315	3720	3185	NA	+2.5	-0.7	-12.1	0.0	NA
416 Rigby	410	2370	2110	1870	1640	NA	5115	4050	3165	2455	NA	+2.5	-2.4	-17.3	0.0	$110
416 Rem. Mag.*	350	2520	2270	2034	1814	1611	4935	4004	3216	2557	2017	+2.5	-0.8	-12.6	-35.0	$82
416 Rem. Mag.*	400	2400	2175	1962	1763	1579	5115	4201	3419	2760	2214	+2.5	-1.5	-14.6	0.0	$80
416 Wea. Mag.*	400	2700	2397	2115	1852	1613	6474	5104	3971	3047	2310	+2.5	0.0	-10.1	-30.4	$96
10.57 (416) Meteor	400	2730	2532	2342	2161	1987	6621	5695	4874	4147	3508	+1.9	0.0	-8.3	-24.0	NA
404 Jeffrey	400	2150	1924	1716	1525	NA	4105	3289	2614	2064	NA	+2.5	-4.0	-22.1	0.0	NA
425, 44																
425 Express	400	2400	2160	1934	1725	NA	5115	4145	3322	2641	NA	+2.5	-1.0	-14.0	0.0	NA
44-40 Win.	200	1190	1006	900	822	756	629	449	360	300	254	0.0	-33.3	0.0	0.0	$36**
44 Rem. Mag.	210	1920	1477	1155	982	880	1719	1017	622	450	361	0.0	-17.6	0.0	0.0	$14
44 Rem. Mag.	240	1760	1380	1114	970	878	1650	1015	661	501	411	0.0	-17.6	0.0	0.0	$13
444 Marlin	240	2350	1815	1377	1087	941	2942	1753	1001	630	472	+2.5	-15.1	-31.0	0.0	$22
444 Marlin	265	2120	1733	1405	1160	1012	2644	1768	1162	791	603	+2.5	-6.0	-32.2	0.0	Disc.
444 Marlin Light Mag	265	2335	1913	1551	1266		3208	2153	1415	943		2.0	-4.90	-26.5	0.0	NA
444 Mar. Lever Evolution	265	2325	1971	1652	1380	NA	3180	2285	1606	1120	NA	3.00	-1.40	-18.6	NA	NA
45																
45-70 Govt.	300	1810	1497	1244	1073	969	2182	1492	1031	767	625	0.0	-14.8	0.0	0.0	$21
45-70 Govt. Supreme	300	1880	1558	1292	1103	988	2355	1616	1112	811	651	0.0	-12.9	-46.0	-105.0	NA
45-70 Lever Evolution	325	2050	1729	1450	1225	NA	3032	2158	1516	1083	NA	3.00	-4.10	-27.8	NA	NA
45-70 Govt. CorBon	350	1800	1526	1296			2519	1810	1307			0.0	-14.6	0.0	0.0	NA
45-70 Govt.	405	1330	1168	1055	977	918	1590	1227	1001	858	758	0.0	-24.6	0.0	0.0	$21
45-70 Govt. PMC Cowboy	405	1550	1193				1639	1280				0.0	-23.9	0.0	0.0	NA
45-70 Govt. Garrett	415	1850					3150					3.0	-7.0	0.0	0.0	NA

Many manufacturers do not supply suggested retail prices. Others did not get their pricing to us before press time. All pricing can vary dependent on the exact brand and style of ammo selected and/or the retail outlet from which you make your purchase. Pricing has been rounded to the nearest dollar and represents our best estimate of average pricing. An * after the cartridge means these loads are available with Nosler Partition or Swift A-Frame bullets. Listed pricing may or may not reflect this bullet type. ** = these are packed 50 to box, all others are 20 to box. Wea. Mag.= Weatherby Magnum. Spfd. = Springfield. A-Sq. = A-Square. N.E.=Nitro Express.

Cartridge	Bullet Wgt. Grs.	VELOCITY (fps)					ENERGY (ft. lbs.)					TRAJ. (in.)				Est. Price/ box
		Muzzle	100 yds.	200 yds.	300 yds.	400 yds.	Muzzle	100 yds.	200 yds.	300 yds.	400 yds.	100 yds.	200 yds.	300 yds.	400 yds.	
45-70 Govt. Garrett	530	1550	1343	1178	1062	982	2828	2123	1633	1327	1135	0.0	-17.8	0.0	0.0	NA
450 Bushmaster	250	2200	1831	1508	1480	1073	2686	1860	1262	864	639	0.00	-9.00	-33.5	0.00	NA
450 Marlin	350	2100	1774	1488	1254	1089	3427	2446	1720	1222	922	0.0	-9.7	-35.2	0.0	NA
450 Mar. Lever Evolution	325	2225	1887	1585	1331	NA	3572	2569	1813	1278	NA	3.00	-2.20	-21.3	NA	NA
458 Win. Magnum	350	2470	1990	1570	1250	1060	4740	3065	1915	1205	870	+2.5	-2.5	-21.6	0.0	$43
458 Win. Magnum	400	2380	2170	1960	1770	NA	5030	4165	3415	2785	NA	+2.5	-0.4	-13.4	0.0	$73
458 Win. Magnum	465	2220	1999	1791	1601	NA	5088	4127	3312	2646	NA	+2.5	-2.0	-17.7	0.0	NA
458 Win. Magnum	500	2040	1823	1623	1442	1237	4620	3689	2924	2308	1839	+2.5	-3.5	-22.0	0.0	$61
458 Win. Magnum	510	2040	1770	1527	1319	1157	4712	3547	2640	1970	1516	+2.5	-4.1	-25.0	0.0	$41
450 Dakota	500	2450	2235	2030	1838	1658	6663	5544	4576	3748	3051	+2.5	-0.6	-12.0	-33.8	NA
450 N.E. 3-1/4"	465	2190	1970	1765	1577	NA	4952	4009	3216	2567	NA	+2.5	-3.0	-20.0	0.0	NA
450 N.E. 3-1/4"	500	2150	1920	1708	1514	NA	5132	4093	3238	2544	NA	+2.5	-4.0	-22.9	0.0	NA
450 No. 2	465	2190	1970	1765	1577	NA	4952	4009	3216	2567	NA	+2.5	-3.0	-20.0	0.0	NA
450 No. 2	500	2150	1920	1708	1514	NA	5132	4093	3238	2544	NA	+2.5	-4.0	-22.9	0.0	NA
458 Lott	465	2380	2150	1932	1730	NA	5848	4773	3855	3091	NA	+2.5	-1.0	-14.0	0.0	NA
458 Lott	500	2300	2062	1838	1633	NA	5873	4719	3748	2960	NA	+2.5	-1.6	-16.4	0.0	NA
450 Ackley Mag.	465	2400	2169	1950	1747	NA	5947	4857	3927	3150	NA	+2.5	-1.0	-13.7	0.0	NA
450 Ackley Mag.	500	2320	2081	1855	1649	NA	5975	4085	3820	3018	NA	+2.5	-1.2	-15.0	0.0	NA
460 Short A-Sq.	500	2420	2175	1943	1729	NA	6501	5250	4193	3319	NA	+2.5	-0.8	-12.8	0.0	NA
460 Wea. Mag.	500	2700	2404	2128	1869	1635	8092	6416	5026	3878	2969	+2.5	+0.6	-8.9	-28.0	$72
475																
500/465 N.E.	480	2150	1917	1703	1507	NA	4926	3917	3089	2419	NA	+2.5	-4.0	-22.2	0.0	NA
470 Rigby	500	2150	1940	1740	1560	NA	5130	4170	3360	2695	NA	+2.5	-2.8	-19.4	0.0	NA
470 Nitro Ex.	480	2190	1954	1735	1536	NA	5111	4070	3210	2515	NA	+2.5	-3.5	-20.8	0.0	NA
470 Nitro Ex.	500	2150	1890	1650	1440	1270	5130	3965	3040	2310	1790	+2.5	-4.3	-24.0	0.0	$177
475 No. 2	500	2200	1955	1728	1522	NA	5375	4243	3316	2573	NA	+2.5	-3.2	-20.9	0.0	NA
50, 58																
505 Gibbs	525	2300	2063	1840	1637	NA	6166	4922	3948	3122	NA	+2.5	-3.0	-18.0	0.0	NA
500 N.E.-3"	570	2150	1928	1722	1533	NA	5850	4703	3752	2975	NA	+2.5	-3.7	-22.0	0.0	NA
500 N.E.-3"	600	2150	1927	1721	1531	NA	6158	4947	3944	3124	NA	+2.5	-4.0	-22.0	0.0	NA
495 A-Square	570	2350	2117	1896	1693	NA	5850	4703	3752	2975	NA	+2.5	-1.0	-14.5	0.0	NA
495 A-Square	600	2280	2050	1833	1635	NA	6925	5598	4478	3562	NA	+2.5	-2.0	-17.0	0.0	NA
500 A-Square	600	2380	2144	1922	1766	NA	7546	6126	4920	3922	NA	+2.5	-3.0	-17.0	0.0	NA
500 A-Square	707	2250	2040	1841	1567	NA	7947	6530	5318	4311	NA	+2.5	-2.0	-17.0	0.0	NA
500 BMG PMC	660	3080	2854	2639	2444	2248	13688		500 yd. zero			+3.1	+3.9	+4.7	+2.8	NA
577 Nitro Ex.	750	2050	1793	1562	1360	NA	6990	5356	4065	3079	NA	+2.5	-5.0	-26.0	0.0	NA
577 Tyrannosaur	750	2400	2141	1898	1675	NA	9591	7633	5996	4671	NA	+3.0	0.0	-12.9	0.0	NA
600, 700																
600 N.E.	900	1950	1680	1452	NA	NA	7596	5634	4212	NA	NA	+5.6	0.0	0.0	0.0	NA
700 N.E.	1200	1900	1676	1472	NA	NA	9618	7480	5774	NA	NA	+5.7	0.0	0.0	0.0	NA

Notes: Blanks are available in 32 S&W, 38 S&W and 38 Special. "V" after barrel length indicates test barrel was vented to produce ballistics similar to a revolver with a normal barrel-to-cylinder gap. Ammo prices are per 50 rounds except when marked with an ** which signifies a 20 round box; *** signifies a 25-round box. Not all loads are available from all ammo manufacturers. Listed loads are those made by Remington, Winchester, Federal, and others. DISC. is a discontinued load.
Prices are rounded to the nearest whole dollar and will vary with brand and retail outlet. † = new bullet weight this year; "c" indicates a change in data.

Cartridge	Bullet Wgt. Grs.	VELOCITY (fps)			ENERGY (ft. lbs.)			Mid-Range Traj. (in.)		Bbl. Lgth. (in).	Est. Price/ box
		Muzzle	50 yds.	100 yds.	Muzzle	50 yds.	100 yds.	50 yds.	100 yds.		
22, 25											
221 Rem. Fireball	50	2650	2380	2130	780	630	505	0.2	0.8	10.5"	$15
25 Automatic	35	900	813	742	63	51	43	NA	NA	2"	$18
25 Automatic	45	815	730	655	65	55	40	1.8	7.7	2"	$21
25 Automatic	50	760	705	660	65	55	50	2.0	8.7	2"	$17
30											
7.5mm Swiss	107	1010	NA	NA	240	NA	NA	NA	NA	NA	NEW
7.62mmTokarev	87	1390	NA	NA	365	NA	NA	0.6	NA	4.5"	NA
7.62 Nagant	97	790	NA	NA	134	NA	NA	NA	NA	NA	NEW
7.63 Mauser	88	1440	NA	NA	405	NA	NA	NA	NA	NA	NEW
30 Luger	93†	1220	1110	1040	305	255	225	0.9	3.5	4.5"	$34
30 Carbine	110	1790	1600	1430	785	625	500	0.4	1.7	10"	$28
30-357 AeT	123	1992	NA	NA	1084	NA	NA	NA	NA	10"	NA
32											
32 S&W	88	680	645	610	90	80	75	2.5	10.5	3"	$17
32 S&W Long	98	705	670	635	115	100	90	2.3	10.5	4"	$17
32 Short Colt	80	745	665	590	100	80	60	2.2	9.9	4"	$19
32 H&R Magnum	85	1100	1020	930	230	195	165	1.0	4.3	4.5"	$21
32 H&R Magnum	95	1030	940	900	225	190	170	1.1	4.7	4.5"	$19
327 Federal Magnum	100	1500	1320	1180	500	390	310	-0.2	-4.50	4-V	NA
32 Automatic	60	970	895	835	125	105	95	1.3	5.4	4"	$22
32 Automatic	60	1000	917	849	133	112	96			4"	NA
32 Automatic	65	950	890	830	130	115	100	1.3	5.6	NA	NA
32 Automatic	71	905	855	810	130	115	95	1.4	5.8	4"	$19
8mm Lebel Pistol	111	850	NA	NA	180	NA	NA	NA	NA	NA	NEW
8mm Steyr	112	1080	NA	NA	290	NA	NA	NA	NA	NA	NEW
8mm Gasser	126	850	NA	NA	200	NA	NA	NA	NA	NA	NEW
9mm, 38											
380 Automatic	60	1130	960	NA	170	120	NA	1.0	NA	NA	NA
380 Automatic	85/88	990	920	870	190	165	145	1.2	5.1	4"	$20
380 Automatic	90	1000	890	800	200	160	130	1.2	5.5	3.75"	$10
380 Automatic	95/100	955	865	785	190	160	130	1.4	5.9	4"	$20
38 Super Auto +P	115	1300	1145	1040	430	335	275	0.7	3.3	5"	$26
38 Super Auto +P	125/130	1215	1100	1015	425	350	300	0.8	3.6	5"	$26
38 Super Auto +P	147	1100	1050	1000	395	355	325	0.9	4.0	5"	NA
9x18mm Makarov	95	1000	NA	NA	NA	NA	NA	NA	NA	NA	NEW
9x18mm Ultra	100	1050	NA	NA	240	NA	NA	NA	NA	NA	NEW
9x23mm Largo	124	1190	1055	966	390	306	257	0.7	3.7	4"	NA
9x23mm Win.	125	1450	1249	1103	583	433	338	0.6	2.8	NA	NA
9mm Steyr	115	1180	NA	NA	350	NA	NA	NA	NA	NA	NEW
9mm Luger	88	1500	1190	1010	440	275	200	0.6	3.1	4"	$24
9mm Luger	90	1360	1112	978	370	247	191	NA	NA	4"	$26
9mm Luger	95	1300	1140	1010	350	275	215	0.8	3.4	4"	NA
9mm Luger	100	1180	1080	NA	305	255	NA	0.9	NA	4"	NA
9mm Luger	115	1155	1045	970	340	280	240	0.9	3.9	4"	$21
9mm Luger	123/125	1110	1030	970	340	290	260	1.0	4.0	4"	$23
9mm Luger	140	935	890	850	270	245	225	1.3	5.5	4"	$23
9mm Luger	147	990	940	900	320	290	265	1.1	4.9	4"	$26
9mm Luger +P	90	1475	NA	NA	437	NA	NA	NA	NA	NA	NA
9mm Luger +P	115	1250	1113	1019	399	316	265	0.8	3.5	4"	$27
9mm Federal	115	1280	1130	1040	420	330	280	0.7	3.3	4"V	$24
9mm Luger Vector	115	1155	1047	971	341	280	241	NA	NA	4"	NA
9mm Luger +P	124	1180	1089	1021	384	327	287	0.8	3.8	4"	NA
38											
38 S&W	146	685	650	620	150	135	125	2.4	10.0	4"	$19
38 Short Colt	125	730	685	645	150	130	115	2.2	9.4	6"	$19
39 Special	100	950	900	NA	200	180	NA	1.3	NA	4"V	NA
38 Special	110	945	895	850	220	195	175	1.3	5.4	4"V	$23
38 Special	110	945	895	850	220	195	175	1.3	5.4	4"V	$23
38 Special	130	775	745	710	175	160	120	1.9	7.9	4"V	$22
38 Special Cowboy	140	800	767	735	199	183	168			7.5" V	NA
38 (Multi-Ball)	140	830	730	505	215	130	80	2.0	10.6	4"V	$10**

Notes: Blanks are available in 32 S&W, 38 S&W and 38 Special. "V" after barrel length indicates test barrel was vented to produce ballistics similar to a revolver with a normal barrel-to-cylinder gap. Ammo prices are per 50 rounds except when marked with an ** which signifies a 20 round box; *** signifies a 25-round box. Not all loads are available from all ammo manufacturers. Listed loads are those made by Remington, Winchester, Federal, and others. DISC. is a discontinued load. Prices are rounded to the nearest whole dollar and will vary with brand and retail outlet. † = new bullet weight this year; "c" indicates a change in data.

Cartridge	Bullet Wgt. Grs.	VELOCITY (fps)			ENERGY (ft. lbs.)			Mid-Range Traj. (in.)		Bbl. Lgth. (in).	Est. Price/ box
		Muzzle	50 yds.	100 yds.	Muzzle	50 yds.	100 yds.	50 yds.	100 yds.		
38 Special	148	710	635	565	165	130	105	2.4	10.6	4"V	$17
38 Special	158	755	725	690	200	185	170	2.0	8.3	4"V	$18
38 Special +P	95	1175	1045	960	290	230	195	0.9	3.9	4"V	$23
38 Special +P	110	995	925	870	240	210	185	1.2	5.1	4"V	$23
38 Special +P	125	975	929	885	264	238	218	1	5.2	4"	NA
38 Special +P	125	945	900	860	250	225	205	1.3	5.4	4"V	#23
38 Special +P	129	945	910	870	255	235	215	1.3	5.3	4"V	$11
38 Special +P	130	925	887	852	247	227	210	1.3	5.50	4"V	NA
38 Special +P	147/150(c)	884	NA	NA	264	NA	NA	NA	NA	4"V	$27
38 Special +P	158	890	855	825	280	255	240	1.4	6.0	4"V	$20

357

Cartridge	Bullet Wgt. Grs.	Muzzle	50 yds.	100 yds.	Muzzle	50 yds.	100 yds.	50 yds.	100 yds.	Bbl. Lgth.	Est. Price/box
357 SIG	115	1520	NA	NA	593	NA	NA	NA	NA	NA	NA
357 SIG	124	1450	NA	NA	578	NA	NA	NA	NA	NA	NA
357 SIG	125	1350	1190	1080	510	395	325	0.7	3.1	4"	NA
357 SIG	150	1130	1030	970	420	355	310	0.9	4.0	NA	NA
356 TSW	115	1520	NA	NA	593	NA	NA	NA	NA	NA	NA
356 TSW	124	1450	NA	NA	578	NA	NA	NA	NA	NA	NA
356 TSW	135	1280	1120	1010	490	375	310	0.8	3.5	NA	NA
356 TSW	147	1220	1120	1040	485	410	355	0.8	3.5	5"	NA
357 Mag., Super Clean	105	1650									NA
357 Magnum	110	1295	1095	975	410	290	230	0.8	3.5	4"V	$25
357 (Med.Vel.)	125	1220	1075	985	415	315	270	0.8	3.7	4"V	$25
357 Magnum	125	1450	1240	1090	585	425	330	0.6	2.8	4"V	$25
357 (Multi-Ball)	140	1155	830	665	420	215	135	1.2	6.4	4"V	$11**
357 Magnum	140	1360	1195	1075	575	445	360	0.7	3.0	4"V	$25
357 Magnum FlexTip	140	1440	1274	1143	644	504	406	NA	NA	NA	NA
357 Magnum	145	1290	1155	1060	535	430	360	0.8	3.5	4"V	$26
357 Magnum	150/158	1235	1105	1015	535	430	360	0.8	3.5	4"V	$25
357 Mag. Cowboy	158	800	761	725	225	203	185				NA
357 Magnum	165	1290	1189	1108	610	518	450	0.7	3.1	8-3/8"	NA
357 Magnum	180	1145	1055	985	525	445	390	0.9	3.9	4"V	$25
357 Magnum	180	1180	1088	1020	557	473	416	0.8	3.6	8"V	NA
357 Mag. CorBon F.A.	180	1650	1512	1386	1088	913	767	1.66	0.0		NA
357 Mag. CorBon	200	1200	1123	1061	640	560	500	3.19	0.0		NA
357 Rem. Maximum	158	1825	1590	1380	1170	885	670	0.4	1.7	10.5"	$14**

40, 10mm

Cartridge	Bullet Wgt. Grs.	Muzzle	50 yds.	100 yds.	Muzzle	50 yds.	100 yds.	50 yds.	100 yds.	Bbl. Lgth.	Est. Price/box
40 S&W	135	1140	1070	NA	390	345	NA	0.9	NA	4"	NA
40 S&W	155	1140	1026	958	447	362	309	0.9	4.1	4"	$14***
40 S&W	165	1150	NA	NA	485	NA	NA	NA	NA	4"	$18***
40 S&W	180	985	936	893	388	350	319	1.4	5.0	4"	$14***
40 S&W	180	1015	960	914	412	368	334	1.3	4.5	4"	NA
400 Cor-Bon	135	1450	NA	NA	630	NA	NA	NA	NA	5"	NA
10mm Automatic	155	1125	1046	986	436	377	335	0.9	3.9	5"	$26
10mm Automatic	170	1340	1165	1145	680	510	415	0.7	3.2	5"	$31
10mm Automatic	175	1290	1140	1035	650	505	420	0.7	3.3	5.5"	$11**
10mm Auto. (FBI)	180	950	905	865	361	327	299	1.5	5.4	4"	$16**
10mm Automatic	180	1030	970	920	425	375	340	1.1	4.7	5"	$16**
10mm Auto H.V.	180†	1240	1124	1037	618	504	430	0.8	3.4	5"	$27
10mm Automatic	200	1160	1070	1010	495	510	430	0.9	3.8	5"	$14**
10.4mm Italian	177	950	NA	NA	360	NA	NA	NA	NA	NA	NEW
41 Action Exp.	180	1000	947	903	400	359	326	0.5	4.2	5"	$13**
41 Rem. Magnum	170	1420	1165	1015	760	515	390	0.7	3.2	4"V	$33
41 Rem. Magnum	175	1250	1120	1030	605	490	410	0.8	3.4	4"V	$14**
41 (Med. Vel.)	210	965	900	840	435	375	330	1.3	5.4	4"V	$30
41 Rem. Magnum	210	1300	1160	1060	790	630	535	0.7	3.2	4"V	$33
41 Rem. Magnum	240	1250	1151	1075	833	706	616	0.8	3.3	6.5V	NA

44

Cartridge	Bullet Wgt. Grs.	Muzzle	50 yds.	100 yds.	Muzzle	50 yds.	100 yds.	50 yds.	100 yds.	Bbl. Lgth.	Est. Price/box
44 S&W Russian	247	780	NA	NA	335	NA	NA	NA	NA	NA	NA
44 S&W Special	180	980	NA	NA	383	NA	NA	NA	NA	6.5"	NA
44 S&W Special	180	1000	935	882	400	350	311	NA	NA	7.5"V	NA
44 S&W Special	200†	875	825	780	340	302	270	1.2	6.0	6"	$13**
44 S&W Special	200	1035	940	865	475	390	335	1.1	4.9	6.5"	$13**
44 S&W Special	240/246	755	725	695	310	285	265	2.0	8.3	6.5"	$26
44-40 Win. Cowboy	225	750	723	695	281	261	242				NA

Notes: Blanks are available in 32 S&W, 38 S&W and 38 Special. "V" after barrel length indicates test barrel was vented to produce ballistics similar to a revolver with a normal barrel-to-cylinder gap. Ammo prices are per 50 rounds except when marked with an ** which signifies a 20 round box; *** signifies a 25-round box. Not all loads are available from all ammo manufacturers. Listed loads are those made by Remington, Winchester, Federal, and others. DISC. is a discontinued load. Prices are rounded to the nearest whole dollar and will vary with brand and retail outlet. † = new bullet weight this year; "c" indicates a change in data.

Cartridge	Bullet Wgt. Grs.	VELOCITY (fps)			ENERGY (ft. lbs.)			Mid-Range Traj. (in.)		Bbl. Lgth. (in).	Est. Price/ box
		Muzzle	50 yds.	100 yds.	Muzzle	50 yds.	100 yds.	50 yds.	100 yds.		
44 Rem. Magnum	180	1610	1365	1175	1035	745	550	0.5	2.3	4"V	$18**
44 Rem. Magnum	200	1400	1192	1053	870	630	492	0.6	NA	6.5"	$20
44 Rem. Magnum	210	1495	1310	1165	1040	805	635	0.6	2.5	6.5"	$18**
44 Rem. Mag. FlexTip	225	1410	1240	1111	993	768	617	NA	NA	NA	NA
44 (Med. Vel.)	240	1000	945	900	535	475	435	1.1	4.8	6.5"	$17
44 R.M. (Jacketed)	240	1180	1080	1010	740	625	545	0.9	3.7	4"V	$18**
44 R.M. (Lead)	240	1350	1185	1070	970	750	610	0.7	3.1	4"V	$29
44 Rem. Magnum	250	1180	1100	1040	775	670	600	0.8	3.6	6.5"V	$21
44 Rem. Magnum	250	1250	1148	1070	867	732	635	0.8	3.3	6.5"V	NA
44 Rem. Magnum	275	1235	1142	1070	931	797	699	0.8	3.3	6.5"	NA
44 Rem. Magnum	300	1200	1100	1026	959	806	702	NA	NA	7.5"	$17
44 Rem. Magnum	330	1385	1297	1220	1406	1234	1090	1.83	0.00	NA	NA
440 CorBon	260	1700	1544	1403	1669	1377	1136	1.58	NA	10"	NA

45, 50

Cartridge	Bullet Wgt. Grs.	Muzzle	50 yds.	100 yds.	Muzzle	50 yds.	100 yds.	50 yds.	100 yds.	Bbl. Lgth.	Est. Price/ box
450 Short Colt/450 Revolver	226	830	NA	NA	350	NA	NA	NA	NA	NA	NEW
45 S&W Schofield	180	730	NA	NA	213	NA	NA	NA	NA	NA	NA
45 S&W Schofield	230	730	NA	NA	272	NA	NA	NA	NA	NA	NA
45 G.A.P.	185	1090	970	890	490	385	320	1.0	4.7	5"	NA
45 G.A.P.	230	880	842	NA	396	363	NA	NA	NA	NA	NA
45 Automatic	165	1030	930	NA	385	315	NA	1.2	NA	5"	NA
45 Automatic	185	1000	940	890	410	360	325	1.1	4.9	5"	$28
45 Auto. (Match)	185	770	705	650	245	204	175	2.0	8.7	5"	$28
45 Auto. (Match)	200	940	890	840	392	352	312	2.0	8.6	5"	$20
45 Automatic	200	975	917	860	421	372	328	1.4	5.0	5"	$18
45 Automatic	230	830	800	675	355	325	300	1.6	6.8	5"	$27
45 Automatic	230	880	846	816	396	366	340	1.5	6.1	5"	NA
45 Automatic +P	165	1250	NA	NA	573	NA	NA	NA	NA	NA	NA
45 Automatic +P	185	1140	1040	970	535	445	385	0.9	4.0	5"	$31
45 Automatic +P	200	1055	982	925	494	428	380	NA	NA	5"	NA
45 Super	185	1300	1190	1108	694	582	504	NA	NA	5"	NA
45 Win. Magnum	230	1400	1230	1105	1000	775	635	0.6	2.8	5"	$14**
45 Win. Magnum	260	1250	1137	1053	902	746	640	0.8	3.3	5"	$16**
45 Win. Mag. CorBon	320	1150	1080	1025	940	830	747	3.47			NA
455 Webley MKII	262	850	NA	NA	420	NA	NA	NA	NA	NA	NA
45 Colt	200	1000	938	889	444	391	351	1.3	4.8	5.5"	$21
45 Colt	225	960	890	830	460	395	345	1.3	5.5	5.5"	$22
45 Colt + P CorBon	265	1350	1225	1126	1073	884	746	2.65	0.0		NA
45 Colt + P CorBon	300	1300	1197	1114	1126	956	827	2.78	0.0		NA
45 Colt	250/255	860	820	780	410	375	340	1.6	6.6	5.5"	$27
454 Casull	250	1300	1151	1047	938	735	608	0.7	3.2	7.5"V	NA
454 Casull	260	1800	1577	1381	1871	1436	1101	0.4	1.8	7.5"V	NA
454 Casull	300	1625	1451	1308	1759	1413	1141	0.5	2.0	7.5"V	NA
454 Casull CorBon	360	1500	1387	1286	1800	1640	1323	2.01	0.0		NA
460 S&W	200	2300	2042	1801	2350	1851	1441	0	-1.60	NA	NA
460 S&W	260	2000	1788	1592	2309	1845	1464	NA	NA	7.5"V	NA
460 S&W	250	1450	1267	1127	1167	891	705	NA	NA	8.375-V	NA
460 S&W	250	1900	1640	1412	2004	1494	1106	0	-2.75	NA	NA
460 S&W	395	1550	1389	1249	2108	1691	1369	0	-4.00	NA	NA
475 Linebaugh	400	1350	1217	1119	1618	1315	1112	NA	NA	NA	NA
480 Ruger	325	1350	1191	1076	1315	1023	835	2.6	0.0	7.5"	NA
50 Action Exp.	325	1400	1209	1075	1414	1055	835	0.2	2.3	6"	$24**
500 S&W	275	1665	1392	1183	1693	1184	854	1.5	NA	8.375	NA
500 S&W	350	1400	1231	1106	1523	1178	951	NA	NA	10"	NA
500 S&W	400	1675	1472	1299	2493	1926	1499	1.3	NA	8.375	NA
500 S&W	440	1625	1367	1169	2581	1825	1337	1.6	NA	8.375	NA
500 S&W	500	1425	1281	1164	2254	1823	1505	NA	NA	10"	NA

Note: The actual ballistics obtained with your firearm can vary considerably from the advertised ballistics. Also, ballistics can vary from lot to lot with the same brand and type load.

Cartridge	Bullet Wt. Grs.	Velocity (fps) 22-1/2" Bbl.		Energy (ft. lbs.) 22-1/2" Bbl.		Mid-Range Traj. (in.)	Muzzle Velocity
		Muzzle	100 yds.	Muzzle	100 yds.	100 yds.	6" Bbl.
17 Aguila	20	1850	1267	NA	NA	NA	NA
17 Hornady Mach 2	17	2100	1530	166	88	0.7	NA
17 HMR	17	2550	1902	245	136	NA	NA
17 HMR	20	2375	1776	250	140	NA	NA
5mm Rem. Rimfire Mag.	30	2300	1669	352	188	NA	24
22 Short Blank	—	—	—	—	—	—	—
22 Short CB	29	727	610	33	24	NA	706
22 Short Target	29	830	695	44	31	6.8	786
22 Short HP	27	1164	920	81	50	4.3	1077
22 Colibri	20	375	183	6	1	NA	NA
22 Super Colibri	20	500	441	11	9	NA	NA
22 Long CB	29	727	610	33	24	NA	706
22 Long HV	29	1180	946	90	57	4.1	1031
22 LR Pistol Match	40	1070	890	100	70	4.6	940
22 LR Sub Sonic HP	38	1050	901	93	69	4.7	NA
22 LR Standard Velocity	40	1070	890	100	70	4.6	940
22 LR AutoMatch	40	1200	990	130	85	NA	NA
22 LR HV	40	1255	1016	140	92	3.6	1060
22 LR Silhoutte	42	1220	1003	139	94	3.6	1025
22 SSS	60	950	802	120	86	NA	NA
22 LR HV HP	40	1280	1001	146	89	3.5	1085
22 Velocitor GDHP	40	1435	0	0	0	NA	NA
22 LR Hyper HP	32/33/34	1500	1075	165	85	2.8	NA
22 LR Expediter	32	1640	NA	191	NA	NA	NA
22 LR Stinger HP	32	1640	1132	191	91	2.6	1395
22 LR Lead Free	30	1650	NA	181	NA	NA	NA
22 LR Hyper Vel	30	1750	1191	204	93	NA	NA
22 LR Shot #12	31	950	NA	NA	NA	NA	NA
22 WRF LFN	45	1300	1015	169	103	3	NA
22 Win. Mag. Lead Free	28	2200	NA	301	NA	NA	NA
22 Win. Mag.	30	2200	1373	322	127	1.4	1610
22 Win. Mag. V-Max BT	33	2000	1495	293	164	0.60	NA
22 Win. Mag. JHP	34	2120	1435	338	155	1.4	NA
22 Win. Mag. JHP	40	1910	1326	324	156	1.7	1480
22 Win. Mag. FMJ	40	1910	1326	324	156	1.7	1480
22 Win. Mag. Dyna Point	45	1550	1147	240	131	2.60	NA
22 Win. Mag. JHP	50	1650	1280	300	180	1.3	NA
22 Win. Mag. Shot #11	52	1000	—	NA	—	—	NA

NOTES: * = 10 rounds per box. ** = 5 rounds per box. Pricing variations and number of rounds per box can occur with type and brand of ammunition. Listed pricing is the average nominal cost for load style and box quantity shown. Not every brand is available in all shot size variations. Some manufacturers do not provide suggested list prices. All prices rounded to nearest whole dollar. The price you pay will vary dependent upon outlet of purchase. # = new load spec this year; "C" indicates a change in data.

10 Gauge 3-1/2" Magnum

4-1/2	2-1/4	premium	BB, 2, 4, 5, 6	Win., Fed., Rem.	$33	1205
Max	2	premium	4, 5, 6	Fed., Win.	NA	1300
4-1/4	2	high velocity	BB, 2, 4	Rem.	$22	1210
Max	18 pellets	premium	00 buck	Fed., Win.	$7**	1100
Max	1-7/8	Bismuth	BB, 2, 4	Bis.	NA	1225
Max	1-3/4	high density	BB, 2	Rem.	NA	1300
4-1/4	1-3/4	steel	TT, T, BBB, BB, 1, 2, 3	Win., Rem.	$27	1260
Mag	1-5/8	steel	T, BBB, BB, 2	Win.	$27	1285
Max	1-5/8	Bismuth	BB, 2, 4	Bismuth	NA	1375
Max	1-1/2	steel	T, BBB, BB, 1, 2, 3	Fed.	NA	1450
Max	1-3/8	steel	T, BBB, BB, 1, 2, 3	Fed., Rem.	NA	1500
Max	1-3/8	steel	T, BBB, BB, 2	Fed., Win.	NA	1450
Max	1-3/4	slug, rifled	slug	Fed.	NA	1280
Max	24 pellets	Buckshot	1 Buck	Fed.	NA	1100
Max	54 pellets	Super-X	4 Buck	Win.	NA	1150

12 Gauge 3-1/2" Magnum

Max	2-1/4	premium	4, 5, 6	Fed., Rem., Win.	$13*	1150
Max	2	Lead	4, 5, 6	Fed.	NA	1300
Max	2	Copper plated turkey	4, 5	Rem.	NA	1300
Max	18 pellets	premium	00 buck	Fed., Win., Rem.	$7**	1100
Max	1-7/8	Wingmaster HD	4, 6	Rem.	NA	1225
Max	1-7/8	heavyweight	5, 6	Fed.	NA	1300
Max	1-3/4	high density	BB, 2, 4, 6	Rem.		1300
Max	1-7/8	Bismuth	BB, 2, 4	Bis.	NA	1225
Max	1-5/8	Hevi-shot	T	Hevi-shot	NA	1350
Max	1-5/8	Wingmaster HD	T	Rem.	NA	1350
Max	1-5/8	high density	BB, 2	Fed.	NA	1450
Max	1-3/8	Heavyweight	2, 4, 6	Fed.	NA	1450
Max	1-3/8	steel	T, BBB, BB, 2, 4	Fed., Win., Rem.	NA	1450
Max	1-1/2	FS steel	BBB, BB, 2	Fed.	NA	1500
Max	1-1/2	Supreme H-V	BBB, BB, 2, 3	Win.	NA	1475
Max	1-3/8	H-speed steel	BB, 2	Rem.	NA	1550
Max	1-1/4	Steel	BB, 2	Win.	NA	1625
Max	24 pellets	Premium	1 Buck	Fed.	NA	1100
Max	54 pellets	Super-X	4 Buck	Win.	NA	1050

12 Gauge 3" Magnum

4	2	premium	BB, 2, 4, 5, 6	Win., Fed., Rem.	$9*	1175
4	1-7/8	premium	BB, 2, 4, 6	Win., Fed., Rem.	$19	1210
4	1-7/8	duplex	4x6	Rem.	$9*	1210
Max	1-3/4	turkey	4, 5, 6	Fed., Fio., Win., Rem.	NA	1300
Max	1-3/4	high density	BB, 2, 4	Rem.	NA	1450
Max	1-5/8	high density	BB, 2	Fed.	NA	1450
Max	1-5/8	Wingmaster HD	4, 6	Rem.	NA	1227
Max	1-5/8	high velocity	4, 5, 6	Fed.	NA	1350
4	1-5/8	premium	2, 4, 5, 6	Win., Fed., Rem.	$18	1290
Max	1-1/2	Wingmaster HD	T	Rem.	NA	1300
Max	1-1/2	Hevi-shot	T	Hevi-shot	NA	1300
Max	1-1/2	high density	BB, 2, 4	Rem.	NA	1300
Max	1-5/8	Bismuth	BB, 2, 4, 5, 6	Bis.	NA	1250
4	24 pellets	buffered	1 buck	Win., Fed., Rem.	$5**	1040
4	15 pellets	buffered	00 buck	Win., Fed., Rem.	$6**	1210
4	10 pellets	buffered	000 buck	Win., Fed., Rem.	$6**	1225
4	41 pellets	buffered	4 buck	Win., Fed., Rem.	$6**	1210
Max	1-3/8	heavyweight	5, 6	Fed.	NA	1300
Max	1-3/8	high density	B, 2, 4, 6	Rem. Win.	NA	1450

12 Gauge 3" Magnum (cont.)

Max	1-3/8	slug	slug	Bren.	NA	1476
Max	1-1/4	slug, rifled	slug	Fed.	NA	1600
Max	1-3/16	saboted slug	copper slug	Rem.	NA	1500
Max	7/8	slug, rifled	slug	Rem.	NA	1875
Max	1-1/8	low recoil	BB	Fed.	NA	850
Max	1-1/8	steel	BB, 2, 3, 4	Fed., Win., Rem.	NA	1550
Max	1-1/16	high density	2, 4	Win.	NA	1400
Max	1	steel	4, 6	Fed.	NA	1330
Max	1-3/8	buckhammer	slug	Rem.	NA	1500
Max	1	slug, rifled	slug, magnum	Win., Rem.	$5**	1760
Max	1	saboted slug	slug	Rem., Win., Fed.	$10**	1550
Max	385 grs.	partition gold	slug	Win.	NA	2000
Max	1-1/8	Rackmaster	slug	Win.	NA	1700
Max	300 grs.	XP3	slug	Win.	NA	2100
3-5/8	1-3/8	steel	BBB, BB, 1, 2, 3, 4	Win., Fed., Rem.	$19	1275
Max	1-1/8	steel	BB, 2, 4	Rem.	NA	1500
Max	1-1/8	steel	T, BBB, BB, 2, 4, 5, 6	Fed., Win.	NA	1450
Max	1-1/8	steel	BB, 2	Fed.	NA	1400
4	1-1/4	steel	T, BBB, BB, 1, 2, 3, 4, 6	Win., Fed., Rem.	$18	1400
Max	1-1/4	FS steel	BBB, BB, 2	Fed.	NA	1450

12 Gauge 2-3/4"

Max	1-5/8	magnum	4, 5, 6	Win., Fed.	$8*	1250
Max	1-3/8	lead	4, 5, 6	Fiocchi	NA	1485
Max	1-3/8	turkey	4, 5, 6	Fio.	NA	1250
Max	1-3/8	steel	4, 5, 6	Fed.	NA	1400
Max	1-3/8	Bismuth	BB, 2, 4, 5, 6	Bis.	NA	1300
3-3/4	1-1/2	magnum	BB, 2, 4, 5, 6	Win., Fed., Rem.	$16	1260
Max	1-1/4	Supreme H-V	4, 5, 6, 7-1/2	Win. Rem.	NA	1400
3-3/4	1-1/4	high velocity	BB, 2, 4, 5, 6, 7-1/2, 8, 9	Win., Fed., Rem., Fio.	$13	1330
Max	1-1/4	high density	B, 2, 4	Win.	NA	1450
Max	1-1/4	high density	4, 6	Rem.	NA	1325
3-1/4	1-1/4	standard velocity	6, 7-1/2, 8, 9	Win., Fed., Rem., Fio.	$11	1220
Max	1-1/8	Hevi-shot	5	Hevi-shot	NA	1350
3-1/4	1-1/8	standard velocity	4, 6, 7-1/2, 8, 9	Win., Fed., Rem., Fio.	$9	1255
Max	1-1/8	steel	2, 4	Rem.	NA	1390
Max	1	steel	BB, 2	Fed.	NA	1450
3-1/4	1	standard velocity	6, 7-1/2, 8	Rem., Fed., Fio., Win.	$6	1290
3-1/4	1-1/4	target	7-1/2, 8, 9	Win., Fed., Rem.	$10	1220
3	1-1/8	spreader	7-1/2, 8, 8-1/2, 9	Fio.	NA	1200
3	1-1/8	target	7-1/2, 8, 9, 7-1/2x8	Win., Fed., Rem., Fio.	$7	1200
2-3/4	1-1/8	target	7-1/2, 8, 8-1/2, 9, 7-1/2x8	Win., Fed., Rem., Fio.	$7	1145
2-3/4	1-1/8	low recoil	7-1/2, 8	Rem.	NA	1145
2-1/2	26 grams	low recoil	8	Win.	NA	980
2-1/4	1-1/8	target	7-1/2, 8, 8-1/2, 9	Rem., Fed.	$7	1080
Max	1	spreader	7-1/2, 8, 8-1/2, 9	Fio.	NA	1300
3-1/4	28 grams (1 oz)	target	7-1/2, 8, 9	Win., Fed., Rem., Fio.	$8	1290
3	1	target	7-1/2, 8, 8-1/2, 9	Win., Fio.	NA	1235
2-3/4	1	target	7-1/2, 8, 8-1/2, 9	Fed., Rem., Fio.	NA	1180
3-1/4	24 grams	target	7-1/2, 8, 9	Fed., Win., Fio.	NA	1325
3	7/8	light	8	Fio.	NA	1200
3-3/4	8 pellets	buffered	000 buck	Win., Fed., Rem.	$4**	1325

NOTES: * = 10 rounds per box. ** = 5 rounds per box. Pricing variations and number of rounds per box can occur with type and brand of ammunition. Listed pricing is the average nominal cost for load style and box quantity shown. Not every brand is available in all shot size variations. Some manufacturers do not provide suggested list prices. All prices rounded to nearest whole dollar. The price you pay will vary dependent upon outlet of purchase. # = new load spec this year; "C" indicates a change in data.

12 Gauge 2-3/4" (cont.)

4	12 pellets	premium	00 buck	Win., Fed., Rem.	$5**	1290
3-3/4	9 pellets	buffered	00 buck	Win., Fed., Rem., Fio.	$19	1325
3-3/4	12 pellets	buffered	0 buck	Win., Fed., Rem.	$4**	1275
4	20 pellets	buffered	1 buck	Win., Fed., Rem.	$4**	1075
3-3/4	16 pellets	buffered	1 buck	Win., Fed., Rem.	$4**	1250
4	34 pellets	premium	4 buck	Fed., Rem.	$5**	1250
3-3/4	27 pellets	buffered	4 buck	Win., Fed., Rem., Fio.	$4**	1325
Max	1	saboted slug	slug	Win., Fed., Rem.	$10**	1450
Max	1-1/4	slug, rifled	slug	Fed.	NA	1520
Max	1-1/4	slug	slug	Lightfield		1440
Max	1-1/4	saboted slug	attached sabot	Rem.	NA	1550
Max	1	slug, rifled	slug, magnum	Rem., Fio.	$5**	1680
Max	1	slug, rifled	slug	Win., Fed., Rem.	$4**	1610
Max	1	sabot slug	slug	Sauvestre		1640
Max	7/8	slug, rifled	slug	Rem.	NA	1800
Max	400	plat. tip	sabot slug	Win.	NA	1700
Max	385 grains	Partition Gold Slug	slug	Win.	NA	1900
Max	385 grains	Core-Lokt bonded	sabot slug	Rem.	NA	1900
Max	325 grains	Barnes Sabot	slug	Fed.	NA	1900
Max	300 grains	SST Slug	sabot slug	Hornady	NA	2050
3	1-1/8	steel target	6-1/2, 7	Rem.	NA	1200
2-3/4	1-1/8	steel target	7	Rem.	NA	1145
3	1#	steel	7	Win.	$11	1235
3-1/2	1-1/4	steel	T, BBB, BB, 1, 2, 3, 4, 5, 6	Win., Fed., Rem.	$18	1275
3-3/4	1-1/8	steel	BB, 1, 2, 3, 4, 5, 6	Win., Fed., Rem., Fio.	$16	1365
3-3/4	1	steel	2, 3, 4, 5, 6, 7	Win., Fed., Rem., Fio.	$13	1390
Max	7/8	steel	7	Fio.	NA	1440

16 Gauge 2-3/4"

3-1/4	1-1/4	magnum	2, 4, 6	Fed., Rem.	$16	1260
3-1/4	1-1/8	high velocity	4, 6, 7-1/2	Win., Fed., Rem., Fio.	$12	1295
Max	1-1/8	Bismuth	4, 5	Bis.	NA	1200
2-3/4	1-1/8	standard velocity	6, 7-1/2, 8	Fed., Rem., Fio.	$9	1185
2-1/2	1	dove	6, 7-1/2, 8, 9	Fio., Win.	NA	1165
2-3/4	1		6, 7-1/2, 8	Fio.	NA	1200
Max	15/16	steel	2, 4	Fed., Rem.	NA	1300
Max	7/8	steel	2, 4	Win.	$16	1300
3	12 pellets	buffered	1 buck	Win., Fed., Rem.	$4**	1225
Max	4/5	slug, rifled	slug	Win., Fed., Rem.	$4**	1570
Max	.92	sabot slug	slug	Sauvestre	NA	1560

20 Gauge 3" Magnum

3	1-1/4	premium	2, 4, 5, 6, 7-1/2	Win., Fed., Rem.	$15	1185
Max	1-1/4	Wingmaster HD	4, 6	Rem.	NA	1185
3	1-1/4	turkey	4, 6	Fio.	NA	1200
Max	1-1/4	Hevi-shot	2, 4, 6	Hevi-shot	NA	1250
Max	1-1/8	high density	4, 6	Rem.	NA	1300
Max	18 pellets	buck shot	2 buck	Fed.	NA	1200
Max	24 pellets	buffered	3 buck	Win.	$5**	1150
2-3/4	20 pellets	buck	3 buck	Rem.	$4**	1200
3-1/4	1	steel	1, 2, 3, 4, 5, 6	Win., Fed., Rem.	$15	1330

20 Gauge 3" Magnum (cont.)

Max	7/8	steel	2, 4	Win.	NA	1300
Max	1-1/16	high density	2, 4	Win.	NA	1400
Max	1-1/16	Bismuth	2, 4, 5, 6	Bismuth	NA	1250
Mag	5/8	saboted slug	275 gr.	Fed.	NA	1900

20 Gauge 2-3/4"

2-3/4	1-1/8	magnum	4, 6, 7-1/2	Win., Fed., Rem.	$14	1175
2-3/4	1	high velocity	4, 5, 6, 7-1/2, 8, 9	Win., Fed., Rem., Fio.	$12	1220
Max	1	Bismuth	4, 6	Bis.	NA	1200
Max	1	Hevi-shot	5	Hevi-shot	NA	1250
Max	1	Supreme H-V	4, 6, 7-1/2	Win. Rem.	NA	1300
Max	7/8	Steel	2, 3, 4	Fio.	NA	1500
2-1/2	1	standard velocity	6, 7-1/2, 8	Win., Rem., Fed., Fio.	$6	1165
2-1/2	7/8	clays	8	Rem.	NA	1200
2-1/2	7/8	promotional	6, 7-1/2, 8	Win., Rem., Fio.	$6	1210
2-1/2	1	target	8, 9	Win., Rem.	$8	1165
Max	7/8	clays	7-1/2, 8	Win.	NA	1275
2-1/2	7/8	target	8, 9	Win., Fed., Rem.	$8	1200
Max	3/4	steel	2, 4	Rem.	NA	1425
2-1/2	7/8	steel - target	7	Rem.	NA	1200
Max	1	buckhammer	slug	Rem.	NA	1500
Max	5/8	Saboted Slug	Copper Slug	Rem.	NA	1500
Max	20 pellets	buffered	3 buck	Win., Fed.	$4	1200
Max	5/8	slug, saboted	slug	Win.,	$9**	1400
2-3/4	5/8	slug, rifled	slug	Rem.	$4**	1580
Max	3/4	saboted slug	copper slug	Fed., Rem.	NA	1450
Max	3/4	slug, rifled	slug	Win., Fed., Rem., Fio.	$4**	1570
Max	.9	sabot slug	slug	Sauvestre		1480
Max	260 grains	Partition Gold Slug	slug	Win.	NA	1900
Max	260 grains	Core-Lokt Ultra	slug	Rem.	NA	1900
Max	260 grains	saboted slug	platinum tip	Win.	NA	1700
Max	3/4	steel	2, 3, 4, 6	Win., Fed., Rem.	$14	1425
Max	250 grains	SST slug	slug	Hornady	NA	1800
Max	1/2	rifled, slug	slug	Rem.	NA	1800

28 Gauge 2-3/4"

2	1	high velocity	6, 7-1/2, 8	Win.	$12	1125
2-1/4	3/4	high velocity	6, 7-1/2, 8, 9	Win., Fed., Rem., Fio.	$11	1295
2	3/4	target	8, 9	Win., Fed., Rem.	$9	1200
Max	3/4	sporting clays	7-1/2, 8-1/2	Win.	NA	1300
Max	5/8	Bismuth	4, 6	Bis.	NA	1250
Max	5/8	steel	6, 7	NA	NA	1300

410 Bore 3"

Max	11/16	high velocity	4, 5, 6, 7-1/2, 8, 9	Win., Fed., Rem., Fio.	$10	1135
Max	9/16	Bismuth	4	Bis.	NA	1175
Max	3/8	steel	6	NA	NA	1400

410 Bore 2-1/2"

Max	1/2	high velocity	4, 6, 7-1/2	Win., Fed., Rem.	$9	1245
Max	1/5	slug, rifled	slug	Win., Fed., Rem.	$4**	1815
1-1/2	1/2	target	8, 8-1/2, 9	Win., Fed., Rem., Fio.	$8	1200
Max	1/2	sporting clays	7-1/2, 8, 8-1/2	Win.	NA	1300
Max		Buckshot	5-000 Buck	Win.	NA	1135

2010 GUNS ILLUSTRATED Complete Compact CATALOG

☞ GUNDEX

☞ HANDGUNS

☞ RIFLES

☞ SHOTGUNS

GUNDEX

GUNDEX

GUNDEX

GUNDEX

GUNDEX

GUNDEX

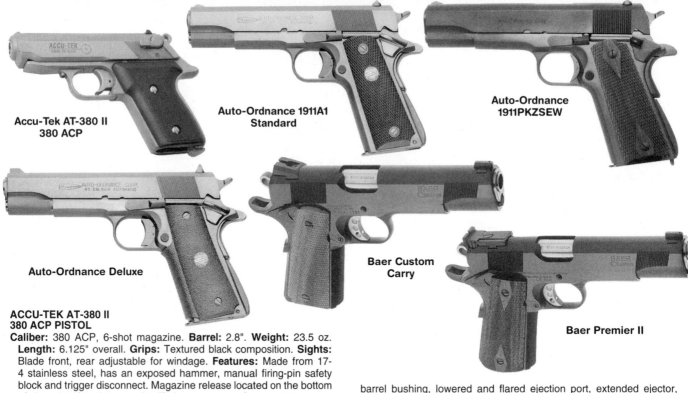

Accu-Tek AT-380 II 380 ACP

Auto-Ordnance 1911A1 Standard

Auto-Ordnance 1911PKZSEW

Auto-Ordnance Deluxe

Baer Custom Carry

Baer Premier II

ACCU-TEK AT-380 II 380 ACP PISTOL
Caliber: 380 ACP, 6-shot magazine. **Barrel:** 2.8". **Weight:** 23.5 oz. **Length:** 6.125" overall. **Grips:** Textured black composition. **Sights:** Blade front, rear adjustable for windage. **Features:** Made from 17-4 stainless steel, has an exposed hammer, manual firing-pin safety block and trigger disconnect. Magazine release located on the bottom of the grip. American made, lifetime warranty. Comes with two 6-round stainless steel magazines and a California-approved cable lock. Introduced 2006. Made in U.S.A. by Excel Industries.
Price: Satin stainless $262.00

ARMALITE AR-24 PISTOL
Caliber: 9mm Para., 10- or 15-shot magazine. **Barrel:** 4.671", 6 groove, right-hand cut rifling. **Weight:** 34.9 oz. **Length:** 8.27" overall. **Grips:** Black polymer. **Sights:** Dovetail front, fixed rear, 3-dot luminous design. **Features:** Machined slide, frame and barrel. Serrations on forestrap and backstrap, external thumb safety and internal firing pin box, half cock. Two 15-round magazines, pistol case, pistol lock, manual and cleaning brushes. Manganese phosphate finish. Compact comes with two 13-round magazines, 3.89" barrel, weighs 33.4 oz. Made in U.S.A. by ArmaLite.
Price: AR-24 Full Size.............................$550.00
Price: AR-24K Compact............................$550.00

AUTO-ORDNANCE 1911A1 AUTOMATIC PISTOL
Caliber: 45 ACP, 7-shot magazine. **Barrel:** 5". **Weight:** 39 oz. **Length:** 8.5" overall. **Grips:** Brown checkered plastic with medallion. **Sights:** Blade front, rear drift-adjustable for windage. **Features:** Same specs as 1911A1 military guns-parts interchangeable. Frame and slide blued; each radius has non-glare finish. Introduced 2002. Made in U.S.A. by Kahr Arms.
Price: 1911PKZSE Parkerized, plastic grips $627.00
Price: 1911PKZSEW Parkerized $662.00
Price: 1911PKZMA Parkerized, Mass. Compliant (2008).....$627.00

AUTO-ORDNANCE TA5 SEMI-AUTO PISTOL
Caliber: 45 ACP, 30-round stick magazine (standard), 50- or 100-round drum magazine optional. **Barrel:** 10.5", finned. **Weight:** 6.5 lbs. **Length:** 25" overall. **Features:** Semi-auto pistol patterned after Thompson Model 1927 semi-auto carbine. Horizontal vertical foregrip, aluminum receiver, top cocking knob, grooved walnut pistolgrip.
Price: $1,143.00

BAER H.C. 40 AUTO PISTOL
Caliber: 40 S&W, 18-shot magazine. **Barrel:** 5". **Weight:** 37 oz. **Length:** 8.5" overall. **Grips:** Wood. **Sights:** Low-mount adjustable rear sight with hidden rear leaf, dovetail front sight. **Features:** Double-stack Caspian frame, beavertail grip safety, ambidextrous thumb safety, 40 S&W match barrel with supported chamber, match stainless steel

barrel bushing, lowered and flared ejection port, extended ejector, match trigger fitted, integral mag well, bead blast blue finish on lower, polished sides on slide. Introduced 2008. Made in U.S.A. by Les Baer Custom, Inc.
Price: $2,960.00

BAER 1911 CUSTOM CARRY AUTO PISTOL
Caliber: 45 ACP, 7- or 10-shot magazine. **Barrel:** 5". **Weight:** 37 oz. **Length:** 8.5" overall. **Grips:** Checkered walnut. **Sights:** Baer improved ramp-style dovetailed front, Novak low-mount rear. **Features:** Baer forged NM frame, slide and barrel with stainless bushing. Baer speed trigger with 4-lb. pull. Partial listing shown. Made in U.S.A. by Les Baer Custom, Inc.
Price: Custom Carry 5", blued $1,995.00
Price: Custom Carry 5", stainless $2,120.00
Price: Custom Carry 4" Commanche length, blued $1,995.00
Price: Custom Carry 4" Commanche length, stainless $2,120.00

BAER 1911 ULTIMATE RECON PISTOL
Caliber: 45 ACP, 7- or 10-shot magazine. **Barrel:** 5". **Weight:** 37 oz. **Length:** 8.5" overall. **Grips:** Checkered cocobolo. **Sights:** Baer improved ramp-style dovetailed front, Novak low-mount rear. **Features:** NM Caspian frame, slide and barrel with stainless bushing. Baer speed trigger with 4-lb. pull. Includes integral Picatinny rail and Sure-Fire X-200 light. Made in U.S.A. by Les Baer Custom, Inc. Introduced 2006.
Price: Bead blast blued $3,070.00
Price: Bead blast chrome $3,390.00

BAER 1911 PREMIER II AUTO PISTOL
Caliber: 38 Super, 400 Cor-Bon, 45 ACP, 7- or 10-shot magazine. **Barrel:** 5". **Weight:** 37 oz. **Length:** 8.5" overall. **Grips:** Checkered rosewood, double diamond pattern. **Sights:** Baer dovetailed front, low-mount Bo-Mar rear with hidden leaf. **Features:** Baer NM forged steel frame and barrel with stainless bushing, deluxe Commander hammer and sear, beavertail grip safety with pad, extended ambidextrous safety; flat mainspring housing; 30 lpi checkered front strap. Made in U.S.A. by Les Baer Custom, Inc.
Price: 5" 45 ACP $1,790.00
Price: 5" 400 Cor-Bon $1,890.00
Price: 5" 38 Super $2,070.00
Price: 6" 45 ACP, 400 Cor-Bon, 38 Super, from.........$1,990.00
Price: Super-Tac, 45 ACP, 400 Cor-Bon, 38 Super, from ..$2,280.00

Baer 1911 Stinger

Beretta 92FS

Beretta Bobcat

Beretta PX4 Storm

Beretta Tomcat

Beretta U22 Neos

Beretta PX4 Storm Sub-Compact

BAER 1911 S.R.P. PISTOL
Caliber: 45 ACP. **Barrel:** 5". **Weight:** 37 oz. **Length:** 8.5" overall. **Grips:** Checkered walnut. **Sights:** Trijicon night sights. **Features:** Similar to the F.B.I. contract gun except uses Baer forged steel frame. Has Baer match barrel with supported chamber, complete tactical action. Has Baer Ultra Coat finish. Introduced 1996. Made in U.S.A. by Les Baer Custom, Inc.
Price: Government or Commanche length **$2,590.00**

BAER 1911 STINGER PISTOL
Caliber: 45 ACP, 7-round magazine. **Barrel:** 5". **Weight:** 34 oz. **Length:** 8.5" overall. **Grips:** Checkered cocobolo. **Sights:** Baer dovetailed front, low-mount Bo-Mar rear with hidden leaf. **Features:** Baer NM frame. Baer Commanche slide, Officer's style grip frame, beveled mag well. Made in U.S.A. by Les Baer Custom, Inc.
Price: Blued **$1,890.00**
Price: Stainless **$1,970.00**

BAER 1911 PROWLER III PISTOL
Caliber: 45 ACP, 8-round magazine. **Barrel:** 5". **Weight:** 34 oz. **Length:** 8.5" overall. **Grips:** Checkered cocobolo. **Sights:** Baer dovetailed front, low-mount Bo-Mar rear with hidden leaf. **Features:** Similar to Premier II with tapered cone stub weight, rounded corners. Made in U.S.A. by Les Baer Custom, Inc.
Price: Blued **$2,580.00**

BERETTA MODEL 92FS PISTOL
Caliber: 9mm Para., 10-shot magazine. **Barrel:** 4.9". **Weight:** 34 oz. **Length:** 8.5" overall. **Grips:** Checkered black plastic. **Sights:** Blade front, rear adjustable for windage. Tritium night sights available. **Features:** Double action. Extractor acts as chamber loaded indicator, squared trigger guard, grooved front and backstraps, inertia firing pin. Matte or blued finish. Introduced 1977. Made in U.S.A.
Price: With plastic grips **$650.00**

BERETTA MODEL 80 CHEETAH SERIES DA PISTOLS
Caliber: 380 ACP, 10-shot magazine (M84); 8-shot (M85); 22 LR, 7-shot (M87). **Barrel:** 3.82". **Weight:** About 23 oz. (M84/85); 20.8 oz. (M87). **Length:** 6.8" overall. **Grips:** Glossy black plastic (wood optional at extra cost). **Sights:** Fixed front, drift-adjustable rear. **Features:** Double action, quick takedown, convenient magazine release. Introduced 1977. Made in U.S.A.
Price: Model 84 Cheetah, plastic grips **$650.00**

BERETTA MODEL 21 BOBCAT PISTOL
Caliber: 22 LR or 25 ACP. Both double action. **Barrel:** 2.4". **Weight:** 11.5 oz.; 11.8 oz. **Length:** 4.9" overall. **Grips:** Plastic. **Features:** Available in nickel, matte, engraved or blue finish. Introduced in 1985.
Price: Bobcat, 22 or 25, blue **$335.00**

Price: Bobcat, 22, Inox **$420.00**
Price: Bobcat, 22 or 25, matte **$335.00**

BERETTA MODEL 3032 TOMCAT PISTOL
Caliber: 32 ACP, 7-shot magazine. **Barrel:** 2.45". **Weight:** 14.5 oz. **Length:** 5" overall. **Grips:** Checkered black plastic. **Sights:** Blade front, drift-adjustable rear. **Features:** Double action with exposed hammer; tip-up barrel for direct loading/unloading; thumb safety; polished or matte blue finish. Made in U.S.A. Introduced 1996.
Price: Matte **$435.00**
Price: Inox **$555.00**

BERETTA MODEL U22 NEOS
Caliber: 22 LR, 10-shot magazine. **Barrel:** 4.5"; 6". **Weight:** 32 oz.; 36 oz. **Length:** 8.8"; 10.3". **Sights:** Target. **Features:** Integral rail for standard scope mounts, light, perfectly weighted, 100 percent American made by Beretta.
Price: **$250.00**
Price: Inox **$350.00**

BERETTA MODEL PX4 STORM
Caliber: 9mm Para., 40 S&W. **Capacity:** 17 (9mm Para.); 14 (40 S&W). **Barrel:** 4". **Weight:** 27.5 oz. **Grips:** Black checkered w/3 interchangeable backstraps. **Sights:** 3-dot system coated in Superluminova; removable front and rear sights. **Features:** DA/SA, manual safety/hammer decocking lever (ambi) and automatic firing pin block safety. Picatinny rail. Comes with two magazines (17/10 in 9mm Para. and 14/10 in 40 S&W). Removable hammer unit. American made by Beretta. Introduced 2005.
Price: **$600.00**
Price: 45 ACP **$650.00**

BERETTA MODEL PX4 STORM SUB-COMPACT
Caliber: 9mm, 40 S&W. **Capacity:** 13 (9mm); 10 (40 S&W). **Barrel:** 3". **Weight:** 26.1 oz. **Length:** 6.2" overall. **Grips:** NA. **Sights:** NA. **Features:** Ambidextrous manual safety lever, interchangeable backstraps included, lock breech and tilt barrel system, stainless steel barrel, Picatinny rail.
Price: **$600.00**

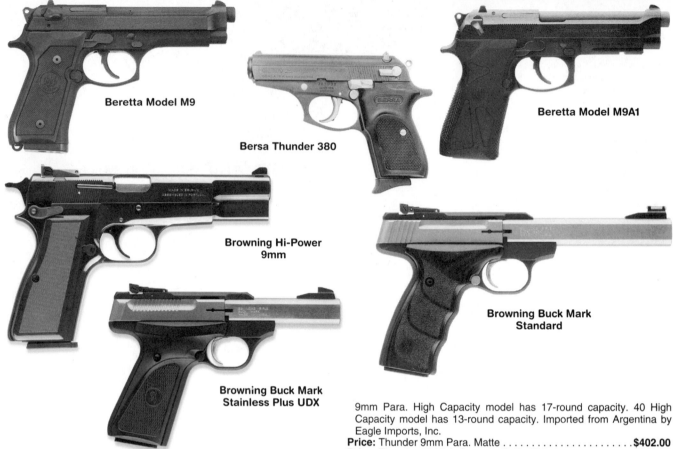

Beretta Model M9

Bersa Thunder 380

Beretta Model M9A1

Browning Hi-Power 9mm

Browning Buck Mark Standard

Browning Buck Mark Stainless Plus UDX

BERETTA MODEL M9
Caliber: 9mm Para. **Capacity:** 15. **Barrel:** 4.9". **Weight:** 32.2-35.3 oz. **Grips:** Plastic. **Sights:** Dot and post, low profile, windage adjustable rear. **Features:** DA/SA, forged aluminum alloy frame, delayed locking-bolt system, manual safety doubles as decocking lever, combat-style trigger guard, loaded chamber indicator. Comes with two magazines (15/10). American made by Beretta. Introduced 2005.
Price: **$650.00**

BERETTA MODEL M9A1
Caliber: 9mm Para. **Capacity:** 15. **Barrel:** 4.9". **Weight:** 32.2-35.3 oz. **Grips:** Plastic. **Sights:** Dot and post, low profile, windage adjustable rear. **Features:** Same as M9, but also includes integral Mil-Std-1913 Picatinny rail, has checkered frontstrap and backstrap. Comes with two magazines (15/10). American made by Beretta. Introduced 2005.
Price: **$750.00**

BERSA THUNDER 45 ULTRA COMPACT PISTOL
Caliber: 45 ACP. **Barrel:** 3.6". **Weight:** 27 oz. **Length:** 6.7" overall. **Grips:** Anatomically designed polymer. **Sights:** White outline rear. **Features:** Double action; firing pin safeties, integral locking system. Available in matte, satin nickel, gold, or duo-tone. Introduced 2003. Imported from Argentina by Eagle Imports, Inc.
Price: Thunder 45, matte blue **$402.00**
Price: Thunder 45, stainless **$480.00**
Price: Thunder 45, satin nickel **$445.00**

BERSA THUNDER 380 SERIES PISTOLS
Caliber: 380 ACP, 7 rounds **Barrel:** 3.5". **Weight:** 23 oz. **Length:** 6.6" overall. **Features:** Otherwise similar to Thunder 45 Ultra Compact. 380 DLX has 9-round capacity. 380 Concealed Carry has 8 round capacity. Imported from Argentina by Eagle Imports, Inc.
Price: Thunder 380 Matte **$310.00**
Price: Thunder 380 Satin Nickel **$336.00**
Price: Thunder 380 Blue DLX **$332.00**
Price: Thunder 380 Matte CC (2006) **$315.00**

BERSA THUNDER 9 ULTRA COMPACT/40 SERIES PISTOLS
Caliber: 9mm Para., 40 S&W. **Barrel:** 3.5". **Weight:** 24.5 oz. **Length:** 6.6" overall. **Features:** Otherwise similar to Thunder 45 Ultra Compact.

9mm Para. High Capacity model has 17-round capacity. 40 High Capacity model has 13-round capacity. Imported from Argentina by Eagle Imports, Inc.
Price: Thunder 9mm Para. Matte **$402.00**
Price: Thunder 40 High Capacity Satin Nickel **$419.00**

BROWNING HI POWER 9MM AUTOMATIC PISTOL
Caliber: 9mm Para., 13-round magazine; 40 S&W, 10-round magazine. **Barrel:** 4-5/8". **Weight:** 32 to 39 oz. **Length:** 7.75" overall. **Metal Finishes:** Blued (Standard); black-epoxy/silver-chrome (Practical); black-epoxy (Mark III). **Grips:** Molded (Mark III); wraparound Pachmayr (Practical); or walnut grips (Standard). **Sights:** Fixed (Practical, Mark III, Standard); low-mount adjustable rear (Standard). Cable lock supplied. **Features:** External hammer with half-cock and thumb safeties. Fixed rear sight model available. Commander-style (Practical) or spur-type hammer, single action. Includes gun lock. Imported from Belgium by Browning.
Price: Mark III **$979.00**
Price: Standard, fixed sights, from **$999.00**
Price: SMark III, Digital green (2009) **$985.00**

BROWNING BUCK MARK PISTOLS
Common Features: Caliber: 22 LR, 10-shot magazine. **Action:** Blowback semi-auto. **Trigger:** Wide grooved style. **Sights:** Ramp front, Browning Pro-Target rear adjustable for windage and elevation. **Grips:** Cocobolo, target-style (Hunter, 5.5 Target, 5.5 Field); polymer (Camper, Camper Stainless, Micro Nickel, Standard, STD Stainless); checkered walnut (Challenge); laminated (Plus and Plus Nickel); laminated rosewood (Bullseye Target, FLD Plus); rubber (Bullseye Standard). **Metal finishes:** Matte blue (Hunter, Camper, Challenge, Plus, Bullseye Target, Bullseye Standard, 5.5 Target, 5.5 Field, FLD Plus); matte stainless (Camper Stainless, STD Stainless, Micro Standard); nickel-plated (Micro Nickel, Plus Nickel, and Nickel). **Features:** Machined aluminum frame. Includes gun lock. Introduced 1985. Hunter, Camper Stainless, STD Stainless, 5.5 Target, 5.5 Field all introduced 2005. Multiple variations, as noted below. Made in U.S.A. From Browning.
Price: Hunter, 7.25" heavy barrel, 38 oz., Truglo sight **$429.00**
Price: Camper, 5.5" heavy barrel, 34 oz. **$329.00**
Price: FLD Camper Stainless URX, 5.5" tapered bull barrel, 34 oz. **$359.00**
Price: Standard URX, 5.5" flat-side bull barrel, 34 oz. **$399.00**
Price: Standard Stainless URX, 5.5" flat-side bull barrel, 34 oz. **$439.00**
Price: Micro Standard URX, 4" flat-side bull barrel, 32 oz. ... **$399.00**

Browning FLD Plus Rosewood UDX

Charles Daly Empire EFS

Charles Daly M-5 Government

Browning Stainless Camper

Cobra Patriot 45

Cobra Patiot 380

BROWNING BUCK MARK PISTOLS *(cont.)*
Price: Micro Standard Stainless URX, 4" flat-side bull barrel,
32 oz. **$439.00**
Price: Challenge, 5.5" lightweight taper barrel, 25 oz. **$399.00**
Price: Contour 5.5 URX, 5.5" barrel, 36 oz. **$469.00**
Price: Contour 7.25 URX, 7.25", 39 oz. **$479.00**
Price: Contour Lite 5.5 URX, 5.5" barrel, 28 oz., adj. sights . **$519.00**
Price: Contour Lite 7.25 URX, 7.25" barrel, 30 oz., adj. sights **$529.00**
Price: Bullseye URX, 7.25" fluted bull barrel, 36 oz. **$549.00**
Price: Bullseye Target Stainless, 7.25" fluted bull barrel,
36 oz. **$719.00**
Price: 5.5 Target, 5.5" round bull barrel, target sights,
35.5 oz. **$579.00**
Price: 5.5 Field, 5.5" round bull barrel, 35 oz. **$579.00**
Price: Plus Stainless UDX (2007). **$509.00**
Price: Plus UDX (2007). **$469.00**
Price: FLD Plus Rosewood UDX (2007). **$469.00**
Price: Stainless Camper, 5.5" tapered bull barrel (2008) **$379.00**
Price: Practical URX Fiber-Optic, 5.5" barrel (2009) **$379.00**
Price: Lite Splash 5.5 URX **$489.00**
Price: Lite Splash 7.25 URX **$509.00**

BUSHMASTER CARBON 15 .223 PISTOL
Caliber: 5.56/223, 30-round. **Barrel:** 7.25" stainless steel. **Weight:** 2.88 lbs. **Length:** 20" overall. **Grips:** Pistol grip, Hogue overmolded unit for ergonomic comfort. **Sights:** A2-type front with dual-aperture slip-up rear. **Features:** AR-style semi-auto pistol with carbon composite receiver, shortenend handguard, full-length optics rail.
Price: . . . . **NA**
Price: Type 97 pistol, without handguard **$1,055.00**

CHARLES DALY ENHANCED 1911 PISTOLS
Caliber: 45 ACP. **Barrel:** 5". **Weight:** 38 oz. **Length:** 8.75" overall. **Grips:** Checkered double diamond hardwood. **Sights:** Dovetailed front and dovetailed snag-free low profile rear sights, 3-dot system. **Features:** Extended high-rise beavertail grip safety, combat trigger, combat hammer, beveled magazine well, flared and lowered ejection port. Field Grade models are satin-finished blued steel. EMS series includes an ambidextrous safety, 4" barrel, 8-shot magazine. ECS series has a contoured left hand safety, 3.5" barrel, 6-shot magazine. Two magazines,

lockable carrying case. Introduced 1998. Empire series are stainless versions. Imported from the Philippines by K.B.I., Inc.
Price: EFS, blued, 39.5 oz., 5" barrel **$649.00**
Price: EMS, blued, 37 oz., 4" barrel **$649.00**
Price: ECS, blued, 34.5 oz., 3.5" barrel **$649.00**

CHARLES DALY M-5 POLYMER-FRAMED HI-CAP 1911 PISTOL
Caliber: 9mm Para., 12-round magazine; 40 S&W 17-round magazine; 45 ACP, 13-round magazine. **Barrel:** 5". **Weight:** 33.5 oz. **Length:** 8.5" overall. **Grips:** Checkered polymer. **Sights:** Blade front, adjustable low-profile rear. **Features:** Stainless steel beaver-tail grip safety, rounded trigger-guard, tapered bull barrel, full-length guide rod, matte blue finish on frame and slide. 40 S&W models in M-5 Govt. 1911, M-5 Commander, and M-5 IPSC introduced 2006; M-5 Ultra X Compact in 9mm Para. and 45 ACP introduced 2006; M-5 IPSC .45 ACP introduced 2006. Made in Israel by BUL, imported by K.B.I., Inc.
Price: M-5 Govt. 1911, 40 S&W/45 ACP, matte blue **$749.00**
Price: M-5 Commander, 40 S&W/45 ACP, matte blue **$749.00**
Price: M-5 Ultra X Compact, 9mm Para., 3.1" barrel,
7" OAL, 28 oz. **$749.00**
Price: M-5 Ultra X Compact, 45 ACP, 3.1" barrel, 7" OAL,
28 oz. **$749.00**

COBRA ENTERPRISES FS32, FS380 AUTO PISTOL
Caliber: 32 ACP, 380 ACP, 7-shot magazine. **Barrel:** 3.5". **Weight:** 2.1 lbs. **Length:** 6-3/8" overall. **Grips:** Black composition. **Sights:** Fixed. **Features:** Choice of bright chrome, satin nickel or black finish. Introduced 2002. Made in U.S.A. by Cobra Enterprises of Utah, Inc.
Price: **$165.00**

COBRA ENTERPRISES PATRIOT 45 PISTOL
Caliber: 45 ACP, 6, 7, or 10-shot magazine. **Barrel:** 3.3". **Weight:** 20 oz. **Length:** 6" overall. **Grips:** Black polymer. **Sights:** Rear adjustable. **Features:** Stainless steel or black melonite slide with load indicator; Semi-auto locked breech, DAO. Made in U.S.A. by Cobra Enterprises of Utah, Inc.
Price: **$380.00**

COBRA ENTERPRISES CA32, CA380 PISTOL
Caliber: 32 ACP, 380 ACP. **Barrel:** 2.8". **Weight:** 22 oz. **Length:** 5.4". **Grips:** Black molded synthetic. **Sights:** Fixed. **Features:** Choice of black, satin nickel, or chrome finish. Made in U.S.A. by Cobra Enterprises of Utah, Inc.
Price: **$157.00**

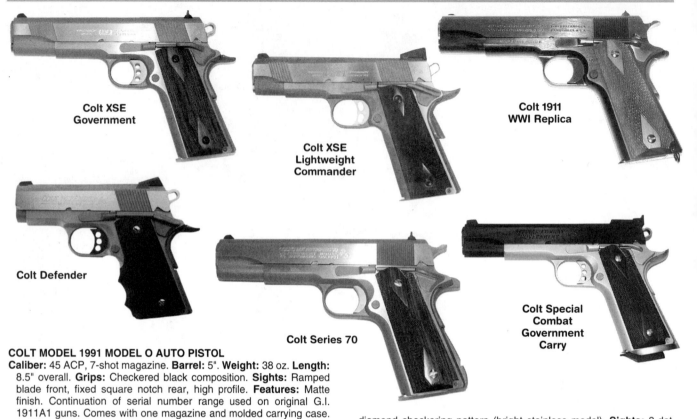

Colt XSE Government

Colt XSE Lightweight Commander

Colt 1911 WWI Replica

Colt Defender

Colt Series 70

Colt Special Combat Government Carry

COLT MODEL 1991 MODEL O AUTO PISTOL
Caliber: 45 ACP, 7-shot magazine. **Barrel:** 5". **Weight:** 38 oz. **Length:** 8.5" overall. **Grips:** Checkered black composition. **Sights:** Ramped blade front, fixed square notch rear, high profile. **Features:** Matte finish. Continuation of serial number range used on original G.I. 1911A1 guns. Comes with one magazine and molded carrying case. Introduced 1991.
Price: Blue **$786.00**
Price: Stainless **$839.00**

COLT XSE SERIES MODEL O AUTO PISTOLS
Caliber: 45 ACP, 8-shot magazine. **Barrel:** 4.25", 5". **Grips:** Checkered, double diamond rosewood. **Sights:** Drift-adjustable 3-dot combat. **Features:** Brushed stainless finish; adjustable, two-cut aluminum trigger; extended ambidextrous thumb safety; upswept beavertail with palm swell; elongated slot hammer. Introduced 1999. From Colt's Mfg. Co., Inc.
Price: XSE Government (5" bbl.) **$944.00**
Price: XSE Government (4.25" bbl.) **$944.00**

COLT XSE LIGHTWEIGHT COMMANDER AUTO PISTOL
Caliber: 45 ACP, 8-shot. **Barrel:** 4.25". **Weight:** 26 oz. **Length:** 7.75" overall. **Grips:** Double diamond checkered rosewood. **Sights:** Fixed, glare-proofed blade front, square notch rear; 3-dot system. **Features:** Brushed stainless slide, nickeled aluminum frame; McCormick elongated slot enhanced hammer, McCormick two-cut adjustable aluminum hammer. Made in U.S.A. by Colt's Mfg. Co., Inc.
Price: Stainless **$944.00**

COLT DEFENDER
Caliber: 45 ACP, 7-shot magazine. **Barrel:** 3". **Weight:** 22-1/2 oz. **Length:** 6.75" overall. **Grips:** Pebble-finish rubber wraparound with finger grooves. **Sights:** White dot front, snag-free Colt competition rear. **Features:** Stainless finish; aluminum frame; combat-style hammer; Hi Ride grip safety, extended manual safety, disconnect safety. Introduced 1998. Made in U.S.A. by Colt's Mfg. Co., Inc.
Price: 07000D, stainless. **$885.00**

COLT SERIES 70
Caliber: 45 ACP. **Barrel:** 5". **Weight:** NA. **Length:** NA. **Grips:** Rosewood with double diamond checkering pattern. **Sights:** Fixed. **Features:** Custom replica of the Original Series 70 pistol with a Series 70 firing system, original rollmarks. Introduced 2002. Made in U.S.A. by Colt's Mfg. Co., Inc.
Price: Blued **$919.00**
Price: Stainless **$950.00**

COLT 38 SUPER
Caliber: 38 Super. **Barrel:** 5". **Weight:** NA. **Length:** 8.5" **Grips:** Checkered rubber (stainless and blue models); wood with double

diamond checkering pattern (bright stainless model). **Sights:** 3-dot. **Features:** Beveled magazine well, standard thumb safety and service-style grip safety. Introduced 2003. Made in U.S.A. by Colt's Mfg. Co., Inc.
Price: Blued **$837.00**
Price: Stainless **$866.00**
Price: Bright Stainless **$1,090.00**

COLT 1918 WWI REPLICA
Caliber: 45 ACP, 2 7-round magazines. **Barrel:** 5". **Weight:** 38 oz. **Length:** 8.5". **Grips:** Checkered walnut with double diamond checkering pattern. **Sights:** Tapered blade front sight, U-shaped rear notch. **Features:** Reproduction based on original 1911 blueprints. Original rollmarks and inspector marks. Smooth mainspring housing with lanyard loop, WWI-style manual thumb and grip safety, black oxide finish. Introduced 2007. Made in U.S.A. by Colt's Mfg. Co., Inc.
Price: Blued **$990.00**

COLT RAIL GUN
Caliber: 45 ACP (8+1). **Barrel:** NA. **Weight:** NA. **Length:** NA. **Grips:** Rosewood double diamond. **Sights:** White dot front and Novak rear. **Features:** 1911-style semi-auto. Stainless steel frame and slide, front and rear slide serrations, skeletonized trigger, integral; accessory rail, Smith & Alexander upswept beavertail grip palm swell safety, tactical thumb safety, National Match barrel.
Price: . . . . **TO BE ANNOUNCED**

COLT NEW AGENT
Caliber: 45 ACP (7+1). **Barrel:** 3". **Weight:** 25 oz. **Length:** 6.75" overall. **Grips:** Double diamond slim fit. **Sights:** Snag free trench style. **Features:** Semi-auto pistol with blued finish and enhanced black anodized aluminum receiver. Skeletonized aluminum trigger, series 80 firing system, front strap serrations, beveled magazine well.
Price: **$885.00**

COLT SPECIAL COMBAT GOVERNMENT CARRY MODEL
Caliber: 45 ACP (8+1), 38 Super (9+1). **Barrel:** 5". **Weight:** NA. **Length:** NA. **Grips:** Black/silver synthetic. **Sights:** Novak front and rear night. **Features:** 1911-style semi-auto. Skeletonized three-hole trigger, slotted hammer, Smith & Alexander upswept beavertail grip palm swell safety and extended magazine well, Wilson tactical ambidextrous safety. Available in blued, hard chrome, or blue/satin nickel finish, depending on chambering.
Price: **$1,676.00**

CZ 75 B 9mm

CZ 75 B Decocker

CZ 75/85 Kadet

CZ 85

CZ 97 B

nut

black polycoat finish, extended beavertail, new grip geometry with checkering on front and back straps, and double or single action operation. Introduced 2005. The Shadow variant designed as an IPSC "production" division competition firearm. Includes competition hammer, competition rear sight and fiber-optic front sight, modified slide release, lighter recoil and main spring for use with "minor power factor" competition ammunition. Includes polycoat finish and slim walnut grips. Finished by CZ Custom Shop. Imported from the Czech Republic by CZ-USA.
Price: SP-01 9mm Para., black polymer, 19+1 . . . .$850.00

CZ 75 B AUTO PISTOL
Caliber: 9mm Para., 40 S&W, 10-shot magazine. **Barrel:** 4.7". **Weight:** 34.3 oz. **Length:** 8.1" overall. **Grips:** High impact checkered plastic. **Sights:** Square post front, rear adjustable for windage; 3-dot system. **Features:** Single action/double action design; firing pin block safety; choice of black polymer, matte or high-polish blue finishes. All-steel frame. B-SA is a single action with a drop-free magazine. Imported from the Czech Republic by CZ-USA.
Price: 75 B, black polymer, 16-shot magazine $597.00
Price: 75 B, dual-tone or satin nickel $617.00
Price: 40 S&W, black polymer, 12-shot magazine $615.00
Price: 40 S&W, glossy blue, dual-tone, satin nickel $669.00
Price: 75 B-SA, 9mm Para./40 S&W, single action $609.00

CZ 75 BD Decocker
Similar to the CZ 75B except has a decocking lever in place of the safety lever. All other specifications are the same. Introduced 1999. Imported from the Czech Republic by CZ-USA.
Price: 9mm Para., black polymer $609.00

CZ 75 B Compact Auto Pistol
Similar to the CZ 75 B except has 14-shot magazine in 9mm Para., 3.9" barrel and weighs 32 oz. Has removable front sight, non-glare ribbed slide top. Trigger guard is squared and serrated; combat hammer. Introduced 1993. Imported from the Czech Republic by CZ-USA.
Price: 9mm Para., black polymer $631.00
Price: 9mm Para., dual tone or satin nickel $651.00
Price: 9mm Para. D PCR Compact, alloy frame $651.00

CZ 75 Champion Pistol
Similar to the CZ 75 B except has a longer frame and slide, rubber grip to accommodate new heavy-duty magazine. Ambidextrous thumb safety, extended magazine release; three-port compensator. Blued slide and stain nickel frame finish. Introduced 2005. Imported from the Czech Republic by CZ-USA.
Price: 40 S&W, 12-shot mag. $1,739.00

CZ 75 Tactical Sport
Similar to the CZ 75 B except the CZ 75 TS is a competition ready pistol designed for IPSC standard division (USPSA limited division). Fixed target sights, tuned single-action operation, lightweight polymer match trigger with adjustments for take-up and overtravel, competition hammer, extended magazine catch, ambidextrous manual safety, checkered walnut grips, polymer magazine well, two tone finish. Introduced 2005. Imported from the Czech Republic by CZ-USA.
Price: 9mm Para., 20-shot mag. $1,338.00
Price: 40 S&W, 16-shot mag. $1,338.00

CZ 75 SP-01 Pistol
Similar to NATO-approved CZ 75 Compact P-01 model. Features an integral 1913 accessory rail on the dust cover, rubber grip panels,

CZ 75 SP-01 Phantom
Similar to the CZ 75 B. 9mm Luger, 19-round magazine, weighs 26 oz. and features a polymer frame with accessory rail, and a forged steel slide with a weight-saving scalloped profile. Two interchangeable grip inserts are included to accommodate users with different-sized hands.
Price: $695.00

CZ 85 B/85 Combat Auto Pistol
Same gun as the CZ 75 except has ambidextrous slide release and safety levers; non-glare, ribbed slide top; squared, serrated trigger guard; trigger stop to prevent overtravel. Introduced 1986. The CZ 85 Combat features a fully adjustable rear sight, extended magazine release, ambidextrous slide stop and safety catch, drop free magazine and overtravel adjustment. Imported from the Czech Republic by CZ-USA.
Price: 9mm Para., black polymer $628.00
Price: Combat, black polymer $702.00
Price: Combat, dual-tone, satin nickel $732.00

CZ 75 KADET AUTO PISTOL
Caliber: 22 LR, 10-shot magazine. **Barrel:** 4.88". **Weight:** 36 oz. **Grips:** High impact checkered plastic. **Sights:** Blade front, fully adjustable rear. **Features:** Single action/double action mechanism; all-steel construction. Introduced 1999. Kadet conversion kit consists of barrel, slide, adjustable sights, and magazine to convert the centerfire 75 to rimfire. Imported from the Czech Republic by CZ-USA.
Price: Black polymer $689.00
Price: Kadet conversion kit $412.00

CZ 83 DOUBLE-ACTION PISTOL
Caliber: 32 ACP, 380 ACP, 12-shot magazine. **Barrel:** 3.8". **Weight:** 26.2 oz. **Length:** 6.8" overall. **Grips:** High impact checkered plastic. **Sights:** Removable square post front, rear adjustable for windage; 3-dot system. **Features:** Single action/double action; ambidextrous magazine release and safety. Blue finish; non-glare ribbed slide top. Imported from the Czech Republic by CZ-USA.
Price: Glossy blue, 32 ACP or 380 ACP $495.00
Price: Satin Nickel $522.00

CZ 97 B AUTO PISTOL
Caliber: 45 ACP, 10-shot magazine. **Barrel:** 4.85". **Weight:** 40 oz. **Length:** 8.34" overall. **Grips:** Checkered walnut. **Sights:** Fixed. **Features:** Single action/double action; full-length slide rails; screw-in barrel bushing; linkless barrel; all-steel construction; chamber loaded indicator; dual transfer bars. Introduced 1999. Imported from the Czech Republic by CZ-USA.
Price: Black polymer $779.00
Price: Glossy blue $799.00

Dan Wesson Pointman

Dan Wesson DW RZ-10

Desert Baby Eagle

EAA Witness

Desert Eagle Mark XIX

CZ 97 BD Decocker
Similar to the CZ 97 B except has a decocking lever in place of the safety lever. Tritium night sights. Rubber grips. All other specifications are the same. Introduced 1999. Imported from the Czech Republic by CZ-USA.
Price: 9mm Para., black polymer $874.00

CZ 2075 RAMI/RAMI P AUTO PISTOL
Caliber: 9mm Para., 40 S&W. **Barrel:** 3". **Weight:** 25 oz. **Length:** 6.5" overall. **Grips:** Rubber. **Sights:** Blade front with dot, white outline rear drift adjustable for windage. **Features:** Single-action/double-action; alloy or polymer frame, steel slide; has laser sight mount. Imported from the Czech Republic by CZ-USA.
Price: 9mm Para., alloy frame, 10 and 14-shot magazines . . .$671.00
Price: 40 S&W, alloy frame, 8-shot magazine $671.00
Price: RAMI P, polymer frame, 9mm Para., 40 S&W $612.00

CZ P-01 AUTO PISTOL
Caliber: 9mm Para., 14-shot magazine. **Barrel:** 3.85". **Weight:** 27 oz. **Length:** 7.2" overall. **Grips:** Checkered rubber. **Sights:** Blade front with dot, white outline rear drift adjustable for windage. **Features:** Based on the CZ 75, except with forged aircraft-grade aluminum alloy frame. Hammer forged barrel, decocker, firing-pin block, M3 rail, dual slide serrations, squared trigger guard, re-contoured trigger, lanyard loop on butt. Serrated front and back strap. Introduced 2006. Imported from the Czech Republic by CZ-USA.
Price: CZ P-01 . . . .$672.00

DAN WESSON FIREARMS POINTMAN SEVEN AUTO PISTOL
Caliber: 10mm, 40 S&W, 45 ACP. **Barrel:** 5". **Grips:** Diamond checkered cocobolo. **Sights:** Bo-Mar style adjustable target sight. **Weight:** 38 oz. **Features:** Stainless-steel frame and serrated slide. Series 70-style 1911, stainless-steel frame, forged stainless-steel slide. One-piece match-grade barrel and bushing. 20-LPI checkered mainspring housing, front and rear slide cocking serrations, beveled magwell, dehorned by hand. Lowered and flared ejection port, Ed Brown slide stop and memory groove grip safety, tactical extended thumb safety. Commander-style match hammer, match grade sear, aluminum trigger with stainless bow, Wolff springs. Introduced 2000. Made in U.S.A. by Dan Wesson Firearms, distributed by CZ-USA.
Price: 45 ACP, 7+1 . . . .$1,158.00
Price: 10mm, 8+1 . . . .$1,191.00
Price: 40 S&W, stainless $1,189.00
Price: 45 ACP, Desert Tan $1,269.00

Dan Wesson Commander Classic Bobtail Auto Pistols
Similar to Pointman Seven, a Commander-sized frame with 4.25" barrel. Available with stainless finish, fixed night sights. Introduced 2005.

Made in U.S.A. by Dan Wesson Firearms, distributed by CZ-USA.
Price: 45 ACP, 7+1, 33 oz. $1,191.00
Price: 10mm, 8+1, 33 oz., stainless $1,224.00
Price: 10mm, 33 oz. two-tone $1,530.00

DAN WESSON DW RZ-10 AUTO PISTOL
Caliber: 10mm, 9-shot. **Barrel:** 5". **Grips:** Diamond checkered cocobolo. **Sights:** Bo-Mar style adjustable target sight. **Weight:** 38.3 oz. **Length:** 8.8" overall. **Features:** Stainless-steel frame and serrated slide. Series 70-style 1911, stainless-steel frame, forged stainless-steel slide. Commander-style match hammer. Reintroduced 2005. Made in U.S.A. by Dan Wesson Firearms, distributed by CZ-USA.
Price: 10mm, 8+1 . . . .$1,191.00

Dan Wesson DW RZ-10 Sportsman
Similar to the RZ-10 Auto except with 8-shot magazine. Weighs 36 oz., length is 8.8" overall.
Price: $1,448.00

Dan Wesson DW RZ-45 Heritage
Similar to the RZ-10 Auto except in 45 ACP with 7-shot magazine. Weighs 36 oz., length is 8.8" overall.
Price: 10mm, 8+1 . . . .$1,141.00

DESERT EAGLE MARK XIX PISTOL
Caliber: 357 Mag., 9-shot; 44 Mag., 8-shot; 50 AE, 7-shot. **Barrel:** 6", 10", interchangeable. **Weight:** 357 Mag.-62 oz.; 44 Mag.-69 oz.; 50 AE-72 oz. **Length:** 10.25" overall (6" bbl.). **Grips:** Polymer; rubber available. **Sights:** Blade on ramp front, combat-style rear. Adjustable available. **Features:** Interchangeable barrels; rotating three-lug bolt; ambidextrous safety; adjustable trigger. Military epoxy finish. Satin, bright nickel, chrome, brushed, matte or black-oxide finishes available. 10" barrel extra. Imported from Israel by Magnum Research, Inc.
Price: Black-6, 6" barrel $1,475.00
Price: Black-10, 10" barrel $1,575.00
Price: Component System Package, 3 barrels,
carrying case, from $2,801.00

DESERT BABY MICRO DESERT EAGLE PISTOL
Caliber: 380 ACP, 6-rounds. **Barrel:** 2.22". **Weight:** 14 oz. **Length:** 4.52" overall. **Grips:** NA. **Sights:** Fixed low-profile. **Features:** Small-frame DAO pocket pistol. Steel slide, aluminum alloy frame, nickel-teflon finish.
Price: $535.00

DESERT BABY EAGLE PISTOLS
Caliber: 9mm Para., 40 S&W, 45 ACP, 10- or 15-round magazines. **Barrel:** 3.64", 3.93", 4.52". **Weight:** 26.8 to 39.8 oz. **Length:** 7.25" to 8.25" overall. **Grips:** Polymer. **Sights:** Drift-adjustable rear, blade front. **Features:** Steel frame and slide; slide safety; decocker. Reintroduced in 1999. Imported from Israel by Magnum Research, Inc.
Price: $619.00

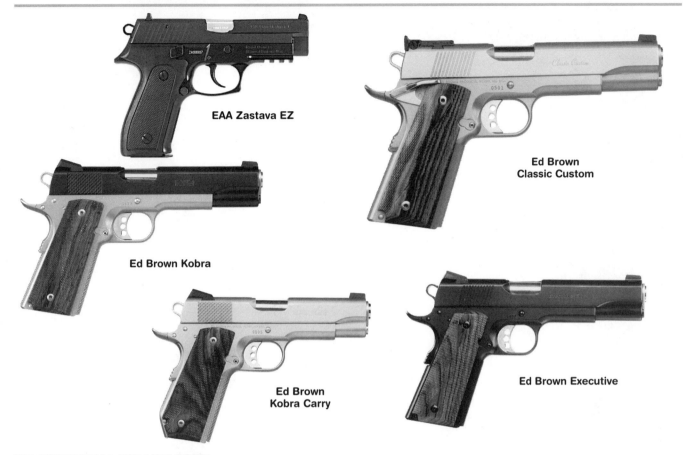

EAA Zastava EZ

Ed Brown Classic Custom

Ed Brown Kobra

Ed Brown Kobra Carry

Ed Brown Executive

EAA WITNESS FULL SIZE AUTO PISTOL

Caliber: 9mm Para., 38 Super, 18-shot magazine; 40 S&W, 10mm, 15-shot magazine; 45 ACP, 10-shot magazine. **Barrel:** 4.50". **Weight:** 35.33 oz. **Length:** 8.10" overall. **Grips:** Checkered rubber. **Sights:** Undercut blade front, open rear adjustable for windage. **Features:** Double-action/single-action trigger system; round trigger guard; frame-mounted safety. Introduced 1991. Polymer frame introduced 2005. Imported from Italy by European American Armory.
Price: 9mm Para., 38 Super, 10mm, 40 S&W, 45 ACP, full-size steel
    frame, Wonder finish **$514.00**
Price: 45/22 22 LR, full-size steel frame, blued **$472.00**
Price: 9mm Para., 40 S&W, 45 ACP, full-size polymer frame . **$472.00**

EAA WITNESS COMPACT AUTO PISTOL

Caliber: 9mm Para., 40 S&W, 10mm, 12-shot magazine; 45 ACP, 8-shot magazine. **Barrel:** 3.6". **Weight:** 30 oz. **Length:** 7.3" overall. Otherwise similar to Full Size Witness. Polymer frame introduced 2005. Imported from Italy by European American Armory.
Price: 9mm Para., 10mm, 40 S&W, 45 ACP, steel frame,
    Wonder finish **$514.00**
Price: 9mm Para., 40 S&W, 45 ACP, polymer frame **$472.00**

EAA WITNESS-P CARRY AUTO PISTOL

Caliber: 10mm, 15-shot magazine; 45 ACP, 10-shot magazine. **Barrel:** 3.6". **Weight:** 27 oz. **Length:** 7.5" overall. Otherwise similar to Full Size Witness. Polymer frame introduced 2005. Imported from Italy by European American Armory.
Price: 10mm, 45 ACP, polymer frame, from **$598.00**

EAA ZASTAVA EZ PISTOL

Caliber: 9mm Para., 15-shot magazine; 40 S&W, 11-shot magazine; 45 ACP, 10-shot magazine. **Barrel:** 3.5" or 4." **Weight:** 30-33 oz. **Length:** 7.25" to 7.5" overall. **Features:** Ambidextrous decocker, slide release and magazine release; three dot sight system, aluminum frame, steel slide, accessory rail, full-length claw extractor, loaded chamber indicator. M88 compact has 3.6" barrel, weighs 28 oz. Introduced 2008. Imported by European American Armory.
Price: 9mm Para. or 40 S&W, blued **$547.00**
Price: 9mm Para. or 40 S&W, chromed **$587.00**
Price: 45 ACP, chromed **$587.00**
Price: M88, from **$292.00**

ED BROWN CLASSIC CUSTOM

Caliber: 45 ACP, 7 shot. **Barrel:** 5". **Weight:** 40 oz. **Grips:** Cocobolo wood. **Sights:** Bo-Mar adjustable rear, dovetail front. **Features:** Single-action, M1911 style, custom made to order, stainless frame and slide available. Special mirror-finished slide.
Price: Model CC-BB, blued **$3,155.00**
Price: Model CC-SB, blued and stainless **$3,155.00**
Price: Model CC-SS, stainless **$3,155.00**

ED BROWN KOBRA AND KOBRA CARRY

Caliber: 45 ACP, 7-shot magazine. **Barrel:** 5" (Kobra); 4.25" (Kobra Carry). **Weight:** 39 oz. (Kobra); 34 oz. (Kobra Carry). **Grips:** Hogue exotic wood. **Sights:** Ramp, front; fixed Novak low-mount night sights, rear. **Features:** Has snakeskin pattern serrations on forestrap and mainspring housing, dehorned edges, beavertail grip safety.
Price: Kobra K-BB, blued **$2,195.00**
Price: Kobra K-SB, stainless and blued **$2,195.00**
Price: Kobra K-SS, stainless **$2,195.00**
Price: Kobra Carry blued, blued/stainless, or stainless from **$2,445.00**

Ed Brown Executive Pistols

Similar to other Ed Brown products, but with 25-lpi checkered frame and mainspring housing.
Price: Elite blued, blued/stainless, or stainless, from **$2,395.00**
Price: Carry blued, blued/stainless, or stainless, from **$2,645.00**
Price: Target blued, blued/stainless, or stainless (2006)
    from **$2,595.00**

Ed Brown Special Forces Pistol

Similar to other Ed Brown products, but with ChainLink treatment on forestrap and mainspring housing. Entire gun coated with Gen III finish. "Square cut" serrations on rear of slide only. Dehorned. Introduced 2006.
Price: From **$2,195.00**

Ed Brown Special Forces Carry Pistol

Similar to the Special Forces basic models. Features a 4.25" Commander model slide, single stack commander Bobtail frame. Weighs approx. 35 oz. Fixed dovetail 3-dot night sights with high visibility white outlines.
Price: From **$2,445.00**

Ed Brown Special Forces

Excel Arms Accelerator MP-22

Firestorm 45 Gov't

Glock 17C

Firestorm Mini

Glock 22

Glock 26

EXCEL ARMS ACCELERATOR MP-17/MP-22 PISTOLS

Caliber: 17 HMR, 22 WMR, 9-shot magazine. **Barrel:** 8.5" bull barrel. **Weight:** 54 oz. **Length:** 12.875" overall. **Grips:** Textured black composition. **Sights:** Fully adjustable target sights. **Features:** Made from 17-4 stainless steel, comes with aluminum rib, integral Weaver base, internal hammer, firing-pin block. American made, lifetime warranty. Comes with two 9-round stainless steel magazines and a California-approved cable lock. 22 WMR Introduced 2006. Made in U.S.A. by Excel Arms.
Price: $433.00
Price: Camo finishes (2008) $520.00

FIRESTORM AUTO PISTOLS

Caliber: 22 LR, 32 ACP, 10-shot magazine; 380 ACP, 7-shot magazine; 9mm Para., 40 S&W, 10-shot magazine; 45 ACP, 7-shot magazine. **Barrel:** 3.5". **Weight:** From 23 oz. **Length:** From 6.6" overall. **Grips:** Rubber. **Sights:** 3-dot. **Features:** Double action. Distributed by SGS Importers International.
Price: 22 LR, matte or duotone, from $309.95
Price: 380, matte or duotone, from $311.95
Price: Mini Firestorm 9mm Para., matte, duotone, nickel, from **$395.00**
Price: Mini Firestorm 40 S&W, matte, duotone, nickel, from . .$395.00
Price: Mini Firestorm 45 ACP, matte, duotone, chrome, from .$402.00

GLOCK 17/17C AUTO PISTOL

Caliber: 9mm Para., 17/19/33-shot magazines. **Barrel:** 4.49". **Weight:** 22.04 oz. (without magazine). **Length:** 7.32" overall. **Grips:** Black polymer. **Sights:** Dot on front blade, white outline rear adjustable for windage. **Features:** Polymer frame, steel slide; double-action trigger with "Safe Action" system; mechanical firing pin safety, drop safety; simple takedown without tools; locked breech, recoil operated action. ILS designation refers to Internal Locking System. Adopted by Austrian armed forces 1983. NATO approved 1984. Imported from Austria by Glock, Inc.
Price: Fixed sight $690.00

GLOCK 19/19C AUTO PISTOL

Caliber: 9mm Para., 15/17/19/33-shot magazines. **Barrel:** 4.02". **Weight:** 20.99 oz. (without magazine). **Length:** 6.85" overall. Compact version of Glock 17. Pricing the same as Model 17. Imported from Austria by Glock, Inc.
Price: Fixed sight $699.00
Price: 19C Compensated (fixed sight) $675.00

GLOCK 20/20C 10MM AUTO PISTOL

Caliber: 10mm, 15-shot magazines. **Barrel:** 4.6". **Weight:** 27.68 oz.

(without magazine). **Length:** 7.59" overall. **Features:** Otherwise similar to Model 17. Imported from Austria by Glock, Inc. Introduced 1990.
Price: Fixed sight, from $700.00

GLOCK MODEL 20 SF SHORT FRAME PISTOL

Caliber: 10mm. **Barrel:** 4.61" with hexagonal rifling. **Weight:** 27.51 oz. **Length:** 8.07" overall. **Sights:** Fixed. **Features:** Otherwise similar to Model 20 but with short-frame design, extended sight radius.
Price: **$664.00**

GLOCK 21/21C AUTO PISTOL

Caliber: 45 ACP, 13-shot magazines. **Barrel:** 4.6". **Weight:** 26.28 oz. (without magazine). **Length:** 7.59" overall. **Features:** Otherwise similar to Model 17. Imported from Austria by Glock, Inc. Introduced 1991. SF version has tactical rail, smaller diameter grip, 10-round magazine capacity. Introduced 2007.
Price: Fixed sight, from **$700.00**

GLOCK 22/22C AUTO PISTOL

Caliber: 40 S&W, 15/17-shot magazines. **Barrel:** 4.49". **Weight:** 22.92 oz. (without magazine). **Length:** 7.32" overall. **Features:** Otherwise similar to Model 17, including pricing. Imported from Austria by Glock, Inc. Introduced 1990.
Price: Fixed sight, from $641.00

GLOCK 23/23C AUTO PISTOL

Caliber: 40 S&W, 13/15/17-shot magazines. **Barrel:** 4.02". **Weight:** 21.16 oz. (without magazine). **Length:** 6.85" overall. **Features:** Otherwise similar to Model 22, including pricing. Compact version of Glock 22. Imported from Austria by Glock, Inc. Introduced 1990.
Price: Fixed sight $641.00
Price: 23C Compensated (fixed sight) $694.00

GLOCK 26 AUTO PISTOL

Caliber: 9mm Para. 10/12/15/17/19/33-shot magazines. **Barrel:** 3.46". **Weight:** 19.75 oz. **Length:** 6.29" overall. Subcompact version of Glock 17. Pricing the same as Model 17. Imported from Austria by Glock, Inc.
Price: Fixed sight $690.00

Glock 35

Glock 30

Glock 31

Heckler & Koch
USP45

Heckler & Koch
USP Compact

GLOCK 27 AUTO PISTOL
Caliber: 40 S&W, 9/11/13/15/17-shot magazines. **Barrel:** 3.46". **Weight:** 19.75 oz. (without magazine). **Length:** 6.29" overall. **Features:** Otherwise similar to Model 22, including pricing. Subcompact version of Glock 22. Imported from Austria by Glock, Inc. Introduced 1996.
Price: Fixed sight **$750.00**

GLOCK 29 AUTO PISTOL
Caliber: 10mm, 10/15-shot magazines. **Barrel:** 3.78". **Weight:** 24.69 oz. (without magazine). **Length:** 6.77" overall. **Features:** Otherwise similar to Model 20, including pricing. Subcompact version of Glock 20. Imported from Austria by Glock, Inc. Introduced 1997.
Price: Fixed sight **$672.00**

GLOCK MODEL 29 SF SHORT FRAME PISTOL
Caliber: 10mm. **Barrel:** 3.78" with hexagonal rifling. **Weight:** 24.52 oz. **Length:** 6.97" overall. **Sights:** Fixed. **Features:** Otherwise similar to Model 29 but with short-frame design, extended sight radius.
Price: **$660.00**

GLOCK 30 AUTO PISTOL
Caliber: 45 ACP, 9/10/13-shot magazines. **Barrel:** 3.78". **Weight:** 23.99 oz. (without magazine). **Length:** 6.77" overall. **Features:** Otherwise similar to Model 21, including pricing. Subcompact version of Glock 21. Imported from Austria by Glock, Inc. Introduced 1997. SF version has tactical rail, octagonal rifled barrel with a 1:15.75 rate of twist, smaller diameter grip, 10-round magazine capacity. Introduced 2008
Price: Fixed sight **$700.00**

GLOCK 31/31C AUTO PISTOL
Caliber: 357 Auto, 15/17-shot magazines. **Barrel:** 4.49". **Weight:** 23.28 oz. (without magazine). **Length:** 7.32" overall. **Features:** Otherwise similar to Model 17. Imported from Austria by Glock, Inc.
Price: Fixed sight, from **$641.00**

GLOCK 32/32C AUTO PISTOL
Caliber: 357 Auto, 13/15/17-shot magazines. **Barrel:** 4.02". **Weight:** 21.52 oz. (without magazine). **Length:** 6.85" overall. **Features:** Otherwise similar to Model 31. Compact. Imported from Austria by Glock, Inc.
Price: Fixed sight **$669.00**

GLOCK 33 AUTO PISTOL
Caliber: 357 Auto, 9/11/13/15/17-shot magazines. **Barrel:** 3.46". **Weight:** 19.75 oz. (without magazine). **Length:** 6.29" overall. **Features:** Otherwise similar to Model 31. Subcompact. Imported from Austria by Glock, Inc.
Price: Fixed sight, from **$641.00**

GLOCK 34 AUTO PISTOL
Caliber: 9mm Para. 17/19/33-shot magazines. **Barrel:** 5.32". **Weight:** 22.9 oz. **Length:** 8.15" overall. Competition version of Glock 17 with extended barrel, slide, and sight radius dimensions. Imported from Austria by Glock, Inc.
Price: Adjustable sight, from **$648.00**

GLOCK 35 AUTO PISTOL
Caliber: 40 S&W, 15/17-shot magazines. **Barrel:** 5.32". **Weight:** 24.52 oz. (without magazine). **Length:** 8.15" overall. **Features:** Otherwise similar to Model 22. Competition version of Glock 22 with extended barrel, slide, and sight radius dimensions. Imported from Austria by Glock, Inc. Introduced 1996.
Price: Adjustable sight **$648.00**

GLOCK 36 AUTO PISTOL
Caliber: 45 ACP, 6-shot magazines. **Barrel:** 3.78". **Weight:** 20.11 oz. (without magazine). **Length:** 6.77" overall. **Features:** Single-stack magazine, slimmer grip than Glock 21/30. Subcompact. Imported from Austria by Glock, Inc. Introduced 1997.
Price: Adjustable sight **$616.00**

GLOCK 37 AUTO PISTOL
Caliber: 45 GAP, 10-shot magazines. **Barrel:** 4.49". **Weight:** 25.95 oz. (without magazine). **Length:** 7.32" overall. **Features:** Otherwise similar to Model 17. Imported from Austria by Glock, Inc. Introduced 2005.
Price: Fixed sight, from **$562.00**

GLOCK 38 AUTO PISTOL
Caliber: 45 GAP, 8/10-shot magazines. **Barrel:** 4.02". **Weight:** 24.16 oz. (without magazine). **Length:** 6.85" overall. **Features:** Otherwise similar to Model 37. Compact. Imported from Austria by Glock, Inc.
Price: Fixed sight **$614.00**

GLOCK 39 AUTO PISTOL
Caliber: 45 GAP, 6/8/10-shot magazines. **Barrel:** 3.46". **Weight:** 19.33 oz. (without magazine). **Length:** 6.3" overall. **Features:** Otherwise similar to Model 37. Subcompact. Imported from Austria by Glock, Inc.
Price: Fixed sight **$614.00**

HECKLER & KOCH USP AUTO PISTOL
Caliber: 9mm Para., 15-shot magazine; 40 S&W, 13-shot magazine; 45 ACP, 12-shot magazine. **Barrel:** 4.25-4.41". **Weight:** 1.65 lbs. **Length:** 7.64-7.87" overall. **Grips:** Non-slip stippled black polymer. **Sights:** Blade front, rear adjustable for windage. **Features:** New HK design with polymer frame, modified Browning action with recoil reduction system, single control lever. Special "hostile environment" finish on all metal parts. Available in SA/DA, DAO, left- and right-hand versions. Introduced 1993. 45 ACP Introduced 1995. Imported from Germany by Heckler & Koch, Inc.
Price: USP 45 . . . . **$919.00**
Price: USP 40 and USP 9mm **$859.00**

**Heckler & Koch
USP45 Compact**

**Heckler & Koch
USP45 Tactical**

**Heckler & Koch Mark
23 Special Operations**

Hi-Point C-9

HECKLER & KOCH USP COMPACT AUTO PISTOL

Caliber: 9mm Para., 13-shot magazine; 40 S&W and .357 SIG, 12-shot magazine; 45 ACP, 8-shot magazine. Similar to the USP except the 9mm Para., 357 SIG, and 40 S&W have 3.58" barrels, measure 6.81" overall, and weigh 1.47 lbs. (9mm Para.). Introduced 1996. 45 ACP measures 7.09" overall. Introduced 1998. Imported from Germany by Heckler & Koch, Inc.
Price: USP Compact 45 . . . .**$959.00**
Price: USP Compact 9mm Para., 40 S&W **$879.00**

HECKLER & KOCH USP45 TACTICAL PISTOL

Caliber: 40 S&W, 13-shot magazine; 45 ACP, 12-shot magazine. **Barrel:** 4.90-5.09". **Weight:** 1.9 lbs. **Length:** 8.64" overall. **Grips:** Non-slip stippled polymer. **Sights:** Blade front, fully adjustable target rear. **Features:** Has extended threaded barrel with rubber O-ring; adjustable trigger; extended magazine floorplate; adjustable trigger stop; polymer frame. Introduced 1998. Imported from Germany by Heckler & Koch, Inc.
Price: USP Tactical 45 . . . .**$1,239.00**
Price: USP Tactical 40 . . . .**$1,179.00**

HECKLER & KOCH USP COMPACT TACTICAL PISTOL

Caliber: 45 ACP, 8-shot magazine. Similar to the USP Tactical except measures 7.72" overall, weighs 1.72 lbs. Introduced 2006. Imported from Germany by Heckler & Koch, Inc.
Price: USP Compact Tactical **$1,179.00**

HECKLER & KOCH MARK 23 SPECIAL OPERATIONS PISTOL

Caliber: 45 ACP, 12-shot magazine. **Barrel:** 5.87". **Weight:** 2.42 lbs. **Length:** 9.65" overall. **Grips:** Integral with frame; black polymer. **Sights:** Blade front, rear drift adjustable for windage; 3-dot. **Features:** Civilian version of the SOCOM pistol. Polymer frame; double action; exposed hammer; short recoil, modified Browning action. Introduced 1996. Imported from Germany by Heckler & Koch, Inc.
Price: **$2,139.00**

HECKLER & KOCH P2000 AUTO PISTOL

Caliber: 9mm Para., 13-shot magazine; 40 S&W and .357 SIG, 12-shot magazine. **Barrel:** 3.62". **Weight:** 1.5 lbs. **Length:** 7" overall. **Grips:** Interchangeable panels. **Sights:** Fixed Patridge style, drift adjustable for windage, standard 3-dot. **Features:** Incorporates features of HK USP Compact pistol, including Law Enforcement Modification (LEM) trigger, double-action hammer system, ambidextrous magazine release, dual slide-release levers, accessory mounting rails, recurved, hook trigger guard, fiber-reinforced polymer frame, modular grip with exchangeable back straps, nitro-carburized finish, lock-out safety device. Introduced 2003. Imported from Germany by Heckler & Koch, Inc.
Price: **$879.00**
Price: P2000 LEM DAO, 357 SIG, intr. 2006 . . . .**$879.00**
Price: P2000 SA/DA, 357 SIG, intr. 2006 . . . .**$879.00**

HECKLER & KOCH P2000 SK AUTO PISTOL

Caliber: 9mm Para., 10-shot magazine; 40 S&W and .357 SIG, 9-shot magazine. **Barrel:** 3.27". **Weight:** 1.3 lbs. **Length:** 6.42" overall. **Sights:** Fixed Patridge style, drift adjustable. **Features:** Standard accessory rails, ambidextrous slide release, polymer frame, polygonal bore profile. Smaller version of P2000. Introduced 2005. Imported from Germany by Heckler & Koch, Inc.
Price: **$919.00**

HI-POINT FIREARMS MODEL 9MM COMPACT PISTOL

Caliber: 9mm Para., 8-shot magazine. **Barrel:** 3.5". **Weight:** 25 oz.

Length: 6.75" overall. **Grips:** Textured plastic. **Sights:** Combat-style adjustable 3-dot system; low profile. **Features:** Single-action design; frame-mounted magazine release; polymer frame. Scratch-resistant matte finish. Introduced 1993. Comps are similar except they have a 4" barrel with muzzle brake/compensator. Compensator is slotted for laser or flashlight mounting. Introduced 1998. Made in U.S.A. by MKS Supply, Inc.
Price: C-9 9mm **$155.00**

Hi-Point Firearms Model 380 Polymer Pistol

Similar to the 9mm Compact model except chambered for 380 ACP, 8-shot magazine, adjustable 3-dot sights. Weighs 25 oz. Polymer frame. Action locks open after last shot. Includes 10-shot and 8-shot magazine; trigger lock. Introduced 1998. Comps are similar except they have a 4" barrel with muzzle compensator. Introduced 2001. Made in U.S.A. by MKS Supply, Inc.
Price: CF-380 . . . .**$135.00**

HI-POINT FIREARMS 40SW/POLY AND 45 AUTO PISTOLS

Caliber: 40 S&W, 8-shot magazine; 45 ACP (9-shot). **Barrel:** 4.5". **Weight:** 32 oz. **Length:** 7.72" overall. **Sights:** Adjustable 3-dot. **Features:** Polymer frames, last round lock-open, grip mounted magazine release, magazine disconnect safety, integrated accessory rail, trigger lock. Introduced 2002. Made in U.S.A. by MKS Supply, Inc.
Price: 40SW-B **$186.00**
Price: 45 ACP **$186.00**

HIGH STANDARD VICTOR 22 PISTOL

Caliber: 22 Long Rifle (10 rounds) or .22 Short (5 rounds). **Barrel:** 4.5"-5.5". **Weight:** 45 oz.-46 oz. **Length:** 8.5"-9.5" overall. **Grips:** Freestyle wood. **Sights:** Frame mounted, adjustable. **Features:** Semi-auto with drilled and tapped barrel, tu-tone or blued finish.
Price: **$845.00**

High Standard 10X Custom 22 Pistol

Similar to the Victor model but with precision fitting, black wood grips, 5.5" barrel only. High Standard Universal Mount, 10-shot magazine, barrel drilled and tapped, certificate of authenticity. Overall length is 9.5". Weighs 44 oz. to 46 oz. From High Standard Custom Shop.
Price: **$1,095.00**

HIGH STANDARD SUPERMATIC TROPHY 22 PISTOL

Caliber: 22 Long Rifle (10 rounds) or .22 Short (5 rounds/Citation version), not interchangable. **Barrel:** 5.5", 7.25". **Weight:** 44 oz., 46 oz. **Length:** 9.5", 11.25" overall. **Grips:** Wood. **Sights:** Adjustable. **Features:** Semi-auto with drilled and tapped barrel, tu-tone or blued finish with gold accents.
Price: 5.5" **$845.00**

Kahr K9094C

Kahr M9093

Kahr PM4543

Kahr KT9093-Novak

Kahr TP4543

High Standard Olympic Military 22 Pistol
Similar to the Supermatic Trophy model but in 22 Short only with 5.5" bull barrel, five-round magazine, aluminum alloy frame, adjustable sights. Overall length is 9.5", weighs 42 oz.
Price: **$875.00**

High Standard Supermatic Citation Series 22 Pistol
Similar to the Supermatic Trophy model but with heavier trigger pull, 10" barrel, and nickel accents. 22 Short conversion unit available. Overall length 14.5", weighs 52 oz.
Price: **$895.00**

HIGH STANDARD SUPERMATIC TOURNAMENT 22 PISTOL
Caliber: 22 LR. **Barrel:** 5.5" bull barrel. **Weight:** 44 oz. **Length:** 9.5" overall. **Features:** Limited edition; similar to High Standard Victor model but with rear sight mounted directly to slide.
Price: **$835.00**

HIGH STANDARD SPORT KING 22 PISTOL
Caliber: 22 LR. **Barrel:** 4.5" or 6.75" tapered barrel. **Weight:** 40 oz. to 42 oz. **Length:** 8.5" to 10.75". **Features:** Sport version of High Standard Supermatic. Two-tone finish, fixed sights.
Price: **$725.00**

KAHR K SERIES AUTO PISTOLS
Caliber: K9: 9mm Para., 7-shot; K40: 40 S&W, 6-shot magazine. **Barrel:** 3.5". **Weight:** 25 oz. **Length:** 6" overall. **Grips:** Wraparound textured soft polymer. **Sights:** Blade front, rear drift adjustable for windage; bar-dot combat style. **Features:** Trigger-cocking double-action mechanism with passive firing pin block. Made of 4140 ordnance steel with matte black finish. Contact maker for complete price list. Introduced 1994. Made in U.S.A. by Kahr Arms.
Price: K9093C K9, matte stainless steel **$855.00**
Price: K9093NC K9, matte stainless steel w/tritium
night sights **$985.00**
Price: K9094C K9 matte blackened stainless steel **$891.00**
Price: K9098 K9 Elite 2003, stainless steel **$932.00**
Price: K4043 K40, matte stainless steel **$855.00**
Price: K4043N K40, matte stainless steel w/tritium
night sights **$985.00**
Price: K4044 K40, matte blackened stainless steel **$891.00**
Price: K4048 K40 Elite 2003, stainless steel **$932.00**

Kahr MK Series Micro Pistols
Similar to the K9/K40 except is 5.35" overall, 4" high, with a 3.08" barrel. Weighs 23.1 oz. Has snag-free bar-dot sights, polished feed ramp, dual recoil spring system, DA-only trigger. Comes with 5-round flush baseplate and 6-shot grip extension magazine. Introduced 1998. Made in U.S.A. by Kahr Arms.
Price: M9093 MK9, matte stainless steel **$855.00**
Price: M9093N MK9, matte stainless steel, tritium
night sights **$958.00**
Price: M9098 MK9 Elite 2003, stainless steel **$932.00**
Price: M4043 MK40, matte stainless steel **$855.00**
Price: M4043N MK40, matte stainless steel, tritium
night sights **$958.00**
Price: M4048 MK40 Elite 2003, stainless steel **$932.00**

KAHR P SERIES PISTOLS
Caliber: 380 ACP, 9x19, 40 S&W, 45 ACP. Similar to K9/K40 steel frame pistol except has polymer frame, matte stainless steel slide. Barrel length 3.5"; overall length 5.8"; weighs 17 oz. Includes two 7-shot magazines, hard polymer case, trigger lock. Introduced 2000. Made in U.S.A. by Kahr Arms.

Price: KP9093 9mm Para. **$739.00**
Price: KP4043 40 S&W **$739.00**
Price: KP4543 45 ACP.............................**$805.00**
Price: KP3833 380 ACP (2008) **$649.00**

KAHR PM SERIES PISTOLS
Caliber: 9x19, 40 S&W, 45 ACP. Similar to P-Series pistols except has smaller polymer frame (Polymer Micro). Barrel length 3.08"; overall length 5.35"; weighs 17 oz. Includes two 7-shot magazines, hard polymer case, trigger lock. Introduced 2000. Made in U.S.A. by Kahr Arms.
Price: PM9093 PM9 ....**$786.00**
Price: PM4043 PM40 ....**$786.00**
Price: PM4543 (2007) **$855.00**

KAHR T SERIES PISTOLS
Caliber: T9: 9mm Para., 8-shot magazine; T40: 40 S&W, 7-shot magazine. **Barrel:** 4". **Weight:** 28.1-29.1 oz. **Length:** 6.5" overall. **Grips:** Checkered Hogue Pau Ferro wood grips. **Sights:** Rear: Novak low profile 2-dot tritium night sight, front tritium night sight. **Features:** Similar to other Kahr makes, but with longer slide and barrel upper, longer butt. Trigger cocking DAO; lock breech; "Browning-type" recoil lug; passive striker block; no magazine disconnect. Comes with two magazines. Introduced 2004. Made in U.S.A. by Kahr Arms.
Price: KT9093 T9 matte stainless steel **$831.00**
Price: KT9093-NOVAK T9, "Tactical 9," Novak night sight ...**$968.00**
Price: KT4043 40 S&W...............................**$831.00**

KAHR TP SERIES PISTOLS
Caliber: TP9: 9mm Para., 7-shot magazine; TP40: 40 S&W, 6-shot magazine. Barrel: 4". **Weight:** 19.1-20.1 oz. **Length:** 6.5-6.7" overall. **Grips:** Textured polymer. Similar to T-series guns, but with polymer frame, matte stainless steel slide. Comes with two magazines. TP40s introduced 2006. Made in U.S.A. by Kahr Arms.
Price: TP9093 TP9 ....**$697.00**
Price: TP9093-Novak TP9 (Novak night sights)...........**$838.00**
Price: TP4043 TP40 ....**$697.00**
Price: TP4043-Novak (Novak night sights) **$838.00**
Price: TP4543 (2007) **$697.00**
Price: TP4543-Novak (4.04 barrel, Novak night sights) **$838.00**

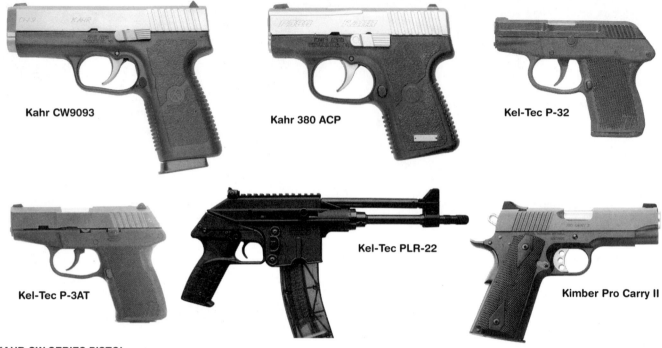

Kahr CW9093

Kahr 380 ACP

Kel-Tec P-32

Kel-Tec P-3AT

Kel-Tec PLR-22

Kimber Pro Carry II

KAHR CW SERIES PISTOL
Caliber: 9mm Para., 7-shot magazine; 40 S&W and 45 ACP, 6-shot magazine. **Barrel:** 3.5-3.64". **Weight:** 17.7-18.7 oz. **Length:** 5.9-6.36" overall. **Grips:** Textured polymer. Similar to P-Series, but CW Series have conventional rifling, metal-injection-molded slide stop lever, no front dovetail cut, one magazine. CW40 introduced 2006. Made in U.S.A. by Kahr Arms.
Price: CW9093 CW9 . . . .**$549.00**
Price: CW4043 CW40 . . . .**$549.00**
Price: CW4543 45 ACP (2008) **$606.00**

KAHR 380 ACP PISTOL
Caliber: 380 ACP, 6+1. **Barrel:** 2.5" Lothar Walther. **Weight:** 11.3 oz. **Length:** 4.9" overall. **Features:** DAO semi-auto with black polymer frame and grips, stainless steel slide.
Price: **$649.00**

KEL-TEC P-11 AUTO PISTOL
Caliber: 9mm Para., 10-shot magazine. **Barrel:** 3.1". **Weight:** 14 oz. **Length:** 5.6" overall. **Grips:** Checkered black polymer. **Sights:** Blade front, rear adjustable for windage. **Features:** Ordnance steel slide, aluminum frame. Double-action-only trigger mechanism. Introduced 1995. Made in U.S.A. by Kel-Tec CNC Industries, Inc.
Price: From **$333.00**

KEL-TEC PF-9 PISTOL
Caliber: 9mm Para.; 7 rounds. **Weight:** 12.7 oz. **Sights:** Rear sight adjustable for windage and elevation. **Barrel Length:** 3.1". **Length:** 5.85". **Features:** Barrel, locking system, slide stop, assembly pin, front sight, recoil springs and guide rod adapted from P-11. Trigger system with integral hammer block and the extraction system adapted from P-3AT. MIL-STD-1913 Picatinny rail. Made in U.S.A. by Kel-Tec CNC Industries, Inc.
Price: From **$333.00**

KEL-TEC P-32 AUTO PISTOL
Caliber: 32 ACP, 7-shot magazine. **Barrel:** 2.68". **Weight:** 6.6 oz. **Length:** 5.07" overall. **Grips:** Checkered composite. **Sights:** Fixed. **Features:** Double-action-only mechanism with 6-lb. pull; internal slide stop. Textured composite grip/frame. Now available in 380 ACP. Made in U.S.A. by Kel-Tec CNC Industries, Inc.
Price: From **$318.00**

KEL-TEC P-3AT PISTOL
Caliber: 380 ACP; 7-rounds. **Weight:** 7.2 oz. **Length:** 5.2". **Features:** Lightest 380 ACP made; aluminum frame, steel barrel.
Price: From **$324.00**

KEL-TEC PLR-16 PISTOL
Caliber: 5.56mm NATO; 10-round magazine. **Weight:** 51 oz. **Sights:** Rear sight adjustable for windage, front sight is M-16 blade. **Barrel Length:** 9.2". **Length:** 18.5". **Features:** Muzzle is threaded 1/2"-28 to accept standard attachments such as a muzzle brake. Except for the barrel, bolt, sights, and mechanism, the PLR-16 pistol is made of high-impact glass fiber reinforced polymer. Gas-operated semi-auto. Conventional gas-piston operation with M-16 breech locking system. MIL-STD-1913 Picatinny rail. Made in U.S.A. by Kel-Tec CNC Industries, Inc.
Price: Blued **$665.00**

Kel-Tec PLR-22 Pistol
Semi-auto pistol chambered in 22 LR; based on centerfire PLR-16 by same maker. Blowback action, 26-round magazine. Open sights and picatinny rail for mounting accessories; threaded muzzle. Overall length is 18.5", weighs 40 oz.
Price: **$390.00**

KIMBER CUSTOM II AUTO PISTOL
Caliber: 45 ACP. **Barrel:** 5". **Weight:** 38 oz. **Length:** 8.7" overall. **Grips:** Checkered black rubber, walnut, rosewood. **Sights:** Dovetailed front and rear, Kimber low profile adj. or fixed sights. **Features:** Slide, frame and barrel machined from steel or stainless steel. Match grade barrel, chamber and trigger group. Extended thumb safety, beveled magazine well, beveled front and rear slide serrations, high ride beavertail grip safety, checkered flat mainspring housing, kidney cut under trigger guard, high cut grip, match grade stainless steel barrel bushing, polished breech face, Commander-style hammer, lowered and flared ejection port, Wolff springs, bead blasted black oxide or matte stainless finish. Introduced in 1996. Made in U.S.A. by Kimber Mfg., Inc.
Price: Custom II **$828.00**
Price: Custom II Walnut (double-diamond
    walnut grips) **$872.00**

Kimber Stainless II Auto Pistols
Similar to Custom II except has stainless steel frame. 9mm Para. chambering and 45 ACP with night sights introduced 2008. Also chambered in 38 Super. Target version also chambered in 10mm.
Price: Stainless II 45 ACP **$964.00**
Price: Stainless II 9mm Para. (2008) **$983.00**
Price: Stainless II 45 ACP w/night sights (2008) **$1,092.00**
Price: Stainless II Target 45 ACP (stainless, adj. sight) **$942.00**

Kimber Pro Carry II Auto Pistol
Similar to Custom II, has aluminum frame, 4" bull barrel fitted directly to the slide without bushing. Introduced 1998. Made in U.S.A. by Kimber Mfg., Inc.
Price: Pro Carry II, 45 ACP **$888.00**
Price: Pro Carry II, 9mm **$929.00**
Price: Pro Carry II w/night sights **$997.00**

Kimber Ultra Carry II

Kimber Gold Match II

Kimber CDP II

Kimber Eclipse II

Kimber Eclipse Pro II

Korth Auto Pistol

Kimber Compact Stainless II Auto Pistol
Similar to Pro Carry II except has stainless steel frame, 4-inch bbl., grip is .400" shorter than standard, no front serrations. Weighs 34 oz. 45 ACP only. Introduced in 1998. Made in U.S.A. by Kimber Mfg., Inc.
Price: **$1,009.00**

Kimber Ultra Carry II Auto Pistol
Lightweight aluminum frame, 3" match grade bull barrel fitted to slide without bushing. Grips .4" shorter. Low effort recoil. Weighs 25 oz. Introduced in 1999. Made in U.S.A. by Kimber Mfg., Inc.
Price: Stainless Ultra Carry II 45 ACP **$980.00**
Price: Stainless Ultra Carry II 9mm Para. (2008) **$1,021.00**
Price: Stainless Ultra Carry II 45 ACP with night sights (2008) **$1,089.00**

Kimber Gold Match II Auto Pistol
Similar to Custom II models. Includes stainless steel barrel with match grade chamber, ambidextrous thumb safety, adjustable sight, premium aluminum trigger, hand-checkered double diamond rosewood grips. Barrel hand-fitted for target accuracy. Made in U.S.A. by Kimber Mfg., Inc.
Price: Gold Match II **$1,345.00**
Price: Gold Match Stainless II 45 ACP **$1,519.00**
Price: Gold Match Stainless II 9mm Para. (2008) **$1,563.00**

Kimber Team Match II Auto Pistol
Similar to Gold Match II. Identical to pistol used by U.S.A. Shooting Rapid Fire Pistol Team, available in 45 ACP and 38 Super. Standard features include 30 lines-per-inch front strap extended and beveled magazine well, red, white and blue Team logo grips. Introduced 2008.
Price: 45 ACP.................................... **$1,539.00**
Price: 9mm...................................... **$1,546.00**

Kimber CDP II Series Auto Pistol
Similar to Custom II, but designed for concealed carry. Aluminum frame. Standard features include stainless steel slide, fixed Meprolight tritium 3-dot (green) dovetail-mounted night sights, match grade barrel and chamber, 30 LPI front strap checkering, two-tone finish, ambidextrous thumb safety, hand-checkered double diamond rosewood grips. Introduced in 2000. Made in U.S.A. by Kimber Mfg., Inc.
Price: Ultra CDP II 9mm Para. (2008) **$1,359.00**
Price: Ultra CDP II 45 ACP **$1,318.00**
Price: Compact CDP II 45 ACP **$1,318.00**
Price: Pro CDP II 45 ACP.......................... **$1,318.00**
Price: Custom CDP II (5" barrel, full length grip) **$1,318.00**

Kimber Eclipse II Series Auto Pistol
Similar to Custom II and other stainless Kimber pistols. Stainless slide and frame, black oxide, two-tone finish. Gray/black laminated grips. 30 lpi front strap checkering. All models have night sights; Target versions have Meprolight adjustable Bar/Dot version. Made in U.S.A. by Kimber Mfg., Inc.

Price: Eclipse Ultra II (3" barrel, short grip) **$1,236.00**
Price: Eclipse Pro II (4" barrel, full length grip) **$1,236.00**
Price: Eclipse Pro Target II (4" barrel, full length grip, adjustable sight) **$1,236.00**
Price: Eclipse Custom II 10mm **$1,291.00**
Price: Eclipse Target II (5" barrel, full length grip, adjustable sight) **$1,345.00**

KIMBER TACTICAL ENTRY II PISTOL
Caliber: 45 ACP, 7-round magazine. **Barrel:** 5". **Weight:** 40 oz. **Length:** 8.7" overall. **Features:** 1911-style semi auto with checkered frontstrap, extended magazine well, night sights, heavy steel frame, tactical rail.
Price: **$1,428.00**

KIMBER TACTICAL CUSTOM HD II PISTOL
Caliber: 45 ACP, 7-round magazine. **Barrel:** 5" match-grade. **Weight:** 39 oz. **Length:** 8.7" overall. **Features:** 1911-style semi auto with night sights, heavy steel frame.
Price: **$1,333.00**

KIMBER SIS AUTO PISTOL
Caliber: 45 ACP, 7-round magazine. **Barrel:** 3", ramped match grade. **Weight:** 31 oz. **Grips:** Stippled black laminate logo grips. **Sights:** SIS fixed tritium Night Sight with cocking shoulder. **Features:** Named for LAPD Special Investigation Section. Stainless-steel slides, frames and serrated mainspring housings. Flat top slide, solid trigger, SIS-pattern slide serrations, black small parts, gray KimPro II finish, black small parts. Bumped and grooved beavertail grip safety, Kimber Service Melt on slide and frame edges, ambidextrous thumb safety, stainless steel KimPro Tac-Mag magazine. Rounded mainspring housing and frame on Ultra version. Introduced 2007. Made in U.S.A. by Kimber Mfg., Inc.
Price: SIS Ultra (2008) **$1,427.00**
Price: SIS Pro (2008) **$1,427.00**
Price: SIS Custom **$1,427.00**
Price: Custom/RL **$1,522.00**

KORTH USA PISTOL SEMI-AUTO
Caliber: 9mm Para., 9x21. **Barrel:** 4", 4.5". **Weight:** 39.9 oz. **Grips:** Walnut, Palisander, Amboinia, Ivory. **Sights:** Fully adjustable. **Features:** DA/SA, 2 models available with either rounded or combat-style trigger guard, recoil-operated, locking block system, forged steel. Available finishes: High polish blue plasma, high polish or matted silver plasma, gray pickled finish, or high polish blue. "Schalldampfer Modell" has special threaded 4.5" barrel and thread protector for a suppressor, many deluxe options available, 10-shot mag. From Korth USA.
Price: From.................................... **$15,000.00**

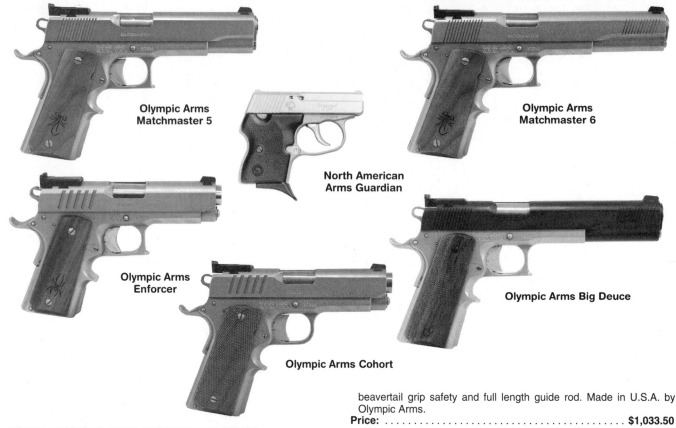

Olympic Arms
Matchmaster 5

North American
Arms Guardian

Olympic Arms
Matchmaster 6

Olympic Arms
Enforcer

Olympic Arms Big Deuce

Olympic Arms Cohort

NORTH AMERICAN ARMS GUARDIAN DAO PISTOL
Caliber: 25 NAA, 32 ACP, 380 ACP, 32 NAA, 6-shot magazine. **Barrel:** 2.49". **Weight:** 20.8 oz. **Length:** 4.75" overall. **Grips:** Black polymer. **Sights:** Low profile fixed. **Features:** Double-action only mechanism. All stainless steel construction. Introduced 1998. Made in U.S.A. by North American Arms.
Price: From **$402.00**

OLYMPIC ARMS MATCHMASTER 5 1911 PISTOL
Caliber: 45 ACP, 7-shot magazine. **Barrel:** 5" stainless steel. **Weight:** 40 oz. **Length:** 8.75" overall. **Grips:** Smooth walnut with laser-etched scorpion icon. **Sights:** Ramped blade, LPA adjustable rear. **Features:** Matched frame and slide, fitted and head-spaced barrel, complete ramp and throat jobs, lowered and widened ejection port, beveled mag well, hand-stoned-to-match hammer and sear, lightweight long-shoe over-travel adjusted trigger, shaped and tensioned extractor, extended thumb safety, wide beavertail grip safety and full-length guide rod. Made in U.S.A. by Olympic Arms, Inc.
Price: **$903.00**

OLYMPIC ARMS MATCHMASTER 6 1911 PISTOL
Caliber: 45 ACP, 7-shot magazine. **Barrel:** 6" stainless steel. **Weight:** 44 oz. **Length:** 9.75" overall. **Grips:** Smooth walnut with laser-etched scorpion icon. **Sights:** Ramped blade, LPA adjustable rear. **Features:** Matched frame and slide, fitted and head-spaced barrel, complete ramp and throat jobs, lowered and widened ejection port, beveled mag well, hand-stoned-to-match hammer and sear, lightweight long-shoe over-travel adjusted trigger, shaped and tensioned extractor, extended thumb safety, wide beavertail grip safety and full length guide rod. Made in U.S.A. by Olympic Arms, Inc.
Price: **$973.00**

OLYMPIC ARMS ENFORCER 1911 PISTOL
Caliber: 45 ACP, 6-shot magazine. **Barrel:** 4" bull stainless steel. **Weight:** 35 oz. **Length:** 7.75" overall. **Grips:** Smooth walnut with etched black widow spider icon. **Sights:** Ramped blade front, LPA adjustable rear. **Features:** Compact Enforcer frame. Bushingless bull barrel with triplex counter-wound self-contained recoil system. Matched frame and slide, fitted and head-spaced barrel, complete ramp and throat jobs, lowered and widened ejection port, beveled mag well, hand-stoned-to-match hammer and sear, lightweight longshoe over-travel adjusted trigger, shaped and tensioned extractor, extended thumb safety, wide

beavertail grip safety and full length guide rod. Made in U.S.A. by Olympic Arms.
Price: **$1,033.50**

OLYMPIC ARMS COHORT PISTOL
Caliber: 45 ACP, 7-shot magazine. **Barrel:** 4" bull stainless steel. **Weight:** 36 oz. **Length:** 7.75" overall. **Grips:** Fully checkered walnut. **Sights:** Ramped blade front, LPA adjustable rear. **Features:** Full size 1911 frame. Bushingless bull barrel with triplex counter-wound self-contained recoil system. Matched frame and slide, fitted and head-spaced barrel, complete ramp and throat jobs, lowered and widened ejection port, beveled mag well, hand-stoned-to-match hammer and sear, lightweight long-shoe over-travel adjusted trigger, shaped and tensioned extractor, extended thumb safety, wide beavertail grip safety and full length guide rod. Made in U.S.A. by Olympic Arms.
Price: **$973.70**

OLYMPIC ARMS BIG DEUCE PISTOL
Caliber: 45 ACP, 7-shot magazine. **Barrel:** 6" stainless steel. **Weight:** 44 oz. **Length:** 9.75" overall. **Grips:** Double diamond checkered exotic cocobolo wood. **Sights:** Ramped blade front, LPA adjustable rear. **Features:** Carbon steel parkerized slide with satin bead blast finish full size frame. Matched frame and slide, fitted and head-spaced barrel, complete ramp and throat jobs, lowered and widened ejection port, beveled mag well, hand-stoned-to-match hammer and sear, lightweight long-shoe over-travel adjusted trigger, shaped and tensioned extractor, extended thumb safety, wide beavertail grip safety and full length guide rod. Made in U.S.A. by Olympic Arms.
Price: **$1,033.50**

OLYMPIC ARMS WESTERNER SERIES 1911 PISTOLS
Caliber: 45 ACP, 7-shot magazine. **Barrel:** 4", 5", 6" stainless steel. **Weight:** 35-43 oz. **Length:** 7.75-9.75" overall. **Grips:** Smooth ivory laser-etched Westerner icon. **Sights:** Ramped blade, LPA adjustable rear. **Features:** Matched frame and slide, fitted and head-spaced barrel, complete ramp and throat jobs, lowered and widened ejection port, beveled mag well, hand-stoned-to-match hammer and sear, lightweight long-shoe over-travel adjusted trigger, shaped and tensioned extractor, extended thumb safety, wide beavertail grip safety and full length guide rod. Entire pistol is fitted and assembled, then disassembled and subjected to the color case hardening process. Made in U.S.A. by Olympic Arms, Inc.
Price: Constable, 4" barrel, 35 oz. **$1,163.50**
Price: Westerner, 5" barrel, 39 oz. **$1,033.50**
Price: Trail Boss, 6" barrel, 43 oz. **$1,103.70**

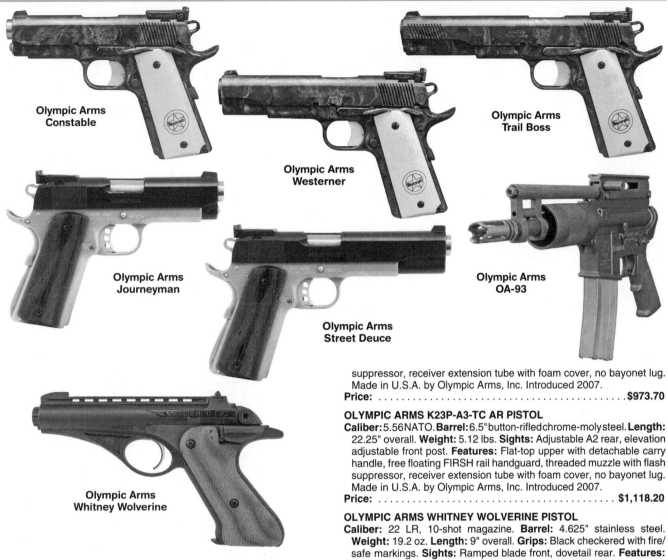

Olympic Arms Constable

Olympic Arms Westerner

Olympic Arms Trail Boss

Olympic Arms Journeyman

Olympic Arms Street Deuce

Olympic Arms OA-93

Olympic Arms Whitney Wolverine

OLYMPIC ARMS SCHUETZEN PISTOL WORKS 1911 PISTOLS

Caliber: 45 ACP, 7-shot magazine. **Barrel:** 4", 5.2", bull stainless steel. **Weight:** 35-38 oz. **Length:** 7.75-8.75" overall. **Grips:** Double diamond checkered exotic cocobolo wood. **Sights:** Ramped blade, LPA adjustable rear. **Features:** Carbon steel parkerized slide with satin bead blast finish full size frame. Matched frame and slide, fitted and head-spaced barrel, complete ramp and throat jobs, lowered and widened ejection port, beveled mag well, hand-stoned-to-match hammer and sear, lightweight long-shoe over-travel adjusted trigger, shaped and tensioned extractor, extended thumb safety, wide beavertail grip safety and full length guide rod. Custom made by Olympic Arms Schuetzen Pistol Works. Parts are hand selected and fitted by expert pistolsmiths. Several no-cost options to choose from. Made in U.S.A. by Olympic Arms Schuetzen Pistol Works.
Price: Journeyman, 4" bull barrel, 35 oz. **$1,293.50**
Price: Street Deuce, 5.2" bull barrel, 38 oz. **$1,293.50**

OLYMPIC ARMS OA-93 AR PISTOL

Caliber: 5.56 NATO. **Barrel:** 6.5" button-rifled stainless steel. **Weight:** 4.46 lbs. **Length:** 17" overall. **Sights:** None. **Features:** Olympic Arms integrated recoil system on the upper receiver eliminates the buttstock, flat top upper, free floating tubular match handguard, threaded muzzle with flash suppressor. Made in U.S.A. by Olympic Arms, Inc.
Price: **$1,202.50**

OLYMPIC ARMS K23P AR PISTOL

Caliber: 5.56 NATO. **Barrel:** 6.5" button-rifled chrome-moly steel. **Length:** 22.25" overall. **Weight:** 5.12 lbs. **Sights:** Adjustable A2 rear, elevation adjustable front post. **Features:** A2 upper with rear sight, free floating tubular match handguard, threaded muzzle with flash

suppressor, receiver extension tube with foam cover, no bayonet lug. Made in U.S.A. by Olympic Arms, Inc. Introduced 2007.
Price: **$973.70**

OLYMPIC ARMS K23P-A3-TC AR PISTOL

Caliber: 5.56 NATO. **Barrel:** 6.5" button-rifled chrome-moly steel. **Length:** 22.25" overall. **Weight:** 5.12 lbs. **Sights:** Adjustable A2 rear, elevation adjustable front post. **Features:** Flat-top upper with detachable carry handle, free floating FIRSH rail handguard, threaded muzzle with flash suppressor, receiver extension tube with foam cover, no bayonet lug. Made in U.S.A. by Olympic Arms, Inc. Introduced 2007.
Price: **$1,118.20**

OLYMPIC ARMS WHITNEY WOLVERINE PISTOL

Caliber: 22 LR, 10-shot magazine. **Barrel:** 4.625" stainless steel. **Weight:** 19.2 oz. **Length:** 9" overall. **Grips:** Black checkered with fire/safe markings. **Sights:** Ramped blade front, dovetail rear. **Features:** Polymer frame with natural ergonomics and ventilated rib. Barrel with 6-groove 1x16 twist rate. All metal magazine shell. Made in U.S.A. by Olympic Arms.
Price: **$291.00**

PARA USA PXT 1911 SINGLE-ACTION SINGLE-STACK AUTO PISTOLS

Caliber: 38 Super, 9mm Para., 45 ACP. **Barrel:** 3.5", 4.25", 5". **Weight:** 28-40 oz. **Length:** 7.1-8.5" overall. **Grips:** Checkered cocobolo, textured composition, Mother of Pearl synthetic. **Sights:** Blade front, low-profile Novak Extreme Duty adjustable rear. High visibility 3-dot system. **Features:** Available with alloy, steel or stainless steel frames. Skeletonized trigger, spurred hammer. Manual thumb, grip and firing pin lock safeties. Full-length guide rod. PXT designates new Para Power Extractor throughout the line. Introduced 2004. Made in U.S.A. by Para USA.
Price: 1911 SSP 9mm Para. (2008) **$959.00**
Price: 1911 SSP 45 ACP (2008) **$959.00**

PARA USA PXT 1911 SINGLE-ACTION HIGH-CAPACITY AUTO PISTOLS

Caliber: 9mm Para., 45 ACP, 10/14/18-shot magazines. **Barrel:** 3", 5". **Weight:** 34-40 oz. **Length:** 7.1-8.5" overall. **Grips:** Textured composition. **Sights:** Blade front, low-profile Novak Extreme Duty adjustable rear or fixed sights. High visibility 3-dot system. **Features:** Available with alloy, steel or stainless steel frames. Skeletonized match trigger, spurred hammer, flared ejection port. Manual thumb, grip and firing pin lock safeties. Full-length guide rod. Introduced 2004. Made in U.S.A. by Para USA.
Price: PXT P14-45 Gun Rights (2008), 14+1, 5" barrel **$1,149.00**
Price: P14-45 (2008), 14+1, 5" barrel **$919.00**

Para Todd Jarrett

Para LDA

Para Warthog

Para Slim-Hawg

Para Nite Hawg

Phoenix Arms HP22

Para USA PXT Limited Pistols

Similar to the PXT-Series pistols except with full-length recoil guide system; fully adjustable rear sight; tuned trigger with over-travel stop; beavertail grip safety; competition hammer; front and rear slide serrations; ambidextrous safety; lowered ejection port; ramped match-grade barrel; dove-tailed front sight. Introduced 2004. Made in U.S.A. by Para USA.
Price: Todd Jarrett 40 S&W, 16+1, stainless **$1,729.00**

Para USA LDA Single-Stack Auto Pistols

Similar to LDA-series with double-action trigger mechanism. Cocobolo and polymer grips. Available in 45 ACP. Introduced 1999. Made in U.S.A. by Para USA.
Price: SSP, 8+1, 5" barrel **$899.00**

Para USA LDA Hi-Capacity Auto Pistols

Similar to LDA-series with double-action trigger mechanism. Polymer grips. Available in 9mm Para., 40 S&W, 45 ACP. Introduced 1999. Made in U.S.A. by Para USA.
Price: High-Cap 45, 14+1 . . . . **$1,279.00**

PARA USA WARTHOG

Caliber: 9mm Para., 45 ACP, 6, 10, or 12-shot magazines. **Barrel:** 3". **Weight:** 24 to 31.5 oz. **Length:** 6.5". **Grips:** Varies by model. **Features:** Single action. Big Hawg (2008) is full-size .45 ACP on lightweight alloy frame, 14+1, match grade ramped barrel, Power extractor, three white-dot fixed sights. Made in U.S.A. by Para USA.
Price: Slim-Hawg (2006) single stack .45 ACP,
   stainless, 6+1 . . . . **$1,099.00**
Price: Nite Hawg .45 ACP, black finish, 10+1 . . . . **$1,099.00**
Price: Warthog .45 ACP, Regal finish, 10+1 . . . .**$959.00**
Price: Warthog Stainless **$1,069.00**
Price: Big Hawg (2008) **$959.00**

PHOENIX ARMS HP22, HP25 AUTO PISTOLS

Caliber: 22 LR, 10-shot (HP22), 25 ACP, 10-shot (HP25). **Barrel:** 3". **Weight:** 20 oz. **Length:** 5.5" overall. **Grips:** Checkered composition. **Sights:** Blade front, adjustable rear. **Features:** Single action, exposed hammer; manual hold-open; button magazine release. Available in satin nickel, matte blue finish. Introduced 1993. Made in U.S.A. by Phoenix Arms.
Price: With gun lock **$130.00**
Price: HP Range kit with 5" bbl., locking case and accessories
   (1 Mag) **$171.00**
Price: HP Deluxe Range kit with 3" and 5" bbls.,
   2 mags, case **$210.00**

PICUDA .17 MACH-2 GRAPHITE PISTOL

Caliber: 17 HM2, 22 LR, 10-shot magazine. **Barrel:** 10" graphite barrel, "French grey" anodizing. **Weight:** 3.2 pounds. **Length:** 20.5" overall. **Grips:** Barracuda nutmeg laminated pistol stock. **Sights:** None, integral

scope base. **Features:** MLP-1722 receiver, target trigger, match bolt kit. Introduced 2008. Made in U.S.A. by Magnum Research, Inc.
Price: **$699.00**

ROCK RIVER ARMS BASIC CARRY AUTO PISTOL

Caliber: 45 ACP. **Barrel:** NA. **Weight:** NA. **Length:** NA. **Grips:** Rosewood, checkered. **Sights:** dovetail front sight, Heinie rear sight. **Features:** NM frame with 20-, 25- or 30-LPI checkered front strap, 5-inch slide with double serrations, lowered and flared ejection port, throated NM Kart barrel with NM bushing, match Commander hammer and match sear, aluminum speed trigger, dehorned, Parkerized finish, one magazine, accuracy guarantee. 3.5 lb. Trigger pull. Introduced 2006. RRA Service Auto 9mm has forged NM frame with beveled mag well, fixed target rear sight and dovetail front sight, KKM match 1:32 twist 9mm Para. barrel with supported ramp. Guaranteed to shoot 1-inch groups at 25 yards with quality 9mm Para. 115-124 grain match ammunition. Intr. 2008. Made in U.S.A. From Rock River Arms.
Price: Basic Carry PS2700 . . . . **$1,600.00**
Price: Limited Match PS2400 . . . . **$2,185.00**
Price: RRA Service Auto 9mm Para. PS2715 . . . . **$1,790.00**

ROCK RIVER ARMS LAR-15/LAR-9 PISTOLS

Caliber: .223/5.56mm NATO chamber 4-shot magazine. **Barrel:** 7", 10.5" Wilson chrome moly, 1:9 twist, A2 flash hider, 1/2-28 thread. **Weight:** 5.1 lbs. (7" barrel), 5.5 lbs. (10.5" barrel). **Length:** 23" overall. **Stock:** Hogue rubber grip. **Sights:** A2 front. **Features:** Forged A2 or A4 upper, single stage trigger, aluminum free-float tube, one magazine. Similar 9mm Para. LAR-9 also available. From Rock River Arms, Inc.
Price: LAR-15 7" A2 AR2115 . . . .**$955.00**
Price: LAR-15 10.5" A4 AR2120 . . . .**$945.00**
Price: LAR-9 7" A2 9MM2115 . . . .**$1,125.00**

ROHRBAUGH R9 SEMI-AUTO PISTOL

Caliber: 9mm Parabellum, 380 ACP. **Barrel:** 2.9". **Weight:** 12.8 oz. **Length:** 5.2" overall. **Features:** Very small double-action-only semi-auto pocket pistol. Stainless steel slide with matte black aluminum frame. Available with or without sights. Available with all-black (Stealth) and partial Diamond Black (Stealth Elite) finish.
Price: **$1,149.00**

RUGER SR9 AUTOLOADING PISTOL

Caliber: 9mm Para. **Barrel:** 4.14". **Weight:** 26.25, 26.5 oz. **Grips:** Glass-filled nylon in two color options—black or OD Green, w/flat or arched reversible backstrap. **Sights:** Adjustable 3-dot, built-in Picatinny-style rail. **Features:** Semi-DA, 6 configurations, striker-fired, through-hardened stainless steel slide, brushed or blackened stainless slide with black grip frame or blackened stainless slide with OD Green grip frame, ambi manual 1911-style safety, ambi mag release, mag disconnect, loaded chamber indicator, Ruger camblock design to absorb recoil, two 10 or 17-shot mags. Intr. 2008. Made in U.S.A. by Sturm, Ruger & Co.
Price: SR9 (17-Round), SR9-10 (SS) **$525.00**
Price: KBSR9 (17-Round), KBSR9-10 (Blackened SS) **$565.00**
Price: KODBSR9 (17-Round), KODBSR9-10
   (OD Green Grip) **$565.00**

Ruger SR9

Ruger LCP

Ruger P90

Ruger KP944D

Ruger KP9515

Ruger KP512 MKIII

Ruger KP45HMKIII

Ruger Mark III Hunter

RUGER LCP
Caliber: .380 ACP. **Barrel:** 2.75" **Weight:** 9.4 oz. **Grips:** Glass-filled nylon. **Sights:** Fixed. **Features:** SA, one configuration, ultra-light compact carry pistol in Ruger's smallest pistol frame, through-hardened stainless steel slide, blued finish, lock breach design, 6-shot mag. Intr. 2008. Made in U.S.A. by Sturm, Ruger & Co.
Price: LCP...**$347.00**

RUGER P90 MANUAL SAFETY MODEL AUTOLOADING PISTOL
Caliber: 45 ACP, 8-shot magazine. **Barrel:** 4.50". **Weight:** 33.5 oz. **Length:** 7.75" overall. **Grips:** Grooved black synthetic composition. **Sights:** Square post front, square notch rear adjustable for windage, both with white dot. **Features:** Double action; ambidextrous slide-mounted safety-levers. Stainless steel only. Introduced 1991.
Price: KP90 with extra mag, loader, case and gunlock **$617.00**
Price: P90 (blue) **$574.00**

Ruger KP944 Autoloading Pistol
Sized midway between full-size P-Series and compact KP94. 4.2" barrel, 7.5" overall length, weighs about 34 oz. KP94 manual safety model. Slide gripping grooves roll over top of slide. KP94 has ambidextrous safety-levers; Stainless slide, barrel, alloy frame. Also blue. Includes hard case and lock, spare magazine. Introduced 1994. Made in U.S.A. by Sturm, Ruger & Co.
Price: P944, blue, manual safety, .40 cal. **$541.00**
Price: KP944 (40-caliber) (manual safety-stainless) **$628.00**

RUGER P95 AUTOLOADING PISTOL
Caliber: 9mm, 15-shot magazine. **Barrel:** 3.9". **Weight:** 30 oz. **Length:** 7.25" overall. **Grips:** Grooved; integral with frame. **Sights:** Blade front, rear drift adjustable for windage; 3-dot system. **Features:** Molded polymer grip frame, stainless steel or chrome-moly slide. Suitable for +P+ ammunition. Safety model, decocker. Introduced 1996. Made in U.S.A. by Sturm, Ruger & Co. Comes with lockable plastic case, spare magazine, loader and lock, Picatinny rails.
Price: KP95PR15 safety model, stainless steel **$424.00**
Price: P95PR15 safety model, blued finish **$395.00**
Price: P95PR 10-round model, blued finish **$393.00**
Price: KP95PR 10-round model, stainless steel...........**$424.00**

RUGER 22 CHARGER PISTOL
Caliber: .22 LR. **Barrel:** 10". **Weight:** 3.5 lbs (w/out bi-pod). **Stock:** Black Laminate. **Sights:** None. **Features:** Rimfire Autoloading, one configuration, 10/22 action, adjustable bi-pod, new mag release for easier removal, precision-rifled barrel, black matte finish, combination Weaver-style and tip-off scope mount, 10-shot mag. Intr. 2008. Made in U.S.A. by Sturm, Ruger & Co.
Price: CHR22-10...................................**$380.00**

RUGER MARK III STANDARD AUTOLOADING PISTOL
Caliber: 22 LR, 10-shot magazine. **Barrel:** 4.5", 4.75", 5.5", 6", or 6-7/8". **Weight:** 33 oz. (4.75" bbl.). **Length:** 9" (4.75" bbl.). **Grips:**

Checkered composition grip panels. **Sights:** Fixed, fiber-optic front, fixed rear. **Features:** Updated design of original Standard Auto and Mark II series. Hunter models have lighter barrels. Target models have cocobolo grips; bull, target, competition, and hunter barrels; and adjustable sights. Introduced 2005.
Price: MKIII4, MKIII6 (blued) **$352.00**
Price: MKIII512 (blued bull barrel) **$417.00**
Price: KMKIII512 (stainless bull barrel) **$527.00**
Price: MKIII678 (blued) **$417.00**
Price: KMKIII678GC (stainless slabside barrel) **$606.00**
Price: KMKIII678H (stainless fluted barrel) **$620.00**
Price: KMKIII45HCL (Crimson Trace Laser Grips, intr. 2008) .**$787.00**
Price: KMKIII454 (2009) **$620.00**

Ruger 22/45 Mark III Pistol
Similar to other 22 Mark III autos except has Zytel grip frame that matches angle and magazine latch of Model 1911 45 ACP pistol. Available in 4" standard, 4.5", 5.5", 6-7/8" bull barrels. Comes with extra magazine, plastic case, lock. Introduced 1992. Hunter introduced 2006.
Price: P4MKIII, 4" bull barrel, adjustable sights **$326.00**
Price: P45GCMKIII, 4.5" bull barrel, fixed sights **$324.00**
Price: P512MKIII (5.5" bull blued barrel, adj. sights) **$326.00**
Price: KP512MKIII (5.5" stainless bull barrel, adj. sights **$435.00**
Price: Hunter KP45HMKIII 4.5" barrel (2007), KP678HMKIII,
6-7/8" stainless fluted bull barrel, adj. sights **$532.00**

Sabre Defence
Sphinx 9mm

Sabre Defence
Sphinx 45 ACP

SIG SAUER
1911 TTT

SIG SAUER 1911
Compact Nitron

SIG SAUER 1911
Blackwater

SIG SAUER
P220

SABRE DEFENCE SPHINX PISTOLS
Caliber: 9mm Para., 45 ACP., 10-shot magazine. **Barrel:** 4.43". **Weight:** 39.15 oz. **Length:** 8.27" overall. **Grips:** Textured polymer. **Sights:** Fixed Trijicon Night Sights. **Features:** CNC engineered from stainless steel billet; grip frame in stainless steel, titanium or high-strength aluminum. Integrated accessory rail, high-cut beavertail, decocking lever. Made in Switzerland. Imported by Sabre Defence Industries.
Price: 45 ACP (2007) **$2,990.00**
Price: 9mm Para. Standard, titanium w/decocker **$2,700.00**

SEECAMP LWS 32/380 STAINLESS DA AUTO
Caliber: 32 ACP, 380 ACP Win. Silvertip, 6-shot magazine. **Barrel:** 2", integral with frame. **Weight:** 10.5 oz. **Length:** 4-1/8" overall. **Grips:** Glass-filled nylon. **Sights:** Smooth, no-snag, contoured slide and barrel top. **Features:** Aircraft quality 17-4 PH stainless steel. Inertia-operated firing pin. Hammer fired double-action-only. Hammer automatically follows slide down to safety rest position after each shot, no manual safety needed. Magazine safety disconnector. Polished stainless. Introduced 1985. From L.W. Seecamp.
Price: 32 . . . . **$446.25**
Price: 380 . . . . **$795.00**

SIG SAUER 250 COMPACT AUTO PISTOL
Caliber: 9mm Para. (16-round magazine), 357 SIG, 40 S&W and 45 ACP. **Barrel:** NA. **Weight:** 24.6 oz. **Length:** 7.2" overall. **Grips:** Interchangeable polymer. **Sights:** Siglite night sights. **Features:** Modular design allows for immediate change in caliber and size; subcompact, compact and full. Six different grip combinations for each size. Introduced 2008. From Sig Sauer, Inc.
Price: P250 . . . . **$750.00**

SIG SAUER 1911 PISTOLS
Caliber: 45 ACP, 8-shot magazine. **Barrel:** 5". **Weight:** 40.3 oz. **Length:** 8.65" overall. **Grips:** Checkered wood grips. **Sights:** Novak night sights. Blade front, drift adjustable rear for windage. **Features:** Single-action 1911. Hand-fitted dehorned stainless-steel frame and slide; match-grade barrel, hammer/sear set and trigger; 25-lpi front strap checkering, 20-lpi mainspring housing checkering. Beavertail grip safety with speed bump, extended thumb safety, firing pin safety and hammer intercept notch. Introduced 2005. XO series has contrast sights, Ergo Grip XT textured polymer grips. Target line features adjustable target night sights, match barrel, custom wood grips, non-railed frame in stainless or Nitron finishes. TTT series is two-tone 1911 with Nitron slide and black controls on stainless frame. Includes burled maple grips, adjustable combat night sights. STX line available from Sig Sauer Custom Shop; two-tone 1911, non-railed, Nitron slide, stainless frame, burled maple grips. Polished cocking serrations, flat-top slide, magwell. Carry line has Novak night sights, lanyard attachment point,

gray diamondwood or rosewood grips, 8+1 capacity. Compact series has 6+1 capacity, 7.7" OAL, 4.25" barrel, slim-profile wood grips, weighs 30.3 oz. RCS line (Compact SAS) is Customs Shop version with anti-snag dehorning. Stainless or Nitron finish, Novak night sights, slim-profile gray diamondwood or rosewood grips. 6+1 capacity. 1911 C3 (2008) is a 6+1 compact .45 ACP, rosewood custom wood grips, two-tone and Nitron finishes. Weighs about 30 ounces unloaded, lightweight alloy frame. Length is 7.7". From SIG SAUER, Inc.
Price: Nitron **$1,200.00**
Price: Stainless **$1,170.00**
Price: XO Black **$1,005.00**
Price: Target Nitron (2006) **$1,230.00**
Price: TTT (2006) **$1,290.00**
Price: STX (2006) **$1,455.00**
Price: Carry Nitron (2006) **$1,200.00**
Price: Compact Nitron **$1,200.00**
Price: RCS Nitron **$1,305.00**
Price: C3 (2008) **$1,200.00**
Price: Platinum Elite **$1,275.00**
Price: Blackwater (2009) **$1,290.00**

SIG SAUER P220 AUTO PISTOLS
Caliber: 45 ACP, (7- or 8-shot magazine). **Barrel:** 4.4". **Weight:** 27.8 oz. **Length:** 7.8" overall. **Grips:** Checkered black plastic. **Sights:** Blade front, drift adjustable rear for windage. Optional Siglite night sights. **Features:** Double action. Stainless-steel slide, Nitron finish, alloy frame, M1913 Picatinny rail; safety system of decocking lever, automatic firing pin safety block, safety intercept notch, and trigger bar disconnector. Squared combat-type trigger guard. Slide stays open after last shot. Introduced 1976. P220 SAS Anti-Snag has dehorned stainless steel slide, front Siglite Night Sight, rounded trigger guard, dust cover, Custom Shop wood grips. Equinox line is Custom Shop product with Nitron stainless-steel slide with a black hard-anodized alloy frame, brush-polished flats and nickel accents. Truglo tritium fiber-optic front sight, rear Siglite night sight, gray laminated wood grips with checkering and stippling. From SIG SAUER, Inc.
Price: P220 Two-Tone, matte-stainless slide,
    black alloy frame **$1,110.00**
Price: P220 Elite Stainless (2008) **$1,350.00**
Price: P220 Two-Tone SAO, single action (2006), from . . . **$1,086.00**
Price: P220 DAK (2006) **$853.00**
Price: P220 Equinox (2006) **$1,200.00**
Price: P220 Elite Dark (2009) **$1,200.00**
Price: P220 Elite Dark, threaded barrel (2009) **$1,305.00**

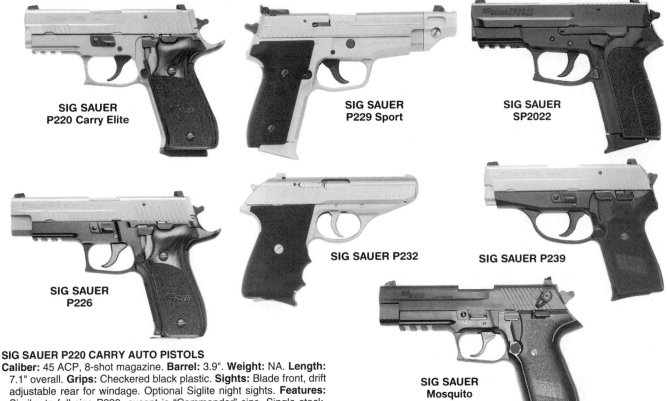

SIG SAUER P220 Carry Elite

SIG SAUER P229 Sport

SIG SAUER SP2022

SIG SAUER P226

SIG SAUER P232

SIG SAUER P239

SIG SAUER Mosquito

SIG SAUER P220 CARRY AUTO PISTOLS

Caliber: 45 ACP, 8-shot magazine. **Barrel:** 3.9". **Weight:** NA. **Length:** 7.1" overall. **Grips:** Checkered black plastic. **Sights:** Blade front, drift adjustable rear for windage. Optional Siglite night sights. **Features:** Similar to full-size P220, except is "Commander" size. Single stack, DA/SA operation, Nitron finish, Picatinny rail, and either post and dot contrast or 3-dot Siglite night sights. Introduced 2005. Many variations availble. From SIG SAUER, Inc.
Price: P220 Carry, from . . . . $975.00; w/night sights $1,050.00
Price: P220 Carry Elite Stainless (2008) $1,350.00

SIG SAUER P229 DA Auto Pistol

Similar to the P228 except chambered for 9mm Para. (10- or 15-round magazines), 40 S&W, 357 SIG (10- or 12-round magazines). Has 3.86" barrel, 7.1" overall length and 3.35" height. Weight is 32.4 oz. Introduced 1991. Frame made in Germany, stainless steel slide assembly made in U.S.; pistol assembled in U.S. Many variations available. From SIG SAUER, Inc.
Price: P229, from . . . . $975.00; w/night sights $1,050.00
Price: P229 Platinum Elite (2008). $1,275.00

SIG SAUER SP2022 PISTOLS

Caliber: 9mm Para., 357 SIG, 40 S&W, 10-, 12-, or 15-shot magazines. **Barrel:** 3.9". **Weight:** 30.2 oz. **Length:** 7.4" overall. **Grips:** Composite and rubberized one-piece. **Sights:** Blade front, rear adjustable for windage. Optional Siglite night sights. **Features:** Polymer frame, stainless steel slide; integral frame accessory rail; replaceable steel frame rails; left- or right-handed magazine release, two interchangeable grips. From SIG SAUER, Inc.
Price: SP2009, Nitron finish $613.00

SIG SAUER P226 Pistols

Similar to the P220 pistol except has 4.4" barrel, measures 7.7" overall, weighs 34 oz. Chambered in 9mm, 357 SIG, or 40 S&W. X-Five series has factory tuned single-action trigger, 5" slide and barrel, ergonomic wood grips with beavertail, ambidextrous thumb safety and stainless slide and frame with magwell, low-profile adjustable target sights, front cocking serrations and a 25-meter factory test target. Many variations available. From SIG SAUER, Inc.
Price: P226, from $975.00
Price: P226 Blackwater Tactical (2009) $1,300.00

SIG SAUER P232 PERSONAL SIZE PISTOL

Caliber: 380 ACP, 7-shot. **Barrel:** 3.6". **Weight:** 17.6-22.4 oz. **Length:** 6.6" overall. **Grips:** Checkered black composite. **Sights:** Blade front, rear adjustable for windage. **Features:** Double action/single action or DAO. Blow-back operation, stationary barrel. Introduced 1997. From SIG SAUER, Inc.
Price: P232, from $660.00

SIG SAUER P239 PISTOL

Caliber: 9mm Para., 8-shot, 357 SIG 40 S&W, 7-shot magazine. **Barrel:** 3.6". **Weight:** 25.2 oz. **Length:** 6.6" overall. **Grips:** Checkered black composite. **Sights:** Blade front, rear adjustable for windage. Optional Siglite night sights. **Features:** SA/DA or DAO; blackened stainless steel slide, aluminum alloy frame. Introduced 1996. Made in U.S.A. by SIG SAUER, Inc.
Price: P239, from $840.00

SIG SAUER MOSQUITO PISTOL

Caliber: 22 LR, 10-shot magazine. **Barrel:** 3.9". **Weight:** 24.6 oz. **Length:** 7.2" overall. **Grips:** Checkered black composite. **Sights:** Blade front, rear adjustable for windage. **Features:** Blowback operated, fixed barrel, polymer frame, slide-mounted ambidextrous safety. Introduced 2005. Made in U.S.A. by SIG SAUER, Inc.
Price: Mosquito, from $375.00

SMITH & WESSON M&P AUTO PISTOLS

Caliber: 9mm Para., 40 S&W, 357 Auto. **Barrel:** 4.25". **Weight:** 24.25 oz. **Length:** 7.5" overall. **Grips:** One-piece Xenoy, wraparound with straight backstrap. **Sights:** Ramp dovetail mount front; tritium sights optional; Novak Lo-mount Carry rear. **Features:** Zytel polymer frame, embedded stainless steel chassis; stainless steel slide and barrel, stainless steel structural components, black Melonite finish, reversible magazine catch, 3 interchangeable palmswell grip sizes, universal rail, sear deactivation lever, internal lock system, magazine disconnect. Ships with 2 magazines. Internal lock models available. Overall height: 5.5"; width: 1.2"; sight radius: 6.4". Introduced November 2005. 45 ACP version introduced 2007, 10+1 or 14+1 capacity. **Barrel:** 4.5". **Length:** 8.05". **Weight:** 29.6 ounces. **Features:** Picatinny-style equipment rail; black or bi-tone, dark-earth-brown frame. Bi-tone M&P45 includes ambidextrous, frame-mounted thumb safety, take down tool with lanyard attachment. Compact 9mm Para./357 SIG/40 S&W versions introduced 2007. Compacts have 3.5" barrel, OAL 6.7". 10+1 or 12+1 capacity. **Weight:** 21.7 ounces. **Features:** Picatinny-style equipment rail. Made in U.S.A. by Smith & Wesson.
Price: Full Size, from. $719.00
Price: Compacts, from $719.00
Price: Midsize, from $758.00
Price: Crimson Trace Lasergrip models, from $988.00
Price: Thumb-safety M&P models, from $719.00

Smith & Wesson M&P

Smith & Wesson M&P Compact

Smith & Wesson M&P 45 Bi-Tone

Smith & Wesson 908

Smith & Wesson 4013TSW

Smith & Wesson 3913 LadySmith

Smith & Wesson SW1911

Smith & Wesson SW1911 Sub-Compact Pro Series

SMITH & WESSON MODEL 908 AUTO PISTOL
Caliber: 9mm Para., 8-shot magazine. **Barrel:** 3.5". **Weight:** 24 oz. **Length:** 6-13/16". **Grips:** One-piece Xenoy, wraparound with straight backstrap. **Sights:** Post front, fixed rear, 3-dot system. **Features:** Aluminum alloy frame, matte blue carbon steel slide; bobbed hammer; smooth trigger. Introduced 1996. Made in U.S.A. by Smith & Wesson.
Price: Model 908, black matte finish **$679.00**
Price: Model 908S, stainless matte finish **$679.00**
Price: Model 908S Carry Combo, with holster **$703.00**

SMITH & WESSON MODEL 4013TSW AUTO
Caliber: 40 S&W, 9-shot magazine. **Barrel:** 3.5". **Weight:** 26.8 oz. **Length:** 6 3/4" overall. **Grips:** Xenoy one-piece wraparound. **Sights:** Novak 3-dot system. **Features:** Traditional double-action system; stainless slide, alloy frame; fixed barrel bushing; ambidextrous decocker; reversible magazine catch, equipment rail. Introduced 1997. Made in U.S.A. by Smith & Wesson.
Price: Model 4013TSW **$1,027.00**

SMITH & WESSON MODEL 910 DA AUTO PISTOL
Caliber: 9mm Para., 10-shot magazine. **Barrel:** 4". **Weight:** 28 oz. **Length:** 7-3/8" overall. **Grips:** One-piece Xenoy, wraparound with straight backstrap. **Sights:** Post front with white dot, fixed 2-dot rear. **Features:** Alloy frame, blue carbon steel slide. Slide-mounted decocking lever. Introduced 1995.
Price: **$648.00**

SMITH & WESSON MODEL 3913 TRADITIONAL DOUBLE ACTIONS
Caliber: 9mm Para., 8-shot magazine. **Barrel:** 3.5". **Weight:** 24.8 oz. **Length:** 6.75" overall. **Grips:** One-piece Delrin wraparound, textured surface. **Sights:** Post front with white dot, Novak LoMount Carry with two dots. **Features:** TSW has aluminum alloy frame, stainless slide. Bobbed hammer with no half-cock notch; smooth .304" trigger with rounded edges. Straight backstrap. Equipment rail. Extra magazine included. Introduced 1989. The 3913-LS Ladysmith has frame that is upswept at the front, rounded trigger guard. Comes in frosted stainless steel with matching gray grips. Grips are ergonomically correct for a woman's hand. Novak LoMount Carry rear sight adjustable for windage. Extra magazine included. Introduced 1990.
Price: 3913TSW **$924.00**
Price: 3913-LS **$909.00**

SMITH & WESSON MODEL SW1911 PISTOLS
Caliber: 45 ACP, 8 rounds. **Barrel:** 5". **Weight:** 39 oz. **Length:** 8.7". **Grips:** Wood or rubber. **Sights:** Novak Lo-Mount Carry, white dot front. **Features:** Large stainless frame and slide with matte finish, single-side external safety. No. 108284 has adjustable target rear sight, ambidextrous safety levers, 20-lpi checkered front strap, comes with two 8-round magazines. DK model (Doug Koenig) also has oversized magazine well, Doug Koenig speed hammer, flat competition speed trigger with overtravel stop, rosewood grips with Smith & Wesson silver medallions, oversized magazine well, special serial number run. No. 108295 has olive drab Crimson Trace lasergrips. No. 108299 has carbon-steel frame and slide with polished flats on slide, standard GI recoil guide, laminated double-diamond walnut grips with silver Smith & Wesson medallions, adjustable target sights. Tactical Rail No. 108293 has a Picatinny rail, black Melonite finish, Novak Lo-Mount Carry Sights, scandium alloy frame. Tactical Rail Stainless introduced 2006. SW1911PD gun is Commander size, scandium-alloy frame, 4.25" barrel, 8" OAL, 28.0 oz., non-reflective black matte finish. Gunsite edition has scandium alloy frame, beveled edges, solid match aluminum trigger, Herrett's logoed tactical oval walnut stocks, special serial number run, brass bead Novak front sight. SC model has 4.25" barrel, scandium alloy frame, stainless-steel slide, non-reflective matte finish.
Price: From **$1,130.00**
Price: Crimson Trace Laser Grips **$1,493.00**

SMITH & WESSON MODEL 1911 SUB-COMPACT PRO SERIES
Caliber: 45 ACP, 7 + 1-shot magazine. **Barrel:** 3". **Weight:** 24 oz. **Length:** 6-7/8". **Grips:** Fully stippled synthetic. **Sights:** Dovetail white dot front, fixed white 2-dot rear. **Features:** Scandium frame with stainless steel slide, matte black finish throughout. Oversized external extractor, 3-hole curved trigger with overtravel stop, full-length guide rod, and cable lock. Introduced 2009.
Price: **$1,264.00**

Springfield Armory EMP

Springfield Armory XD

Springfield Armory XD

Springfield Armory XD 45 ACP Extended

Springfield Armory XD 45 ACP

Springfield Armory 1911A1 Standard

SMITH & WESSON ENHANCED SIGMA SERIES DAO PISTOLS
Caliber: 9mm Para., 40 S&W; 10-, 16-shot magazine. **Barrel:** 4". **Weight:** 24.7 oz. **Length:** 7.25" overall. **Grips:** Integral. **Sights:** White dot front, fixed rear; 3-dot system. Tritium night sights available. **Features:** Ergonomic polymer frame; low barrel centerline; internal striker firing system; corrosion-resistant slide; Teflon-filled, electroless-nickel coated magazine, equipment rail. Introduced 1994. Made in U.S.A. by Smith & Wesson.
Price: From **$482.00**

SMITH & WESSON MODEL CS9 CHIEF'S SPECIAL AUTO
Caliber: 9mm Para., 7-shot magazine. **Barrel:** 3". **Weight:** 20.8 oz. **Length:** 6.25" overall. **Grips:** Hogue wraparound rubber. **Sights:** White dot front, fixed 2-dot rear. **Features:** Traditional double-action trigger mechanism. Alloy frame, stainless slide. Ambidextrous safety. Introduced 1999. Made in U.S.A. by Smith & Wesson.
Price: Stainless **$782.00**

SMITH & WESSON MODEL CS45 CHIEF'S SPECIAL AUTO
Caliber: 45 ACP, 6-shot magazine. **Weight:** 23.9 oz. **Features:** Introduced 1999. Made in U.S.A. by Smith & Wesson.
Price: From **$787.00**

SPRINGFIELD ARMORY EMP ENHANCED MICRO PISTOL
Caliber: 9mm Para., 40 S&W; 9-round magazine. **Barrel:** 3" stainless steel match grade, fully supported ramp, bull. **Weight:** 26 oz. **Length:** 6.5" overall. **Grips:** Thinline cocobolo hardwood. **Sights:** Fixed low profile combat rear, dovetail front, 3-dot tritium. **Features:** Two 9-round stainless steel magazines with slam pads, long aluminum match-grade trigger adjusted to 5 to 6 lbs., forged aluminum alloy frame, black hardcoat anodized; dual spring full-length guide rod, forged satin-finish stainless steel slide. Introduced 2007. From Springfield Armory.
Price: 9mm Para. Compact Bi-Tone **$1,329.00**
Price: 40 S&W Compact Bi-Tone (2008) **$1,329.00**

SPRINGFIELD ARMORY XD POLYMER AUTO PISTOLS
Caliber: 9mm Para., 40 S&W, 45 ACP. **Barrel:** 3", 4", 5". **Weight:** 20.5-31 oz. **Length:** 6.26-8" overall. **Grips:** Textured polymer. **Sights:** Varies by model; Fixed sights are dovetail front and rear steel 3-dot units. **Features:** Three sizes in X-Treme Duty (XD) line: Sub-Compact (3" barrel), Service (4" barrel), Tactical (5" barrel). Three ported models available. Ergonomic polymer frame, hammer-forged barrel, no-tool disassembly, ambidextrous magazine release, visual/tactile loaded chamber indicator, visual/tactile striker status indicator, grip safety, XD gear system included. Introduced 2004. XD 45 introduced 2006. Compact line introduced 2007. Compacts ship with one extended magazine (13) and one compact magazine (10). From Springfield Armory.
Price: Sub-Compact OD Green 9mm Para./40 S&W, fixed sights **$543.00**
Price: Compact 45 ACP, 4" barrel, Bi-Tone finish (2008) **$589.00**
Price: Compact 45 ACP, 4" barrel, OD green frame, stainless slide (2008) **$653.00**
Price: Service Black 9mm Para./40 S&W, fixed sights **$543.00**
Price: Service Dark Earth 45 ACP, fixed sights **$571.00**
Price: Service Black 45 ACP, external thumb safety (2008). . .**$571.00**
Price: V-10 Ported Black 9mm Para./40 S&W **$573.00**
Price: Tactical Black 45 ACP, fixed sights **$616.00**
Price: Service Bi-Tone 40 S&W, Trijicon night sights (2008) . .**$695.00**

SPRINGFIELD ARMORY GI 45 1911A1 AUTO PISTOLS
Caliber: 45 ACP; 6-, 7-, 13-shot magazines. **Barrel:** 3", 4", 5". **Weight:** 28-36 oz. **Length:** 5.5-8.5" overall. **Grips:** Checkered double-diamond walnut, "U.S" logo. **Sights:** Fixed GI style. **Features:** Similar to WWII GI-issue 45s at hammer, beavertail, mainspring housing. From Springfield Armory.
Price: GI .45 4" Champion Lightweight, 7+1, 28 oz. **$619.00**
Price: GI .45 5" High Capacity, 13+1, 36 oz. **$676.00**
Price: GI .45 5" OD Green, 7+1, 36 oz. **$619.00**
Price: GI .45 3" Micro Compact, 6+1, 32 oz. **$667.00**

SPRINGFIELD ARMORY MIL-SPEC 1911A1 AUTO PISTOLS
Caliber: 38 Super, 9-shot magazines; 45 ACP, 7-shot magazines. **Barrel:** 5". **Weight:** 35.6-39 oz. **Length:** 8.5-8.625" overall. **Features:** Similar to GI 45s. From Springfield Armory.
Price: Mil-Spec Parkerized, 7+1, 35.6 oz. **$715.00**
Price: Mil-Spec Stainless Steel, 7+1, 36 oz. **$784.00**
Price: Mil-Spec 38 Super, 9+1, 39 oz. **$775.00**

Springfield Armory Custom Loaded Champion 1911A1 Pistol
Similar to standard 1911A1, slide and barrel are 4". 7.5" OAL. Available in 45 ACP only. Novak Night Sights. Delta hammer and cocobolo grips. Parkerized or stainless. Introduced 1989.
Price: Stainless, 34 oz. **$1,031.00**
Price: Lightweight, 28 oz. **$989.00**

Springfield
Armory
Full-Size
1911A1

Springfield Armory TRP

Taurus 1911B

Taurus PT-22

Springfield Armory Custom Loaded Ultra Compact Pistol
Similar to 1911A1 Compact, shorter slide, 3.5" barrel, 6+1, 7" OAL. Beavertail grip safety, beveled magazine well, fixed sights. Videki speed trigger, flared ejection port, stainless steel frame, blued slide, match grade barrel, rubber grips. Introduced 1996. From Springfield Armory.
Price: Stainless Steel **$1,031.00**

SPRINGFIELD ARMORY CUSTOM LOADED MICRO-COMPACT 1911A1 PISTOL
Caliber: 45 ACP, 6+1 capacity. **Barrel:** 3" 1:16 LH. **Weight:** 24-32 oz. **Length:** 4.7". **Grips:** Slimline cocobolo. **Sights:** Novak LoMount tritium. Dovetail front. **Features:** Aluminum hard-coat anodized alloy frame, forged steel slide, forged barrel, ambi-thumb safety, Extreme Carry Bevel dehorning. Lockable plastic case, 2 magazines.
Price: Lightweight Bi-Tone **$992.00**

SPRINGFIELD ARMORY CUSTOM LOADED LONG SLIDE 1911A1 PISTOL
Caliber: 45 ACP, 7+1 capacity. **Barrel:** 6" 1:16 LH. **Weight:** 41 oz. **Length:** 9.5". **Grips:** Slimline cocobolo. **Sights:** Dovetail front; fully adjustable target rear. **Features:** Longer sight radius, 7.9".
Price: Bi-Tone Operator w/light rail **$1,189.00**

Springfield Armory Tactical Response Loaded Pistols
Similar to 1911A1 except 45 ACP only, checkered front strap and mainspring housing, Novak Night Sight combat rear sight and matching dove-tailed front sight, tuned, polished extractor, oversize barrel link; lightweight speed trigger and combat action job, match barrel and bushing, extended ambidextrous thumb safety and fitted beavertail grip safety. Checkered cocobolo wood grips, comes with two Wilson 7-shot magazines. Frame is engraved "Tactical" both sides of frame with "TRP." Introduced 1998. TRP-Pro Model meets FBI specifications for SWAT Hostage Rescue Team. From Springfield Armory.
Price: 45 TRP Service Model, black Armory Kote finish, fixed Trijicon night sights **$1,741.00**

TAURUS MODEL 800 SERIES
Caliber: 9mm Para., 40 S&W, 45 ACP. **Barrel:** 4". **Weight:** 32 oz. **Length:** 8.25". **Grips:** Checkered. **Sights:** Novak. **Features:** DA/SA. Blue and Stainless Steel finish. Introduced in 2007. Imported from Brazil by Taurus International.
Price: 809B, 9mm Para., Blue, 17+1 . . . . **$623.00**

TAURUS MODEL 1911
Caliber: 45 ACP, 8+1 capacity. **Barrel:** 5". **Weight:** 33 oz. **Length:** 8.5". **Grips:** Checkered black. **Sights:** Heinie straight 8. **Features:** SA. Blue, stainless steel, duotone blue, and blue/gray finish. Standard/picatinny rail, standard frame, alloy frame, and alloy/picatinny rail. Introduced in 2007. Imported from Brazil by Taurus International.
Price: 1911B, Blue **$719.00**
Price: 1911SS, Stainless Steel **$816.00**
Price: 1911SS-1, Stainless Steel **$847.00**
Price: 1911 DT, Duotone Blue **$795.00**

TAURUS MODEL 917
Caliber: 9mm Para., 19+1 capacity. **Barrel:** 4.3". **Weight:** 32.2 oz. **Length:** 8.5". **Grips:** Checkered rubber. **Sights:** Fixed. **Features:** SA/

DA. Blue and stainless steel finish. Medium frame. Introduced in 2007. Imported from Brazil by Taurus International.
Price: 917B-20, Blue **$542.00**
Price: 917SS-20, Stainless Steel **$559.00**

TAURUS MODEL PT-22/PT-25 AUTO PISTOLS
Caliber: 22 LR, 8-shot (PT-22); 25 ACP, 9-shot (PT-25). **Barrel:** 2.75". **Weight:** 12.3 oz. **Length:** 5.25" overall. **Grips:** Smooth rosewood or mother-of-pearl. **Sights:** Fixed. **Features:** Double action. Tip-up barrel for loading, cleaning. Blue, nickel, duo-tone or blue with gold accents. Introduced 1992. Made in U.S.A. by Taurus International.
Price: PT-22B or PT-25B, checkered wood grips **$248.00**

Taurus Model 22PLY Small Polymer Frame Pistols
Similar to Taurus Models PT-22 and PT-25 but with lightweight polymer frame. Features include 22 LR (9+1) or 25 ACP (8+1) chambering. 2.33" tip-up barrel, matte black finish, extended magazine with finger lip, manual safety. Overall length is 4.8". Weighs 10.8 oz.
Price: . . . . **TO BE ANNOUNCED**

TAURUS MODEL 24/7
Caliber: 9mm Para., 40 S&W, 45 ACP. **Barrel:** 4". **Weight:** 27.2 oz. **Length:** 7-1/8". **Grips:** "Ribber" rubber-finned overlay on polymer. **Sights:** Adjustable. **Features:** SA/DA; accessory rail, four safeties, blue or stainless finish. One-piece guide rod, flush-fit magazine, flared bushingless barrel, Picatinny accessory rail, manual safety, user changeable sights, loaded chamber indicator, tuned ejector and lowered port, one piece guide rod and flat wound captive spring. Introduced 2003. Long Slide models have 5" barrels, measure 8-1/8" overall, weigh 27.2 oz. Imported from Brazil by Taurus International.
Price: 40BP, 40 S&W, blued, 10+1 or 15+1 . . . . **$452.00**
Price: 24/7-PRO Standard Series: 4" barrel; stainless, duotone or blued finish **$452.00**
Price: 24/7-PRO Compact Series; 3.2" barrel; stainless, titanium or blued finish **$467.00**
Price: 24/7-PRO Long Slide Series: 5.2" barrel; matte stainless, blued or stainless finish **$506.00**
Price: 24/7PLS, 5" barrel, chambered in 9mm Parabellum, 38 Super and 40 S&W **$506.00**

Taurus Model 2045 Large Frame Pistol
Similar to Taurus Model 24/7 but chambered in 45 ACP only. Features include polymer frame, blued or matte stainless steel slide, 4.2" barrel, ambidextrous "memory pads" to promote safe finger position during loading, ambi three-position safety/decocker. Picatinny rail system, fixed sights. Overall length is 7.34". Weighs 31.5 oz.
Price: **$577.00**

TAURUS MODEL 58 PISTOL
Caliber: 380 ACP (19+1). **Barrel:** 3.25". **Weight:** 18.7 oz. **Length:** 6.125" overall. **Grips:** Polymer. **Sights:** Fixed. **Features:** SA/DA semi-auto. Scaled-down version of the full-size Model 92; steel slide, alloy frame, frame-mounted ambi safety, blued or stainless finish, and extended magazine.
Price: 58HCB **$602.00**
Price: 58HCSS **$617.00**

Taurus 92

Taurus 99SS

Taurus 100

Taurus 132
Millennium Pro

Taurus 138
Millennium Pro

Taurus 140
Millennium Pro

Taurus 738 TCP

TAURUS MODEL 92 AUTO PISTOL
Caliber: 9mm Para., 10- or 17-shot mags. Barrel: 5". Weight: 34 oz. Length: 8.5" overall. Grips: Checkered rubber, rosewood, mother-of-pearl. Sights: Fixed notch rear. 3-dot sight system. Also offered with micrometer-click adjustable night sights. Features: Double action, ambidextrous 3-way hammer drop safety, allows cocked & locked carry. Blue, stainless steel, blue with gold highlights, stainless steel with gold highlights, forged aluminum frame, integral key-lock. .22 LR conversion kit available. Imported from Brazil by Taurus International.
Price: 92B $542.00
Price: 92SS $559.00

Taurus Model 99 Auto Pistol
Similar to Model 92, fully adjustable rear sight.
Price: 99B $559.00

Taurus Model 90-Two Semi-Auto Pistol
Similar to Model 92 but with one-piece wraparound grips, automatic disassembly lathc, internal recoil buffer, addition slide serrations, picatinny rail with removable cover, 10- and 17-round magazine (9mm) or 10- and 12-round magazines (40 S&W). Overall length is 8.5". Weight is 32.5 oz.
Price: $725.00

TAURUS MODEL 100/101 AUTO PISTOL
Caliber: 40 S&W, 10- or 11-shot mags. Barrel: 5". Weight: 34 oz. Length: 8.5". Grips: Checkered rubber, rosewood, mother-of-pearl. Sights: 3-dot fixed or adjustable; night sights available. Features: Single/double action with three-position safety/decocker. Reintroduced in 2001. Imported by Taurus International.
Price: 100B $542.00

TAURUS MODEL 111 MILLENNIUM PRO AUTO PISTOL
Caliber: 9mm Para., 10- or 12-shot mags. Barrel: 3.25". Weight: 18.7 oz. Length: 6-1/8" overall. Grips: Checkered polymer. Sights: 3-dot fixed; night sights available. Low profile, 3-dot combat. Features: Double action only, polymer frame, matte stainless or blue steel slide, manual safety, integral key-lock. Deluxe models with wood grip inserts.
Price: 111BP, 111BP-12. . . . . $419.00
Price: 111PTi titanium slide $592.00

TAURUS 132 MILLENNIUM PRO AUTO PISTOL
Caliber: 32 ACP, 10-shot mag. Barrel: 3.25". Weight: 18.7 oz. Grips: Polymer. Sights: 3-dot fixed; night sights available. Features: Double-action-only, polymer frame, matte stainless or blue steel slide, manual safety, integral key-lock action. Introduced 2001.
Price: 132BP. $419.00

TAURUS 138 MILLENNIUM PRO SERIES
Caliber: 380 ACP, 10- or 12-shot mags. Barrel: 3.25". Weight: 18.7 oz. Grips: Polymer. Sights: Fixed 3-dot fixed. Features: Double-action-only, polymer frame, matte stainless or blue steel slide, manual safety, integral key-lock.
Price: 138BP. $419.00

TAURUS 140 MILLENNIUM PRO AUTO PISTOL
Caliber: 40 S&W, 10-shot mag. Barrel: 3.25". Weight: 18.7 oz. Grips: Checkered polymer. Sights: 3-dot fixed; night sights available. Features: Double action only; matte stainless or blue steel slide, black polymer frame, manual safety, integral key-lock action. From Taurus International.
Price: 140BP $436.00

TAURUS 145 MILLENNIUM PRO AUTO PISTOL
Caliber: 45 ACP, 10-shot mag. Barrel: 3.27". Weight: 23 oz. Stock: Checkered polymer. Sights: 3-dot fixed; night sights available. Features: Double-action only, matte stainless or blue steel slide, black polymer frame, manual safety, integral key-lock. Compact model is 6+1 with a 3.25" barrel, weighs 20.8 oz. From Taurus International.
Price: 145BP, blued $436.00
Price: 145SSP, stainless, ... $453.00

Taurus Model 609Ti-Pro
Similar to other Millennium Pro models but with titanium slide. Chambered in 9mm Parabellum. Weighs 19.7 oz. Overall length is 6.125". Features include 13+1 capacity, 3.25" barrel, checkered polymer grips, and Heinie Straight-8 sights.
Price: $608.00

TAURUS MODEL 738 TCP COMPACT PISTOL
Caliber: 380 ACP, 6+1 (standard magazine) or 8+1 (extended magazine). Barrel: 3.3". Weight: 9 oz. (titanium slide) to 10.2 oz. Length: 5.19". Sights: Low-profile fixed. Features: Lightweight DAO semi-auto with polymer frame; blued (738B), stainless (738SS) or titanium (738Ti) slide; concealed hammer; ambi safety; loaded chamber indicator.
Price: . . . . $623.00 to $686.00

TAURUS MODEL 911B AUTO PISTOL
Caliber: 9mm Para., 10-shot mag. Barrel: 4". Weight: 28.2 oz. Length: 7" overall. Grips: Checkered rubber, rosewood, mother-of-pearl. Sights: Fixed, 3-dot blue or stainless; night sights optional. Features: Double action, semi-auto ambidextrous 3-way hammer drop safety, allows cocked & locked carry. Blue, stainless steel, blue with gold highlights, or stainless steel with gold highlights, forged aluminum frame, integral key-lock.
Price: From. $584.00

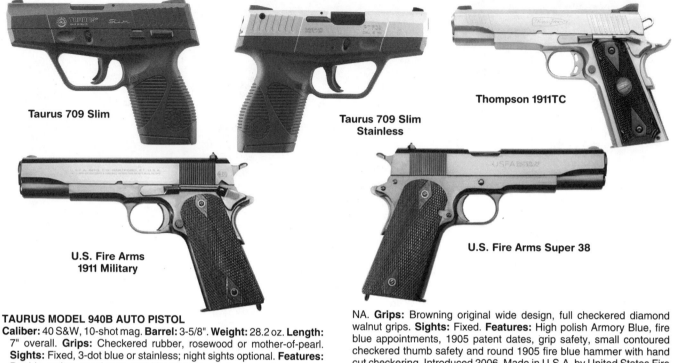

Taurus 709 Slim

Taurus 709 Slim Stainless

Thompson 1911TC

U.S. Fire Arms 1911 Military

U.S. Fire Arms Super 38

TAURUS MODEL 940B AUTO PISTOL
Caliber: 40 S&W, 10-shot mag. **Barrel:** 3-5/8". **Weight:** 28.2 oz. **Length:** 7" overall. **Grips:** Checkered rubber, rosewood or mother-of-pearl. **Sights:** Fixed, 3-dot blue or stainless; night sights optional. **Features:** Double action, semi-auto ambidextrous 3-way hammer drop safety, allows cocked & locked carry. Blue, stainless steel, blue with gold highlights, or stainless steel with gold highlights, forged aluminum frame, integral key-lock.
Price: From $584.00

TAURUS MODEL 945B/38S SERIES
Caliber: 45 ACP, 8-shot mag. **Barrel:** 4.25". **Weight:** 28.2/29.5 oz. **Length:** 7.48" overall. **Grips:** Checkered rubber, rosewood or mother-of-pearl. **Sights:** Fixed, 3-dot; night sights optional. **Features:** Double-action with ambidextrous 3-way hammer drop safety allows cocked & locked carry. Forged aluminum frame, 945C has ported barrel/slide. Blue, stainless, blue with gold highlights, stainless with gold highlights, integral key-lock. Introduced 1995. 38 Super line based on 945 frame introduced 2005. 38S series is 10+1, 30 oz., 7.5" overall. Imported by Taurus International.
Price: From $625.00

TAURUS MODEL 709 "SLIM"
Caliber: 9mm Parabellum, 7+1. **Barrel:** 3.2". **Weight:** 10 oz. **Length:** 6.2" overall. **Grips:** Checkered polymer. **Sights:** Fixed. **Features:** Semi-auto pistol, single/double action. Streamlined profile, choice of blued (709B) or stainless (709SS) slide.
Price: $436.00

THOMPSON CUSTOM 1911A1 AUTOMATIC PISTOL
Caliber: 45 ACP, 7-shot magazine. **Barrel:** 4.3". **Weight:** 34 oz. **Length:** 8" overall. **Grips:** Checkered laminate grips with a Thompson bullet logo inlay. **Sights:** Front and rear sights are black with serrations and are dovetailed into the slide. **Features:** Machined from 420 stainless steel, matte finish. Thompson bullet logo on slide. Flared ejection port, angled front and rear serrations on slide, 20-lpi checkered mainspring housing and frontstrap. Adjustable trigger, combat hammer, stainless steel full-length recoil guide rod, extended beavertail grip safety; extended magazine release; checkered slide-stop lever. Made in U.S.A. by Kahr Arms.
Price: 1911TC, 5", 39 oz., 8.5" overall, stainless frame $813.00

THOMPSON TA5 1927A-1 LIGHTWEIGHT DELUXE PISTOL
Caliber: 45 ACP, 50-round drum magazine. **Barrel:** 10.5" 1:16 right-hand twist. **Weight:** 94.5 oz. **Length:** 23.3" overall. **Grips:** Walnut, horizontal foregrip **Sights:** Blade front, open rear adjustable. **Features:** Based on Thompson machine gun design. Introduced 2008. Made in U.S.A. by Kahr Arms.
Price: TA5 (2008) $1,237.00

U.S. FIRE ARMS 1910 COMMERCIAL MODEL AUTOMATIC PISTOL
Caliber: 45 ACP, 7-shot magazine. **Barrel:** 5". **Weight:** NA. **Length:**
NA. **Grips:** Browning original wide design, full checkered diamond walnut grips. **Sights:** Fixed. **Features:** High polish Armory Blue, fire blue appointments, 1905 patent dates, grip safety, small contoured checkered thumb safety and round 1905 fire blue hammer with hand cut checkering. Introduced 2006. Made in U.S.A. by United States Fire Arms Mfg. Co.
Price: $1,895.00

U.S. FIRE ARMS 1911 MILITARY MODEL AUTOMATIC PISTOL
Caliber: 45 ACP, 7-shot magazine. **Barrel:** 5". **Weight:** NA. **Length:** NA. **Grips:** Browning original wide design, full checkered diamond walnut grips. **Sights:** Fixed. **Features:** Military polish Armory Blue, fire blue appointments, 1905 patent dates, grip safety, small contoured checkered thumb safety and round 1905 fire blue hammer with hand cut checkering. Introduced 2006. Made in U.S.A. by United States Fire Arms Mfg. Co.
Price: $1,895.00

U.S. FIRE ARMS SUPER 38 AUTOMATIC PISTOL
Caliber: 38 Auto, 9-shot magazine. **Barrel:** 5". **Weight:** NA. **Length:** NA. **Grips:** Browning original wide design, full checkered diamond walnut grips. **Sights:** Fixed. **Features:** Armory blue, fire blue appointments, 1913 patent date, grip safety, small contoured checkered thumb safety and spur 1911 hammer with hand cut checkering. Supplied with two Super 38 Auto. mags. Super .38 roll mark on base. Introduced 2006. Made in U.S.A. by United States Fire Arms Mfg. Co.
Price: $1,895.00

U.S. FIRE ARMS ACE .22 LONG RIFLE AUTOMATIC PISTOL
Caliber: 22 LR, 10-shot magazine. **Barrel:** 5". **Weight:** NA. **Length:** NA. **Grips:** Browning original wide design, full checkered diamond walnut grips. **Sights:** Fixed. **Features:** Armory blue commercial finish, fire blue appointments, 1913 patent date, grip safety, small contoured checkered thumb safety and spur 1911 hammer with hand cut checkering. Supplied with two magazines. Ace roll mark on base. Introduced 2006. Made in U.S.A. by United States Fire Arms Mfg. Co.
Price: $1,995.00

WALTHER PPS PISTOL
Caliber: 9mm Para., 40 S&W. 6-, 7-, 8-shot magazines for 9mm Para.; 5-, 6-, 7-shot magazines for 40 S&W. **Barrel:** 3.2". **Weight:** 19.4 oz. **Length:** 6.3" overall. **Stocks:** Stippled black polymer. **Sights:** Picatinny-style accessory rail, 3-dot low-profile contoured sight. **Features:** PPS-"Polizeipistole Schmal," or Police Pistol Slim. Measures 1.04 inches wide. Ships with 6- and 7-round magazines. Striker-fired action, flat slide stop lever, alternate backstrap sizes. QuickSafe feature decocks striker assembly when backstrap is removed. Loaded chamber indicator. First Edition model, limited to 1,000 units, has anthracite grey finish, aluminum gun case. Introduced 2008. Made in U.S.A. by Smith & Wesson.
Price: $713.00
Price: First Edition.................................$665.00

Walther PPK/S

Walther P99

Walther P22

WALTHER PPK/S AMERICAN AUTO PISTOL
Caliber: 32 ACP, 380 ACP, 7-shot magazine. **Barrel:** 3.27". **Weight:** 23-1/2 oz. Length: 6.1" overall. Stocks: Checkered plastic. **Sights:** Fixed, white markings. **Features:** Double action; manual safety blocks firing pin and drops hammer; chamber loaded indicator on 32 and 380; extra finger rest magazine provided. Made in the United States. Introduced 1980. Made in U.S.A. by Smith & Wesson.
Price: **$605.00**

WALTHER P99 AUTO PISTOL
Caliber: 9mm Para., 9x21, 40 S&W, 10-shot magazine. **Barrel:** 4". **Weight:** 25 oz. Length: 7" overall. **Grips:** Textured polymer. **Sights:** Blade front (comes with three interchangeable blades for elevation adjustment), micrometer rear adjustable for windage. **Features:** Double-action mechanism with trigger safety, decock safety, internal striker safety; chamber loaded indicator; ambidextrous magazine release levers; polymer frame with interchangeable backstrap inserts. Comes with two magazines. Introduced 1997. Made in U.S.A. by Smith & Wesson.
Price: From **$799.00**

WALTHER P22 PISTOL
Caliber: 22 LR. **Barrel:** 3.4", 5". **Weight:** 19.6 oz. (3.4"), 20.3 oz. (5"). **Length:** 6.26", 7.83". **Grips:** NA. **Sights:** Interchangeable white dot, front, 2-dot adjustable, rear. **Features:** A rimfire version of the Walther P99 pistol, available in nickel slide with black frame, or green frame with black slide versions. Made in U.S.A. by Smith & Wesson.
Price: From **$362.00**

WILSON COMBAT ELITE PROFESSIONAL
Caliber: 9mm Para., 38 Super, 40 S&W; 45 ACP, 8-shot magazine. **Barrel:** Compensated 4.1" hand-fit, heavy flanged cone match grade. **Weight:** 36.2 oz. Length: 7.7" overall. **Grips:** Cocobolo. **Sights:** Combat Tactical yellow rear tritium inserts, brighter green tritium front insert. **Features:** High-cut front strap, 30-lpi checkering on front strap and flat mainspring housing, High-Ride Beavertail grip safety. Dehorned, ambidextrous thumb safety, extended ejector, skeletonized ultralight hammer, ultralight trigger, Armor-Tuff finish on frame and slide. Introduced 1997. Made in U.S.A. by Wilson Combat.
Price: From **$2,600.00**

Includes models suitable for several forms of competition and other sporting purposes.

Baer 1911 Ultimate Master

Colt Special Combat Government

Baer 1911 Bullseye Wadcutter

Competitor Single Shot

CZ 75 Champion

BAER 1911 ULTIMATE MASTER COMBAT PISTOL

Caliber: 38 Super, 400 Cor-Bon 45 ACP (others available), 10-shot magazine. **Barrel:** 5", 6"; Baer NM. **Weight:** 37 oz. **Length:** 8.5" overall. **Grips:** Checkered cocobolo. **Sights:** Baer dovetail front, low-mount Bo-Mar rear with hidden leaf. **Features:** Full-house competition gun. Baer forged NM blued steel frame and double serrated slide; Baer triple port, tapered cone compensator; fitted slide to frame; lowered, flared ejection port; Baer reverse recoil plug; full-length guide rod; recoil buff; beveled magazine well; Baer Commander hammer, sear; Baer extended ambidextrous safety, extended ejector, checkered slide stop, beavertail grip safety with pad, extended magazine release button; Baer speed trigger. Made in U.S.A. by Les Baer Custom, Inc.
Price: 45 ACP Compensated **$2,790.00**
Price: 38 Super Compensated **$2,940.00**

BAER 1911 NATIONAL MATCH HARDBALL PISTOL

Caliber: 45 ACP, 7-shot magazine. **Barrel:** 5". **Weight:** 37 oz. **Length:** 8.5" overall. **Grips:** Checkered walnut. **Sights:** Baer dovetail front with under-cut post, low-mount Bo-Mar rear with hidden leaf. **Features:** Baer NM forged steel frame, double serrated slide and barrel with stainless bushing; slide fitted to frame; Baer match trigger with 4-lb. pull; polished feed ramp, throated barrel; checkered front strap, arched mainspring housing; Baer beveled magazine well; lowered, flared ejection port; tuned extractor; Baer extended ejector, checkered slide stop; recoil buff. Made in U.S.A. by Les Baer Custom, Inc.
Price: **$1,890.00**

Baer 1911 Bullseye Wadcutter Pistol

Similar to National Match Hardball except designed for wadcutter loads only. Polished feed ramp and barrel throat; Bo-Mar rib on slide; full length recoil rod; Baer speed trigger with 3-1/2-lb. pull; Baer deluxe hammer and sear; Baer beavertail grip safety with pad; flat mainspring housing checkered 20 lpi. Blue finish; checkered walnut grips. Made in U.S.A. by Les Baer Custom, Inc.
Price: From **$1,890.00**

BF CLASSIC PISTOL

Caliber: Customer orders chamberings. **Barrel:** 8-15" Heavy Match Grade with 11-degree target crown. **Weight:** Approx 3.9 lbs. **Length:** From 16" overall. **Grips:** Thumbrest target style. **Sights:** Bo-Mar/Bond ScopeRib I Combo with hooded post front adjustable for height and width, rear notch available in .032", .062", .080" and .100" widths; 1/2-MOA clicks. **Features:** Hand fitted and headspaced, drilled and tapped for scope mount. Etched receiver; gold-colored trigger. Introduced 1988. Made in U.S.A. by E. Arthur Brown Co. Inc.
Price: **$699.00**

COLT GOLD CUP TROPHY PISTOL

Caliber: 45 ACP, 8-shot + 1 magazine. **Barrel:** 5". **Weight:** NA. **Length:** 8.5". **Grips:** Checkered rubber composite with silver-plated medallion. **Sights:** (O5070X) Dovetail front, Champion rear; (O5870CS) Patridge Target Style front, Champion rear. **Features:** Adjustable aluminum trigger, Beavertail grip safety, full length recoil spring and target recoil spring, available in blued finish and stainless steel.
Price: O5070X **$1,022.00**
Price: O5870CS **$1,071.00**

COLT SPECIAL COMBAT GOVERNMENT

Caliber: 45 ACP, 38 Super. **Barrel:** 5". **Weight:** 39 oz. **Length:** 8.5". **Grips:** Rosewood w/double diamond checkering pattern. **Sights:** Clark dovetail, front; Bo-Mar adjustable, rear. **Features:** A competition-ready pistol with enhancements such as skeletonized trigger, upswept grip safety, custom tuned action, polished feed ramp. Blue or satin nickel finish. Introduced 2003. Made in U.S.A. by Colt's Mfg. Co.
Price: **$1,676.00**

COMPETITOR SINGLE-SHOT PISTOL

Caliber: 22 LR through 50 Action Express, including belted magnums. **Barrel:** 14" standard; 10.5" silhouette; 16" optional. **Weight:** About 59 oz. (14" bbl.). **Length:** 15.12" overall. **Grips:** Ambidextrous; synthetic (standard) or laminated or natural wood. **Sights:** Ramp front, adjustable rear. **Features:** Rotary cannon-type action cocks on opening; cammed ejector; interchangeable barrels, ejectors. Adjustable single stage trigger, sliding thumb safety and trigger safety. Matte blue finish. Introduced 1988. From Competitor Corp., Inc.
Price: 14", standard calibers, synthetic grip **$660.00**

CZ 75 CHAMPION COMPETITION PISTOL

Caliber: 9mm Para., 40 S&W, 16-shot mag. **Barrel:** 4.4". **Weight:** 2.5 lbs. **Length:** 9.4" overall. **Grips:** Black rubber. **Sights:** Blade front, fully adjustable rear. **Features:** Single-action trigger mechanism; three-port compensator (40 S&W, 9mm Para. have two port) full-length guide rod; extended magazine release; ambidextrous safety; flared magazine well; fully adjustable match trigger. Introduced 1999. Imported from the Czech Republic by CZ-USA.
Price: Dual-tone finish **$1,691.00**

EAA Witness
Gold Team

Freedom Arms 83 22
Silhouette Class

Hammerli SP 20

High Standard Trophy

High Standard Victor

EAA WITNESS ELITE GOLD TEAM AUTO
Caliber: 9mm Para., 9x21, 38 Super, 40 S&W, 45 ACP. **Barrel:** 5.1".
Weight: 44 oz. **Length:** 10.5" overall. **Grips:** Checkered walnut,
competition-style. **Sights:** Square post front, fully adjustable rear.
Features: Triple-chamber cone compensator; competition SA trigger;
extended safety and magazine release; competition hammer; beveled
magazine well; beavertail grip. Hand-fitted major components. Hard
chrome finish. Match-grade barrel. From E.A.A. Custom Shop.
Introduced 1992. Limited designed for IPSC Limited Class competition.
Features include full-length dust-cover frame, funneled magazine
well, interchangeable front sights. Stock (2005) designed for IPSC
Production Class competition. Match introduced 2006. Made in Italy,
imported by European American Armory.
Price: Gold Team **$1,902.00**
Price: Limited, 4.5" barrel, 18+1 capacity **$1,219.00**
Price: Stock, 4.5" barrel, hard-chrome finish **$930.00**
Price: Match, 4.75" barrel, two-tone finish **$632.00**

**FREEDOM ARMS MODEL 83 22 FIELD GRADE SILHOUETTE
CLASS**
Caliber: 22 LR, 5-shot cylinder. **Barrel:** 10". **Weight:** 63 oz. **Length:**
15.5" overall. **Grips:** Black micarta. **Sights:** Removable Patridge
front blade; Iron Sight Gun Works silhouette rear, click adjustable for
windage and elevation (optional adj. front sight and hood). **Features:**
Stainless steel, matte finish, manual sliding-bar safety system; dual
firing pins, lightened hammer for fast lock time, pre-set trigger stop.
Introduced 1991. Made in U.S.A. by Freedom Arms.
Price: Silhouette Class **$1,860.00**

FREEDOM ARMS MODEL 83 CENTERFIRE SILHOUETTE MODELS
Caliber: 357 Mag., 41 Mag., 44 Mag.; 5-shot cylinder. **Barrel:** 10",
9" (357 Mag. only). **Weight:** 63 oz. (41 Mag.). **Length:** 15.5", 14.5"
(357 only). **Grips:** Pachmayr Presentation. **Sights:** Iron Sight Gun
Works silhouette rear sight, replaceable adjustable front sight blade
with hood. **Features:** Stainless steel, matte finish, manual sliding-bar
safety system. Made in U.S.A. by Freedom Arms.
Price: Silhouette Models, from **$1,741.65**

HAMMERLI SP 20 TARGET PISTOL
Caliber: 22 LR, 32 S&W. **Barrel:** 4.6". **Weight:** 34.6-41.8 oz. **Length:**
11.8" overall. **Grips:** Anatomically shaped synthetic Hi-Grip available
in five sizes. **Sights:** Integral front in three widths, adjustable rear with
changeable notch widths. **Features:** Extremely low-level sight line;
anatomically shaped trigger; adjustable JPS buffer system for different
recoil characteristics. Receiver available in red, blue, gold, violet or
black. Introduced 1998. Imported from Switzerland by Larry's Guns
of Maine.
Price: Hammerli 22 LR **$1,539.00**

HIGH STANDARD SUPERMATIC TROPHY TARGET PISTOL
Caliber: 22 LR, 9-shot mag. **Barrel:** 5.5" bull or 7.25" fluted. **Weight:** 44-
46 oz. **Length:** 9.5-11.25" overall. **Stock:** Checkered hardwood with
thumbrest. **Sights:** Undercut ramp front, frame-mounted micro-click
rear adjustable for windage and elevation; drilled and tapped for scope
mounting. **Features:** Gold-plated trigger, slide lock, safety-lever and
magazine release; stippled front grip and backstrap; adjustable trigger
and sear. Barrel weights optional. From High Standard Manufacturing
Co., Inc.
Price: 5.5" barrel, adjustable sights **$795.00**
Price: 7.25", adjustable sights **$845.00**

HIGH STANDARD VICTOR TARGET PISTOL
Caliber: 22 LR, 10-shot magazine. **Barrel:** 4.5" or 5.5" polished blue;
push-button takedown. **Weight:** 46 oz. **Length:** 9.5" overall. **Stock:**
Checkered walnut with thumbrest. **Sights:** Undercut ramp front,
micro-click rear adjustable for windage and elevation. Also available
with scope mount, rings, no sights. **Features:** Stainless steel frame.
Full-length vent rib. Gold-plated trigger, slide lock, safety-lever and
magazine release; stippled front grip and backstrap; polished blue
slide; adjustable trigger and sear. Comes with barrel weight. From High
Standard Manufacturing Co., Inc.
Price: 4.5" or 5.5" barrel, vented sight rib,
    universal scope base **$795.00**

KIMBER SUPER MATCH II
Caliber: 45 ACP, 8-shot magazine. **Barrel:** 5". **Weight:** 38 oz. **Length:**
8.7" overall. **Grips:** Rosewood double diamond. **Sights:** Blade front,
Kimber fully adjustable rear. **Features:** Guaranteed shoot 1" group
at 25 yards. Stainless steel frame, black KimPro slide; two-piece
magazine well; premium aluminum match-grade trigger; 30 lpi front
strap checkering; stainless match-grade barrel; ambidextrous safety;
special Custom Shop markings. Introduced 1999. Made in U.S.A. by
Kimber Mfg., Inc.
Price: **$2,225.00**

Kimber Super Match II

Smith & Wesson Model 22A

Ruger MKIII512

Springfield Armory 1911A1 Trophy Match

STI Executive

KIMBER RIMFIRE TARGET

Caliber: 22LR, 10-shot magazine. **Barrel:** 5". **Weight:** 23oz. **Length:** 8.7" overall. **Grips:** Rosewood, Kimber logo, double diamond checkering, or black synthetic double diamond. **Sights:** Blade front, Kimber fully adjustable rear. **Features:** Bumped beavertail grip safety, extended thumb safety, extended magazine release button. Serrated flat top slide with flutes, machined aluminum slide and frame, matte black or satin silver finishes. 30 lines-per-inch checkering on frontstrap and under trigger guard; aluminum trigger, test target, accuracy guarantee. No slide lock-open after firing the last round in the magazine. Introduced 1999. Made in U.S.A. by Kimber Mfg., Inc.
Price: **$833.00**

RUGER MARK III TARGET MODEL AUTOLOADING PISTOL

Caliber: 22 LR, 10-shot magazine. **Barrel:** 5.5" to 6-7/8". **Weight:** 41 to 45 oz. **Length:** 9.75" to 11-1/8" overall. **Grips:** Checkered cocobolo, laminate. **Sights:** .125" blade front, micro-click rear, adjustable for windage and elevation, loaded chamber indicator; integral lock, magazine disconnect. Plastic case with lock included. Mark II series introduced 1982, discontinued 2004. Mark III introduced 2005.
Price: MKIII512 (bull barrel, blued) **$417.00**
Price: KMKIII512 (bull barrel, stainless) **$527.00**
Price: MKIII678 (blued Target barrel, 6-7/8") **$417.00**
Price: KMKIII678GC (stainless slabside barrel) **$606.00**
Price: KMKIII678H (stainless fluted barrel) **$620.00**
Price: KMKIII45HCL (Crimson Trace Laser Grips, intr. 2008) .**$787.00**
Price: KMKIII45H (2009) **$620.00**

SMITH & WESSON MODEL 41 TARGET

Caliber: 22 LR, 10-shot clip. **Barrel:** 5.5", 7". **Weight:** 41 oz. (5.5" barrel). **Length:** 10.5" overall (5.5" barrel). **Grips:** Checkered walnut with modified thumbrest, usable with either hand. **Sights:** 1/8" Patridge on ramp base; micro-click rear adjustable for windage and elevation. **Features:** 3/8" wide, grooved trigger; adjustable trigger stop drilled and tapped.
Price: S&W Bright Blue, either barrel **$1,288.00**

SMITH & WESSON MODEL 22A PISTOLS

Caliber: 22 LR, 10-shot magazine. **Barrel:** 4", 5.5" bull. **Weight:** 28-39 oz. **Length:** 9.5" overall. **Grips:** Dymondwood with ambidextrous thumbrests and flared bottom or rubber soft touch with thumbrest. **Sights:** Patridge front, fully adjustable rear. **Features:** Sight bridge with Weaver-style integral optics mount; alloy frame, stainless barrel and slide; blue/black finish. Introduced 1997. The 22S is similar to the Model 22A except has stainless steel frame. Introduced 1997. Made in U.S.A. by Smith & Wesson.
Price: from **$308.00**
Price: Realtree APG camo finish (2008). **$356.00**

SPRINGFIELD ARMORY LEATHAM LEGEND TGO SERIES PISTOLS

Three models of 5" barrel, 45 ACP 1911 pistols built for serious competition. TGO 1 has deluxe low mount Bo-Mar rear sight, Dawson fiber optics front sight, 3.5 lb. trigger pull.
Price: TGO 1 . . . .**$3,095.00**

Springfield Armory Trophy Match Pistol

Similar to Springfield Armory's Full Size model, but designed for bullseye and action shooting competition. Available with a Service Model 5" frame with matching slide and barrel in 5" and 6" lengths. Fully adjustable sights, checkered frame front strap, match barrel and bushing. In 45 ACP only. From Springfield Inc.
Price: **$1,573.00**

STI EAGLE 5.0, 6.0 PISTOL

Caliber: 9mm Para., 9x21, 38 & 40 Super, 40 S&W, 10mm, 45 ACP, 10-shot magazine. **Barrel:** 5", 6" bull. **Weight:** 34.5 oz. **Length:** 8.62" overall. **Grips:** Checkered polymer. **Sights:** STI front, Novak or Heinie rear. **Features:** Standard frames plus 7 others; adjustable match trigger; skeletonized hammer; extended grip safety with locator pad. Introduced 1994. Made in U.S.A. by STI International.
Price: . . . . (5.0 Eagle) **$1,940.12**, (6.0 Eagle), **$1,049.98**

STI EXECUTIVE PISTOL

Caliber: 40 S&W. **Barrel:** 5" bull. **Weight:** 39 oz. **Length:** 8-5/8". **Grips:** Gray polymer. **Sights:** Dawson fiber optic, front; STI adjustable rear. **Features:** Stainless mag. well, front and rear serrations on slide. Made in U.S.A. by STI.
Price: **$2,464.00**

STI TROJAN

Caliber: 9mm Para., 38 Super, 40 S&W, 45 ACP. **Barrel:** 5", 6". **Weight:** 36 oz. **Length:** 8.5". **Grips:** Rosewood. **Sights:** STI front with STI adjustable rear. **Features:** Stippled front strap, flat top slide, one-piece steel guide rod.
Price: (Trojan 5") **$1,110.00**
Price: (Trojan 6", not available in 38 Super) **$1,419.60**

Includes models suitable for hunting and competitive courses of fire, both police and international.

Charter Arms Bulldog

Charter Arms Off Duty

Charter Arms Undercover

Charter Arms Mag Pug

Comanche III

EAA Windicator

CHARTER ARMS BULLDOG REVOLVER

Caliber: 44 Special. **Barrel:** 2.5". **Weight:** NA. **Sights:** Blade front, notch rear. **Features:** 6-round cylinder, soft-rubber pancake-style grips, shrouded ejector rod, wide trigger and hammer spur. American made by Charter Arms, distributed by MKS Supply.
Price: Blued **$455.00**
Price: Stainless **$465.00**
Price: Target Bulldog, 4" barrel, 23 oz. **$459.00**

CHARTER ARMS OFF DUTY REVOLVER

Caliber: 38 Spec. **Barrel:** 2". **Weight:** 12.5 oz. **Sights:** Blade front, notch rear. **Features:** 5-round cylinder, aluminum casting, DAO. American made by Charter Arms, distributed by MKS Supply.
Price: Aluminum **$438.00**

CHARTER ARMS UNDERCOVER REVOLVER

Caliber: **Barrel:** 2". **Weight:** 12 oz. **Sights:** Blade front, notch rear. **Features:** 6-round cylinder. American made by Charter Arms, distributed by MKS Supply.
Price: Blued **$438.00**

CHARTER ARMS UNDERCOVER SOUTHPAW REVOLVER

Caliber: 38 Spec. +P. **Barrel:** 2". **Weight:** 12 oz. **Sights:** NA. **Features:** Cylinder release is on the right side and the cylinder opens to the right side. Exposed hammer for both single and double-action firing. 5-round cylinder. American made by Charter Arms, distributed by MKS Supply.
Price: Blued **$469.00**

CHARTER ARMS MAG PUG REVOLVER

Caliber: 357 Mag. **Barrel:** 2.2". **Weight:** 23 oz. **Sights:** Blade front, notch rear. **Features:** Five-round cylinder. American made by Charter Arms, distributed by MKS Supply.
Price: Blued or stainless **$409.00**

CHARTER ARMS PINK LADY REVOLVER

Caliber: 32 H&R Magnum, 38 Special +P. **Barrel:** 2". **Weight:** 12 oz. **Grips:** Rubber Pachmayr-style. **Sights:** Fixed. **Features:** Snubnose, five-round cylinder. Pink anodized aluminum alloy frame.
Price: **$438.00**
Price: Lavender Lady, lavender frame **$438.00**
Price: Goldfinger, gold anodized frame, matte black barrel
and cylinder assembly **$438.00**

CHARTER ARMS SOUTHPAW REVOLVER

Caliber: 38 Special +P. **Barrel:** 2". **Weight:** 12 oz. **Grips:** Rubber Pachmayr-style. **Sights:** NA. **Features:** Snubnose, five-round cylinder, matte black aluminum alloy frame with stainless steel cylinder. Cylinder latch and crane assembly are on right side of frame for convenience to left-hand shooters.
Price: **$469.00**

COMANCHE I, II, III DA REVOLVERS

Caliber: 22 LR, 9 shot. 38 Spec., 6 shot. 357 Mag, 6 shot. **Barrel:** 6", 22 LR; 2" and 4", 38 Spec.; 2" and 3", 357 Mag. **Weight:** 39 oz. **Length:** 10.8" overall. **Grips:** Rubber. **Sights:** Adjustable rear. **Features:** Blued or stainless. Distributed by SGS Importers.
Price: I Blue **$236.95**
Price: I Alloy **$258.95**
Price: II 38 Spec., 3" bbl., 6-shot, stainless, intr. 2006 . . . . . .**$236.95**
Price: II 38 Spec., 4" bbl., 6-shot, stainless **$219.95**
Price: III 357 Mag., 3" bbl., 6-shot, blue **$253.95**
Price: III 357 Mag., 4" bbl., 6-shot, blue **$274.95**

EAA WINDICATOR REVOLVERS

Caliber: 38 Spec., 6-shot; 357 Mag., 6-shot. **Barrel:** 2", 4". **Weight:** 30 oz. (4"). **Length:** 8.5" overall (4" bbl.). **Grips:** Rubber with finger grooves. **Sights:** Blade front, fixed or adjustable on rimfires; fixed only on 32, 38. **Features:** Swing-out cylinder; hammer block safety; blue finish. Introduced 1991. Imported from Germany by European American Armory.
Price: 38 Spec. 2" barrel, alloy frame **$277.00**
Price: 38 Spec. 4" barrel, alloy frame **$292.00**
Price: 357 Mag, 2" barrel, steel frame **$292.00**
Price: 357 Mag, 4" barrel, steel frame **$311.00**

KORTH USA REVOLVERS

Caliber: 22 LR, 22 WMR, 32 S&W Long, 38 Spec., 357 Mag., 9mm Para. **Barrel:** 3", 4", 5.25", 6". **Weight:** 36-52 oz. **Grips:** Combat, Sport: Walnut, Palisander, Amboinia, Ivory. Grips, Target: German Walnut, matte with oil finish, adjustable ergonomic competition style. **Sights:** Adjustable Patridge (Sport) or Baughman (Combat), interchangeable and adjustable rear w/Patridge front (Target) in blue and matte. **Features:** DA/SA, 3 models, over 50 configurations, externally adjustable trigger stop and weight, interchangeable cylinder, removable wide-milled trigger shoe on Target model. Deluxe models are highly engraved editions. Available finishes include high polish blue finish, plasma coated in high polish or matted silver, gold, blue, or charcoal. Many deluxe options available. 6-shot. From Korth USA.
Price: From **$8,000.00**
Price: Deluxe Editions, from **$12,000.00**

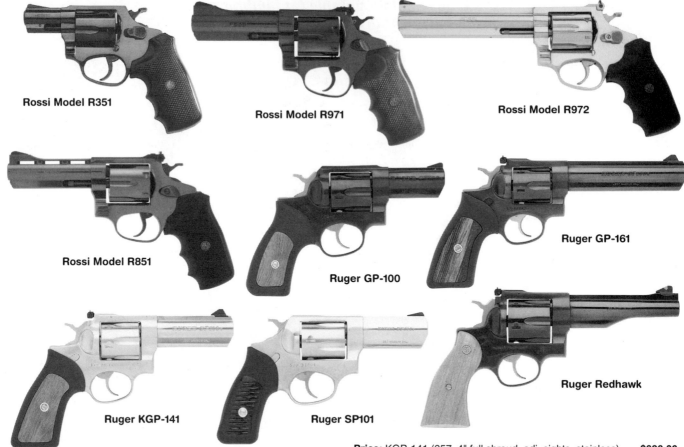

Rossi Model R351

Rossi Model R971

Rossi Model R972

Rossi Model R851

Ruger GP-100

Ruger GP-161

Ruger KGP-141

Ruger SP101

Ruger Redhawk

ROSSI R461/R462/R971/R972
Caliber: .357 Mag. **Barrel:** 2" (R46), 4" (R971), 6" (R972). **Weight:** 26-35 oz. **Grips:** Rubber. **Sights:** Fixed (R46), Fully Adjustable (R972). **Features:** DA/SA, 4 models available, +P rated frame, blue carbon or high polish stainless steel, patented Taurus Security System, 6-shot.
Price: From **$352.00**

ROSSI MODEL R351/R352/R851 REVOLVERS
Caliber: .38 Spec. **Barrel:** 2" (R35), 4" (R851). **Weight:** 24-32 oz. **Grips:** Rubber. **Sights:** Fixed (R35), Fully Adjustable (R851). **Features:** DA/SA, 3 models available, +P rated frame, blue carbon or high polish stainless steel, patented Taurus Security System, 5-shot (R35) 6-shot (R851).
Price: From **$352.00**

ROSSI MODEL R971/R972 REVOLVERS
Caliber: 357 Mag. +P, 6-shot. **Barrel:** 4", 6". **Weight:** 32 oz. **Length:** 8.5" or 10.5" overall. **Grips:** Rubber. **Sights:** Blade front, adjustable rear. **Features:** Single/double action. Patented key-lock Taurus Security System; forged steel frame. Introduced 2001. Made in Brazil by Amadeo Rossi. Imported by BrazTech/Taurus.
Price: Model R971 (blued finish, 4" bbl.) **$406.00**
Price: Model R972 (stainless steel finish, 6" bbl.) **$460.00**

Rossi Model 851
Similar to Model R971/R972, chambered for 38 Spec. +P. Blued finish, 4" barrel. Introduced 2001. Made in Brazil by Amadeo Rossi. From BrazTech/Taurus.
Price: **$352.00**

RUGER GP100 REVOLVERS
Caliber: 38 Spec. +P, 357 Mag., 6-shot. **Barrel:** 3" full shroud, 4" full shroud, 6" full shroud. **Weight:** 3" full shroud-36 oz., 4" full shroud-38 oz. **Sights:** Fixed; adjustable on 4" full shroud, all 6" barrels. **Grips:** Ruger Santoprene Cushioned Grip with Goncalo Alves inserts. **Features:** Uses action, frame features of both the Security-Six and Redhawk revolvers. Full length, short ejector shroud. Satin blue and stainless steel.
Price: GP-141 (357, 4" full shroud, adj. sights, blue) **$616.00**
Price: GP-161 (357, 6" full shroud, adj. sights, blue), 46 oz. . .**$616.00**

Price: KGP-141 (357, 4" full shroud, adj. sights, stainless) . . .**$680.00**
Price: KGP-161 (357, 6" full shroud, adj. sights, stainless) 46 oz. **$680.00**
Price: KGPF-331 (357, 3" full shroud, stainless) **$659.00**

RUGER SP101 REVOLVERS
Caliber: 327 Federal, 6-shot; 38 Spec. +P, 357 Mag., 5-shot. **Barrel:** 2.25", 3-1/16". **Weight:** (38 & 357 mag models) 2.25"-25 oz.; 3-1/16"-27 oz. **Sights:** Adjustable on 327, fixed on others. **Grips:** Ruger Cushioned Grip with inserts. **Features:** Compact, small frame, double-action revolver. Full-length ejector shroud. Stainless steel only. Introduced 1988.
Price: KSP-321X (2.25", 357 Mag.) **$589.00**
Price: KSP-331X (3-1/16", 357 Mag.) **$589.00**
Price: KSP-821X (2.25", 38 Spec.) **$589.00**
Price: KSP-32731X (3-1/16", 327 Federal, intr. 2008) **$589.00**
Price: KSP-321X-LG (Crimson Trace Laser Grips, intr. 2008) .**$839.00**

Ruger SP101 Double-Action-Only Revolver
Similar to standard SP101 except double-action-only with no single-action sear notch. Spurless hammer, floating firing pin and transfer bar safety system. Available with 2.25" barrel in 357 Mag. Weighs 25 oz., overall length 7". Natural brushed satin, high-polish stainless steel. Introduced 1993.
Price: KSP321XL (357 Mag.) **$589.00**
Price: KSP321XL-LG (357 Mag., Crimson Trace Laser Grips, intr. 2008) **$839.00**

RUGER REDHAWK
Caliber: 44 Rem. Mag., 45 Colt, 6-shot. **Barrel:** 4", 5.5", 7.5". **Weight:** About 54 oz. (7.5" bbl.). **Length:** 13" overall (7.5" barrel). **Grips:** Square butt cushioned grip panels. **Sights:** Interchangeable Patridge-type front, rear adjustable for windage and elevation. **Features:** Stainless steel, brushed satin finish, blued ordnance steel. 9.5" sight radius. Introduced 1979.
Price: KRH-44, stainless, 7.5" barrel **$861.00**
Price: KRH-44R, stainless 7.5" barrel w/scope mount **$915.00**
Price: KRH-445, stainless 5.5" barrel **$861.00**
Price: KRH-444, stainless 4" barrel (2007) **$861.00**
Price: KRH-45-4, Hogue Monogrip, 45 Colt (2008) **$861.00**

Ruger Redhawk KRH-444

Ruger Super Redhawk

Smith & Wesson Model 357

Smith & Wesson Model 638

Smith & Wesson Model 442

Smith & Wesson Model 60 Chief's Special

RUGER SUPER REDHAWK REVOLVER

Caliber: 44 Rem. Mag., 45 Colt, 454 Casull, 480 Ruger, 5 or 6-shot. **Barrel:** 2.5", 5.5", 7.5", 9.5". **Weight:** About 54 oz. (7.5" bbl.). **Length:** 13" overall (7.5" barrel). **Grips:** Hogue Tamer Monogrip. **Features:** Similar to standard Redhawk except has heavy extended frame with Ruger Integral Scope Mounting System on wide topstrap. Wide hammer spur lowered for better scope clearance. Incorporates mechanical design features and improvements of GP-100. Ramp front sight base has Redhawk-style Interchangeable Insert sight blades, adjustable rear sight. Satin stainless steel and low-glare stainless finishes. Introduced 1987.
Price: KSRH-2454, 2.5" 454 Casull/45 Colt, Hogue Tamer
Monogrip, Alaskan Model **$992.00**
Price: KSRH-7, 7.5" 44 Mag, Ruger grip **$915.00**
Price: KSRH-7454, 7.5" 45 Colt/454 Casull **$992.00**
Price: KSRH-9, 9" 44 Mag, Ruger grip **$915.00**
Price: KSRH-9480-5, 9.5", 480 Ruger, intr. 2008 . . . .**$963.00**
Price: KSRH-2, 2.5" 44 Mag, Alaskan Model, intr. 2008 . . . . .**$992.00**

SMITH & WESSON MODEL 14 CLASSIC

Caliber: 38 Spec. +P, 6-shot. **Barrel:** 6". **Weight:** 35 oz. **Length:** 11.5". Grips: Wood. Sights: Pinned Patridge front, micro adjustable rear. Features: Recreation of the vintage Model 14 revolver. Carbon steel frame and cylinder with blued finish.
Price: **$995.00**
Price: Model 14 150253, nickel finish **$1,074.00**

SMITH & WESSON M&P REVOLVERS

Caliber: 38 Spec., 357 Mag., 5 rounds (Centennial), 8 rounds (large frame). **Barrel:** 1.87" (Centennial), 5" (large frame). **Weight:** 13.3 oz. (Centennial), 36.3 oz. (large frame). **Length:** 6.31" overall (small frame), 10.5" (large frame). **Grips:** Synthetic. **Sights:** Integral U-Notch rear, XS Sights 24/7 Tritium Night. **Features:** Scandium alloy frame, stainless steel cylinder, matte black finish. Made in U.S.A. by Smith & Wesson.
Price: M&P 340, double action **$869.00**
Price: M&P 340CT, Crimson Trace Lasergrips. **$1,122.00**
Price: M&P R8 large frame. **$1,311.00**

SMITH & WESSON NIGHT GUARD REVOLVERS

Caliber: 357 Mag., 38 Spec. +P, 5-, 6-, 7-, 8-shot. **Barrel:** 2.5 or 2.75" (45 ACP). **Weight:** 24.2 oz. (2.5" barrel). **Length:** 7.325" overall (2.5" barrel). **Grips:** Pachmayr Compac Custom. **Sights:** XS Sight 24/7 Standard Dot Tritium front, Cylinder & Slide Extreme Duty fixed rear. **Features:** Scandium alloy frame, stainless PVD cylinder, matte black finish. Introduced 2008. Made in U.S.A. by Smith & Wesson.
Price: Model 310, 10mm/40 S&W (interchangeable), 2.75" barrel,
large-frame snubnose **$1,153.00**
Price: Model 315, 38 Special +P, 2.5" barrel,
medium-frame snubnose **$995.00**
Price: Model 325, 45 ACP, 2.75" barrel, large-frame
snubnose **$1,153.00**
Price: Model 327, 38/357, 2.5" barrel, large-frame
snubnose **$1,153.00**
Price: Model 329, 44 Magnum/38 Special (interchangeable),
2.5" barrel, large-frame snubnose **$1,153.00**

Price: Model 357, 41 Magnum, 2.75" barrel, large-frame
snubnose **$1,153.00**
Price: Model 386, 357 Magnum/44 Special +P (interchangeable),
2.5" barrel, medium-frame snubnose. **$1,074.00**
Price: Model 396, 44 Special, 2.5" barrel, medium-frame
snubnose **$1,074.00**

SMITH & WESSON J-FRAME REVOLVERS

The smallest S&W wheelguns come in a variety of chamberings, barrel lengths, and materials, as noted in the individual model listings.

SMITH & WESSON 60LS/642LS LADYSMITH REVOLVERS

Caliber: .38 Spec. +P, 357 Mag., 5-shot. **Barrel:** 1-7/8" (642LS); 2-1/8" (60LS) **Weight:** 14.5 oz. (642LS); 21.5 oz. (60LS); **Length:** 6.6" overall (60LS); . **Grips:** Wood. **Sights:** Black blade, serrated ramp front, fixed notch rear. **Features:** 60LS model has a Chiefs Special-style frame. 642LS has Centennial-style frame, frosted matte finish, smooth combat wood grips. Introduced 1996. Comes in a fitted carry/storage case. Introduced 1989. Made in U.S.A. by Smith & Wesson.
Price: From **$782.00**

SMITH & WESSON MODEL 63

Caliber: 22 LR, 8-shot. **Barrel:** 5". **Weight:** 28.8 oz. **Length:** 9.5" overall. **Grips:** Black rubber. **Sights:** Black ramp front sight, adjustable black blade rear sight. **Features:** Stainless steel construction throughout. Made in U.S.A. by Smith & Wesson.
Price: **$845.00**

SMITH & WESSON MODEL 442/637/638/642 AIRWEIGHT REVOLVERS

Caliber: 38 Spec. +P, 5-shot. **Barrel:** 1-7/8". **Weight:** 15 oz. (37, 442); 20 oz. (3); 21.5 oz.; **Length:** 6-3/8" overall. **Grips:** Soft rubber. **Sights:** Fixed, serrated ramp front, square notch rear. **Features:** Aluminum-alloy frames. Models 37, 637; Chiefs Special-style frame with exposed hammer. Introduced 1996. Models 442, 642; Centennial-style frame, enclosed hammer. Model 638, Bodyguard style, shrouded hammer. Comes in a fitted carry/storage case. Introduced 1989. Made in U.S.A. by Smith & Wesson.
Price: From **$600.00**

SMITH & WESSON MODEL 60 CHIEF'S SPECIAL

Caliber: 357 Mag., 38 Spec. +P, 5-shot. **Barrel:** 2-1/8", 3" or 5". **Weight:** 22.5 oz. (2-1/8" barrel). **Length:** 6-5/8" overall (2-1/8" barrel). **Grips:** Rounded butt synthetic grips. **Sights:** Fixed, serrated ramp front, square notch rear. **Features:** Stainless steel construction, satin finish, internal lock. Introduced 1965. The 5"-barrel model has target semi-lug barrel, rosewood grip, red ramp front sight, adjustable rear sight. Made in U.S.A. by Smith & Wesson.
Price: 2-1/8" barrel, intr. 2005 . . . .**$798.00**
Price: 3" barrel, 7.5" OAL, 24 oz. **$830.00**

Smith & Wesson
Model 317 AirLite

Smith & Wesson
Model 340

Smith & Wesson
Model 360 PD Airlite
SC Chief's Special

Smith & Wesson
Model 438

Smith & Wesson
Model 632

Smith & Wesson
Model 10

SMITH & WESSON MODEL 317 AIRLITE REVOLVERS
Caliber: 22 LR, 8-shot. **Barrel:** 1-7/8", 3". **Weight:** 10.5 oz. **Length:** 6.25" overall (1-7/8" barrel). **Grips:** Rubber. **Sights:** Serrated ramp front, fixed notch rear. **Features:** Aluminum alloy, carbon and stainless steels, Chiefs Special-style frame with exposed hammer. Smooth combat trigger. Clear Cote finish. Introduced 1997. Made in U.S.A. by Smith & Wesson.
Price: Model 317, 1-7/8" barrel **$766.00**
Price: Model 317 w/HiViz front sight, 3" barrel, 7.25 OAL **$830.00**

SMITH & WESSON MODEL 340/340PD AIRLITE SC CENTENNIAL
Caliber: 357 Mag., 38 Spec. +P, 5-shot. **Barrel:** 1-7/8". **Weight:** 12 oz. **Length:** 6-3/8" overall (1-7/8" barrel). **Grips:** Rounded butt rubber. **Sights:** Black blade front, rear notch **Features:** Centennial-style frame, enclosed hammer. Internal lock. Matte silver finish. Scandium alloy frame, titanium cylinder, stainless steel barrel liner. Made in U.S.A. by Smith & Wesson.
Price: Model 340 ....**$1,051.00**
Price: Model 340PD **$1,122.00**

SMITH & WESSON MODEL 351PD REVOLVER
Caliber: 22 Mag., 7-shot. **Barrel:** 1-7/8". **Weight:** 10.6 oz. **Length:** 6.25" overall (1-7/8" barrel). **Sights:** HiViz front sight, rear notch. **Grips:** Wood. **Features:** Seven-shot, aluminum-alloy frame. Chiefs Special-style frame with exposed hammer. Nonreflective matte-black finish. Internal lock. Made in U.S.A. by Smith & Wesson.
Price: **$830.00**

SMITH & WESSON MODEL 360/360PD AIRLITE CHIEF'S SPECIAL
Caliber: 357 Mag., 38 Spec. +P, 5-shot. **Barrel:** 1-7/8". **Weight:** 12 oz. **Length:** 6-3/8" overall (1-7/8" barrel). **Grips:** Rounded butt rubber. **Sights:** Black blade front, fixed rear notch. **Features:** Chief's Special-style frame with exposed hammer. Internal lock. Scandium alloy frame, titanium cylinder, stainless steel barrel. Made in U.S.A. by Smith & Wesson.
Price: 360PD **$988.00**

SMITH & WESSON MODEL 438
Caliber: 38 Spec. +P, 5-shot. **Barrel:** 1-7/8". **Weight:** 15.1 oz. **Length:** 6.31" overall. **Grips:** Synthetic. **Sights:** Fixed front and rear. **Features:** Aluminum alloy frame, stainless steel cylinder. Matte black finish throughout. Made in U.S.A. by Smith & Wesson.
Price: **$624.00**

SMITH & WESSON MODEL 632 POWERPORT PRO SERIES
Caliber: 327 Mag., 6-shot. **Barrel:** 3". **Weight:** 24.5 oz. **Length:** 7.5". **Grips:** Synthetic. **Sights:** Pinned serrated ramp front, adjustable rear. **Features:** Full-lug ported barrel with full-length extractor. Stainless steel frame and cylinder. Introduced 2009.
Price: **$980.00**

SMITH & WESSON MODEL 637
Caliber: 38 Spec. +P, 5-shot. **Barrel:** 1-7/8". **Weight:** 15 oz. **Length:** 6-3/8" overall. **Grips:** Rubber. **Sights:** Integral front sight, fixed rear sight. **Features:** Aluminum alloy frame with stainless steel cylinder.

Matte silver finish. Made in U.S.A. by Smith & Wesson.
Price: **$600.00**
Price: Model 637CT, Crimson Trace lasergrips **$877.00**

SMITH & WESSON MODEL 640 CENTENNIAL DA ONLY
Caliber: 357 Mag., 38 Spec. +P, 5-shot. **Barrel:** 2-1/8". **Weight:** 23 oz. **Length:** 6.75" overall. **Grips:** Uncle Mike's Boot grip. **Sights:** Serrated ramp front, fixed notch rear. **Features:** Stainless steel. Fully concealed hammer, snag-proof smooth edges. Internal lock. Introduced 1995 in 357 Mag.
Price: **$798.00**

SMITH & WESSON MODEL 642
Caliber: 38 Spec. +P, 5-shot. **Barrel:** 1-7/8". **Weight:** 15 oz. **Length:** 6-3/8" overall. **Grips:** Rubber. **Sights:** Fixed front and rear. **Features:** Aluminum alloy frame, stainless steel cylinder. Matte silver finish. Made in U.S.A. by Smith & Wesson.
Price: **$600.00**

SMITH & WESSON MODEL 649 BODYGUARD REVOLVER
Caliber: 357 Mag., 38 Spec. +P, 5-shot. **Barrel:** 2-1/8". **Weight:** 23 oz. **Length:** 6-5/8" overall. **Grips:** Uncle Mike's Combat. **Sights:** Black pinned ramp front, fixed notch rear. **Features:** Stainless steel construction, satin finish. Internal lock. Bodyguard style, shrouded hammer. Made in U.S.A. by Smith & Wesson.
Price: **$798.00**

SMITH & WESSON K-FRAME/L-FRAME REVOLVERS
These mid-size S&W wheelguns come in a variety of chamberings, barrel lengths, and materials, as noted in individual model listings.

SMITH & WESSON MODEL 10 REVOLVER
Caliber: 38 Spec. +P, 6-shot. **Barrel:** 4". **Weight:** 36 oz. **Length:** 8-7/8" overall. **Grips:** Soft rubber; square butt. **Sights:** Fixed; black blade front, square notch rear. Blued carbon steel frame.
Price: Blue **$758.00**

SMITH & WESSON MODEL 64/67 REVOLVERS
Caliber: 38 Spec. +P, 6-shot. **Barrel:** 3". **Weight:** 33 oz. **Length:** 8-7/8" overall. **Grips:** Soft rubber. **Sights:** Fixed, 1/8" serrated ramp front, square notch rear. Model 67 (**Weight:** 36 oz. **Length:** 8-7/8") similar to Model 64 except for adjustable sights. **Features:** Satin finished stainless steel, square butt.
Price: From **$758.00**

SMITH & WESSON MODEL 617 REVOLVERS
Caliber: 22 LR, 6- or 10-shot. **Barrel:** 4". **Weight:** 41 oz. (4" barrel). **Length:** 9-1/8" (4" barrel). **Grips:** Soft rubber. **Sights:** Patridge front, adjustable rear. Drilled and tapped for scope mount. **Features:** Stainless steel with satin finish; 4" has .312" smooth trigger, .375" semi-target hammer; 6" has either .312" combat or .400" serrated trigger, .375" semi-target or .500" target hammer; 8-3/8" with .400" serrated trigger, .500" target hammer. Introduced 1990.
Price: From **$916.00**

Smith & Wesson Model 686 SSR

Smith & Wesson Model 21

Smith & Wesson Model 329

Smith & Wesson Model 625

Smith & Wesson Model 500

Smith & Wesson Model 460V

SMITH & WESSON MODELS 620 REVOLVERS
Caliber: 38 Spec. +P; 357 Mag., 7 rounds. **Barrel:** 4". **Weight:** 37.5 oz. **Length:** 9.5". **Grips:** Rubber. **Sights:** Integral front blade, fixed rear notch on the 619; adjustable white-outline target style rear, red ramp front on 620. **Features:** Replaces Models 65 and 66. Two-piece semi-lug barrel. Satin stainless frame and cylinder. Made in U.S.A. by Smith & Wesson.
Price: **$893.00**

SMITH & WESSON MODEL 686/686 PLUS REVOLVERS
Caliber: 357 Mag., 38 S&W Special; 6 rounds. **Barrel:** 2.5", 4", 6". **Weight:** 35 oz. (2.5" barrel). **Length:** 7.5", (2.5" barrel). **Grips:** Rubber. **Sights:** White outline adjustable rear, red ramp front. **Features:** Satin stainless frame and cylinder. Plus series guns have 7-shot cylinders. Introduced 1996. Powerport (PP) has Patridge front, adjustable rear sight. Introduced early 1980s. Stock Service Revolver (SSR) intr. 2007. **Capacity:** 6. **Barrel:** 4". **Sights:** Interchangeable front, adjustable rear. **Grips:** Wood. **Finish:** Satin stainless frame and cylinder. **Weight:** 38.3 oz. **Features:** Chamfered charge holes, custom barrel w/recessed crown, bossed mainspring. High-hold ergonomic grip. Made in U.S.A. by Smith & Wesson.
Price: 686 . . . .**$909.00**
Price: Plus, 7 rounds **$932.00**
Price: PP, 6" barrel, 6 rounds, 11-3/8" OAL **$877.00**
Price: SSR **$1,059.00**

SMITH & WESSON N-FRAME REVOLVERS
These large-frame S&W wheelguns come in a variety of chamberings, barrel lengths, and materials, as noted in the individual model listings.

SMITH & WESSON MODEL 21
Caliber: 44 Special, 6-round. **Barrel:** 4" tapered. **Weight:** NA. **Length:** NA. **Grips:** Smooth wood. **Sights:** Pinned half-moon service front; service rear. **Features:** Carbon steel frame, blued finish.
Price: **$924.00**

SMITH & WESSON MODEL 29 CLASSIC
Caliber: 44 Mag, 6-round. **Barrel:** 6.5". **Weight:** 48.5 oz. **Length:** 12". **Grips:** Altamont service walnut. **Sights:** Adjustable white-outline rear, red ramp front. **Features:** Carbon steel frame, polished-blued or nickel finish. Has integral key lock safety feature to prevent accidental discharges. Alo available with 3" barrel. Original Model 29 made famous by "Dirty Harry" character created in 1971 by Clint Eastwood.
Price: **$1240.00**

SMITH & WESSON MODEL 329PD AIRLITE REVOLVERS
Caliber: 44 Spec., 44 Mag., 6-round. **Barrel:** 4". **Weight:** 26 oz. **Length:** 9.5". **Grips:** Wood. **Sights:** Adj. rear, HiViz orange-dot front. **Features:** Scandium alloy frame, blue/black finish.
Price: From **$1,264.00**

SMITH & WESSON MODEL 625/625JM REVOLVERS
Caliber: 45 ACP, 6-shot. **Barrel:** 4", 5". **Weight:** 43 oz. (4" barrel). **Length:** 9-3/8" overall (4" barrel). **Grips:** Soft rubber; wood optional. **Sights:** Patridge front on ramp, S&W micrometer click rear adjustable for windage and elevation. **Features:** Stainless steel construction with .400" semi-target hammer, .312" smooth combat trigger; full lug barrel. Glass beaded finish. Introduced 1989. "Jerry Miculek" Professional (JM) Series has .265"-wide grooved trigger, special wooden Miculek Grip, five full moon clips, gold bead Patridge front sight on interchangeable front sight base, bead blast finish. Unique serial number run. Mountain Gun has 4" tapered barrel, drilled and tapped, Hogue Rubber Monogrip, pinned black ramp front sight, micrometer click-adjustable rear sight, satin stainless frame and barrel, weighs 39.5 oz.
Price: 625JM **$1,074.00**

SMITH & WESSON MODEL 629 REVOLVERS
Caliber: 44 Magnum, 44 S&W Special, 6-shot. **Barrel:** 4", 5", 6.5". **Weight:** 41.5 oz. (4" bbl.). **Length:** 9-5/8" overall (4" bbl.). **Grips:** Soft rubber; wood optional. **Sights:** 1/8" red ramp front, white outline rear, internal lock, adjustable for windage and elevation. Classic similar to standard Model 629, except Classic has full-lug 5" barrel, chamfered front of cylinder, interchangeable red ramp front sight with adjustable white outline rear, Hogue grips with S&W monogram, drilled and tapped for scope mounting. Factory accurizing and endurance packages. Introduced 1990. Classic Power Port has Patridge front sight and adjustable rear sight. Model 629CT has 5" barrel, Crimson Trace Hoghunter Lasergrips, 10.5" OAL, 45.5 oz. weight. Introduced 2006.
Price: From **$1,035.00**

SMITH & WESSON X-FRAME REVOLVERS
These extra-large X-frame S&W wheelguns come in a variety of chamberings, barrel lengths, and materials, as noted in individual model listings.

SMITH & WESSON MODEL S&W500 (163565)
Caliber: 500 S&W Mag., 5 rounds. **Barrel:** 6.5". **Weight:** 60.7 oz. **Length:** 12.875". **Grips:** Synthetic. **Sights:** Red Ramp front sights, adjustable white outline rear. **Features:** Similar to other S&W500 models but with integral compensator and half-length ejector shroud. Made in U.S.A. by Smith & Wesson.
Price: From **$1,375.00**

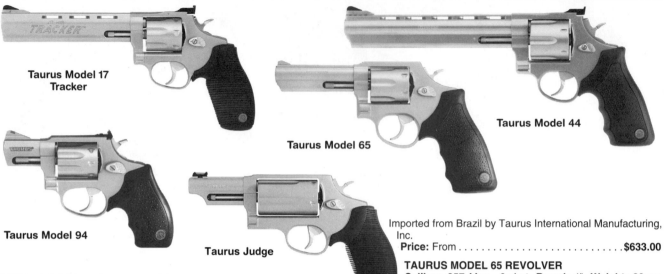

Taurus Model 17 Tracker

Taurus Model 65

Taurus Model 44

Taurus Model 94

Taurus Judge

SMITH & WESSON MODEL 460V REVOLVERS

Caliber: 460 S&W Mag., 5-shot. Also chambers 454 Casull, 45 Colt. **Barrel:** 8-3/8" gain-twist rifling. **Weight:** 62.5 oz. **Length:** 11.25". **Grips:** Rubber. **Sights:** Adj. rear, red ramp front. **Features:** Satin stainless steel frame and cylinder, interchangeable compensator. 460XVR (X-treme Velocity Revolver) has black blade front sight with interchangeable green Hi-Viz tubes, adjustable rear sight. 7.5"-barrel version has Lothar-Walther barrel, 360-degree recoil compensator, tuned Performance Center action, pinned sear, integral Weaver base, non-glare surfaces, scope mount accessory kit for mounting full-size scopes, flashed-chromed hammer and trigger, Performance Center gun rug and shoulder sling. Interchangeable Hi-Viz green dot front sight, adjustable black rear sight, Hogue Dual Density Monogrip, matte-black frame and shroud finish with glass-bead cylinder finish, 72 oz. Compensated Hunter has tear drop chrome hammer, .312 chrome trigger, Hogue Dual Density Monogrip, satin/matte stainless finish, HiViz interchangeable front sight, adjustable black rear sight. XVR introduced 2006.
Price: 460V **$1,446.00**
Price: 460XVR, from **$1,446.00**

SMITH & WESSON MODEL 500 REVOLVERS

Caliber: 500 S&W Mag., 5 rounds. **Barrel:** 4", 8-3/8". **Weight:** 72.5 oz. **Length:** 15" (8-3/8" barrel). **Grips:** Hogue Sorbothane Rubber. **Sights:** Interchangeable blade, front, adjustable rear. **Features:** Recoil compensator, ball detent cylinder latch, internal lock. 6.5"-barrel model has orange-ramp dovetail Millett front sight, adjustable black rear sight, Hogue Dual Density Monogrip, .312" chrome trigger with over-travel stop, chrome tear-drop hammer, glassbead finish. 10.5"-barrel model has red ramp front sight, adjustable rear sight, .312 chrome trigger with overtravel stop, chrome tear drop hammer with pinned sear, hunting sling. Compensated Hunter has .400 orange ramp dovetail front sight, adjustable black blade rear sight, Hogue Dual Density Monogrip, glassbead finish w/black clear coat. Made in U.S.A. by Smith & Wesson.
Price: From **$1,375.00**

SUPER SIX CLASSIC BISON BULL

Caliber: 45-80 Government, 6-shot. **Barrel:** 10" octagonal with 1:14 twist. **Weight:** 6 lbs. **Length:** 17.5"overall. **Grips:** NA. **Sights:** Ramp front sight with dovetailed blade, click-adjustable rear. **Features:** Manganese bronze frame. Integral scope mount, manual crossbolt safety.
Price: . . . . **Appx. $1,100.00**

TAURUS MODEL 17 "TRACKER"

Caliber: 17 HMR, 7-shot. **Barrel:** 6.5". **Weight:** 45.8 oz. **Grips:** Rubber. **Sights:** Adjustable. **Features:** Double action, matte stainless, integral key-lock.
Price: From **$453.00**

TAURUS MODEL 44 REVOLVER

Caliber: 44 Mag., 6-shot. **Barrel:** 4", 6.5", 8-3/8". **Weight:** 44-3/4 oz. **Grips:** Rubber. **Sights:** Adjustable. **Features:** Double-action. Integral key-lock. Introduced 1994. New Model 44S12 has 12" vent rib barrel.

Imported from Brazil by Taurus International Manufacturing, Inc.
Price: From **$633.00**

TAURUS MODEL 65 REVOLVER

Caliber: 357 Mag., 6-shot. **Barrel:** 4". **Weight:** 38 oz. **Length:** 10.5" overall. **Grips:** Soft rubber. **Sights:** Fixed. **Features:** Double action, integral key-lock. Seven models for 2006 Imported by Taurus International.
Price: From **$419.00**

Taurus Model 66 Revolver

Similar to Model 65, 4" or 6" barrel, 7-shot cylinder, adjustable rear sight. Integral key-lock action. Imported by Taurus International.
Price: From **$469.00**

TAURUS MODEL 82 HEAVY BARREL REVOLVER

Caliber: 38 Spec., 6-shot. **Barrel:** 4", heavy. **Weight:** 36.5 oz. **Length:** 9-1/4" overall (4" bbl.). **Grips:** Soft black rubber. **Sights:** Serrated ramp front, square notch rear. **Features:** Double action, solid rib, integral key-lock. Imported by Taurus International.
Price: From **$403.00**

TAURUS MODEL 85 REVOLVER

Caliber: 38 Spec., 5-shot. **Barrel:** 2". **Weight:** 17-24.5 oz., titanium 13.5-15.4 oz. **Grips:** Rubber, rosewood or mother-of-pearl. **Sights:** Ramp front, square notch rear. **Features:** Blue, matte stainless, blue with gold accents, stainless with gold accents; rated for +P ammo. Integral keylock. Some models have titantium frame. Introduced 1980. Imported by Taurus International.
Price: From **$403.00**

Taurus 851 & 651 Revolvers

Small frame SA/DA revolvers similar to Taurus Model 85 but with Centennial-style concealed-hammer frame. Chambered in 38 Special +P (Model 851) or 357 Magnum (Model 651). Features include five-shot cylinder; 2" barrel; fixed sights; blue, matte blue, titanium or stainless finish; Taurus security lock. Overall length is 6.5". Weighs 15.5 oz. (titanium) to 25 oz. (blued and stainless).
Price: From **$411.00**

TAURUS MODEL 94 REVOLVER

Caliber: 22 LR, 9-shot cylinder; 22 Mag, 8-shot cylinder **Barrel:** 2", 4", 5". **Weight:** 18.5-27.5 oz. **Grips:** Soft black rubber. **Sights:** Serrated ramp front, click-adjustable rear. **Features:** Double action, integral key-lock. Introduced 1989. Imported by Taurus International.
Price: From **$369.00**

TAURUS MODEL 4510 JUDGE

Caliber: 3" .410/45 LC, 2.5" .410/45 LC. **Barrel:** 3", 6.5" (blued finish). **Weight:** 35.2 oz., 22.4 oz. **Length:** 7.5". **Grips:** Ribber. **Sights:** Fiber Optic. **Features:** DA/SA. Matte Stainless and Ultra-Lite Stainless finish. Introduced in 2007. Imported from Brazil by Taurus International.
Price: 4510T TrackerSS Matte Stainless **$569.00**
Price: 4510TKR-3B Judge **$558.00**
Price: 4510TKR-SSR, ported barrel, tactical rail **$608.00**

TAURUS RAGING BULL MODEL 416

Caliber: 41 Magnum, 6-shot. **Barrel:** 6.5". **Weight:** 61.9 oz. **Grips:** Rubber. **Sights:** Adjustable. **Features:** Double-action, ported, ventilated rib, matte stainless, integral key-lock.
Price: **$706.00**

Taurus 444 Ultra-Lite

Taurus Model 605

Taurus Model 444 Raging Bull

Taurus Model 608

Taurus Model 651

Taurus Model 650

Taurus Model 970 Tracker

TAURUS MODEL 425 TRACKER REVOLVERS
Caliber: 357 Mag., 7-shot; 41 Mag., 5-shot.
Barrel: 4" and 6". **Weight:** 28.8-40 oz. (titanium) 24.3-28. (6"). **Grips:** Rubber. **Sights:** Fixed front, adjustable rear. **Features:** Double-action stainless steel, Shadow Gray or Total Titanium; vent rib (steel models only); integral key-lock action. Imported by Taurus International.
Price: From $569.00

TAURUS MODEL 444 ULTRA-LIGHT
Caliber: 44 Mag, 5-shot. **Barrel:** 4". **Weight:** 28.3 oz. **Length:** 9.8"overall. **Grips:** Cushioned inset rubber. **Sights:** Fixed red-fiber optic front, adjustable rear. **Features:** UltraLite titanium blue finish, titanium/alloy frame built on Raging Bull design. Smooth trigger shoe, 1.760" wide, 6.280" tall. Barrel rate of twist 1:16", 6 grooves. Introduced 2005. Imported by Taurus International.
Price: $666.00

TAURUS MODEL 416/444/454 RAGING BULL REVOLVERS
Caliber: 41 Mag., 44 Mag., 454 Casull. **Barrel:** 2.25" (454 Casull only), 5", 6.5", 8-3/8". **Weight:** 53-63 oz. **Length:** 12" overall (6.5" barrel). **Grips:** Soft black rubber. **Sights:** Patridge front, adjustable rear. **Features:** Double-action, ventilated rib, ported, integral key-lock. Introduced 1997. Imported by Taurus International.
Price: From $641.00

TAURUS MODEL 605 REVOLVER
Caliber: 357 Mag., 5-shot. **Barrel:** 2". **Weight:** 24 oz. **Grips:** Rubber. **Sights:** Fixed. **Features:** Double-action, blue or stainless or titanium, concealed hammer models DAO, porting optional, integral key-lock. Introduced 1995. Imported by Taurus International.
Price: From $403.00

TAURUS MODEL 608 REVOLVER
Caliber: 357 Mag. 38 Spec., 8-shot. **Barrel:** 4", 6.5", 8-3/8". **Weight:** 44-57 oz. **Length:** 9-3/8" overall. **Grips:** Soft black rubber. **Sights:** Adjustable. **Features:** Double-action, integral key-lock action. Available in blue or stainless. Introduced 1995. Imported by Taurus International.
Price: From. $584.00

TAURUS MODEL 617 REVOLVER
Caliber: 357 Mag., 7-shot. **Barrel:** 2". **Weight:** 28.3 oz. **Length:** 6.75" overall. **Grips:** Soft black rubber. **Sights:** Fixed. **Features:** Double-action, blue, Shadow Gray, bright spectrum blue or matte stainless steel, integral key-lock. Available with porting, concealed hammer. Introduced 1998. Imported by Taurus International.
Price: $436.00

TAURUS MODEL 650 CIA REVOLVER
Caliber: 357 Mag., 5-shot. **Barrel:** 2". **Weight:** 24.5 oz. **Grips:** Rubber. **Sights:** Ramp front, square notch rear. **Features:** Double-action only, blue or matte stainless steel, integral key-lock, internal hammer. Introduced 2001. From Taurus International.
Price: From $411.00

TAURUS MODEL 651 PROTECTOR REVOLVER
Caliber: 357 Mag., 5-shot. **Barrel:** 2". **Weight:** 17-24.5 oz. **Grips:** Rubber. **Sights:** Fixed. **Features:** Concealed single-action/double-action design. Shrouded cockable hammer, blue, matte stainless, Shadow Gray, Total Titanium, integral key-lock. Made in Brazil. Imported by Taurus International Manufacturing, Inc.
Price: From $411.00

Taurus Model 731 Revolver
Similar to the Taurus Model 605, except in .32 Magnum.
Price: $469.00

TAURUS MODEL 817 ULTRA-LITE REVOLVER
Caliber: 38 Spec., 7-shot. **Barrel:** 2". **Weight:** 21 oz. **Length:** 6.5" overall. **Grips:** Soft rubber. **Sights:** Fixed. **Features:** Double-action, integral key-lock. Rated for +P ammo. Introduced 1999. Imported from Brazil by Taurus International.
Price: From $436.00

TAURUS MODEL 850 CIA REVOLVER
Caliber: 38 Spec., 5-shot. **Barrel:** 2". **Weight:** 17-24.5 oz. **Grips:** Rubber, mother-of-pearl. **Sights:** Ramp front, square notch rear. **Features:** Double-action only, blue or matte stainless steel, rated for +P ammo, integral key-lock, internal hammer. Introduced 2001. From Taurus International.
Price: From $411.00

TAURUS MODEL 941 REVOLVER
Caliber: 22 LR (Mod. 94), 22 WMR (Mod. 941), 8-shot. **Barrel:** 2", 4", 5". **Weight:** 27.5 oz. (4" barrel). **Grips:** Soft black rubber. **Sights:** Serrated ramp front, rear adjustable. **Features:** Double-action, integral key-lock. Introduced 1992. Imported by Taurus International.
Price: From $386.00

TAURUS MODEL 970/971 TRACKER REVOLVERS
Caliber: 22 LR (Model 970), 22 Magnum (Model 971); 7-shot. **Barrel:** 6". **Weight:** 53.6 oz. **Grips:** Rubber. **Sights:** Adjustable. **Features:** Double barrel, heavy barrel with ventilated rib; matte stainless finish, integral key-lock. Introduced 2001. From Taurus International.
Price: $453.00
Price: Model 17SS6, chambered in 17 HMR $453.00

Both classic six-shooters and modern adaptations for hunting and sport.

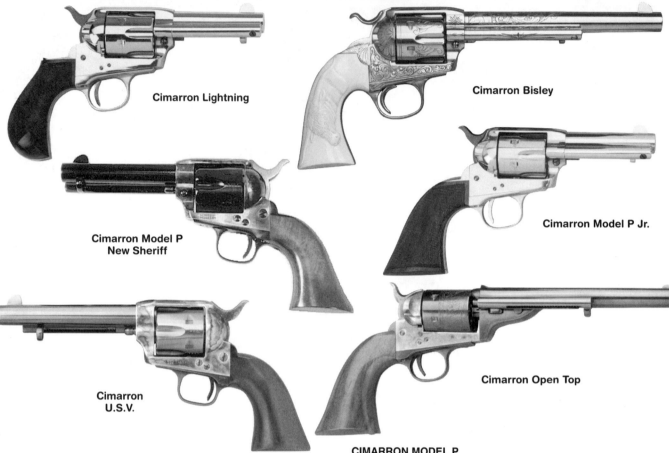

Cimarron Lightning

Cimarron Bisley

Cimarron Model P
New Sheriff

Cimarron Model P Jr.

Cimarron
U.S.V.

Cimarron Open Top

BERETTA STAMPEDE SINGLE-ACTION REVOLVER
Caliber: 357 Mag, 45 Colt, 6-shot. Barrel: 4.75", 5.5", 7.5", blued. Weight: 36.8 oz. (4.75" barrel). Length: 9.5" overall (4.75" barrel). Grips: Wood, walnut, black polymer. Sights: Blade front, notch rear. Features: Transfer-bar safety. Introduced 2003. Stampede Inox (2004) is stainless steel with black polymer grips. Compact Stampede Marshall (2004) has birdshead-style walnut grips, 3.5" barrel, color-case-hardened frame, blued barrel and cylinder. Manufactured for Beretta by Uberti.
Price: Nickel, 45 Colt $630.00
Price: Blued, 45 Colt, 357 Mag, 4.75", 5-1/2" $575.00
Price: Deluxe, 45 Colt, 357 Mag. 4.75", 5-1/2" $675.00
Price: Marshall, 45 Colt, 357 Mag. 3.5" $575.00
Price: Bisley nickel, 4.75", 5.5" $775.00
Price: Bisley, 4.75", 5.5" $675.00
Price: Stampede Deluxe, 45 Colt 7.5" $775.00
Price: Stampede Blued, 45 Colt 7.5" $575.00
Price: Marshall Old West, 45 Colt 3.5" $650.00

CHARTER ARMS DIXIE DERRINGER
Caliber: 22 LR, 22 Magnum, 22 LR/Magnum convertible. Barrel: 1-1/8". Weight: 6 oz. Grips: NA. Sights: NA. Features: Single-action minigun, five-round cylinder, hammer block safety, stainless steel construction.
Price: $469.00

CIMARRON LIGHTNING SA
Caliber: 22 LR, 32-20, 32 H&R, 38 Colt, Barrel: 3.5", 4.75", 5.5". Grips: Smooth or checkered walnut. Sights: Blade front. Features: Replica of the Colt 1877 Lightning DA. Similar to Cimarron Thunderer, except smaller grip frame to fit smaller hands. Standard blue, charcoal blue or nickel finish with forged, old model, or color case hardened frame. Introduced 2001. From Cimarron F.A. Co.
Price: From $480.70

CIMARRON MODEL P
Caliber: 32 WCF, 38 WCF, 357 Mag., 44 WCF, 44 Spec., 45 Colt, 45 LC and 45 ACP. Barrel: 4.75", 5.5", 7.5". Weight: 39 oz. Length: 10" overall (4" barrel). Grips: Walnut. Sights: Blade front, fixed or adjustable rear. Features: Uses "old model" black powder frame with "Bullseye" ejector or New Model frame. Imported by Cimarron F.A. Co.
Price: from $494.09
Price: Laser Engraved, from $879.00
Price: New Sheriff, from $494.09

Cimarron Bisley Model Single-Action Revolvers
Similar to 1873 Model P, special grip frame and trigger guard, knurled wide-spur hammer, curved trigger. Available in 357 Mag., 44 WCF, 44 Spl., 45 Colt. Introduced 1999. Imported by Cimarron F.A. Co.
Price: From $574.43

CIMARRON MODEL "P" JR.
Caliber: 32-20, 32 H&R, Barrel: 3.5", 4.75", 5.5". Grips: Checkered walnut. Sights: Blade front. Features: Styled after 1873 Colt Peacemaker, except 20 percent smaller. Blue finish with color case-hardened frame; Cowboy action. Introduced 2001. From Cimarron F.A. Co.
Price: $400.36

CIMARRON U.S.V. ARTILLERY MODEL SINGLE-ACTION
Caliber: 45 Colt. Barrel: 5.5". Weight: 39 oz. Length: 11.5" overall. Grips: Walnut. Sights: Fixed. Features: U.S. markings and cartouche, case-hardened frame and hammer; 45 Colt only. Imported by Cimarron F.A. Co.
Price: $547.65

CIMARRON 1872 OPEN TOP REVOLVER
Caliber: 38, 44 Special, 44 Colt, 44 Russian, 45 LC, 45 S&W Schofield. Barrel: 5.5" and 7.5". Grips: Walnut. Sights: Blade front, fixed rear. Features: Replica of first cartridge-firing revolver. Blue, charcoal blue, nickel or Original finish; Navy-style brass or steel Army-style frame. Introduced 2001 by Cimarron F.A. Co.
Price: $467.31

Cimarron Thunderer

Colt Single-Action Army

EAA Bounty Hunter

EMF 1875 Outlaw

EMF 1890 Police

CIMARRON THUNDERER REVOLVER
Caliber: 357 Mag., 44 WCF, 45 Colt, 6-shot. **Barrel:** 3.5", 4.75", with ejector. **Weight:** 38 oz. (3.5" barrel). **Grips:** Smooth or checkered walnut. **Sights:** Blade front, notch rear. **Features:** Thunderer grip. Introduced 1993. Imported by Cimarron F.A. Co.
Price: Stainless.....................................$534.26

COLT SINGLE-ACTION ARMY REVOLVER
Caliber: 357 Mag., 38 Spec., .32/20, 44-40, 45 Colt, 6-shot. **Barrel:** 4.75", 5.5", 7.5". **Weight:** 40 oz. (4.75" barrel). **Length:** 10.25" overall (4.75" barrel). **Grips:** Black Eagle composite. **Sights:** Blade front, notch rear. **Features:** Available in full nickel finish with nickel grip medallions, or Royal Blue with color case-hardened frame. Reintroduced 1992. Sheriff's Model and Frontier Six introduced 2008.
Price: P1540, 32-20, 4.75" barrel, color case-hardened/blued
   finish...**$1,290.00**
Price: P1656, 357 Mag., 5.5" barrel, nickel finish..........**$1,490.00**
Price: P1876, 45 LC, 7.5" barrel, nickel finish **$1,490.00**
Price: P2830S SAA Sheriff's, 3" barrel, 45 LC (2008) **$1,290.00**
Price: P2950FSS Frontier Six Shooter, 5.5" barrel, 44-40
   (2008).......................................**$1,350.00**

EAA BOUNTY HUNTER SA REVOLVERS
Caliber: 22 LR/22 WMR, 357 Mag., 44 Mag., 45 Colt, 6-shot. **Barrel:** 4.5", 7.5". **Weight:** 2.5 lbs. **Length:** 11" overall (4-5/8" barrel). **Grips:** Smooth walnut. **Sights:** Blade front, grooved topstrap rear. **Features:** Transfer bar safety; 3-position hammer; hammer forged barrel. Introduced 1992. Imported by European American Armory.
Price: Blue or case-hardened, from $392.00
Price: Nickel $432.00
Price: 22 LR/22 WMR, blue $292.00
Price: As above, nickel $325.00

EMF MODEL 1873 FRONTIER MARSHAL
Caliber: 357 Mag., 45 Colt. **Barrel:** 4.75", 5-1/2", 7.5". **Weight:** 39 oz. **Length:** 10.5" overall. **Grips:** One-piece walnut. **Sights:** Blade front, notch rear. Features: Bright brass trigger guard and backstrap, color case-hardened frame, blued barrel and cylinder. Introduced 1998. Imported from Italy.
Price: **$485.00**

EMF HARTFORD SINGLE-ACTION REVOLVERS
Caliber: 357 Mag., 32-20, 38-40, 44-40, 44 Spec., 45 Colt. **Barrel:** 4.75", 5.5", 7.5". **Weight:** 45 oz. **Length:** 13" overall (7.5" barrel). **Grips:** Smooth walnut. **Sights:** Blade front, fixed rear. **Features:** Identical to the original Colts. All major parts serial numbered using original Colt-style lettering, numbering. Bullseye ejector head and color case-hardening on old model frame and hammer. Introduced 1990. Imported by E.M.F. Co.
Price: Old Model **$489.90**
Price: Case-hardened New Model frame **$489.90**

EMF Great Western II Express Single-Action Revolver
Same as the regular model except uses grip of the Colt Lightning revolver. Barrel lengths of 4.75". Introduced 2006. Imported by E.M.F. Co.
Price: Stainless, Ultra Ivory grips **$715.00**
Price: Walnut grips **$690.00**

EMF 1875 OUTLAW REVOLVER
Caliber: 357 Mag., 44-40, 45 Colt. **Barrel:** 7.5", 9.5". **Weight:** 46 oz. **Length:** 13.5" overall. **Grips:** Smooth walnut. **Sights:** Blade front, fixed groove rear. **Features:** Authentic copy of 1875 Remington with firing pin in hammer; color case-hardened frame, blue cylinder, barrel, steel backstrap and trigger guard. Also available in nickel, factory engraved. Imported by E.M.F. Co.
Price: All calibers **$479.90**
Price: Laser Engraved **$684.90**

EMF 1890 Police Revolver
Similar to the 1875 Outlaw except has 5.5" barrel, weighs 40 oz., with 12.5" overall length. Has lanyard ring in butt. No web under barrel. Calibers: 45 Colt. Imported by E.M.F. Co.
Price: **$489.90**

EMF 1873 GREAT WESTERN II
Caliber: .357, 45 LC, 44/40. **Barrel:** 4 3/4", 5.5", 7.5". **Weight:** 36 oz. **Length:** 11" (5.5"). **Grips:** Walnut. **Sights:** Blade front, notch rear. **Features:** Authentic reproduction of the original 2nd generation Colt single-action revolver. Standard and bone case hardening. Coil hammer spring. Hammer-forged barrel.
Price: 1873 Californian **$520.00**
Price: 1873 Custom series, bone or nickel, ivory-like grips .. **$689.90**
Price: 1873 Stainless steel, ivory-like grips **$589.90**

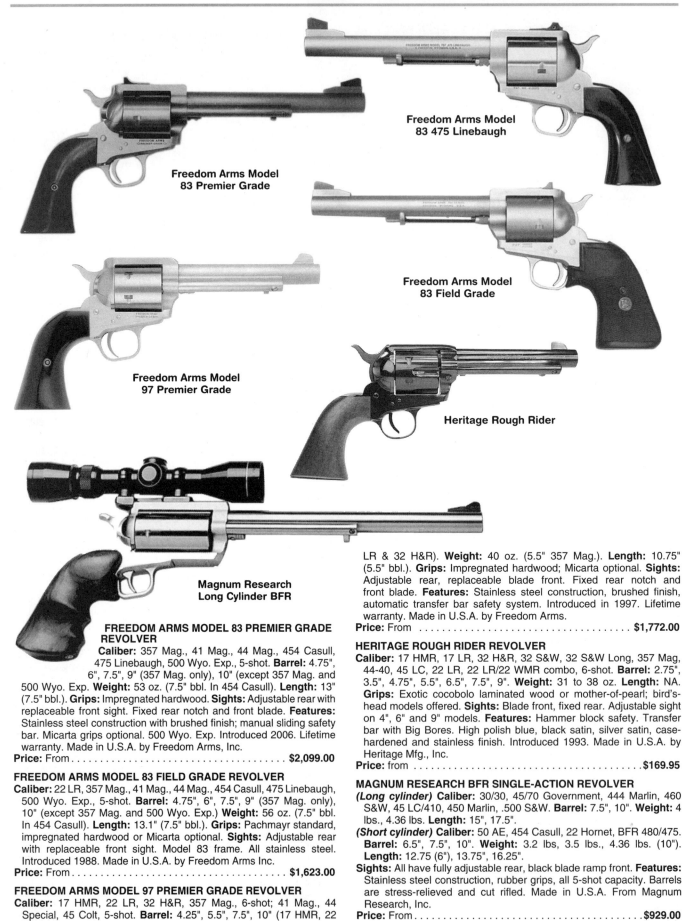

Freedom Arms Model
83 475 Linebaugh

Freedom Arms Model
83 Premier Grade

Freedom Arms Model
83 Field Grade

Freedom Arms Model
97 Premier Grade

Heritage Rough Rider

Magnum Research
Long Cylinder BFR

FREEDOM ARMS MODEL 83 PREMIER GRADE REVOLVER
Caliber: 357 Mag., 41 Mag., 44 Mag., 454 Casull, 475 Linebaugh, 500 Wyo. Exp., 5-shot. **Barrel:** 4.75", 6", 7.5", 9" (357 Mag. only), 10" (except 357 Mag. and 500 Wyo. Exp. **Weight:** 53 oz. (7.5" bbl. In 454 Casull). **Length:** 13" (7.5" bbl.). **Grips:** Impregnated hardwood. **Sights:** Adjustable rear with replaceable front sight. Fixed rear notch and front blade. **Features:** Stainless steel construction with brushed finish; manual sliding safety bar. Micarta grips optional. 500 Wyo. Exp. Introduced 2006. Lifetime warranty. Made in U.S.A. by Freedom Arms, Inc.
Price: From **$2,099.00**

FREEDOM ARMS MODEL 83 FIELD GRADE REVOLVER
Caliber: 22 LR, 357 Mag., 41 Mag., 44 Mag., 454 Casull, 475 Linebaugh, 500 Wyo. Exp., 5-shot. **Barrel:** 4.75", 6", 7.5", 9" (357 Mag. only), 10" (except 357 Mag. and 500 Wyo. Exp.) **Weight:** 56 oz. (7.5" bbl. In 454 Casull). **Length:** 13.1" (7.5" bbl.). **Grips:** Pachmayr standard, impregnated hardwood or Micarta optional. **Sights:** Adjustable rear with replaceable front sight. Model 83 frame. All stainless steel. Introduced 1988. Made in U.S.A. by Freedom Arms Inc.
Price: From **$1,623.00**

FREEDOM ARMS MODEL 97 PREMIER GRADE REVOLVER
Caliber: 17 HMR, 22 LR, 32 H&R, 357 Mag., 6-shot; 41 Mag., 44 Special, 45 Colt, 5-shot. **Barrel:** 4.25", 5.5", 7.5", 10" (17 HMR, 22 LR & 32 H&R). **Weight:** 40 oz. (5.5" 357 Mag.). **Length:** 10.75" (5.5" bbl.). **Grips:** Impregnated hardwood; Micarta optional. **Sights:** Adjustable rear, replaceable blade front. Fixed rear notch and front blade. **Features:** Stainless steel construction, brushed finish, automatic transfer bar safety system. Introduced in 1997. Lifetime warranty. Made in U.S.A. by Freedom Arms.
Price: From **$1,772.00**

HERITAGE ROUGH RIDER REVOLVER
Caliber: 17 HMR, 17 LR, 32 H&R, 32 S&W, 32 S&W Long, 357 Mag, 44-40, 45 LC, 22 LR, 22 LR/22 WMR combo, 6-shot. **Barrel:** 2.75", 3.5", 4.75", 5.5", 6.5", 7.5", 9". **Weight:** 31 to 38 oz. **Length:** NA. **Grips:** Exotic cocobolo laminated wood or mother-of-pearl; bird's-head models offered. **Sights:** Blade front, fixed rear. Adjustable sight on 4", 6" and 9" models. **Features:** Hammer block safety. Transfer bar with Big Bores. High polish blue, black satin, silver satin, case-hardened and stainless finish. Introduced 1993. Made in U.S.A. by Heritage Mfg., Inc.
Price: from **$169.95**

MAGNUM RESEARCH BFR SINGLE-ACTION REVOLVER
(Long cylinder) **Caliber:** 30/30, 45/70 Government, 444 Marlin, 460 S&W, 45 LC/410, 450 Marlin, .500 S&W. **Barrel:** 7.5", 10". **Weight:** 4 lbs., 4.36 lbs. **Length:** 15", 17.5".
(Short cylinder) **Caliber:** 50 AE, 454 Casull, 22 Hornet, BFR 480/475. **Barrel:** 6.5", 7.5", 10". **Weight:** 3.2 lbs., 3.5 lbs., 4.36 lbs. (10"). **Length:** 12.75 (6"), 13.75", 16.25".
Sights: All have fully adjustable rear, black blade ramp front. **Features:** Stainless steel construction, rubber grips, all 5-shot capacity. Barrels are stress-relieved and cut rifled. Made in U.S.A. From Magnum Research, Inc.
Price: From **$929.00**

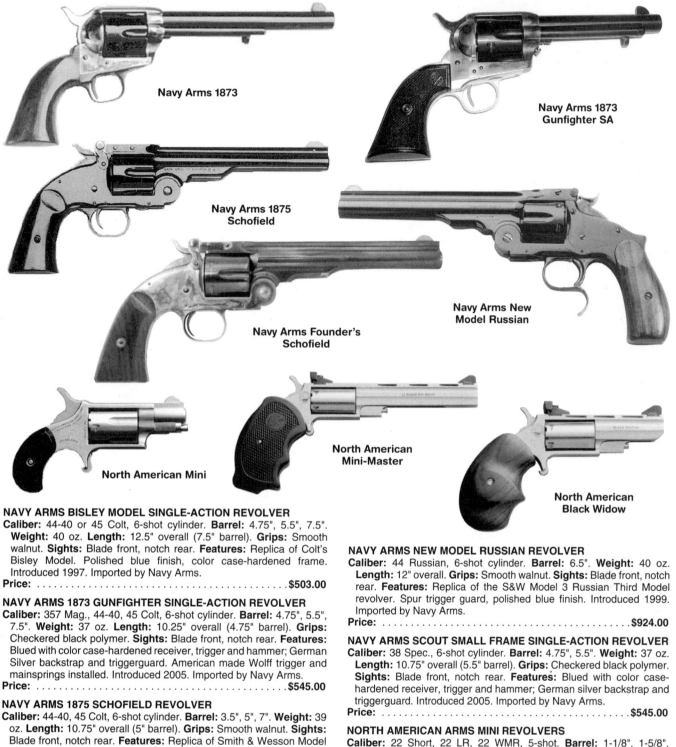

Navy Arms 1873

Navy Arms 1873
Gunfighter SA

Navy Arms 1875
Schofield

Navy Arms New
Model Russian

Navy Arms Founder's
Schofield

North American Mini

North American
Mini-Master

North American
Black Widow

NAVY ARMS BISLEY MODEL SINGLE-ACTION REVOLVER
Caliber: 44-40 or 45 Colt, 6-shot cylinder. **Barrel:** 4.75", 5.5", 7.5".
Weight: 40 oz. **Length:** 12.5" overall (7.5" barrel). **Grips:** Smooth
walnut. **Sights:** Blade front, notch rear. **Features:** Replica of Colt's
Bisley Model. Polished blue finish, color case-hardened frame.
Introduced 1997. Imported by Navy Arms.
Price: $503.00

NAVY ARMS 1873 GUNFIGHTER SINGLE-ACTION REVOLVER
Caliber: 357 Mag., 44-40, 45 Colt, 6-shot cylinder. **Barrel:** 4.75", 5.5",
7.5". **Weight:** 37 oz. **Length:** 10.25" overall (4.75" barrel). **Grips:**
Checkered black polymer. **Sights:** Blade front, notch rear. **Features:**
Blued with color case-hardened receiver, trigger and hammer; German
Silver backstrap and triggerguard. American made Wolff trigger and
mainsprings installed. Introduced 2005. Imported by Navy Arms.
Price: $545.00

NAVY ARMS 1875 SCHOFIELD REVOLVER
Caliber: 44-40, 45 Colt, 6-shot cylinder. **Barrel:** 3.5", 5", 7". **Weight:** 39
oz. **Length:** 10.75" overall (5" barrel). **Grips:** Smooth walnut. **Sights:**
Blade front, notch rear. **Features:** Replica of Smith & Wesson Model
3 Schofield. Single-action, top-break with automatic ejection. Polished
blue finish. Introduced 1994. Imported by Navy Arms.
Price: Hideout Model, 3.5" barrel $882.00
Price: Wells Fargo, 5" barrel $882.00
Price: U.S. Cavalry model, 7" barrel, military markings $882.00

NAVY ARMS FOUNDER'S MODEL SCHOFIELD REVOLVER
Caliber: 45 Colt, 38 Spl., 6-shot cylinder. **Barrel:** 7.5". **Weight:** 41 oz.
Length: 13.75". **Grips:** Deluxe hand-rubbed walnut with cartouching.
Sights: Blade front, notch rear. **Features:** Charcoal blued with bone
color case-hardened receiver, trigger, hammer and backstrap. Limited
production "VF" serial number prefix. Introduced 2005. Imported by
Navy Arms.
Price: $924.00

NAVY ARMS NEW MODEL RUSSIAN REVOLVER
Caliber: 44 Russian, 6-shot cylinder. **Barrel:** 6.5". **Weight:** 40 oz.
Length: 12" overall. **Grips:** Smooth walnut. **Sights:** Blade front, notch
rear. **Features:** Replica of the S&W Model 3 Russian Third Model
revolver. Spur trigger guard, polished blue finish. Introduced 1999.
Imported by Navy Arms.
Price: $924.00

NAVY ARMS SCOUT SMALL FRAME SINGLE-ACTION REVOLVER
Caliber: 38 Spec., 6-shot cylinder. **Barrel:** 4.75", 5.5". **Weight:** 37 oz.
Length: 10.75" overall (5.5" barrel). **Grips:** Checkered black polymer.
Sights: Blade front, notch rear. **Features:** Blued with color case-
hardened receiver, trigger and hammer; German silver backstrap and
triggerguard. Introduced 2005. Imported by Navy Arms.
Price: $545.00

NORTH AMERICAN ARMS MINI REVOLVERS
Caliber: 22 Short, 22 LR, 22 WMR, 5-shot. **Barrel:** 1-1/8", 1-5/8".
Weight: 4 to 6.6 oz. **Length:** 3-5/8" to 6-1/8" overall. **Grips:** Laminated
wood. **Sights:** Blade front, notch fixed rear. **Features:** All stainless
steel construction. Polished satin and matte finish. Engraved models
available. From North American Arms.
Price: 22 Short, 22 LR $229.00

NORTH AMERICAN ARMS MINI-MASTER
Caliber: 22 LR, 22 WMR, 5-shot cylinder. **Barrel:** 4". **Weight:** 10.7 oz.
Length: 7.75" overall. **Grips:** Checkered hard black rubber. **Sights:**
Blade front, white outline rear adjustable for elevation, or fixed.
Features: Heavy vented barrel; full-size grips. Non-fluted cylinder.
Introduced 1989.
Price: Fixed sight $284.00
Price: Adjustable sight $314.00

Ruger New Model Blackhawk 50th Anniversary

Ruger Bisley Single-Action

Ruger Super Blackhawk Hunter

Ruger New Model Blackhawk

Ruger New Vaquero

Ruger New Bearcat

North American Arms Black Widow Revolver

Similar to Mini-Master, 2" heavy vent barrel. Built on 22 WMR frame. Non-fluted cylinder, black rubber grips. Available with Millett Low Profile fixed sights or Millett sight adjustable for elevation only. Overall length 5-7/8", weighs 8.8 oz. From North American Arms.
Price: Adjustable sight, 22 LR or 22 WMR **$299.00**
Price: Fixed sight, 22 LR or 22 WMR **$269.00**

NORTH AMERICAN ARMS "THE EARL" SINGLE-ACTION REVOLVER

Caliber: 22 Magnum with 22 LR accessory cylinder, 5-shot cylinder. **Barrel:** 4" octagonal. **Weight:** 6.8 oz. **Length:** 7-3/4" overall. **Grips:** Wood. **Sights:** Barleycorn front and fixed notch rear. **Features:** Single-action mini-revolver patterned after 1858-style Remington percussion revolver. Includes a spur trigger and a faux loading lever that serves as cylinder pin release.
Price: . . . . **$289.00** (22 Magnum only); **$324.00** (convertible)

RUGER NEW MODEL SINGLE SIX & NEW MODEL .32 H&R SINGLE SIX REVOLVERS

Caliber: 17 HMR, 22 LR, 22 Mag. **Barrel:** 4-5/8", 5.5", 6.5", 7.5", 9.5". 6-shot. **Grips:** Rosewood, black laminate. **Sights:** Adjustable or fixed. **Features:** Blued or stainless metalwork, short grips available, convertible models available. Introduced 2003 in 17 HMR.
Price: 17 HMR (blued) **$519.00**
Price: 22 LR/22 Mag., from **$506.00**

RUGER NEW MODEL BLACKHAWK/BLACKHAWK CONVERTIBLE

Caliber: 30 Carbine, 357 Mag./38 Spec., 41 Mag., 45 Colt, 6-shot. **Barrel:** 4-5/8", 5.5", 6.5", 7.5" (30 carbine and 45 Colt). **Weight:** 36 to 45 oz. Lengths: 10-3/8" to 13.5". **Grips:** Rosewood or black checkered. **Sights:** 1/8" ramp front, micro-click rear adjustable for windage and elevation. **Features:** Rosewood grips, Ruger transfer bar safety system, independent firing pin, hardened chrome-moly steel frame, music wire springs through-out. Case and lock included. Convertibles come with extra cylinder.
Price: 30 Carbine, 7.5" (BN31, blued) **$541.00**
Price: 357 Mag. (blued or satin stainless), from **$541.00**
Price: 41 Mag. (blued) **$541.00**
Price: 45 Colt (blued or satin stainless), from **$541.00**
Price: 357 Mag./9mm Para. Convertible (BN34XL, BN36XL) **$617.00**
Price: 45 Colt/45 ACP Convertible (BN44X, BN455XL) **$617.00**

Ruger Bisley Single-Action Revolver

Similar to standard Blackhawk, hammer is lower with smoothly curved, deeply checkered wide spur. The trigger is strongly curved with wide smooth surface. Longer grip frame. Adjustable rear sight, ramp-style front. Unfluted cylinder and roll engraving, adjustable sights. Chambered for 44 Mag. and 45 Colt; 7.5" barrel; overall length 13.5"; weighs 48-51 oz. Plastic lockable case. Orig. fluted cylinder introduced 1985; discontinued 1991. Unfluted cylinder introduced 1986.
Price: RB-44W (44 Mag), RB45W (45 Colt) **$683.00**

RUGER NEW MODEL SUPER BLACKHAWK

Caliber: 44 Mag., 6-shot. Also fires 44 Spec. **Barrel:** 4-5/8", 5.5", 7.5", 10.5" bull. **Weight:** 45-55 oz. **Length:** 10.5" to 16.5" overall. **Grips:** Rosewood. **Sights:** 1/8" ramp front, micro-click rear adjustable for windage and elevation. **Features:** Ruger transfer bar safety system, fluted or unfluted cylinder, steel grip and cylinder frame, round or square back trigger guard, wide serrated trigger, wide spur hammer. With case and lock.
Price: Blue, 4-5/8", 5.5", 7.5" (S-458N, S-45N, S-47N) **$650.00**
Price: Blue, 10.5" bull barrel (S-411N) **$667.00**
Price: Stainless, 4-5/8", 5.5", 7.5" (KS-458N, KS-45N, KS-47N) **$667.00**
Price: Stainless, 10.5" bull barrel (KS-411N) **$694.00**
Price: Super Blackhawk 50th Anniversary: Gold highlights, ornamentation; commemorates 50-year anniversary of Super Blackhawk **$729.00**

RUGER NEW MODEL SUPER BLACKHAWK HUNTER

Caliber: 44 Mag., 6-shot. **Barrel:** 7.5", full-length solid rib, unfluted cylinder. **Weight:** 52 oz. **Length:** 13-5/8". **Grips:** Black laminated wood. **Sights:** Adjustable rear, replaceable front blade. **Features:** Reintroduced Ultimate SA revolver. Includes instruction manual, high-impact case, set 1" medium scope rings, gun lock, ejector rod as standard.
Price: Hunter model, satin stainless, 7.5" (KS-47NHNN) **$781.00**
Price: Hunter model, Bisley frame, satin stainless 7.5" (KS-47NHB) **$781.00**

RUGER NEW VAQUERO SINGLE-ACTION REVOLVER

Caliber: 357 Mag., 45 Colt, 6-shot. **Barrel:** 4-5/8", 5.5", 7.5". **Weight:** 39-45 oz. **Length:** 10.5" overall (4-5/8" barrel). **Grips:** Rubber with Ruger medallion. **Sights:** Fixed blade front, fixed notch rear. **Features:** Transfer bar safety system and loading gate interlock. Blued model color case-hardened finish on frame, rest polished and blued. Engraved model available. Gloss stainless. Introduced 2005.
Price: 357 Mag., blued or stainless **$659.00**
Price: 45 Colt, blued or stainless **$659.00**
Price: 357 Mag., 45 Colt, ivory grips, 45 oz. (2009) **$729.00**

Taurus Gaucho 357

Taurus Gaucho 45

Uberti 1873 Cattleman

Uberti Bisley

Uberti 1875 Outlaw

Ruger New Model Bisley Vaquero

Similar to New Vaquero but with Bisley-style hammer and grip frame. Chambered in 357 and 45 Colt. Features include a 5.5" barrel, simulated ivory grips, fixed sights, six-shot cylinder. Overall length is 11.12", weighs 45 oz.
Price: **$729.00**

RUGER NEW BEARCAT SINGLE-ACTION

Caliber: 22 LR, 6-shot. **Barrel:** 4". **Weight:** 24 oz. **Length:** 9" overall. **Grips:** Smooth rosewood with Ruger medallion. **Sights:** Blade front, fixed notch rear. **Features:** Reintroduction of the Ruger Bearcat with slightly lengthened frame, Ruger transfer bar safety system. Available in blue only. Rosewood grips. Introduced 1996 (blued), 2003 (stainless). With case and lock.
Price: SBC-4, blued **$501.00**
Price: KSBC-4, satin stainless **$540.00**

STI TEXICAN SINGLE-ACTION REVOLVER

Caliber: 45 Colt, 6-shot. **Barrel:** 5.5", 4140 chrome-moly steel by Green Mountain Barrels. 1:16 twist, air gauged to .0002". Chamber to bore alignment less than .001". Forcing cone angle, 3 degrees. **Weight:** 36 oz. **Length:** 11". **Grips:** "No crack" polymer. **Sights:** Blade front, fixed notch rear. **Features:** Parts made by ultra-high speed or electron discharge machined processes from chrome-moly steel forgings or bar stock. Competition sights, springs, triggers and hammers. Frames, loading gates, and hammers are color case hardened by Turnbull Restoration. Frame, back strap, loading gate, trigger guard, cylinders made of 4140 re-sulphurized Maxell 3.5 steel. Hammer firing pin (no transfer bar). S.A.S.S. approved. Introduced 2008. Made in U.S.A. by STI International.
Price: 5.5" barrel **$1,299.99**

TAURUS SINGLE-ACTION GAUCHO REVOLVERS

Caliber: 38 Spl, 357 Mag, 44-40, 45 Colt, 6-shot. **Barrel:** 4.75", 5.5", 7.5", 12". **Weight:** 36.7-37.7 oz. **Length:** 13". **Grips:** Checkered black polymer. **Sights:** Blade front, fixed notch rear. **Features:** Integral transfer bar; blue, blue with case hardened frame, matte stainless and the hand polished "Sundance" stainless finish. Removable cylinder, half-cock notch. Introduced 2005. Imported from Brazil by Taurus International.
Price: S/A-357-B, 357 Mag., Sundance blue finish,
5.5" barrel **$520.00**
Price: S/A-357-S/S7, 357 Mag., polished stainless,
7.5" barrel **$536.00**
Price: S/A-45-B7 .... **$520.00**

UBERTI 1851-1860 CONVERSION REVOLVERS

Caliber: 38 Spec., 45 Colt, 6-shot engraved cylinder. **Barrel:** 4.75", 5.5", 7.5", 8" **Weight:** 2.6 lbs. (5.5" bbl). **Length:** 13" overall (5.5" bbl.). **Grips:** Walnut. **Features:** Brass backstrap, trigger guard; color case-hardened frame, blued barrel, cylinder. Introduced 2007. Imported from Italy by Stoeger Industries.
Price: 1851 Navy **$519.00**
Price: 1860 Army **$549.00**

UBERTI 1871-1872 OPEN TOP REVOLVERS

Caliber: 38 Spec., 45 Colt, 6-shot engraved cylinder. **Barrel:** 4.75", 5.5", 7.5". **Weight:** 2.6 lbs. (5.5" bbl). **Length:** 13" overall (5.5" bbl.). **Grips:** Walnut. **Features:** Blued backstrap, trigger guard; color case-hardened frame, blued barrel, cylinder. Introduced 2007. Imported from Italy by Stoeger Industries.
Price: **$499.00**

UBERTI 1873 CATTLEMAN SINGLE-ACTION

Caliber: 45 Colt; 6-shot fluted cylinder. **Barrel:** 4.75", 5.5", 7.5". **Weight:** 2.3 lbs. (5.5" bbl). **Length:** 11" overall (5.5" bbl). **Grips:** Styles: Frisco (pearl styled); Desperado (buffalo horn styled); Chisholm (checkered walnut); Gunfighter (black checkered), Cody (ivory styled), one-piece walnut. **Sights:** Blade front, groove rear. **Features:** Steel or brass backstrap, trigger guard; color case-hardened frame, blued barrel, cylinder. NM designates New Model plunger style frame; OM designates Old Model screw cylinder pin retainer. Imported from Italy by Stoeger Industries.
Price: 1873 Cattleman Frisco **$789.00**
Price: 1873 Cattleman Desperado (2006) **$789.00**
Price: 1873 Cattleman Chisholm (2006) **$539.00**
Price: 1873 Cattleman NM, blued 4.75" barrel **$479.00**
Price: 1873 Cattleman NM, Nickel finish, 7.5" barrel **$609.00**
Price: 1873 Cattleman Cody.......................... **$789.00**

UBERTI 1873 CATTLEMAN BIRD'S HEAD SINGLE ACTION

Caliber: 357 Mag., 45 Colt; 6-shot fluted cylinder **Barrel:** 3.5", 4", 4.75", 5.5". **Weight:** 2.3 lbs. (5.5" bbl). **Length:** 10.9" overall (5.5" bbl). **Grips:** One-piece walnut. **Sights:** Blade front, groove rear. **Features:** Steel or brass backstrap, trigger guard; color case-hardened frame, blued barrel, cylinder. Imported from Italy by Stoeger Industries.
Price: 1873 Cattleman Bird's Head OM 3.5" barrel **$539.00**

UBERTI 1873 BISLEY SINGLE-ACTION REVOLVER

Caliber: 357 Mag., 45 Colt (Bisley); 22 LR and 38 Spec. (Stallion), both with 6-shot fluted cylinder. **Barrel:** 4.75", 5.5", 7.5". **Weight:** 2 to 2.5 lbs. **Length:** 12.7" overall (7.5" barrel). **Grips:** Two-piece walnut. **Sights:** Blade front, notch rear. **Features:** Replica of Colt's Bisley Model. Polished blue finish, color case-hardened frame. Introduced 1997. Imported by Stoeger Industries.
Price: 1873 Bisley, 7.5" barrel **$569.00**

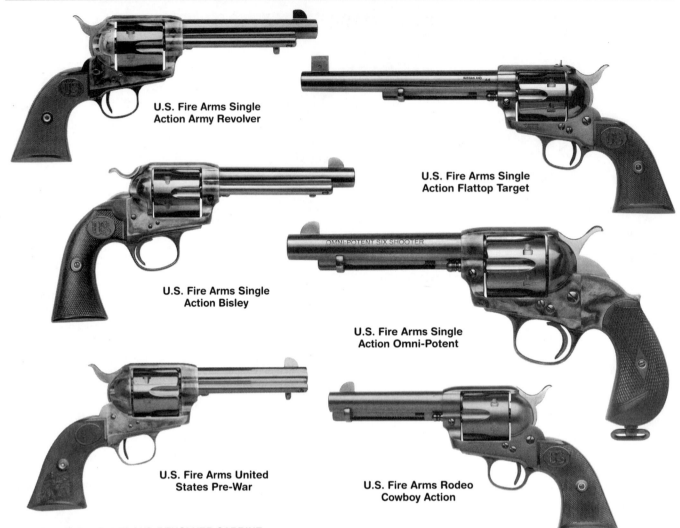

U.S. Fire Arms Single Action Army Revolver

U.S. Fire Arms Single Action Flattop Target

U.S. Fire Arms Single Action Bisley

U.S. Fire Arms Single Action Omni-Potent

U.S. Fire Arms United States Pre-War

U.S. Fire Arms Rodeo Cowboy Action

UBERTI 1873 BUNTLINE AND REVOLVER CARBINE SINGLE-ACTION

Caliber: 357 Mag., 44-40, 45 Colt; 6-shot fluted cylinder **Barrel:** 18". **Length:** 22.9" to 34". **Grips:** Walnut pistol grip or rifle stock. **Sights:** Fixed or adjustable. **Features:** Imported from Italy by Stoeger Industries.
Price: 1873 Revolver Carbine, 18" barrel, 34" OAL **$729.00**
Price: 1873 Catttleman Buntline Target, 18" barrel, 22.9" OAL **$639.00**

UBERTI OUTLAW, FRONTIER, AND POLICE REVOLVERS

Caliber: 45 Colt, 6-shot fluted cylinder. **Barrel:** 5.5", 7.5". **Weight:** 2.5 to 2.8 lbs. **Length:** 10.8" to 13.6" overall. **Grips:** Two-piece smooth walnut. **Sights:** Blade front, notch rear. **Features:** Cartridge version of 1858 Remington percussion revolver. Nickel and blued finishes. Imported by Stoeger Industries.
Price: 1875 Outlaw nickel finish **$629.00**
Price: 1875 Frontier, blued finish **$539.00**
Price: 1890 Police, blued finish **$549.00**

UBERTI 1870 SCHOFIELD-STYLE TOP BREAK REVOLVER

Caliber: 38, 44 Russian, 44-40, 45 Colt, 6-shot cylinder. **Barrel:** 3.5", 5", 7". **Weight:** 2.4 lbs. (5" barrel) **Length:** 10.8" overall (5" barrel). **Grips:** Two-piece smooth walnut or pearl. **Sights:** Blade front, notch rear. **Features:** Replica of Smith & Wesson Model 3 Schofield. Single-action, top break with automatic ejection. Polished blue finish (first model). Introduced 1994. Imported by Stoeger Industries.
Price: No. 3-2nd Model, nickel finish **$1,369.00**

U.S. FIRE ARMS SINGLE-ACTION REVOLVER

Caliber: 45 Colt (standard); 32 WCF, 38 WCF, 38 Spec., 44 WCF, 44 Special, 6-shot cylinder. **Barrel:** 4.75", 5.5", 7.5". **Weight:** 37 oz.

Length: NA. **Grips:** Hard rubber. **Sights:** Blade front, notch rear. **Features:** Recreation of original guns; 3" and 4" have no ejector. Available with all-blue, blue with color case-hardening, or full nickel-plate finish. Other models include Custer Battlefield Gun ($1,625, 7.5" barrel), Flattop Target ($1,625), Sheriff's Model ($875, with barrel lengths starting at 2"), Snubnose ($1,475, barrel lengths 2", 3", 4"), Omni-Potent Six-Shooter and Omni-Target Six-Shooter (from $1,625), Bisley ($1,350, introduced 2006). Made in U.S.A. by United States Fire Arms Mfg. Co.
Price: Blue/cased-colors **$875.00**
Price: Nickel **$1,220.00**

U.S. FIRE ARMS RODEO COWBOY ACTION REVOLVER

Caliber: 45 Colt, **Barrel:** 4.75", 5.5". **Grips:** Rubber. **Features:** Historically correct Armory bone case hammer, blue satin finish, transfer bar safety system, correct solid firing pin. Entry level basic cowboy SASS gun. Other models include the Gunslinger ($1,145). 2006 version includes brown-rubber stocks.
Price: **$550.00**
Price: New Rodeo 2 (2007) **$605.00**

U.S. FIRE ARMS U.S. PRE-WAR

Caliber: 45 Colt (standard); 32 WCF, 38 WCF, 38 Spec., 44 WCF, 44 Special. **Barrel:** 4.75", 5.5", 7.5". **Grips:** Hard rubber. **Features:** Armory bone case/Armory blue finish standard, cross-pin or black powder frame. Introduced 2002. Made in U.S.A. by United States Firearms Mfg. Co.
Price: **$1,270.00**

Specially adapted single-shot and multi-barrel arms.

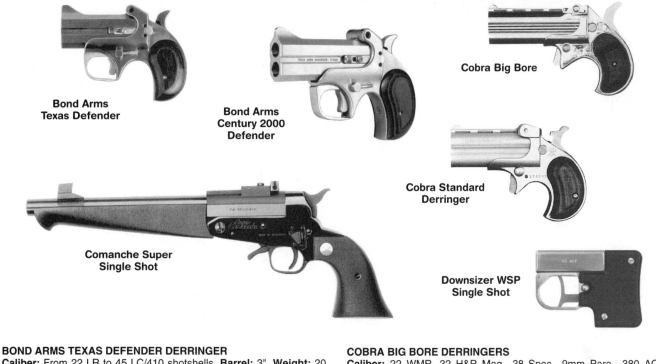

Bond Arms Texas Defender

Bond Arms Century 2000 Defender

Cobra Big Bore

Cobra Standard Derringer

Comanche Super Single Shot

Downsizer WSP Single Shot

BOND ARMS TEXAS DEFENDER DERRINGER
Caliber: From 22 LR to 45 LC/.410 shotshells. **Barrel:** 3". **Weight:** 20 oz. **Length:** 5". **Grips:** Rosewood. **Sights:** Blade front, fixed rear. **Features:** Interchangeable barrels, stainless steel firing pins, cross-bolt safety, automatic extractor for rimmed calibers. Stainless steel construction, brushed finish. Right or left hand.
Price: $399.00
Price: Interchangeable barrels, 22 LR thru 45 LC, 3" $139.00
Price: Interchangeable barrels, 45 LC, 3.5" . . . . .$159.00 to $189.00

BOND ARMS RANGER
Caliber: 45 LC/.410 shotshells. **Barrel:** 4.25". **Weight:** 23.5 oz. **Length:** 6.25". **Features:** Similar to Snake Slayer except no trigger guard. Intr. 2008. From Bond Arms.
Price: $649.00

BOND ARMS CENTURY 2000 DEFENDER
Caliber: 45 LC/.410 shotshells. **Barrel:** 3.5". **Weight:** 21 oz. **Length:** 5.5". **Features:** Similar to Defender series.
Price: $420.00

BOND ARMS COWBOY DEFENDER
Caliber: From 22 LR to 45 LC/.410 shotshells. **Barrel:** 3". **Weight:** 19 oz. **Length:** 5.5". **Features:** Similar to Defender series. No trigger guard.
Price: $399.00

BOND ARMS SNAKE SLAYER
Caliber: 45 LC/.410 shotshell (2.5" or 3"). **Barrel:** 3.5". **Weight:** 21 oz. **Length:** 5.5". **Grips:** Extended rosewood. **Sights:** Blade front, fixed rear. **Features:** Single-action; interchangeable barrels; stainless steel firing pin. Introduced 2005.
Price: $469.00

BOND ARMS SNAKE SLAYER IV
Caliber: 45 LC/.410 shotshell (2.5" or 3"). **Barrel:** 4.25". **Weight:** 22 oz. **Length:** 6.25". **Grips:** Extended rosewood. **Sights:** Blade front, fixed rear. **Features:** Single-action; interchangeable barrels; stainless steel firing pin. Introduced 2006.
Price: $499.00

CHARTER ARMS DIXIE DERRINGERS
Caliber: 22 LR, 22 WMR. **Barrel:** 1.125". **Weight:** 6 oz. **Length:** 4" overall. **Grips:** Black polymer **Sights:** Blade front, fixed notch rear. **Features:** Stainless finish. Introduced 2006. Made in U.S.A. by Charter Arms, distributed by MKS Supply.
Price: $215.00

COBRA BIG BORE DERRINGERS
Caliber: 22 WMR, 32 H&R Mag., 38 Spec., 9mm Para., 380 ACP. **Barrel:** 2.75". **Weight:** 14 oz. **Length:** 4.65" overall. **Grips:** Textured black or white synthetic or laminated rosewood. **Sights:** Blade front, fixed notch rear. **Features:** Alloy frame, steel-lined barrels, steel breech block. Plunger-type safety with integral hammer block. Black, chrome or satin finish. Introduced 2002. Made in U.S.A. by Cobra Enterprises of Utah, Inc.
Price: $165.00

COBRA LONG-BORE DERRINGERS
Caliber: 22 WMR, 38 Spec., 9mm Para. **Barrel:** 3.5". **Weight:** 16 oz. **Length:** 5.4" overall. **Grips:** Black or white synthetic or rosewood. **Sights:** Fixed. **Features:** Chrome, satin nickel, or black Teflon finish. Introduced 2002. Made in U.S.A. by Cobra Enterprises of Utah, Inc.
Price: $165.00

COBRA STANDARD SERIES DERRINGERS
Caliber: 22 LR, 22 WMR, 25 ACP, 32 ACP. **Barrel:** 2.4". **Weight:** 9.5 oz. **Length:** 4" overall. **Grips:** Laminated wood or pearl. **Sights:** Blade front, fixed notch rear. **Features:** Choice of black powder coat, satin nickel or chrome finish. Introduced 2002. Made in U.S.A. by Cobra Enterprises of Utah, Inc.
Price: $145.00

COMANCHE SUPER SINGLE-SHOT PISTOL
Caliber: 45 LC, .410 **Barrel:** 10". **Sights:** Adjustable. **Features:** Blue finish, not available for sale in CA, MA. Distributed by SGS Importers International, Inc.
Price: $200.00

MAXIMUM SINGLE-SHOT PISTOL
Caliber: 22 LR, 22 Hornet, 22 BR, 22 PPC, 223 Rem., 22-250, 6mm BR, 6mm PPC, 243, 250 Savage, 6.5mm-35M, 270 MAX, 270 Win., 7mm TCU, 7mm BR, 7mm-35, 7mm INT-R, 7mm-08, 7mm Rocket, 7mm Super-Mag., 30 Herrett, 30 Carbine, 30-30, 308 Win., 30x39, 32-20, 350 Rem. Mag., 357 Mag., 357 Maximum, 358 Win., 375 H&H, 44 Mag., 454 Casull. **Barrel:** 8.75", 10.5", 14". **Weight:** 61 oz. (10.5" bbl.); 78 oz. (14" bbl.). **Length:** 15", 18.5" overall (with 10.5" and 14" bbl., respectively). **Grips:** Smooth walnut stocks and forend. Also available with 17" finger groove grip. **Sights:** Ramp front, fully adjustable open rear. **Features:** Falling block action; drilled and tapped for M.O.A. scope mounts; integral grip frame/receiver; adjustable trigger; Douglas barrel (interchangeable). Introduced 1983. Made in U.S.A. by M.O.A. Corp.
Price: Stainless receiver, blue barrel $839.00
Price: Stainless receiver, stainless barrel $937.00

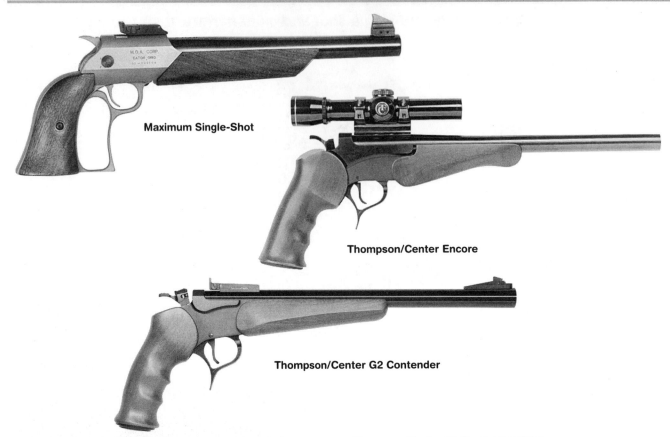

Maximum Single-Shot

Thompson/Center Encore

Thompson/Center G2 Contender

THOMPSON/CENTER ENCORE PISTOL
Caliber: 22-250, 223, 204 Ruger, 6.8 Rem., 260 Rem., 7mm-08, 243, 308, 270, 30-06, 375 JDJ, 204 Ruger, 44 Mag., 454 Casull, 480 Ruger, 444 Marlin single shot, 450 Marlin with muzzle tamer, no sights. **Barrel:** 12", 15", tapered round. **Weight:** NA. **Length:** 21" overall with 12" barrel. **Grips:** American walnut with finger grooves, walnut forend. **Sights:** Blade on ramp front, adjustable rear, or none. **Features:** Interchangeable barrels; action opens by squeezing the trigger guard; drilled and tapped for scope mounting; blue finish. Announced 1996. Made in U.S.A. by Thompson/Center Arms.
Price: $615.00

Thompson/Center G2 Contender Pistol
A second generation Contender pistol maintaining the same barrel interchangeability with older Contender barrels and their corresponding forends (except Herrett forend). The G2 frame will not accept old-style grips due to the change in grip angle. Incorporates an automatic hammer block safety with built-in interlock. Features include trigger adjustable for overtravel, adjustable rear sight; ramp front sight blade, blued steel finish.
Price: $600.00

Both classic arms and recent designs in American-style repeaters for sport and field shooting.

Armalite M15A2

Armalite AR-10A4

Armalite AR-180B

ARMALITE M15A2 CARBINE
Caliber: 223 Rem., 30-round magazine. **Barrel:** 16" heavy chrome lined; 1:9" twist. **Weight:** 7 lbs. **Length:** 35-11/16" overall. **Stock:** Green or black composition. **Sights:** Standard A2. **Features:** Upper and lower receivers have push-type pivot pin; hard coat anodized; A2-style forward assist; M16A2-type raised fence around magazine release button. Made in U.S.A. by ArmaLite, Inc.
Price: Green **$1,150.00**
Price: Black. **$1,150.00**

ARMALITE AR-10A4 SPECIAL PURPOSE RIFLE
Caliber: 308 Win., 10- and 20-round magazine. **Barrel:** 20" chrome-lined, 1:11.25" twist. **Weight:** 9.6 lbs. **Length:** 41" overall. **Stock:** Green or black composition. **Sights:** Detachable handle, front sight, or scope mount available; comes with international style flattop receiver with Picatinny rail. **Features:** Forged upper receiver with case deflector. Receivers are hard-coat anodized. Introduced 1995. Made in U.S.A. by ArmaLite, Inc.
Price: Green **$1,557.00**
Price: Black. **$1,557.00**

ArmaLite AR-10A2
Utilizing the same 20" double-lapped, heavy barrel as the ArmaLite AR10A4 Special Purpose Rifle. Offered in 308 Win. only. Made in U.S.A. by ArmaLite, Inc.
Price: AR-10A2 rifle or carbine **$1,561.00**

ARMALITE AR-10B RIFLE
Caliber: 308 Win. **Barrel:** 20" chrome lined. **Weight:** 9.5 lbs. **Length:** 41". **Stock:** Synthetic. **Sights:** Rear sight adjustable for windage, small and large apertures. **Features:** Early-style AR-10. Lower and upper receivers made of forged aircraft alloy. Brown Sudanese-style furniture, elevation scale window. Charging handle in carry handle. Made in U.S.A. by Armalite.
Price: **$1,699.00**

ARSENAL, INC. SLR-107F
Caliber: 7.62x39mm. **Barrel:** 16.25". **Weight:** 7.3 lbs. **Stock:** Left-side folding polymer stock. **Sights:** Adjustable rear. **Features:** Stamped receiver, 24mm flash hider, bayonet lug, accessory lug, stainless steel heat shield, two-stage trigger. Introduced 2008. Made in U.S.A. by Arsenal, Inc.
Price: SLR-107FR, includes scope rail **$1,035.00**

ARSENAL, INC. SLR-107CR
Caliber: 7.62x39mm. **Barrel:** 16.25". **Weight:** 6.9 lbs. **Stock:** Left-side folding polymer stock. **Sights:** Adjustable rear. **Features:** Stamped receiver, front sight block/gas block combination, 500-meter rear sight, cleaning rod, stainless steel heat shield, scope rail, and removable muzzle attachment. Introduced 2007. Made in U.S.A. by Arsenal, Inc.
Price: SLR-107CR **$1,200.00**

ARSENAL, INC. SLR-106CR
Caliber: 5.56 NATO. **Barrel:** 16.25", Steyr chrome-lined barrel, 1:7 twist rate. **Weight:** 6.9 lbs. **Stock:** Black polymer folding stock with cutout for scope rail. Stainless-steel heatshield handguard. **Sights:** 500-meter rear sight and rear sight block calibrated for 5.56 NATO. Warsaw Pact scope rail. **Features:** Uses Arsenal, Bulgaria, Mil-Spec receiver, two-stage trigger, hammer and disconnector. Polymer magazines in 5- and 10-round capacity in black and green, with Arsenal logo. Others are 30-round black waffles, 20- and 30-round versions in clear/smoke waffle, featuring the "10" in a double-circle logo of Arsenal, Bulgaria. Ships with 5-round magazine, sling, cleaning kit in a tube, 16" cleaning rod, oil bottle. Introduced 2007. Made in U.S.A. by Arsenal, Inc.
Price: SLR-106CR **$1,200.00**

AUTO-ORDNANCE 1927A-1 THOMPSON
Caliber: 45 ACP. **Barrel:** 16.5". **Weight:** 13 lbs. **Length:** About 41" overall (Deluxe). **Stock:** Walnut stock and vertical forend. **Sights:** Blade front, open rear adjustable for windage. **Features:** Recreation of Thompson Model 1927. Semi-auto only. Deluxe model has finned barrel, adjustable rear sight and compensator; Standard model has plain barrel and military sight. From Auto-Ordnance Corp.
Price: Deluxe **$1,420.00**
Price: Lightweight model (9.5 lbs.) **$1,145.00**

Auto-Ordnance 1927A-1 Thompson

Benelli R1

Benelli R1 APG Camo

Barrett Model 82A-1

Beretta CX4 Carbine

Auto-Ordnance Thompson M1/M1-C
Similar to the 1927 A-1 except is in the M-1 configuration with side cocking knob, horizontal forend, smooth unfinned barrel, sling swivels on butt and forend. Matte-black finish. Introduced 1985.
Price: M1 semi-auto carbine **$1,334.00**
Price: M1-C lightweight semi-auto **$1,065.00**

Auto-Ordnance 1927 A-1 Commando
Similar to the 1927 A-1 except has Parkerized finish, black-finish wood butt, pistol grip, horizontal forend. Comes with black nylon sling. Introduced 1998. Made in U.S.A. by Auto-Ordnance Corp.
Price: T1-C **$1,393.00**

BARRETT MODEL 82A-1 SEMI-AUTOMATIC RIFLE
Caliber: 50 BMG, 10-shot detachable box magazine. **Barrel:** 29". **Weight:** 28.5 lbs. **Length:** 57" overall. **Stock:** Composition with energy-absorbing recoil pad. **Sights:** Scope optional. **Features:** Semi-automatic, recoil operated with recoiling barrel. Three-lug locking bolt; muzzle brake. Adjustable bipod. Introduced 1985. Made in U.S.A. by Barrett Firearms.
Price: From **$8,900.00**

BENELLI R1 RIFLE
Caliber: 300 Win. Mag., 300 WSM, 270 WSM (24" barrel); 30-06 Spfl., 308 Win. (22" barrel); 300 Win. Mag., 30-06 Spfl., (20" barrel). **Weight:** 7.1 lbs. **Length:** 43.75" to 45.75". **Stock:** Select satin walnut or synthetic. **Sights:** None. **Features:** Auto-regulating gas-operated system, three-lug rotary bolt, interchangeable barrels, optional recoil pads. Introduced 2003. Imported from Italy by Benelli USA.
Price: Synthetic with ComforTech gel recoil pad **$1,549.00**
Price: Satin walnut **$1,379.00**
Price: APG HD camo, 30-06 (2008) **$1,689.00**

BERETTA CX4/PX4 STORM CARBINE
Caliber: 9mm Para., 40 S&W, 45 ACP. **Weight:** 5.75 lbs. Barrel **Length:** 16.6", chrome lined, rate of twist 1:16 (40 S&W) or 1:10 (9mm Para.). **Length:** NA. **Stock:** Black synthetic. **Sights:** NA. **Features:** Introduced 2005. Imported from Italy by Beretta USA.
Price: **$900.00**

Browning Mark II Safari

Browning BAR Shorttrac Mossy Oak

Browning BAR LongTrac Digital Green

Browning Lightweight Stalker

Browning Lightweight Stalker

BROWNING BAR SAFARI AND SAFARI W/BOSS SEMI-AUTO RIFLES

Caliber: Safari: 243 Win., 25-06 Rem., 270 Win., 7mm Rem. Mag.., 30-06 Spfl., 308 Win., 300 Win. Mag. Safari w/BOSS: 270 Win., 7mm Rem. Mag., 30-06 Spfl., 300 Win. Mag., 338 Win. Mag., plus 270 WSM, 7mm WSM, 300 WSM. **Barrel:** 22-24" round tapered. **Weight:** 7.4-8.2 lbs. **Length:** 43-45" overall. **Stock:** French walnut pistol grip stock and forend, hand checkered. **Sights:** No sights. **Features:** Has new bolt release lever; removable trigger assembly with larger trigger guard; redesigned gas and buffer systems. Detachable 4-round box magazine. Scroll-engraved receiver is tapped for scope mounting. BOSS barrel vibration modulator and muzzle brake system available. Mark II Safari introduced 1993. Imported from Belgium by Browning.
Price: BAR MK II Safari, from **$1,109.00**
Price: BAR Safari w/BOSS, from **$1,229.00**

BROWNING BAR SHORTTRAC/LONGTRAC AUTO RIFLES

Caliber: (ShortTrac models) 270 WSM, 7mm WSM, 300 WSM, 243 Win., 308 Win., 325 WSM; (LongTrac models) 270 Win., 30-06 Spfl., 7mm Rem. Mag., 300 Win. Mag. **Barrel:** 23". **Weight:** 6 lbs. 10 oz. to 7 lbs. 4 oz. **Length:** 41.5" to 44". **Stock:** Satin-finish walnut, pistol-grip, fluted forend. **Sights:** Adj. rear, bead front standard, no sights on BOSS chamberings. Gas-operated, blued finish, rotary bolt design (LongTrac models).
Price: BAR ShortTrac, 243 Win., 308 Win. from **$1,079.00**
Price: BAR ShortTrac Left-Hand, intr. 2007, from **$1,129.00**

Price: BAR ShortTrac Mossy Oak New Break-up
. . . . **$1,249.00 to $1,349.00**
Price: BAR LongTrac Left Hand, 270 Win., 30-06 Spfl.,
from **$1,129.00**
Price: BAR LongTrac, from **$1,079.00**
Price: BAR LongTrac Mossy Oak Break Up, intr. 2007,
from **$1,249.00**
Price: Bar LongTrac, Digital Green camo (2009)
. . . . **$1,247.00 to $1,347.00**

BROWNING BAR STALKER AUTO RIFLES

Caliber: 243 Win., 308 Win., 270 Win., 30-06 Spfl., 270 WSM, 7mm WSM, 300 WSM, 300 Win. Mag., 338 Win. Mag. **Barrel:** 20-24". **Weight:** 7.1-7.75 LBS. **Length:** 41-45" overall. **Stock:** Black composite stock and forearm. **Sights:** Hooded front and adjustable rear. **Features:** Gas-operated action with seven-lug rotary bolt; dual action bars; 2-, 3- or 4-shot magazine (depending on cartridge). Introduced 2001. Imported by Browning.
Price: BAR ShortTrac or LongTrac Stalker, from **$1,119.00**
Price: BAR Lightweight Stalker, from **$1,099.00**

BUSHMASTER SUPERLIGHT CARBINES

Caliber: 223 Rem., 30-shot magazine. **Barrel:** 16", heavy; 1:9" twist. **Weight:** 6.25 lbs. **Length:** 31.25-34.5" overall. **Stock:** 6-position telestock or Stubby (7.25" length). **Sights:** Fully adjustable M16A2 sight system. **Features:** Adapted from original G.I. pencil-barrel profile. Chrome-lined barrel with manganese phosphate finish. "Shorty" handguards. Has forged aluminum receivers with pushpin. Made in U.S.A. by Bushmaster Firearms, Inc.
Price: From **$1, 250.00**

Bushmaster XM15 E2S Carbine

Bushmaster Varminter

Bushmaster XM15 E2S Dissipator Carbine
Similar to the XM15 E2S Shorty carbine except has full-length "Dissipator" handguards. Weighs 7.6 lbs.; 34.75" overall; forged aluminum receivers with push-pin style takedown. Made in U.S.A. by Bushmaster Firearms, Inc.
Price: From **$1,240.00**

Bushmaster XM15 E25 AK Shorty Carbine
Similar to the XM15 E2S Shorty except has 14.5" barrel with an AK muzzle brake permanently attached giving 16" barrel length. Weighs 7.3 lbs. Introduced 1999. Made in U.S.A. by Bushmaster Firearms, Inc.
Price: From **$1,215.00**

Bushmaster M4 Post-Ban Carbine
Similar to the XM15 E2S except has 14.5" barrel with Mini Y compensator, and fixed telestock. MR configuration has fixed carry handle.
Price: **$1,190.00**

BUSHMASTER VARMINTER RIFLE
Caliber: 223 Rem., 5-shot. **Barrel:** 24", 1:9" twist, fluted, heavy, stainless. **Weight:** 8.75 lbs. **Length:** 42.25". **Stock:** Rubberized pistol grip. **Sights:** 1/2" scope risers. **Features:** Gas-operated, semi-auto, two-stage trigger, slotted free floater forend, lockable hard case.
Price: **$1,360.00**
Price: Bushmaster Predator: 20" 1:8 barrel, 223 Rem. **$1,245.00**
Price: Bushmaster Stainless Varmint Special: Same as
Varminter but with 24" stainless barrel **$1,277.00**

BUSHMASTER 6.8 SPC CARBINE
Caliber: 6.8 SPC, 26-shot mag. **Barrel:** 16" M4 profile. **Weight:** 6.57 lbs. **Length:** 32.75" overall. **Features:** Semi-auto AR-style with Izzy muzzle brake, six-position telestock. Available in A2 (fixed carry handle) or A3 (removable carry handle) configuration.
Price: **$1,500.00**

BUSHMASTER ORC CARBINE
Caliber: 5.56/223. **Barrel:** 16" M4 profile. **Weight:** 6 lbs. **Length:** 32.5" overall. **Features:** AR-style carbine with chrome-lined barrel, fixed carry handle, receiver-length picatinny optics rail, heavy oval M4-style handguards.
Price: **$1,085.00**

BUSHMASTER 11.5" BARREL CARBINE
Caliber: 5.56/223, 30-shot mag. **Barrel:** 11.5". **Weight:** 6.46 lbs. or 6.81 lbs. **Length:** 31.625" overall. **Features:** AR-style carbine with chrome-lined barrel with permanently attached BATF-approved 5.5" flash suppressor, fixed or removable carry handle, optional optics rail.
Price: **$1,215.00**

BUSHMASTER HEAVY-BARRELED CARBINE
Caliber: 5.56/223. **Barrel:** 16". **Weight:** 6.93 lbs. to 7.28 lbs. **Length:** 32.5" overall. **Features:** AR-style carbine with chrome-lined heavy profile vanadium steel barrel, fixed or removable carry handle, six-position telestock.
Price: **$1,215.00**

BUSHMASTER MODULAR CARBINE
Caliber: 5.56/223, 30-shot mag. **Barrel:** 16". **Weight:** 7.3 lbs. **Length:** 36.25" overall. **Features:** AR-style carbine with chrome-lined chrome-moly vanadium steel barrel, skeleton stock or six-position telestock, clamp-on front sight and detachable flip-up dual aperature rear.
Price: **$1,745.00**

BUSHMASTER CARBON 15 TOP LOADER RIFLE
Caliber: 5.56/223, internal 10-shot mag. **Barrel:** 16" chrome-lined M4 profile. **Weight:** 5.8 lbs. **Length:** 32.75" overall. **Features:** AR-style carbine with standard A2 front sight, dual aperture rear sight, receiver-length optics rail, lightweight carbon fiber receiver, six-position telestock. Will not accept detachable box magazines.
Price: **$1,070.00**

BUSHMASTER CARBON 15 FLAT-TOP CARBINE
Caliber: 5.56/223, 30-shot mag. **Barrel:** 16" M4 profile. **Weight:** 5.77 lbs. **Length:** 32.75" overall. **Features:** AR-style carbine Izzy flash suppressor, AR-type front sight, dual aperture flip, lightweight carbon composite receiver with receiver-length optics rail.
Price: **$1,155.00**
Price: Carbon 15 9mm, chambered in 9mm Parabellum . . . **$1,025.00**

BUSHMASTER 450 RIFLE AND CARBINE
Caliber: 450 Bushmaster. **Barrel:** 20" (rifle), 16" (carbine), five-round mag. **Weight:** 8.3 lbs. (rifle), 8.1 lbs. (carbine). **Length:** 39.5" overall (rifle), 35.25" overall (carbine). **Features:** AR-style with chrome-lined chrome-moly barrel, synthetic stock, Izzy muzzle brake.
Price: **$1,350.00**

BUSHMASTER GAS PISTON RIFLE
Caliber: 223, 30-shot mag. **Barrel:** 16". **Weight:** 7.46 lbs. **Length:** 32.5" overall. **Features:** Semi-auto AR-style with telescoping stock, carry handle, piston assembly rather than direct gas impingement.
Price: **$1,795.00**

BUSHMASTER TARGET RIFLE
Caliber: 5.56/223, 30-shot mag. **Barrel:** 20" or 24" heavy or standard. **Weight:** 8.43 lbs. to 9.29 lbs. **Length:** 39.5" or 43.5" overall. **Features:** Semi-auto AR-style with chrome-lined or stainless steel 1:9 barrel, fixed or removable carry handle, manganese phosphate finish.
Price: **$1,195.00**

BUSHMASTER M4A3 TYPE CARBINE
Caliber: 5.56/223, 30-shot mag. **Barrel:** 16". **Weight:** 6.22 to 6.7 lbs. **Length:** 31" to 32.5" overall. **Features:** AR-style carbine with chrome-moly vanadium steel barrel, Izzy-type flash-hider, six-position telestock, various sight options, standard or multi-rail handguard, fixed or removable carry handle.
Price: **$1,270.00**
Price: Patrolman's Carbine: Standard mil-style sights **$1,270.00**
Price: State Compliance Carbine: Compliant with various state
regulations **$1,270.00**

Century International AES-10 Hi-Cap with bipod

Century International
WASR-10 Hi-Cap

Century International WASR-2 Hi-Cap

Century International M70AB2 Sporter

CENTURY INTERNATIONAL AES-10 HI-CAP RIFLE
Caliber: 7.62x39mm. 30-shot magazine. **Barrel:** 23.2". **Weight:** NA. **Length:** 41.5" overall. **Stock:** Wood grip, forend. **Sights:** Fixed-notch rear, windage-adjustable post front. **Features:** RPK-style, accepts standard double-stack AK-type mags. Side-mounted scope mount, integral carry handle, bipod. Imported by Century Arms Int'l.
Price: AES-10, from $450.00

CENTURY INTERNATIONAL GP WASR-10 HI-CAP RIFLE
Caliber: 7.62x39mm. 30-shot magazine. **Barrel:** 16.25", 1:10 right-hand twist. **Weight:** 7.2 lbs. **Length:** 34.25" overall. **Stock:** Wood laminate or composite, grip, forend. **Sights:** Fixed-notch rear, windage-adjustable post front. **Features:** Two 30-rd. detachable box magazines, cleaning kit, bayonet. Version of AKM rifle; U.S.-parts added for BATFE compliance. Threaded muzzle, folding stock, bayonet lug, compensator, Dragunov stock available. Made in Romania by Cugir Arsenal. Imported by Century Arms Int'l.
Price: GP WASR-10, from $350.00

CENTURY INTERNATIONAL WASR-2 HI-CAP RIFLE
Caliber: 5.45x39mm. 30-shot magazine. **Barrel:** 16.25". **Weight:** 7.5 lbs. **Length:** 34.25" overall. Stocks: Wood laminate. **Sights:** Fixed-notch rear, windage-adjustable post front. **Features:** 1 30-rd. detachable box magazine, cleaning kit, sling. WASR-3 HI-CAP chambered in 223 Rem. Imported by Century Arms Int'l.
Price: GP WASR-2/3, from $250.00

CENTURY INTERNATIONAL M70AB2 SPORTER RIFLE
Caliber: 7.62x39mm. 30-shot magazine. **Barrel:** 16.25". **Weight:** 7.5 lbs. **Length:** 34.25" overall. Stocks: Metal grip, wood forend. **Sights:** Fixed-notch rear, windage-adjustable post front. **Features:** 2 30-rd. double-stack magazine, cleaning kit, compensator, bayonet lug and bayonet. Paratrooper-style Kalashnikov with under-folding stock. Imported by Century Arms Int'l.
Price: M70AB2, from. $480.00

COLT MATCH TARGET MODEL RIFLE
Caliber: 223 Rem., 5-shot magazine. **Barrel:** 16.1" or 20". **Weight:** 7.1 to 8.5 lbs. **Length:** 34.5" to 39" overall. **Stock:** Composition stock, grip, forend. **Sights:** Post front, rear adjustable for windage and elevation. **Features:** 5-round detachable box magazine, flash suppressor, sling swivels. Forward bolt assist included. Introduced 1991. Made in U.S.A. by Colt's Mfg. Co., Inc.
Price: Match Target HBAR MT6601 . . . . $1,182.00

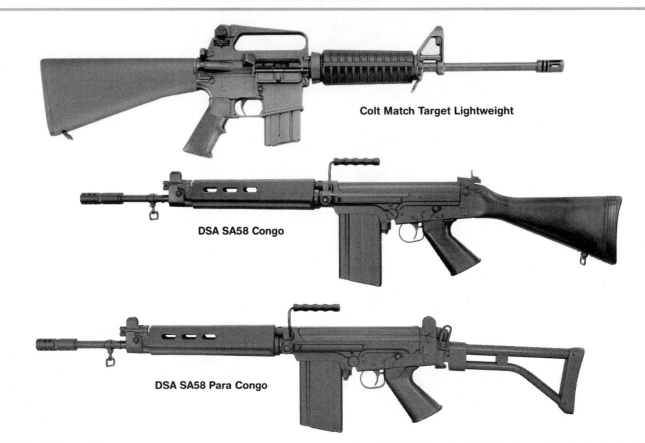

Colt Match Target Lightweight

DSA SA58 Congo

DSA SA58 Para Congo

Colt Match Target M4
Similar to above but with carbine-length barrel.
Price: .... **NA**

DPMS PANTHER ARMS AR-15 RIFLES
Caliber: 223 Rem., 7.62x39. **Barrel:** 16" to 24". **Weight:** 7.75 to 11.75 lbs. **Length:** 34.5" to 42.25" overall. **Stock:** Black Zytel composite. **Sights:** Square front post, adjustable A2 rear. **Features:** Steel or stainless steel heavy or bull barrel; hardcoat anodized receiver; aluminum free-float tube handguard; many options. From DPMS Panther Arms.
Price: Panther Bull Twenty (20" stainless bull bbl.) $920.00
Price: Arctic Panther...............................$1,099.00
Price: Panther Classic................................$799.00
Price: Panther Bull Sweet Sixteen (16" stainless bull bbl.) ...$885.00
Price: DCM Panther (20" stainless heavy bbl., n.m. sights) $1,099.00
Price: Panther 7.62x39 (20" steel heavy bbl.) $859.00

DPMS PANTHER ARMS CLASSIC AUTO RIFLE
Caliber: 5.56x45mm. **Barrel:** Heavy 16" to 20" w/flash hider. **Weight:** 7 to 9 lbs. **Length:** 34-11/16" to 38-7/16". **Sights:** Adj. rear and front. **Stock:** Black Zytel w/trap door assembly. **Features:** Gas operated rotating bolt, mil spec or Teflon black finish.
Price: Panther A2 Tactical 16" $814.00
Price: Panther Lite 16 ....$725.00
Price: Panther Carbine $799.00
Price: Panther The Agency Rifle....................$1,999.00

DSA Z4 GTC CARBINE WITH C.R.O.S.
Caliber: 5.56 NATO **Barrel:** 16" 1:9 twist M4 profile fluted chrome lined heavy barrel with threaded Vortec flash hider. **Weight:** 7.6 lbs. **Stock:** 6 position collapsible M4 stock, Predator P4X free float tactical rail. **Sights:** Chrome lined Picatinny gas block w/removable front sight. **Features:** The Corrosion Resistant Operating System incorporates the new P.O.F. Gas Trap System with removable gas plug eliminates problematic features of standard AR gas system, Forged 7075T6 DSA lower receiver. Introduced 2006. Made in U.S.A. by DSA, Inc.
Price: $1,800.00

DSA CQB MRP, STANDARD MRP
Caliber: 5.56 NATO **Barrel:** 16" or 18" 1:7 twist chrome-lined or stainless steel barrel with A2 flash hider **Stock:** 6 position collapsible M4 stock. **Features:** LMT 1/2" MRP upper receiver with 20.5" Standard quad rail or 16.5" CQB quad rail, LMT-enhanced bolt with dual extractor springs, free float barrel, quick change barrel system, forged 7075T6 DSA lower receiver. EOTech and vertical grip additional. Introduced 2006. Made in U.S.A. by DSA, Inc.
Price: CQB MRP w/16" chrome-lined barrel **$2,420.00**
Price: CQB MRP w/16" stainless steel barrel............ **$2,540.00**
Price: Standard MRP w/16" chrome-lined barrel **$2,620.00**
Price: Standard MRP w/16" or 18" stainless steel barrel ... **$2,740.00**

DSA STD CARBINE
Caliber: 5.56 NATO. **Barrel:** 16" 1:9 twist D4 w/A2 flash hider. **Weight:** 6.25 lbs. **Length:** 31". **Stock:** A2 buttstock, D4 handguard w/heatshield. **Sights:** Forged A2 front sight with lug. **Features:** Forged 7075T6 DSA lower receiver, forged A2 or flattop upper receiver. Introduced 2006. Made in U.S.A. by DSA, Inc.
Price: A2 or Flattop STD Carbine..................... **$1,025.00**
Price: With LMT SOPMOD stock **$1,267.00**

DSA 1R CARBINE
Caliber: 5.56 NATO. **Barrel:** 16" 1:9 twist D4 w/A2 flash hider. **Weight:** 6.25 lbs. **Length:** Variable. **Stock:** 6 position collapsible M4 stock, D4 handguard w/heatshield. **Sights:** Forged A2 front sight with lug. **Features:** Forged 7075T6 DSA lower receiver, forged A2 or flattop upper receiver. Introduced 2006. Made in U.S.A. by DSA, Inc.
Price: A2 or Flattop 1R Carbine **$1,055.00**
Price: With VLTOR ModStock **$1,175.00**

DSA XM CARBINE
Caliber: 5.56 NATO. **Barrel:** 11.5" 1:9 twist D4 with 5.5" permanently attached flash hider. **Weight:** 6.25 lbs. **Length:** Variable. **Stock:** Collapsible, Handguard w/heatshield. **Sights:** Forged A2 front sight with lug. **Features:** Forged 7075T6 DSA lower receiver, forged A2 upper receiver. Introduced 2006. Made in U.S.A. by DSA, Inc.
Price: **$1,055.00**

DSA STANDARD
Caliber: 5.56 NATO. **Barrel:** 20" 1:9 twist heavy barrel w/A2 flash hider. **Weight:** 6.25 lbs. **Length:** 38-7/16". **Stock:** A2 buttstock, A2 handguard w/heatshield. **Sights:** Forged A2 front sight with lug. **Features:** Forged 7075T6 DSA lower receiver, forged A2 or flattop upper receiver. Introduced 2006. Made in U.S.A. by DSA, Inc.
Price: A2 or Flattop Standard **$1,025.00**

DSA SA58 Gray Wolf

DSA SA58 Predator

DSA SA58 T48

DSA SA58 G1

DSA DCM RIFLE

Caliber: 223 Wylde Chamber. **Barrel:** 20" 1:8 twist chrome moly match grade Badger Barrel. **Weight:** 10 lbs. **Length:** 39.5". **Stock:** DCM freefloat handguard system, A2 buttstock. **Sights:** Forged A2 front sight with lug. **Features:** NM two stage trigger, NM rear sight, forged 7075T6 DSA lower receiver, forged A2 upper receiver. Introduced 2006. Made in U.S.A. by DSA, Inc.
Price: **$1,520.00**

DSA S1

Caliber: 223 Rem. Match Chamber. **Barrel:** 16", 20" or 24" 1:8 twist stainless steel bull barrel. **Weight:** 8.0, 9.5 and 10 lbs. **Length:** 34.25", 38.25" and 42.25". **Stock:** A2 buttstock with free float aluminum handguard. **Sights:** Picatinny gas block sight base. **Features:** Forged 7075T6 DSA lower receiver, Match two stage trigger, forged flattop upper receiver, fluted barrel optional. Introduced 2006. Made in U.S.A. by DSA, Inc.
Price: **$1,155.00**

DSA SA58 CONGO, PARA CONGO

Caliber: 308 Win. **Barrel:** 18" w/short Belgian short flash hider. **Weight:** 8.6 lbs. (Congo); 9.85 lbs. (Para Congo). **Length:** 39.75" **Stock:** Synthetic w/military grade furniture (Congo); Synthetic with non-folding steel para stock (Para Congo). **Sights:** Elevation adjustable protected post front sight, windage adjustable rear peep (Congo); Belgian type Para Flip Rear (Para Congo). **Features:** Fully-adjustable gas system, high-grade steel upper receiver with carry handle. Made in U.S.A. by DSA, Inc.
Price: Congo. **$1,850.00**
Price: Para Congo **$2,095.00**

DSA SA58 GRAY WOLF

Caliber: 308 Win. **Barrel:** 21" match-grade bull w/target crown. **Weight:** 13 lbs. **Length:** 41.75". **Stock:** Synthetic. **Sights:** Elevation-adjustable post front sight, windage-adjustable match rear peep. **Features:** Fully-adjustable gas system, high-grade steel upper receiver, Picatinny scope mount, DuraCoat finish. Made in U.S.A. by DSA, Inc.
Price: **$2,120.00**

DSA SA58 PREDATOR

Caliber: 243 Win., 260 Rem., 308 Win. **Barrel:** 16" and 19" w/target crown. **Weight:** 9 to 9.3 lbs. **Length:** 36.25" to 39.25". **Stock:** Green synthetic. **Sights:** Elevation-adjustable post front; windage-adjustable match rear peep. **Features:** Fully-adjustable gas system, high-grade steel upper receiver, Picatinny scope mount, DuraCoat solid and camo finishes. Made in U.S.A. by DSA, Inc.
Price: 243 Win., 260 Rem. **$1,695.00**
Price: 308 Win. **$1,640.00**

DSA SA58 T48

Caliber: 308 Win. **Barrel:** 21" with Browning long flash hider. **Weight:** 9.3 lbs. **Length:** 44.5". **Stock:** European walnut. **Sights:** Elevation-adjustable post front, windage adjustable rear peep. **Features:** Gas-operated semi-auto with fully adjustable gas system, high grade steel upper receiver with carry handle. DuraCoat finishes. Made in U.S.A. by DSA, Inc.
Price: **$1,995.00**

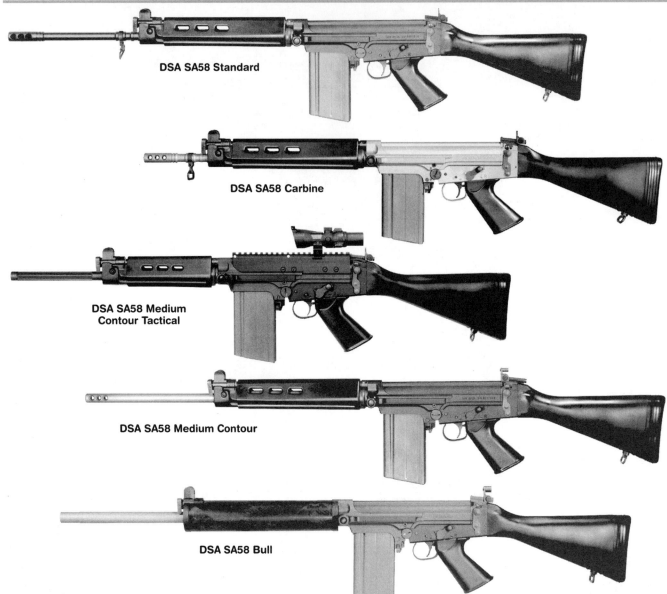

DSA SA58 Standard

DSA SA58 Carbine

DSA SA58 Medium
Contour Tactical

DSA SA58 Medium Contour

DSA SA58 Bull

DSA SA58 G1
Caliber: 308 Win. **Barrel:** 21" with quick-detach flash hider. **Weight:** 10.65 lbs. **Length:** 44". **Stock:** Steel bipod cut handguard with hardwood stock and synthetic pistol grip. **Sights:** Elevation-adjustable post front, windage adjustable rear peep. **Features:** Gas-operated semi-auto with fully adjustable gas system, high grade steel upper receiver with carry handle, original GI steel lower receiver with GI bipod. DuraCoat finishes. Made in U.S.A. by DSA, Inc.
Price: **$1,850.00**

DSA SA58 STANDARD
Caliber: 308 Win. **Barrel:** 21" bipod cut w/threaded flash hider. **Weight:** 8.75 lbs. **Length:** 43". **Stock:** Synthetic, X-Series or optional folding para stock. **Sights:** Elevation-adjustable post front, windage-adjustable rear peep. **Features:** Fully adjustable short gas system, high grade steel or 416 stainless upper receiver. Made in U.S.A. by DSA, Inc.
Price: High-grade steel. **$1,595.00**
Price: Folding para stock **$1,845.00**

DSA SA58 CARBINE
Caliber: 308 Win. **Barrel:** 16.25" bipod cut w/threaded flash hider. **Weight:** 8.35 lbs. **Length:** 37.5". **Stock:** Synthetic, X-Series or optional folding para stock. **Sights:** Elevation-adjustable post front, windage-adjustable rear peep. **Features:** Fully adjustable short gas system, high grade steel or 416 stainless upper receiver. Made in U.S.A. by DSA, Inc.
Price: High-grade steel. **$1,595.00**

Price: Stainless steel **$1,850.00**

DSA SA58 TACTICAL CARBINE
Caliber: 308 Win. **Barrel:** 16.25" fluted with A2 flash hider. **Weight:** 8.25 lbs. **Length:** 36.5". **Stock:** Synthetic, X-Series or optional folding para stock. **Sights:** Elevation-adjustable post front, windage-adjustable match rear peep. **Features:** Shortened fully adjustable short gas system, high grade steel or 416 stainless upper receiver. Made in U.S.A. by DSA, Inc.
Price: High-grade steel. **$1,595.00**
Price: Stainless steel **$1,850.00**

DSA SA58 MEDIUM CONTOUR
Caliber: 308 Win. **Barrel:** 21" w/threaded flash hider. **Weight:** 9.75 lbs. **Length:** 43". **Stock:** Synthetic military grade. **Sights:** Elevation-adjustable post front, windage-adjustable match rear peep. **Features:** Gas-operated semi-auto with fully adjustable gas system, high grade steel receiver. Made in U.S.A. by DSA, Inc.
Price: **$1,595.00**

DSA SA58 BULL BARREL RIFLE
Caliber: 308 Win. **Barrel:** 21". **Weight:** 11.1 lbs. **Length:** 41.5". **Stock:** Synthetic, free floating handguard. **Sights:** Elevation-adjustable windage-adjustable post front, match rear peep. **Features:** Gas-operated semi-auto with fully adjustable gas system, high grade steel or stainless upper receiver. Made in U.S.A. by DSA, Inc.

DSA SA58 OSW

Excel Arms Accelerator

Heckler & Koch USC

Hi-Point Carbine

Les Baer Flattop

Price: . . . .
$1,745.00
Price: Stainless steel . . . .
$1,995.00

DSA SA58 MINI OSW

Caliber: 308 Win. **Barrel:** 11" or 13" w/A2 flash hider. **Weight:** 9 to 9.35 lbs. **Length:** 32.75" to 35". **Stock:** Fiberglass reinforced short synthetic handguard, para folding stock and synthetic pistol grip. **Sights:** Adjustable post front, para rear sight. **Features:** Semi-auto or select fire with fully adjustable short gas system, optional FAL rail handguard, SureFire Vertical Foregrip System, EOTech HOLOgraphic Sight and ITC cheekrest. Made in U.S.A. by DSA, Inc.
Price: **$1,845.00**

EXCEL ARMS ACCELERATOR RIFLES

Caliber: 17 HMR, 22 WMR, 17M2, 22 LR, 9-shot magazine. **Barrel:** 18" fluted stainless steel bull barrel. **Weight:** 8 lbs. **Length:** 32.5" overall. **Grips:** Textured black polymer. **Sights:** Fully adjustable target sights. **Features:** Made from 17-4 stainless steel, aluminum shroud w/ Weaver rail, manual safety, firing-pin block, last-round bolt-hold-open feature. Four packages with various equipment available. American made, lifetime warranty. Comes with one 9-round stainless steel magazine and a California-approved cable lock. Introduced 2006. Made in U.S.A. by Excel Arms.
Price: MR-17 17 HMR. **$488.00**
Price: MR-22 22 WMR **$523.00**

HECKLER & KOCH USC CARBINE

Caliber: 45 ACP, 10-shot magazine. **Barrel:** 16". **Weight:** 8.6 lb. **Length:**

35.4" overall. **Stock:** Skeletonized polymer thumbhole. **Sights:** Blade front with integral hood, fully adjustable diopter. **Features:** Based on German UMP submachine gun. Blowback operation; almost entirely constructed of carbon fiber-reinforced polymer. Free-floating heavy target barrel. Introduced 2000. From H&K.
Price: **$1,249.00**

HI-POINT 9MM CARBINE

Caliber: 9mm Para., 40 S&W, 10-shot magazine. **Barrel:** 16.5" (17.5" for 40 S&W). **Weight:** 4.5 lbs. **Length:** 31.5" overall. **Stock:** Black polymer, camouflage. **Sights:** Protected post front, aperture rear. Integral scope mount. **Features:** Grip-mounted magazine release. Black or chrome finish. Sling swivels. Available with laser or red dot sights. Introduced 1996. Made in U.S.A. by MKS Supply, Inc.
Price: 995-B (black) **$220.00**
Price: 995-CMO (camo) **$235.00**

LES BAER CUSTOM ULTIMATE AR 223 RIFLES

Caliber: 223. **Barrel:** 18", 20", 22", 24". **Weight:** 7.75 to 9.75 lb. **Length:** NA. **Stock:** Black synthetic. **Sights:** None furnished; Picatinny-style flattop rail for scope mounting. **Features:** Forged receiver; Ultra single-stage trigger (Jewell two-stage trigger optional); titanium firing pin; Versa-Pod bipod; chromed National Match carrier; stainless steel, hand-lapped and cryo-treated barrel; guaranteed to shoot 1/2 or 3/4 MOA, depending on model. Made in U.S.A. by Les Baer Custom Inc.
Price: Super Varmint Model **$2,390.00**
Price: Super Match Model (introduced 2006) **$2,490.00**

Les Baer IPSC

Olympic Arms K9 Carbine

Olympic Arms K3B

Olympic Arms Plinker Plus AR15

Price: M4 Flattop model **$2,360.00**
Price: Police Special 16" (2008) **$1,690.00**
Price: IPSC Action Model **$2,640.00**

LR 300 RIFLES
Caliber: 5.56 NATO, 30-shot magazine. **Barrel:** 16.5"; 1:9" twist. **Weight:** 7.4-7.8 lbs. **Length:** NA. **Stock:** Folding. **Sights:** YHM flip front and rear. **Features:** Flattop receive, full length top picatinny rail. Phantom flash hider, multi sling mount points, field strips with no tools. Made in U.S.A. from Z-M Weapons.
Price: AXL, AXLT **$2,139.00**
Price: NXL **$2,208.00**

MERKEL MODEL SR1 SEMI-AUTOMATIC RIFLE
Caliber: 308 Win., 300 Win Mag. **Features:** Streamlined profile, checkered walnut stock and forend, 19.7- (308) or 20-8" (300 SM) barrel, two- or five-shot detachable box magazine. Adjustable front and rear iron sights with Weaver-style optics rail included. Imported from Germany by Merkel USA.
Price: **$1,595.00**

OLYMPIC ARMS K9, K10, K40, K45 PISTOL-CALIBER AR15 CARBINES
Caliber: 9mm Para., 10mm, 40 S&W, 45 ACP; 32/10-shot modified magazines. **Barrel:** 16" button rifled stainless steel, 1x16 twist rate. **Weight:** 6.73 lbs. **Length:** 31.625" overall. **Stock:** A2 grip, M4 6-point collapsible stock. **Features:** A2 upper with adjustable rear sight, elevation adjustable front post, bayonet lug, sling swivel, threaded muzzle, flash suppressor, carbine length handguards. Made in U.S.A. by Olympic Arms, Inc.

Price: K9GL, 9mm Para., Glock lower **$1,092.00**
Price: K10, 10mm, modified 10-round Uzi magazine **$1,006.20**
Price: K40, 40 S&W, modified 10-round Uzi magazine **$1,006.20**
Price: K45, 45 ACP, modified 10-round Uzi magazine **$1,006.20**

OLYMPIC ARMS K3B SERIES AR15 CARBINES
Caliber: 5.56 NATO, 30-shot magazines. **Barrel:** 16" button rifled chrome-moly steel, 1x9 twist rate. **Weight:** 5-7 lbs. **Length:** 31.75" overall. **Stock:** A2 grip, M4 6-point collapsible buttstock. **Features:** A2 upper with adjustable rear sight, elevation adjustable front post, bayonet lug, sling swivel, threaded muzzle, flash suppressor, carbine length handguards. Made in U.S.A. by Olympic Arms, Inc.
Price: K3B base model, A2 upper **$815.00**
Price: K3B-M4 M4 contoured barrel & handguards **$1,038.70**
Price: K3B-M4-A3-TC A3 upper, M4 barrel, FIRSH rail handguard **$1,246.70**
Price: K3B-CAR 11.5" barrel with 5.5" permanent flash suppressor **$968.50**
Price: K3B-FAR 16" featherweight contoured barrel **$1,006.20**

OLYMPIC ARMS PLINKER PLUS AR15 MODELS
Caliber: 5.56 NATO, 30-shot magazine. **Barrel** 16" or 20" button-rifled chrome-moly steel, 1x9 twist. **Weight:** 7.5-8.5 lbs. **Length:** 35.5"-39.5" overall. **Stock:** A2 grip, A2 buttstock with trapdoor. **Sights:** A1 windage

Olympic Arms Plinker Plus 20

Ruger Mini-14/5 Ranch

Ruger Mini-14 ATI Stock

Ruger Mini-14 Tactical

rear, elevation-adjustable front post. **Features:** A1 upper, fiberlite handguards, bayonet lug, threaded muzzle and flash suppressor. Made in U.S.A. by Olympic Arms, Inc.

Price: Plinker Plus $713.70
Price: Plinker Plus 20 . . . .$843.70

REMINGTON MODEL R-15 MODULAR REPEATING RIFLE

Caliber: 223 and 30 Rem. AR, five-shot magazine. **Barrel:** 18" (carbine), 22", 24". **Weight:** 6.75 to 7.75 lbs. **Length:** 36.25" to 42.25". **Stock:** Camo. **Features:** AR-style with optics rail, aluminum alloy upper and lower.

Price: R-15 Hunter: 30 Rem. AR, 22" barrel, Realtree AP HD
 camo **$1,225.00**
Price: R-15 VTR Byron South Edition: 223, 18" barrel, Advantage
 MAX-1 HD camo **$1,772.00**
Price: R-15 VTR SS Varmint: Same as Byron South Edition but
 with 24" stainless steel barrel **$1,412.00**
Price: R-15 VTR Thumbhole: Similar to R-15 Hunter but with
 thumbhole stock **$1,412.00**
Price: R-15 VYR Predator: 204 Ruger or .223, 22" barrel . . **$1,225.00**
Price: R-15 Predator Carbine: Similar to above but with
 18" barrel **$1,225.00**

REMINGTON MODEL R-25 MODULAR REPEATING RIFLE

Caliber: 243, 7mm-08, 308 Win., four-shot magazine. **Barrel:** 20" chrome-moly. **Weight:** 7.75 lbs. **Length:** 38.25" overall. **Features:** AR-style semi-auto with single-stage trigger, aluminum alloy upper and lower, Mossy Oak Treestand camo finish overall.

Price: **$1,567.00**

REMINGTON MODEL 750 WOODSMASTER

Caliber: 243 Win., 270 Win., 308 Win., 30-06 Spfl., 35 Whelen. 4-shot magazine. **Barrel:** 22" round tapered. **Weight:** 7.5 lbs. **Length:** 42.6" overall. **Stock:** Restyled American walnut forend and stock with machine-cut checkering. Satin finish. **Sights:** Gold bead front sight on

ramp; step rear sight with windage adjustable. **Features:** Replaced wood-stocked Model 7400 line introduced 1981. Gas action, SuperCell recoil pad. Positive cross-bolt safety. Carbine chambered in 308 Win., 30-06 Spfl., 35 Whelen. Receiver tapped for scope mount. Introduced 2006. Made in U.S.A. by Remington Arms Co.

Price: 750 Woodsmaster **$879.00**
Price: 750 Woodsmaster Carbine (18.5" bbl.) **$879.00**
Price: 750 Synthetic stock (2007). **$773.00**

ROCK RIVER ARMS STANDARD A2 RIFLE

Caliber: 45 ACP. **Barrel:** NA. **Weight:** 8.2 lbs. **Length:** NA. **Stock:** Thermoplastic. **Sights:** Standard AR-15 style sights. **Features:** Two-stage, national match trigger; optional muzzle brake. Pro-Series Government package includes side-mount sling swivel, chrome-lined 1:9 twist barrel, mil-spec forged lower receiver, Hogue rubber grip, NM two-stage trigger, 6-position tactical CAR stock, Surefire M73 quad rail handguard, other features. Made in U.S.A. From Rock River Arms.

Price: Standard A2 AR1280 . . . .**$945.00**
Price: Pro-Series Government Package GOVT1001 (2008) **$2,290.00**
Price: Elite Comp AR1270 (2008). **$1,145.00**

RUGER MINI-14 RANCH RIFLE AUTOLOADING RIFLE

Caliber: 223 Rem., 5-shot detachable box magazine. **Barrel:** 18.5". Rifling twist 1:9". **Weight:** 6.75 to 7 lbs. **Length:** 37.25" overall. **Stock:** American hardwood, steel reinforced, or synthetic. **Sights:** Protected blade front, fully adjustable Ghost Ring rear. **Features:** Fixed piston gas-operated, positive primary extraction. New buffer system, redesigned ejector system. Ruger S100RM scope rings included on Ranch Rifle. Heavier barrels added in 2008, 20-round magazine added in 1009.

Price: Mini-14/5, Ranch Rifle, blued, scope rings **$855.00**
Price: K-Mini-14/5, Ranch Rifle, stainless, scope rings **$921.00**
Price: K-Mini-6.8/5P, All-Weather Ranch Rifle, stainless,
 synthetic stock (2008) **$921.00**
Price: Mini-14 Target Rifle: laminated thumbhole stock,
 heavy crowned 22" stainless steel barrel, other

Sabre Defence Competition Extreme

Sabre Defence M5 Tactical

Sabre Defence Heavy Bench Target

Sabre Defence Varmint

refinements **$1,066.00**
Price: Mini-14 ATI Stock: Tactical version of Mini-14 but with six-position collapsible stock or folding stock, grooved pistol grip. multiple picatinny optics/accessory rails . . . **$872.00**
Price: Mini-14 Tactical Rifle: Similar to Mini-14 but with 16-21" barrel with flash hider, black synthetic stock, adjustable sights **$894.00**

Ruger NRA Mini-14 Rifle
Similar to the Mini-14 Ranch Rifle except comes with two 20-round magazines and special Black Hogue OverMolded stock with NRA gold-tone medallion in grip cap. Special serial number sequence (NRA8XXXXX). For 2008 only.
Price: M-14/20C-NRA. **$1,035.00**
Price: M-14/5C-NRA (5-round magazines). **$1,035.00**

Ruger Mini Thirty Rifle
Similar to the Mini-14 Ranch Rifle except modified to chamber the 7.62x39 Russian service round. **Weight:** 6.75 lbs. Has 6-groove barrel with 1:10" twist, Ruger Integral Scope Mount bases and protected blade front, fully adjustable Ghost Ring rear. Detachable 5-shot staggered box magazine. Stainless w/synthetic stock. Introduced 1987.

Price: Stainless, scope rings **$921.00**

SABRE DEFENCE SABRE RIFLES
Caliber: 5.56 NATO, 6.5 Grendel, 30-shot magazines. **Barrel:** 20" 410 stainless steel, 1x8 twist rate; or 18" vanadium alloy, chrome-lined barrel with Sabre Gill-Brake. **Weight:** 6.77 lbs. **Length:** 31.75" overall. **Stock:** SOCOM 3-position stock with Samson M-EX handguards. **Sights:** Flip-up front and rear sights. **Features:** Fluted barrel, Harris bipod, and two-stage match trigger, Ergo Grips; upper and matched lower CNC machined from 7075-T6 forgings. SOCOM adjustable stock, Samson tactical handguards, M4 contour barrels available in 14.5" and 16" are made of MIL-B-11595 vanadium alloy and chrome lined. Introduced 2002. From Sabre Defence Industries.
Price: 6.5 Grendel, from **$1,409.00**
Price: Competition Extreme, 20" barrel, from **$2,189.00**
Price: Competition Deluxe, from **$2,299.00**
Price: Competition Special, 5.56mm, 18" barrel, from **$1,899.00**
Price: SPR Carbine, from **$2,499.00**
Price: M4 Tactical, from **$1,969.00**
Price: M4 Carbine, 14.5" barrel, from **$1,399.00**
Price: M4 Flat-top Carbine, 16" barrel, from **$1,349.00**

SIG 556 Classic

SIG 556 DMR

SIG 556 SCM

SIG 556 SWAT

standard AR magazines. Polymer forearm, three integrated Picatinny rails, forward mount for right- or left-side sling attachment. Aircraft-grade aluminum alloy trigger housing, hard-coat anodized finish; two-stage trigger, ambidextrous safety, 30-round polymer magazine, battery compartments, pistol-grip rubber-padded watertight adjustable butt stock with sling-attachment points. SIG 556 SWAT model has flat-top Picatinny railed receiver, tactical quad rail. SIG 556 HOLO sight options include front combat sight, flip-up rear sight, and red-dot style holographic sighting system with four illuminated reticle patterns. DMR features a 24" military grade cold hammer-forged heavy contour barrel, 5.56mm NATO, target crown. Imported by Sig Sauer, Inc.

Price: M5 Flat-top, 16" barrel, from $1,399.00
Price: M5 Tactical, 14.5" barrel, from $2,099.00
Price: M5 Carbine, from $1,309.00
Price: Precision Marksman, 20" barrel, from $2,499.00
Price: A4 Rifle, 20" barrel, from $1,349.00
Price: A3 National Match, 20" barrel $1,699.00
Price: Heavy Bench Target, 24" barrel, from $1,889.00
Price: Varmint, 20" barrel $1,709.00

Price: SIG 556 . . . . $2,099.00
Price: SIG 556 HOLO (2008) $1,832.00
Price: SIG 556 DMR (2008) $2,400.00
Price: SIG 556 SWAT $2,000.00
Price: SIG 556 SCM $1,838.00

SIG 556 AUTOLOADING RIFLE

Caliber: 223 Rem., 30-shot detachable box magazine. **Barrel:** 16". Rifling twist 1:9". **Weight:** 6.8 lbs. **Length:** 36.5" overall. **Stock:** Polymer, folding style. **Sights:** Flip-up front combat sight, adjustable for windage and elevation. **Features:** Based on SG 550 series rifle. Two-position adjustable gas piston operating rod system, accepts

SMITH & WESSON M&P15 RIFLES

Caliber: 5.56mm NATO/223, 30-shot steel magazine. **Barrel:** 16", 1:9 **Weight:** 6.74 lbs., w/o magazine. **Length:** 32-35" overall. **Stock:** Black synthetic. **Sights:** Adjustable post front sight, adjustable dual

Springfield M1A

Winchester Super X

aperture rear sight. **Features:** 6-position telescopic stock, thermo-set M4 handguard. 14.75" sight radius. 7-lbs. (approx.) trigger pull. 7075 T6 aluminum upper, 4140 steel barrel. Chromed barrel bore, gas key, bolt carrier. Hard-coat black-anodized receiver and barrel finish. Introduced 2006. Made in U.S.A. by Smith & Wesson.
Price: M&P15 No. 811000 . . . . **$1,406.00**
Price: M&P15T No. 811001, free float modular rail forend . **$1,888.00**
Price: M&P15A No. 811002, folding battle rear sight **$1,422.00**
Price: M&P15A No. 811013, optics ready compliant (2008). **$1,169.00**

SMITH & WESSON MODEL M&P15VTAC VIKING TACTICS MODEL
Caliber: 223 Remington/5.56 NATO, 30-round magazine. **Barrel:** 16". **Weight:** 6.5 lbs. **Length:** 35" extended, 32" collapsed, overall. **Features:** Six-position CAR stock. Surefire flash-hider and G2 light with VTAC light mount; VTAC/JP handguard; JP single-stage match trigger and speed hammer; three adjustable picatinny rails; VTAC padded two-point adjustable sling.
Price: **$2,196.00**

SMITH & WESSON M&P15PC CAMO
Caliber: 223 Rem/5.56 NATO, A2 configuration, 10-round mag. **Barrel:** 20" stainless with 1:8 twist. **Weight:** 8.2 lbs. **Length:** 38.5" overall. **Features:** AR-style, no sights but integral front and rear optics rails. Two-stage trigger, aluminum lower. Finished in Realtree Advantage Max-1 camo.
Price: **$2,046.00**

SPRINGFIELD ARMORY M1A RIFLE
Caliber: 7.62mm NATO (308), 5- or 10-shot box magazine. **Barrel:** 25-1/16" with flash suppressor, 22" without suppressor. **Weight:** 9.75 lbs. **Length:** 44.25" overall. **Stock:** American walnut with walnut-colored heat-resistant fiberglass handguard. Matching walnut handguard available. Also available with fiberglass stock. **Sights:** Military, square blade front, full click-adjustable aperture rear. **Features:** Commercial equivalent of the U.S. M-14 service rifle with no provision for automatic firing. From Springfield Armory
Price: SOCOM 16 . . . . **$1,855.00**
Price: SOCOM II, from **$2,090.00**
Price: Scout Squad, from **$1,726.00**
Price: Standard M1A, from **$1,608.00**
Price: Loaded Standard, from **$1,759.00**

Price: National Match, from **$2,249.00**
Price: Super Match (heavy premium barrel) about **$2,818.00**
Price: Tactical, from **$3,780.00**

STONER SR-15 M-5 RIFLE
Caliber: 223. **Barrel:** 20". **Weight:** 7.6 lbs. **Length:** 38" overall. **Stock:** Black synthetic. **Sights:** Post front, fully adjustable rear (300-meter sight). **Features:** Modular weapon system; two-stage trigger. Black finish. Introduced 1998. Made in U.S.A. by Knight's Mfg.
Price: **$1,695.00**

STONER SR-25 CARBINE
Caliber: 7.62 NATO, 10-shot steel magazine. **Barrel:** 16" free-floating **Weight:** 7.75 lbs. **Length:** 35.75" overall. **Stock:** Black synthetic. **Sights:** Integral Weaver-style rail. Scope rings, iron sights optional. **Features:** Shortened, non-slip handguard; removable carrying handle. Matte black finish. Introduced 1995. Made in U.S.A. by Knight's Mfg. Co.
Price: **$3,345.00**

WILSON COMBAT TACTICAL RIFLES
Caliber: 5.56mm NATO, accepts all M-16/AR-15 Style Magazines, includes one 20-round magazine. **Barrel:** 16.25", 1:9 twist, match-grade fluted. **Weight:** 6.9 lbs. **Length:** 36.25" overall. **Stock:** Fixed or collapsible. **Features:** Free-float ventilated aluminum quad-rail handguard, Mil-Spec parkerized barrel and steel components, anodized receiver, precision CNC-machined upper and lower receivers, 7075 T6 aluminum forgings. Single stage JP Trigger/ Hammer Group, Wilson Combat Tactical Muzzle Brake, nylon tactical rifle case. M-4T version has flat-top receiver for mounting optics, OD green furniture, 16.25" match-grade M-4 style barrel. SS-15 Super Sniper Tactical Rifle has 1-in-8 twist, heavy 20" match-grade fluted stainless steel barrel. Made in U.S.A by Wilson Combat.
Price: UT-15 Tactical Carbine. **$1,785.00**
Price: M4-TP Tactical Carbine **$1,575.00**

Both classic arms and recent designs in American-style repeaters for sport and field shooting.

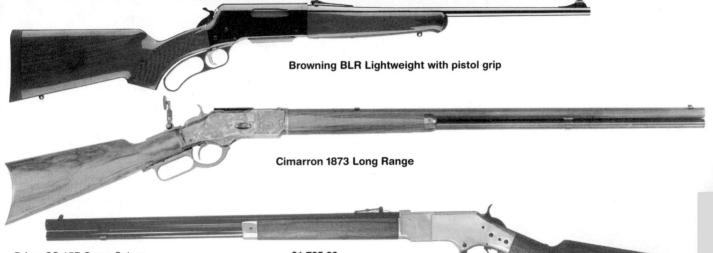

Browning BLR Lightweight with pistol grip

Cimarron 1873 Long Range

Cimarron 1866
Winchester Replica

Price: SS-15P Super Sniper **$1,795.00**

WINCHESTER SUPER X RIFLE
Caliber: 270 WSM, 30-06 Spfl., 300 Win. Mag., 300 WSM, 4-shot steel magazine. **Barrel:** 22", 24", 1:10", blued. **Weight:** 7.25 lbs. **Length:** up to 41-3/8". **Stock:** Walnut, 14-1/8"x 7/8"x 1.25". **Sights:** None. **Features:** Gas operated, removable trigger assembly, detachable box magazine, drilled and tapped, alloy receiver, enlarged trigger guard, crossbolt safety. Reintroduced 2008. Made in U.S.A. by Winchester Repeating Arms.
Price: Super X Rifle, from **$949.00**

BERETTA 1873 RENEGADE SHORT LEVER-ACTION RIFLE
Caliber: 45 Colt, 357 Magnum. **Barrel:** 20" round or 24-1/2" octagonal. **Features:** Blued finish, checkered walnut buttstock and forend, adjustable rear sight and fixed blade front, ten-round tubular magazine.
Price: **$1,350.00**

BERETTA GOLD RUSH SLIDE-ACTION RIFLE AND CARBINE
Caliber: 357 Magnum, 45 Colt. **Barrel:** 20" round or 24-1/2"octagonal. **Features:** External replica of old Colt Lightning Magazine Rifle. Case-hardened receiver, walnut buttstock and forend, crescent buttplate, 13-round (rifle) or 10-round (carbine) magazine. Available as Standard Carbine, Standard Rifle, or Deluxe Rifle.
Price: Standard Carbine **$1,375.00**
Price: Standard Rifle **$1,425.00**
Price: Deluxe Rifle **$11,950.00**

BROWNING BLR RIFLES
Action: Lever action with rotating bolt head, multiple-lug breech bolt with recessed bolt face, side ejection. Rack-and-pinion lever. Flush-mounted detachable magazines, with 4+1 capacity for magnum cartridges, 5+1 for standard rounds. **Barrel:** Button-rifled chrome-moly steel with crowned muzzle. **Stock:** Buttstocks and forends are American walnut with grip and forend checkering. Recoil pad installed. Trigger: Wide-groove design, trigger travels with lever. Half-cock hammer safety; fold-down hammer. **Sights:** Gold bead on ramp front; low-profile square-notch adjustable rear. **Features:** Blued barrel and receiver, high-gloss wood finish. Receivers are drilled and tapped for scope mounts, swivel studs included. Action lock provided. Introduced 1996. Imported from Japan by Browning.

BROWNING BLR LIGHTWEIGHT W/PISTOL GRIP, SHORT AND LONG ACTION; LIGHTWEIGHT '81, SHORT AND LONG ACTION
Calibers: Short Action, 20" Barrel: 22-250 Rem., 243 Win., 7mm-08 Rem., 308 Win., 358, 450 Marlin. Calibers: Short Action, 22" Barrel: 270 WSM, 7mm WSM, 300 WSM, 325 WSM. Calibers: Long Action 22" Barrel: 270 Win., 30-06. Calibers: Long Action 24" Barrel: 7mm Rem. Mag., 300 Win. Mag. **Weight:** 6.5-7.75 lbs. **Length:** 40-45" overall. **Stock:** New checkered pistol grip and Schnabel forearm. Lightweight '81 differs from Pistol Grip models with a Western-style straight grip stock and banded forearm. Lightweight w/Pistol Grip Short Action and Long Action introduced 2005. Model '81 Lightning Long Action introduced 1996.
Price: Lightweight w/Pistol Grip Short Action, from **$879.00**
Price: Lightweight w/Pistol Grip Long Action **$929.00**
Price: Lightweight '81 Short Action **$839.00**
Price: Lightweight '81 Long Action **$889.00**

Dixie 1873

Marlin 336C

Marlin 338MXLR

Price: Lightweight '81 Takedown Short Action, intr. 2007,
from **$949.00**
Price: Lightweight '81 Takedown Long Action, intr. 2007,
from **$999.00**

CHARLES DALY MODEL 1892 LEVER-ACTION RIFLES

Caliber: 45 Colt; 5-shot magazine with removable plug. **Barrel:** 24.25" octagonal. **Weight:** 6.8 lbs. **Length:** 42" overall. **Stock:** Two-piece American walnut, oil finish. **Sights:** Post front, adjustable open rear. **Features:** Color case-hardened receiver, lever, buttplate, forend cap. Introduced 2007. Imported from Italy by K.B.I., Inc.
Price: 1892 Rifle **$1,094.00**
Price: Take Down Rifle **$1,249.00**

CIMARRON 1860 HENRY RIFLE CIVIL WAR MODEL

Caliber: 44 WCF, 45 LC; 12-shot magazine. **Barrel:** 24" (rifle). **Weight:** 9.5 lbs. **Length:** 43" overall (rifle). **Stock:** European walnut. **Sights:** Bead front, open adjustable rear. **Features:** Brass receiver and buttplate. Uses original Henry loading system. Copy of the original rifle. Charcoal blue finish optional. Introduced 1991. Imported by Cimarron F.A. Co.
Price: From **$1,444.78**

CIMARRON 1866 WINCHESTER REPLICAS

Caliber: 38 Spec., 357, 45 LC, 32 WCF, 38 WCF, 44 WCF. **Barrel:** 24" (rifle), 20" (short rifle), 19" (carbine), 16" (trapper). **Weight:** 9 lbs. **Length:** 43" overall (rifle). **Stock:** European walnut. **Sights:** Bead front, open adjustable rear. **Features:** Solid brass receiver, buttplate, forend cap. Octagonal barrel. Copy of the original Winchester '66 rifle. Introduced 1991. Imported by Cimarron F.A. Co.
Price: 1866 Sporting Rifle, 24" barrel, from **$1,096.64**
Price: 1866 Short Rifle, 20" barrel, from **$1,096.64**
Price: 1866 Carbine, 19" barrel, from **$1,123.42**
Price: 1866 Trapper, 16" barrel, from **$1,069.86**

CIMARRON 1873 SHORT RIFLE

Caliber: 357 Mag., 38 Spec., 32 WCF, 38 WCF, 44 Spec., 44 WCF, 45 Colt. **Barrel:** 20" tapered octagon. **Weight:** 7.5 lbs. **Length:** 39" overall. **Stock:** Walnut. **Sights:** Bead front, adjustable semi-buckhorn rear. **Features:** Has half "button" magazine. Original-type markings, including caliber, on barrel and elevator and "Kings" patent. From Cimarron F.A. Co.
Price: **$1,203.76**

Cimarron 1873 Deluxe Sporting Rifle

Similar to the 1873 Short Rifle except has 24" barrel with half-magazine.
Price: **$1,324.70**

CIMARRON 1873 LONG RANGE RIFLE

Caliber: 44 WCF, 45 Colt. **Barrel:** 30", octagonal. **Weight:** 8.5 lbs. **Length:** 48" overall. **Stock:** Walnut. **Sights:** Blade front, semi-buckhorn ramp rear. Tang sight optional. **Features:** Color case-hardened frame;

choice of modern blue-black or charcoal blue for other parts. Barrel marked "Kings Improvement." From Cimarron F.A. Co.
Price: **$1,284.10**

DIXIE ENGRAVED 1873 SPORTING RIFLE

Caliber: 44-40, 13-shot magazine. **Barrel:** 24.25", tapered octagon. **Weight:** 8.25 lbs. **Length:** 43.25" overall. **Stock:** Walnut. **Sights:** Blade front, adjustable rear. **Features:** Engraved frame polished bright (casehardened on plain). Replica of Winchester 1873. Made in Italy. From Dixie Gun Works.
Price: Plain, blued rifle in .44/40, .45 LC, .32/20, .38/40. . . . **$1,050.00**

DIXIE 1873 DELUXE SPORTING RIFLE

Caliber: .44-40, .45 LC, .32-20 and .38-40, 13-shot magazine. **Barrel:** 24.25", tapered octagon. **Weight:** 8.25 lbs. **Length:** 43.25" overall. **Stock:** Walnut. Checkered pistol grip buttstock and forearm. **Sights:** Blade front, adjustable rear. **Features:** Color casehardened frame. Engraved frame polished bright. Replica of Winchester 1873. Made in Italy. From Dixie Gun Works.
Price: . . . . **$1,050.00 to $1,100.00**

DIXIE LIGHTNING RIFLE AND CARBINE

Caliber: .44-40 or .45 LC, 10-shot magazine. **Barrel:** 26" round or octagon, 1:16" or 1:36" twist. **Weight:** 7.25 lbs. **Length:** 43" overall. **Stock:** Walnut. **Sights:** Blade front, open adjustable rear. **Features:** Checkered forearm, blued steel furniture. Made by Pedersoli in Italy. Imported by Dixie Gun Works.
Price: **$1,095.00**
Price: Carbine **$1,225.00**

EMF 1860 HENRY RIFLE

Caliber: 44-40 or 45 Colt. **Barrel:** 24". **Weight:** About 9 lbs. **Length:** About 43.75" overall. **Stock:** Oil-stained American walnut. **Sights:** Blade front, rear adjustable for elevation. **Features:** Reproduction of the original Henry rifle with brass frame and buttplate, rest blued. Imported by EMF.
Price: Brass frame **$1,149.90**
Price: Casehardened frame **$1,229.90**

EMF 1866 YELLOWBOY LEVER ACTIONS

Caliber: 38 Spec., 44-40, 45 LC. **Barrel:** 19" (carbine), 24" (rifle). **Weight:** 9 lbs. **Length:** 43" overall (rifle). **Stock:** European walnut. **Sights:** Bead front, open adjustable rear. **Features:** Solid brass frame, blued barrel, lever, hammer, buttplate. Imported from Italy by EMF.
Price: Rifle **$1,044.90**
Price: Border Rifle, Short **$969.90**

EMF MODEL 1873 LEVER-ACTION RIFLE

Caliber: 32/20, 357 Mag., 38/40, 44-40, 45 Colt. **Barrel:** 18", 20", 24", 30". **Weight:** 8 lbs. **Length:** 43.25" overall. **Stock:** European walnut. **Sights:** Bead front, rear adjustable for windage and elevation. **Features:** Color case-hardened frame (blue on carbine). Imported by EMF.
Price: **$1,099.90**

Marlin 308MX

Marlin 308MX

Marlin 1894 Cowboy

Marlin 1895

EMF MODEL 1873 REVOLVER CARBINE
Caliber: 357 Mag., 45 Colt. **Barrel:** 18". **Weight:** 4 lbs., 8 oz. **Length:** 43-3/4" overall. **Stock:** One-piece walnut. **Sights:** Blade front, notch rear. **Features:** Color case-hardened frame, blue barrel, backstrap and trigger guard. Introduced 1998. Imported from Italy by EMF.
Price: Standard . . . . $979.90 to $1,040.00

HENRY BIG BOY LEVER-ACTION CARBINE
Caliber: 357 Magnum, 44 Magnum, 45 Colt, 10-shot tubular magazine. **Barrel:** 20" octagonal, 1:38 right-hand twist. **Weight:** 8.68 lbs. **Length:** 38.5" overall. **Stock:** Straight-grip American walnut, brass buttplate. **Sights:** Marbles full adjustable semi-buckhorn rear, brass bead front. **Features:** Brasslite receiver not tapped for scope mount. Made in U.S.A. by Henry Repeating Arms.
Price: H006 44 Magnum, walnut, blued barrel **$899.95**
Price: H006DD Deluxe 44 Magnum, engraved receiver. . . . **$1,995.95**

Henry .30/30 Lever-Action Carbine
Same as the Big Boy except has straight grip American walnut, 30-30 only, 6-shot. Receivers are drilled and tapped for scope mount. Made in U.S.A. by Henry Repeating Arms.
Price: H009 Blued receiver, round barrel **$749.95**
Price: H009B Brass receiver, octagonal barrel. **$969.95**

MARLIN MODEL 336C LEVER-ACTION CARBINE
Caliber: 30-30 or 35 Rem., 6-shot tubular magazine. **Barrel:** 20" Micro-Groove. **Weight:** 7 lbs. **Length:** 38.5" overall. **Stock:** Checkered American black walnut, capped pistol grip. Mar-Shield finish; rubber buttpad; swivel studs. **Sights:** Ramp front with Wide-Scan hood, semi-buckhorn folding rear adjustable for windage and elevation. **Features:** Hammer-block safety. Receiver tapped for scope mount, offset hammer spur; top of receiver sandblasted to prevent glare. Includes safety lock.
Price: $530.00

Marlin Model 336SS Lever-Action Carbine
Same as the 336C except receiver, barrel and other major parts are machined from stainless steel. 30-30 only, 6-shot; receiver tapped for scope. Includes safety lock.
Price: $650.00

Marlin Model 336W Lever-Action Rifle
Similar to the Model 336C except has walnut-finished, cut-checkered Maine birch stock; blued steel barrel band has integral sling swivel; no front sight hood; comes with padded nylon sling; hard rubber buttplate. Introduced 1998. Includes safety lock. Made in U.S.A. by Marlin.
Price: $452.00
Price: With 4x scope and mount $495.00

Marlin Model XLR Lever-Action Rifles
Similar to Model 336C except has an 24" stainless barrel with Ballard-type cut rifling, stainless steel receiver and other parts, laminated hardwood stock with pistol grip, nickel-plated swivel studs. Chambered for 30-30 Win. with Hornady spire-pointed Flex-Tip cartridges. Includes safety lock. Introduced 2006. Similar models chambered for 308 Marlin Express introduced in 2007
Price: Model 336XLR $816.00

MARLIN MODEL 338MXLR
Caliber: 338 Marlin Express. **Barrel:** 24" stainless steel. **Weight:** 7.5 lbs. **Length:** 42.5" overall. **Features:** Stainless steel receiver, lever and magazine tube. Black/gray laminated checkered stock and forend. Hooded ramp front sight and adjustable semi-buckhorn rear; drilled and tapped for scope mounts. Receiver-mounted crossbolt safety.
Price: Model 338MXLR $806.00
Price: Model 308MXLR: 308 Marlin Express $806.00
Price: Model 338MX: Similar to Model 338MXLR but with blued metal and walnut stock and forend $611.00
Price: Model 308MX: 308 Marlin Express $611.00

MARLIN MODEL 444 LEVER-ACTION SPORTER
Caliber: 444 Marlin, 5-shot tubular magazine. **Barrel:** 22" deep cut Ballard rifling. **Weight:** 7.5 lbs. **Length:** 40.5" overall. **Stock:** Checkered American black walnut, capped pistol grip, rubber rifle buttpad. Mar-Shield finish; swivel studs. **Sights:** Hooded ramp front, folding semi-buckhorn rear adjustable for windage and elevation. **Features:** Hammer-block safety. Receiver tapped for scope mount;

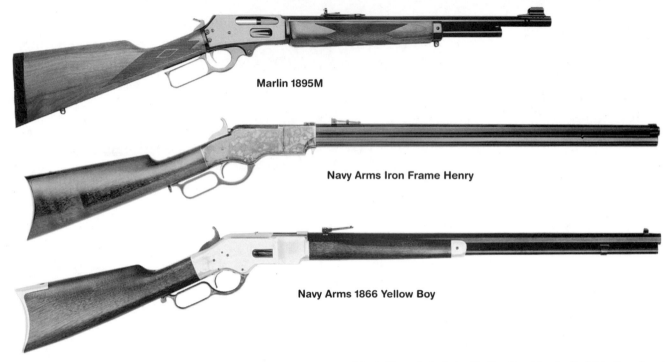

Marlin 1895M

Navy Arms Iron Frame Henry

Navy Arms 1866 Yellow Boy

offset hammer spur. Includes safety lock.
Price: **$619.00**

Marlin Model 444XLR Lever-Action Rifle
Similar to Model 444 except has an 24" stainless barrel with Ballard-type cut rifling, stainless steel receiver and other parts, laminated hardwood stock with pistol grip, nickel-plated swivel studs. Chambered for 444 Marlin with Hornady Evolution spire-pointed Flex-Tip cartridges. Includes safety lock. Introduced 2006.
Price: (Model 444XLR) **$816.00**

MARLIN MODEL 1894 LEVER-ACTION CARBINE
Caliber: 44 Spec./44 Mag., 10-shot tubular magazine. **Barrel:** 20" Ballard-type rifling. **Weight:** 6 lbs. **Length:** 37.5" overall. **Stock:** Checkered American black walnut, straight grip and forend. Mar-Shield finish. Rubber rifle buttpad; swivel studs. **Sights:** Wide-Scan hooded ramp front, semi-buckhorn folding rear adjustable for windage and elevation. **Features:** Hammer-block safety. Receiver tapped for scope mount, offset hammer spur, solid top receiver sand blasted to prevent glare. Includes safety lock.
Price: **$576.00**

Marlin Model 1894C Carbine
Similar to the standard Model 1894 except chambered for 38 Spec./357 Mag. with full-length 9-shot magazine, 18.5" barrel, hammer-block safety, hooded front sight. Introduced 1983. Includes safety lock.
Price: **$576.00**

MARLIN MODEL 1894 COWBOY
Caliber: 357 Mag., 44 Mag., 45 Colt, 10-shot magazine. **Barrel:** 20" tapered octagon, deep cut rifling. **Weight:** 7.5 lbs. **Length:** 41.5" overall. **Stock:** Straight grip American black walnut, hard rubber buttplate, Mar-Shield finish. **Sights:** Marble carbine front, adjustable Marble semi-buckhorn rear. **Features:** Squared finger lever; straight grip stock; blued steel forend tip. Designed for Cowboy Shooting events. Introduced 1996. Includes safety lock. Made in U.S.A. by Marlin.
Price: **$822.00**

Marlin Model 1894SS
Similar to Model 1894 except has stainless steel barrel, receiver, lever, guard plate, magazine tube and loading plate. Nickel-plated swivel studs.
Price: **$704.00**

MARLIN MODEL 1895 LEVER-ACTION RIFLE
Caliber: 45-70 Govt., 4-shot tubular magazine. **Barrel:** 22" round. **Weight:** 7.5 lbs. **Length:** 40.5" overall. **Stock:** Checkered American black walnut, full pistol grip. Mar-Shield finish; rubber buttpad; quick detachable swivel studs. **Sights:** Bead front with Wide-Scan hood, semi-buckhorn folding rear adjustable for windage and elevation. **Features:** Hammer-block safety. Solid receiver tapped for scope mounts or receiver sights; offset hammer spur. Includes safety lock.
Price: **$619.00**

Marlin Model 1895G Guide Gun Lever-Action Rifle
Similar to Model 1895 with deep-cut Ballard-type rifling; straight-grip walnut stock. Overall length is 37", weighs 7 lbs. Introduced 1998. Includes safety lock. Made in U.S.A. by Marlin.
Price: **$630.00**

Marlin Model 1895GS Guide Gun
Similar to Model 1895G except receiver, barrel and most metal parts are machined from stainless steel. Chambered for 45-70 Govt., 4-shot, 18.5" barrel. Overall length is 37", weighs 7 lbs. Introduced 2001. Includes safety lock. Made in U.S.A. by Marlin.
Price: **$752.00**

Marlin Model 1895 SBLR
Similar to Model 1895GS Guide Gun but with stainless steel barrel (18.5"), receiver, large loop lever and magazine tube. Black/gray laminated buttstock and forend, XS ghost ring rear sight, hooded ramp front sight, receiver/barrel-mounted top rail for mounting accessory optics. Chambered in 45-70 Government. Overall length is 42.5", weighs 7.5 lbs.
Price: **$979.00**

Marlin Model 1895 Cowboy Lever-Action Rifle
Similar to Model 1895 except has 26" tapered octagon barrel with Ballard-type rifling, Marble carbine front sight and Marble adjustable semi-buckhorn rear sight. Receiver tapped for scope or receiver sight. Overall length is 44.5", weighs about 8 lbs. Introduced 2001. Includes safety lock. Made in U.S.A. by Marlin.
Price: **$785.00**

Marlin Model 1895XLR Lever-Action Rifle
Similar to Model 1895 except has an 24" stainless barrel with Ballard-type cut rifling, stainless steel receiver and other parts, laminated hardwood stock with pistol grip, nickel-plated swivel studs. Chambered for 45-70 Govt. Government with Hornady Evolution spire-pointed Flex-Tip cartridges. Includes safety lock. Introduced 2006.
Price: (Model 1895MXLR) **$816.00**

Marlin Model 1895M Lever-Action Rifle
Similar to Model 1895G except has an 18.5" barrel with Ballard-type cut rifling. Chambered for 450 Marlin. Includes safety lock.
Price: (Model 1895M) **$678.00**

Rossi R92

Uberti 1873 Sporting

Uberti 1866 Yellowboy

Marlin Model 1895MXLR Lever-Action Rifle

Similar to Model 1895M except has an 24" stainless barrel with Ballard-type cut rifling, stainless steel receiver and other parts, laminated hardwood stock with pistol grip, nickel-plated swivel studs. Chambered for 450 Marlin with Hornady Evolution spire-pointed Flex-Tip cartridges. Includes safety lock. Introduced 2006.

Price: (Model 1895MXLR) **$874.00**

MOSSBERG 464 LEVER ACTION RIFLE

Caliber: 30-30 Win., 6-shot tubular magazine. **Barrel:** 20" round. **Weight:** 6.7 lbs. **Length:** 38.5" overall. **Stock:** Hardwood, quick detachable swivel studs. **Sights:** Folding rear sight, adjustable for windage and elevation. **Features:** Blued receiver and barrel, receiver drilled and tapped, two-position top-tang safety. Available with straight grip or semi-pistol grip. Introduced 2008. From O.F. Mossberg & Sons, Inc.

Price: **$497.00**

NAVY ARMS 1874 SHARPS #2 CREEDMORE RIFLE

Caliber: .45-70 Govt. **Barrel:** 30" octagon. **Weight:** 10 lbs. **Length:** 48" overall. **Sights:** Soule target grade rear tang sight, front globe with 12 inserts. **Features:** Highly polished nickel receiver and action, double-set triggers. From Navy Arms.

Price: Model SCR072 (2008) **$1,816.00**

NAVY ARMS MILITARY HENRY RIFLE

Caliber: 44-40 or 45 Colt, 12-shot magazine. **Barrel:** 24.25". **Weight:** 9 lbs., 4 oz. **Stock:** European walnut. **Sights:** Blade front, adjustable ladder-type rear. **Features:** Brass frame, buttplate, rest blued. Replica of the model used by cavalry units in the Civil War. Has full-length magazine tube, sling swivels; no forend. Imported from Italy by Navy Arms.

Price: **$1,199.00**

Navy Arms Iron Frame Henry

Similar to the Military Henry Rifle except receiver is blued or color case-hardened steel. Imported by Navy Arms.

Price: Blued **$1,247.00**

NAVY ARMS 1866 YELLOW BOY RIFLE

Caliber: 38 Spec., 44-40, 45 Colt, 12-shot magazine. **Barrel:** 20" or 24", full octagon. **Weight:** 8.5 lbs. **Length:** 42.5" overall. **Stock:** Walnut. **Sights:** Blade front, adjustable ladder-type rear. **Features:** Brass frame, forend tip, buttplate, blued barrel, lever, hammer. Introduced 1991. Imported from Italy by Navy Arms.

Price: Yellow Boy Rifle, 24.25" barrel **$915.00**
Price: Yellow Boy Carbine, 19" barrel **$882.00**

NAVY ARMS 1873 WINCHESTER-STYLE RIFLE

Caliber: 357 Mag., 44-40, 45 Colt, 12-shot magazine. **Barrel:** 24.25". **Weight:** 8.25 lbs. **Length:** 43" overall. **Stock:** European walnut. **Sights:** Blade front, buckhorn rear. **Features:** Color case-hardened frame, rest blued. Full-octagon barrel. Imported by Navy Arms.

Price: **$1,047.00**
Price: 1873 Carbine, 19" barrel **$1,024.00**
Price: 1873 Sporting Rifle (octagonal bbl., checkered
  walnut stock and forend) **$1,183.00**
Price: 1873 Border Model, 20" octagon barrel **$1,047.00**
Price: 1873 Deluxe Border Model **$1,183.00**

PUMA MODEL 92 RIFLES AND CARBINES

Caliber: 17 HMR (XP and Scout models, only; intr. 2008), 38 Spec./357 Mag., 44 Mag., 45 Colt, 454 Casull, 480 Ruger (.44-40 in 20" octagonal barrel). **Barrel:** 16" and 20" round; 20" and 24" octagonal. 1:30" rate of twist (exc. 17 HMR is 1:9"). **Weight:** 7.7 lbs. **Stock:** Walnut stained hardwood. **Sights:** Blade front, V rear, buckhorn sights sold separately. **Features:** Finishes available in blue/blue, blue/case colored and stainless/stainless with matching crescent butt plates. .454 and .480 calibers have rubber recoil pads. Full-length magazines, thumb safety. Large lever loop or HiViz sights available on select models. Magazine capacity is 12 rounds with 24" bbl.; 10 rounds with 20" barrel; 8 rounds in 16" barrel. Introduced in 2002. Scout includes long-eye-relief scope, rail, elevated cheekpiece, intr. 2008. XP chambered in 17 HMR, 38 Spec./357 Mag. and 44 Mag., loads through magazine tube or loading gate, intr. 2008. Imported from Brazil by Legacy Sports International.

Price: From **$959.00**
Price: Scout Model, w/2.5x32 Nikko-Stirling Nighteater
  scope, intr. 2008, from **$739.00**
Price: XP Model, tube feed magazine, intr. 2008, from **$613.00**

Uberti 1860 Henry

U.S. Fire Arms Lightning Premium Carbine

U.S. Fire Arms Standard Lightning

Winchester Model 1895 Safari Centennial High Grade

REMINGTON MODEL 7600/7615 PUMP ACTION

Caliber: 243 Win., 270 Win., 30-06 Spfl., 308; 223 Rem. (7615 only). **Barrel:** 22" round tapered. **Weight:** 7.5 lbs. **Length:** 42.6" overall. **Stock:** Cut-checkered walnut pistol grip and forend, Monte Carlo with full cheekpiece. Satin or high-gloss finish. Also, black synthetic. **Sights:** Gold bead front sight on matted ramp, open step adjustable sporting rear. **Features:** Redesigned and improved version of the Model 760. Detachable 4-shot clip. Cross-bolt safety. Receiver tapped for scope mount. Introduced 1981. Model 7615 Tactical chambered in 223 Rem. **Features:** Knoxx SpecOps NRS (Non Recoil Suppressing) adjustable stock, parkerized finish, 10-round detachable magazine box, sling swivel studs. Introduced 2007.

Price: 7600 Wood **$792.00**
Price: 7600 Synthetic. **$665.00**
Price: 7615 Ranch Carbine **$955.00**
Price: 7615 Camo Hunter. **$1,009.00**
Price: 7615 Tactical 223 Rem., 16.5" barrel, 10-rd.
    magazine (2008). **$932.00**

ROSSI R92 LEVER-ACTION CARBINE

Caliber: 38 Special/357 Mag, 44 Mag., 44-40 Win., 45 Colt, 454 Casull. **Barrel:** 16" or 20" with round barrel, 20" or 24" with octagon barrel. **Weight:** 4.8 lbs. to 7 lbs. **Length:** 34" to 41.5". **Features:** Blued or stainless finish. Various options available in selected chamberings (large lever loop, fiber optic sights, cheekpiece, etc.).
Price: From **$499.00**

TAURUS THUNDERBOLT PUMP ACTION

Caliber: 38/.357, 45 Long Colt, 12 or 14 rounds. **Barrel:** 26" blue or polished stainless. **Weight:** 8.1 lbs. **Length:** 43" overall. **Stock:** Hardwood stock and forend. Gloss finish. **Sights:** Longhorn adjustable rear. Introduced 2004. Imported from Brazil by Taurus International.
Price: C45BR (blued) **$705.00**
Price: C45SSR (stainless) **$813.00**

TRISTAR SHARPS 1874 SPORTING RIFLE

Caliber: 45-70 Govt. **Barrel:** 28", 32", 34" octagonal. **Weight:** 9.75 lbs. **Length:** 44.5" overall. **Stock:** Walnut. **Sights:** Dovetail front, adjustable rear. **Features:** Cut checkering, case colored frame finish.
Price: **$1,099.00**

Barrett Model 95

Blaser R93 Classic

Browning A-Bolt Hunter

Browning A-Bolt Target

UBERTI 1873 SPORTING RIFLE

Caliber: 357 Mag., 44-40, 45 Colt. **Barrel:** 19" to 24.25". **Weight:** Up to 8.2 lbs. **Length:** Up to 43.3" overall. **Stock:** Walnut, straight grip and pistol grip. **Sights:** Blade front adjustable for windage, open rear adjustable for elevation. **Features:** Color case-hardened frame, blued barrel, hammer, lever, buttplate, brass elevator. Imported by Stoeger Industries.

Price: 1873 Carbine, 19" round barrel **$1,199.00**
Price: 1873 Short Rifle, 20" octagonal barrel **$1,249.00**
Price: 1873 Special Sporting Rifle, 24.25" octagonal barrel **$1,379.00**

UBERTI 1866 YELLOWBOY CARBINE, SHORT RIFLE, RIFLE

Caliber: 38 Spec., 44-40, 45 Colt. **Barrel:** 24.25", octagonal. **Weight:** 8.2 lbs. **Length:** 43.25" overall. **Stock:** Walnut. **Sights:** Blade front adjustable for windage, rear adjustable for elevation. **Features:** Frame, buttplate, forend cap of polished brass, balance charcoal blued. Imported by Stoeger Industries.

Price: 1866 Yellowboy Carbine, 19" round barrel. **$1,079.00**
Price: 1866 Yellowboy Short Rifle, 20" octagonal barrel . . . **$1,129.00**
Price: 1866 Yellowboy Rifle, 24.25" octagonal barrel **$1,129.00**

UBERTI 1860 HENRY RIFLE

Caliber: 44-40, 45 Colt. **Barrel:** 24.25", half-octagon. **Weight:** 9.2 lbs. **Length:** 43.75" overall. **Stock:** American walnut. **Sights:** Blade front, rear adjustable for elevation. Imported by Stoeger Industries.

Price: 1860 Henry Trapper, 18.5" barrel, brass frame **$1,329.00**
Price: 1860 Henry Rifle Iron Frame, 24.25" barrel **$1,419.00**

UBERTI LIGHTNING RIFLE

Caliber: 357 Mag., 45 Colt, 10+1. **Barrel:** 20" to 24.25". **Stock:** Walnut. Finish: Blue or case-hardened. Introduced 2006. Imported by Stoeger Industries.

Price: 1875 Lightning Rifle, 24.25" barrel **$1,259.00**
Price: 1875 Lightning Short Rifle, 20" barrel **$1,259.00**
Price: 1875 Lightning Carbine, 20" barrel **$1,179.00**

UBERTI SPRINGFIELD TRAPDOOR RIFLE

Caliber: 4-70, single shot. **Barrel:** 22" or 32.5". **Stock:** Walnut. Finish: Blue and case-hardened. Introduced 2006. Imported by Stoeger Industries.

Price: Springfield Trapdoor Carbine, 22" barrel **$1,429.00**
Price: Springfield Trapdoor Army, 32.5" barrel **$1,669.00**

U.S. FIRE ARMS STANDARD LIGHTNING MAGAZINE RIFLE

Caliber: 45 Colt, 44 WCF, 44 Spec., 38 WCF, 15-shot. **Barrel:** 26". **Stock:** Oiled walnut. Finish: High polish blue. Nickel finish also available. Introduced 2002. Made in U.S.A. by United States Fire-Arms Manufacturing Co.

Price: Round barrel. **$1,480.00**
Price: Octagonal barrel, checkered forend **$1,750.00**
Price: Half-round barrel, checkered forend **$1,995.00**
Price: Premium Carbine, 20" round barrel **$1,480.00**
Price: Baby Carbine, 20" special taper barrel **$1,995.00**
Price: Deluxe Lightning **$2,559.00**

WINCHESTER MODEL 1895 SAFARI CENTENNIAL HIGH GRADE

Caliber: 405 Win. **Barrel:** 24" blued round, four-round box mag. **Weight:**

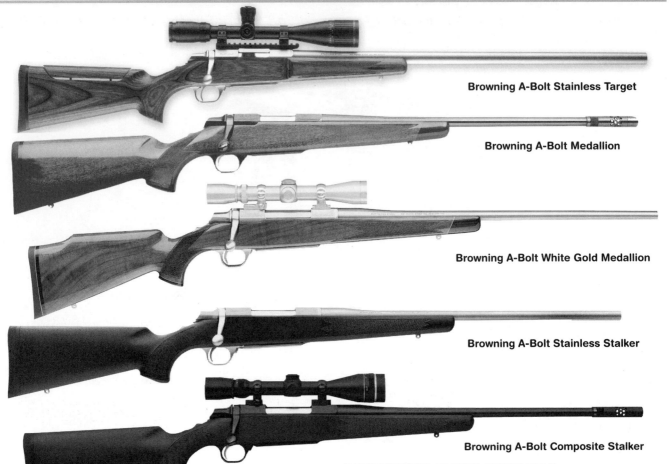

Browning A-Bolt Stainless Target

Browning A-Bolt Medallion

Browning A-Bolt White Gold Medallion

Browning A-Bolt Stainless Stalker

Browning A-Bolt Composite Stalker

8 lbs. **Length:** NA. **Features:** Patterned after original Winchester Model 1895. Commemorates Theodore Roosevelt's 1909 African safari. Checkered walnut forend and buttstock with inlaid "TR" medallion, engraved and silvered receiver.
Price: **$1,749.00**
Price: Custom Grade: Jeweled hammer, fancier wood and angraving, gold-filled highlights and numerous accessories. Production limited to 100 sets **$3,649.00**

BARRETT MODEL 95 BOLT-ACTION RIFLE
Caliber: 50 BMG, 5-shot magazine. **Barrel:** 29". **Weight:** 23.5 lbs. **Length:** 45" overall. **Stock:** Energy-absorbing recoil pad. **Sights:** Scope optional. **Features:** Bolt-action, bullpup design. Disassembles without tools; extendable bipod legs; match-grade barrel; muzzle brake. Introduced 1995. Made in U.S.A. by Barrett Firearms Mfg., Inc.
Price: From **$6,500.00**

BLASER R93 BOLT-ACTION RIFLE
Caliber: 22-250 Rem., 243 Win., 6.5x55, 270 Win., 7x57, 7mm-08 Rem., 308 Win., 30-06 Spfl., 257 Wby. Mag., 7mm Rem. Mag., 300 Win. Mag., 300 Wby. Mag., 338 Win. Mag., 375 H&H, 416 Rem. Mag. **Barrel:** 22" (standard calibers), 26" (magnum). **Weight:** 7 lbs. **Length:** 40" overall (22" barrel). **Stock:** Two-piece European walnut. **Sights:** None furnished; drilled and tapped for scope mounting. **Features:** Straight pull-back bolt action with thumb-activated safety slide/cocking mechanism; interchangeable barrels and bolt heads. Introduced 1994. Imported from Germany by Blaser USA.
Price: R93 Prestige, wood grade 3 . . . . **$3,275.00**
Price: R93 Luxus **$4,460.00**
Price: R93 Professional **$2,950.00**
Price: R93 Grand Luxe **$8,163.00**
Price: R93 Attache **$6,175.00**

BROWNING A-BOLT RIFLES
Common Features: Short-throw (60") fluted bolt, three locking lugs, plunger-type ejector; adjustable trigger is grooved. Chrome-plated trigger sear. Hinged floorplate, detachable box magazine. Slide tang safety. Receivers are drilled and tapped for scope mounts, swivel studs included. Barrel is free-floating and glass-bedded, recessed muzzle. Safety is top-tang sliding button. Engraving available for bolt sleeve or rifle body. Introduced 1985. Imported from Japan by Browning.

BROWNING A-BOLT HUNTER
Calibers: 22" Barrel: 223 Rem., 22-250 Rem., 243 Win., 270 Win., 30-06 Spfl., 7mm-08 Rem., 308 Win. **Barrel:** 270 WSM, 7mm WSM, 300 WSM, 325 WSM (intr. 2005). **Calibers:** 24" Barrel: 25-06 Rem. **Calibers:** 26" Barrel: 7mm Rem. Mag., 300 Win. Mag., 338 Win. Mag. **Weight:** 6.25-7.2 lbs. **Length:** 41.25-46.5" overall. **Stock:** Sporter-style

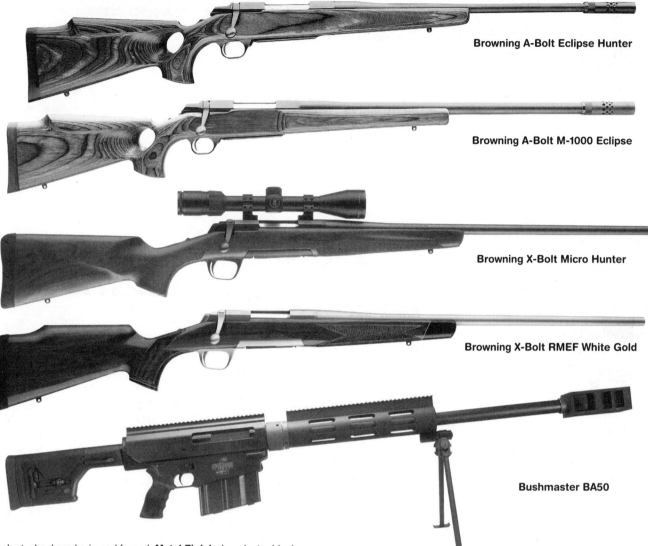

Browning A-Bolt Eclipse Hunter

Browning A-Bolt M-1000 Eclipse

Browning X-Bolt Micro Hunter

Browning X-Bolt RMEF White Gold

Bushmaster BA50

walnut; checkered grip and forend. **Metal Finish:** Low-luster blueing.
Price: Hunter, left-hand, from **$819.00**

BROWNING A-BOLT HUNTER FLD
Caliber: 23" Barrel: 270 WSM, 7mm WSM, 300 WSM, 325 WSM (intr. 2005). **Weight:** 6.6 lbs. **Length:** 42.75" overall. **Features:** FLD has low-luster blueing and select Monte Carlo stock with right-hand palm swell, double-border checkering. Otherwise similar to A-Bolt Hunter.
Price: FLD **$899.00**

Browning A-Bolt Target
Similar to A-Bolt Hunter but with 28" heavy bull blued barrel, blued receiver, satin finish gray laminated stock with adjustable comb and semi-beavertail forend. Chambered in 223, 308 Winchester and 300 WSM. Available also with stainless receiver and barrel.
Price: From **$1,269.00**
Price: Stainless, from **$1,489.00**

BROWNING A-BOLT MOUNTAIN TI
Caliber: 223 WSSM, 243 WSSM, 25 WSSM (all added 2005); 270 WSM, 7mm WSM, 300 WSM. **Barrel:** 22" or 23". **Weight:** 5.25-5.5 lbs. **Length:** 41.25-42.75" overall. **Stock:** Lightweight fiberglass Bell & Carlson model in Mossy-Oak New Break Up camo. Metal Finish: Stainless barrel, titanium receiver. **Features:** Pachmayr Decelerator recoil pad. Introduced 1999.
Price: From **$1,819.00**

BROWNING A-BOLT MICRO HUNTER AND MICRO HUNTER LEFT-HAND
Calibers: 20" Barrel: 22-250 Rem., 243 Win., 308 Win., 7mm-08. 22" Barrel: 22 Hornet, 270 WSM, 7mm WSM, 300 WSM, 325 WSM (2005). **Weight:** 6.25-6.4 lbs. **Length:** 39.5-41.5" overall. **Features:** Classic

walnut stock with 13.3" LOP. Otherwise similar to A-Bolt Hunter.
Price: Micro Hunter, from **$759.00**
Price: Micro Hunter left-hand, from **$799.00**

BROWNING A-BOLT MEDALLION
Calibers: 22" Barrel: 223 Rem., 22-250 Rem., 243 Win., 308 Win., 270 Win., 280 Rem., 30-06.; 23" Barrel: 270 WSM, 7mm WSM, 300 WSM, 325 WSM (intr. 2005); 24" Barrel: 25-06 Rem.; 26" Barrel: 7mm Rem. Mag., 300 Win. Mag., 338 Win. Mag., 375 H&H. **Weight:** 6.25-7.1 lbs. **Length:** 41.25-46.5" overall. **Stock:** Select walnut stock, glossy finish, rosewood grip and forend caps, checkered grip and forend. Metal Finish: Engraved high-polish blued receiver.
Price: Medallion, from **$909.00**
Price: Medallion WSM **$959.00**
Price: Medallion w/BOSS, intr. 1987, from **$1,009.00**

BROWNING A-BOLT WHITE GOLD MEDALLION, RMEF WHITE GOLD, WHITE GOLD MEDALLION W/BOSS
Calibers: 22" Barrel: 270 Win., 30-06. Calibers: 23" Barrel: 270 WSM, 7mm WSM, 300 WSM, 325 WSM (intr. 2005). Calibers: 26" Barrel: 7mm Rem. Mag., 300 Win. Mag. **Weight:** 6.4-7.7 lbs. **Length:** 42.75-46.5" overall. **Stock:** select walnut stock with brass spacers between rubber recoil pad and between the rosewood gripcap and forend tip; gold-filled barrel inscription; palm-swell pistol grip, Monte Carlo comb, 22 lpi checkering with double borders. **Metal Finish:** Engraved high-polish stainless receiver and barrel. BOSS version chambered in 270 Win. and 30-06 (22" barrel) and 7mm Rem. Mag. and 300 Win. Mag. (26" barrel). Introduced 1988. RMEF version has engraved gripcap, continental cheekpiece; gold engraved, stainless receiver and bbl.

Cooper Model 21 Bolt

CZ 527 Lux

CZ 527 FS

CZ 527 American

Introduced 2004.
Price: White Gold Medallion, from $1,309.00
Price: Rocky Mt. Elk Foundation White Gold, 325 WSM,
    intr. 2007 . . . . $1,399.00

BROWNING A-BOLT STAINLESS STALKER, STAINLESS STALKER LEFT-HAND

Calibers: 22" Barrel: 223 Rem., 243 Win., 270 Win., 280 Rem., 7mm-08 Rem., 30-06 Spfl., 308 Win. Calibers: 23" Barrel: 270 WSM, 7mm WSM, 300 WSM, 325 WSM (intr. 2005). Calibers: 24" Barrel: 25-06 Rem. Calibers: 26" Barrel: 7mm Rem. Mag., 300 Win. Mag., 338 Win. Mag., 375 H&H. **Weight:** 6.1-7.2 lbs. **Length:** 40.9-46.5" overall. **Features:** Similar to the A-Bolt Hunter model except receiver and barrel are made of stainless steel; other exposed metal surfaces are finished silver-gray matte. Graphite-fiberglass composite textured stock. No sights are furnished, except on 375 H&H, which comes with open sights. Introduced 1987.
Price: Stainless Stalker left-hand, from $1,029.00
Price: Stainless Stalker w/Boss, from. $1,119.00

BROWNING A-BOLT COMPOSITE STALKER

Calibers: 22 Barrel: 270 Win., 30-06 Sprg.; 23" Barrel: 270 WSM, 7mm WSM, 300 WSM, 325 WSM; 24" Barrel: 25-06 Rem.; 26" Barrel: 7mm Rem. Mag., 300 Win. Mag., 338 Win. Mag. **Weight:** 6.6-7.3 lbs. **Length:** 42.5-46.5" overall. **Features:** Similar to the A-Bolt Stainless Stalker except has black composite stock with textured finish and matte-blued finish on all exposed metal surfaces except bolt sleeve. No sights are furnished.
Price: Composite Stalker w/BOSS, from $869.00
Price: Stainless Stalker $1,009.00
Price: Stainless Stalker w/Boss, from. $1,079.00

BROWNING A-BOLT ECLIPSE HUNTER W/BOSS, M-1000 ECLIPSE W/BOSS, M-1000 ECLIPSE WSM, STAINLESS M-1000 ECLIPSE WSM

Calibers: 22" Barrel: 270 Win., 30-06. Calibers: 26" Barrel: 7mm Rem. Mag., 300 Win. Mag., 270 WSM, 7mm WSM, 300 WSM. **Weight:** 7.5-9.9 lbs. **Length:** 42.75-46.5" overall. **Features:** All models have gray/black laminated thumbhole stock. Introduced 1996. Two versions have BOSS barrel vibration modulator and muzzle brake. Hunter has sporter-weight barrel. M-1000 Eclipses have long actions and heavy target barrels, adjustable triggers, bench-style forends, 3-shot magazines. Introduced 1997.
Price: Eclipse Hunter w/BOSS, from $1,259.00
Price: M-1000 Eclipse, from $1,169.00
Price: M-1000 Eclipse w/BOSS, from $1,259.00
Price: Stainless M-1000 Eclipse WSM, from $1,399.00
Price: Stainless M-1000 Eclipse w/BOSS, from $1,489.00

BROWNING X-BOLT HUNTER

Calibers: 223, 22-250, 243 Win., 25-06 Rem., 270 Win., 270 WSM, 280 Rem., 30-06 Spfl., 300 Win. Mag., 300 WSM, 308 Win., 325 WSM, 338 Win. Mag., 375 H&H Mag., 7mm Rem. Mag., 7mm WSM, 7mm-08 Rem. **Barrels:** 22", 23", 24", 26", varies by model. Matte blued or stainless free-floated barrel, recessed muzzle crown. **Weight:** 6.3-7 lbs. **Stock:** Hunter and Medallion models have wood stocks; Composite Stalker and Stainless Stalker models have composite stocks. Inflex Technology recoil pad. **Sights:** None, drilled and tapped receiver, X-Lock scope mounts. **Features:** Adjustable three-lever Feather Trigger system, polished hard-chromed steel components, factory pre-set at 3.5 lbs., alloy trigger housing. Bolt unlock button, detachable rotary magazine, 60-degree bolt lift, three locking lugs, top-tang safety, sling swivel studs. Medallion has metal engraving, gloss finish walnut stock, rosewood fore-end grip and pistol grip cap. Introduced 2008. From Browning.

Browning X-Bolt Micro Hunter

Similar to Browning X-Bolt Hunter but with compact dimensions (13-15/16 length of pull, 41-1/4 overall length).
Price: Standard chamberings $839.00
Price: Magnum $869.00

Browning X-Bolt Varmint Stalker

Similar to Browning X-Bolt Stalker but with medium-heavy free-floated barrel, target crown, composite stock. Chamberings available: 223, 22-250, 243 Winchester and 308 Winchester only.
Price: $1,019.00

Browning X-Bolt RMEF White Gold

Similar to X-Bolt Medallion but with gold-engraved matte stainless finish and Rocky Mountain Elk Foundation grip cap. Chambered in 325 WSM only.
Price: $1,399.00

Browning X-Bolt RMEF Special Hunter

Similar to above but with matte blued finish without gold highlights.
Price: $919.00

BUSHMASTER BA50 BOLT-ACTION RIFLE

Caliber: 50 Browning BMG. **Barrel:** 30" (rifle), 22" (carbine), 10-round

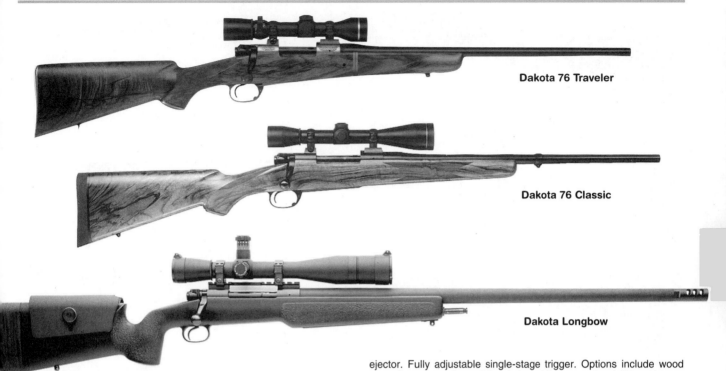

Dakota 76 Traveler

Dakota 76 Classic

Dakota Longbow

mag. **Weight:** 30 lbs. (rifle), 27 lbs. (carbine). **Length:** 58" overall (rifle), 50" overall (carbine). **Features:** Free-floated Lother Walther barrel with muzzle brake, Magpul PRS adjustable stock.
Price: **$4,895.00**

CARBON ONE BOLT-ACTION RIFLE
Caliber: 22-250 to 375 H&H. **Barrel:** Up to 28". **Weight:** 5.5 to 7.25 lbs. **Length:** Varies. **Stock:** Synthetic or wood. **Sights:** None furnished. **Features:** Choice of Remington, Browning or Winchester action with free-floated Christensen graphite/epoxy/steel barrel, trigger pull tuned to 3 to 3.5 lbs. Made in U.S.A. by Christensen Arms.
Price: Carbon One Hunter Rifle, 6.5 to 7 lbs. **$1,775.00**
Price: Carbon One Custom, 5.5 to 6.5 lbs., Shilen trigger .. **$3,900.00**
Price: Carbon Extreme **$2,450.00**

CENTURY INTERNATIONAL M70 SPORTER DOUBLE-TRIGGER BOLT ACTION RIFLE
Caliber: 22-250 Rem., 270 Win., 300 Win. Mag, 308 Win., 24" barrel. **Weight:** 7.95 lbs. **Length:** 44.5". **Sights:** Flip-up U-notch rear sight, hooded blade front sight. **Features:** Mauser M98-type action; 5-rd fixed box magazine. 22-250 has hinged floorplate. Monte Carlo stock, oil finish. Adjustable trigger on double-trigger models. 300 Win. Mag. Has 3-rd. fixed box magazine. 308 Win. holds 5 rounds. 300 and 308 have buttpads. Manufactured by Zastava in Yugoslavia, imported by Century International.
Price: M70 Sporter Double-Trigger. **$500.00**
Price: M70 Sporter Double-Trigger 22-250 .... **$475.00**
Price: M70 Sporter Single-Trigger .300 Win. Mag. **$475.00**
Price: M70 Sporter Single/Double Trigger 308 Win. **$500.00**

CHEYTAC M-200
Caliber: 408 CheyTac, 7-round magazine. **Barrel:** 30". **Length:** 55", stock extended. **Weight:** 27 lbs. (steel barrel); 24 lbs. (carbon fiber barrel). **Stock:** Retractable. **Sights:** None, scope rail provided. **Features:** CNC-machined receiver, attachable Picatinny rail M-1913, detachable barrel, integral bipod, 3.5-lb. trigger pull, muzzle brake. Made in U.S. by CheyTac, LLC.
Price: **$13,795.00**

COOPER MODEL 21 BOLT-ACTION RIFLE
Caliber: 17 Rem., 19-223, Tactical 20, .204 Ruger, 222 Rem, 222 Rem. Mag., 223 Rem, 223 Rem A.I., 6x45, 6x47. **Barrel:** 22" or 24" in Classic configurations, 24"-26" in Varminter configurations. **Weight:** 6.5-8.0 lbs., depending on type. **Stock:** AA-AAA select claro walnut, 20 lpi checkering. **Sights:** None furnished. **Features:** Three front locking-lug bolt-action single shot. Action: 7.75" long, Sako extractor. Button

ejector. Fully adjustable single-stage trigger. Options include wood upgrades, case-color metalwork, barrel fluting, custom LOP, and many others.
Price: From **$1,395.00**

COOPER MODEL 22 BOLT-ACTION RIFLE
Caliber: 22-250 Rem., 22-250 Rem. AI, 25-06 Rem., 25-06 Rem. AI, 243 Win., 243 Win. AI, 220 Swift, 250/3000 AI, 257 Roberts, 257 Roberts AI, 7mm-08 Rem., 6mm Rem., 260 Rem., 6 x 284, 6.5 x 284, 22 BR, 6mm BR, 308 Win. **Barrel:** 24" or 26" stainless match in Classic configurations. 24" or 26" in Varminter configurations. **Weight:** 7.5 to 8.0 lbs. depending on type. **Stock:** AA-AAA select claro walnut, 20 lpi checkering. **Sights:** None furnished. **Features:** Three front locking-lug bolt-action single shot. Action: 8.25" long, Sako style extractor. Button ejector. Fully adjustable single-stage trigger. Options include wood upgrades, case-color metalwork, barrel fluting, custom LOP, and many others.
Price: From..................................... **$1,495.00**

COOPER MODEL 38 BOLT-ACTION RIFLE
Caliber: 17 Squirrel, 17 He Bee, 17 Ackley Hornet, 17 Mach IV, 19 Calhoon, 20 VarTarg, 221 Fireball, 22 Hornet, 22 K-Hornet, 22 Squirrel, 218 Bee, 218 Mashburn Bee. **Barrel:** 22" or 24" in Classic configurations, 24" or 26" in Varminter configurations. **Weight:** 6.5-8.0 lbs. depending on type. **Stock:** AA-AAA select claro walnut, 20 lpi checkering. **Sights:** None furnished. **Features:** Three front locking-lug bolt-action single shot. Action: 7" long, Sako style extractor. Button ejector. Fully adjustable single-stage trigger. Options include wood upgrades, case-color metalwork, barrel fluting, custom LOP, and many others.
Price: From..................................... **$1,395.00**

CZ 527 LUX BOLT-ACTION RIFLE
Caliber: 204 Ruger, 22 Hornet, 222 Rem., 223 Rem., detachable 5-shot magazine. **Barrel:** 23.5"; standard or heavy barrel. **Weight:** 6 lbs., 1 oz. **Length:** 42.5" overall. **Stock:** European walnut with Monte Carlo. **Sights:** Hooded front, open adjustable rear. **Features:** Improved mini-Mauser action with non-rotating claw extractor; single set trigger; grooved receiver. Imported from the Czech Republic by CZ-USA.
Price: Brown laminate stock **$718.00**
Price: Model FS, full-length stock, cheekpiece **$827.00**

CZ 527 American Bolt-Action Rifle
Similar to the CZ 527 Lux except has classic-style stock with 18 lpi checkering; free-floating barrel; recessed target crown on barrel. No sights furnished. Introduced 1999. Imported from the Czech Republic by CZUSA.
Price: From..................................... **$751.00**

DSA DS-MP1

Ed Brown Savanna

Howa M-1500 Varmint Supreme

CZ 550 AMERICAN CLASSIC BOLT-ACTION RIFLE
Caliber: 22-250 Rem., 243 Win., 6.5x55, 7x57, 7x64, 308 Win., 9.3x62, 270 Win., 30-06. **Barrel:** free-floating barrel; recessed target crown. **Weight:** 7.48 lbs. **Length:** 44.68" overall. **Stock:** American classic-style stock with 18 lpi checkering or FS (Mannlicher). **Sights:** No sights furnished. **Features:** Improved Mauser-style action with claw extractor, fixed ejector, square bridge dovetailed receiver; single set trigger. Introduced 1999. Imported from the Czech Republic by CZ-USA.
Price: FS (full stock) **$894.00**
Price: American, from **$827.00**

CZ 550 Safari Magnum/American Safari Magnum Bolt-Action Rifles
Similar to CZ 550 American Classic. Chambered for 375 H&H Mag., 416 Rigby, 458 Win. Mag., 458 Lott. Overall length is 46.5"; barrel length 25"; weighs 9.4 lbs., 9.9 lbs (American). Hooded front sight, express rear with one standing, two folding leaves. Imported from the Czech Republic by CZ-USA.
Price: **$1,179.00**
Price: American **$1,261.00**
Price: American Kevlar **$1,714.00**

CZ 550 Varmint Bolt-Action Rifle
Similar to CZ 550 American Classic. Chambered for 308 Win. and 22-250. Kevlar, laminated stocks. Overall length is 46.7"; barrel length 25.6"; weighs 9.1 lbs. Imported from the Czech Republic by CZ-USA.
Price: **$841.00**
Price: Kevlar **$1,037.00**
Price: Laminated **$966.00**

CZ 550 Magnum H.E.T. Bolt-Action Rifle
Similar to CZ 550 American Classic. Chambered for 338 Lapua, 300 Win. Mag., 300 RUM. Overall length is 52"; barrel length 28"; weighs 14 lbs. Adjustable sights, satin blued barrel. Imported from the Czech Republic by CZ-USA.
Price: **$3,673.00**

CZ 550 Ultimate Hunting Bolt-Action Rifle
Similar to CZ 550 American Classic. Chambered for 300 Win Mag. Overall length is 44.7"; barrel length 23.6"; weighs 7.7 lbs. Imported from the Czech Republic by CZ-USA.
Price: **$4,242.00**

CZ 750 SNIPER RIFLE
Caliber: 308 Winchester, 10-shot magazine. **Barrel:** 26". **Weight:** 11.9 lbs. **Length:** 48" overall. **Stock:** Polymer thumbhole. **Sights:** None furnished; permanently attached Weaver rail for scope mounting. **Features:** 60-degree bolt throw; oversized trigger guard and bolt handle for use with gloves; full-length equipment rail on forend; fully adjustable trigger. Introduced 2001. Imported from the Czech Republic by CZ-USA.
Price: **$2,404.00**

DAKOTA 76 TRAVELER TAKEDOWN RIFLE
Caliber: 257 Roberts, 25-06 Rem., 7x57, 270 Win., 280 Rem., 30-06 Spfl., 338-06, 35 Whelen (standard length); 7mm Rem. Mag., 300 Win. Mag., 338 Win. Mag., 416 Taylor, 458 Win. Mag. (short magnums); 7mm, 300, 330, 375 Dakota Magnums. **Barrel:** 23". **Weight:** 7.5 lbs. **Length:** 43.5" overall. **Stock:** Medium fancy-grade walnut in classic style. Checkered grip and forend; solid buttpad. **Sights:** None furnished; drilled and tapped for scope mounts. **Features:** Threadless disassembly. Uses modified Model 76 design with many features of the Model 70 Winchester. Left-hand model also available. Introduced 1989. African chambered for 338 Lapua Mag., 404 Jeffery, 416 Rigby, 416 Dakota, 450 Dakota, 4-round magazine, select wood, two stock cross-bolts. 24" barrel, weighs 9-10 lbs. Ramp front sight, standing leaf rear. Introduced 1989.Made in U.S.A. by Dakota Arms, Inc.
Price: Classic **$6,095.00**
Price: Safari **$7,895.00**
Price: African **$9,495.00**

DAKOTA 76 CLASSIC BOLT-ACTION RIFLE
Caliber: 257 Roberts, 270 Win., 280 Rem., 30-06 Spfl., 7mm Rem. Mag., 338 Win. Mag., 300 Win. Mag., 375 H&H, 458 Win. Mag. **Barrel:** 23". **Weight:** 7.5 lbs. **Length:** 43.5" overall. **Stock:** Medium fancy grade walnut in classic style. Checkered pistol grip and forend; solid buttpad. **Sights:** None furnished; drilled and tapped for scope mounts. **Features:** Has many features of the original Winchester Model 70. One-piece rail trigger guard assembly; steel gripcap. Model 70-style trigger. Many options available. Left-hand rifle available at same price. Introduced 1988. From Dakota Arms, Inc.
Price: From **$4,595.00**

DAKOTA LONGBOW T-76 TACTICAL RIFLE
Caliber: 300 Dakota Magnum, 330 Dakota Magnum, 338 Lapua Magnum. **Barrel:** 28", .950" at muzzle **Weight:** 13.7 lbs. **Length:** 50" to 52" overall. **Stock:** Ambidextrous McMillan A-2 fiberglass, black or olive green color; adjustable cheekpiece and buttplate. **Sights:** None furnished. Comes with Picatinny one-piece optical rail. **Features:** Uses the Dakota 76 action with controlled-round feed; three-position firing pin block safety; claw extractor; Model 70-style trigger. Comes

with bipod, case tool kit. Introduced 1997. Made in U.S.A. by Dakota Arms, Inc.

Price: **$4,795.00**

DAKOTA MODEL 97 BOLT-ACTION RIFLE

Caliber: 22-250 to 330. **Barrel:** 22" to 24". **Weight:** 6.1 to 6.5 lbs. **Length:** 43" overall. **Stock:** Fiberglass. **Sights:** Optional. **Features:** Matte blue finish, black stock. Right-hand action only. Introduced 1998. Made in U.S.A. by Dakota Arms, Inc.

Price: From **$3,395.00**

DAKOTA PREDATOR RIFLE

Caliber: 17 VarTarg, 17 Rem., 17 Tactical, 20 VarTarg, 20 Tactical, .20 PPC, 204 Ruger, 221 Rem Fireball, 222 Remington, 22 PPC, 223 Rem., 6mm PPC, 6.5 Grendel. **Barrel:** 22" match grade stainless;. **Weight:** NA. **Length:** NA. **Stock:** Special select walnut, sporter-style stock, 23 lpi checkering on forend and grip. **Sights:** None furnished. Drilled and tapped for scope mounting. **Features:** 13-5/8" LOP, 1/2" black presentation pad, 11" recessed target crown. Serious Predator includes XXX walnut varmint style stock w/semi-beavertail forend, stainless receiver. All-Weather Predator includes varmint style composite stock w/semi-beavertail forend, stainless receiver. Introduced 2007. Made in U.S.A. by Dakota Arms, Inc.

Price: Classic **$4,295.00**
Price: Serious **$3,295.00**
Price: All-Weather.............................. **$1,995.00**

DSA DS-MP1

Caliber: 308 Win. match chamber. **Barrel:** 22", 1:10 twist, hand-lapped stainless-steel match-grade Badger Barrel with recessed target crown. **Weight:** 11.5 lbs. **Length:** 41.75". **Stock:** Black McMillan A5 pillar bedded in Marine-Tex with 13.5" length of pull. **Sights:** Tactical Picatinny rail. **Features:** Action, action threads and action bolt locking shoulder completely trued, Badger Ordnance precision ground heavy recoil lug, machined steel Picatinny rail sight mount, trued action threads, action bolt locking shoulder, bolt face and lugs, 2.5-lb. trigger pull, barrel and action finished in Black DuraCoat, guaranteed to shoot 1/2 MOA at 100 yards with match-grade ammo. Introduced 2006. Made in U.S.A. by DSA, Inc.

Price: **$2,800.00**

EAA/ZASTAVA M-93 BLACK ARROW RIFLE

Caliber: 50 BMG. **Barrel:** 36". **Weight:** 7 to 8.5 lbs. **Length:** 60". **Stock:** Synthetic. **Sights:** Scope rail and iron sights. **Features:** **Features:** Mauser action, developed in early 1990s by Zastava Arms Factory. Fluted heavy barrel with recoil reducing muzzle brake, self-leveling and adjustable folding integral bipod, back up iron sights, heavy duty carry handle, detachable 5 round box magazine, and quick detachable scope mount. Imported by EAA. Imported from Russia by EAA Corp.

Price: **$6,986.25**

ED BROWN HUNTING SERIES RIFLES

Caliber: Many calibers available. **Barrel:** 24" (Savanna, Express, Varmint); 23-24" (Damara); 22" (Compact Varmint). **Weight:** 8 to 8.5 lbs. (Savanna); 6.2 to 6.9 lbs. (Damara); 9 lbs. (Express); 10 lbs. (Varmint), 8.75 lbs. (Compact Varmint). **Stock:** Fully glass-bedded McMillan fiberglass sporter. **Sights:** None furnished. Talley scope mounts utilizing heavy-duty 8-40 screws. **Features:** Custom action with machined steel trigger guard and hinged floor plate.

Price: Savanna................................. **$3,895.00**
Price: Damara .... **$3,995.00 to $4,095.00**
Price: Express **$4,995.00**
Price: Varmint & Compact Varmint................... **$3,895.00**

ED BROWN MODEL 704 BUSHVELD

Caliber: 338 Win. Mag., 375 H&H, 416 Rem. Mag., 458 Win. Mag., 458 Lott and all Ed Brown Savanna long action calibers. **Barrel:** 24" medium or heavy weight. **Weight:** 8.25 lbs. **Stock:** Fully bedded McMillan fiberglass with Monte Carlo style cheekpiece, Pachmayr Decelerator recoil pad. **Sights:** None furnished. Talley scope mounts utilizing heavy-duty 8-40 screws. **Features:** Stainless steel barrel, additional calibers: iron sights.

Price: From **$2,995.00**

ED BROWN MODEL 704 EXPRESS

Caliber: 375 H&H, 416 Rem, 458 Lott, other calibers available. **Barrel:** 24" #4 Stainless barrel with black Gen III coating for superior rust

protection. **Weight:** 9 lbs. **Stocks:** Hand-bedded McMillan fiberglass stock. Monte Carlo style with cheek piece and full 1" thick Pachmayr Decel recoil pad. **Sights:** Adjustable iron sights. **Features:** Ed Brown controlled feed action. A special dropped box magazine ensures feeding and allows a full four-round capacity in the magazine, plus one in the chamber. Barrel band is standard for lower profile when carrying the rifle through heavy brush.

Price: From **$3,695.00**

HOWA M-1500 RANCHLAND COMPACT

Caliber: 223 Rem., 22-250 Rem., 243 Win., 308 Win. and 7mm-08. **Barrel:** 20" #1 contour, blued finish. **Weight:** 7 lbs. **Stock:** Hogue Overmolded in black, OD green, Coyote Sand colors. 13.87" LOP. **Sights:** None furnished; drilled and tapped for scope mounting. **Features:** Three-position safety, hinged floor plate, adjustable trigger, forged one-piece bolt, M-16 style extractor, forged flat-bottom receiver. Also available with Nikko-Stirling Nighteater 3-9x42 riflescope. Introduced in 2008. Imported from Japan by Legacy Sports International.

Price: Rifle Only, (2008) **$479.00**
Price: Rifle with 3-9x42 Nighteater scope (2008) **$599.00**

HOWA M-1500 THUMBHOLE SPORTER

Caliber: 204, 223 Rem., 22-250 Rem., 243 Win., 6.5x55 (2008) 25-06 Rem., 270 Win., 7mm Rem. Mag., 308 Win., 30-06 Spfl., 300 Win. Mag., 338 Win. Mag., 375 Ruger. Similar to Camo Lightning except stock. **Weight:** 7.6 to 7.7 lbs. **Stock:** S&K laminated wood in nutmeg (brown/black) or pepper (grey/black) colors, raised comb with forward taper, flared pistol grip and scalloped thumbhole. **Sights:** None furnished; drilled and tapped for scope mounting. **Features:** Three-position safety, hinged floor plate, adjustable trigger, forged one-piece bolt, M-16 style extractor, forged flat-bottom receiver. Introduced in 2001. Imported from Japan by Legacy Sports International.

Price: Blue/Nutmeg, standard calibers ....**$649.00 to $669.00**
Price: Stainless/Pepper, standard calibers ......**$749.00 to $769.00**

HOWA M-1500 VARMINTER SUPREME AND THUMBHOLE VARMINTER SUPREME

Caliber: 204, 223 Rem., 22-250 Rem., 243 Win., 308 Win. **Stock:** Varminter Supreme: Laminated wood in nutmeg (brown), pepper (grey) colors, raised comb and rollover cheekpiece, full pistol grip with palm-filling swell and broad beavertail forend with six vents for barrel cooling. Thumbhole Varminter Supreme similar, adds a high, straight comb, more vertical pistol grip. **Sights:** None furnished; drilled and tapped for scope mounting. **Features:** Three-position safety, hinged floor plate, adjustable trigger, forged one-piece bolt, M-16 style extractor, forged flat-bottom receiver, hammer forged bull barrel and recessed muzzle crown; overall length, 43.75", 9.7 lbs. Introduced 2001. Barreled actions imported by Legacy Sports International; stocks by S&K Gunstocks.

Price: Varminter Supreme, Blue/Nutmeg **$679.00**
Price: Varminter Supreme, Stainless/Pepper **$779.00**
Price: Thumbhole Varminter Supreme, Blue/Nutmeg.......**$679.00**
Price: Thumbhole Varminter Supreme, Stainless/Pepper **$779.00**

HOWA CAMO LIGHTNING M-1500

Caliber: 204, 223 Rem., 22-250 Rem., 243 Win., 25-06 Rem., 270 Win., 308 Win., 30-06 Spfl., 300 Win. Mag., 338 Win. Mag., 7mm Rem. Mag. **Barrel:** 22" standard calibers; 24" magnum calibers; #2 and #6 contour; blue and stainless. **Weight:** 7.6 to 9.3 lbs. **Length:** 42" to 44.5" overall. **Stock:** Synthetic with molded cheek piece, checkered grip and forend. **Sights:** None furnished; drilled and tapped for scope mounting. **Features:** Three-position safety, hinged floor plate, adjustable trigger, forged one-piece bolt, M-16 style extractor, forged flat bottom receiver. Introduced in 1993. Barreled actions imported by Legacy Sports International.

Price: Blue, #2 barrel, standard calibers..................**$377.00**
Price: Stainless, #2 barrel, standard calibers **$479.00**
Price: Blue, #2 barrel, magnum calibers **$390.00**
Price: Stainless, #2 barrel, magnum calibers **$498.00**
Price: Blue, #6 barrel, standard calibers **$425.00**
Price: Stainless, #6 barrel, standard calibers **$498.00**

HOWA/HOGUE M-1500

Caliber: 204, 223 Rem., 22-250 Rem., 243 Win., 6.5x5 (2008), 25-06 Rem., 270 Win., 308 Win., 30-06 Spfl., 300 Win. Mag., 338 Win. Mag., 7mm Rem. Mag., 375 Ruger (2008). **Barrel:** Howa barreled action;

Kimber 8400

L.A.R. Grizzly

Magnum Research Mountain Eagle

Magnum Research Tactical

stainless or blued, 22" #2 contour. **Weight:** 7.4 to 7.6 lbs. **Stock:** Hogue Overmolded, black, or OD green; ambidextrous palm swells. **Sights:** None furnished; drilled and tapped for scope mounting. **Length:** 42" to 44.5" overall. **Features:** Three-position safety, hinged floor plate, adjustable trigger, forged one-piece bolt, M-16 style extractor, forged flat bottom receiver, aluminum pillar bedding and free-floated barrels. Introduced in 2006. Available w/3-10x42 Nikko-Stirling Nighteater scope, rings, bases (2008). from Imported from Japan by Legacy Sports International.
Price: Blued, rifle only . . . .$479.00 to $499.00
Price: Blue, rifle with scope package (2008) . . . . .$599.00 to $619.00
Price: Stainless, rifle only . . . .$625.00 to $675.00

HOWA/HOGUE M-1500 COMPACT HEAVY BARREL VARMINTER
Chambered in 223 Rem., 308 Win., has 20" #6 contour heavy barrel, recessed muzzle crown. **Stock:** Hogue Overmolded, black, or OD green; ambidextrous palm swells. **Sights:** None furnished; drilled and tapped for scope mounting. **Length:** 44.0" overall. **Features:** Three-position safety, hinged floor plate, adjustable trigger, forged one-piece bolt, M-16 style extractor, forged flat bottom receiver, aluminum pillar bedding and free-floated barrels. **Weight:** 9.3 lbs. Introduced 2008. Imported from Japan by Legacy Sports International.
Price: From $559.00

HOWA/AXIOM M-1500
Caliber: 204, 223 Rem., 22-250 Rem., 243 Win., 6.5x55 (2008), 25-06 Rem. (2008), 270 Win., 308 Win., 30-06 Spfl., 7mm Rem, 300 Win. Mag., 338 Win. Mag., 375 Ruger standard barrel; 204, 223 Rem., 243 Win. and 308 Win. heavy barrel. **Barrel:** Howa barreled action, 22" contour standard barrel, 20" #6 contour heavy barrel, and 24" #6 contour heavy barrel. **Weight:** 8.6-10 lbs. **Stock:** Knoxx Industries Axiom V/S synthetic, black or camo. Adjustable length of pull from 11.5" to 15.5". **Sights:** None furnished; drilled and tapped for scope mounting. **Features:** Three-position safety, adjustable trigger, hinged floor plate, forged receiver with large recoil lug, forged one-piece

bolt with dual locking lugs Introduced in 2007. Standard-barrel scope packages come with 3-10x42 Nikko-Stirling Nighteater scope, rings, bases (2008). Heavy barrels come with 4-16x44 Nikko-Stirling scope. Imported from Japan by Legacy Sports International.
Price: Axiom Standard Barrel, black stock, from $699.00
Price: Axiom 20" and 24" Varminter, black or
camo stock, from $799.00
Price: Axiom 20" and 24" Varminter, camo stock
w/scope (2008), from $819.00

HOWA M-1500 ULTRALIGHT 2-N-1 YOUTH
Caliber: 223 Rem., 22-250 Rem., 243 Win., 308 Win., 7mm-08. **Barrel:** 20" #1 contour, blued. **Weight:** 6.8 lbs. **Length:** 39.25" overall. **Stock:** Hogue Overmolded w/adult-size Hogue Overmolded in OD green. **Sights:** None furnished; drilled and tapped for scope mounting. **Features:** Bolt and receiver milled to reduce weight, three-position safety, hinged floor plate, adjustable trigger, forged one-piece bolt, M-16 style extractor, forged flat-bottom receiver. Scope package includes 3-9x42 Nikko-Stirling riflescope with bases and rings. Imported from Japan by Legacy Sports International.
Price: Blue, Youth Rifle. $539.00
Price: w/Scope package (2008) $589.00

H-S PRECISION PRO-SERIES BOLT-ACTION RIFLES
Caliber: 30 chamberings, 3- or 4-round magazine. **Barrel:** 20", 22", 24" or 26", sporter contour Pro-Series 10X match-grade stainless steel barrel. Optional muzzle brake on 30 cal. or smaller. **Weight:** 7.5 lbs. **Length:** NA. **Stock:** Pro-Series synthetic stock with full-length bedding block chassis system, sporter style. **Sights:** None; drilled and tapped for bases. **Features:** Accuracy guarantee: up to 30 caliber, 1/2 minute of angle (3 shots at 100 yards), test target supplied. Stainless steel action, stainless steel floorplate with detachable magazine, matte black Teflon finish. Made in U.S.A. by H-S Precision, Inc.
Price: SPR $2,680.00
Price: SPL Lightweight (2008) $2,825.00

KEL-TEC RFB
Caliber: 7.62 NATO (308 Win.). **Barrels:** 18" to 32". **Weight:** 11.3 lbs. (unloaded). **Length:** 40" overall. **Features:** Gas-operated semi-auto bullpup-style, forward-ejecting. Fully ambidextrous controls, adjustable

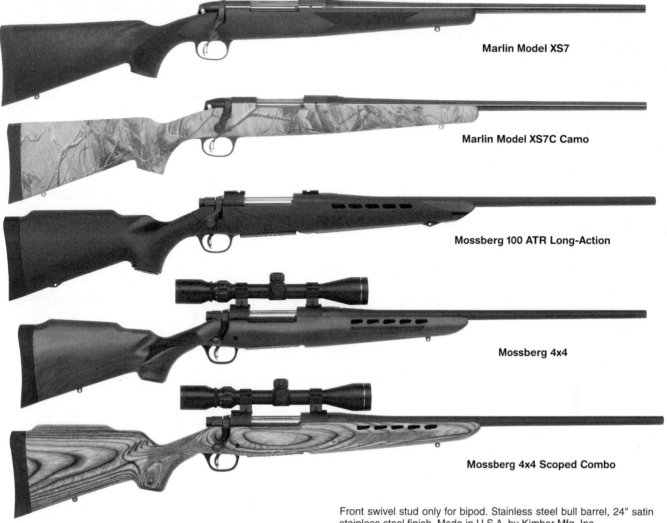

Marlin Model XS7

Marlin Model XS7C Camo

Mossberg 100 ATR Long-Action

Mossberg 4x4

Mossberg 4x4 Scoped Combo

trigger mechanism, no open sights, four-sided picatinny forend. Accepts standard FAL-type magazines. Production of the RFB has been delayed due to redesign but was expected to begin first quarter 2009.
Price: **$1,800.00**

KENNY JARRETT BOLT-ACTION RIFLE
Caliber: 223 Rem., 243 Improved, 243 Catbird, 7mm-08 Improved, 280 Remington, .280 Ackley Improved, 7mm Rem. Mag., 284 Jarrett, 30-06 Springfield, 300 Win. Mag., .300 Jarrett, 323 Jarrett, 338 Jarrett, 375 H&H, 416 Rem., 450 Rigby., other modern cartridges. **Barrel:** NA. **Weight:** NA. **Length:** NA. **Stock:** NA. **Features:** Tri-Lock receiver. Talley rings and bases. Accuracy guarantees and custom loaded ammunition.
Price: Signature Series............................. **$7,640.00**
Price: Wind Walker **$7,380.00**
Price: Original Beanfield (customer's receiver) **$5,380.00**
Price: Professional Hunter **$10,400.00**
Price: SA/Custom **$6,630.00**

KIMBER MODEL 8400 BOLT-ACTION RIFLE
Caliber: 25-06 Rem., 270 Win., 7mm, 30-06 Spfl., 300 Win. Mag., 338 Win. Mag., or 325 WSM, 4 shot. **Barrel:** 24". **Weight:** 6 lbs. 3 oz. to 6 lbs 10 oz. **Length:** 43.25". **Stock:** Claro walnut or Kevlar-reinforced fiberglass. **Sights:** None; drilled and tapped for bases. **Features:** Mauser claw extractor, two-position wing safety, action bedded on aluminum pillars and fiberglass, free-floated barrel, match grade adjustable trigger set at 4 lbs., matte or polished blue or matte stainless finish. Introduced 2003. Sonora model (2008) has brown laminated stock, hand-rubbed oil finish, chambered in 25-06 Rem., 30-06 Spfl., and 300 Win. Mag. Weighs 8.5 lbs., measures 44.50" overall length.

Front swivel stud only for bipod. Stainless steel bull barrel, 24" satin stainless steel finish. Made in U.S.A. by Kimber Mfg. Inc.
Price: Classic **$1,172.00**
Price: Classic Select Grade, French walnut stock (2008). . . **$1,359.00**
Price: SuperAmerica, AAA walnut stock. **$2,240.00**
Price: Sonora **$1,359.00**
Price: Police Tactical, synthetic stock, fluted barrel
(300 Win. Mag only) **$2,575.00**

Kimber Model 8400 Caprivi Bolt-Action Rifle
Similar to 8400 bolt rifle, but chambered for .375 H&H and 458 Lott, 4-shot magazine. Stock is Claro walnut or Kevlar-reinforced fiberglass. Features twin steel crossbolts in stock, AA French walnut, pancake cheekpiece, 24 lines-per-inch wrap-around checkering, ebony forend tip, hand-rubbed oil finish, barrel-mounted sling swivel stud, 3-leaf express sights, Howell-type rear sling swivel stud and a Pachmayr Decelerator recoil pad in traditional orange color. Introduced 2008. Made in U.S.A. by Kimber Mfg. Inc.
Price: **$3,196.00**

Kimber Model 8400 Talkeetna Bolt-Action Rifle
Similar to 8400 bolt rifle, but chambered for .375 H&H, 4-shot magazine. Weighs 8 lbs, overall length is 44.5". Stock is synthetic. Features free-floating match grade barrel with tapered match grade chamber and target crown, three-position wing safety acts directly on the cocking piece for greatest security, and Pacmayr Decelerator. Made in U.S.A. by Kimber Mfg. Inc.
Price: **$2,108.00**

KIMBER MODEL 84M BOLT-ACTION RIFLE
Caliber: 22-250 Rem., 204 Ruger, 223 Rem., 243 Win., 260 Rem., 7mm-08 Rem., 308 Win., 5-shot. **Barrel:** 22", 24", 26". **Weight:** 5 lbs., 10 oz. to 10 lbs. **Length:** 41" to 45". **Stock:** Claro walnut, checkered with steel gripcap; synthetic or gray laminate. **Sights:** None; drilled

Remington 700 CDL

Remington 700 CDL SF

Remington 700 BDL

Remington 700 SPS Varmint

Remington Model 700 LSS

and tapped for bases. **Features:** Mauser claw extractor, three-position wing safety, action bedded on aluminum pillars, free-floated barrel, match-grade trigger set at 4 lbs., matte blue finish. Includes cable lock. Introduced 2001. Montana (2008) has synthetic stock, Pachmayr Decelerator recoil pad, stainless steel 22" sporter barrel. Made in U.S.A. by Kimber Mfg. Inc.

Price: Classic (243 Win., 260, 7mm-08 Rem., 308) **$1,114.00**
Price: Varmint (22-250) **$1,224.00**
Price: Montana **$1,276.00**
Price: Classic Stainless, matte stainless steel receiver
    and barrel (243 Win., 7mm-08, 308 Win.) **$1,156.00**

L.A.R. GRIZZLY 50 BIG BOAR RIFLE
Caliber: 50 BMG, single shot. **Barrel:** 36". **Weight:** 30.4 lbs. **Length:** 45.5" overall. **Stock:** Integral. Ventilated rubber recoil pad. **Sights:** None furnished; scope mount. **Features:** Bolt-action bullpup design, thumb and bolt stop safety. All-steel construction. Introduced 1994. Made in U.S.A. by L.A.R. Mfg., Inc.
Price: From **$2,350.00**

MAGNUM RESEARCH MOUNTAIN EAGLE MAGNUMLITE RIFLES
Caliber: 22-250 Rem., 223 Rem., 280 Rem., 7mm WSM, 30-06 Spfl., 308 Win., 300 WSM, 300 Win. Mag., 3-shot magazine. **Barrel:** 24" sport taper graphite; 26" bull barrel graphite. **Weight:** 7.1-9.2 lbs. **Length:** 44.5-48.25" overall (adjustable on Tactical model). **Stock:** Hogue OverMolded synthetic, H-S Precision Tactical synthetic, H-S Precision Varmint synthetic. **Sights:** None. **Features:** Remington Model 700 receiver. Introduced in 2001. From Magnum Research, Inc.
Price: MLR3006ST24 Hogue stock **$2,295.00**
Price: MLR7MMBST24 Hogue stock **$2,295.00**
Price: MLRT22250 H-S Tactical stock, 26" bull barrel **$2,400.00**

Price: MLRT300WI Tactical **$2,400.00**

MARLIN XL7 BOLT ACTION RIFLE
Caliber: 25-06 Rem. 270 Win., 30-06 Spfl., 4-shot magazine. **Barrel:** 22" 1:10" right-hand twist, recessed barrel crown. **Weight:** 6.5 lbs. **Length:** 42.5" overall. **Stock:** Black synthetic or Realtree APG-HD camo, Soft-Tech recoil pad, pillar bedded. **Sights:** None. **Features:** Pro-Fire trigger is user adjustable down to 2.5 lbs. Fluted bolt, steel sling swivel studs, high polished blued steel, checkered bolt handle, molded checkering, one-piece scope base. Introduced in 2008. From Marlin Firearms, Inc.
Price: Black Synthetic. **$326.00**
Price: Camouflaged **$356.00**

Marlin XS7 Short-Action Bolt-Action Rifle
Similar to Model XL7 but chambered in 7mm-08, 243 Winchester and 308 Winchester.
Price: . . . . **NA**
Price: XS7Y Youth **$341.00**
Price: XS7C Camo, Realtree APG HD camo stock **$341.00**

MERKEL KR1 BOLT-ACTION RIFLE
Caliber: 223 Rem., 243 Rem., 6.5x55, 7mm-08, 308 Win., 270 Win., 30-06, 9.3x62, 7mm Rem. Mag., 300 Win. Mag., 270 WSM, 300 WSM, 338 Win. Mag. **Features:** Short lock, short bolt movement, take-down design with interchangeable barrel assemblies, three-position safety, detachable box magazine, fine trigger with set feature, checkered walnut pistol-grip semi-schnable stock. Adjustable iron sights with quick release mounts. Imported from Germany by Merkel USA.
Price: **$1,995.00**
Price: Model KR1 Stutzen Antique: 20.8" barrel, case-colored receiver,
    Mannlicher-style stock **$3,395.00**

MOSSBERG 100 ATR BOLT-ACTION RIFLE
Caliber: 243 Win. (2006), 270 Win., 308 Win. (2006), 30-06 Spfl., 4-round magazine. **Barrel:** 22", 1:10 twist, free-floating, button-rifled,

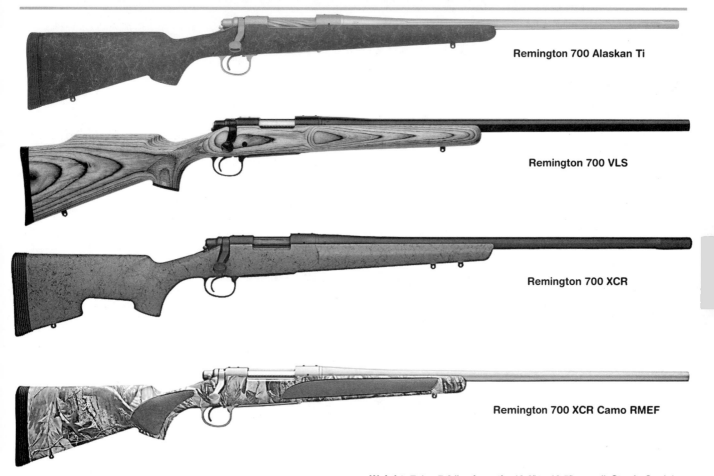

Remington 700 Alaskan Ti

Remington 700 VLS

Remington 700 XCR

Remington 700 XCR Camo RMEF

recessed muzzle crown. **Weight:** 6.7 to 7.75 lbs. **Length:** 42"-42.75" overall. **Stock:** Black synthetic, walnut, Mossy Oak New Break Up camo, Realtree AP camo. **Sights:** Factory-installed Weaver-style scope bases; scoped combos include 3x9 factory-mounted, bore-sighted scopes. **Features:** Marinecote and matte blue metal finishes, free gun lock, side lever safety. Introduced 2005. Night Train (2008)comes with Picatinny rail and factory-mounted 4-16x50mm variable scope. From O.F. Mossberg & Sons, Inc.

Price: Short-Action 243 Win., wood stock, matte blue, from. . . **$424.00**
Price: Long-Action 270 Win., Mossy Oak New Break Up
camo, matte blue, from **$424.00**
Price: Scoped Combo 30-06 Spfl., Walnut-Dura-Wood stock,
Marinecote finish, from **$481.00**
Price: Bantam Short Action 308 Win., 20" barrel **$471.00**
Price: Night Train Short-Action Scoped Combo (2008) **$567.00**

MOSSBERG 4X4 BOLT-ACTION RIFLE

Caliber: 25-06 Rem, 270 Win., 30-06 Spfl., 7mm Rem. Mag., .300 Win. Mag., .338 Win. Mag., detachable box magazine, 4 rounds standard, 3 rounds magnum. **Barrel:** 24", 1:10 twist, free-floating, button-rifled, recessed muzzle crown. **Weight:** 7+ lbs. **Length:** 42" overall. **Stock:** Skeletonized synthetic laminate (2008); black synthetic, laminated, select American black walnut. **Sights:** Factory-installed Weaver-style scope bases. **Features:** Marinecote and matte blue metal finishes, free gun lock, side lever safety. Scoped combos include factory-mounted, bore-sighted 3-9x40mm variable. Introduced 2007. From O.F. Mossberg & Sons, Inc.

Price: 25-06 Rem., walnut stock, matte blue, from **$505.00**
Price: 300 Win. Mag., synthetic laminate stock (2008), from . . **$505.00**
Price: 4X4 Classic Stock Synthetic: Black synthetic stock and
Marinecote metal surfaces **$654.00**
Price: 4X4 Scoped Combo: Matte blue finish and 3x9 scope   **$654.00**
Price: 4X4 Classic Walnut Stock: Checkered walnut stock . . **$654.00**

REMINGTON MODEL 700 CDL CLASSIC DELUXE RIFLE

Caliber: 223 Rem., 243 Win., 25-06 Rem., 270 Win., 7mm-08 Rem., 7mm Rem. Mag., 7mm Rem. Ultra Mag., 30-06 Spfl., 300 Rem. Ultra Mag., 300 Win. Mag., 35 Whelen. **Barrel:** 24" or 26" round tapered.

Weight: 7.4 to 7.6 lbs. **Length:** 43.6" to 46.5" overall. **Stock:** Straight-comb American walnut stock, satin finish, checkering, right-handed cheek piece, black fore-end tip and grip cap, sling swivel studs. **Sights:** None. **Features:** Satin blued finish, jeweled bolt body, drilled and tapped for scope mounts. Hinged-floorplate magazine capacity: 4, standard calibers; 3, magnum calibers. SuperCell recoil pad, cylindrical receiver, integral extractor. Introduced 2004. CDL SF (stainless fluted) chambered for 260 Rem., 257 Wby. Mag., 270 Win., 270 WSM, 7mm-08 Rem., 7mm Rem. Mag., 30-06 Spfl., 300 WSM. Left-hand versions introduced 2008 in six calibers. Made in U.S. by Remington Arms Co., Inc.

Price: Standard Calibers: 24" barrel **$959.00**
Price: Magnum Calibers: 26" barrel **$987.00**
Price: CDL SF (2007), from **$1,100.00**
Price: CDL LH (2008), from **$987.00**
Price: CDL High Polish Blued (2008), from **$959.00**
Price: CDL SF (2009), 257 Roberts . . . . **NA**

REMINGTON MODEL 700 BDL RIFLE

Caliber: 243 Win., 270 Win., 7mm Rem. Mag. 30-06 Spfl., 300 Rem Ultra Mag. **Barrel:** 22, 24, 26" round tapered. **Weight:** 7.25-7.4 lbs. **Length:** 41.6-46.5" overall. **Stock:** Walnut. Gloss-finish pistol grip stock with skip-line checkering, black forend tip and gripcap with white line spacers. Quick-release floorplate. **Sights:** Gold bead ramp front; hooded ramp, removable step-adjustable rear with windage screw. **Features:** Side safety, receiver tapped for scope mounts, matte receiver top, quick detachable swivels.

Price: 243 Win., 270 Win., 30-06 . . . . **$927.00**
Price: 7mm Rem. Mag. 300 Rem Ultra Mag. **$955.00**

REMINGTON MODEL 700 SPS RIFLES

Caliber: 17 Rem. Fireball, 204 Ruger, 22-250 Rem., 6.8 Rem SPC, 223 Rem., 243 Win., 270 Win. 270 WSM, 7mm-08 Rem., 7mm Rem. Mag., 7mm Rem. Ultra Mag., 30-06 Spfl., 308 Win., 300 WSM, 300 Win. Mag., 300 Rem. Ultra Mag. **Barrel:** 20", 24" or 26" carbon steel. **Weight:** 7 to 7.6 lbs. **Length:** 39.6" to 46.5" overall. **Stock:** Black synthetic, sling swivel studs, SuperCell recoil pad. **Sights:** None. Introduced 2005. SPS Stainless replaces Model 700 BDL Stainless Synthetic. **Barrel:**

Remington 700 XHR

Remington 700 Target Tactical

Remington 700 Varmint SF

Remington 770

Remington Seven CDL

Bead-blasted 416 stainless steel. **Features:** Plated internal fire control component. SPS DM features detachable box magazine. Buckmaster Edition versions feature Realtree Hardwoods HD camouflage and Buckmasters logo engraved on floorplate. SPS Varmint includes X-Mark Pro trigger, 26" heavy contour barrel, vented beavertail forend, dual front sling swivel studs. Made in U.S. by Remington Arms Co., Inc.

Price: SPS, from $639.00
Price: SPS DM (2005) $672.00
Price: SPS Youth, 20" barrel (2007) 243 Win., 7mm-08. . . . . .$604.00
Price: SPS Varmint (2007). $665.00
Price: SPS Stainless, (2005), from $732.00
Price: SPS Buckmasters Youth (2008), 243 Win. $707.00
Price: SPS Youth LH (2008), 243 Win., 7mm-08 . . . .$620.00
Price: SPS Varmint LH (2008) $692.00
Price: SPS Synthetic Left-Hand . . . . NA

REMINGTON MODEL 700 MOUNTAIN LSS RIFLES

Caliber: 270 Win., 280 Rem., 7mm-08 Rem., 30-06. **Barrel:** 22" satin stainless steel. **Weight:** 6.6 lbs. **Length:** 41.6" to 42.5" overall. **Stock:** Brown laminated, sling swivel studs, SuperCell recoil pad, black forend tip. **Sights:** None. **Barrel:** Bead-blasted 416 stainless steel, lightweight contour. Made in U.S. by Remington Arms Co., Inc.

Price: $1,052.00

7mm Rem. Mag., 30-06 Spfl., 300 WSM, 300 Win. Mag. **Barrel:** 24" round tapered. **Weight:** 6 lbs. **Length:** 43.6" to 44.5" overall. **Stock:** Bell & Carlson carbon-fiber synthetic, sling swivel studs, SuperCell gel recoil pad. **Sights:** None. **Features:** Formerly Model 700 Titanium, introduced 2001. Titanium receiver, spiral-cut fluted bolt, skeletonized bolt handle, X-Mark Pro trigger, satin stainless finish. Drilled and tapped for scope mounts. Hinged-floorplate magazine capacity: 4, standard calibers; 3, magnum calibers. Introduced 2007. Made in U.S. by Remington Arms Co., Inc.

Price: From. $2,225.00

REMINGTON MODEL 700 VLS/VLSS TH RIFLES

Caliber: 204 Ruger, 223 Rem., 22-250 Rem., 243 Win., 308 Win. **Barrel:** 26" heavy contour barrel (0.820" muzzle O.D.), concave target-style barrel crown **Weight:** 9.4 lbs. **Length:** 45.75" overall. **Stock:** Brown laminated stock, satin finish, with beavertail forend, gripcap, rubber buttpad. **Sights:** None. **Features:** Introduced 1995. VLSS TH (varmint laminate stock stainless) thumbhole model introduced 2007. Made in U.S. by Remington Arms Co., Inc.

Price: VLS. $979.00
Price: VL SS TH $1,085.00

REMINGTON MODEL 700 VSSF-II/SENDERO SF II RIFLES

Caliber: 17 Rem. Fireball, 204 Ruger, 220 Swift, 223 Rem., 22-250 Rem., 308 Win. **Barrel:** satin blued 26" heavy contour (0.820" muzzle

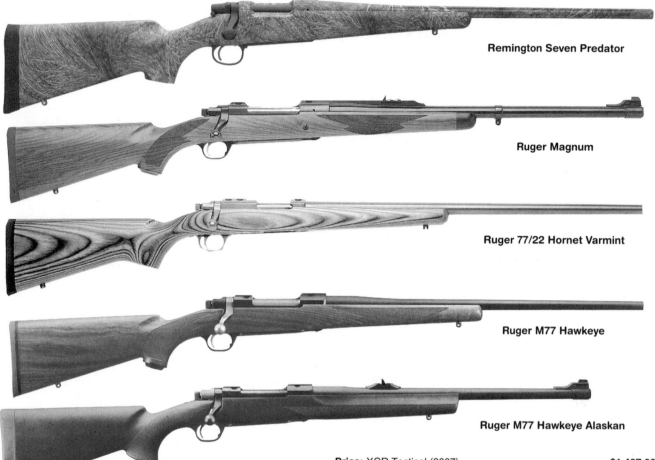

Remington Seven Predator

Ruger Magnum

Ruger 77/22 Hornet Varmint

Ruger M77 Hawkeye

Ruger M77 Hawkeye Alaskan

O.D.). VSSF has satin-finish stainless barreled action with 26" fluted barrel. **Weight:** 8.5 lbs. **Length:** 45.75" overall. **Stock:** H.S. Precision composite reinforced with aramid fibers, black (VSSF-II) Contoured beavertail fore-end with ambidextrous finger grooves, palm swell, and twin front tactical-style swivel studs. **Sights:** None. **Features:** Aluminum bedding block, drilled and tapped for scope mounts, hinged floorplate magazines. Introduced 1994. Sendero model is similar to VSSF-II except chambered for 264 Win. Mag, 7mm Rem. Mag., 7mm Rem. Ultra Mag., 300 Win. Mag., 300 Rem. Ultra Mag. Polished stainless barrel. Introduced 1996. Made in U.S. by Remington Arms Co., Inc.

Price: VSSF-II **$1,332.00**
Price: Sendero SF II **$1,359.00**

REMINGTON MODEL 700 XCR RIFLE

Caliber: 25-06 Rem., 270 Win., 270 WSM, 7mm-08 Rem., 7mm Rem. Mag., 7mm Rem Ultra Mag., 30-06 Spfl., 300 WSM, 300 Win. Mag., 300 Rem. Ultra Mag., 338 Rem. Ultra Mag., 338 Win. Mag., 375 H&H Mag., 375 Rem. Ultra Mag. **Barrel:** 24" standard caliber; 26" magnum. **Weight:** 7.4 to 7.6 lbs. **Length:** 43.6" to 46.5" overall. **Stock:** Black synthetic, SuperCell recoil pad, rubber overmolded grip and forend. **Sights:** None. **Features:** XCR (Xtreme Conditions Rifle) includes TriNyte Corrosion Control System; drilled and tapped for scope mounts. 375 H&H Mag., 375 Rem. Ultra Mag. chamberings come with iron sights. Introduced 2005. XCR Tactical model introduced 2007. **Features:** Bell & Carlson OD green tactical stock, beavertail forend, recessed thumbhook behind pistol grip, TriNyte coating over stainless steel barrel, LTR fluting. Chambered in 223 Rem., 300 Win. Mag., 308 Win. 700XCR Left Hand introduced 2008 in 270 Win., 7mm Rem. Mag., 30-06 Spfl., 300 Rem Ultra Mag. Made in U.S. by Remington Arms Co., Inc.

Price: From **$1,065.00**

Price: XCR Tactical (2007) **$1,407.00**
Price: XCR Left Hand (2008) **$1,092.00**
Price: XCR Compact Tactical (2008), 223 Rem., 308 Win. . . **$1,434.00**

Remington Model 700 XCR Camo RMEF

Similar to Model 700 XCR but with stainless barrel and receiver, AP HD camo stock, TriNyte coating overall, 7mm Remington Ultra Mag chambering.

Price: **$1,199.00**

REMINGTON 700 XHR EXTREME HUNTING RIFLE

Caliber: 243 Win., 25-06, 270 Win., 7mm-08, 7mm Rem. Mag., 300 Win. Mag., 7mm Rem. Ultra Mag. **Barrel:** 24", 25", or 26" triangular magnum-contour counterbored. **Weight:** 7-1/4 to 7-5/8 lbs. **Length:** 41-5/8 to 46-1/2 overall. **Features:** Adjustable trigger, synthetic stock finished in Realtree AG HD camo, satin black oxide finish on exposed metal surfaces, hinged floorplate, SuperCell recoil pad.

Price: . . . . **$879.00 to $927.00**

REMINGTON MODEL 700 XCR TARGET TACTICAL RIFLE

Caliber: 308 Win. **Barrel:** 26" triangular counterbored, 1:11-1/2 rifling. **Weight:** 11.75 lbs. **Length:** 45-3/4" overall. **Features:** Textured green Bell & Carlson varmint/tactical stock with adjustable comb and length of pull, adjustable trigger, satin black oxide finish on exposed metal surfaces, hinged floorplate, SuperCell recoil pad, matte blue on exposed metal surfaces.

Price: **$1,407.00**

REMINGTON MODEL 700 VTR VARMINT/TACTICAL RIFLE

Caliber: 17 Rem. Fireball, 204 Ruger, 22-250, 223 Rem., 243 Win., 308 Win. **Barrel:** 22" triangular counterbored. **Weight:** 7.5 lbs. **Length:** 41-5/8" overall. **Features:** Olive drab overmolded or Digital Tiger TSP Desert Camo stock with vented semi-beavertail forend, tactical-style dual swivel mounts for bipod, matte blue on exposed metal surfaces.

Price: **$1,972.00**
Price: VTR Desert Recon, Digital Desert Camo stock, 223 and 308 Win. only **$1,972.00**

Ruger M77 Standard Left-Hand

Ruger M77 Hawkeye Compact

Ruger M77 Hawkeye Tactical

Ruger M77 Hawkeye Predator

Sako 85 Grey Wolf

REMINGTON MODEL 700 VARMINT SF RIFLE

Caliber: 17 Rem. Fireball, 204 Ruger, 22-250, 223, 220 Swift. **Barrel:** 26" stainless steel fluted. **Weight:** 8.5 lbs. **Length:** 45.75". **Features:** Synthetic stock with ventilated forend, stainless steel/triggerguard/ floorplate, dual tactical swivels for bipod attachment.
Price: $825.00

REMINGTON MODEL 770 BOLT-ACTION RIFLE

Caliber: 243 Win., 270 Win., 7mm Rem. Mag., 7mm-08 Rem., 308 Win., 30-06 Spfl., 300 Win. Mag. **Barrel:** 22" or 24", button rifled. **Weight:** 8.5 lbs. **Length:** 42.5" to 44.5" overall. **Stock:** Black synthetic. **Sights:** Bushnell Sharpshooter 3-9x scope mounted and bore-sighted. **Features:** Upgrade of Model 710 introduced 2001. Unique action locks bolt directly into barrel; 60-degree bolt throw; 4-shot dual-stack magazine; all-steel receiver. Introduced 2007. Made in U.S.A. by Remington Arms Co.
Price: $460.00
Price: Youth, 243 Win. $460.00
Price: Stainless Camo (2008), stainless barrel, nickel-plated bolt,
    Realtree camo stock. $540.00

REMINGTON MODEL SEVEN CDL/CDL MAGNUM

Caliber: 17 Rem. Fireball, 243 Win., 260 Rem., 270 WSM, 7mm-08 Rem., 308 Win., 300 WSM, 350 Rem. Mag. **Barrel:** 20"; 22" magnum. **Weight:** 6.5 to 7.4 lbs. **Length:** 39.25" to 41.25" overall. **Stock:** American walnut, SuperCell recoil pad, satin finished. **Sights:** None. **Features:** Satin finished carbon steel barrel and action, 3- or 4-round magazine, hinged magazine floorplate. Furnished with iron sights and sling swivel studs, drilled and tapped for scope mounts. CDL versions introduced 2007. Made in U.S.A. by Remington Arms Co.
Price: CDL $959.00
Price: CDL Magnum $1,01200
Price: Predator (2008) $825.00
Price: 25th Anniversary (2008), 7mm-08 . . . . $969.00

REMINGTON MODEL 798/799 BOLT-ACTION RIFLES

Caliber: 243 Win., 270 Win., 7mm Rem. Mag., 308 Win., .30-06 Spfl., .300 Win. Mag., .375 H&H Mag., .458 Win. Mag. **Barrel:** 20" to 26". **Weight:** 7.75 lbs. **Length:** 39.5" to 42.5" overall. **Stock:** Brown or green laminated, 1-inch rubber butt pad. **Sights:** None. Receiver drilled and tapped for standard Mauser 98 (long- and short-action) scope mounts. **Features:** Model 98 Mauser action (square-bridge Mauser 98). Claw extractor, sporter style 2-position safety, solid steel hinged floorplate magazine. Introduced 2006. Made in U.S.A. by Remington Arms Co.
Price: Model 798 SPS, black synthetic stock (2008), from. . . . **$527.00**
Price: Model 798 Satin Walnut Stock (2008), from. **$648.00**
Price: Model 798 Safari Grade (2008), from. **$1,141.00**
Price: Model 799, from **$648.00**

RUGER MAGNUM RIFLE

Caliber: 375 H&H, 416 Rigby, 458 Lott. **Barrel:** 23". **Weight:** 9.5 to 10.25 lbs. **Length:** 44". **Stock:** AAA Premium Grade Circassian walnut with live-rubber recoil pad, metal gripcap, and studs for mounting sling swivels. **Sights:** Blade, front; V-notch rear express sights (one stationary, two folding) drift-adjustable for windage. **Features:** Floorplate latch secures the hinged floorplate against accidental dumping of cartridges; one-piece bolt has a non-rotating Mauser-type controlled-feed extractor; fixed-blade ejector.

Sako 85 Finnlight

Sako 75 Hunter

Sako 75 Deluxe

Sako 75 Varmint

Savage Model 12FV

Price: M77RSM MKII **$2,334.00**

RUGER COMPACT MAGNUMS

Caliber: .338 RCM, .300 RCM; 3-shot magazine. **Barrel:** 20". **Weight:** 6.75 lbs. **Length:** 39.5-40" overall. **Stock:** American walnut and black synthetic; stainless steel and Hawkeye Matte blued finishes. **Sights:** Adjustable Williams "U" notch rear sight and brass bead front sight. **Features:** Based on a shortened .375 Ruger case, the .300 and .338 RCMs match the .300 and .338 Win. Mag. in performance; RCM stock is 1/2 inch shorter than standard M77 Hawkeye stock; LC6 trigger; steel floor plate engraved with Ruger logo and "Ruger Compact Magnum"; Red Eagle recoil pad; Mauser-type controlled feeding; claw extractor; 3-position safety; hammer-forged steel barrels; Ruger scope rings. Walnut stock includes extensive cut-checkering and rounded profiles. Intr. 2008. Made in U.S.A. by Sturm, Ruger & Co.
Price: HM77RCM (walnut/Hawkeye matte blued) **$995.00**
Price: HKM77PRCM (synthetic/SS) **$995.00**

RUGER 77/22 BOLT-ACTION RIFLE

Caliber: 22 Hornet, 6-shot rotary magazine. **Barrel:** 20" or 24". **Weight:** About 6.25 to 7.5 lbs. **Length:** 39.5" to 43.5" overall. **Stock:** Checkered American walnut, black rubber buttpad; brown laminate. **Sights:** None. **Features:** Same basic features as rimfire model except slightly lengthened receiver. Uses Ruger rotary magazine. Three-position safety. Comes with 1" Ruger scope rings. Introduced 1994.
Price: 77/22-RH (rings only, no sights) **$754.00**
Price: K77/22-VHZ Varmint, laminated stock, no sights **$836.00**

RUGER M77 HAWKEYE RIFLES

Caliber: 204 Ruger, 223 Rem., 22-250 Rem., 243 Win., 257 Roberts, 25-06 Rem., 270 Win., 280 Rem., 7mm/08, 7mm Rem. Mag., 308 Win., 30-06 Spfl., 300 Win. Mag., 338 Win. Mag., 338 Federal, 358 Win. Mag., 416 Ruger, 375 Ruger, 300 Ruger Compact Magnum, 338 Ruger Compact Magnum; 4-shot magazine, except 3-shot magazine

for magnums; 5-shot magazine for 204 Ruger and 223 Rem. **Barrel:** 22", 24". **Weight:** 6.75 to 8.25 lbs. **Length:** 42-44.4" overall. **Stock:** American walnut. **Sights:** None furnished. Receiver has Ruger integral scope mount base, Ruger 1" rings. **Features:** Includes Ruger LC6 trigger, new red rubber recoil pad, Mauser-type controlled feeding, claw extractor, 3-position safety, hammer-forged steel barrels, Ruger scope rings. Walnut stock includes wrap-around cut checkering on the forearm and, more rounded contours on stock and top of pistol grips. Matte stainless version features synthetic stock. Hawkeye Alaskan and African chambered in 375 Ruger. Alaskan features matte-black finish, 20" barrel, Hogue OverMolded synthetic stock. African has 23" blued barrel, checkered walnut stock, left-handed model. 375's have windage-adjustable shallow "V" notch rear sight, white bead front sights. Introduced 2007. Left-hand models available 2008.

RUGER M77 HAWKEYE RIFLES *(cont.)*
Price: Standard, right- and left-hand. **$803.00**
Price: All-Weather. **$803.00**
Price: Laminate, left-hand **$862.00**
Price: Ultra Light **$862.00**
Price: All-Weather Ultra Light **$803.00**
Price: Compact **$803.00**
Price: Laminate Compact **$862.00**
Price: Compact Magnum **$899.00**
Price: African **$1,079.00**
Price: Alaskan **$1,079.00**
Price: Sporter **$862.00**
Price: Tactical **$1,138.00**
Price: Predator **$935.00**
Price: International **$939.00**

RUGER M77VT TARGET RIFLE

Caliber: 22-250 Rem., 223 Rem., 204 Ruger, 243 Win., 25-06 Rem., 308 Win. **Barrel:** 26" heavy stainless steel with target grey finish. **Weight:** 9 to 9.75 lbs. **Length:** Approx. 45.75" to 46.75" overall. **Stock:**

Savage Model 116FSAK

Savage Model 111F

Savage Model 11FCNS

Laminated American hardwood with beavertail forend, steel swivel studs; no checkering or gripcap. **Sights:** Integral scope mount bases in receiver. **Features:** Ruger diagonal bedding system. Ruger steel 1" scope rings supplied. Fully adjustable trigger. Steel floorplate and trigger guard. New version introduced 1992.
Price: KM77VT MKII **$935.00**

SAKO A7 AMERICAN BOLT-ACTION RIFLE
Caliber: 22-250, 243 Win., 25-06, 260 Rem., 270 Win., 270 WSM, 300 WSM, 30-06, 7mm Rem. Mag., 7mm-08. **Barrel:** 22-7/16" standard, 24-3/8" magnum. **Weight:** 6 lbs. 3 oz. to 6 lbs. 13 oz. **Length:** 42-5/16" to 44-5/16" overall. **Features:** Blued or stainless barrel and receiver, black composite stock with sling swivels and recoil pad, two-position safety, adjustable trigger, detachable 3+1 box magazine.
Price: From . . . . $850.00 (blued); $950.00 (stainless)

SAKO TRG-42 BOLT-ACTION RIFLE
Caliber: 338 Lapua Mag. and 300 Win. Mag. **Barrel:** 27-1/8". **Weight:** 11.25 lbs. **Length:** NA. **Stock:** NA. **Sights:** NA. **Features:** 5-shot magazine, fully adjustable stock and competition trigger. Imported from Finland by Beretta USA.
Price: **$2,775.00**

SAKO MODEL 85 BOLT-ACTION RIFLES
Caliber: 22-250 Rem., 243 Win., 25-06 Rem., 260, 6.5x55mm, 270 Win., 270 WSM, 7mm-08 Rem., 308 Win., 30-06; 7mm WSM, 300 WSM, 338 Federal. **Barrel:** 22.4", 22.9", 24.4". **Weight:** 7.75 lbs. **Length:** NA. **Stock:** Polymer, laminated or high-grade walnut, straight comb, shadow-line cheekpiece. **Sights:** None furnished. **Features:** Controlled-round feeding, adjustable trigger, matte stainless or nonreflective satin blue. Quad model is polymer/stainless with four interchangeable barrels in 22 LR, 22 WMR 17 HMR and 17 Mach 2; 50-degree bolt-lift, ambidextrous palm-swell, adjustable butt-pad. Introduced 2006. Imported from Finland by Beretta USA.
Price: Sako 85 Hunter, walnut/blued $1,700.00
Price: Sako 85 Grey Wolf, laminated/stainless $1,575.00
Price: Sako 85 Quad, polymer/stainless $925.00
Price: Sako 85 Quad Combo, four barrels $2,175.00

Sako 85 Finnlight
Similar to Model 85 but chambered in 243 Win., 25-06, 260 Rem., 270 Win., 270 WSM, 300 WSM, 30-06, 300 WM, 308 Win., 6.5x55mm, 7mm Rem Mag., 7mm-08. Weighs 6 lbs., 3 oz. to 6 lbs. 13 oz. Stainless steel barrel and receiver, black synthetic stock.
Price: **$1,600.00**

SAKO 75 HUNTER BOLT-ACTION RIFLE
Caliber: 223 Rem., 22-250 Rem., 243 Win., 25-06 Rem., 260, 270 Win., 270 WSM, 280 Rem., 300 Win. Mag., 30-06; 7mm-08 Rem., 308 Win., 270 Wby. Mag., 7mm Rem. Mag., 7mm STW, 7mm Wby. Mag., 300 Wby. Mag., 338 Win. Mag., 340 Wby. Mag., 375 H&H. **Barrel:** 22", standard calibers; 24", 26" magnum calibers. **Weight:** About 6 lbs. **Length:** NA. **Stock:** European walnut with matte lacquer finish. **Sights:** None furnished; dovetail scope mount rails. **Features:** New design with three locking lugs and a mechanical ejector, key locks firing pin and bolt, cold hammer-forged barrel is free-floating, two-position safety, hinged floorplate or detachable magazine that can be loaded from the top, short 70-degree bolt lift. Five action lengths. Introduced 1997. Imported from Finland by Beretta USA.
Price: From **$1,375.00**

Sako 75 Deluxe Rifle
Similar to 75 Hunter except select wood rosewood gripcap and forend tip. Available in 17 Rem., 222, 223 Rem., 25-06 Rem., 243 Win., 7mm-08 Rem., 308 Win., 25-06 Rem., 270 Win., 280 Rem., 30-06; 270 Wby. Mag., 7mm Rem. Mag., 7mm STW, 7mm Wby. Mag., 300 Win. Mag., 300 Wby. Mag., 338 Win. Mag., 340 Wby. Mag., 375 H&H, 416 Rem. Mag. Introduced 1997. Imported from Finland by Beretta USA.
Price: From **$2,175.00**

Sako 75 Varmint Rifle
Similar to Model 75 Hunter except chambered only for 17 Rem., 222 Rem., 223 Rem., 22-250 Rem., 22 PPC and 6mm PPC, 24" heavy barrel with recessed crown; set trigger; beavertail forend. Introduced 1998. Imported from Finland by Beretta USA.
Price: **$1,850.00**

SAVAGE MODEL 25 BOLT ACTION RIFLES
Caliber: 204 Ruger, 223 Rem., 4-shot magazine. **Barrel:** 24", medium-contour fluted barrel with recessed target crown, free-floating sleeved barrel, dual pillar bedding. **Weight:** 8.25 lbs. **Length:** 43.75" overall. **Stock:** Brown laminate with beavertail-style forend. **Sights:** Weaver-style bases installed. **Features:** Diameter-specific action built around the 223 Rem. bolthead dimension. Three locking lugs, 60-degree bolt lift, AccuTrigger adjustable from 2.5 to 3.25 lbs. Model 25 Classic Sporter has satin lacquer American walnut with contrasting forend tip, wraparound checkering, 22" blued barrel. **Weight:** 7.15 lbs. **Length:** 41.75". Introduced 2008. Made in U.S.A. by Savage Arms, Inc.
Price: Model 25 Lightweight Varminter. $641.00
Price: Model 25 Lightweight Varminter Thumbhole $691.00
Price: Model 25 Classic Sporter $672.00

SAVAGE CLASSIC SERIES MODEL 14/114 RIFLES
Caliber: 204 Ruger, 223 Rem., 22-250 Rem., 243 Win., 7mm-08 Rem., 308 Win., 270 WSM, 300 WSM (short action Model 14), 2- or 4-shot

Savage Model 10 BAS

Savage Model 10 BAT/S

Savage Model 10FP

Savage Model 10FCP

Savage Model 10 Precision Carbine

Savage Model 10 Predator

magazine; 270 Win., 7mm Rem. Mag., 30-06 Spfl., 300 Win. Mag. (long action Model 114), 3- or 4-shot magazine. **Barrel:** 22" or 24". **Weight:** 7 to 7.5 lbs. **Length:** 41.75" to 43.75" overall (Model 14); 43.25" to 45.25" overall (Model 114). **Stock:** Satin lacquer American walnut with ebony forend, wraparound checkering, Monte Carlo Comb and cheekpiece. **Sights:** None furnished. Receiver drilled and tapped for scope mounting. **Features:** AccuTrigger, high luster blued barreled action, hinged floorplate. From Savage Arms, Inc.

Price: Model 14 or 114 Classic, from $826.00
Price: Model 14 or 114 American Classic, detachable box
    magazine, from. $779.00
Price: Model 14 or 114 Euro Classic, oil finish, from $875.00
Price: Model 14 Left Hand, 250 Savage and 300 Savage only $779.00

SAVAGE MODEL 12 SERIES VARMINT RIFLES
Caliber: 204 Ruger, 223 Rem., 22-250 Rem. 4-shot magazine. **Barrel:** 26" stainless barreled action, heavy fluted, free-floating and button-rifled barrel. **Weight:** 10 lbs. **Length:** 46.25" overall. **Stock:** Dual pillar bedded, low profile, laminated stock with extra-wide beavertail forend. **Sights:** None furnished; drilled and tapped for scope mounting. **Features:** Recessed target-style muzzle. AccuTrigger, oversized bolt handle, detachable box magazine, swivel studs. Model 112BVSS has heavy target-style prone laminated stock with high comb, Wundhammer palm swell, internal box magazine. Model 12FVSS has black synthetic stock, additional chamberings in 308 Win., 270 WSM, 300 WSM. Model 12FV has blued receiver. Model 12BTCSS has brown laminate vented thumbhole stock. Made in U.S.A. by Savage Arms, Inc.
Price: Model 12 Varminter, from. $991.00

Price: Model 12BVSS. $899.00
Price: Model 12FVSS, from $815.00
Price: Model 12FV $658.00
Price: Model 12BTCSS (2008) $1,041.00
Price: Model 12 Long Range (2008). $1,239.00
Price: Model 12 LRPV, single-shot only with right bolt/left
    port or left load/right eject receiver $1,273.00

SAVAGE MODEL 16/116 WEATHER WARRIORS
Caliber: 204 Ruger, 223 Rem., 22-250 Rem., 243 Win., 7mm-08 Rem., 308 Win., 270 WSM, 7mm WSM, 300 WSM (short action Model 16), 2- or 4-shot magazine; 270 Win., 7mm Rem. Mag., 30-06 Spfl., 300 Win. Mag., 338 Win. Mag. (long action Model 114), 3- or 4-shot magazine. **Barrel:** 22", 24"; stainless steel with matte finish, free-floated barrel. **Weight:** 6.5 to 6.75 lbs. **Length:** 41.75" to 43.75" overall (Model 16); 42.5" to 44.5" overall (Model 116). **Stock:** Graphite/fiberglass filled composite. **Sights:** None furnished; drilled and tapped for scope mounting. **Features:** Quick-detachable swivel studs; laser-etched bolt. Left-hand models available. Model 116FSS introduced 1991; 116FSAK introduced 1994. Made in U.S.A. by Savage Arms, Inc.
Price: Model 16FHSS or 116FHSS, hinged floorplate magazine,
    from. $755.00
Price: Model 16FLHSS or 116FLHSS, left hand models, from. $755.00
Price: Model 16FSS or 116FSS, internal box magazine, from . $678.00
Price: Model 16FCSS or 116FCSS, detachable box magazine,
    from. $755.00
Price: Model 16FHSAK or 116FHSAK, adjustable muzzle
    brake. $822.00

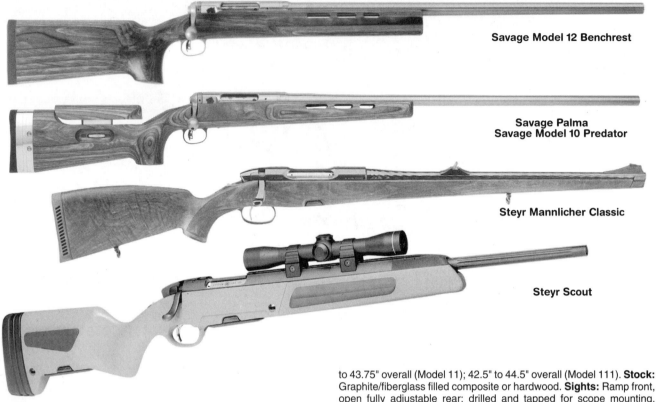

Savage Model 12 Benchrest

Savage Palma
Savage Model 10 Predator

Steyr Mannlicher Classic

Steyr Scout

SAVAGE MODEL 10GXP3, 110GXP3 PACKAGE GUNS

Caliber: 223 Rem., 22-250 Rem., 243 Win., 7mm-08 Rem., 308 Win., 300 WSM (10GXP3). 25-06 Rem., 270 Win., 30-06 Spfl., 7mm Rem. Mag., 300 Win. Mag., 300 Rem. Ultra Mag. (110GXP3). **Barrel:** 22" 24", 26". **Weight:** 7.5 lbs. average. **Length:** 43" to 47". **Stock:** Walnut Monte Carlo with checkering. **Sights:** 3-9x40mm scope, mounted & bore sighted. **Features:** Blued, free floating and button rifled, internal box magazines, swivel studs, leather sling. Left-hand available.
Price: AccuTrigger, from.............................$669.00

SAVAGE MODEL 11FXP3, 111FXP3, 111FCXP3, 11FYXP3 (YOUTH) PACKAGE GUNS

Caliber: 223 Rem., 22-250 Rem., 243 Win., 308 Win., 300 WSM (11FXP3). 270 Win., 30-06 Spfl., 25-06 Rem., 7mm Rem. Mag., 300 Win. Mag., 338 Win. Mag., 300 Rem. Ultra Mag. (11FCXPE & 111FXP3). **Barrel:** 22" to 26". **Weight:** 6.5 lbs. **Length:** 41" to 47". **Stock:** Synthetic checkering, dual pillar bed. **Sights:** 3-9X40mm scope, mounted & bore sighted. **Features:** Blued, free floating and button rifled, Top loading internal box mag (except 111FXCP3 has detachable box magazine). Nylon sling and swivel studs. Some left-hand available.
Price: Model 11FXP3, from..........................$640.00
Price: Model 111FCXP3 ....$519.00
Price: Model 11FYXP3, 243 Win., 12.5" pull (youth) $519.00
Price: Model 11FLYXP3 Youth: Left-handed configuration of Model 11FYXP3 Youth $640.00

SAVAGE MODEL 16FXP3, 116FXP3 SS ACTION PACKAGE GUNS

Caliber: 223 Rem., 243 Win., 308 Win., 300 WSM, 270 Win., 30-06 Spfl., 7mm Rem. Mag., 300 Win. Mag., 338 Win. Mag., 375 H&H, 7mm S&W, 7mm Rem. Ultra Mag., 300 Rem. Ultra Mag. **Barrel:** 22", 24", 26". **Weight:** 6.75 lbs. average. **Length:** 41" to 46". **Stock:** Synthetic checkering, dual pillar bed. **Sights:** 3-9X40mm scope, mounted & bore sighted. **Features:** Free floating and button rifled. Internal box magazine, nylon sling and swivel studs.
Price: From....................................$736.00

SAVAGE MODEL 11/111 HUNTER SERIES BOLT ACTIONS

Caliber: 223 Rem., 22-250 Rem., 243 Win., 7mm-08 Rem., 308 Win., 270 WSM, 7mm WSM, 300 WSM (short action Model 11), 2- or 4-shot magazine; 25-06 Rem., 270 Win., 7mm Rem. Mag., 30-06 Spfl., 300 Win. Mag., (long action Model 111), 3- or 4-shot magazine. **Barrel:** 22" or 24"; blued free-floated barrel. **Weight:** 6.5 to 6.75 lbs. **Length:** 41.75"

to 43.75" overall (Model 11); 42.5" to 44.5" overall (Model 111). **Stock:** Graphite/fiberglass filled composite or hardwood. **Sights:** Ramp front, open fully adjustable rear; drilled and tapped for scope mounting. **Features:** Three-position top tang safety, double front locking lugs. Introduced 1994. Made in U.S.A. by Savage Arms, Inc.
Price: Model 11FL or 111FL $564.00
Price: Model 11FL or 111FL, left hand models, from $564.00
Price: Model 11FCNS or 111FCNS, detachable box magazine, from......................................$591.00

SAVAGE MODEL 11/111 HUNTER SERIES BOLT ACTIONS *(cont.)*
Price: Model 11FLNS or 111FLNS $564.00
Price: Model 11G or 111G, hardwood stock, from $582.00
Price: Model 11BTH or 111BTH, laminate thumbhole stock (2008) $779.00
Price: Model 11FNS Model FLNS $591.00
Price: Model 11FHNS or 111FHNS....................$656.00
Price: Model 11FYCAK Youth $691.00
Price: Model 11GNS or 111GNS $618.00
Price: Model 11GLNS or 111GLSN $618.00
Price: Model 11GCNS or 111GCNS $659.00

SAVAGE MODEL 10 BAS LAW ENFORCEMENT BOLT-ACTION RIFLE

Caliber: 380 Win. **Barrel:** 24" fluted heavy with muzzle brake. **Weight:** 13.4 lbs. **Length:** NA. **Features:** Bolt-action repeater based on Model 10 action but with M4-style collapsible buttstock, pistolgrip with palm swell, all-aluminum Accustock, picatinny rail for mounting optics.
Price: $1,852.00
Price: 10 BAT/S, multi-adjustable buttstock $1,991.00

SAVAGE MODEL 10FP/110FP LAW ENFORCEMENT SERIES RIFLES

Caliber: 223 Rem., 308 Win. (Model 10), 4-shot magazine; 25-06 Rem., 300 Win. Mag., (Model 110), 3- or 4-shot magazine. **Barrel:** 24"; matte blued free-floated heavy barrel and action. **Weight:** 6.5 to 6.75 lbs. **Length:** 41.75" to 43.75" overall (Model 10); 42.5" to 44.5" overall (Model 110). **Stock:** Black graphite/fiberglass composition, pillar-bedded, positive checkering. **Sights:** None furnished. Receiver drilled and tapped for scope mounting. **Features:** Black matte finish on all metal parts. Double swivel studs on the forend for sling and/or bipod mount. Right- or left-hand. Model 110FP introduced 1990. Model 10FP introduced 1998. Model 10FCPXP has HS Precision black synthetic tactical stock with molded alloy bedding system, Leupold 3.5-10x40mm black matte scope with Mil Dot reticle, Farrell Picatinny Rail Base, flip-open lens covers, 1.25" sling with QD swivels, Harris bipod, Storm heavy duty case. Made in U.S.A. by Savage Arms, Inc.

Thompson/Center Icon

Tikka T3 Hunter

Weatherby Mark V Lazermark

Price: Model 10FP, 10FLP (left hand), 110FP $649.00
Price: Model 10FP folding Choate stock. $896.00
Price: Model 10FCP McMillan, McMillan fiberglass tactical
  stock $1,178.00
Price: Model 10FCP-HS HS Precision, HS Precision tactical
  stock $984.00
Price: Model 10FPXP-HS Precision $2,715.00
Price: Model 10FCP $866.00
Price: Model 10FLCP, left-hand model, standard stock
  or Accu-Stock $866.00
Price: Model 110FCP $866.00
Price: Model 10 Precision Carbine, 20" medium contour barrel,
  synthetic camo Accu-Stock, 223/308 . . . . $829.00
Price: Model 10 FCM Scout $646.00

Savage Model 110-50th Anniversary Rifle
  Same action as 110-series rifles, except offered in 300 Savage, limited edition of 1,000 rifles. Has high-luster blued barrel and action, unique checkering pattern, high-grade hinged floorplate, scroll pattern on receiver, 24-karat gold-plated double barrel bands, 24-karat gold-plated AccuTrigger, embossed recoil pad. Introduced 2008. Made in U.S.A. from Savage Arms, Inc.
Price: Model 110 50th Anniversary. $1,724.00

SAVAGE MODEL 10 PREDATOR SERIES
Caliber: 223, 22-250, 243, 204 Ruger. **Barrel:** 22", medium-contour. **Weight:** 7.25 lbs. **Length:** 43"overall. **Stock:** Synthetic with rounded forend and oversized bolt handle. **Features:** Entirely covered in either Mossy Oak Brush or Realtree Hardwoods Snow pattern camo. Also features AccuTrigger, detachable box magazine.
Price: $806.00

Savage Model 10XP Predator Hunting Bolt-Action Rifle Package
  Similar to Model 10 but chambered in 223, 204, 22-250 or 243 Win. Includes 4-12x40 scope, 22" barrel, AccuTrigger, choice of Realtree Snow or Mossy Oak Brush camo overall.
Price: $839.00

SAVAGE MODEL 12 PRECISION TARGET SERIES BENCHREST RIFLE
Caliber: 308 Win, 6.5x284 Norman, 6mm Norma BR. **Barrel:** 29" ultra-heavy. **Weight:** 12.75 lbs. **Length:** 50" overall. **Stock:** Gray laminate. Features: New Left-Load, Right-Eject target action, Target AccuTrigger adjustable from approx 6 oz to 2.5 lbs, oversized bolt handle, stainless extra-heavy free-floating and button-rifled barrel.
Price: $1,375.00

Savage Model 12 Precision Target Palma Rifle
  Similar to Model 12 Benchrest but in 308 Palma only, 30" barrel, multi-adjustable stock, weighs 13.3 lbs.
Price: $1,798.00

Savage Model 12 F Class Target Rifle
  Similar to Model 12 Benchrest but in 6.5x284 Norma, 6 Norma BR, 30" barrel, weighs 11.5 lbs.
Price: $1,341.00

Savage Model 12 F/TR Target Rifle
  Similar to Model 12 Benchrest but in 308 Win. only, 30" barrel, weighs 12.65 lbs.
Price: $1,265.00

SMITH & WESSON I-BOLT RIFLES
Caliber: 25-06 Rem., 270 Win., 30-06 Win. (4-round magazine), 7mm Rem. Mag., 300 Win. Mag. (3-round magazine). **Barrel:** 23", 1:10" right-hand twist, 1:9" right-hand twist for 7mm Mag. Thompson/Center barrel. Blued and stainless. **Weight:** 6.75 lbs. **Stock:** Black synthetic, Realtree AP camo, walnut. Length of pull, 13-5/8", drop at comb, 7/8". Monte Carlo cheekpiece. **Sights:** Adjustable post front sight, adjustable dual aperture rear sight. **Features:** Adjustable Tru-Set Trigger. Introduced 2008. Made in U.S.A. by Smith & Wesson.
Price: Black synthetic stock, weather shield finish $588.00
Price: Camo stock, weather shield finish $658.00

STEVENS MODEL 200 BOLT-ACTION RIFLES
Caliber: 223, 22-250, 243, 7mm-08, 308 Win. (short action) or 25-06, 270 Win., 30-06, 7mm Rem. Mag., 300 Win Mag. **Barrel:** 22" (short action) or 24" (long action blued). **Weight:** 6.5 lbs. **Length:** 41.75" overall. **Stock:** Black synthetic or camo. **Sights:** None. **Features:** Free-floating and button-rifled barrel, top loading internal box magazine, swivel studs.
Price: . . . . $399.00 (standard); $439.00 (camo)
Price: Model 200XP Long or Short Action
  Package Rifle with 4x12 scope. $449.00
Price: Model 200XP Camo, camo stock $499.00

STEYR MANNLICHER CLASSIC RIFLE
Caliber: 222 Rem., 223 Rem., 243 Win., 25-06 Rem., 308 Win., 6.5x55, 6.5x57, 270 Win., 270 WSM, 7x64 Brenneke, 7mm-08 Rem., 7.5x55, 30-06 Spfl., 9.3x62, 6.5x68, 7mm Rem. Mag., 300 WSM, 300 Win. Mag., 8x68S, 4-shot magazine. **Barrel:** 23.6" standard; 26" magnum; 20" full stock standard calibers. **Weight:** 7 lbs. **Length:** 40.1" overall. **Stock:** Hand-checkered fancy European oiled walnut with standard forend. **Sights:** Ramp front adjustable for elevation, V-notch rear adjustable for windage. **Features:** Single adjustable trigger; 3-position roller safety with "safe-bolt" setting; drilled and tapped for Steyr factory scope mounts. Introduced 1997. Imported from Austria by Steyr Arms, Inc.
Price: Half stock, standard calibers $3,799.00

Weatherby Mark V Sporter

Weatherby Mark V Synthetic

Weatherby Mark V Accumark

Weatherby Mark V SVR

Price: Full stock, standard calibers **$4,199.00**

Steyr Pro Hunter Rifle

Similar to the Classic Rifle except has ABS synthetic stock with adjustable butt spacers, straight comb without cheekpiece, palm swell, Pachmayr 1" swivels. Special 10-round magazine conversion kit available. Introduced 1997. Imported from Austria by Steyr Arms, Inc.
Price: From **$1,500.00**

STEYR SCOUT BOLT-ACTION RIFLE

Caliber: 308 Win., 5-shot magazine. **Barrel:** 19", fluted. **Weight:** NA. **Length:** NA. **Stock:** Gray Zytel. **Sights:** Pop-up front & rear, Leupold M8 2.5x28 IER scope on Picatinny optic rail with Steyr mounts. **Features:** luggage case, scout sling, two stock spacers, two magazines. Introduced 1998. Imported from Austria by Steyr Arms, Inc.
Price: From **$2,199.00**

STEYR SSG 69 PII BOLT-ACTION RIFLE

Caliber: 22-250 Rem., 243 Win., 308 Win., detachable 5-shot rotary magazine. **Barrel:** 26". **Weight:** 8.5 lbs. **Length:** 44.5" overall. **Stock:** Black ABS Cycolac with spacers for length of pull adjustment. **Sights:** Hooded ramp front adjustable for elevation, V-notch rear adjustable for windage. **Features:** Sliding safety; NATO rail for bipod; 1" swivels; Parkerized finish; single or double-set triggers. Imported from Austria by Steyr Arms, Inc.
Price: **$1,889.00**

THOMPSON/CENTER ICON BOLT-ACTION RIFLE

Caliber: 22-250 Rem., 243 Win., 308 Win., 30TC, 3-round box magazine. **Barrel:** 24", button rifled. **Weight:** 7.5 lbs. **Length:** 44.5" overall. **Stock:** Walnut, 20-lpi grip and forend cut checkering with ribbon detail. **Sights:** None; integral Weaver style scope mounts. **Features:** Interchangeable bolt handle, 60-degree bolt lift, Interlok Bedding System, 3-lug bolt with T-Slot extractor, cocking indicator, adjustable trigger, preset to 3 to 3.5 lbs of pull. Introduced 2007. From Thompson/Center Arms.
Price: **$1,025.00**

Thompson/Center ICON Precision Hunter Rifle

Similar to the basic ICON model. Available in 204 Ruger, 223 Rem., 22-250 Rem., 243 Win. and 308 Win. 22" heavy barrel, blued finish, varminter-style stock. Introduced 2009.
Price: **$1,149.00**

THOMPSON/CENTER VENTURE BOLT-ACTION RIFLE

Caliber: 270 Win., 7mm Rem. Mag., 30-06 Springfield, 300 Win. Mag.,
3-round magazine. **Barrel:** 24". **Weight:** NA. **Length:** NA. **Stock:** Composite. **Sights:** NA. **Features:** Nitride fat bolt design, externally adjustable trigger, two-position safety, textured grip. Introduced 2009.
Price: **$489.00**

TIKKA T3 HUNTER

Caliber: 223 Rem., 22-250 Rem., 243 Win., 308 Win., 25-06 Rem., 270 Win., 30-06 Spfl., 300 Win. Mag., 338 Win. Mag., 270 WSM, 300 WSM, 6.5x55 Swedish Mauser, 7mm Rem. Mag. **Stock:** Walnut. **Sights:** None furnished. **Barrel:** 22-7/16", 24-3/8". **Features:** Detachable magazine, aluminum scope rings. Introduced 2005. Imported from Finland by Beretta USA.
Price: **$675.00**

Tikka T3 Stainless Synthetic

Similar to the T3 Hunter except stainless steel, synthetic stock. Available in 243 Win., 2506, 270 Win., 308 Win., 30-06 Spfl., 270 WSM, 300 WSM, 7mm Rem. Mag., 300 Win. Mag., 338 Win. Mag. Introduced 2005. Imported from Finland by Beretta USA.
Price: **$700.00**

Tikka T3 Lite Bolt-Action Rifle

Similar to the T3 Hunter, available in 223 Rem., 22-250 Rem., 308 Win., 243 Win., 25-06 Rem., 270 Win., 270 WSM, 30-06 Sprg., 300 Win Mag., 300 WSM, 338 Federal, 338 Win Mag., 7mm Rem. Mag., 7mm-08 Rem. Barrel lengths vary from 22-7/16" to 24-3/8". Made in Finland by Sako. Imported by Beretta USA.
Price: **$695.00**
Price: Stainless steel synthetic **$600.00**
Price: Stainless steel synthetic, left-hand **$700.00**

Tikka T3 Varmint/Super Varmint Rifle

Similar to the T3 Hunter, available in 223 Rem., 22-250 Rem., 308 Win. Length is 23-3/8" (Super Varmint). Made in Finland by Sako. Imported by Beretta USA.
Price: **$900.00**
Price: Super Varmint **$1,425.00**

ULTRA LIGHT ARMS BOLT-ACTION RIFLES

Caliber: 17 Rem. to 416 Rigby. **Barrel:** Douglas, length to order. **Weight:** 4.75 to 7.5 lbs. **Length:** Varies. **Stock:** Kevlar graphite composite, variety of finishes. **Sights:** None furnished; drilled and tapped for scope mounts. **Features:** Timney trigger, hand-lapped action, button-rifled barrel, hand-bedded action, recoil pad, sling-swivel studs, optional Jewell trigger. Made in U.S.A. by New Ultra Light Arms.
Price: Model 20 (short action) **$3,000.00**
Price: Model 24 (long action) **$3,100.00**

**Winchester Model 70
Extreme Weather SS**

**Winchester Model 70
Super Grade**

**Winchester Model 70
Coyote Light**

**Winchester Model 70
Featherweight**

**Winchester Model 70
Sporter**

**Winchester Model 70
Ultimate Shadow**

Price: Model 28 (magnum action) **$3,400.00**
Price: Model 40 (300 Wby. Mag., 416 Rigby) **$3,400.00**
Price: Left-hand models, add **$100.00**

WEATHERBY MARK V BOLT-ACTION RIFLES

Caliber: Deluxe version comes in all Weatherby calibers plus 243 Win., 270 Win., 7mm-08 Rem., 30-06 Spfl., 308 Win. **Barrel:** 24", 26", 28". **Weight:** 6.75 to 10 lbs. **Length:** 44" to 48.75" overall. **Stock:** Walnut, Monte Carlo with cheekpiece; high luster finish; checkered pistol grip and forend; recoil pad. **Sights:** None furnished. **Features:** 4 models with Mark V action and wood stocks; other common elements include cocking indicator; adjustable trigger; hinged floorplate, thumb safety; quick detachable sling swivels. Ultramark has hand-selected exhibition-grade walnut stock, maplewood/ebony spacers, 20-lpi checkering. Chambered for 257 and 300 Wby Mags. Lazermark same as Mark V Deluxe except stock has extensive oak leaf pattern laser carving on pistol grip and forend; chambered in Wby. Magnums—257, 270 Win., 7mm., 300, 340, with 26" barrel. Introduced 1981. Sporter is same as the Mark V Deluxe without the embellishments. Metal has low-luster blue, stock is Claro walnut with matte finish, Monte Carlo comb, recoil pad. Chambered for these Wby. Mags: 257, 270 Win., 7mm, 300, 340. Other chamberings: 7mm Rem. Mag., 300 Win. Introduced 1993. Six Mark V models come with synthetic stocks. Ultra Lightweight rifles weigh 5.75 to 6.75 lbs.; 24", 26" fluted stainless barrels with recessed target crown; Bell & Carlson stock with CNC-machined aluminum bedding plate and tan "spider web" finish, skeletonized handle and sleeve. Available in 243 Win., Wby. Mag., 25-06 Rem., 270 Win., 7mm-08 Rem., 7mm Rem. Mag., 280 Rem., 308 Win., 30-06 Spfl., 300 Win. Mag. Wby. Mag chamberings: 240, 257, 270 Win., 7mm, 300. Introduced 1998. Accumark uses Mark V action with heavy-contour 26" and 28" stainless barrels with black oxidized flutes, muzzle diameter of .705". No sights, drilled and tapped for scope mounting. Stock is composite with matte gel-coat finish, full length aluminum bedding Hasblock. Weighs 8.5 lbs. Chambered for these Wby. Mags: 240 (2007), 257, 270, 7mm, 300, 340, 338-378, 30-378. Other chamberings: 22-250 (2007), 243 Win. (2007), 25-06 Rem. (2007), 270 Win. (2007), 308 Win.(2007), 7mm Rem. Mag., 300 Win. Mag. Introduced 1996. SVM (Super VarmintMaster) has 26" fluted stainless barrel, spiderweb-pattern tan laminated synthetic stock, fully adjustable trigger. Chambered for 223 Rem., 22-250 Rem., 243. Mark V Synthetic has lightweight injection-molded synthetic stock with raised Monte Carlo comb, checkered grip and forend, custom floorplate release. Weighs 6.5-8.5 lbs., 24-28" barrels. Available in 22-250 Rem., 243 Win., 25-06 Rem., 270 Win., 7mm-08 Rem., 7mm Rem., Mag, 280 Rem., 308 Win., 30-06 Spfl., 308 Win., 300 Win. Mag., 375 H&H Mag, and these Wby. Magnums: 240, 257, 270 Win., 7mm, 300, 30-378, 338-378, 340. Introduced 1997. Fibermark composites are similar to other Mark V models except has black Kevlar and fiberglass composite stock and bead-bead-blast blue or stainless finish. Chambered for 9 standard and magnum calibers. Introduced 1983; reintroduced 2001. SVR comes with 22" button-rifled chrome-moly barrel, .739 muzzle diameter. Composite stock w/bedding block, gray spiderweb pattern. Made in U.S.A. From Weatherby.

Price: Mark V Deluxe **$2,199.00**
Price: Mark V Ultramark **$2,979.00**
Price: Mark V Lazermark **$2,479.00**
Price: Mark V Sporter **$1,499.00**
Price: Mark V SVM **$1,959.00**
Price: Mark V Ultra Lightweight **$1,879.00**
Price: Mark V Ultra Lightweight LH **$1,911.00**
Price: Mark V Accumark **$1,879.00**
Price: Mark V Synthetic **$1,209.00**
Price: Mark V Fibermark Composite **$1,449.00**
Price: Mark V SVR Special Varmint Rifle **$1,259.00**

Ballard No. 7

WEATHERBY VANGUARD BOLT-ACTION RIFLES

Caliber: 257, 300 Wby Mags; 223 Rem., 22-250 Rem., 243 Win., 25-06 Rem. (2007), 270 Win., 270 WSM, 7mm Rem. Mag., 308 Win., 30-06 Spfl., 300 Win. Mag., 300 WSM, 338 Win. Mag. **Barrel:** 24" barreled action, matte black. **Weight:** 7.5 to 8.75 lbs. **Length:** 44" to 46-3/4" overall. **Stock:** Raised comb, Monte Carlo, injection-molded composite stock. **Sights:** None furnished. **Features:** One-piece forged, fluted bolt body with three gas ports, forged and machined receiver, adjustable trigger, factory accuracy guarantee. Vanguard Stainless has 410-Series stainless steel barrel and action, bead blasted matte metal finish. Vanguard Deluxe has raised comb, semi-fancy grade Monte Carlo walnut stock with maplewood spacers, rosewood forend and grip cap, polished action with high-gloss-blued metalwork. Vanguard Synthetic Package includes Vanguard Synthetic rifle with Bushnell Banner 3-9x40mm scope mounted and boresighted, Leupold Rifleman rings and bases, Uncle Mikes nylon sling, and Plano PRO-MAX injection-molded case. Sporter has Monte Carlo walnut stock with satin urethane finish, fineline diamond point checkering, contrasting rosewood forend tip, matte-blued metalwork. Sporter SS metalwork is 410 Series bead-blasted stainless steel. Vanguard Youth/Compact has 20" No. 1 contour barrel, short action, scaled-down non-reflective matte black hardwood stock with 12.5" length of pull and full-size, injection-molded composite stock. Chambered for 223 Rem., 22-250 Rem., 243 Win., 7mm-08 Rem., 308 Win. Weighs 6.75 lbs.; OAL 38.9". Sub-MOA Matte and Sub-MOA Stainless models have pillar-bedded Fiberguard composite stock (Aramid, graphite unidirectional fibers and fiberglass) with 24" barreled action; matte black metalwork, Pachmayr Decelerator recoil pad. Sub-MOA Stainless metalwork is 410 Series bead-blasted stainless steel. Sub-MOA Varmint guaranteed to shoot 3-shot group of .99" or less when used with specified Weatherby factory or premium (non-Weatherby calibers) ammunition. Hand-laminated, tan Monte Carlo composite stock with black spiderwebbing; CNC-machined aluminum bedding block, 22" No. 3 contour barrel, recessed target crown. Varmint Special has tan injection-molded Monte Carlo composite stock, pebble grain finish, black spiderwebbing. 22" No. 3 contour barrel (.740 muzzle dia.), bead blasted matte black finish, recessed target crown. Made in U.S.A. From Weatherby.

Price: Vanguard Synthetic $399.00
Price: Vanguard Stainless $709.00
Price: Vanguard Deluxe, 7mm Rem. Mag., 300 Win. Mag.
    (2007). $989.00
Price: Vanguard Synthetic Package, 25-06 Rem. (2007). $552.00
Price: Vanguard Sporter $689.00
Price: Vanguard Sporter SS $869.00
Price: Vanguard Youth/Compact $649.00
Price: Vanguard Sub-MOA Matte, 25-06 Rem. (2007). $929.00
Price: Vanguard Sub-MOA Stainless, 270 WSM $1,079.00
Price: Vanguard Sub-MOA Varmint, 204 Ruger (2007) $1,009.00

WINCHESTER MODEL 70 BOLT-ACTION RIFLES

Caliber: Varies by model. **Barrel:** Blued, or free-floating, fluted stainless hammer-forged barrel, 22", 24", 26". Recessed target crown. **Weight:** 6.75 to 7.25 lbs. **Length:** 41 to 45.75 " overall. **Stock:** Walnut (three models) or Bell and Carlson composite; textured charcoal-grey matte finish, Pachmayr Decelerator recoil pad. **Sights:** None. **Features:** Claw extractor, three-position safety, M.O.A. three-lever trigger system, factory-set at 3.75 lbs. Super Grade features fancy grade walnut stock, contrasting black fore-end tip and pistol grip cap, and sculpted shadowline cheekpiece. Featherweight Deluxe has angled-comb walnut stock, Schnabel fore-end, satin finish, cut checkering. Sporter Deluxe has satin-finished walnut stock, cut checkering, sculpted cheekpiece. Extreme Weather SS has composite stock, drop @ comb, 0.5"; drop @ heel, 0.5". Introduced 2008. Made in U.S.A. from Winchester Repeating Arms.

Price: Extreme Weather SS, 270 Win., 270 WSM, 30-06 Spfl., 300
    Win. Mag., 300 WSM, 308 Win., 325 WSM, 243 Winchester,
    7mm WSM, from. $1,069.00
Price: Super Grade, 30-06 Sprg., 300 Win. Mag., 270 WSM, 300
    WSM, 270 Winchester, from. $1,139.00
Price: Featherweight Deluxe, 243 Win., 270 Win., 270 WSM,
    30-06 Spfl., 300 Win. Mag., 300 WSM, 308 Win.,
    325 WSM, 7mm-08 Rem., from $999.00
Price: Sporter Deluxe, 270 Win., 270 WSM, 30-06 Spfl.,
    300 Win. Mag., 300 WSM, 325 WSM, from $999.00

WINCHESTER MODEL 70 COYOTE LIGHT

Caliber: 22-250, 243 Winchester, 308 Winchester, 270 WSM, 300 WSM and 325 WSM, five-shot magazine (3-shot in 270 WSM, 300 WSM and 325 WSM). **Barrel:** 22" fluted stainless barrel (24" in 270 WSM, 300 WSM and 325 WSM). **Weight:** 7.5 lbs. **Length:** NA. **Features:** Composite Bell and Carlson stock, Pachmayr Decelerator pad. Controlled round feeding. No sights but drilled and tapped for mounts.
Price: $1,099.00

WINCHESTER MODEL 70 FEATHERWEIGHT

Caliber: 22-250, 243, 7mm-08, 308, 270 WSM, 7mm WSM, 300 WSM, 325 WSM, 25-06, 270, 30-06, 7mm Rem. Mag., 300 Win. Mag., 338 Win. Mag. Capacity 5 rounds (short action) or 3 rounds (long action). **Barrel:** 22" blued barrel (24" in magnum chamberings). **Weight:** 6-1/2 to 7-1/4 lbs. **Length:** NA. **Features:** Satin-finished checkered Grade I walnut stock, controlled round feeding. Pachmayr Decelerator pad. No sights but drilled and tapped for scope mounts.
Price: Short action $799.00
Price: Long action and magnum) $839.00

WINCHESTER MODEL 70 SPORTER

Caliber: 270 WSM, 7mm WSM, 300 WSM, 325 WSM, 25-06, 270, 30-06, 7mm Rem. Mag., 300 Win. Mag., 338 Win. Mag. Capacity 5 rounds (short action) or 3 rounds (long action). Barrel: 22", 24" or 26" blued. Weight: 6-1/2 to 7-1/4 lbs. Length: NA. Features: Satin-finished checkered Grade I walnut stock with sculpted cheekpiece, controlled round feeding. Pachmayr Decelerator pad. No sights but drilled and tapped for scope mounts.
Price: Short action $799.00
Price: Long action and magnum) $839.00

WINCHESTER MODEL 70 ULTIMATE SHADOW

Caliber: 243, 308, 270 WSM, 7mm WSM, 300 WSM, 325 WSM, 270, 30-06, 7mm Rem. Mag., 300 Win. Mag. Capacity 5 rounds (short action) or 3 rounds (long action). **Barrel:** 22" matte stainless (24" or 26" in magnum chamberings). **Weight:** 6-1/2 to 7-1/4 lbs. **Length:** NA. **Features:** Synthetic stock with WinSorb recoil pad, controlled round feeding. Pachmayr Decelerator pad. No sights but drilled and tapped for scope mounts.
Price: Standard. $739.00
Price: Magnum $769.00

Prices given are believed to be accurate at time of publication however, many factors affect retail pricing so exact prices are not possible.

Cabela's Sharps

Cimarron Billy Dixon

Cimarron Quigley

Cimarron 1885 High Wall

ARMALITE AR-50 RIFLE
Caliber: 50 BMG **Barrel:** 31". **Weight:** 33.2 lbs. **Length:** 59.5" **Stock:** Synthetic. **Sights:** None furnished. **Features:** A single-shot bolt-action rifle designed for long-range shooting. Available in left-hand model. Made in U.S.A. by Armalite.
Price: $3,359.00

BALLARD 1875 1 1/2 HUNTER RIFLE
Caliber: NA. **Barrel:** 26-30". **Weight:** NA **Length:** NA. **Stock:** Hand-selected classic American walnut. **Sights:** Blade front, Rocky Mountain rear. **Features:** Color case-hardened receiver, breechblock and lever. Many options available. Made in U.S.A. by Ballard Rifle & Cartridge Co.
Price: $3,250.00

BALLARD 1875 #3 GALLERY SINGLE SHOT RIFLE
Caliber: NA. **Barrel:** 24-28" octagonal with tulip. **Weight:** NA. **Length:** NA. **Stock:** Hand-selected classic American walnut. **Sights:** Blade front, Rocky Mountain rear. **Features:** Color case-hardened receiver, breechblock and lever. Many options available. Made in U.S.A. by Ballard Rifle & Cartridge Co.
Price: $3,300.00

BALLARD 1875 #4 PERFECTION RIFLE
Caliber: 22 LR, 32-40, 38-55, 40-65, 40-70, 45-70 Govt., 45-90, 45-110, 50-70, 50-90. **Barrel:** 30" or 32" octagon, standard or heavyweight. **Weight:** 10.5 lbs. (standard) or 11.75 lbs. (heavyweight bbl.). **Length:** NA. **Stock:** Smooth walnut. **Sights:** Blade front, Rocky Mountain rear. **Features:** Rifle or shotgun-style buttstock, straight grip action, single or double-set trigger, "S" or right lever, hand polished and lapped Badger barrel. Made in U.S.A. by Ballard Rifle & Cartridge Co.
Price: $3,950.00

BALLARD 1875 #7 LONG RANGE RIFLE
Caliber: 32-40, 38-55, 40-65, 40-70 SS, 45-70 Govt., 45-90, 45-110. **Barrel:** 32", 34" half-octagon. **Weight:** 11.75 lbs. **Length:** NA. **Stock:** Walnut; checkered pistol grip shotgun butt, ebony forend

cap. **Sights:** Globe front. **Features:** Designed for shooting up to 1000 yards. Standard or heavy barrel; single or double-set trigger; hard rubber or steel buttplate. Introduced 1999. Made in U.S.A. by Ballard Rifle & Cartridge Co.
Price: From $3,600.00

BALLARD 1875 #8 UNION HILL RIFLE
Caliber: 22 LR, 32-40, 38-55, 40-65 Win., 40-70 SS. **Barrel:** 30" half-octagon. **Weight:** About 10.5 lbs. **Length:** NA. **Stock:** Walnut; pistol grip butt with cheekpiece. **Sights:** Globe front. **Features:** Designed for 200-yard offhand shooting. Standard or heavy barrel; double-set triggers; full loop lever; hook Schuetzen buttplate. Introduced 1999. Made in U.S.A. by Ballard Rifle & Cartridge Co.
Price: From $4,175.00

BALLARD MODEL 1885 LOW WALL SINGLE SHOT RIFLE
Caliber: NA. **Barrel:** 24-28". **Weight:** NA. **Length:** NA. **Stock:** Hand-selected classic American walnut. **Sights:** Blade front, sporting rear. **Features:** Color case hardened receiver, breech block and lever. Many options available. Made in U.S.A. by Ballard Rifle & Cartridge Co.
Price: $3,300.00

BALLARD MODEL 1885 HIGH WALL STANDARD SPORTING SINGLE SHOT RIFLE
Caliber: 17 Bee, 22 Hornet, 218 Bee, 219 Don Wasp, 219 Zipper, 22 Hi-Power, 225 Win., 25-20 WCF, 25-35 WCF, 25 Krag, 7mmx57R, 30-30, 30-40 Krag, 303 British, 33 WCF, 348 WCF, 35 WCF, 35-30/30, 9.3x74R, 405 WCF, 50-110 WCF, 500 Express, 577 Express. **Barrel:** Lengths to 34". **Weight:** NA. **Stock:** Straight-grain American walnut. **Sights:** Buckhorn or flattop rear, blade front. **Features:** Faithful copy of original Model 1885 High Wall; parts interchange with original rifles; variety of options available. Introduced 2000. Made in U.S.A. by Ballard Rifle & Cartridge Co.
Price: $3,300.00

BALLARD MODEL 1885 HIGH WALL SPECIAL SPORTING SINGLE SHOT RIFLE
Caliber: NA. **Barrel:** 28-30" octagonal. **Weight:** NA. **Length:** NA. **Stock:** Hand-selected classic American walnut. **Sights:** Blade front,

Dakota Single Shot

H&R Ultra Varmint

H&R CR-45LC

H&R Ultra Hunter

sporting rear. **Features:** Color case hardened receiver, breech block and lever. Many options available. Made in U.S.A. by Ballard Rifle & Cartridge Co.
Price: $3,600.00

BARRETT MODEL 99 SINGLE SHOT RIFLE
Caliber: 50 BMG. **Barrel:** 33". **Weight:** 25 lbs. **Length:** 50.4" overall. **Stock:** Anodized aluminum with energy-absorbing recoil pad. **Sights:** None furnished; integral M1913 scope rail. **Features:** Bolt action; detachable bipod; match-grade barrel with high-efficiency muzzle brake. Introduced 1999. Made in U.S.A. by Barrett Firearms.
Price: From $4,000.00

BROWN MODEL 97D SINGLE SHOT RIFLE
Caliber: 17 Ackley Hornet through 45-70 Govt. **Barrel:** Up to 26", air gauged match grade. **Weight:** About 5 lbs., 11 oz. **Stock:** Sporter style with pistol grip, cheekpiece and Schnabel forend. **Sights:** None furnished; drilled and tapped for scope mounting. **Features:** Falling block action gives rigid barrel-receiver matting; polished blue/black finish. Hand-fitted action. Many options. Made in U.S.A. by E. Arthur Brown Co., Inc.
Price: From $999.00

BROWNING MODEL 1885 HIGH WALL SINGLE SHOT RIFLE
Caliber: 22-250 Rem., 30-06 Spfl., 270 Win., 7mm Rem. Mag., 454 Casull, 45-70 Govt. **Barrel:** 28". **Weight:** 8 lbs., 12 oz. **Length:** 43.5" overall. **Stock:** Walnut with straight grip, Schnabel forend. **Sights:** None furnished; drilled and tapped for scope mounting. **Features:** Replica of J.M. Browning's high-wall falling block rifle. Octagon barrel with recessed muzzle. Imported from Japan by Browning. Introduced 1985.
Price: $1,260.00

C. SHARPS ARMS MODEL 1875 TARGET & SPORTING RIFLE
Caliber: 38-55, 40-65, 40-70 Straight or Bottlenecks, 45-70, 45-90. Barrel: 30" heavy taperred round. **Weight:** 11 lbs. **Length:** NA. **Stock:** American walnut. **Sights:** Globe with post front sight. **Features:** Long Range Vernier tang sight with windage adjustments. Pistol grip stock with cheek rest; checkered steel buttplate. Introduced 1991. From C. Sharps Arms Co.
Price: Without sights. $1,325.00
Price: With blade front & Buckhorn rear barrel sights. $1,420.00
Price: With standard Tang & Globe w/post & ball front
    sights $1,615.00
Price: With deluxe vernier Tang & Globe w/spirit level &
    aperture sights $1,730.00
Price: With single set trigger, add $125.00

C. Sharps Arms 1875 Classic Sharps
Similar to New Model 1875 Sporting Rifle except 26", 28" or 30" full octagon barrel, crescent buttplate with toe plate, Hartford-style forend with cast German silver nose cap. Blade front sight, Rocky Mountain buckhorn rear. Weighs 10 lbs. Introduced 1987. From C. Sharps Arms Co.
Price: $1,670.00

C. SHARPS ARMS 1874 BRIDGEPORT SPORTING RIFLE
Caliber: 38-55 TO 50-3.25. **Barrel:** 26", 28", 30" tapered octagon. **Weight:** 10.5 lbs. **Length:** 47". **Stock:** American black walnut; shotgun butt with checkered steel buttplate; straight grip, heavy forend with Schnabel tip. **Sights:** Blade front, buckhorn rear. Drilled and tapped for tang sight. **Features:** Double-set triggers. Made in U.S.A. by C. Sharps Arms.
Price: $1,895.00

C. SHARPS ARMS NEW MODEL 1885 HIGHWALL RIFLE
Caliber: 22 LR, 22 Hornet, 219 Zipper, 25-35 WCF, 32-40 WCF, 38-55 WCF, 40-65, 30-40 Krag, 40-50 ST or BN, 40-70 ST or BN, 40-90 ST or BN, 45-70 Govt. 2-1/10" ST, 45-90 2-4/10" ST, 45-100 2-6/10" ST, 45-110 2-7/8" ST, 45-120 3-1/4" ST. **Barrel:** 26", 28", 30", tapered full octagon. **Weight:** About 9 lbs., 4 oz. **Length:** 47" overall. **Stock:** Oil-

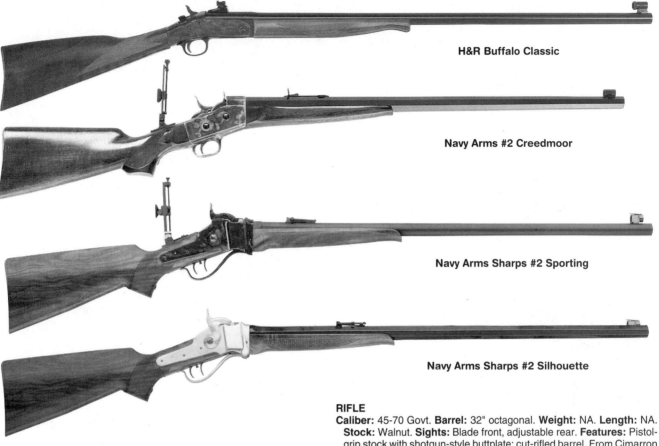

H&R Buffalo Classic

Navy Arms #2 Creedmoor

Navy Arms Sharps #2 Sporting

Navy Arms Sharps #2 Silhouette

finished American walnut; Schnabel-style forend. **Sights:** Blade front, buckhorn rear. Drilled and tapped for optional tang sight. **Features:** Single trigger; octagonal receiver top; checkered steel buttplate; color case-hardened receiver and buttplate, blued barrel. Many options available. Made in U.S.A. by C. Sharps Arms Co.
Price: From **$1,750.00**

C. SHARPS ARMS CUSTOM NEW MODEL 1877 LONG RANGE TARGET RIFLE
Caliber: 44-90 Sharps/Rem., 45-70 Govt., 45-90, 45-100 Sharps. **Barrel:** 32", 34" tapered round with Rigby flat. **Weight:** About 10 lbs. **Stock:** Walnut checkered. Pistol grip/forend. **Sights:** Classic long range with windage. **Features:** Custom production only.
Price: From **$7,250.00**

CABELA'S 1874 SHARPS SPORTING RIFLE
Caliber: 45-70. **Barrel:** 32", tapered octabon. **Weight:** 10.5 lbs. **Length:** 49.25" overall. **Stock:** Checkered walnut. **Sights:** Blade front, open adjustable rear. **Features:** Color case-hardened receiver and hammer, rest blued. Introduced 1995. Imported by Cabela's.
Price: 45-70 . . . . **$1,399.99**
Price: Quigley Sharps, 45-70 Govt., 45-120, 45-110 . . . . . **$1,699.99**

CIMARRON BILLY DIXON 1874 SHARPS SPORTING RIFLE
Caliber: 40-40, 50-90, 50-70, 45-70 Govt. **Barrel:** 32" tapered octagonal. **Weight:** NA. **Length:** NA. **Stock:** European walnut. **Sights:** Blade front, Creedmoor rear. **Features:** Color case-hardened frame, blued barrel. Hand-checkered grip and forend; hand-rubbed oil finish. Introduced 1999. Imported by Cimarron F.A. Co.
Price: From **$1,987.70**

CIMARRON QUIGLEY MODEL 1874 SHARPS SPORTING RIFLE
Caliber: 45-110, 50-70, 50-40, 45-70 Govt., 45-90, 45-120. **Barrel:** 34" octagonal. **Weight:** NA. **Length:** NA. **Stock:** Checkered walnut. **Sights:** Blade front, adjustable rear. **Features:** Blued finish; double-set triggers. From Cimarron F.A. Co.
Price: From **$2,156.70**

CIMARRON SILHOUETTE MODEL 1874 SHARPS SPORTING

RIFLE
Caliber: 45-70 Govt. **Barrel:** 32" octagonal. **Weight:** NA. **Length:** NA. **Stock:** Walnut. **Sights:** Blade front, adjustable rear. **Features:** Pistol-grip stock with shotgun-style buttplate; cut-rifled barrel. From Cimarron F.A. Co.
Price: **$1,597.70**

CIMARRON MODEL 1885 HIGH WALL RIFLE
Caliber: 38-55, 40-65, 45-70 Govt., 45-90, 45-120, 30-40 Krag, 348 Winchester. **Barrel:** 30" octagonal. **Weight:** NA. **Length:** NA. **Stock:** European walnut. **Sights:** Bead front, semi-buckhorn rear. **Features:** Replica of the Winchester 1885 High Wall rifle. Color case-hardened receiver and lever, blued barrel. Curved buttplate. Optional double-set triggers. Introduced 1999. Imported by Cimarron F.A. Co.
Price: From **$1,002.91**
Price: With pistol grip, from **$1,136.81**

DAKOTA MODEL 10 SINGLE SHOT RIFLE
Caliber: Most rimmed and rimless commercial calibers. **Barrel:** 23". **Weight:** 6 lbs. **Length:** 39.5" overall. **Stock:** Medium fancy grade walnut in classic style. Checkered grip and forend. **Sights:** None furnished. Drilled and tapped for scope mounting. **Features:** Falling block action with underlever. Top tang safety. Removable trigger plate for conversion to single set trigger. Introduced 1990. Made in U.S.A. by Dakota Arms.
Price: From **$4,695.00**
Price: Action only **$1,875.00**
Price: Magnum action only **$1,875.00**

EMF PREMIER 1874 SHARPS RIFLE
Caliber: 45/70, 45/110, 45/120. **Barrel:** 32", 34". **Weight:** 11-13 lbs. **Length:** 49", 51" overall. **Stock:** Pistol grip, European walnut. **Sights:** Blade front, adjustable rear. **Features:** Superb quality reproductions of the 1874 Sharps Sporting Rifles; casehardened locks; double-set triggers; blue barrels. Imported from Pedersoli by EMF.
Price: Business Rifle. **$1,199.90**
Price: "Quigley", Patchbox, heavy barrel **$1,799.90**
Price: Silhouette, pistol-grip **$1,499.90**
Price: Super Deluxe Hand Engraved **$3,500.00**

HARRINGTON & RICHARDSON ULTRA VARMINT/ULTRA HUNTER RIFLES
Caliber: 204 Ruger, 22 WMR, 22-250 Rem., 223 Rem., 243 Win., 25-06 Rem., 30-06. **Barrel:** 22" to 26" heavy taper. **Weight:** About 7.5

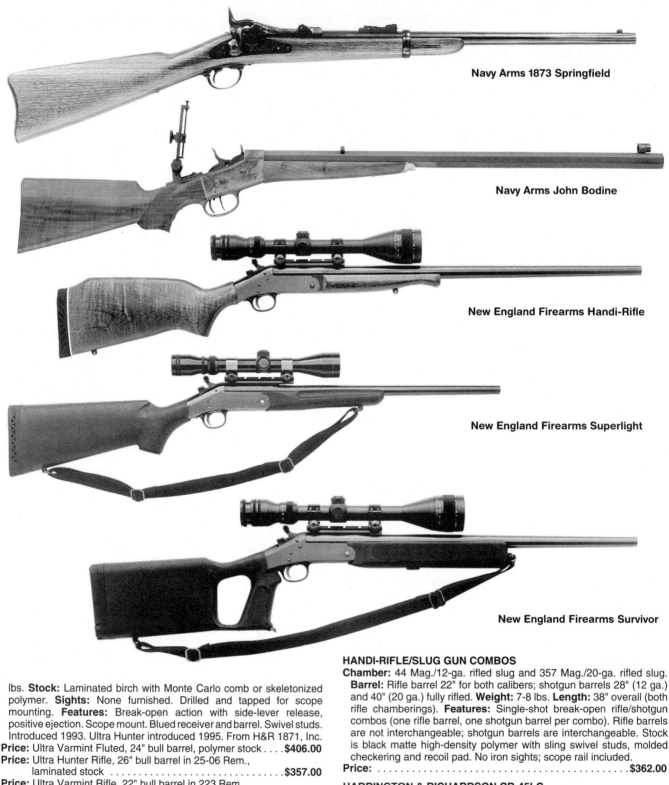

Navy Arms 1873 Springfield

Navy Arms John Bodine

New England Firearms Handi-Rifle

New England Firearms Superlight

New England Firearms Survivor

lbs. **Stock:** Laminated birch with Monte Carlo comb or skeletonized polymer. **Sights:** None furnished. Drilled and tapped for scope mounting. **Features:** Break-open action with side-lever release, positive ejection. Scope mount. Blued receiver and barrel. Swivel studs. Introduced 1993. Ultra Hunter introduced 1995. From H&R 1871, Inc.
Price: Ultra Varmint Fluted, 24" bull barrel, polymer stock **$406.00**
Price: Ultra Hunter Rifle, 26" bull barrel in 25-06 Rem.,
  laminated stock **$357.00**
Price: Ultra Varmint Rifle, 22" bull barrel in 223 Rem.,
  laminated stock **$357.00**

HARRINGTON & RICHARDSON/NEW ENGLAND FIREARMS STAINLESS ULTRA HUNTER WITH THUMBHOLE STOCK
Caliber: 45-70 Govt. **Barrel:** 24". **Weight:** 8 lbs. **Length:** 40". **Features:** Stainless steel barrel and receiver with scope mount rail, hammer extension, cinnamon laminate thumbhole stock.
Price: $439.00

HARRINGTON & RICHARDSON/NEW ENGLAND FIREARMS

HANDI-RIFLE/SLUG GUN COMBOS
Chamber: 44 Mag./12-ga. rifled slug and 357 Mag./20-ga. rifled slug. **Barrel:** Rifle barrel 22" for both calibers; shotgun barrels 28" (12 ga.) and 40" (20 ga.) fully rifled. **Weight:** 7-8 lbs. **Length:** 38" overall (both rifle chamberings). **Features:** Single-shot break-open rifle/shotgun combos (one rifle barrel, one shotgun barrel per combo). Rifle barrels are not interchangeable; shotgun barrels are interchangeable. Stock is black matte high-density polymer with sling swivel studs, molded checkering and recoil pad. No iron sights; scope rail included.
Price: **$362.00**

HARRINGTON & RICHARDSON CR-45LC
Caliber: 45 Colt. **Barrel:** 20". **Weight:** 6.25 lbs. **Length:** 34"overall. Features: Single-shot break-open carbine. Cut-checkered American black walnut with case-colored crescent steel buttplate, open sights, case-colored receiver.
Price: $407.00

HARRINGTON & RICHARDSON BUFFALO CLASSIC RIFLE
Caliber: 45-70 Govt. **Barrel:** 32" heavy. **Weight:** 8 lbs. **Length:** 46" overall. **Stock:** Cut-checkered American black walnut. **Sights:** Williams receiver sight; Lyman target front sight with 8 aperture inserts. **Features:**

Remington No. 1 Mid-Range

Rossi Single Shot

Rossi Matched Pairs

Ruger No. 1-B

Ruger K1-B-BBZ

Color case-hardened Handi-Rifle action with exposed hammer; color case-hardened crescent buttplate; 19th century checkering pattern. Introduced 1995. Made in U.S.A. by H&R 1871, Inc.
Price: Buffalo Classic Rifle **$449.00**

KRIEGHOFF HUBERTUS SINGLE-SHOT RIFLE
Caliber: 222, 243 Win., 270 Win., 308 Win., 30-06 Spfl., 5.6x50R Mag., 5.6x52R, 6x62R Freres, 6.5x57R, 6.5x65R, 7x57R, 7x65R, 8x57JRS, 8x75RS, 9.3x74R, 7mm Rem. Mag., 300 Win. Mag. **Barrel:** 23.5". **Weight:** 6.5 lbs. **Length:** 40.5. **Stock:** High-grade walnut. **Sights:** Blade front, open rear. **Features:** Break-open loading with manual cocking lever on top tang; takedown; extractor; Schnabel forearm; many options. Imported from Germany by Krieghoff International Inc.
Price: Hubertus single shot, from **$5,995.00**
Price: Hubertus, magnum calibers **$6,995.00**

MEACHAM HIGHWALL SILHOUETTE OR SCHUETZEN RIFLE
Caliber: any rimmed cartridge. **Barrel:** 26-34". **Weight:** 8-15 lbs. **Sights:** none. Tang drilled for Win. base, 3/8 dovetail slot front. **Stock:** Fancy eastern walnut with cheekpiece; ebony insert in forearm tip. **Features:** Exact copy of 1885 Winchester. With most Winchester factory options available, including double set triggers. Introduced 1994. Made in U.S.A. by Meacham T&H Inc.
Price: From **$4,999.00**

MERKEL K1 MODEL LIGHTWEIGHT STALKING RIFLE
Caliber: 243 Win., 270 Win., 7x57R, 308 Win., 30-06 Spfl., 7mm Rem. Mag., 300 Win. Mag., 9.3x74R. **Barrel:** 23.6". **Weight:** 5.6 lbs. unscoped. **Stock:** Satin-finished walnut, fluted and checkered; sling-swivel studs. **Sights:** None (scope base furnished). **Features:** Franz Jager single-shot break-open action, cocking/uncocking slide-type

safety, matte silver receiver, selectable trigger pull weights, integrated, quick detach 1" or 30mm optic mounts (optic not included). Imported from Germany by Merkel USA.
Price: Jagd Stutzen Carbine **$3,795.00**

MERKEL K-2 CUSTOM SINGLE-SHOT "WEIMAR" STALKING RIFLE
Caliber: 308 Win., 30-06 Spfl., 7mm Rem. Mag., 300 Win. Mag. **Features:** Franz Jager single-shot break-open action, cocking.uncocking slide safety, deep relief engraved hunting scenes on silvered receiver, octagin barrel, deluxe walnut stock. Includes front and reare adjustable iron sights, scope rings. Imported from Germany by Merkel USA.
Price: Jagd Stutzen Carbine **$15,595.00**

NAVY ARMS 1874 SHARPS "QUIGLEY" RIFLE
Caliber: .45-70 Govt. **Barrel:** 34" octagon. **Weight:** 10 lbs. **Length:** 50" overall. **Grips:** Walnut checkered at wrist and forend. **Sights:** High blade front, full buckhorn rear. **Features:** Color case-hardened receiver, trigger, military patchbox, hammer and lever. Double-set triggers, German silver gripcap. Reproduction of rifle from "Quigley Down Under" movie.
Price: Model SQR045 (20087) **$2,026.00**

NAVY ARMS 1874 SHARPS #2 CREEDMOOR RIFLE
Caliber: 45/70. **Barrel:** 30" tapered round. **Stock:** Walnut. **Sights:** Front globe, "soule" tang rear. **Features:** Nickel receiver and action. Lightweight sporting rifle.
Price: **$1,816.00**

Navy Arms Sharps Sporting Rifle
Same as the Navy Arms Sharps Plains Rifle except has pistol grip stock. Introduced 1997. Imported by Navy Arms.
Price: 45-70 Govt. only **$1,711.00**

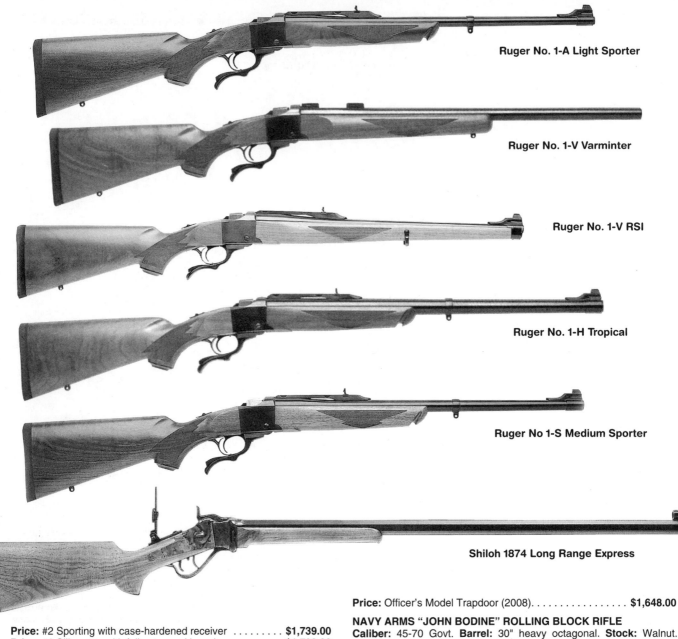

Ruger No. 1-A Light Sporter

Ruger No. 1-V Varminter

Ruger No. 1-V RSI

Ruger No. 1-H Tropical

Ruger No 1-S Medium Sporter

Shiloh 1874 Long Range Express

Price: #2 Sporting with case-hardened receiver $1,739.00
Price: #2 Silhouette with full octagonal barrel $1,739.00

NAVY ARMS 1885 HIGH WALL RIFLE
Caliber: 45-70 Govt.; others available on special order. **Barrel:** 28" round, 30" octagonal. **Weight:** 9.5 lbs. **Length:** 45.5" overall (30" barrel). **Stock:** Walnut. **Sights:** Blade front, vernier tang-mounted peep rear. **Features:** Replica of Winchester's High Wall designed by Browning. Color case-hardened receiver, blued barrel. Introduced 1998. Imported by Navy Arms.
Price: 28", round barrel, target sights $1,120.00
Price: 30" octagonal barrel, target sights $1,212.00

NAVY ARMS 1873 SPRINGFIELD CAVALRY CARBINE
Caliber: 45-70 Govt. **Barrel:** 22". **Weight:** 7 lbs. **Length:** 40.5" overall. **Stock:** Walnut. **Sights:** Blade front, military ladder rear. **Features:** Blued lockplate and barrel; color case-hardened breechblock; saddle ring with bar. Replica of 7th Cavalry gun. Officer's Model Trapdoor has single-set trigger, bone case-hardened buttplate, trigger guard and breechblock. Deluxe walnut stock hand-checkered at the wrist and forend. German silver forend cap and rod tip. Adjustable rear peep target sight. Authentic flip-up 'Beech' front target sight. Imported by Navy Arms.
Price: Model STC073 . . . . $1,261.00

Price: Officer's Model Trapdoor (2008). **$1,648.00**

NAVY ARMS "JOHN BODINE" ROLLING BLOCK RIFLE
Caliber: 45-70 Govt. **Barrel:** 30" heavy octagonal. **Stock:** Walnut. **Sights:** Globe front, "soule" tang rear. **Features:** Double-set triggers.
Price: **$1,928.00**
Price: (#2 with deluxe nickel finished receiver) **$1,928.00**

NAVY ARMS 1874 SHARPS NO. 3 LONG RANGE RIFLE
Caliber: 45-70 Govt. **Barrel:** 34" octagon. **Weight:** 10 lbs., 14 oz. **Length:** 51.2". **Stock:** Deluxe walnut. **Sights:** Globe target front and match grade rear tang. **Features:** Shotgun buttplate, German silver forend cap, color case hardened receiver. Imported by Navy Arms.
Price: **$2,432.00**

NEW ENGLAND FIREARMS HANDI-RIFLE
Caliber: 204 Ruger, 22 Hornet, 223 Rem., 243 Win., 30-30, 270 Win., 280 Rem., 7mm-08 Rem., 308 Win., 7.62x39 Russian, 30-06 Spfl., 357 Mag., 35 Whelen, 44 Mag., 45-70 Govt., 500 S&W. **Barrel:** From 20" to 26", blued or stainless. **Weight:** 5.5 to 7 lbs. **Stock:** Walnut-finished hardwood or synthetic. **Sights:** Vary by model, but most have ramp front, folding rear, or are drilled and tapped for scope mount. **Features:** Break-open action with side-lever release. Swivel studs on all models. Blue finish. Introduced 1989. From H&R 1871, Inc.
Price: Various cartridges. **$292.00**
Price: 7.62x39 Russian, 35 Whelen, intr. 2006 . . . .**$292.00**
Price: Youth, 37" OAL, 11.75" LOP, 6.75 lbs. **$292.00**

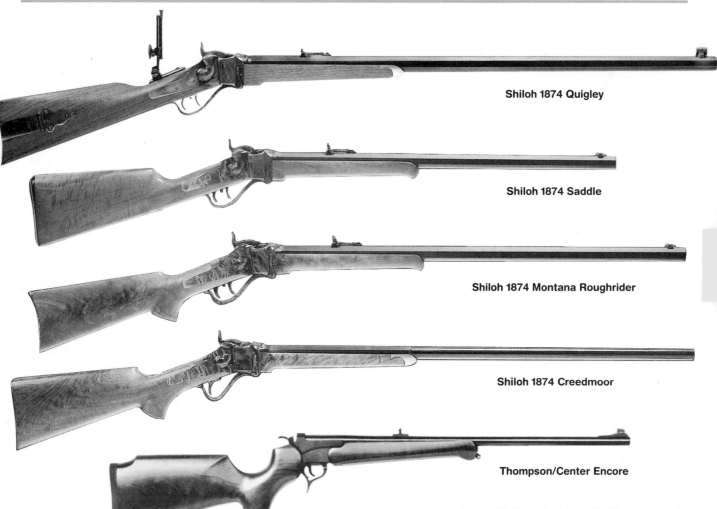

Shiloh 1874 Quigley

Shiloh 1874 Saddle

Shiloh 1874 Montana Roughrider

Shiloh 1874 Creedmoor

Thompson/Center Encore

Price: Handi-Rifle/Pardner combo, 20 ga. synthetic, intr. 2006 . . . . **$325.00**
Price: Handi-Rifle/Pardner Superlight, 20 ga., 5.5 lbs., intr. 2006 . . . . **$325.00**
Price: Synthetic **$302.00**
Price: Stainless **$364.00**
Price: Superlight, 20" barrel, 35.25" OAL, 5.5 lbs. **$302.00**

NEW ENGLAND FIREARMS SURVIVOR RIFLE
Caliber: 223 Rem., 308 Win., .410 shotgun, 45 Colt, single shot. **Barrel:** 20" to 22". **Weight:** 6 lbs. **Length:** 34.5" to 36" overall. **Stock:** Black polymer, thumbhole design. **Sights:** None furnished; scope mount provided. **Features:** Receiver drilled and tapped for scope mounting. Stock and forend have storage compartments for ammo, etc.; comes with integral swivels and black nylon sling. Introduced 1996. Made in U.S.A. by H&R 1871, Inc.
Price: Blue or nickel finish. **$304.00**

NEW ENGLAND FIREARMS SPORTSTER/VERSA PACK RIFLE
Caliber: 17M2, 17 HMR, 22 LR, 22 WMR, .410 bore single shot. **Barrel:** 20" to 22". **Weight:** 5.4 to 7 lbs. **Length:** 33" to 38.25" overall. **Stock:** Black polymer. **Sights:** Adjustable rear, ramp front. **Features:** Receiver drilled and tapped for scope mounting. Made in U.S.A. by H&R 1871, Inc.
Price: Sportster 17M2, 17 HMR **$193.00**
Price: Sportster **$161.00**
Price: Sportster Youth **$161.00**

REMINGTON MODEL SPR18 SINGLE SHOT RIFLES
Caliber: 223 Rem., 243 Win., 270 Win., .30-06 Spfl., 308 Win., 7.62x39mm. **Barrel:** 23.5" chrome-lined hammer forged, all steel receiver, spiral-cut fluting. **Weight:** 6.75 lbs. **Stock:** Walnut stock and fore-end, swivel studs. **Sights:** adjustable, with 11mm scope rail. **Length:** 39.75" overall. **Features:** Made in U.S. by Remington Arms Co., Inc.
Price: Blued/walnut (2008) **$277.00**
Price: Nickel/walnut (2008) **$326.00**

REMINGTON NO. 1 ROLLING BLOCK MID-RANGE SPORTER
Caliber: 45-70 Govt. **Barrel:** 30" round. **Weight:** 8.75 lbs. **Length:** 46.5" overall. **Stock:** American walnut with checkered pistol grip and forend. **Sights:** Beaded blade front, adjustable center-notch buckhorn rear. **Features:** Recreation of the original. Polished blue metal finish. Many options available. Introduced 1998. Made in U.S.A. by Remington.
Price: **$2,927.00**
Price: Silhouette model with single-set trigger, heavy barrel **$3,366.00**

ROSSI SINGLE-SHOT RIFLES
Caliber: 17, 223 Rem., 243 Win., 270 Win., .30-06, 308 Win., 7.62x39, 22-250. **Barrel:** 22" (Youth), 23". **Weight:** 6.25-7 lbs. **Stocks:** Wood, Black Synthetic (Youth). **Sights:** Adjustable sights, drilled and tapped for scope. **Features:** Single-shot break open, 13 models available, positive ejection, internal transfer bar mechanism, manual external safety, trigger block system, Taurus Security System, Matte blue finish, youth models available.
Price: **$238.00**

ROSSI MATCHED PAIRS
Gauge/Caliber: 12, 20, .410, 22 Mag, 22 LR, 17 HMR, 223 Rem, 243 Win., 270 Win., .30-06, 308Win., .50 (black powder). **Barrel:** 23", 28". **Weight:** 5-6.3 lbs. **Stocks:** Wood or black synthetic. **Sights:** Bead front on shotgun barrel, fully adjustable front and rear on rifle barrel, drilled and tapped for scope, fully adjustable fiber optic sights (black powder). **Features:** Single-shot break open, 27 models available, internal transfer bar mechanism, manual external safety, blue finish, trigger block system, Taurus Security System, youth models available.
Price: Rimfire/Shotgun, from. **$178.00**

Thompson/Center Encore "Katahdin"

Thompson/Center Contender

Traditions 1874 Sharps Deluxe

Traditions 1874 Sharps Sporting Deluxe

Uberti 1885 High-Wall Single Shot

Price: Centerfire/Shotgun **$299.00**
Price: Black Powder Matched Pair, from **$262.00**

RUGER NO. 1-B SINGLE SHOT
Caliber: 223 Rem., 204 Ruger, 25-06 Rem., 270 Win., 30-06 Spfl., 7mm Rem. Mag., 300 Win. Mag., 308 Win. **Barrel:** 26" round tapered with quarter-rib; with Ruger 1" rings. **Weight:** 8.25 lbs. **Length:** 42.25" overall. **Stock:** Walnut, two-piece, checkered pistol grip and semi-beavertail forend. **Sights:** None, 1" scope rings supplied for integral mounts. **Features:** Under-lever, hammerless falling block design has auto ejector, top tang safety.
Price: 1-B $1,093.00
Price: K1-B-BBZ stainless steel, laminated stock 25-06 Rem.,
    7mm Rem. Mag., 270, 300 Win. Mag., 243 Win.,
    30-06 . . . . $1,186.00

RUGER NO. 1-A LIGHT SPORTER
Caliber: 243 Win., 270 Win., 7x57, 30-06, 300 Ruger Compact Magnum. **Weight:** 7.25 lbs. Similar to the No. 1-B Standard Rifle except has lightweight 22" barrel, Alexander Henry-style forend, adjustable folding leaf rear sight on quarter-rib, dovetailed ramp front with gold bead.
Price: No. 1A. $1,147.00

Ruger No. 1-V Varminter
Similar to the No. 1-B Standard Rifle except has 24" heavy barrel. Semi-beavertail forend, barrel ribbed for target scope block, with 1" Ruger scope rings. Calibers 204 Ruger (26" barrel), 22-250 Rem., 223

Rem., 25-06 Rem. Weight about 9 lbs.
Price: No. 1-V $1,147.00

Ruger No. 1 RSI International
Similar to the No. 1-B Standard Rifle except has lightweight 20" barrel, full-length International-style forend with loop sling swivel, adjustable folding leaf rear sight on quarter-rib, ramp front with gold bead. Calibers 30-06 Spfl., 270 and 7x57. Weight is about 7.25 lbs.
Price: No. 1 RSI $1,186.00

Ruger No. 1-H Tropical Rifle
Similar to the No. 1-B Standard Rifle except has Alexander Henry forend, adjustable folding leaf rear sight on quarter-rib, ramp front with dovetail gold bead, 24" heavy barrel. Calibers 375 H&H, 416 Rigby, 458 Lott, 405 Win., 450/400 Nitro Express 3" (weighs about 9 lbs.), 416 Ruger.
Price: No. 1H $1,147.00

Ruger No. 1-S Medium Sporter
Similar to the No. 1-B Standard Rifle except has Alexander Henry-style forend, adjustable folding leaf rear sight on quarter-rib, ramp front sight base and dovetail-type gold bead front sight. Calibers include 9.3x74R, 45-70 Govt. with 22" barrel, 338 Ruger Compact Magnum, 375 Ruger, 460 S&W Magnum, 480 Ruger/475 Linebaugh. Weighs about 7.25 lbs.
Price: No. 1-S $1,147.00
Price: K1-S-BBZ, S/S, 45-70 Govt. $1,186.00

Designs for sporting and utility purposes worldwide.

Beretta Express SSO

Beretta Model 455 SxS

CZ 584 Solo

Hoenig Rotary Round Action Double Rifle

SHILOH RIFLE CO. SHARPS 1874 LONG RANGE EXPRESS
Caliber: 40-50 BN, 40-70 BN, 40-90 BN, 45-70 Govt. ST, 45-90 ST, 45-110 ST, 50-70 ST, 50-90 ST, 38-55, 40-70 ST, 40-90 ST. **Barrel:** 34" tapered octagon. **Weight:** 10.5 lbs. **Length:** 51" overall. **Stock:** Oil-finished walnut (upgrades available) with pistol grip, shotgun-style butt, traditional cheek rest, Schnabel forend. **Sights:** Customer's choice. **Features:** Re-creation of the Model 1874 Sharps rifle. Double-set triggers. Made in U.S.A. by Shiloh Rifle Mfg. Co.
Price: **$1,902.00**
Price: Sporter Rifle No. 1 (similar to above except with 30" barrel, blade front, buckhorn rear sight) **$1,902.00**
Price: Sporter Rifle No. 3 (similar to No. 1 except straight-grip stock, standard wood) **$1,800.00**

SHILOH RIFLE CO. SHARPS 1874 QUIGLEY
Caliber: 45-70 Govt., 45-110. **Barrel:** 34" heavy octagon. **Stock:** Military-style with patch box, standard grade American walnut. **Sights:** Semi buckhorn, interchangeable front and midrange vernier tang sight with windage. **Features:** Gold inlay initials, pewter tip, Hartford collar, case color or antique finish. Double-set triggers.
Price: **$3,298.00**

SHILOH RIFLE CO. SHARPS 1874 SADDLE RIFLE
Caliber: 38-55, 40-50 BN, 40-65 Win., 40-70 BN, 40-70 ST, 40-90 BN, 40-90 ST, 44-77 BN, 44-90 BN, 45-70 Govt. ST, 45-90 ST, 45-100 ST, 45-110 ST, 45-120 ST, 50-70 ST, 50-90 ST. **Barrel:** 26" full or half octagon. **Stock:** Semi fancy American walnut. Shotgun style with cheekrest. **Sights:** Buckhorn and blade. **Features:** Double-set trigger, numerous custom features can be added.
Price: **$1,852.00**

SHILOH RIFLE CO. SHARPS 1874 MONTANA ROUGHRIDER
Caliber: 38-55, 40-50 BN, 40-65 Win., 40-70 BN, 40-70 ST, 40-90 BN, 40-90 ST, 44-77 BN, 44-90 BN, 45-70 Govt., 45-90 ST, 45-100 ST, 45-110 ST, 45-120 ST, 50-70 ST, 50-90 ST. **Barrel:** 30" full or half octagon. **Stock:** American walnut in shotgun or military style. **Sights:** Buckhorn and blade. **Features:** Double-set triggers, numerous custom features can be added.
Price: **$1,902.00**

SHILOH RIFLE CO. SHARPS CREEDMOOR TARGET
Caliber: 38-55, 40-50 BN, 40-65 Win., 40-70 BN, 40-70 ST, 40-90 BN, 40-90 ST, 44-77 BN, 44-90 BN, 45-70 Govt. ST, 45-90 ST, 45-100 ST, 45-110 ST, 45-120 ST, 50-70 ST, 50-90 ST. **Barrel:** 32", half round-half octagon. **Stock:** Extra fancy American walnut. Shotgun style with pistol grip. **Sights:** Customer's choice. **Features:** Single trigger, AA finish on stock, polished barrel and screws, pewter tip.
Price: **$2,743.00**

THOMPSON/CENTER ENCORE RIFLE
Caliber: 22-250 Rem., 223 Rem., 243 Win., 204 Ruger, 6.8 Rem. Spec., 25-06 Rem., 270 Win., 7mm-08 Rem., 308 Win., 30-06 Spfl., 7mm Rem. Mag., 300 Win. Mag. **Barrel:** 24", 26". **Weight:** 6 lbs., 12 oz. (24" barrel). **Length:** 38.5" (24" barrel). **Stock:** American walnut. Monte Carlo style; Schnabel forend or black composite. **Sights:** Ramp-style white bead front, fully adjustable leaf-type rear. **Features:** Interchangeable barrels; action opens by squeezing trigger guard; drilled and tapped for T/C scope mounts; polished blue finish. Introduced 1996. Made in U.S.A. by Thompson/Center Arms.
Price: . . . .**$604.00 to $663.00**
Price: Extra barrels **$277.00**

Thompson/Center Stainless Encore Rifle
Similar to blued Encore except stainless steel with blued sights, black composite stock and forend. Available in 22-250 Rem., 223 Rem., 7mm-08 Rem., 30-06 Spfl., 308 Win. Introduced 1999. Made in U.S.A. by Thompson/Center Arms.
Price: . . . .**$680.00 to $738.00**

THOMPSON/CENTER ENCORE "KATAHDIN" CARBINE
Caliber: 45-70 Govt., 450 Marlin. **Barrel:** 18" with muzzle tamer. **Stock:** Composite.
Price: **$619.00**

Thompson/Center G2 Contender Rifle
Similar to the G2 Contender pistol, but in a compact rifle format.

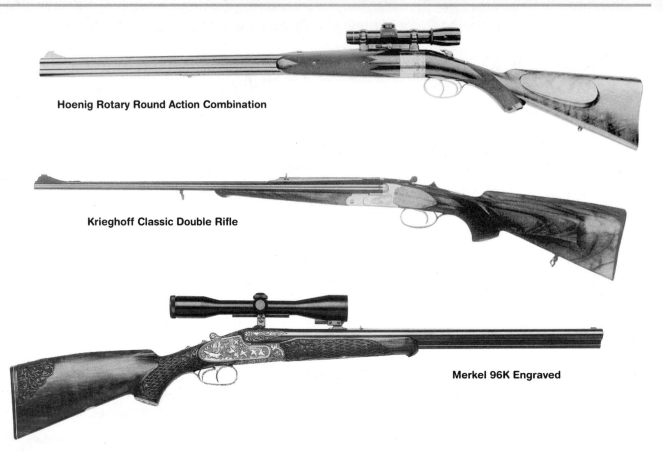

Hoenig Rotary Round Action Combination

Krieghoff Classic Double Rifle

Merkel 96K Engraved

Weighs 5.5 lbs. Features interchangeable 23" barrels, chambered for 17 HMR, 22 LR, 223 Rem., 30/30 Win. and 45/70 Govt.; plus a 45 cal. muzzleloading barrel. All of the 16.25" and 21" barrels made for the old-style Contender will fit. Introduced 2003. Made in U.S.A. by Thompson/Center Arms.
Price: . . . .**$622.00 to $637.00**

TRADITIONS 1874 SHARPS DELUXE RIFLE
Caliber: 45-70 Govt. **Barrel:** 32" octagonal; 1:18" twist. **Weight:** 11.67 lbs. **Length:** 48.8" overall. **Stock:** Checkered walnut with German silver nose cap and steel buttplate. **Sights:** Globe front, adjustable Creedmore rear with 12 inserts. **Features:** Color case-hardened receiver; double-set triggers. Introduced 2001. Imported from Pedersoli by Traditions.
Price: **$1,545.00**

Traditions 1874 Sharps Sporting Deluxe Rifle
Similar to Sharps Deluxe but custom silver engraved receiver, European walnut stock and forend, satin finish, set trigger, fully adjustable.
Price: **$2,796.00**

Traditions 1874 Sharps Standard Rifle
Similar to 1874 Sharps Deluxe except has blade front and adjustable buckhorn-style rear sight. Weighs 10.67 pounds. Introduced 2001. Imported from Pedersoli by Traditions.
Price: **$1,324.00**

TRADITIONS ROLLING BLOCK SPORTING RIFLE
Caliber: 45-70 Govt. **Barrel:** 30" octagonal; 1:18" twist. **Weight:** 11.67 lbs. **Length:** 46.7" overall. **Stock:** Walnut. **Sights:** Blade front, adjustable rear. **Features:** Antique silver, color case-hardened receiver, drilled and tapped for tang/globe sights; brass buttplate and trigger guard. Introduced 2001. Imported from Pedersoli by Traditions.
Price: **$1,029.00**

UBERTI 1874 SHARPS SPORTING RIFLE
Caliber: 45-70 Govt. **Barrel:** 30", 32", 34" octagonal. **Weight:** 10.57

lbs. with 32" barrel. **Length:** 48.9" with 32" barrel. **Stock:** Walnut. **Sights:** Dovetail front, Vernier tang rear. **Features:** Cut checkering, case-colored finish on frame, buttplate, and lever. Imported by Stoeger Industries.
Price: Standard Sharps (2006), 30" barrel **$1,459.00**
Price: Special Sharps (2006) 32" barrel **$1,729.00**
Price: Deluxe Sharps (2006) 34" barrel **$2,749.00**
Price: Down Under Sharps (2006) 34" barrel **$2,249.00**
Price: Long Range Sharps (2006) 34" barrel **$2,279.00**
Price: Buffalo Hunters Sharps, 32" barrel **$2,219.00**
Price: Calvary Carbine Sharps, 22" barrel **$1,569.00**
Price: Sharps Extra Deluxe, 32" barrel (2009) **$4,199.00**
Price: Sharps Hunter, 28" barrel **$1,459.00**

UBERTI 1885 HIGH-WALL SINGLE-SHOT RIFLES
Caliber: 45-70 Govt., 45-90, 45-120 single shot. **Barrel:** 28" to 23". **Weight:** 9.3 to 9.9 lbs. **Length:** 44.5" to 47" overall. **Stock:** Walnut stock and forend. **Sights:** Blade front, fully adjustable open rear. **Features:** Based on Winchester High-Wall design by John Browning. Color case-hardened frame and lever, blued barrel and buttplate. Imported by Stoeger Industries.
Price: 1885 High-Wall, 28" round barrel **$969.00**
Price: 1885 High-Wall Sporting, 30" octagonal barrel **$1,029.00**
Price: 1885 High-Wall Special Sporting, 32" octagonal
barrel **$1,179.00**

Designs for hunting, utility and sporting purposes, including training for competition.

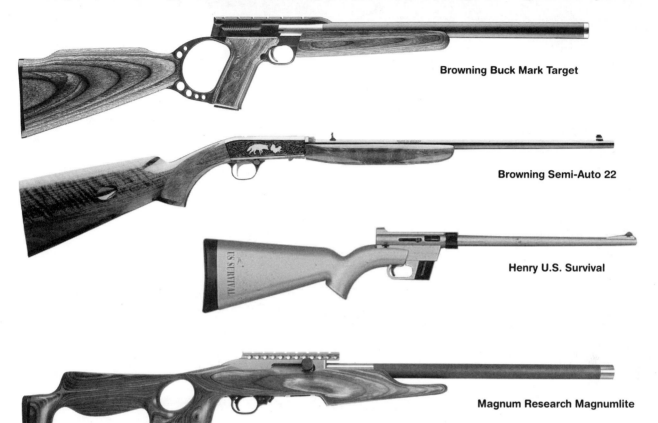

Browning Buck Mark Target

Browning Semi-Auto 22

Henry U.S. Survival

Magnum Research Magnumlite

BERETTA EXPRESS SSO O/U DOUBLE RIFLES
Caliber: 375 H&H, 458 Win. Mag., 9.3x74R. **Barrel:** 25.5". **Weight:** 11 lbs. **Stock:** European walnut with hand-checkered grip and forend. **Sights:** Blade front on ramp, open V-notch rear. **Features:** Sidelock action with color case-hardened receiver (gold inlays on SSO6 Gold). Ejectors, double triggers, recoil pad. Introduced 1990. Imported from Italy by Beretta U.S.A.
Price: SSO6 . . . . **$21,000.00**
Price: SSO6 Gold **$23,500.00**

BERETTA MODEL 455 SXS EXPRESS RIFLE
Caliber: 375 H&H, 458 Win. Mag., 470 NE, 500 NE 3", 416 Rigby. **Barrel:** 23.5" or 25.5". **Weight:** 11 lbs. **Stock:** European walnut with hand-checkered grip and forend. **Sights:** Blade front, folding leaf V-notch rear. **Features:** Sidelock action with easily removable sideplates; color case-hardened finish (455), custom big game or floral motif engraving (455EELL). Double triggers, recoil pad. Introduced 1990. Imported from Italy by Beretta U.S.A.
Price: Model 455 . . . . **$36,000.00**
Price: Model 455EELL **$47,000.00**

CZ 584 SOLO COMBINATION GUN
Caliber/Gauge: 7x57R; 12, 2-3/4" chamber. **Barrel:** 24.4". **Weight:** 7.37 lbs. **Length:** 45.25" overall. **Stock:** Circassian walnut. **Sights:** Blade front, open rear adjustable for windage. **Features:** Kersten-style double lump locking system; double-trigger Blitz-type mechanism with drop safety and adjustable set trigger for the rifle barrel; auto safety, dual extractors; receiver dovetailed for scope mounting. Imported from the Czech Republic by CZ-USA.
Price: **$851.00**

CZ 589 STOPPER OVER/UNDER GUN
Caliber: 458 Win. Magnum. **Barrels:** 21.7". **Weight:** 9.3 lbs. **Length:** 37.7" overall. **Stock:** Turkish walnut with sling swivels. **Sights:** Blade

front, fixed rear. **Features:** Kersten-style action; Blitz-type double trigger; hammer-forged, blued barrels; satin-nickel, engraved receiver. Introduced 2001. Imported from the Czech Republic by CZ USA.
Price: **$2,999.00**
Price: Fully engraved model **$3,999.00**

DAKOTA DOUBLE RIFLE
Caliber: 470 Nitro Express, 500 Nitro Express. **Barrel:** 25". **Stock:** Exhibition-grade walnut. **Sights:** Express-style. **Features:** Round action; selective ejectors; recoil pad; Americase. From Dakota Arms Inc.
Price: **$25,000.00**

GARBI EXPRESS DOUBLE RIFLE
Caliber: 7x65R, 9.3x74R, 375 H&H. **Barrel:** 24.75". **Weight:** 7.75 to 8.5 lbs. **Length:** 41.5" overall. **Stock:** Turkish walnut. **Sights:** Quarter-rib with express sight. **Features:** Side-by-side double; H&H-pattern sidelock ejector with reinforced action, chopper lump barrels of Boehler steel; double triggers; fine scroll and rosette engraving, or full coverage ornamental; coin-finished action. Introduced 1997. Imported from Spain by Wm. Larkin Moore.
Price: **$25,000.00**

HOENIG ROTARY ROUND ACTION DOUBLE RIFLE
Caliber: Most popular calibers from 225 Win. to 9.3x74R. **Barrel:** 22" to 26". **Stock:** English Walnut; to customer specs. **Sights:** Swivel hood front with button release (extra bead stored in trap door gripcap), express-style rear on quarter-rib adjustable for windage and elevation; scope mount. **Features:** Round action opens by rotating barrels, pulling forward. Inertia extractor system, rotary safety blocks strikers. Single lever quick-detachable scope mount. Simple takedown without removing forend. Introduced 1997. Made in U.S.A. by George Hoenig.
Price: **$19,980.00**

HOENIG ROTARY ROUND ACTION COMBINATION
Caliber: 28 ga. **Barrel:** 26". **Weight:** 7 lbs. **Stock:** English Walnut to customer specs. **Sights:** Front ramp with button release blades. Foldable aperture tang sight windage and elevation adjustable. Quarter-rib with scope mount. **Features:** Round action opens by rotating barrels, pulling forward. Inertia extractor; rotary safety blocks

Marlin Model 60

Marlin Model 70PSS Papoose

Marlin 795

Remington 552 BDL Speedmaster

Remington 597

strikers. Simple takedown without removing forend. Made in U.S.A. by George Hoenig.

Price: **$25,000.00**

KRIEGHOFF CLASSIC DOUBLE RIFLE

Caliber: 7x57R, 7x65R, 308 Win., 30-06 Spfl., 8x57 JRS, 8x75RS, 9.3x74R, 375NE, 500/416NE, 470NE, 500NE. **Barrel:** 23.5". **Weight:** 7.3 to 8 lbs; 10-11 lbs. Big 5. **Stock:** High grade European walnut. Standard model has conventional rounded cheekpiece, Bavaria model has Bavarian-style cheekpiece. **Sights:** Bead front with removable, adjustable wedge (375 H&H and below), standing leaf rear on quarter-rib. **Features:** Boxlock action; double triggers; short opening angle for fast loading; quiet extractors; sliding, self-adjusting wedge for secure bolting; Purdey-style barrel extension; horizontal firing pin placement. Many options available. Introduced 1997. Imported from Germany by Krieghoff International.

Price: With small Arabesque engraving **$8,950.00**
Price: With engraved sideplates **$12,300.00**
Price: For extra barrels **$5,450.00**
Price: Extra 20-ga., 28" shotshell barrels **$3,950.00**

Krieghoff Classic Big Five Double Rifle

Similar to the standard Classic except available in 375 Flanged Mag. N.E., 500/416 NE, 470 NE, 500 NE. Has hinged front trigger, non-removable muzzle wedge (models larger than 375 caliber), Universal Trigger System, Combi Cocking Device, steel trigger guard, specially weighted stock bolt for weight and balance. Many options available. Introduced 1997. Imported from Germany by Krieghoff International. Imperial Model introduced 2006.

Price: **$11,450.00**
Price: With engraved sideplates **$14,800.00**

LEBEAU-COURALLY EXPRESS RIFLE SXS

Caliber: 7x65R, 8x57JRS, 9.3x74R, 375 H&H, 470 N.E. **Barrel:** 24" to 26". **Weight:** 7.75 to 10.5 lbs. **Stock:** Fancy French walnut with cheekpiece. **Sights:** Bead on ramp front, standing left express rear on quarter-rib. **Features:** Holland & Holland-type sidelock with automatic ejectors; double triggers. Built to order only. Imported from Belgium by Wm. Larkin Moore.

Price: **$50,000.00**

MERKEL DRILLINGS

Caliber/Gauge: 12, 20, 3" chambers, 16, 2-3/4" chambers; 22 Hornet, 5.6x50R Mag., 5.6x52R, 222 Rem., 243 Win., 6.5x55, 6.5x57R, 7x57R, 7x65R, 308 Win., 30-06 Spfl., 8x57JRS, 9.3x74R, 375 H&H. **Barrel:** 25.6". **Weight:** 7.9 to 8.4 lbs. depending upon caliber. **Stock:** Oil-finished walnut with pistol grip; cheekpiece on 12-, 16-gauge. **Sights:** Blade front, fixed rear. **Features:** Double barrel locking lug with Greener cross bolt; scroll-engraved, case-hardened receiver; automatic trigger safety; Blitz action; double triggers. Imported from Germany by Merkel USA.

Price: Model 96K (manually cocked rifle system), from **$8,495.00**
Price: Model 96K engraved (hunting series on receiver) . . . **$9,795.00**

MERKEL BOXLOCK DOUBLE RIFLES

Caliber: 5.6x52R, 243 Winchester, 6.5x55, 6.5x57R, 7x57R, 7x65R, 308 Win., 30-06 Springfield, 8x57 IRS, 9.3x74R. **Barrel:** 23.6". **Weight:** 7.7 oz. **Length:** NA. **Stock:** Walnut, oil finished, pistol grip. **Sights:** Fixed 100 meter. **Features:** Anson & Deely boxlock action with cocking indicators, double triggers, engraved color case-hardened receiver. Introduced 1995. Imported from Germany by Merkel USA.

Price: Model 140-2, from **$11,995.00**
Price: Model 141 Small Frame SXS Rifle; built on smaller

Remington 597 FLX

Ruger 10/22 Deluxe Sporter

Ruger 10/22 Target

frame, chambered for 7mm Mauser, 30-06, or
9.3x74R **$8,195.00**
Price: Model 141 Engraved; fine hand-engraved hunting
scenes on silvered receiver **$9,495.00**

RIZZINI EXPRESS 90L DOUBLE RIFLE
Caliber: 30-06 Spfl., 7x65R, 9.3x74R. **Barrel:** 24". **Weight:** 7.5 lbs.
Length: 40" overall. **Stock:** Select European walnut with satin oil
finish; English-style cheekpiece. **Sights:** Ramp front, quarter-rib
with express sight. **Features:** Color case-hardened boxlock action;
automatic ejectors; single selective trigger; polished blue barrels. Extra
20 gauge shotgun barrels available. Imported for Italy by Wm. Larkin
Moore.
Price: With case **$3,850.00**

BROWNING BUCK MARK SEMI-AUTO RIFLES
Caliber: 22 LR, 10+1. Action: A rifle version of the Buck Mark Pistol;
straight blowback action; machined aluminum receiver with integral rail
scope mount; manual thumb safety. **Barrel:** Recessed crowns. **Stock:**
Stock and forearm with full pistol grip. **Features:** Action lock provided.
Introduced 2001. Four model name variations for 2006, as noted below.
Sights: FLD Target, FLD Carbon, and Target models have integrated
scope rails. Sporter has Truglo/Marble fiber optic sights. Imported from
Japan by Browning.
Price: FLD Target, 5.5 lbs., bull barrel, laminated stock **$659.00**
Price: Target, 5.4 lbs., blued bull barrel, wood stock **$639.00**
Price: Sporter, 4.4 lbs., blued sporter barrel w/sights **$639.00**

BROWNING SA-22 SEMI-AUTO 22 RIFLES
Caliber: 22 LR, 11+1. **Barrel:** 16.25". **Weight:** 5.2 lbs. **Length:** 37" overall.
Stock: Checkered select walnut with pistol grip and semi-beavertail
forend. **Sights:** Gold bead front, folding leaf rear. **Features:** Engraved
receiver with polished blue finish; cross-bolt safety; tubular magazine
in buttstock; easy takedown for carrying or storage. The Grade VI is
available with either grayed or blued receiver with extensive engraving
with gold-plated animals: right side pictures a fox and squirrel in a
woodland scene; left side shows a beagle chasing a rabbit. On top is a
portrait of the beagle. Stock and forend are of high-grade walnut with
a double-bordered cut checkering design. Introduced 1987. Imported
from Japan by Browning.
Price: Grade I, scroll-engraved blued receiver **$619.00**

Classic and modern models for sport and utility, including training.

Browning BL-22

Henry Lever-Action 22

Henry Golden Boy 22

Henry Pump-Action 22

Marlin Model 39A

Price: Grade VI BL, gold-plated engraved blued receiver . . **$1,329.00**

CZ 513 RIFLE
Caliber: 22 LR, 5-shot magazine. **Barrel:** 20.9". **Weight:** 5.7 lbs. **Length:** 39" overall. **Stock:** Beechwood. **Sights:** Tangent iron. **Features:** Simplified version of the CZ 452, no checkering on stock, simple non-adjustable trigger. Imported from the Czech Republic by CZ-USA.
Price: **$328.00**

HENRY U.S. SURVIVAL RIFLE AR-7 22
Caliber: 22 LR, 8-shot magazine. **Barrel:** 16" steel lined. **Weight:** 2.25 lbs. **Stock:** ABS plastic. **Sights:** Blade front on ramp, aperture rear. **Features:** Takedown design stores barrel and action in hollow stock. Light enough to float. Silver, black or camo finish. Comes with two magazines. Introduced 1998. From Henry Repeating Arms Co.
Price: H002S Silver finish **$245.00**
Price: H002B Black finish **$245.00**
Price: H002C Camo finish **$310.00**

KEL-TEC SU-22CA
Caliber: 22 LR. **Features:** Blowback action, cross bolt safety, adjustable front and rear sights with integral picatinny rail. Threaded muzzle, 26-round magazine.
Price: . . . . **Appx. $400.00**

MAGNUM RESEARCH MAGNUMLITE RIFLES
Caliber: 22 WMR, 17 HMR, 22 LR 17M2, 10-shot magazine. **Barrel:** 17" graphite. **Weight:** 4.45 lbs. **Length:** 35.5" overall. **Stock:** Hogue OverMolded synthetic or walnut. **Sights:** Integral scope base. **Features:** Magnum Lite graphite barrel, French grey anodizing, match bolt, target trigger. 22 LR/17M2 rifles use factory Ruger 10/22 magazines. 4-5 lbs. average trigger pull. Graphite carbon-fiber barrel weighs approx. 13.04 ounces in 22 LR, 1:16 twist. Introduced: 2007. From Magnum Research, Inc.

Price: MLR22H 22 LR. **$640.00**

MARLIN MODEL 60 AUTO RIFLE
Caliber: 22 LR, 14-shot tubular magazine. **Barrel:** 19" round tapered. **Weight:** About 5.5 lbs. **Length:** 37.5" overall. **Stock:** Press-checkered, walnut-finished Maine birch with Monte Carlo, full pistol grip; Mar-Shield finish. **Sights:** Ramp front, open adjustable rear. **Features:** Matted receiver is grooved for scope mount. Manual bolt hold-open; automatic last-shot bolt hold-open. Model 60C is similar except has hardwood Monte Carlo stock with Mossy Oak Break-Up camouflage pattern. From Marlin.
Price: **$179.00**
Price: With 4x scope **$186.00**
Price: Model 60C camo **$211.00**

Marlin Model 60SS Self-Loading Rifle
Same as the Model 60 except breech bolt, barrel and outer magazine tube are made of stainless steel; most other parts are either nickel-plated or coated to match the stainless finish. Monte Carlo stock is of black/gray Maine birch laminate, and has nickel-plated swivel studs, rubber buttpad. Introduced 1993. From Marlin.
Price: **$283.00**

MARLIN 70PSS PAPOOSE STAINLESS RIFLE
Caliber: 22 LR, 7-shot magazine. **Barrel:** 16.25" stainless steel, Micro-Groove rifling. **Weight:** 3.25 lbs. **Length:** 35.25" overall. **Stock:** Black fiberglass-filled synthetic with abbreviated forend, nickel-plated swivel studs, molded-in checkering. **Sights:** Ramp front with orange post, cut-away Wide Scan hood; adjustable open rear. Receiver grooved for scope mounting. **Features:** Takedown barrel; cross-bolt safety; manual bolt hold-open; last shot bolt hold-open; comes with padded carrying case. Introduced 1986. Made in U.S.A. by Marlin.
Price: **$284.00**

MARLIN MODEL 795 AUTO RIFLE
Caliber: 22. **Barrel:** 18" with 16-groove Micro-Groove rifling. Ramp front sight, adjustable rear. Receiver grooved for scope mount. **Stock:** Black synthetic, hardwood, synthetic thumbhole, solid pink, pink camo, or

Remington Model 572 BDL Feluxe Fieldmaster

Ruger Model 96/22

Taurus 62R

Mossy Oak New Break-up camo finish. **Features:** 10-round magazine, last shot hold-open feature. Introduced 1997. SS is similar to Model 795 except stainless steel barrel. Most other parts nickel-plated. Adjustable folding semi-buckhorn rear sights, ramp front high-visibility post and removable cutaway wide scan hood. Made in U.S.A. by Marlin Firearms Co.

Price: 795 . . . . **$157.00**
Price: 795SS **$227.00**

MOSSBERG MODEL 702 PLINKSTER AUTO RIFLE

Caliber: 22 LR, 10-round detachable magazine. **Barrel:** 18" free-floating. **Weight:** 4.1 to 4.6 lbs. **Sights:** Adjustable rifle. Receiver grooved for scope mount. **Stock:** Solid pink or pink marble finish synthetic. **Features:** Ergonomically placed magazine release and safety buttons, crossbolt safety, free gun lock. Made in U.S.A. by O.F. Mossberg & Sons, Inc.

Price: Pink Plinkster (2008) **$199.00**

REMINGTON MODEL 552 BDL DELUXE SPEEDMASTER RIFLE

Caliber: 22 S (20), L (17) or LR (15) tubular magazine. **Barrel:** 21" round tapered. **Weight:** 5.75 lbs. **Length:** 40" overall. **Stock:** Walnut.

Checkered grip and forend. **Sights:** Big game. **Features:** Positive cross-bolt safety, receiver grooved for tip-off mount.
Price: **$593.00**
Price: Smoothbore model (2007) **$633.00**

REMINGTON 597 AUTO RIFLE

Caliber: 22 LR, 10-shot clip; 22 WMR, 8-shot clip. **Barrel:** 20". **Weight:** 5.5 lbs. **Length:** 40" overall. **Stock:** Black synthetic. **Sights:** Big game. **Features:** Matte black finish, nickel-plated bolt. Receiver is grooved and drilled and tapped for scope mounts. Introduced 1997. Made in U.S.A. by Remington.

Price: Synthetic Scope Combo (2007) **$239.00**
Price: Model 597 Magnum **$492.00**
Price: Model 597 w/Mossy Oak Blaze Pink or Orange, 22 LR (2008) **$260.00**
Price: Model 597 Stainless TVP, 22 LR (2008) **$552.00**

Includes models for a variety of sports, utility and competitive shooting.

Anschutz 1710D

Browning T-Bolt

Browning T-Bolt Sporter
Left-Hand

Browning T-Bolt Composite
Sporter Left-Hand

Price: Model 597 TVP: Skeletonized laminated stock with
undercut forend, optics rail **$552.00**
Price: Model 597 FLX: Similar to Model 597, Blaze/Pink camo
but with FLX Digital Camo stock **$260.00**

RUGER 10/22 AUTOLOADING CARBINE
Caliber: 22 LR, 10-shot rotary magazine. **Barrel:** 18.5" round tapered.
Weight: 5 lbs. **Length:** 37.25" overall. **Stock:** American hardwood
with pistol grip and barrel band or synthetic. **Sights:** Brass bead
front, folding leaf rear adjustable for elevation. **Features:** Detachable
rotary magazine fits flush into stock, cross-bolt safety, receiver tapped
and grooved for scope blocks or tip-off mount. Scope base adaptor
furnished with each rifle.
Price: Model 10/22-RB (black matte) **$269.00**
Price: Model 10/22-CRR Compact RB (black matte), 2006 . . .**$307.00**

Ruger 10/22 Deluxe Sporter
Same as 10/22 Carbine except walnut stock with hand checkered pistol
grip and forend; straight buttplate, no barrel band, has sling swivels.
Price: Model 10/22-DSP **$355.00**

Ruger 10/22-T Target Rifle
Similar to the 10/22 except has 20" heavy, hammer-forged barrel with
tight chamber dimensions, improved trigger pull, laminated hardwood
stock dimensioned for optical sights. No iron sights supplied. Introduced 1996. Made in U.S.A. by Sturm, Ruger & Co.
Price: 10/22-T **$485.00**
Price: K10/22-T, stainless steel **$533.00**

Ruger K10/22-RPF All-Weather Rifle
Similar to the stainless K10/22/RB except has black composite stock of
thermoplastic polyester resin reinforced with fiberglass; checkered grip
and forend. Brushed satin, natural metal finish with clear hardcoat finish. Weighs 5 lbs., measures 37" overall. Introduced 1997. From Sturm,
Ruger & Co.
Price: **$318.00**

SAVAGE MODEL 64G AUTO RIFLE
Caliber: 22 LR, 10-shot magazine. **Barrel:** 20", 21". **Weight:** 5.5 lbs.
Length: 40", 41". **Stock:** Walnut-finished hardwood with Monte Carlo-
type comb, checkered grip and forend. **Sights:** Bead front, open

adjustable rear. Receiver grooved for scope mounting. **Features:**
Thumb-operated rotating safety. Blue finish. Side ejection, bolt hold-
open device. Introduced 1990. Made in Canada, from Savage Arms.
Price: From **$187.00**

THOMPSON/CENTER 22 LR CLASSIC RIFLE
Caliber: 22 LR, 8-shot magazine. **Barrel:** 22" match-grade. **Weight:** 5.5
pounds. **Length:** 39.5" overall. **Stock:** Satin-finished American walnut
with Monte Carlo-type comb and pistol gripcap, swivel studs. **Sights:**
Ramp-style front and fully adjustable rear, both with fiber optics.
Features: All-steel receiver drilled and tapped for scope mounting;
barrel threaded to receiver; thumb-operated safety; trigger guard safety
lock included. New 22 Classic Benchmark TGT target rifle variant has
18" heavy barrel, brown laminated target stock, blued with matte finish,
10-shot magazine and no sights; drilled and tapped.
Price: T/C 22 LR Classic (blue) **$396.00**
Price: T/C 22 LR Classic Benchmark **$505.00**

Cooper Model 57 Classic

Cooper Custom Classic

CZ 452 Lux

CZ 452 Varmint

CZ 452 American Classic

Marlin 917V

BROWNING BL-22 RIFLES

Action: Short-throw lever action, side ejection. Rack-and-pinion lever. Tubular magazines, with 15+1 capacity for 22 LR. **Barrel:** Recessed muzzle. **Stock:** Walnut, two-piece straight grip Western style. Trigger: Half-cock hammer safety; fold-down hammer. **Sights:** Bead post front, folding-leaf rear. Steel receiver grooved for scope mount. **Weight:** 5-5.4 lbs. **Length:** 36.75-40.75" overall. **Features:** Action lock provided. Introduced 1996. FLD Grade II Octagon has octagonal 24" barrel, silver nitride receiver with scroll engraving, gold-colored trigger. FLD Grade I has satin-nickel receiver, blued trigger, no stock checkering. FLD Grade II has satin-nickel receivers with scroll engraving; gold-colored trigger, cut checkering. Both introduced 2005. Grade I has blued receiver and trigger, no stock checkering. Grade II has gold-colored trigger, cut checkering, blued receiver with scroll engraving. Imported from Japan by Browning.

Price: BL-22 Grade I/II, from. **$529.00**
Price: BL-22 FLD Grade I/II, from **$569.00**
Price: BL-22 FLD, Grade II Octagon **$839.00**

HENRY LEVER-ACTION RIFLES

Caliber: 22 Long Rifle (15 shot), 22 Magnum (11 shots), 17 HMR (11 shots). **Barrel:** 18.25" round. **Weight:** 5.5 to 5.75 lbs. **Length:** 34" overall (22 LR). **Stock:** Walnut. **Sights:** Hooded blade front, open adjustable rear. **Features:** Polished blue finish; full-length tubular magazine; side ejection; receiver grooved for scope mounting. Introduced 1997. Made in U.S.A. by Henry Repeating Arms Co.

Price: H001 Carbine 22 LR. **$325.00**
Price: H001L Carbine 22 LR, Large Loop Lever. **$340.00**

Price: H001Y Youth model (33" overall, 11-round 22 LR) **$325.00**
Price: H001M 22 Magnum, 19.25" octagonal barrel, deluxe walnut stock **$475.00**
Price: H001V 17 HMR, 20" octagonal barrel, Williams Fire Sights **$549.95**

Henry Lever Octagon Frontier Model

Same as Lever rifles except chambered in 17 HMR, 22 Short/22 Long/22 LR, 22 Magnum; 20" octagonal barrel **Sights:** Marbles full adjustable semi-buckhorn rear, brass bead front. Weighs 6.25 lbs. Made in U.S.A. by Henry Repeating Arms Co.
Price: H001T Lever Octagon **$425.00**
Price: H001TM Lever Octagon 22 Magnum. **$539.95**

HENRY GOLDEN BOY 22 LEVER-ACTION RIFLE

Caliber: 17 HMR, 22 LR (16-shot), 22 Magnum. **Barrel:** 20" octagonal. **Weight:** 6.25 lbs. **Length:** 38" overall. **Stock:** American walnut. **Sights:** Blade front, open rear. **Features:** Brasslite receiver, brass buttplate, blued barrel and lever. Introduced 1998. Made in U.S.A. from Henry Repeating Arms Co.
Price: H004 22 LR **$515.00**
Price: H004M 22 Magnum **$595.00**
Price: H004V 17 HMR **$615.00**
Price: H004DD 22 LR Deluxe, engraved receiver **$1,200.00**

HENRY PUMP-ACTION 22 PUMP RIFLE

Caliber: 22 LR, 15-shot. **Barrel:** 18.25". **Weight:** 5.5 lbs. **Length:** NA. **Stock:** American walnut. **Sights:** Bead on ramp front, open adjustable rear. **Features:** Polished blue finish; receiver grooved for scope mount;

Marlin Model 915YN "Little Buckaroo"

Marlin 983T

grooved slide handle; two barrel bands. Introduced 1998. Made in U.S.A. from Henry Repeating Arms Co.

Price: H003T 22 LR $515.00
Price: H003TM 22 Magnum $595.00

MARLIN MODEL 39A GOLDEN LEVER-ACTION RIFLE

Caliber: 22, S (26), L (21), LR (19), tubular magazine. **Barrel:** 24" Micro-Groove. **Weight:** 6.5 lbs. **Length:** 40" overall. **Stock:** Checkered American black walnut; Mar-Shield finish. Swivel studs; rubber buttpad. **Sights:** Bead ramp front with detachable Wide-Scan hood, folding rear semi-buckhorn adjustable for windage and elevation. **Features:** Hammer block safety; rebounding hammer. Takedown action, receiver tapped for scope mount (supplied), offset hammer spur, gold-colored steel trigger. From Marlin Firearms.
Price: $593.00

MOSSBERG MODEL 464 RIMFIRE LEVER-ACTION RIFLE

Caliber: 22 LR. **Barrel:** 20" round blued. **Weight:** 5.6 lbs. **Length:** 35-3/4" overall. **Features:** Adjustable sights, straight grip stock, 124-shot tubular magazine, plain hardwood straight stock and forend.
Price: .... NA; apparently not yet in production

REMINGTON 572 BDL DELUXE FIELDMASTER PUMP RIFLE

Caliber: 22 S (20), L (17) or LR (15), tubular magazine. **Barrel:** 21" round tapered. **Weight:** 5.5 lbs. **Length:** 40" overall. **Stock:** Walnut with checkered pistol grip and slide handle. **Sights:** Big game. **Features:** Cross-bolt safety; removing inner magazine tube converts rifle to single shot; receiver grooved for tip-off scope mount.
Price: $607.00

RUGER MODEL 96 LEVER-ACTION RIFLE

Caliber: 22 WMR, 9 rounds; 17 HMR, 9 rounds. **Barrel:** 18.5". **Weight:** 5.25 lbs. **Length:** 37-3/8". **Stock:** Hardwood. **Sights:** Gold bead front, folding leaf rear. **Features:** Sliding cross button safety, visible cocking indicator; short-throw lever action. Introduced 1996. Made in U.S.A. by Sturm, Ruger & Co.
Price: 96/22M, 22 WMR or 17 HMR.....................$451.00

TAURUS MODEL 62 PUMP RIFLE

Caliber: 22 LR, 12- or 13-shot. **Barrel:** 16.5" or 23" round. **Weight:** 72 oz. to 80 oz. **Length:** 39" overall. **Stock:** Premium hardwood. **Sights:** Adjustable rear, bead blade front, optional tang. **Features:** Blue, case hardened or stainless, bolt-mounted safety, pump action, manual firing pin block, integral security lock system. Imported from Brazil by Taurus International.
Price: From...$299.00

Taurus Model 72 Pump Rifle

Same as Model 62 except chambered in 22 Magnum or 17 HMR; 16.5" barrel holds 10-12 shots, 23" barrel holds 11-13 shots. Weighs 72 oz. to 80 oz. Introduced 2001. Imported from Brazil by Taurus International.
Price: From...$329.00

ANSCHUTZ 1416D/1516D CLASSIC RIFLES

Caliber: 22 LR (1416D888), 22 WMR (1516D), 5-shot clip. **Barrel:** 22.5". **Weight:** 6 lbs. **Length:** 41" overall. **Stock:** European hardwood with walnut finish; classic style with straight comb, checkered pistol grip and forend. **Sights:** Hooded ramp front, folding leaf rear. **Features:** Uses Match 64 action. Adjustable single-stage trigger. Receiver grooved for scope mounting. Imported from Germany by Merkel USA.
Price: 1416D KL, 22 LR $899.00
Price: 1416D KL Classic left-hand $949.00
Price: 1516D KL, 22 WMR $919.00

ANSCHUTZ 1710D CUSTOM RIFLE

Caliber: 22 LR, 5-shot clip. **Barrel:** 24.25". **Weight:** 7-3/8 lbs. **Length:** 42.5" overall. **Stock:** Select European walnut. **Sights:** Hooded ramp front, folding leaf rear; drilled and tapped for scope mounting. **Features:** Match 54 action with adjustable single-stage trigger; roll-over Monte Carlo cheekpiece, slim forend with Schnabel tip, Wundhammer palm swell on pistol grip, rosewood gripcap with white diamond insert; skip-line checkering on grip and forend. Introduced 1988. Imported from Germany by Merkel USA.
Price: $1,649.00

BROWNING T-BOLT RIMFIRE RIFLE

Caliber: 22 LR, 10-round rotary box Double Helix magazine. **Barrel:** 22", free-floating, semi-match chamber, target muzzle crown. **Weight:** 4.8 lbs. **Length:** 40.1" overall. **Stock:** Walnut, satin finish, cut checkering, synthetic buttplate. **Sights:** None. **Features:** Straight-pull bolt-action, three-lever trigger adjustable for pull weight, dual action screws, sling swivel studs. Crossbolt lockup, enlarged bolt handle, one-piece dual extractor with integral spring and red cocking indicator band, gold-tone trigger. Top-tang, thumb-operated two-position safety, drilled and tapped for scope mounts. Varmint model has raised Monte Carlo comb, heavy barrel, wide forearm. Introduced 2006. Imported from Japan by Browning. Left-hand models added in 2009.
Price: Sporter $679.00
Price: Sporter, left-hand, from $689.00
Price: Sporter, 17 HMR, 22 Mag., intr. 2008...........$709.00
Price: Target/Varmint, intr 2007 ....$709.00
Price: Composite Target/Varmint, intr. 2008 ....$709.00
Price: Composite Target/Varmint left-hand, from $689.00
Price: Composite Sporter, 17 HMR, 22 Mag., intr. 2008 ....$709.00
Price: Composite Sporter left-hand, from $689.00

BUSHMASTER DCM-XR COMPETITION RIFLE

Caliber: 223 Rem, 10-shot mag. (2). **Barrel:** Heavy 1"-diameter free-floating match. **Weight:** 13.5 lbs. **Length:** 38.5" overall. **Features:** Fitted bolt, aperture rear sight that accepts four different inserts, choice of two front sight blades, two-stage competition trigger, weighted buttstock. Available in pre-and post-ban configurations.
Price: From... NA

BUSHMASTER PIT VIPER 3-GUN COMPETITION RIFLE

Caliber: 5.56/223 Rem, 20-shot mag. (2). **Barrel:** Lapped/crowned 18" A2-profile 1:8. **Weight:** 7.5 lbs. **Length:** 38" overall. **Features:** AR-style semi-auto rifle designed for three-gun competition. Hybrid chambering to accept mil-spec ammunition, titanium nitride-coated bolt, free-floating handguard with two 3" rails and two 4" rails, JR tactical sight.
Price: From... NA

COOPER MODEL 57-M BOLT-ACTION RIFLE

Caliber: 22 LR, 22 WMR, 17 HMR, 17 Mach 2. **Barrel:** 22" or 24" stainless steel or 4140 match grade. **Weight:** 6.5-7.5 lbs. **Stock:** AA-AAA select Claro walnut, 22 lpi hand checkering. **Sights:** None

Prices given are believed to be accurate at time of publication however, many factors affect retail pricing so exact prices are not possible.

Rossi Matched Pair

Ruger 77/17

Savage Mark I-G

Savage Mark II-BV

furnished. **Features:** Three rear locking lug, repeating bolt-action with 5-shot magazine. for 22 LR and 17M2; 4-shot magazine for 22 WMR and 17 HMR. Fully adjustable trigger. Left-hand models add $150 to base rifle price. 1/4"-group rimfire accuracy guarantee at 50 yards; 0.5"-group centerfire accuracy guarantee at 100 yards. Options include wood upgrades, case-color metalwork, barrel fluting, custom LOP, and many others.

Price: Classic **$1,400.00**
Price: LVT **$1,595.00**
Price: Custom Classic **$2,395.00**
Price: Western Classic **$3,295.00**
Price: TRP-3 (22 LR only, benchrest style) **$1,395.00**
Price: Jackson Squirrel Rifle **$1,595.00**
Price: Jackson Hunter (synthetic) **$1,495.00**

CZ 452 LUX BOLT-ACTION RIFLE
Caliber: 22 LR, 22 WMR, 5-shot detachable magazine. **Barrel:** 24.8". **Weight:** 6.6 lbs. **Length:** 42.63" overall. **Stock:** Walnut with checkered pistol grip. **Sights:** Hooded front, fully adjustable tangent rear. **Features:** All-steel construction, adjustable trigger, polished blue finish. Imported from the Czech Republic by CZ-USA.
Price: 22 LR, 22 WMR **$427.00**

CZ 452 Varmint Rifle
Similar to the Lux model except has heavy 20.8" barrel; stock has beavertail forend; weighs 7 lbs.; no sights furnished. Available in 22 LR, 22 WMR, 17HMR, 17M2. Imported from the Czech Republic by CZ-USA.
Price: From **$497.00**

CZ 452 American Bolt-Action Rifle
Similar to the CZ 452 M 2E Lux except has classic-style stock of Circassian walnut; 22.5" free-floating barrel with recessed target crown; receiver dovetail for scope mounting. No open sights furnished. Introduced 1999. Imported from the Czech Republic by CZ-USA.

Price: 22 LR, 22 WMR **$463.00**

DAVEY CRICKETT SINGLE SHOT RIFLE
Caliber: 22 LR, 22 WMR, single shot. **Barrel:** 16-1/8". **Weight:** About 2.5 lbs. **Length:** 30" overall. **Stock:** American walnut. **Sights:** Post on ramp front, peep rear adjustable for windage and elevation. **Features:** Drilled and tapped for scope mounting using special Chipmunk base ($13.95). Engraved model also available. Made in U.S.A. Introduced 1982. Formerly Chipmunk model. From Keystone Sporting Arms.
Price: From **$220.00**

HENRY ACU-BOLT RIFLE
Caliber: 22, 22 Mag., 17 HMR; single shot. **Barrel:** 20". **Weight:** 4.15 lbs. **Length:** 36". **Stock:** One-piece fiberglass synthetic. **Sights:** Scope mount and 4x scope included. **Features:** Stainless barrel and receiver, bolt-action.
Price: H007 22 LR, ... **$399.95**

HENRY "MINI" BOLT ACTION 22 RIFLE
Caliber: 22 LR, single shot youth gun. **Barrel:** 16" stainless, 8-groove rifling. **Weight:** 3.25 lbs. **Length:** 30", LOP 11.5". **Stock:** Synthetic, pistol grip, wraparound checkering and beavertail forearm. **Sights:** William Fire sights. **Features:** One-piece bolt configuration manually operated safety.
Price: H005 22 LR, black fiberglass stock **$249.95**
Price: H005S 22 LR, orange fiberglass stock **$249.95**

MARLIN MODEL 917 BOLT-ACTION RIFLES
Caliber: 17 HMR, 4- and 7-shot clip. **Barrel:** 22". **Weight:** 6 lbs., stainless 7 lbs. **Length:** 41". **Stock:** Checkered walnut Monte Carlo SS, laminated black/grey. **Sights:** No sights but receiver grooved. **Features:** Swivel studs, positive thumb safety, red cocking indicator, safety lock, SS 1" brushed aluminum scope rings.
Price: 917 . . . . **$240.00**
Price: 917VS Stainless steel barrel **$287.00**
Price: 917VT Laminated thumbhole stock (2008), from **$382.00**
Price: 917VST, stainless-finish metal, gray/black laminated
thumbhole stock **$426.00**

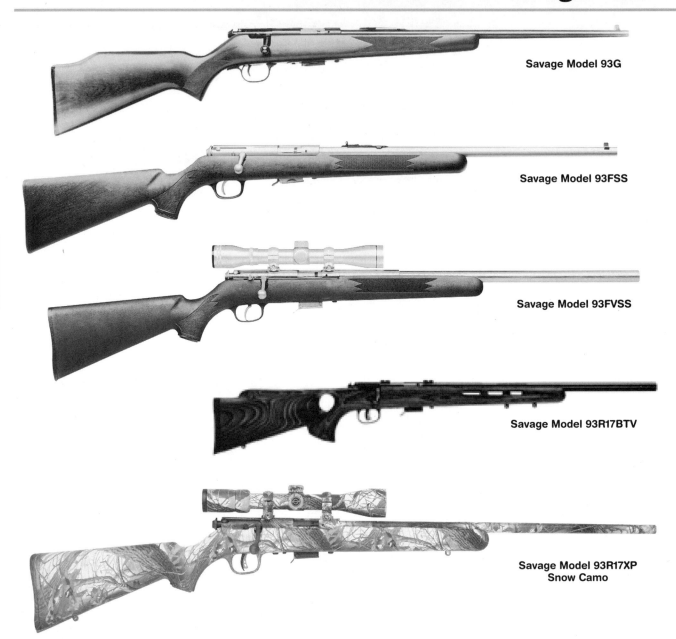

Savage Model 93G

Savage Model 93FSS

Savage Model 93FVSS

Savage Model 93R17BTV

Savage Model 93R17XP
Snow Camo

Price: 917VSF, fluted barrel **$397.00**
Price: 917VS-CF, carbon fiber-patterned stock **$358.00**

MARLIN MODEL 915YN "LITTLE BUCKAROO"
Caliber: 22 S, L, LR, single shot. **Barrel:** 16.25" Micro-Groove. **Weight:** 4.25 lbs. **Length:** 33.25" overall. **Stock:** One-piece walnut-finished, press-checkered Maine birch with Monte Carlo; Mar-Shield finish. **Sights:** Ramp front, adjustable open rear. **Features:** Beginner's rifle with thumb safety, easy-load feed throat, red cocking indicator. Receiver grooved for scope mounting. Introduced 1989.
Price: **$203.00**
Price: 915YS (stainless steel with fire sights) **$227.00**

MARLIN MODEL 982 BOLT-ACTION RIFLE
Caliber: 22 WMR. **Barrel:** 22" Micro-Groove. **Weight:** 6 lbs. **Length:** 41" overall. **Stock:** Walnut Monte Carlo genuine American black walnut with swivel studs; full pistol grip; classic cut checkering; rubber rifle butt pad; tough Mar-Shield finish. **Sights:** Adjustable semi-buckhorn folding rear, ramp front sight with brass bead and Wide-Scan front sight hood. **Features:** 7-shot clip, thumb safety, red cocking indicator, receiver grooved for scope mount. 982S has stainless steel front breech bolt, barrel, receiver and bolt knob. All other parts are either stainless steel or nickel-plated. Has black Monte Carlo stock of fiberglass-filled polycarbonate with molded-in checkering, nickel-plated swivel studs.

Introduced 2005. Made in U.S.A. by Marlin Firearms Co.
Price: 982VS (heavy stainless barrel, 7 lbs). **$309.00**
Price: 982VS-CF (carbon fiber stock). **$350.00**

Marlin Model 925M Bolt-Action Rifles
Similar to the Model 982 except chambered for 22 WMR. Has 7-shot clip magazine, 22" Micro-Groove barrel, checkered walnut-finished Maine birch stock. Introduced 1989.
Price: 925M. **$234.00**
Price: 925RM, black fiberglass-filled synthetic stock **$220.95**

MARLIN MODEL 983 BOLT-ACTION RIFLE
Caliber: 22 WMR. **Barrel:** 22"; 1:16" twist. **Weight:** 6 lbs. **Length:** 41" overall. **Stock:** Walnut Monte Carlo with sling swivel studs, rubber buttpad. **Sights:** Ramp front with brass bead, removable hood; adjustable semi-buckhorn folding rear. **Features:** Thumb safety, red cocking indicator, receiver grooved for scope mount. 983S is same as the Model 983 except front breech bolt, striker knob, trigger stud, cartridge lifter stud and outer magazine tube are of stainless steel; other parts are nickel-plated. Introduced 1993. 983T has a black Monte Carlo fiberglass-filled synthetic stock with sling swivel studs. Introduced 2001.Made in U.S.A. by Marlin Firearms Co.
Price: 983 . . . .**$308.00**
Price: 983S (stainless barrel) **$337.00**

Savage Model 30G Stevens "Favorite"

Savage Cub G Youth

Winchester Wildcat Bolt Action 22

Price: 983T (fiberglass stock) **$245.00**

MEACHAM LOW-WALL RIFLE
Caliber: Any rimfire cartridge. **Barrel:** 26-34". **Weight:** 7-15 lbs. **Sights:** none. Tang drilled for Win. base, 3/8" dovetail slot front. **Stock:** Fancy eastern walnut with cheekpiece; ebony insert in forearm tip. **Features;** Exact copy of 1885 Winchester. With most Winchester factory options available including double set triggers. Introduced 1994. Made in U.S.A. by Meacham T&H Inc.
Price: From **$4,999.00**

MOSSBERG MODEL 817 VARMINT BOLT-ACTION RIFLE
Caliber: 17 HMR, 5-round magazine. **Barrel:** 21"; free-floating bull barrel, recessed muzzle crown. **Weight:** 4.9 lbs. (black synthetic), 5.2 lbs. (wood). **Stock:** Black synthetic or wood; length of pull, 14.25". **Sights:** Factory-installed Weaver-style scope bases. **Features:** Blued or brushed chrome metal finishes, crossbolt safety, gun lock. Introduced 2008. Made in U.S.A. by O.F. Mossberg & Sons, Inc.
Price: Black synthetic stock, chrome finish (2008) **$279.00**

MOSSBERG MODEL 801/802 BOLT RIFLES
Caliber: 22 LR, 10-round detachable magazine. **Barrel:** 18" free-floating. **Weight:** 4.1 to 4.6 lbs. **Sights:** Adjustable rifle. Receiver grooved for scope mount. **Stock:** Solid pink or pink marble finish synthetic. **Features:** Ergonomically placed magazine release and safety buttons, crossbolt safety, free gun lock. 801 Half Pint has 12.25" length of pull, 16" barrel, and weighs 4 lbs. Hardwood stock; removable magazine plug. Made in U.S.A. by O.F. Mossberg & Sons, Inc.

Includes models for classic American and ISU target competition and other sporting and competitive shooting.

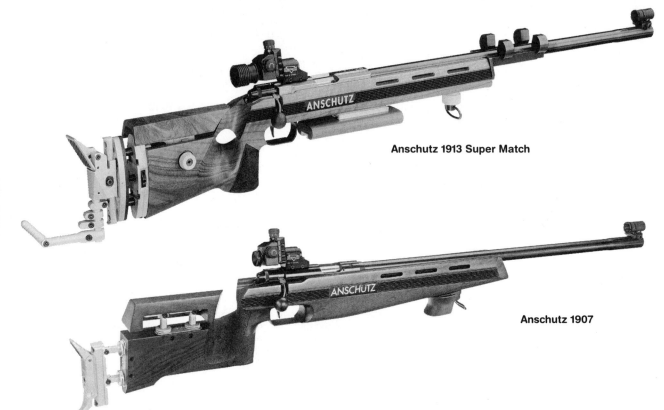

Anschutz 1913 Super Match

Anschutz 1907

Price: Pink Plinkster (2008) **$199.00**
Price: Half Pint (2008)................................**$199.00**

NEW ENGLAND FIREARMS SPORTSTER SINGLE-SHOT RIFLES
Caliber: 22 LR, 22 WMR, 17 HMR, single-shot. **Barrel:** 20". **Weight:** 5.5 lbs. **Length:** 36.25" overall. **Stock:** Black polymer. **Sights:** None furnished; scope mount included. **Features:** Break open, side-lever release; automatic ejection; recoil pad; sling swivel studs; trigger locking system. Introduced 2001. Made in U.S.A. by New England Firearms.
Price: **$149.00**
Price: Youth model (20" barrel, 33" overall, weighs 5-1/3 lbs.) **$149.00**
Price: Sportster 17 HMR **$180.00**

NEW ULTRA LIGHT ARMS 20RF BOLT-ACTION RIFLE
Caliber: 22 LR, single shot or repeater. **Barrel:** Douglas, length to order. **Weight:** 5.25 lbs. **Length:** Varies. **Stock:** Kevlar/graphite composite, variety of finishes. **Sights:** None furnished; drilled and tapped for scope mount. **Features:** Timney trigger, hand-lapped action, button-rifled barrel, hand-bedded action, recoil pad, sling-swivel studs, optional Jewell trigger. Made in U.S.A. by New Ultra Light Arms.
Price: 20 RF single shot **$1,300.00**
Price: 20 RF repeater **$1,350.00**

REMINGTON MODEL FIVE SERIES
Caliber: 17 HMR, 22 LR, 22 WMR. **Barrel:** 16.5" (Youth), 22". **Barrel:** Carbon-steel, hammer-forged barrel, 1:16 twist, polished blue finish. **Weight:** 5.5 to 6.75 lbs. **Stock:** Hardwood, laminate, European Walnut. **Length:** 35.25" to 40.75" overall. **Features:** Detachable, steel magazine box with five-round capacity; steel trigger guard; chrome-plated bolt body; single stage trigger with manual two-position safety; buttplate; sling swivel studs (excluding Youth version); adjustable big game-style rifle sights; and dovetail-style receiver. Introduced 2006. Model Five Youth (22 LR) has 12.4-inch length of pull, 16.5-inch barrel, single-shot adapter. Model Five Laminate has weather-resistant brown laminate stock. Model Five European Walnut has classic satin-finish stock. Made in U.S.A. by Remington.

Price: Model Five Youth, 22 LR (2008). **$237.00**
Price: Model Five Laminate, 17 HMR (2008), 22 LR, 22 WMR **$363.00**
Price: Model Five European Walnut, 22 LR (2008) **$279.00**

ROSSI MATCHED PAIR SINGLE-SHOT RIFLE/SHOTGUN
Caliber: 17 HMR, 22 LR, 22 Mag. **Barrel:** 18.5" or 23". **Weight:** 6 lbs. **Stock:** Hardwood (brown or black finish). **Sights:** Fully adjustable front and rear. **Features:** Break-open breech, transfer-bar manual safety, includes matched 410-, 20 or 12 gauge shotgun barrel with bead front sight. Introduced 2001. Imported by BrazTech/Taurus.
Price: S121280RS **$160.00**
Price: S121780RS **$200.00**
Price: S122280RS **$160.00**
Price: S201780RS **$200.00**

RUGER K77/22 VARMINT RIFLE
Caliber: 22 LR, 10-shot, 22 WMR, 9-shot detachable rotary magazine. **Barrel:** 24", heavy. **Weight:** 7.25 lbs. **Length:** 43.25" overall. **Stock:** Laminated hardwood with rubber buttpad, quick-detachable swivel studs. **Sights:** None furnished. Comes with Ruger 1" scope rings. **Features:** Stainless steel or blued finish. Three-position safety, dual extractors. Stock has wide, flat forend. Introduced 1993.
Price: K77/22VBZ, 22 LR.............................**$836.00**
Price: K77/22VMBZ, 22 WMR **$836.00**

RUGER 77/22 RIMFIRE BOLT-ACTION RIFLE
Caliber: 22 LR, 10-shot rotary magazine; 22 WMR, 9-shot rotary magazine. **Barrel:** 20". **Weight:** About 6 lbs. **Length:** 39.25" overall. **Stock:** Checkered American walnut, laminated hardwood, or synthetic stocks, stainless sling swivels. **Sights:** Plain barrel with 1" Ruger rings. **Features:** Mauser-type action uses Ruger's rotary magazine. Three-position safety, simplified bolt stop, patented bolt locking system. Uses the dual-screw barrel attachment system of the 10/22 rifle. Integral scope mounting system with 1" Ruger rings. Blued model introduced 1983. Stainless steel and blued with synthetic stock introduced 1989.
Price: 77/22R (no sights, rings, walnut stock). **$754.00**
Price: K77/22RP (stainless, no sights, rings, synthetic stock) .**$754.00**
Price: 77/22RM (22 WMR, blued, walnut stock) **$754.00**

Armalite AR-10(T)

Armalite AR-10 338 Federal

Bushmaster A2

Bushmaster DCM-XR

Price: K77/22RMP (22 WMR, stainless, synthetic stock) **$754.00**

RUGER 77/17 RIMFIRE BOLT-ACTION RIFLE
Caliber: 17 HMR (9-shot rotary magazine. **Barrel:** 22" to 24". **Weight:** 6.5-7.5 lbs. **Length:** 41.25-43.25" overall. **Stock:** Checkered American walnut, laminated hardwood; stainless sling swivels. **Sights:** Plain barrel with 1" Ruger rings. **Features:** Mauser-type action uses Ruger's rotary magazine. Three-position safety, simplified bolt stop, patented bolt locking system. Uses the dual-screw barrel attachment system of the 10/22 rifle. Integral scope mounting system with 1" Ruger rings. Introduced 2002.
Price: 77/17-RM (no sights, rings, walnut stock) **$754.00**
Price: K77/17-VMBBZ (Target grey bbl, black laminate stock) **$836.00**

SAVAGE MARK I-G BOLT-ACTION RIFLE
Caliber: 22 LR, single shot. **Barrel:** 20.75". **Weight:** 5.5 lbs. **Length:** 39.5" overall. **Stock:** Walnut-finished hardwood with Monte Carlo-type comb, checkered grip and forend. **Sights:** Bead front, open adjustable rear. Receiver grooved for scope mounting. **Features:** Thumb-operated rotating safety. Blue finish. Rifled or smooth bore. Introduced 1990. Made in Canada, from Savage Arms Inc.
Price: Mark I-G, rifled or smooth bore, right- or left-handed . . . **$226.00**
Price: Mark I-GY (Youth), 19" barrel, 37" overall, 5 lbs. **$226.00**

SAVAGE MARK II BOLT-ACTION RIFLE
Caliber: 22 LR, 10-shot magazine. **Barrel:** 20.5". **Weight:** 5.5 lbs. **Length:** 39.5" overall. **Stock:** Walnut-finished hardwood with Monte Carlo-type comb, checkered grip and forend. **Sights:** Bead front, open adjustable rear. Receiver grooved for scope mounting. **Features:** Thumb-operated rotating safety. Blue finish. Introduced 1990. Made in Canada, from Savage Arms, Inc.
Price: Mark II-BV. **$342.00**
Price: Mark II-GY (youth), 19" barrel, 37" overall, 5 lbs. **$226.00**
Price: Mark II-GL, left-hand **$226.00**
Price: Mark II-F, 17 HM2 . . . . **$202.00**
Price: Mark II XP Camo Scope Package (2008). **$400.00**
Price: Mark II Classic T, thumbhole walnut stock (2008) **$559.00**
Price: Mark II BTV: laminated thumbhole vent stock,
AccuTrigger, blued receiver and bull barrel **$393.00**
Price: Mark II BVTS: stainless barrel/receiver;
available in right- or left-hand (BTVLS) configuration
. . . . **$393.00** (standard); **$441.00** (left hand)

Savage Mark II-FSS Stainless Rifle
Similar to the Mark II except has stainless steel barreled action and black synthetic stock with positive checkering, swivel studs, and 20.75" free-floating and button-rifled barrel with detachable magazine. Weighs 5.5 lbs. Introduced 1997. Imported from Canada by Savage Arms, Inc.
Price: **$273.00**

SAVAGE MODEL 93G MAGNUM BOLT-ACTION RIFLE
Caliber: 22 WMR, 5-shot magazine. **Barrel:** 20.75". **Weight:** 5.75 lbs. **Length:** 39.5" overall. **Stock:** Walnut-finished hardwood with Monte Carlo-type comb, checkered grip and forend. **Sights:** Bead front, adjustable open rear. Receiver grooved for scope mount. **Features:** Thumb-operated rotary safety. Blue finish. Introduced 1994. Made in

Colt Match Target HBAR

Colt Match Target HBAR II

Colt Accurized

Ed Brown Marine Sniper

Canada, from Savage Arms.
Price: Model 93G $260.00
Price: Model 93F (as above with black graphite/fiberglass
    stock) $241.00
Price: Model 93 Classic, American walnut stock (2008).....$566.00
Price: Model 93 Classic T, American walnut thumbhole stock
    (2008) $604.00

Savage Model 93FSS Magnum Rifle
Similar to Model 93G except stainless steel barreled action and black synthetic stock with positive checkering. Weighs 5.5 lbs. Introduced 1997. Imported from Canada by Savage Arms, Inc.
Price: $306.00

Savage Model 93FVSS Magnum Rifle
Similar to Model 93FSS Magnum except 21" heavy barrel with recessed target-style crown, satin-finished stainless barreled action, black graphite/fiberglass stock. Drilled and tapped for scope mounting; comes with Weaver-style bases. Introduced 1998. Imported from Canada by Savage Arms, Inc.
Price: $347.00

Savage Model 93R17 Bolt-Action Rifles
Similar to Model 93G Magnum but chambered in 17 HMR. Features include standard synthetic, hardwood or walnut stock or thumbhole stock with cheekpiece, 21" or 22" barrel, no sights, detachable box magazine.
Price: Model 93R17BTV: Laminted ventilated thumbhole
    stock, blued barrel/receiver **$393.00**
Price: Model 93R17BV: Standard brown laminate stock,

heavy barrel **$342.00**
Price: Model 93R17GV: Checkered hardwood stock **$278.00**
Price: Model 93R17GLV: Left-hand configuration **$278.00**
Price: Model 93R17 Classic T: Checkered walnut thumbhole
    stock with unvented forend, blued barrel/receiver **$559.00**
Price: Model 93R17 Classic: Standard walnut stock **$559.00**
Price: Model 93R17BTVS: Laminated thumbhole vent stock,
    stainless steel barrel and receiver **$441.00**
Price: Model 93R17BLTVS: Left-hand **$441.00**
Price: Model 93R17BVSS: Similar to Model 93R17BTVS but
    with gray laminated non-thumbhole stock **$411.00**
Price: Model 93R17FVS: Black synthetic stock, AccuTrigger,
    blued or stainless heavy barrel **$347.00**

SAVAGE MODEL 30G STEVENS "FAVORITE"
Caliber: 22 LR, 22 WMR Model 30GM, 17 HMR Model 30R17. **Barrel:** 21". **Weight:** 4.25 lbs. **Length:** 36.75". **Stock:** Walnut, straight grip, Schnabel forend. **Sights:** Adjustable rear, bead post front. **Features:** Lever action falling block, inertia firing pin system, Model 30G half octagonal barrel, Model 30GM full octagonal barrel.
Price: Model 30G **$344.00**
Price: Model 30 Takedown **$360.00**

SAVAGE CUB T MINI YOUTH
Caliber: 22 S, L, LR; 17 Mach 2. **Barrel:** 16". **Weight:** 3.5 lbs. **Length:** 33". **Stock:** Walnut finished hardwood thumbhole stock. **Sights:** Bead post, front; peep, rear. **Features:** Mini single-shot bolt action, free-floating button-rifled barrel, blued finish. From Savage Arms.
Price: Cub T Thumbhole, walnut stained laminated **$266.00**
Price: Cub T Pink Thumbhole (2008) **$280.00**

WINCHESTER WILDCAT BOLT ACTION 22
Caliber: 22 S, L, LR; one 5-round and three 10-round magazines. **Barrel:** 21". **Weight:** 6.5 lbs. **Length:** 38-3/8". **Stock:** Checkered hardwood stock, checkered black synthetic Winchester buttplate, Schnabel fore-end. **Sights:** Bead post, front; buckhorn rear. **Features:**

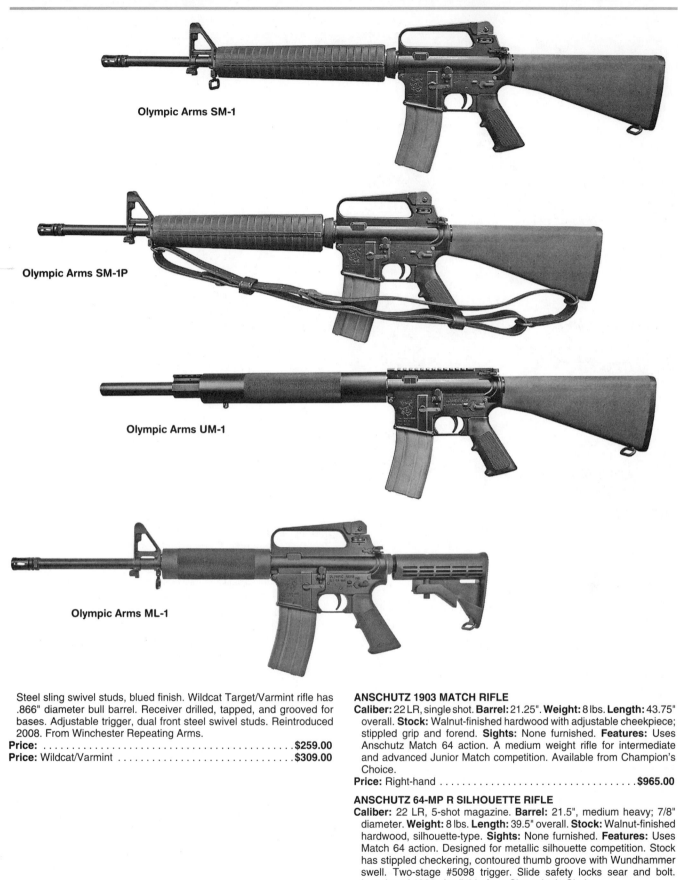

Olympic Arms SM-1

Olympic Arms SM-1P

Olympic Arms UM-1

Olympic Arms ML-1

Steel sling swivel studs, blued finish. Wildcat Target/Varmint rifle has .866" diameter bull barrel. Receiver drilled, tapped, and grooved for bases. Adjustable trigger, dual front steel swivel studs. Reintroduced 2008. From Winchester Repeating Arms.

Price: **$259.00**
Price: Wildcat/Varmint **$309.00**

ANSCHUTZ 1903 MATCH RIFLE

Caliber: 22 LR, single shot. **Barrel:** 21.25". **Weight:** 8 lbs. **Length:** 43.75" overall. **Stock:** Walnut-finished hardwood with adjustable cheekpiece; stippled grip and forend. **Sights:** None furnished. **Features:** Uses Anschutz Match 64 action. A medium weight rifle for intermediate and advanced Junior Match competition. Available from Champion's Choice.

Price: Right-hand **$965.00**

ANSCHUTZ 64-MP R SILHOUETTE RIFLE

Caliber: 22 LR, 5-shot magazine. **Barrel:** 21.5", medium heavy; 7/8" diameter. **Weight:** 8 lbs. **Length:** 39.5" overall. **Stock:** Walnut-finished hardwood, silhouette-type. **Sights:** None furnished. **Features:** Uses Match 64 action. Designed for metallic silhouette competition. Stock has stippled checkering, contoured thumb groove with Wundhammer swell. Two-stage #5098 trigger. Slide safety locks sear and bolt. Introduced 1980. Available from Champion's Choice.

Price: 64-MP R **$950.00**
Price: 64-S BR Benchrest (2008) **$1,175.00**

Remington 40-XB Rangemaster

Sako TRG-22

Springfield Armory M1A Super Match

Springfield Armory M1A/M-21

Anschutz 2007 Match Rifle
Uses same action as the Model 2013, but has a lighter barrel. European walnut stock in right-hand, true left-hand or extra-short models. Sights optional. Available with 19.6" barrel with extension tube, or 26", both in stainless or blue. Introduced 1998. Available from Champion's Choice.
Price: Right-hand, blue, no sights. **$2,410.90**

ANSCHUTZ 1827BT FORTNER BIATHLON RIFLE
Caliber: 22 LR, 5-shot magazine. **Barrel:** 21.7". **Weight:** 8.8 lbs. with sights. **Length:** 40.9" overall. **Stock:** European walnut with cheekpiece, stippled pistol grip and forend. **Sights:** Optional globe front specially designed for Biathlon shooting, micrometer rear with hinged snow cap. **Features:** Uses Super Match 54 action and nine-way adjustable trigger; adjustable wooden buttplate, biathlon butthook, adjustable hand-stop rail. Uses Anschutz/Fortner system straight-pull bolt action, blued or stainless steel barrel. Introduced 1982. Available from Champion's Choice.
Price: Nitride finish with sights, about. **$2,895.00**

ANSCHUTZ SUPER MATCH SPECIAL MODEL 2013 RIFLE
Caliber: 22 LR, single shot. **Barrel:** 25.9". **Weight:** 13 lbs. **Length:** 41.7" to 42.9". **Stock:** Adjustable aluminum. **Sights:** None furnished. **Features:** 2313 aluminum-silver/blue stock, 500mm barrel, fast lock time, adjustable cheek piece, heavy action and muzzle tube, w/ handstop and standing riser block. Introduced in 1997. Available from Champion's Choice.
Price: Right-hand **$3,195.00**

ANSCHUTZ 1912 SPORT RIFLE
Caliber: 22 LR. **Barrel:** 26" match. **Weight:** 11.4 lbs. **Length:** 41.7" overall. **Stock:** Non-stained thumbhole stock adjustable in length

with adjustable butt plate and cheek piece adjustment. Flat forend raiser block 4856 adjustable in height. Hook butt plate. **Sights:** None furnished. **Features:** "Free rifle" for women. Smallbore model 1907 with 1912 **stock:** Match 54 action. Delivered with: Hand stop 6226, forend raiser block 4856, screw driver, instruction leaflet with test target. Available from Champion's Choice.
Price: **$2,595.00**

Anschutz 1913 Super Match Rifle
Same as the Model 1911 except European walnut International-type stock with adjustable cheekpiece, or color laminate, both available with straight or lowered forend, adjustable aluminum hook buttplate, adjustable hand stop, weighs 13 lbs., 46" overall. Stainless or blue barrel. Available from Champion's Choice.
Price: Right-hand, blue, no sights, walnut stock. **$2,695.00**

Anschutz 1907 Standard Match Rifle
Same action as Model 1913 but with 7/8" diameter 26" barrel (stainless or blue). Length is 44.5" overall, weighs 10.5 lbs. Choice of stock configurations. Vented forend. Designed for prone and position shooting ISU requirements; suitable for NRA matches. Also available with walnut flat-forend stock for benchrest shooting. Available from Champion's Choice.
Price: Right-hand, blue, no sights. **$1,655.00**

ARMALITE AR-10(T) RIFLE
Caliber: 308 Win., 10-shot magazine. **Barrel:** 24" target-weight Rock 5R custom. **Weight:** 10.4 lbs. **Length:** 43.5" overall. **Stock:** Green or black composition; N.M. fiberglass handguard tube. **Sights:** Detachable handle, front sight, or scope mount available. Comes with international-style flattop receiver with Picatinny rail. **Features:** National Match two-stage trigger. Forged upper receiver. Receivers hard-coat anodized. Introduced 1995. Made in U.S.A. by ArmaLite, Inc.
Price: Black **$1,912.00**
Price: AR-10, 338 Federal **$1,912.00**

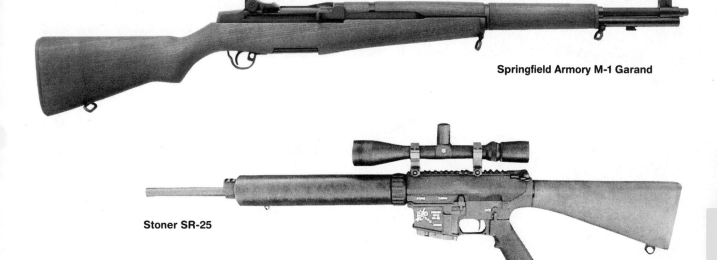

Springfield Armory M-1 Garand

Stoner SR-25

ARMALITE M15A4(T) EAGLE EYE RIFLE
Caliber: 223 Rem., 10-round magazine. **Barrel:** 24" heavy stainless; 1:8" twist. **Weight:** 9.2 lbs. **Length:** 42-3/8" overall. **Stock:** Green or black butt, N.M. fiberglass handguard tube. **Sights:** One-piece international-style flattop receiver with Weaver-type rail, including case deflector. **Features:** Detachable carry handle, front sight and scope mount (30mm or 1") available. Upper and lower receivers have push-type pivot pin, hard coat anodized. Made in U.S.A. by ArmaLite, Inc.
Price: Green or black furniture **$1,296.00**

ARMALITE M15 A4 CARBINE 6.8 & 7.62X39
Caliber: 6.8 Rem, 7.62x39. **Barrel:** 16" chrome-lined with flash suppressor. **Weight:** 7 lbs. **Length:** 26.6". **Features:** Front and rear picatinny rails for mounting optics, two-stage tactical trigger, anodized aluminum/phosphate finish.

Price: **$1,107.00**

BLASER R93 LONG RANGE SPORTER 2 RIFLE
Caliber: 308 Win., 10-shot detachable box magazine. **Barrel:** 24". **Weight:** 10.4 lbs. **Length:** 44" overall. **Stock:** Aluminum with synthetic lining. **Sights:** None furnished; accepts detachable scope mount. **Features:** Straight-pull bolt action with adjustable trigger; fully adjustable stock; quick takedown; corrosion resistant finish. Introduced 1998. Imported from Germany by Blaser USA.
Price: **$3,848.00**

BUSHMASTER A2/A3 TARGET RIFLE
Caliber: 5.56mm, 223 Rem., 30-round magazine **Barrel:** 20", 24". **Weight:** 8.43 lbs. (A2); 8.78 lbs. (A3). **Length:** 39.5" overall (20" barrel). **Stock:** Black composition; A2 type. **Sights:** Adjustable post front, adjustable aperture rear. **Features:** Patterned after Colt M-16A2. Chrome-lined barrel with manganese phosphate exterior. Available in stainless barrel. Made in U.S.A. by Bushmaster Firearms Co.
Price: (A3 type) **$1,135.00**

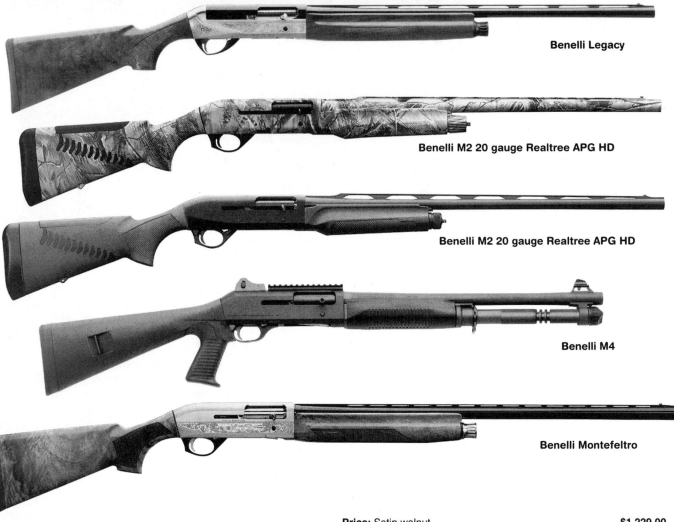

Benelli Legacy

Benelli M2 20 gauge Realtree APG HD

Benelli M2 20 gauge Realtree APG HD

Benelli M4

Benelli Montefeltro

BENELLI LEGACY SHOTGUN

Gauge: 12, 20, 2-3/4" and 3" chamber. **Barrel:** 24", 26", 28" (Full, Mod., Imp. Cyl., Imp. Mod., cylinder choke tubes). Mid-bead sight. **Weight:** 5.8 to 7.4 lbs. **Length:** 49-5/8" overall (28" barrel). **Stock:** Select AA European walnut with satin finish. **Features:** Uses the rotating bolt inertia recoil operating system with a two-piece steel/aluminum etched receiver (bright on lower, blue upper). Drop adjustment kit allows the stock to be custom fitted without modifying the stock. Introduced 1998. Ultralight model has gloss-blued finish receiver. Weight is 6.0 lbs., 24" barrel, 45.5" overall length. WeatherCoat walnut stock. Introduced 2006. Imported from Italy by Benelli USA, Corp.

Price: Legacy **$1,689.00**
Price: Sport (2008) **$2,269.00**

BENELLI ULTRA LIGHT SHOTGUN

Gauge: 12, 20, 3" chamber. **Barrel:** 28". Mid-bead sight. **Weight:** 5.2 to 6 lbs. **Features:** Similar to Legacy line. Drop adjustment kit allows the stock to be custom fitted without modifying the stock. WeatherCoat walnut stock. Lightened receiver, shortened magazine tube, carbon-fiber rib and grip cap. Introduced 2008. Imported from Italy by Benelli USA, Corp.

Price: 12 gauge. **$1,539.00**

BENELLI M2 FIELD SHOTGUNS

Gauge: 20 ga., 12 ga., 3" chamber. **Barrel:** 21", 24", 26", 28". **Weight:** 5.4 to 7.2 lbs. **Length:** 42.5 to 49.5" overall. **Stock:** Synthetic, Advantage Max-4 HD, Advantage Timber HD, APG HD. **Sights:** Red bar. **Features:** Uses the Inertia Driven bolt mechanism. Vent rib. Comes with set of five choke tubes. Imported from Italy by Benelli USA.

Price: Synthetic ComforTech gel recoil pad **$1,319.00**
Price: Camo ComforTech gel recoil pad. **$1,335.00**

Price: Satin walnut **$1,229.00**
Price: Rifled slug synthetic **$1,380.00**
Price: Camo turkey model w/SteadyGrip stock **$1,429.00**
Price: Realtree APG HD ComforTech stock (2007) **$1,429.00**
Price: Realtree APG HD ComforTech 20 ga. (2007) **$1,429.00**
Price: Realtree APG HD LH ComforTech (2007) **$1,429.00**
Price: Realtree APG HD ComforTech Slug (2007). **$1,429.00**
Price: Realtree APG HD w/SteadyGrip stock (2007) **$1,429.00**
Price: Black Synthetic Grip Tight 20 ga. (2007) **$1,319.00**

BENELLI M4 TACTICAL SHOTGUN

Gauge: 12 ga., 3" chamber. **Barrel:** 18.5". **Weight:** 7.8 lbs. **Length:** 40" overall. **Stock:** Synthetic. **Sights:** Ghost Ring rear, fixed blade front. **Features:** Auto-regulating gas-operated (ARGO) action, choke tube, Picatinny rail, standard and collapsible stocks available, optional LE tactical gun case. Introduced 2006. Imported from Italy by Benelli USA.

Price: Pistol grip stock, black synthetic. **$1,699.00**
Price: Desert camo pistol grip (2007) **$1,829.00**

BENELLI MONTEFELTRO SHOTGUNS

Gauge: 12 and 20 ga. Full, Imp. Mod., Mod., Imp. Cyl., Cyl. choke tubes. **Barrel:** 24", 26", 28". **Weight:** 5.3 to 7.1 lbs. **Stock:** Checkered walnut with satin finish. **Length:** 43.6 to 49.5" overall. **Features:** Uses the Inertia Driven rotating bolt system with a simple inertia recoil design. Finish is blue. Introduced 1987.

Price: 24", 26", 28" **$1,219.00**
Price: Left hand. **$1,229.00**
Price: 20 ga. **$1,219.00**
Price: 20 ga. short stock (LOP: 12.5") **$1,120.00**
Price: Silver (AA walnut; nickel-blue receiver) **$1,649.00**
Price: Silver 20 ga. **$1,649.00**

Benelli Super Black Eagle II Realtree APG HD Slug

Benelli Super Black Eagle II

Beretta 3901 Citizen

Beretta UGB

BENELLI SUPER BLACK EAGLE II SHOTGUNS

Gauge: 12, 3-1/2" chamber. **Barrel:** 24", 26", 28" (Cyl. Imp. Cyl., Mod., Imp. Mod., Full choke tubes). **Weight:** 7.1 to 7.3 lbs. **Length:** 45.6 to 49.6" overall. **Stock:** European walnut with satin finish, polymer, or camo. Adjustable for drop. **Sights:** Red bar front. **Features:** Uses Benelli inertia recoil bolt system. Vent rib. Advantage Max-4 HD, Advantage Timber HD camo patterns. Features ComforTech stock. Introduced 1991. Left-hand models available. Imported from Italy by Benelli USA.

Price: Satin walnut, non-ComforTech **$1,549.00**
Price: Camo stock, ComforTech gel recoil pad **$1,759.00**
Price: Black Synthetic stock **$1,649.00**
Price: Max-4 HD Camo stock **$1,759.00**
Price: Timber HD turkey model w/SteadyGrip stock **$1,680.00**
Price: Realtree APG HD w/ComforTech stock (2007) **$1,759.00**
Price: Realtree APG HD LH ComforTech stock (2007) **$1,759.00**
Price: Realtree APG HD Slug Gun (2007) **$1,730.00**

BENELLI CORDOBA SHOTGUN

Gauge: 20; 12; 3" chamber. **Barrel:** 28" and 30", ported, 10mm sporting rib. **Weight:** 7.2 to 7.3 lbs. **Length:** 49.6 to 51.6". **Features:** Designed for high-volume sporting clays and Argentina dove shooting. Inertia-driven action, Extended Sport CrioChokes, 4+1 capacity. Ported. Imported from Italy by Benelli USA.

Price: Black synthetic GripTight ComforTech stock **$1,869.00**
Price: Black synthetic GripTight ComforTech stock, 20 ga.,
(2007) **$1,869.00**
Price: Max-4 HD ComforTech stock (2007) **$2,039.00**

BENELLI SUPERSPORT & SPORT II SHOTGUNS

Gauge: 20; 12; 3" chamber. **Barrel:** 28" and 30", ported, 10mm sporting rib. **Weight:** 7.2 to 7.3 lbs. **Length:** 49.6 to 51.6". **Stock:** Carbon fiber, ComforTech (Supersport) or walnut (Sport II). **Sights:** Red bar front, metal midbead. Sport II is similar to the Legacy model except has nonengraved dual tone blue/silver receiver, ported wide-rib barrel, adjustable buttstock, and functions with all loads. Walnut stock with satin finish. Introduced 1997. **Features:** Designed for high-volume sporting clays. Inertia-driven action, Extended CrioChokes, 4+1

capacity. Ported. Imported from Italy by Benelli USA.
Price: Carbon fiber ComforTech stock **$1,979.00**
Price: Carbon fiber ComforTech stock, 20 ga. (2007) **$1,979.00**
Price: Sport II 20 ga. (2007) **$1,699.00**

BERETTA 3901 SHOTGUNS

Gauge: 12, 20 gauge; 3" chamber, semi-auto. **Barrel:** 26", 28". **Weight:** 6.55 lbs. (20 ga.), 7.2 lbs. (12 ga.). **Length:** NA. **Stock:** Wood, X-tra wood (special process wood enhancement), and polymer. **Features:** Based on A390 shotgun introduced in 1996. Mobilchokes, removable trigger group. 3901 Target RL uses gas operating system; Sporting style flat rib with steel front bead and mid-bead, walnut stock and forearm, satin matte finish, adjustable LOP from 12P13", adjustable for cast on/off, Beretta's Memory System II to adjust the parallel comb. Weighs 7.2 lbs. 3901 Citizen has polymer stock. 3901 Statesman has basic wood and checkering treatment. 3901 Ambassador has X-tra wood stock and fore end; high-polished receiver with engraving, Gel-Tek recoil pad, optional TruGlo fiber-optic front sight. 3901 Rifled Slug Shotgun has black high-impact synthetic stock and fore end, 24" barrel,1:28 twist, Picatinny cantilever rail. Introduced 2006. Made in U.S. by Beretta USA.

Price: 3901 Target RL. **$900.00**
Price: 3901 Citizen, synthetic or wood, from **$750.00**
Price: 3901 Statesman **$900.00**
Price: 3901 Rifled Slug Shotgun. **$800.00**

BERETTA UGB25 XCEL SEMI-AUTO SHOTGUN

Gauge: 12, 2-3/4" chambers. **Barrel:** 28", 30", 32"; competition-style interchangeable vent rib; Optima choke tubes. **Weight:** 7.7-9 lbs. **Stock:** High-grade walnut with oil finish; hand-checkered grip and forend, adjustable. **Features:** Break-open semiautomatic. High-resistance fiberglass-reinforced technopolymer trigger plate, self-lubricating firing mechanism. Rounded alloy receiver, polished sides, external cartridge carrier and feeding port, bottom eject. two technopolymer recoil dampers on breech bolt, double recoil dampers located in the receiver, Beretta Recoil Reduction System, recoil-absorbing Beretta Gel Tek recoil pad. Optima-Bore barrel with a lengthened forcing cone, Optimachoke and Extended Optimachoke tubes. Steel-shot capable, interchangeable aluminum alloy top rib. Introduced 2006. Imported from Italy by Beretta USA.
Price: **$3,875.00**

Beretta AL391 Urika Sporting

Beretta AL391 Urika Gold Sporting

Beretta A391 Xtrema2 3.5

BERETTA AL391 TEKNYS SHOTGUNS
Gauge: 12, 20 gauge; 3" chamber, semi-auto. **Barrel:** 26", 28". **Weight:** 5.9 lbs. (20 ga.), 7.3 lbs. (12 ga.). **Length:** NA. **Stock:** X-tra wood (special process wood enhancement). **Features:** Flat 1/4 rib, TruGlo Tru-Bead sight, recoil reducer, stock spacers, overbored bbls., flush choke tubes. Comes with fitted, lined case.
Price: From **$2,050.00**

BERETTA AL391 URIKA AND URIKA 2 AUTO SHOTGUNS
Gauge: 12, 20 gauge; 3" chamber. **Barrel:** 22", 24", 26", 28", 30"; five Mobilchoke choke tubes. **Weight:** 5.95 to 7.28 lbs. **Length:** Varies by model. **Stock:** Walnut, black or camo synthetic; shims, spacers and interchangeable recoil pads allow custom fit. **Features:** Self-compensating gas op-eration handles full range of loads; recoil re-ducer in receiver; enlarged trigger guard; re-duced-weight receiver, barrel and forend; hard-chromed bore. Introduced 2000. AL391 Urika 2 (2007) has self-cleaning action, X-Tra Grain stock finish. AL391 Urika 2 Gold has higher-grade select oil-finished wood stock, upgraded engrav-ing (gold-filled gamebirds on field models, gold-filled laurel leaf on competition version). Kick-Off recoil reduction system available in Syn-thetic, Realtree Advantage Max-4 and AP models. Imported from Italy by Beretta USA.
Price: Urika 2 X-tra Grain, from **$1,400.00**
Price: Urika 2 Gold, from **$1,550.00**
Price: Urika 2 Synthetic **$975.00**
Price: Urika 2 Realtree AP Kick-Off, ... **$1,350.00**

BERETTA A391 XTREMA2 3.5 AUTO SHOTGUNS
Gauge: 12 ga. 3.5" chamber. **Barrel:** 24", 26", 28". **Weight:** 7.8 lbs. **Stock:** Synthetic. **Features:** Semi-auto goes with two-lug rotating bolt and self-compensating gas valve, extended tang, cross bolt safety, self-cleaning, with case.
Price: From **$1,250.00**

BREDA GRIZZLY
Gauge: 12, 3.5" chamber. **Barrel:** 28". **Weight:** 7.2 lbs. **Stock:** Black synthetic or Advantage Timber with matching metal parts. **Features:** Chokes tubes are Mod., IC, Full; inertia-type action, four-round magazine. Imported from Italy by Legacy Sports International.
Price: Blued/black (2008) **$1,826.00**
Price: Advantage Timber Camo (2008) **$2,121.00**

BREDA XANTHOS
Gauge: 12, 3" chamber. **Barrel:** 28". **Weight:** 6.5 lbs. **Stock:** High grade walnut. **Features:** Chokes tubes are Mod., IC, Full; inertia-type action, four-round magazine, spark engraving with hand-engraved details and hand-gilding figures on receiver. Blued, Grey or Chrome finishes. Imported from Italy by Legacy Sports International.
Price: Blued (2007) **$2,309.00**

Price: Grey (2007) **$2,451.00**
Price: Chrome (2007) **$3,406.00**

BREDA ECHO
Gauge: 12, 20. 3" chamber. **Barrel:** 28". **Weight:** 6.0-6.5 lbs. **Stock:** Walnut. **Features:** Chokes tubes are Mod., IC, Full; inertia-type action, four-round magazine, blue, grey or nickel finishes, modern engraving, fully checkered pistol grip. Imported from Italy by Legacy Sports International.
Price: Blued, 12 ga. (2008) **$1,897.00**
Price: Grey, 12 ga. (2008) **$1,969.00**
Price: Nickel, 12 ga. (2008) **$2,214.00**
Price: Nickel, 20 ga. (2008) **$2,214.00**

BREDA ALTAIR
Gauge: 12, 20. 3" chamber. **Barrel:** 28". **Weight:** 5.7-6.1 lbs. **Stock:** Oil-rubbed walnut. **Features:** Chokes tubes are Mod., IC, Full; gas-actuated action, four-round magazine, blued finish, lightweight frame. Imported from Italy by Legacy Sports International.
Price: Blued, 12 ga. (2008) **$1,320.00**
Price: Grey, 20 ga. (2008) **$1,320.00**

BROWNING GOLD AUTO SHOTGUNS
Gauge: 12, 3" or 3-1/2" chamber; 20, 3" chamber. **Barrel:** 12 ga.-26", 28", 30", Invector Plus choke tubes; 20 ga.-26", 30", Invector choke tubes. **Weight:** 7 lbs., 9 oz. (12 ga.), 6 lbs., 12 oz. (20 ga.). **Length:** 46.25" overall (20 ga., 26" barrel). **Stock:** 14"x1.5"x2-1/3"; select walnut with gloss finish; palm swell grip. **Features:** Self-regulating, self-cleaning gas system shoots all loads; lightweight receiver with special non-glare deep black finish; large reversible safety button; large rounded trigger guard, gold trigger. The 20 gauge has slightly smaller dimensions; 12 gauge have back-bored barrels, Invector Plus tube system. Introduced 1994. Gold Evolve shotguns have new rib design, HiViz sights. Imported by Browning.
Price: Gold Evolve Sporting, 12 ga., 2-3/4" chamber **$1,326.00**
Price: Gold Superlite Hunter, 12 or 20 ga., 26" or
28" barrel, 6.6 lbs. **$1,161.00**

BROWNING GOLD NWTF TURKEY SERIES AND MOSSY OAK SHOTGUNS
Gauge: 12, 10, 3-1/2" chamber. Similar to the Gold Hunter except has specialized camouflage patterns, including National Wild Turkey Federation design. Includes extra-full choke tube and HiViz fiber-optic sights on some models and Dura-Touch coating. Camouflage patterns include Mossy Oak New Break-Up (NBU) or Mossy Oak New Shadow Grass (NSG). NWTF models include NWTF logo on stock. Introduced 2001. From Browning.
Price: NWFT Gold Ultimate Turkey, 24" barrel, 12 ga.
3-1/2" chamber **$1,513.00**
Price: NWFT Gold 10 Gauge, 24" barrel, 3-1/2" chamber . . **$1,639.00**

Browning NWTF Mossy Oak® Break-Up™

Browning Gold Light 10 gauge

Browning Silver Rifled Deer Satin

Browning Silver Stalker

Browning Maxus Stalker

Browning Maxus Mossy Oak Duck Blind

BROWNING GOLD GOLDEN CLAYS AUTO SHOTGUNS

Gauge: 12, 2-3/4" chamber. **Barrel:** 28", 30", Invector Plus choke tubes. **Weight:** about 7.75 lbs. **Length:** From 47.75 to 50.5". **Stock:** Select walnut with gloss finish; palm swell grip, shim adjustable. **Features:** Ported barrels, "Golden Clays" models feature gold inlays and engraving. Imported by Browning.
Price: Gold "Golden Clays" Sporting Clays, intr. 2005 . . . . . **$1,941.00**

Browning Gold Light 10 Gauge Auto Shotgun

Similar to the Gold Hunter except has an alloy receiver that is 1 lb. lighter than standard model. Offered in 26" or 28" bbls. With Mossy Oak Break-Up or Shadow Grass coverage; 5-shot magazine. Weighs 9 lbs., 10 oz. (28" bbl.). Introduced 2001. Imported by Browning.
Price: Camo model only **$1,509.00**

BROWNING SILVER AUTO SHOTGUNS

Gauge: 12, 3" or 3-1/2" chamber; 20, 3" chamber. **Barrel:** 12 ga.-26", 28", 30", Invector Plus choke tubes. **Weight:** 7 lbs., 9 oz. (12 ga.), 6 lbs., 7 oz. (20 ga.). **Stock:** Satin finish walnut. **Features:** Active Valve gas system, semi-humpback receiver. Invector Plus tube system, three choke tubes. Imported by Browning.
Price: Silver Hunter, 12 ga., 3.5" chamber **$1,239.00**
Price: Silver Hunter, 20 ga., 3" chamber, intr. 2008 . . . . **$1,079.00**

Price: Silver Micro, 20 ga., 3" chamber, intr. 2008 . . . . **$1,079.00**
Price: Silver Sporting, 12 ga., 2-3/4" chamber,
intr. 2009 . . . . **$1,199.00**
Price: Silver Sporting Micro, 12 ga., 2-3/4" chamber,
intr. 2008. . . . . **$1,199.00**
Price: Silver Rifled Deer, Mossy Oak New Break-Up,
12 ga., 3" chamber, intr. 2008 . . . . **$1,319.00**
Price: Silver Rifled Deer Stalker, 12 ga., 3" chamber,
intr. 2008. . . . . **$1,169.00**
Price: Silver Rifled Deer Satin, satin-finished aluminum
alloy receiver and satin-finished walnut buttstock
and forend **$1,229.00**
Price: Silver Stalker, black composite buttstock and forend **$1,179.00**

BROWNING MAXUS

Gauge: 12; 3" or 3.5" chambers. **Barrel:** 26" or 28". **Weight:** 6-7/8 lbs. **Length:** 47.25" to 49.25". **Stock:** Composite with close radius pistol grip. **Features:** Aluminum receiver, lightweight profile barrel with vent rib, Vector Pro lengthened forcing cone, DuraTouch Armor Coating overall. Handles shorter shells interchangeably.
Price: Stalker, matte black finish overall, 3-1/2" **$1,379.00**
Price: Stalker, matte black finish overall, 3" **$1,199.00**
Price: Mossy Oak Duck Blind overall, 3-1/2" **$1,499.00**
Price: Mossy Oak Duck Blind overall, 3" **$1,339.00**

Charles Daly Field Pump

Charles Daly Maxi-Mag Field Hunter VR-MC

Charles Daly Superior II

Escort Model AS

Franchi 48AL Deluxe

CHARLES DALY FIELD SEMI-AUTO SHOTGUNS
Gauge: 12, 20, 28. **Barrel:** 22", 24", 26", 28" or 30". **Stock:** Synthetic black, Realtree Hardwoods or Advantage Timber. **Features:** Interchangeable barrels handle all loads including steel shot. Slug model has adjustable sights. Maxi-Mag is 3.5" chamber.
Price: Field Hunter, from $489.00

CHARLES DALY SUPERIOR II SEMI-AUTO SHOTGUNS
Gauge: 12, 20, 28. **Barrel:** 26", 28" or 30". **Stock:** Select Turkish walnut. **Features:** Factory ported interchangeable barrels; wide vent rib on Trap and Sport models; fluorescent red sights.
Price: Superior II Hunter, from $649.00
Price: Superior II Sport $709.00
Price: Superior II Trap. $739.00

ESCORT SEMI-AUTO SHOTGUNS
Gauge: 12, 20; 3" or 3.5" chambers. **Barrel:** 22" (Youth), 26" and 28". **Weight:** 6.7-7.8 lbs. **Stock:** Polymer in black, Shadow Grass® or Obsession® camo finish, Turkish walnut, select walnut. **Sights:** Optional HiViz Spark front. **Features:** Black-chrome or dipped-camo metal parts, top of receiver dovetailed for sight mounts, gold plated trigger, trigger guard safety, magazine cut-off. Three choke tubes (IC, M, F) except the Waterfowl/Turkey Combo, which adds a .665 turkey choke to the standard three. Waterfowl/Turkey combo is two-barrel set, 24"/26" and 26"/28". Several models have Trio recoil pad. Models are: AS, AS Select, AS Youth, AS Youth Select, PS, PS Spark and Waterfowl/Turkey. Introduced 2002. Camo introduced 2003. Youth, Slug and Obsession camo introduced 2005. Imported from Turkey by Legacy Sports International.
Price: . . . . $425.00 to $589.00

FRANCHI INERTIA I-12 SHOTGUN
Gauge: 12, 3" chamber. **Barrel:** 24", 26", 28" (Cyl., IC, Mod., IM, F choke tubes). **Weight:** 7.5 to 7.7. lbs. **Length:** 45" to 49". **Stock:** 14-3.8" LOP, satin walnut with checkered grip and forend, synthetic, Advantage Timber HD or Max-4 camo patterns. **Features:** Inertia-Driven action. AA walnut stock. Red bar front sight, metal mid sight. Imported from Italy by Benelli USA.
Price: Synthetic. $839.00
Price: Camo $949.00
Price: Satin walnut $949.00

FRANCHI MODEL 720 SHOTGUNS
Gauge: 20, 3" chamber. **Barrel:** 24", 26", 28" w/(IC, Mod., F choke tubes). **Weight:** 5.9 to 6.1 lbs. **Length:** 43.25" to 49". **Stock:** WeatherCoat finish walnut, Max-4 and Timber HD camo. **Sights:** Front bead. **Features:** Made in Italy and imported by Benelli USA.
Price: $1,049.00
Price: Walnut, 12.5" LOP, 43.25" OAL $999.00

FRANCHI 48AL FIELD AND DELUXE SHOTGUNS
Gauge: 20 or 28, 2-3/4" chamber. **Barrel:** 24", 26", 28" (Full, Cyl., Mod., choke tubes). **Weight:** 5.4 to 5.7 lbs. **Length:** 42.25" to 48". **Stock:** Walnut with checkered grip and forend. **Features:** Long recoil-operated action. Chrome-lined bore; cross-bolt safety. Imported from Italy by Benelli USA.
Price: AL Field 20 ga. $839.00
Price: AL Deluxe 20 ga., A grade walnut $1,099.00
Price: AL Field 28 ga. $999.00

FRANCHI 720 COMPETITION SHOTGUN
Gauge: 20; 4+1. **Barrel:** 28" ported; tapered target rib and bead front sight. **Weight:** 6.2 lbs. **Stock:** Walnut with WeatherCoat. **Features:** Gas-operated, satin nickel receiver.
Price: $1,149.00

Remington Model 105 CTi

Remington Model 1100 G3

HARRINGTON & RICHARDSON EXCELL AUTO 5 SHOTGUNS
Gauge: 12, 3" chamber. **Barrel:** 22", 24", 28", four screw-in choke tubes (IC, M, IM, F). **Weight:** About 7 lbs. **Length:** 42.5" to 48.5" overall, depending on barrel length. **Stock:** American walnut with satin finish; cut checkering; ventilated buttpad. Synthetic stock or camo-finish. **Sights:** Metal bead front or fiber-optic front and rear. **Features:** Ventilated rib on all models except slug gun. Imported by H&R 1871, Inc.
Price: Synthetic, black, 28" barrel, 48.5" OAL **$415.00**
Price: Walnut, checkered grip/forend, 28" barrel, 48.5" OAL . . **$461.00**
Price: Waterfowl, camo finish **$521.00**
Price: Turkey, camo finish, 22" barrel, fiber optic sights **$521.00**
Price: Combo, synthetic black stock, with slug barrel **$583.00**

LANBER SEMI-AUTOMATIC SHOTGUNS
Gauge: 12, 3". **Barrel:** 26", 28", chrome-moly alloy steel, welded, ventilated top and side ribs. **Weight:** 6.8 lbs. **Length:** 48-3/8". **Stock:** Walnut, oiled finish, laser checkering, rubber buttplate. **Sights:** Fiber-optic front. **Features:** Extractors or automatic ejectors, control and unblocking button. Rated for steel shot. Lanber Polichokes. Imported by Lanber USA.
Price: Model 2533 . . . . **$635.00**

MOSSBERG 930 AUTOLOADER
Gauge: 12, 3" chamber, 4-shot magazine. **Barrel:** 24", 26", 28", over-bored to 10-gauge bore dimensions; factory ported, Accu-Choke tubes. **Weight:** 7.5 lbs. **Length:** 44.5" overall (28" barrel). **Stock:** Walnut or synthetic. Adjustable stock drop and cast spacer system. **Sights:** "Turkey Taker" fiber-optic, adjustable windage and elevation. Front bead fiber-optic front on waterfowl models. **Features:** Self-regulating gas system, dual gas-vent system and piston, EZ-Empty magazine button, cocking indicator. Interchangeable Accu-Choke tube set (IC, Mod, Full) for waterfowl and field models. XX-Full turkey Accu-Choke tube included with turkey models. Ambidextrous thumb-operated safety, Uni-line stock and receiver. Receiver drilled and tapped for scope base attachment, free gun lock. Introduced 2008. From O.F. Mossberg & Sons, Inc.
Price: Turkey, from **$545.00**
Price: Waterfowl, from **$545.00**
Price: Combo, from **$604.00**
Price: Field, from **$568.00**
Price: Slugster, from **$539.00**
Price: Turkey Pistolgrip; full pistolgrip stock, matte black or Mossy Oak Obsession camo finish overall **$628.00**
Price: Tactical; 18.5" tactical barrel, black synthetic stock and matte black finish **$653.00**
Price: Road Blocker; includes muzzle brake **$697.00**
Price: SPX; no muzzle brake, M16-style front sight, ghost ring rear sight, full pistolgrip stock, eight-round extended magazine **$667.00**
Price: SPX; conventional synthetic stock **$700.00**
Price: Home Security/Field Combo; 18.5" Cylinder bore barrel and 28" ported Field barrel; black synthetic stock and matte black finish **$604.00**

MOSSBERG MODEL 935 MAGNUM AUTOLOADING SHOTGUNS
Gauge: 12; 3" and 3.5" chamber, interchangeable. **Barrel:** 22", 24", 26", 28". **Weight:** 7.25 to 7.75 lbs. **Length:** 45" to 49" overall. **Stock:** Synthetic. **Features:** Gas-operated semi-auto models in blued or camo finish. Fiber optics sights, drilled and tapped receiver, interchangeable Accu-Mag choke tubes.
Price: 935 Magnum Turkey: Realtree Hardwoods, Mossy Oak New Break-up or Mossy Oak Obsession camo overall, 24" barrel **$732.00**
Price: 935 Magnum Turkey Pistolgrip; full pistolgrip stock . . **$831.00**
Price: 935 Magnum Grand Slam: 22" barrel, Realtree Hardwoods or Mossy Oak New Break-up camo overall **$747.00**
Price: 935 Magnum Flyway: 28" barrel and Advantage Max-4 camo overall **$781.00**
Price: 935 Magnum Waterfowl: 26"or 28" barrel, matte black, Mossy Oak New Break-up, Advantage Max-4 or Mossy Oak Duck Blind cam overall . . . . **$613.00 to $725.00**
Price: 935 Magnum Slugster: 24" fully rifled barrel, rifle sights, Realtree AP camo overall **$747.00**
Price: 935 Magnum Turkey/Deer Combo: interchangeable 24" Turkey barrel, Mossy Oak New Break-up camo overall **$807.00**
Price: 935 Magnum Waterfowl/Turkey Combo: 24" Turkey and 28" Waterfowl barrels, Mossy Oak New Break-up finish overall **$807.00**

REMINGTON MODEL 105 CTI SHOTGUN
Gauge: 12, 3" chamber, 4-shot magazine. **Barrel:** 26", 28" (IC, Mod., Full ProBore chokes). **Weight:** 7 lbs. **Length:** 46.25" overall (26" barrel). **Stock:** Walnut with satin finish. Checkered grip and forend. **Sights:** Front bead. **Features:** Aircraft-grade titanium receiver body, skeletonized receiver with carbon fiber shell. Bottom feed and eject, target grade trigger, R3 recoil pad, FAA-approved lockable hard case, .735" overbored barrel with lengthened forcing cones. TriNyte coating; carbon/aramid barrel rib. Introduced 2006.
Price: **$1,559.00**

REMINGTON MODEL SPR453 SHOTGUN
Gauge: 12; 3.5" chamber, 4+1 capacity. **Barrel:** 24", 26", 28" vent rib. **Weight:** 8 to 8.25 lbs. **Stock:** Black synthetic. **Features:** Matte finish, dual extractors, four extended screw-in SPR choke tubes (improved cylinder, modified, full and super-full turkey). Introduced 2006. From Remington Arms Co.
Price: Black synthetic **$497.00**

REMINGTON MODEL 11-87 SPORTSMAN SHOTGUNS
Gauge: 12, 20, 3" chamber. **Barrel:** 26", 28", RemChoke tubes. Standard contour, vent rib. **Weight:** About 7.75 to 8.25 lbs. **Length:** 46" to 48" overall. **Stock:** Black synthetic or Mossy Oak Break Up Mossy Oak Duck Blind, and Realtree Hardwoods HD and AP Green HD camo finishes. **Sights:** Single bead front. **Features:** Matte-black metal finish, magazine cap swivel studs. Sportsman Deer gun has 21-inch fully rifled barrel, cantilever scope mount.
Price: Sportsman Camo (2007), 12 or 20 ga. **$879.00**
Price: Sportsman black synthetic, 12 or 20 ga. **$772.00**
Price: Sportsman Deer FR Cantilever, 12 or 20 ga. **$892.00**
Price: Sportsman Youth Synthetic 20 ga., (2008) **$772.00**
Price: Sportsman Youth Camo 20 ga., (2008) **$879.00**
Price: Sportsman Super Magnum 12 ga., 28" barrel (2008) . . . **$825.00**
Price: Sportsman Super Magnum Shurshot Turkey 12 ga., (2008) **$972.00**
Price: Sportsman Super Magnum Waterfowl 12 ga., (2008) . . **$959.00**
Price: Sportsman Compact Synthetic; black synthetic but with reduced overall dimensions **$772.00**

Remington Model 1100 Sporting 12

Remington Model 1100 Sporting 28

Remington Model SP-10

Remington Model SP-10 Thumbhole

REMINGTON MODEL 1100 G3 SHOTGUN

Gauge: 20, 12; 3" chamber. **Barrel:** 26", 28". **Weight:** 6.75-7.6 lbs. **Stock:** Realwood semi-Fancy carbon fiber laminate stock, high gloss finish, machine cut checkering. **Features:** Gas operating system, pressure compensated barrel, solid carbon-steel engraved receiver, titanium coating. Action bars, trigger and extended carrier release, action bar sleeve, action spring, locking block, hammer, sear and magazine tube have nickel-plated, Teflon coating. R3 recoil pad, overbored (.735" dia.) vent rib barrels, ProBore choke tubes. 20 gauge have Rem Chokes. Comes with lockable hard case. Introduced 2006.

Price: G3, 12 or 20 ga. **$1,239.00**
Price: G3 Left Hand, 12 ga. 28" barrel (2008) **$1,329.00**

REMINGTON MODEL 1100 TARGET SHOTGUNS

Gauge: .410 bore, 28, 20, 12. **Barrel:** 26", 27", 28", 30" light target contoured vent rib barrel with twin bead target sights. **Stock:** Semi-fancy American walnut stock and forend, cut checkering, high gloss finish. **Features:** Gold-plated trigger. Four extended choke tubes: Skeet, Improved Cylinder, Light Modified and Modified. 1100 Tournament Skeet (20 and 12 gauge) receiver is roll-marked with "Tournament Skeet." 26" light contour, vent rib barrel has twin bead sights, Extended Target Choke Tubes (Skeet and Improved Cylinder). Model 1100 Premier Sporting (2008) has polished nickel receiver, gold accents, light target contoured vent rib Rem Choke barrels. Wood is semi-fancy American walnut stock and forend, high-gloss finish, cut checkering, sporting clays-style recoil pad. Gold trigger, available in 12, 20, 28 and .410 bore options, Briley extended choke tubes, Premier Sporting hard case. Competition model (12 gauge) has overbored (0.735" bore diameter) 30" barrel. **Weight:** 8 lbs. 10mm target-style rib with twin beads. Extended ProBore choke tubes in Skeet, Improved Cylinder, Light-Modified, Modified and Full. Semi-fancy American walnut stock and forend. Classic Trap model has polished blue receiver with scroll engraving, gold accents, 30" low-profile, light-target contoured vent rib barrel with standard .727" dimensions. Comes with specialized Rem Choke trap tubes: Singles (.027"), Mid Handicap (.034"), and Long Handicap (.041"). Monte Carlo stock of semi-fancy American walnut, deep-cut checkering, high-gloss finish.

Price: Sporting 12, 28" barrel, 8 lbs. **$1,105.00**
Price: Sporting 20, 28" barrel, 7 lbs. **$1,105.00**
Price: Sporting 28, 27" barrel, 6.75 lbs. **$1,159.00**
Price: Sporting 410, 27" barrel, 6.75 lbs. **$1,159.00**
Price: Classic Trap, 12 ga. 30" barrel, ... **$1,159.00**
Price: Premier Sporting (2008), from. **$1,359.00**
Price: Competition, standard stock, 12 ga. 30" barrel **$1,692.00**
Price: Competition, adjustable comb **$1,692.00**

Remington Model 1100 TAC-4

Similar to Model 1100 but with 18" or 22" barrel with ventilated rib; 12 gauge 2-3/4"only; standard black synthetic stock or Knoxx SpecOps SpeedFeed IV pistolgrip stock; RemChoke tactical choke tube; matte black finish overall. Length is 42-1/2" and weighs 7-3/4 lbs.

Price: **$945.00**

REMINGTON MODEL SP-10 MAGNUM SHOTGUN

Gauge: 10, 3-1/2" chamber, 2-shot magazine. **Barrel:** 23", 26", 30" (full and mod. RemChokes). **Weight:** 10.75 to 11 lbs. **Length:** 47.5" overall (26" barrel). **Stock:** Walnut with satin finish (30" barrel) or camo synthetic (26" barrel). Checkered grip and forend. **Sights:** Twin bead. **Features:** Stainless steel gas system with moving cylinder; 3/8" vent rib. Receiver and barrel have matte finish. Brown recoil pad. Comes with padded Cordura nylon sling. Introduced 1989. SP-10 Magnum Camo has buttstock, forend, receiver, barrel and magazine cap covered with Mossy Oak Duck Blind Obsession camo finish; bolt body and trigger guard have matte black finish. RemChoke tube, 26" vent rib barrel with mid-rib bead and Bradley-style front sight, swivel studs and quick-detachable swivels, non-slip Cordura carrying sling. Introduced 1993.

Price: SP-10 Magnum, satin finish walnut stock. **$1,772.00**
Price: SP-10 Magnum Full Camo **$1,932.00**
Price: SP-10 Magnum Waterfowl **$1,945.00**

SAIGA AUTOLOADING SHOTGUN

Gauge: 12, 20, .410; 3" chamber. **Barrel:** 19", 24". **Weight:** 7.9 lbs. **Length: Stock:** Black synthetic. **Sights:** Fixed or adjustable leaf. **Features:** Magazine fed, 2- or 5-round capacity. Imported from Russia by Russian American Armory Co.

Price: **$347.95**

Smith & Wesson 1012

Smith & Wesson 1020

Stoeger Model 2000

Traditions ALS 2100

SMITH & WESSON 1000/1020/1012 SUPER SEMI-AUTO SHOTGUNS
Gauge: 12, 20; 3" in 1000; 3-1/2" chamber in Super. **Barrel:** 24", 26", 28", 30". **Stock:** Walnut. Synthetic finishes are satin, black, Realtree MAX-4, Realtree APG. **Sights:** TruGlo fiber-optic. **Features:** 29 configurations. Gas operated, dual-piston action; chrome-lined barrels, five choke tubes, shim kit for adjusting stock. 20-ga. models are Model 1020 or Model 1020SS (short stock). Lifetime warranty. Introduced 2007. Imported from Turkey by Smith & Wesson.
Price: From **$623.00**

STOEGER MODEL 2000 SHOTGUNS
Gauge: 12, 3" chamber, set of five choke tubes (C, IC, M, F, XFT). **Barrel:** 24", 26", 28", 30". **Stock:** Walnut, synthetic, Timber HD, Max-4. **Sights:** Red bar front. **Features:** Inertia-recoil. Minimum recommended load: 3 dram, 1-1/8 oz. Imported by Benelli USA.
Price: Walnut **$499.00**
Price: Synthetic. **$499.00**
Price: Max-4 . . . .**$549.00**
Price: Black synthetic pistol grip (2007) **$499.00**
Price: APG HD camo pistol grip (2007), 18.5" barrel **$549.00**

TRISTAR VIPER SEMI-AUTOMATIC SHOTGUNS
Gauge: 12, 20; shoots 2-3/4" or 3" interchangeably. **Barrel:** 26", 28" barrels (carbon fiber only of-fered in 12-ga. 28" and 20-ga. 26"). **Stock:** Wood, black synthetic, Mossy Oak Duck Blind camouflage, faux carbon fiber finish (2008) with the new Comfort Touch technology. **Features:** Magazine cut-off, vent rib with matted sight plane, brass front bead (camo models have fiber-optic front sight), five round magazine-shot plug included, and 3 Beretta-style choke tubes (IC, M, F). Viper synthetic, Viper camo have swivel studs. Five-year warranty. Viper Youth models have shortened length of pull and 24" barrel. Imported by Tristar Sporting Arms Ltd.
Price: From **$469.00**
Price: Camo models (2008), from. **$569.00**

TRADITIONS ALS 2100 SERIES SEMI-AUTOMATIC SHOTGUNS
Gauge: 12, 3" chamber; 20, 3" chamber. **Barrel:** 24", 26", 28" (Imp. Cyl., Mod. and Full choke tubes). **Weight:** 5 lbs., 10 oz. to 6 lbs., 5 oz. **Length:** 44" to 48" overall. **Stock:** Walnut or black composite. **Features:** Gas-operated; vent rib barrel with Beretta-style threaded muzzle. Introduced 2001 by Traditions.
Price: Field Model (12 or 20 ga., 26" or 28" bbl., walnut stock) **$479.00**
Price: Youth Model (12 or 20 ga., 24" bbl., walnut stock). **$479.00**
Price: (12 or 20 ga., 26" or 28" barrel, composite stock) **$459.00**

Traditions ALS 2100 Turkey Semi-Automatic Shotgun
Similar to ALS 2100 Field Model except chambered in 12 gauge, 3" only with 26" barrel and Mossy Oak Break Up camo finish. Weighs 6 lbs.; 46" overall.
Price: **$519.00**

Traditions ALS 2100 Waterfowl Semi-Automatic Shotgun
Similar to ALS 2100 Field Model except chambered in 12 gauge, 3" only with 28" barrel and Advantage Wetlands camo finish. Weighs 6.25 lbs.; 48" overall. Multi chokes.
Price: **$529.00**

Traditions ALS 2100 Hunter Combo
Similar to ALS 2100 Field Model except 2 barrels, 28" vent rib and 24" fully rifled deer. Weighs 6 to 6.5 lbs.; 48" overall. Choice TruGlo adj. sights or fixed cantilever mount on rifled barrel. Multi chokes.
Price: Walnut, rifle barrel **$609.00**
Price: Walnut, cantilever. **$629.00**
Price: Synthetic. **$579.00**

Traditions ALS 2100 Slug Hunter Shotgun
Similar to ALS 2100 Field Model, 12 ga., 24" barrel, overall length 44"; weighs 6.25 lbs. Designed specifically for the deer hunter. Rifled barrel has 1 in 36" twist. Fully adjustable fiber-optic sights.
Price: Walnut, rifle barrel **$529.00**
Price: Synthetic, rifle barrel. **$499.00**
Price: Walnut, cantilever. **$549.00**
Price: Synthetic, cantilever **$529.00**

Traditions ALS 2100 Home Security Shotgun
Similar to ALS 2100 Field Model, 12 ga., 20" barrel, overall length 40", weighs 6 lbs. Can be reloaded with one hand while shouldered and ontarget. Swivel studs installed in stock.
Price: **$399.00**

Winchester Super X3 Waterfowl

Winchester X2 NWTF Turkey

Winchester Super X2 Sporting Clays

VERONA MODEL 401 SERIES SEMI-AUTO SHOTGUNS
Gauge: 12. **Barrel:** 26", 28". **Weight:** 6.5 lbs. **Stock:** Walnut, black composite. **Sights:** Red dot. **Features:** Aluminum receivers, gas-operated, 2-3/4" or 3" Magnum shells without adj. or Mod., 4 screw-in chokes and wrench included. Sling swivels, gold trigger. Blued barrel. Imported from Italy by Legacy Sports International.
Price: **$1,199.00**
Price: 406 Series **$1,199.00**

WINCHESTER SUPER X3 SHOTGUNS
Gauge: 12, 3" and 3.5" chambers. **Barrel:** 26", 28", .742" back-bored; Invector Plus choke tubes. **Weight:** 7 to 7.25 lbs. **Stock:** Composite, 14.25"x1.75"x2". Mossy Oak New Break-Up camo with Dura-Touch Armor Coating. Pachmayr Decelerator buttpad with hard heel insert, customizable length of pull. **Features:** Alloy magazine tube, gunmetal grey Perma-Cote UT finish, self-adjusting Active Valve gas action, lightweight recoil spring system. Electroless nickel-plated bolt, three choke tubes, two length-of-pull stock spacers, drop and cast adjustment spacers, sling swivel studs. Introduced 2006. Made in Belgium, assembled in Portugal by U.S. Repeating Arms Co.
Price: Composite . . . .$1,119.00 to $1.239.00
Price: Cantilever Deer. **$1,179.00**
Price: Waterfowl w/Mossy Oak Brush camo, intr. 2007 . . . . **$1,439.00**
Price: Field model, walnut stock, intr. 2007 . . . . **$1,439.00**
Price: Gray Shadow **$1,299.00**
Price: All-Purpose Field **$1,439.00**

Price: Classic Field **$1,159.00**
Price: NWTF Cantiliever Extreme Turkey **$1,499.00**

WINCHESTER SUPER X3 FLANIGUN EXHIBITION/SPORTING
Similar to X3 but .742" backbored barrel, red-toned receiver, black Dura-Touch Armor Coated synthetic stock.
Price: **$1,459.00**

WINCHESTER SUPER X2 AUTO SHOTGUNS
Gauge: 12, 3", 3-1/2" chamber. **Barrel:** Belgian, 24", 26", 28"; Invector Plus choke tubes. **Weight:** 7-1/4 to 7.5 lbs. **Stock:** 14.25"x1.75"x2". Walnut or black synthetic. **Features:** Gas-operated action shoots all loads without adjustment; vent rib barrels; 4-shot magazine. Introduced 1999. Assembled in Portugal by U.S. Repeating Arms Co.
Price: Universal Hunter T **$1,252.00**
Price: NWTF Turkey, 3-1/2", Mossy Oak Break-Up camo . . **$1,236.00**
Price: Universal Hunter Model **$1,252.00**

Winchester Super X2 Sporting Clays Auto Shotguns
Similar to the Super X2 except has two gas pistons (one for target loads, one for heavy 3" loads), adjustable comb system and high-post rib. Back-bored barrel with Invector Plus choke tubes. Offered in 28" and 30" barrels. Introduced 2001. From U.S. Repeating Arms Co.
Price: Super X2 sporting clays **$999.00**
Price: Signature red stock. **$1,015.00**
Price: Practical MK I, composite stock, TruGlo sights **$1,116.00**

Includes a wide variety of sporting guns and guns suitable for competitive shooting.

Benelli Nova Pump

Benelli Nova Pump Slug

Browning BPS Trap

Browning BPS Rifled Deer
Mossy Oak New Break-Up

Browning BPS Micro Trap

BENELLI SUPERNOVA PUMP SHOTGUNS
Gauge: 12; 3.5" chamber. **Barrel:** 24", 26", 28". **Length:** 45.5-49.5". **Stock:** Synthetic; Max-4 , Timber, APG HD (2007). **Sights:** Red bar front, metal midbead. **Features:** 2-3/4", 3" chamber (3-1/2" 12 ga. only). Montefeltro rotating bolt design with dual action bars, magazine cut-off, synthetic trigger assembly, adjustable combs, shim kit, choice of buttstocks. 4-shot magazine. Introduced 2006. Imported from Italy by Benelli USA.
Price: Synthetic ComforTech $499.00
Price: Camo ComforTech $599.00
Price: SteadyGrip . . . . $599.00 to $619.00
Price: Tactical, Ghost Ring sight. . . . .$459.00 to $499.00
Price: Rifled Slug ComforTech, synthetic stock (2007) $670.00
Price: Tactical desert camo pistol grip, 18" barrel (2007) $589.00

BENELLI NOVA PUMP SHOTGUNS
Gauge: 12, 20. **Barrel:** 24", 26", 28". **Stock:** Black synthetic, Max-4, Timber and APG HD. **Sights:** Red bar. **Features:** 2-3/ 4", 3" chamber (3-1/2" 12 ga. only). Montefeltro rotating bolt design with dual action bars, magazine cut-off, synthetic trigger assembly, 4-shot magazine. Introduced 1999. Field & Slug Combo has 24" barrel and rifled bore; open rifle sights; synthetic stock; weighs 8.1 lbs. Imported from Italy by Benelli USA.
PrPrice: Max-4 HD camo stock $499.00
Price: H₂0 model, black synthetic, matte nickel finish $599.00
Price: APG HD stock , 20 ga. (2007) $529.00
Price: Tactical, 18.5" barrel, Ghost Ring sight $429.00
Price: Black synthetic youth stock, 20 ga. $429.00
Price: APG HD stock (2007), 20 ga.. . . . . $529.00

BROWNING BPS PUMP SHOTGUNS
Gauge: 10, 12, 3-1/2" chamber; 12, 16, or 20, 3" chamber (2-3/4" in target guns), 28, 2-3/4" cham-ber, 5-shot magazine, .410, 3" chamber. **Barrel:** 10 ga.-24" Buck Special, 28", 30", 32" Invector; 12, 20 ga.-22", 24", 26", 28", 30", 32" (Imp. Cyl., Mod. or Full), .410-26" barrel. (Imp. Cyl., Mod.

and Full choke tubes.) Also available with Invector choke tubes, 12 or 20 ga.; Upland Special has 22" barrel with Invector tubes. BPS 3" and 3-1/2" have back-bored barrel. **Weight:** 7 lbs., 8 oz. (28" barrel). **Length:** 48.75" overall (28" barrel). **Stock:** 14.25"x1.5"x2.5". Select walnut, semi-beavertail forend, full pistol grip stock. **Features:** All 12 gauge 3" guns except Buck Special and game guns have back-bored barrels with Invector Plus choke tubes. Bottom feeding and ejection, receiver top safety, high post vent rib. Double action bars eliminate binding. Vent rib barrels only. All 12 and 20 gauge guns with 3" chamber available with fully engraved receiver flats at no extra cost. Each gauge has its own unique game scene. Introduced 1977. Stalker is same gun as the standard BPS except all exposed metal parts have a matte blued finish and the stock has a black finish with a black recoil pad. Available in 10 ga. (3-1/2") and 12 ga. with 3" or 3-1/2" chamber, 22", 28", 30" barrel with In-vector choke system. Introduced 1987. Rifled Deer Hunter is similar to the standard BPS except has newly designed receiver/magazine tube/barrel mounting system to eliminate play, heavy 20.5" barrel with rifle-type sights with adjustable rear, solid receiver scope mount, "rifle" stock dimensions for scope or open sights, sling swivel studs. Gloss or matte finished wood with checkering, polished blue metal. Introduced 1992. Imported from Japan by Browning.
Price: Stalker (black syn. stock), 12 ga., from $549.00
Price: Rifled Deer Hunter (22" rifled bbl., cantilever mount),
   intr. 2007. . . . . $699.00
Price: Trap, intr. 2007. . . . . $729.00
Price: Hunter, 16 ga., intr. 2008 . . . . $569.00
Price: Upland Special, 16 ga., intr. 2008 . . . . $569.00
Price: Mossy Oak New Breakup, 3", 12 ga. only $679.00
Price: Mossy Oak New Breakup, 3-1/2", 12 ga. only $799.00
Price: Mossy Oak Duck Blind finish overall, 3" $679.00
Price: Mossy Oak Duck Blind finish overall, 3-1/2" $799.00
Price: Rifled Deer Mossy Oak New Break-Up, 12 ga. $719.00
Price: Rifled Deer Mossy Oak New Break-Up, 20 ga. $839.00
Price: Micro Trap, similar to BPS Trap but with compact
   dimensions (13-3/4" length of pull, 48-1/4" overall
   length), 12 gauge only $729.00

Browning BPS 10 gauge Mossy Oak Shadow Grass

Browning BPS 10 gauge

Charles Daly Maxi-Mag Turkey

Escort AimGuard

Escort Field Hunter

Browning BPS 10 Gauge Camo Pump Shotgun
Similar to the standard BPS except completely covered with Mossy Oak Shadow Grass camouflage. Available with 26" and 28" barrel. Introduced 1999. Imported by Browning
Price: **$799.00**

Browning BPS NWTF Turkey Series Pump Shotgun
Similar to the standard BPS except has full coverage Mossy Oak Break-Up camo finish on synthetic stock, forearm and exposed metal parts. Offered in 12 gauge, 3" or 3-1/2" chamber; 24" bbl. has extra-full choke tube and HiViz fiber-optic sights. Introduced 2001. From Browning.
Price: 12 ga., 3-1/2" chamber **$859.00**
Price: 12 ga., 3" chamber **$709.00**

Browning BPS Micro Pump Shotgun
Similar to the BPS Stalker except 20 ga. only, 22" Invector barrel, stock has pistol grip with recoil pad. Length of pull is 13.25"; weighs 6 lbs., 12 oz. Introduced 1986.
Price: **$569.00**

CHARLES DALY FIELD PUMP SHOTGUNS
Gauge: 12, 20. **Barrel:** Interchangeable 18.5", 24", 26", 28", 30" multi-choked. **Weight:** NA. **Stock:** Synthetic, various finishes, recoil pad. **Receiver:** Machined aluminum. **Features:** Field Tactical and Slug models come with adustable sights; Youth models may be upgraded to full size. Imported from Turkey by K.B.I., Inc.
Price: Field Tactical **$274.00**
Price: Field Hunter **$499.00**
Price: Field Hunter, Realtree Hardwood **$289.00**
Price: Field Hunter Advantage **$289.00**

CHARLES DALY MAXI-MAG PUMP SHOTGUNS
Gauge: 12 gauge, 3-1/2". **Barrel:** 24", 26", 28"; multi-choke system. **Weight:** NA. **Stock:** Synthetic black, Realtree Hardwoods, or Advantage Timber receiver, aluminum alloy. **Features:** Handles 2-3/4", 3" and 3-1/2" loads. Interchangeable ported barrels; Turkey package includes sling, HiViz sights, XX Full choke. Imported from Turkey by K.B.I., Inc.
Price: Field Hunter **$329.00**
Price: Field Hunter Advantage **$319.00**
Price: Field Hunter Hardwoods **$319.00**
Price: Field Hunter Turkey **$434.00**

EMF OLD WEST PUMP (SLIDE ACTION) SHOTGUN
Gauge: 12. **Barrel:** 20". **Weight:** 7 lbs. **Length:** 39-1/2" overall. **Stock:** Smooth walnut with cushioned pad. **Sights:** Front bead. **Features:** Authentic reproduction of Winchester 1897 pump shotgun; blue receiver and barrel; standard modified choke. Introduced 2006. Imported from China for EMF by TTN.
Price: **$449.90**

ESCORT PUMP SHOTGUNS
Gauge: 12, 20; 3" chamber. **Barrel:** 18" (AimGuard and MarineGuard), 22" (Youth Pump), 26", and 28" lengths. **Weight:** 6.7-7.0 lbs. **Stock:** Polymer in black, Shadow Grass® camo or Obsession® camo finish. Two adjusting spacers included. Youth model has Trio recoil pad. **Sights:** Bead or Spark front sights, depending on model. AimGuard and MarineGuard models have blade front sights. **Features:** Black-chrome or dipped camo metal parts, top of receiver dovetailed for sight mounts, gold plated trigger, trigger guard safety, magazine cut-off. Three choke tubes (IC, M, F) except AimGuard/MarineGuard which are cylinder bore. Models include: FH, FH Youth, AimGuard and Marine Guard. Introduced in 2003. Imported from Turkey by Legacy Sports International.
Price: . . . . **$389.00 to $469.00**

Mossberg Model 835 Mossy Oak Camo

Mossberg Model 500 Sporting

Mossberg Model 500 Bantam

Remington 870 Wingmaster

HARRINGTON & RICHARDSON
PARDNER PUMP FIELD GUN FULL-DIP CAMO
Gauge: 12, 20; 3" chamber. **Barrel:** 28" fully rifled. **Weight:** 7.5 lbs. **Length:** 48-1/8" overall. **Stock:** Synthetic or hardwood. **Sights:** NA. **Features:** Steel receiver, double action bars, cross-bolt safety, easy take-down, vent rib, screw-in Modified choke tube. Ventilated recoil pad and grooved forend with Realtree APG-HDTM full camo dip finish.
Price: Full camo version **$278.00**

IAC MODEL 87W-1 LEVER-ACTION SHOTGUN
Gauge: 12; 2-3/4" chamber only. **Barrel:** 20" with fixed Cylinder choke. **Weight:** NA. **Length:** NA. **Stock:** American walnut. **Sights:** Bead front. **Features:** Modern replica of Winchester Model 1887 lever-action shotgun. Includes five-shot tubular magazine, pivoting split-lever design to meet modern safety requirements. Imported by Interstate Arms Corporation.
Price: **$429.95**

ITHACA GUN COMPANY DEERSLAYER III SLUG SHOTGUN
Gauge: 12, 20; 3" chamber. **Barrel:** 26" fully rifled, heavy fluted with 1:28 twist for 12 ga.; 1:24 for 20 ga. **Weight:** 8.14 lbs. to 9.5 lbs. with scope mounted. **Length:** 45.625" overall. **Stock:** Fancy black walnut stock and forend. **Sights:** NA. **Features:** Updated, slug-only version of the classic Model 37. Bottom ejection, blued barrel and receiver.
Price: **$1,189.00**

ITHACA GUN COMPANY MODEL 37 28 GAUGE SHOTGUN
Gauge: 28. **Barrel:** 26" or 28". **Weight:** NA. **Length:** NA. **Stock:** Black walnut stock and forend. **Sights:** NA. **Features:** Scaled down receiver with traditional Model 37 bottom ejection and easy takedown. Available in Fancy "A," Fancy "AA," and Fancy "AAA" grades with increasingly elaborate receiver engraving and decoration. Special order only.
Price: Fancy "A" grade **$999.00**

MOSSBERG MODEL 835 ULTI-MAG PUMP SHOTGUNS
Gauge: 12, 3-1/2" chamber. **Barrel:** Ported 24" rifled bore, 24", 28", Accu-Mag choke tubes for steel or lead shot. **Weight:** 7.75 lbs. **Length:** 48.5" overall. **Stock:** 14"x1.5"x2.5". Dual Comb. Cut-checkered hardwood or camo synthetic; both have recoil pad. **Sights:** White bead front, brass mid-bead; fiber-optic rear. **Features:** Shoots 2-3/4", 3" or 3-1/2" shells. Back-bored and ported barrel to reduce recoil, improve patterns. Ambidextrous thumb safety, twin extractors, dual slide bars. Mossberg Cablelock included. Introduced 1988.
Price: Thumbhole Turkey **$674.00**
Price: Tactical Turkey. **$636.00**
Price: Synthetic Thumbhole Turkey, from. **$493.00**

Price: Turkey, from **$487.00**
Price: Waterfowl, from **$437.00**
Price: Combo, from **$559.00**

MOSSBERG MODEL 500 SPORTING PUMP SHOTGUNS
Gauge: 12, 20, .410, 3" chamber. **Barrel:** 18.5" to 28" with fixed or Accu-Choke, plain or vent rib. **Weight:** 6-1/4 lbs. (.410), 7-1/4 lbs. (12). **Length:** 48" overall (28" barrel). **Stock:** 14"x1.5"x2.5". Walnut-stained hardwood, black synthetic, Mossy Oak Advantage camouflage. Cut-checkered grip and forend. **Sights:** White bead front, brass mid-bead; fiber-optic. **Features:** Ambidextrous thumb safety, twin extractors, disconnecting safety, dual action bars. Quiet Carry forend. Many barrels are ported. From Mossberg.
Price: Turkey. **$410.00**
Price: Waterfowl, from **$406.00**
Price: Combo, from **$391.00**
Price: Field, from. **$354.00**
Price: Slugster, from. **$354.00**

Mossberg Model 500 Bantam Pump Shotgun
Same as the Model 500 Sporting Pump except 12 or 20 gauge, 22" vent rib Accu-Choke barrel with choke tube set; has 1" shorter stock, reduced length from pistol grip to trigger, reduced forend reach. Introduced 1992.
Price: **$354.00**
Price: Super Bantam (2008), from **$338.00**

NEW ENGLAND PARDNER PUMP SHOTGUN
Gauge: 12 ga., 3". **Barrel:** 28" vent rib, screw-in Modified choke tube. **Weight:** 7.5 lbs. **Length:** 48.5". **Stock:** American walnut, grooved forend, ventilated recoil pad. **Sights:** Bead front. **Features:** Machined steel receiver, double action bars, five-shot magazine.
Price: **$200.00**

REMINGTON MODEL 870 WINGMASTER SHOTGUNS
Gauge: 12, 20, 28 ga., .410 bore. **Barrel:** 25", 26", 28", 30" (RemChokes). **Weight:** 7-1/4 lbs. **Length:** 46", 48". **Stock:** Walnut, hardwood. **Sights:** Single bead (Twin bead Wingmaster). **Features:** Light contour barrel. Double action bars, cross-bolt safety, blue finish. LW is 28 gauge and .410-bore only, 25" vent rib barrel with RemChoke tubes, high-gloss wood finish. Limited Edition Model 870 Wingmaster 100th Anniversary Commemorative Edition (2008 only) is 12 gauge with gold centennial logo, "100 Years of Remington Pump Shotguns" banner. Gold-plated trigger, American B Grade walnut stock and forend, high-gloss finish. fleur-de-lis checkering.
Price: Wingmaster, walnut, blued. **$785.00**
Price: LW .410-bore **$839.00**
Price: 100th Anniversary (2008), 12 ga., 28" barrel **$1,035.00**

Remington Model 870 Windmaster LW

Remington Model 870 Marine Magnum

Remington Model 870 Express Deer Gun

Remington Model 870 Express Turkey Gun

Remington Model 870 Express Youth Turkey Gun

Remington Model 870 Express Compact Camo

Remington Model 870 Marine Magnum Shotgun
Similar to 870 Wingmaster except all metal plated with electroless nickel, black synthetic stock and forend. Has 18" plain barrel (cyl.), bead front sight, 7-shot magazine. Introduced 1992. XCS version with TriNyte corrosion control introduced 2007.
Price: **$772.00**

Remington Model 870 Classic Trap Shotgun
Similar to Model 870 Wingmaster except has 30" vent rib, light contour barrel, singles, mid- and long-handicap choke tubes, semi-fancy American walnut stock, high-polish blued receiver with engraving. Chamber 2.75". From Remington Arms Co.
Price: **$1,039.00**
Price: XCS (2007). **$899.00**

Remington Model 870 Express Shotguns
Similar to Model 870 Wingmaster except laminate, syn-thetic black, or camo stock with solid, black recoil pad and pressed checkering on grip and forend. Out-side metal surfaces have black oxide finish. Comes with 26" or 28" vent rib barrel with mod. RemChoke tube. ShurShot Turkey (2008) has ShurShot synthetic pistol-grip thumbhole design, extended forend, Mossy Oak Obsession camouflage, matte black met-al finish, 21" vent rib barrel, twin beads, Turkey Extra Full Rem Choke tube. Receiver drilled and tapped for mounting optics. ShurShot FR CL

(Fully Rifled Cantilever, 2008) includes compact 23" fully-rifled barrel with integrated cantilever scope mount.
Price: 12 and 20 ga., laminate or synthetic right-hand stock . .**$383.00**
Price: 12 or 20 ga., laminate or synthetic left-hand stock **$409.00**
Price: Express Synthetic, 12 ga., 18" barrel (2007) **$383.00**
Price: Express Synthetic, 20 ga., 7 round capacity, from **$385.00**
Price: Express Synthetic Deer FR 12 ga., rifle sights **$425.00**
Price: Express Laminate Deer FR 12 ga., rifle sights **$416.00**
Price: Express Synthetic or Laminate Turkey 12 ga.,
21" barrel **$388.00**
Price: Express Camo Turkey 12 ga., 21" barrel **$445.00**
Price: Express Combo Turkey/Deer Camo 12 ga. **$612.00**
Price: Express Synthetic Youth Combo 20 ga. **$543.00**
Price: Express Magnum ShurShot Turkey (2008) **$492.00**
Price: Express Magnum ShurShot FR CL (2008). **$500.00**
Price: Express ShurShot Synthetic Cantilever; 12 or 20 ga.
with ShurShot stock and cantilever scope mount **$532.00**
Price: Express Compact Deer; 20 ga., similar to 870 Express
Laminate Deer but with smaller dimensions **$395.00**
Price: Express Compact Pink Camo; 20 ga. **$429.00**
Price: Express Compact Synthetic; matte black synthetic
stock **$383.00**
Price: Express Compact Camo; camo buttstock and forend . **$429.00**
Price: Express Compact Jr.; Shorter barrel and LOP **$383.00**

**Remington Model 870 Express
Super Magnum**

Remington Model 870 Express Tactical

**Remington Model 870 Express Tactical
with Ghost Ring Sights**

**Remington Model 870 SPS Shurshot
Synthetic Super Slug**

Remington Model 870 Express Super Magnum Shotgun
Similar to Model 870 Express except 28" vent rib barrel with 3-1/2" chamber, vented recoil pad. Introduced 1998. Model 870 Express Super Magnum Waterfowl (2008) is fully camouflaged with Mossy Oak Duck Blind pattern, 28-inch vent rib Rem Choke barrel, "Over Decoys" Choke tube (.007") fiber-optic HiViz single bead front sight; front and rear sling swivel studs, padded black sling.
Price: **$431.00**
Price: Super Magnum synthetic, 26" **$431.00**
Price: Super Magnum turkey camo (full-coverage
 RealTree Advantage camo), 23" **$564.00**
Price: Super Magnum combo (26" with Mod. RemChoke
 and 20" fully rifled deer barrel with 3" chamber
 and rifle sights; wood stock) **$577.00**
Price: Super Magnum Waterfowl (2008) **$577.00**

Remington Model 870 Special Purpose Shotguns (SPS)
Similar to the Model 870 Express synthetic, chambered for 12 ga. 3" and 3-1/2" shells, has Realtree Hardwoods HD or APG HD camo-synthetic stock and metal treatment, TruGlo fiber-optic sights. Intro-duced 2001. SPS Max Gobbler introduced 2007. Knoxx SpecOps adjustable stock, Williams Fire Sights fiber-optic sights, R3 recoil pad, Realtree APG HD camo. Drilled and tapped for Weaver-style rail
Price: SPS 12 ga. 3" **$671.00**
Price: SPS Super Mag Max Gobbler (2007) **$819.00**

Price: SPS Super Mag Max Turkey ShurShot 3-1/2" (2008) . .**$644.00**
Price: SPS Synthetic ShurShot FR Cantilever 3" (2008) **$671.00**

Remington Model 870 Express Tactical
Similar to Model 870 but in 12 gauge only (2-2/4" and 3" interchange-ably) with 18.5" barrel, Tactical RemChoke extended/ported choke tube, black synthetic buttstock and forend, extended magazine tube, gray powdercoat finish overall. 38.5" overall length, weighs 7.5 lbs.
Price: **$372.00**
Price: Model 870 TAC Desert Recon; desert camo stock and
 sand-toned metal surfaces **$692.00**
Price: Model 870 Express Tactical with Ghost Ring Sights; Top-
 mounted accessories rail and XS ghost ring rear sight **$505.00**

REMINGTON MODEL 870 SPS SHURSHOT SYNTHETIC SUPER SLUG
Gauge: 12; 2-3/4" and 3" chamber, interchangeable. **Barrel:** 25.5" extra-heavy, fully rifled pinned to receiver. **Weight:** 7-7/8 lbs. **Length:** 47" overall. **Features:** Pump-action model based on 870 platform. SuperCell recoil pad. Drilled and tapped for scope mounts with Weaver rail included. Matte black metal surfaces, Mossy Oak Treestand Shurshot buttstock and forend.
Price: . . . .**NA**
Price: 870 SPS ShurShot Synthetic Cantilever; cantilever scope mount
 and Realtree Hardwoods camo buttstock and forend . **$532.00**
Price: 870 SPS ShurShot Synthetic Turkey; adjustable sights and APG
 HD camo buttstock and forend **$532.00**

Remington Model 887 Nitro Mag Pump

Remington Model 887 Nitro Mag Pump Waterfowl

Winchester Super X Pump Black Shadow Field

Winchester Super X Pump Defender

REMINGTON MODEL 887 NITRO MAG PUMP SHOTGUN

Gauge: 12; 3.5", 3", and 2-3/4" chambers. **Barrel:** 28". **Features:** Pump-action model based on the Model 870. Interchangeable shells, black matte ArmoLokt rustproof coating throughout. SuperCell recoil pad. Solid rib and Hi-Viz front sight with interchangeable light tubes. Black synthetic stock with contoured grip panels.
Price: **$399.00**
Price: Model 887 Nitro Mag Waterfowl, Advantage
Max-4 camo overall **$532.00**

STOEGER MODEL P350 SHOTGUNS

Gauge: 12, 3.5" chamber, set of five choke tubes (C, IC, M, IM, XF). **Barrel:** 18.5",24", 26", 28". **Stock:** Black synthetic, Timber HD, Max-4 HD, APG HD camos. **Sights:** Red bar front. **Features:** Inertia-recoil, mercury recoil reducer, pistol grip stocks. Imported by Benelli USA.
Price: Synthetic. **$329.00**
Price: Max-4, Timber HD **$429.00**
Price: Black synthetic pistol grip (2007) **$329.00**
Price: APG HD camo pistol grip (2007) **$429.00**

WINCHESTER SUPER X PUMP SHOTGUNS

Gauge: 12, 3" chambers. **Barrel:** 18"; 26" and 28" barrels are .742" back-bored, chrome plated; Invector Plus choke tubes. **Weight:** 7 lbs. **Stock:** Walnut or composite. **Features:** Rotary bolt, four lugs, dual steel action bars. Walnut Field has gloss-finished walnut stock and forearm, cut checkering. Black Shadow Field has composite stock and forearm, non-glare matte finish barrel and receiver. Speed Pump Defender has composite stock and forearm, chromed plated, 18" cylinder choked barrel, non-glare metal surfaces, five-shot magazine, grooved forearm. Weight, 6.5 lbs. Reintroduced 2008. Made in U.S.A. from Winchester Repeating Arms Co.
Price: Black Shadow Field **$359.00**
Price: Defender. **$319.00**

Includes a variety of game guns and guns for competitive shooting.

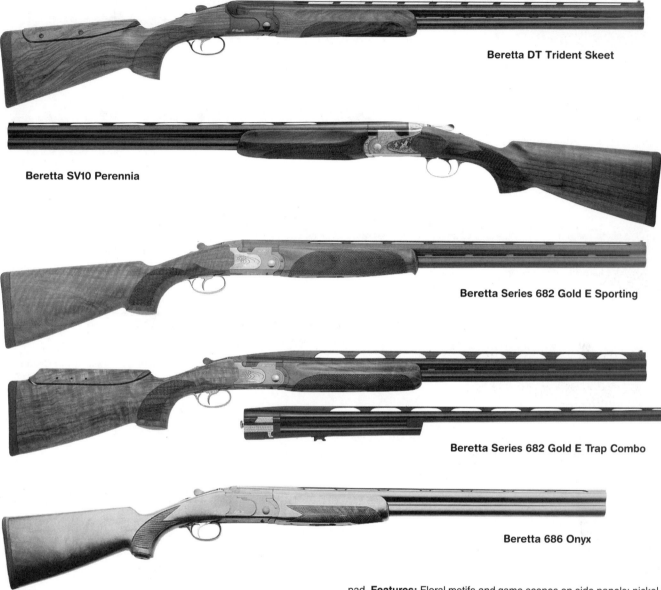

Beretta DT Trident Skeet

Beretta SV10 Perennia

Beretta Series 682 Gold E Sporting

Beretta Series 682 Gold E Trap Combo

Beretta 686 Onyx

BERETTA DT10 TRIDENT SHOTGUNS
Gauge: 12, 2-3/4", 3" chambers. **Barrel:** 28", 30", 32", 34"; competition-style vent rib; fixed or Optima choke tubes. **Weight:** 7.9 to 9 lbs. **Stock:** High-grade walnut stock with oil finish; hand-checkered grip and forend, adjustable stocks available. **Features:** Detachable, adjustable trigger group, raised and thickened receiver, forend iron has adjustment nut to guarantee wood-to-metal fit. Introduced 2000. Imported from Italy by Beretta USA.
Price: DT10 Trident Trap, adjustable stock. **$7,400.00**
Price: DT10 Trident Skeet **$7,900.00**
Price: DT10 Trident Sporting, from. **$6,975.00**

BERETTA SV10 PERENNIA O/U SHOTGUN
Gauge: 12, 3" chambers. **Barrel:** 26", 28", 30". Optima-Bore profile, polished blue. Bore diameter 18.6mm (0.73 in.) Self-adjusting dual conical longitudinal locking lugs, oversized monobloc bearing shoulders, replaceable hinge pins. Ventilated top rib, 6x6mm. Long guided extractors, automatic ejection or mechanical extraction. Optimachoke tubes. **Weight:** 7.3 lbs. **Stock:** Quick take-down stock with pistol grip or English straight stock. Kick-off recoil reduction system available on request on Q-Stock. **Length of pull:** 14.7", drop at comb, 1.5", drop at heel, 2.36" or 1.38"/2.17". Semibeavertail forend with elongated forend lever. New checkering pattern, matte oil finish, rubber

pad. **Features:** Floral motifs and game scenes on side panels; nickel-based protective finish, arrowhead-shaped sideplates, solid steel alloy billet. Kick-Off recoil reduction mechanism available on select models. Fixed chokes on request, removable trigger group, titanium single selective trigger. Manual or automatic safety, newly designed safety and selector lever. Gel-Tek recoil pad available on re-quest. Polypropylene case, 5 chokes with spanner, sling swivels, plastic pad, Beretta gun oil. In-troduced 2008. Imported from Italy by Beretta USA.
Price: From **$3,250.00**

BERETTA SERIES 682 GOLD E SKEET, TRAP, SPORTING O/U SHOTGUNS
Gauge: 12, 2-3/4" chambers. **Barrel:** skeet-28"; trap-30" and 32", Imp. Mod. & Full and Mobilchoke; trap mono shotguns-32" and 34" Mobilchoke; trap top single guns-32" and 34" Full and Mobilchoke; trap combo sets-from 30" O/U, to 32" O/U, 34" top single. **Stock:** Close-grained walnut, hand checkered. **Sights:** White Bradley bead front sight and center bead. **Features:** Receiver has Greystone gunmetal gray finish with gold accents. Trap Monte Carlo stock has deluxe trap recoil pad. Various grades available. Imported from Italy by Beretta USA.
Price: 682 Gold E Trap with adjustable stock. **$4,425.00**
Price: 682 Gold E Trap Unsingle **$4,825.00**
Price: 682 Gold E Sporting **$4,075.00**
Price: 682 Gold E Skeet, adjustable stock **$4,425.00**

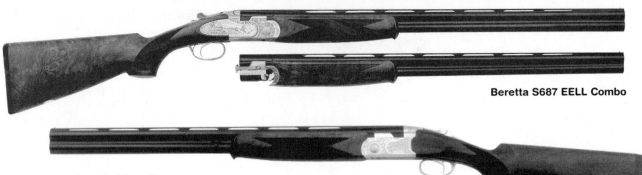

Beretta S687 EELL Combo

Beretta Silver Pigeon

Beretta Silver Pigeon II

Browning Cynergy Classic Field Grade III

Browning Cynergy Classic Field Grade VI

BERETTA 686 ONYX O/U SHOTGUNS
Gauge: 12, 20, 28; 3", 3.5" chambers. **Barrel:** 26", 28" (Mobilchoke tubes). **Weight:** 6.8-6.9 lbs. **Stock:** Checkered American walnut. **Features:** Intended for the beginning sporting clays shooter. Has wide, vented target rib, radiused recoil pad. Polished black finish on receiver and barrels. Introduced 1993. Imported from Italy by Beretta U.S.A.
Price: White Onyx **$1,975.00**
PPrice: White Onyx Sporting **$2,175.00**

BERETTA SILVER PIGEON O/U SHOTGUNS
Gauge: 12, 20, 28, 3" chambers (2-3/4" 28 ga.). .410 bore, 3" chamber. **Barrel:** 26", 28". **Weight:** 6.8 lbs. **Stock:** Checkered walnut. **Features:** Interchangeable barrels (20 and 28 ga.), single selective gold-plated trigger, boxlock action, auto safety, Schnabel forend.
Price: Silver Pigeon S **$2,400.00**
Price: Silver Pigeon II **$3,150.00**
Price: Silver Pigeon III **$3,275.00**
Price: Silver Pigeon IV **$3,200.00**
Price: Silver Pigeon V **$3,675.00**

BERETTA ULTRALIGHT O/U SHOTGUNS
Gauge: 12, 2-3/4" chambers. **Barrel:** 26", 28", Mobilchoke tubes. **Weight:** About 5 lbs., 13 oz. **Stock:** Select American walnut with checkered grip and forend. **Features:** Low-profile aluminum alloy receiver with titanium breech face insert. Electroless nickel receiver with game scene engraving. Single selective trigger; automatic safety. Introduced 1992. Ultralight Deluxe except has matte electroless nickel finish receiver with gold game scene engraving; matte oil-finished, select walnut stock and forend. Imported from Italy by Beretta U.S.A.
Price: **$2,075.00**
Price: Ultralight Deluxe **$2,450.00**

BERETTA COMPETITION SHOTGUNS
Gauge: 12, 20, 28, and .410 bore, 2-3/4", 3" and 3-1/2" chambers. **Barrel:** 26" and 28" (Mobilchoke tubes). **Stock:** Close-grained walnut. **Features:** Highly-figured, American walnut stocks and forends, and a unique, weather-resistant finish on barrels. Silver designates standard 686, 687 models with silver receivers; 686 Silver Pigeon has enhanced engraving pattern, Schnabel forend; Gold indicates higher grade 686EL, 687EL models with full sideplates. Imported from Italy by Beretta U.S.A.
Price: S687 EELL Gold Pigeon Sporting (D.R. engraving). . **$7,675.00**

BILL HANUS 16-GAUGE BROWNING CITORI M525 FIELD
Gauge: 16. **Barrel:** 26" and 28". **Weight:** 6-3/4 pounds. **Stock:** 1-1/2" x 2-3/8" x 14-1/4" and cast neutral. Adjusting for cast-on for left-handed shooters or cast-off for right-handed shooters, $300 extra. Oil finish. **Features:** Full pistol grip with a graceful Schnable forearm and built on a true 16-gauge frame. Factory supplies three Invector choke tubes: IC-M-F and Bill Hanus models come with two Briley-made skeet chokes for close work over dogs and clay-target games.
Price: **$1,795.00**

BROWNING CYNERGY O/U SHOTGUNS
Gauge: 12, 20, 28. **Barrel:** 26", 28", 30", 32". **Stock:** Walnut or composite. **Sights:** White bead front most models; HiViz Pro-Comp sight on some models; mid bead. **Features:** Mono-Lock hinge, recoil-reducing interchangeable Inflex recoil pad, silver nitride receiver; striker-based trigger, ported barrel option. Models include: Cynergy Sporting, Adjustable Comb; Cynergy Sporting Composite CF; Cynergy Field, Composite; Cynergy Classic Sporting; Cynergy Classic Field; Cynergy Camo Mossy Oak New Shadow Grass; Cynergy Camo Mossy

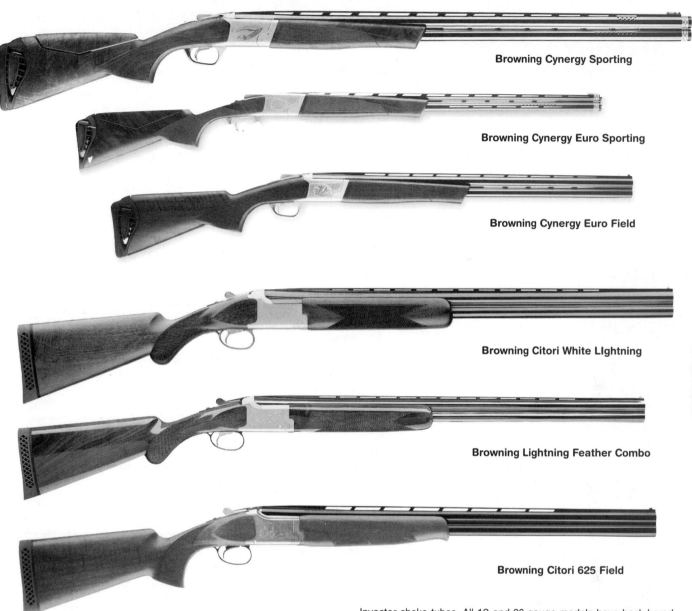

Browning Cynergy Sporting

Browning Cynergy Euro Sporting

Browning Cynergy Euro Field

Browning Citori White LIghtning

Browning Lightning Feather Combo

Browning Citori 625 Field

BROWNING CYNERGY O/U SHOTGUNS (cont.)

Oak New Break-Up; and Cynergy Camo Mossy Oak Brush. Imported from Japan by Browning.

Price: Cynergy Classic Field, 12 ga., from **$2,399.00**
Price: Cynergy Classic Field Grade III, similar to Cynergy Classic Field but with full coverage high-relief engraving on reciever and top lever, gloss finish Grade III/IV walnut., from **$3,499.00**
Price: Cyergy Classic Field Grade VI, similar to Cynergy Classic Field Grade III but with more extensive, gold-highlighted engraving, from **$5,229.00**
Price: Cynergy Classic Sporting, from **$3,499.00**
Price: Cynergy Euro Sporting, 12 ga.; 28", 30", or 32" barrels **$3,719.00**
Price: Cynergy Euro Sporting Composite 12 ga. **$3,499.00**
Price: Cynergy Euro Sporting, adjustable comb, intr. 2006 . **$4,079.00**
Price: Cynergy Feather, 12 ga. intr. 2007 . . . . **$2,579.00**
Price: Cynergy Feather, 20, 28 ga., .410, intr. 2008 . . . . . . **$2,599.00**
Price: Cynergy Euro Sporting, 20 ga., intr. 2008 . . . . **$3,739.00**
Price: Cynergy Euro Field, Invector Plus tubes in 12 and 20 gauge, standard Invector tubes on 28 gauge and 410 . . . . **$2,509.00**

BROWNING CITORI O/U SHOTGUNS

Gauge: 12, 20, 28 and .410. **Barrel:** 26", 28" in 28 and .410. Offered with Invector choke tubes. All 12 and 20 gauge models have back-bored barrels and Invector Plus choke system. **Weight:** 6 lbs., 8 oz. (26" .410) to 7 lbs., 13 oz. (30" 12 ga.). **Length:** 43" overall (26" bbl.). **Stock:** Dense walnut, hand checkered, full pistol grip, beavertail forend. Field-type recoil pad on 12 ga. field guns and trap and skeet models. **Sights:** Medium raised beads, German nickel silver. **Features:** Barrel selector integral with safety, automatic ejectors, three-piece takedown. Citori 625 Field (intr. 2008) includes Vector Pro extended forcing cones, new wood checkering patterns, silver-nitride finish with high-relief engraving, gloss oil finish with Grade II/III walnut with radius pistol grip, Schnabel forearm, 12 gauge, three Invector Plus choke tubes. Citori 625 Sporting (intr. 2008) includes standard and adjustable combs, 32", 30", and 28" barrels, five Diamond Grade extended Invector Plus choke tubes. Triple Trigger System allows adjusting length of pull and choice of wide checkered, narrow smooth, and wide smooth canted trigger shoe. HiViz Pro-Comp fiber-optic front sights. Imported from Japan by Browning.

Price: Lightning, from **$1,763.00**
Price: White Lightning, from **$1,836.00**
Price: Superlight Feather **$2,098.00**
Price: Lightning Feather, combo 20 and 28 ga. **$1,869.00**
Price: 625 Field, 12, 20 or 28 ga. and .410. Weighs 6 lbs. 12 oz. to 7 lbs. 14 oz. **$2,339.00**
Price: 625 Sporting, 12, 20 or 28 ga. and .410, standard comb, intr. 2008 . . . . **$3,329.00**
Price: 625 Sporting, 12 ga., adj. comb, intr. 2008 . . . . **$3,639.00**

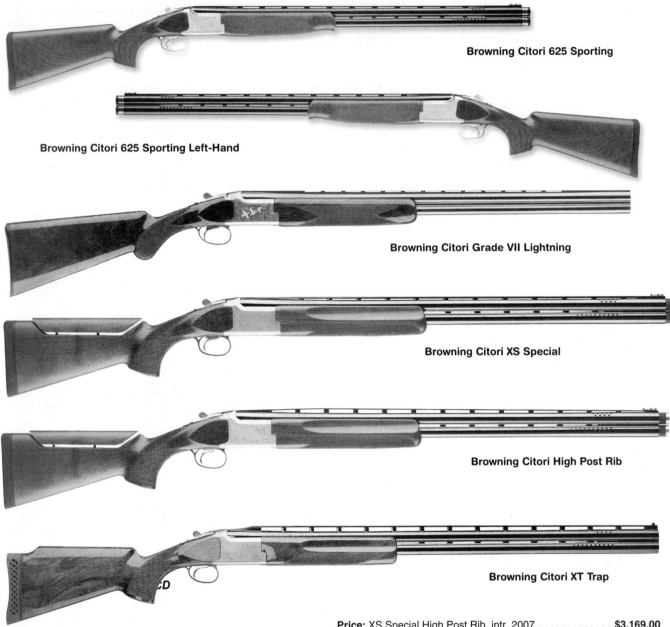

Browning Citori 625 Sporting

Browning Citori 625 Sporting Left-Hand

Browning Citori Grade VII Lightning

Browning Citori XS Special

Browning Citori High Post Rib

Browning Citori XT Trap

Browning Citori High Grade Shotguns

Similar to standard Citori except has engraved hunting scenes and gold inlays, high-grade, hand-oiled walnut stock and forearm. Introduced 2000. From Browning.

Price: Grade IV Lightning, engraved gray receiver,
introduced 2005, from **$2,999.00**
Price: Grade VII Lightning, engraved gray or blue receiver,
introduced 2005, from **$4,769.00**
Price: GTS High Grade, intr. 2007 . . . . **$4,309.00**

Browning Citori XS Sporting O/U Shotguns

Similar to the standard Citori except available in 12, 20, 28 or .410 with 28", 30", 32" ported barrels with various screw-in choke combinations: S (Skeet), C (Cylinder), IC (Improved Cylinder), M (Modified), and IM (Improved Modified). Has pistol grip stock, rounded or Schnabel forend. Weighs 7.1 lbs. to 8.75 lbs. Introduced 2004. Ultra XS Prestige (intr. 2008) has silver-nitride finish receiver with gold accented, high-relief Ultra XS Special engraving. Also, single selective trigger, hammer ejectors, gloss oil finish walnut stock with right-hand palm swell, adjustable comb, Schnabel forearm. Comes with five Invector-Plus Midas Grade choke tubes.

Price: XS Special, 12 ga.; 30", 32" barrels **$3,169.00**
Price: XS Skeet, 12 or 20 ga. **$2,829.00**

Price: XS Special High Post Rib, intr. 2007 . . . . **$3,169.00**
Price: Ultra XS Prestige, intr. 2008 . . . . **$4,759.00**

Browning Citori XT Trap O/U Shotgun

Similar to the Citori XS Special except has engraved silver nitride receiver with gold highlights, vented side barrel rib. Available in 12 gauge with 30" or 32" barrels, Invector-Plus choke tubes, adjustable comb and buttplate. Introduced 1999. Imported by Browning.

Price: XT Trap **$2,639.00**
Price: XT Trap w/adjustable comb **$2,959.00**
Price: XT Trap Gold w/adjustable comb, introduced 2005 . . **$4,899.00**

CHARLES DALY MODEL 206 O/U SHOTGUN

Gauge: 12, 3" chambers. **Barrel:** 26", 28", 30", chrome-moly steel. **Weight:** 8 lbs. **Stock:** Check-ered select Turkish walnut stocks. **Features:** Single selective trigger, extractors or selective automatic ejectors. Sporting model has 10mm ventilated rib and side ventilated ribs. Trap model comes with 10mm top rib and side ventilated ribs and includes a Monte Carlo Trap buttstock. Both competition ribs have mid-brass bead and front fluorescent sights. Five Multi-Choke tubes. Introduced 2008. Imported from Turkey by K.B.I., Inc.

Price: Field, 26" or 28", extractors **$759.00**
Price: Field, 26" or 28", auto-eject **$884.00**
Price: Sporting, 28" or 30" ported, ... **$999.00**
Price: Trap, 28" or 30" ported, ... **$1,064.00**

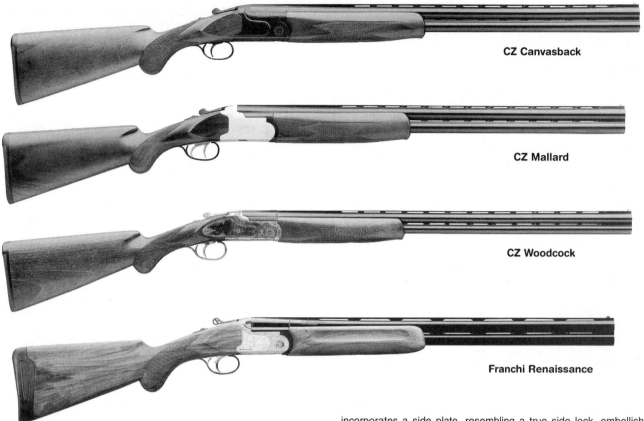

CZ Canvasback

CZ Mallard

CZ Woodcock

Franchi Renaissance

CZ SPORTING OVER/UNDER
Gauge: 12, 3" chambers. **Barrel:** 30", 32" chrome-lined, back-bored with extended forcing cones. **Weight:** 9 lbs. **Length:** NA. **Stock:** Neutral cast stock with an adjustable comb, trap style forend, pistol grip and ambidextrous palm swells. #3 grade Circassian walnut. At lowest position, drop at comb: 1-5/8"; drop at heel: 2-3/8"; length of pull: 14-1/2". **Features:** Designed for Sporting Clays and FITASC competition. Hand engraving, satin black-finished receiver. Tapered rib with center bead and a red fiber-optic front bead, 10 choke tubes with wrench, single selective trigger, automatic ejectors, thin rubber pad with slick plastic top. Introduced 2008. From CZ-USA.
Price: **$2,509.00**

CZ CANVASBACK
Gauge: 12, 20, 3" chambers. **Barrel:** 26", 28". **Length:** NA. **Stock:** Round-knob pistol grip, Schnabel forend, Turkish walnut. **Features:** Single selective trigger, set of 5 screw-in chokes, black chrome finished receiver. From CZ-USA.
Price: **$819.00**

CZ MALLARD
Gauge: 12, 20, 28, .410, 3" chambers. **Barrel:** 26". **Weight:** 7.7 lbs. **Length:** NA. **Stock:** Round-knob pistol grip, Schnabel forend, Turkish walnut. **Features:** Double triggers and extractors, coin finished receiver, multi chokes. From CZ-USA.
Price: **$562.00**

CZ REDHEAD
Gauge: 12, 20, 3" chambers. **Barrel:** 28". **Weight:** 7.4 lbs. **Length:** NA. **Stock:** Round-knob pistol grip, Schnabel forend, Turkish walnut. **Features:** Single selective triggers and extractors (12 & 20 ga.), screw-in chokes (12, 20, 28 ga.) choked IC and Mod (.410), coin finished receiver, multi chokes. From CZ-USA.
Price: **$965.00**

CZ WOODCOCK
Gauge: 12, 20, 28, .410, 3" chambers. **Barrel:** 26". **Weight:** 7.7 lbs. **Length:** NA. **Stock:** Round-knob pistol grip, Schnabel forend, Turkish walnut. **Features:** Single selective triggers and extractors (auto ejectors on 12 & 20 ga.), screw-in chokes (12, 20, 28 ga.) choked IC and Mod (.410), coin finished receiver, multi chokes. The sculptured frame incorporates a side plate, resembling a true side lock, embellished with hand engraving and finished with color casehardening. From CZ-USA.
Price: **$1,246.00**

ESCORT OVER/UNDER SHOTGUNS
Gauge: 12, 3" chamber. **Barrel:** 28". **Weight:** 7.4 lbs. **Stock:** Walnut or select walnut with Trio recoil pad; synthetic stock with adjustable comb. Three adjustment spacers. **Sights:** Bronze front bead. **Features:** Blued barrels, blued or nickel receiver. Trio recoil pad. Five interchangeable chokes (SK, IC, M, IM, F); extractors or ejectors (new, 2008), barrel selector. Hard case available. Introduced 2007. Imported from Turkey by Legacy Sports International.
Price: **$599.00**

FRANCHI RENAISSANCE AND RENAISSANCE SPORTING O/U SHOTGUNS
Gauge: 12, 20, 28, 3" chamber. **Barrel:** 26", 28". **Weight:** 5.0 to 6.0 lbs. **Length:** 42-5/8" to 44-5/8". **Stock:** 14.5" LOP, European oil-finished walnut with standard grade A grade, and AA grade choices. Prince of Wales grip. **Features:** TSA recoil pad, interchangeable chokes, hard case. Introduced 2006. *Sporting model:* **Gauge:** 12 , 3". **Barrel:** 30" ported. **Weight:** 7.9 lbs. **Length:** 46 5/8". **Stock:** 14.5" LOP, A-grade European oil-finished walnut. **Features:** TSA recoil pad, adjustable comb, lengthened forcing cones, extended choke tubes (C, IC, M and wrench), hard case. Introduced 2007. Imported from Italy by Benelli USA.
Price: Field **$1,729.00**
Price: Classic **$1,899.00**
Price: Elite. **$2,399.00**
Price: Sporting **$2,249.00**

KIMBER MARIAS O/U SHOTGUN
Gauge: 20, 16; 3". **Barrel:** 26", 28", 30". **Weight:** 6.5 lbs. **Length:** NA. **Stock:** Turkish walnut stocks, 24-lpi checkering, oil finish. **LOP:** 14.75". **Features:** Hand-detachable back-action sidelock, bone-charcoal case coloring. Hand-engraving on receiver and locks, Belgian rust blue barrels, chrome lined. Five thinwall choke tubes, automatic ejectors, ventilated rib. Gold line cocking indicators on locks. Grade I has 28" barrels, Prince of Wales stock in grade three Turkish walnut in either 12 or 20 gauge. Grade II shas grade four Turkish walnut stocks, 12 gauge in Prince of Wales and 20 with either Prince of Wales or English profiles. Introduced 2008. Imported from Italy by Kimber Mfg., Inc.
Price: Grade II. **$5,799.00**

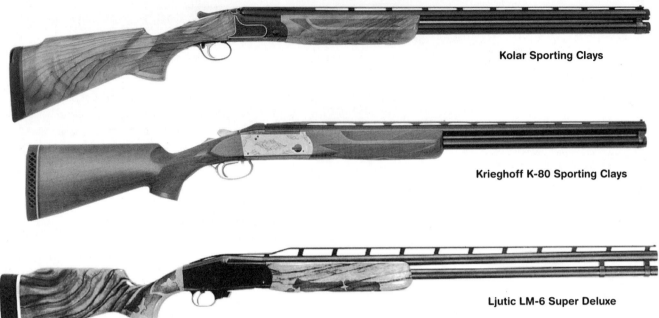

Kolar Sporting Clays

Krieghoff K-80 Sporting Clays

Ljutic LM-6 Super Deluxe

KOLAR SPORTING CLAYS O/U SHOTGUNS
Gauge: 12, 2-3/4" chambers. **Barrel:** 30", 32", 34"; extended choke tubes. **Stock:** 14-5/8"x2.5"x1-7/8"x1-3/8". French walnut. Four stock versions available. **Features:** Single selective trigger, detachable, adjustable for length; overbored barrels with long forcing cones; flat tramline rib; matte blue finish. Made in U.S. by Kolar.
Price: Standard **$9,595.00**
Price: Prestige **$14,190.00**
Price: Elite Gold **$16,590.00**
Price: Legend **$17,090.00**
Price: Select **$22,590.00**
Price: Custom . . . . **Price on request**

Kolar AAA Competition Trap O/U Shotgun
Similar to the Sporting Clays gun except has 32" O/U /34" Unsingle or 30" O/U /34" Unsingle barrels as an over/under, unsingle, or combination set. Stock dimensions are 14.5"x2.5"x1.5"; American or French walnut; step parallel rib standard. Contact maker for full listings. Made in U.S.A. by Kolar.
Price: Over/under, choke tubes, standard **$9,595.00**
Price: Combo (30"/34", 32"/34"), standard **$12,595.00**

Kolar AAA Competition Skeet O/U Shotgun
Similar to the Sporting Clays gun except has 28" or 30" barrels with Kolarite AAA sub gauge tubes; stock of American or French walnut with matte finish; flat tramline rib; under barrel adjustable for point of impact. Many options available. Contact maker for complete listing. Made in U.S.A. by Ko-lar.
Price: Standard, choke tubes **$10,995.00**
Price: Standard, choke tubes, two-barrel set **$12,995.00**

KRIEGHOFF K-80 SPORTING CLAYS O/U SHOTGUN
Gauge: 12. **Barrel:** 28", 30", 32", 34" with choke tubes. **Weight:** About 8 lbs. **Stock:** #3 Sporting stock designed for gun-down shooting. **Features:** Standard receiver with satin nickel finish and classic scroll engraving. Selective mechanical trigger adjustable for position. Choice of tapered flat or 8mm parallel flat barrel rib. Free-floating barrels. Aluminum case. Imported from Germany by Krieghoff International, Inc.
Price: Standard grade with five choke tubes, from **$9,395.00**

KRIEGHOFF K-80 SKEET O/U SHOTGUNS
Gauge: 12, 2-3/4" chambers. **Barrel:** 28", 30", 32", (skeet & skeet), optional choke tubes). **Weight:** About 7.75 lbs. **Stock:** American skeet or straight skeet stocks, with palm-swell grips. Walnut. **Features:** Satin gray receiver finish. Selective mechanical trigger adjustable for position. Choice of ventilated 8mm parallel flat rib or ventilated 8-12mm tapered flat rib. Introduced 1980. Imported from Germany by Krieghoff International, Inc.

Price: Standard, skeet chokes **$8,375.00**
Price: Skeet Special (28", 30", 32" tapered flat rib, skeet & skeet choke tubes) **$9,100.00**

KRIEGHOFF K-80 TRAP O/U SHOTGUNS
Gauge: 12, 2-3/4" chambers. **Barrel:** 30", 32" (Imp. Mod. & Full or choke tubes). **Weight:** About 8.5 lbs. **Stock:** Four stock dimensions or adjustable stock available; all have palm-swell grips. Checkered European walnut. **Features:** Satin nickel receiver. Selective mechanical trigger, adjustable for position. Ventilated step rib. Introduced 1980. Imported from Germany by Krieghoff International, Inc.
Price: K-80 O/U (30", 32", Imp. Mod. & Full), from **$8,850.00**
Price: K-80 Unsingle (32", 34", Full), standard, from **$10,080.00**
Price: K-80 Combo (two-barrel set), standard, from **$13,275.00**

Krieghoff K-20 O/U Shotgun
Similar to the K-80 except built on a 20-gauge frame. Designed for skeet, sporting clays and field use. Offered in 20, 28 and .410; 28", 30" and 32" barrels. Imported from Germany by Krieghoff International Inc.
Price: K-20, 20 gauge, from **$9,575.00**
Price: K-20, 28 gauge, from **$9,725.00**
Price: K-20, .410, from **$9,725.00**

LEBEAU-COURALLY BOSS-VEREES O/U SHOTGUN
Gauge: 12, 20, 2-3/4" chambers. **Barrel:** 25" to 32". **Weight:** To customer specifications. **Stock:** Exhibition-quality French walnut. **Features:** Boss-type sidelock with automatic ejectors; single or double triggers; chopper lump barrels. A custom gun built to customer specifications. Imported from Belgium by Wm. Larkin Moore.
Price: From **$96,000.00**

LJUTIC LM-6 SUPER DELUXE O/U SHOTGUNS
Gauge: 12. **Barrel:** 28" to 34", choked to customer specs for live birds, trap, international trap. **Weight:** To customer specs. **Stock:** To customer specs. Oil finish, hand checkered. **Features:** Custom-made gun. Hollow-milled rib, pull or release trigger, push-button opener in front of trigger guard. From Ljutic Industries.
Price: Super Deluxe LM-6 O/U **$19,995.00**
Price: Over/Under combo (interchangeable single barrel, two trigger guards, one for single trigger, one for doubles) **$27,995.00**
Price: Extra over/under barrel sets, 29"-32" **$6,995.00**

MARLIN L. C. SMITH O/U SHOTGUNS
Gauge: 12, 20. **Barrel:** 26", 28". **Stock:** Checkered walnut w/recoil pad. **Length:** 45". **Weight:** 7.25 lbs. **Features:** 3" chambers; 3 choke tubes (IC, Mod., Full), single selective trigger, selective automatic ejectors; vent rib; bead front sight. Imported from Italy by Marlin. Introduced 2005.
Price: LC12-OU (12 ga., 28" barrel) **$1,254.00**
Price: LC20-OU (20 ga., 26" barrel, 6.25 lbs., OAL 43") . . . **$1,254.00**

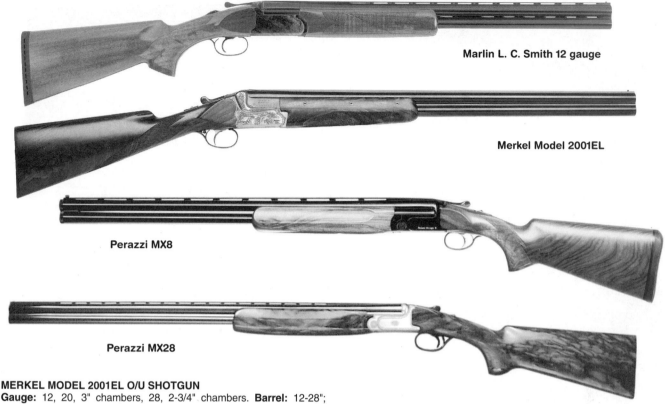

Marlin L. C. Smith 12 gauge

Merkel Model 2001EL

Perazzi MX8

Perazzi MX28

MERKEL MODEL 2001EL O/U SHOTGUN
Gauge: 12, 20, 3" chambers, 28, 2-3/4" chambers. **Barrel:** 12-28"; 20, 28 ga.-26.75". **Weight:** About 7 lbs. (12 ga.). **Stock:** Oil-finished walnut; English or pistol grip. **Features:** Self-cocking Blitz boxlock action with cocking indicators; Kersten double cross-bolt lock; silver-grayed receiver with engraved hunting scenes; coil spring ejectors; single selective or double triggers. Imported from Germany by Merkel USA.
Price: **$9,995.00**
Price: Model 2001EL Sporter; full pistol grip stock **$9,995.00**

Merkel Model 2000CL O/U Shotgun
Similar to Model 2001EL except scroll-engraved case-hardened receiver; 12, 20, 28 gauge. Imported from Germany by Merkel USA.
Price: **$8,495.00**
Price: Model 2016 CL; 16 gauge **$8,495.00**

PERAZZI MX8/MX8 SPECIAL TRAP, SKEET O/U SHOTGUNS
Gauge: 12, 2-3/4" chambers. **Barrel:** Trap: 29.5" (Imp. Mod. & Extra Full), 31.5" (Full & Extra Full). Choke tubes optional. Skeet: 27-5/8" (skeet & skeet). **Weight:** About 8.5 lbs. (trap); 7 lbs., 15 oz. (skeet). **Stock:** Interchangeable and custom made to customer specs. **Features:** Has detachable and interchangeable trigger group with flat V springs. Flat 7/16" vent rib. Many options available. Imported from Italy by Perazzi U.S.A., Inc.
Price: MX Trap Single. **$10,934.00**

Perazzi MX8 Special Skeet O/U Shotgun
Similar to the MX8 Skeet except has adjustable four-position trigger, skeet stock dimensions. Imported from Italy by Perazzi U.S.A., Inc.
Price: From **$11,166.00**

PERAZZI MX8 O/U SHOTGUNS
Gauge: 12, 2-3/4" chambers. **Barrel:** 28-3/8" (Imp. Mod. & Extra Full), 29.5" (choke tubes). **Weight:** 7 lbs., 12 oz. **Stock:** Special specifications. **Features:** Has single selective trigger; flat 7/16" x 5/16" vent rib. Many options available. Imported from Italy by Perazzi U.S.A., Inc.
Price: Standard. **$12,532.00**
Price: Sporting **$11,166.00**
Price: Trap Double Trap (removable trigger group) **$15,581.00**
Price: Skeet **$12,756.00**
Price: SC3 grade (variety of engraving patterns) . . . . **$23,000.00+**
Price: SCO grade (more intricate engraving, gold inlays). **$39,199.00+**

Perazzi MX8/20 O/U Shotgun
Similar to the MX8 except has smaller frame and has a removable trigger mechanism. Available in trap, skeet, sporting or game models with fixed chokes or choke tubes. Stock is made to customer specifications. Introduced 1993. Imported from Italy by Perazzi U.S.A., Inc.
Price: From **$11,731.00**

PERAZZI MX12 HUNTING O/U SHOTGUNS
Gauge: 12, 2-3/4" chambers. **Barrel:** 26.75", 27.5", 28-3/8", 29.5" (Mod. & Full); choke tubes available in 27-5/8", 29.5" only (MX12C). **Weight:** 7 lbs., 4 oz. **Stock:** To customer specs; interchangeable. **Features:** Single selective trigger; coil springs used in action; Schnabel forend tip. Imported from Italy by Perazzi U.S.A., Inc.
Price: From **$11,166.00**
Price: MX12C (with choke tubes). From **$11,960.00**

Perazzi MX20 Hunting O/U Shotguns
Similar to the MX12 except 20 ga. frame size. Non-removable trigger group. Available in 20, 28, .410 with 2-3/4" or 3" chambers. 26" standard, and choked Mod. & Full. Weight is 6 lbs., 6 oz. Imported from Italy by Perazzi U.S.A., Inc.
Price: From **$11,166.00**
Price: MX20C (as above, 20 ga. only, choke tubes). From **$11,960.00**

PERAZZI MX10 O/U SHOTGUN
Gauge: 12, 2-3/4" chambers. **Barrel:** 29.5", 31.5" (fixed chokes). **Weight:** NA. **Stock:** Walnut; cheekpiece adjustable for elevation and cast. **Features:** Adjustable rib; vent side rib. Externally selective trigger. Available in single barrel, combo, over/under trap, skeet, pigeon and sporting models. Introduced 1993. Imported from Italy by Perazzi U.S.A., Inc.
Price: MX200410 . . . . **$18,007.00**

PERAZZI MX28, MX410 GAME O/U SHOTGUN
Gauge: 28, 2-3/4" chambers, .410, 3" chambers. **Barrel:** 26" (Imp. Cyl. & Full). **Weight:** NA. **Stock:** To customer specifications. **Features:** Made on scaled-down frames proportioned to the gauge. Introduced 1993. Imported from Italy by Perazzi U.S.A., Inc.
Price: From **$22,332.00**

PIOTTI BOSS O/U SHOTGUN
Gauge: 12, 20. **Barrel:** 26" to 32", chokes as specified. **Weight:** 6.5 to 8 lbs. **Stock:** Dimensions to customer specs. Best quality figured walnut. **Features:** Essentially a custom-made gun with many options. Introduced 1993. Imported from Italy by Wm. Larkin Moore.
Price: From **$69,000.00**

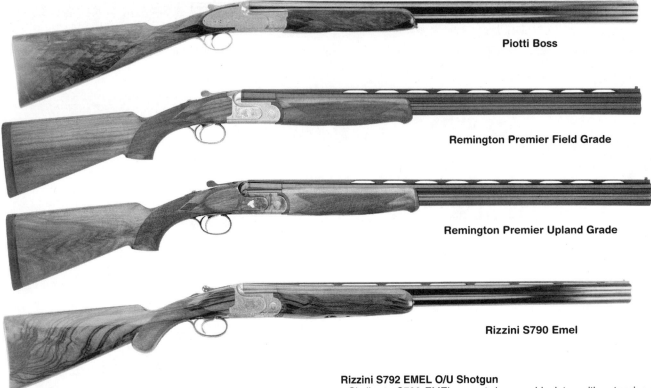

Piotti Boss

Remington Premier Field Grade

Remington Premier Upland Grade

Rizzini S790 Emel

POINTER OVER/UNDER SHOTGUN

Gauge: 12, 20, 28, .410, 3" chambers. **Barrel:** 28", blued. **Weight:** 6.1 to 7.6 lbs. **Stock:** Turkish Walnut. **Sights:** Fiber-optic front, bronze mid-bead. **Choke:** IC/M/F. **Features:** Engraved nickel receiver, automatic ejectors, fitted hard plastic case. Clays model has oversized fiber-optic front sight and palm swell pistol grip. Introduced 2007. Imported from Turkey by Legacy Sports International.
Price: . . . .**$1,299.00 to $1,499.00**

REMINGTON PREMIER OVER/UNDER SHOTGUNS

Gauge: 12, 20, 28, 3" chambers; 28, 2-3/4" chambers. **Barrel:** 26", 28", 30" in 12 gauge; overbored (.735), polished blue; 7mm vent rib. **Sights:** Ivory front bead, steel mid bead. **Weight:** 6.5 to 7.5 lbs. **Stock:** Walnut, cut checkering, Schnabel forends. Checkered pistol grip, checkered forend, satin finish, rubber butt pad. Right-hand palm swell. **Features:** Single selective mechanical trigger, selective automatic ejectors; serrated free-floating vent rib. Five flush mount ProBore choke tubes for 12s and 20s; 28-gauge equipped with 3 flush mount ProBore choke tubes. Hard case included. Introduced 2006. Made in Italy, imported by Remington Arms Co.
Price: Premier Field, nickel-finish receiver, from **$2,086.00**
Price: Premier Upland, case-colored receiver finish, from . . **$2,226.00**
Price: Premier Competition STS (2007) **$2,540.00**
Price: Premier Competition STS Adj. Comb (2007) **$2,890.00**

REMINGTON SPR310 OVER/UNDER SHOTGUNS

Gauge: 12, 20, 28, .410 bore, 3" chambers; 28, 2-3/4" chambers. **Barrel:** 26", 28", 29.5"; blued chrome-lined. **Weight:** 7.25 to 7.5 lbs. **Stock:** Checkered walnut stock and forend, 14.5" LOP; 1.5" drop at comb; 2.5" drop at heel. **Features:** Nickel finish or blued receiver. Single selective mechanical trigger, selective automatic ejectors; serrated free-floating vent rib. SC-4 choke tube set on most models. Sporting has ported barrels, right-hand palm swell, target forend, wide rib. Introduced 2008. Imported by Remington Arms Co.
Price: SPR310, from **$598.00**
Price: SPR310 Sporting **$770.00**

RIZZINI S790 EMEL O/U SHOTGUN

Gauge: 20, 28, .410. **Barrel:** 26", 27.5" (Imp. Cyl. & Imp. Mod.). **Weight:** About 6 lbs. **Stock:** 14"x1.5"x2-1/8". Extra fancy select walnut. **Features:** Boxlock action with profuse engraving; automatic ejectors; single selective trigger; silvered receiver. Comes with Nizzoli leather case. Introduced 1996. Imported from Italy by Wm. Larkin Moore & Co.
Price: From **$14,600.00**

Rizzini S792 EMEL O/U Shotgun

Similar to S790 EMEL except dummy sideplates with extensive engraving coverage. Nizzoli leather case. Introduced 1996. Imported from Italy by Wm. Larkin Moore & Co.
Price: From **$15,500.00**

RIZZINI UPLAND EL O/U SHOTGUN

Gauge: 12, 16, 20, 28, .410. **Barrel:** 26", 27.5", Mod. & Full, Imp. Cyl. & Imp. Mod. choke tubes. **Weight:** About 6.6 lbs. **Stock:** 14.5"x1-1/2"x2.25". **Features:** Boxlock action; single selective trigger; ejectors; profuse engraving on silvered receiver. Comes with fitted case. Introduced 1996. Imported from Italy by Wm. Larkin Moore & Co.
Price: From **$5,200.00**

Rizzini Artemis O/U Shotgun

Same as Upland EL model except dummy sideplates with extensive game scene engraving. Fancy European walnut stock. Fitted case. Introduced 1996. Imported from Italy by Wm. Larkin Moore & Co.
Price: From **$3.260.00**

RIZZINI S782 EMEL O/U SHOTGUN

Gauge: 12, 2-3/4" chambers. **Barrel:** 26", 27.5" (Imp. Cyl. & Imp. Mod.). **Weight:** About 6.75 lbs. **Stock:** 14.5"x1.5"x2.25". Extra fancy select walnut. **Features:** Boxlock action with dummy sideplates, extensive engraving with gold inlaid game birds, silvered receiver, automatic ejectors, single selective trigger. Nizzoli leather case. Introduced 1996. Imported from Italy by Wm. Larkin Moore & Co.
Price: From **$18,800.00**

RUGER RED LABEL O/U SHOTGUNS

Gauge: 12, 20, 3" chambers; 28 2-3/4" chambers. **Barrel:** 26", 28", 30" in 12 gauge. **Weight:** About 7 lbs. (20 ga.); 7.5 lbs. (12 ga.). **Length:** 43" overall (26" barrels). **Stock:** 14"x1.5"x2.5". Straight grain American walnut. Checkered pistol grip or straight grip, checkered forend, rubber butt pad. **Features:** Stainless steel receiver. Single selective mechanical trigger, selective automatic ejectors; serrated free-floating vent rib. Comes with two skeet, one Imp. Cyl., one Mod., one Full choke tube and wrench. Made in U.S. by Sturm, Ruger & Co.
Price: Red Label with pistol grip stock **$1,956.00**
Price: English Field with straight-grip stock **$1,956.00**
Price: Sporting clays (30" bbl.) **$1,956.00**

Ruger Engraved Red Label O/U Shotgun

Similar to Red Label except scroll engraved receiver with 24-carat gold game bird (pheasant in 12 gauge, grouse in 20 gauge, woodcock in 28 gauge). Introduced 2000.
Price: Engraved Red Label, pistol grip only **$2,180.00**

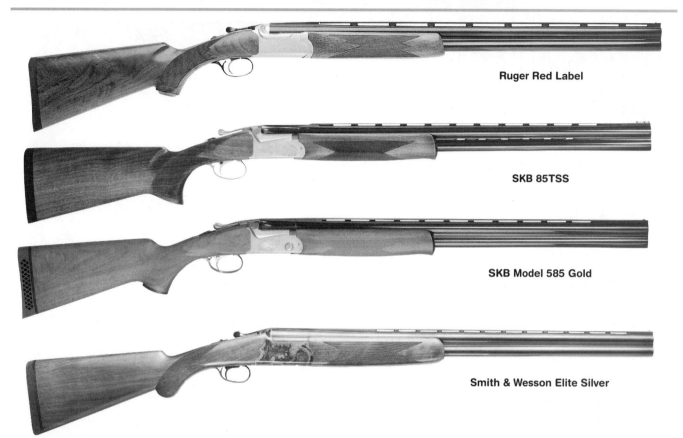

Ruger Red Label

SKB 85TSS

SKB Model 585 Gold

Smith & Wesson Elite Silver

SAVAGE MILANO O/U SHOTGUNS
Gauge: 12, 20, 28, and 410, 2-3/4" (28 ga.) and 3" chambers. **Barrel:** 28"; chrome lined, elongated forcing cones, automatic ejectors. 12, 20, and 28 come with 3 Interchokes (F-M-IC); 410 has fixed chokes (M-IC). **Weight:** 12 ga., 7.5 lbs; 20, 28 gauge, .410, 6.25 lbs. **Length:** NA. **Stock:** Satin finish Turkish walnut stock with laser-engraved checkering, solid rubber recoil pad, Schnabel forend. **Features:** Single selective, mechanical set trigger, fiber-optic front sight with brass mid-rib bead. Introduced 2006. Imported from It-aly by Savage Arms, Inc.
Price: **$1,714.00**

SKB MODEL GC7 O/U SHOTGUNS
Gauge: 12 or 20, 3"; 28, 2-3/4"; .410, 3". **Barrel:** 26", 28", Briley internal chokes. **Weight:** NA. **Length:** NA. **Stock:** Grade II and Grade III American black walnut, high-gloss finish, finger-groove forend. **Sights:** Top ventilated rib, sloped with matte surface (Game). **Features:** Low-profile boxlock action; Greener crossbolt locking action, silver-nitride finish; automatic ejec-tors, single selective trigger. Introduced 2008. Imported from Japan by SKB Shotguns, Inc.
Price: GC7 Game Bird Grade 1, from............... **$1,569.00**
Price: GC7 Clays Grade 1, from.................... **$1,679.00**

SKB MODEL 85TSS O/U SHOTGUNS
Gauge: 12, 20, .410: 3"; 28, 2-3/4". **Barrel:** Chrome lined 26", 28", 30", 32" (w/choke tubes). **Weight:** 7 lbs., 7 oz. to 8 lbs., 14 oz. **Stock:** Hand-checkered American walnut with matte finish, Schnabel or grooved forend. Target stocks available in various styles. **Sights:** HiViz competition sights. **Features:** Low profile boxlock action with Greener-style cross bolt; single selective trigger; manual safety. Back-bored barrels with lengthened forcing cones. Introduced 2004. Imported from Japan by SKB Shotguns, Inc.
Price: Sporting Clays, Skeet, fixed comb, from **$2,199.00**
Price: Sporting clays, Skeet, adjustable comb, from **$2,429.00**
Price: Trap, standard or Monte Carlo.................. **$2,329.00**
Price: Trap adjustable comb........................ **$2,529.00**
Price: Trap Unsingle (2007) **$2,799.00**

SKB MODEL 585 O/U SHOTGUNS
Gauge: 12 or 20, 3"; 28, 2-3/4"; .410, 3". **Barrel:** 12 ga.-26", 28", (InterChoke tubes); 20 ga.-26", 28" (InterChoke tubes); 28-26", 28" (InterChoke tubes); .410-26", 28" (InterChoke tubes). **Weight:** 6.6 to 8.5 lbs. **Length:** 43" to 51-3/8" overall. **Stock:** 14-1/8"x1.5"x2-3/16".

Hand checkered walnut with matte finish. **Sights:** Metal bead front (field). **Features:** Boxlock action; silver nitride finish; manual safety, automatic ejectors, single selective trigger. All 12-gauge barrels are back-bored, have lengthened forcing cones and longer choke tube system. Introduced 1992. Imported from Japan by SKB Shotguns, Inc.
Price: Field **$1,699.00**
Price: Two-barrel field set, 12 & 20................... **$2,749.00**
Price: Two-barrel field set, 20 & 28 or 28 & .410 .... **$2,829.00**

SMITH & WESSON ELITE SILVER SHOTGUNS
Gauge: 12, 3" chambers. **Barrel:** 26", 28", 30", rust-blued chopper-lump. **Weight:** 7.8 lbs. **Length:** 46-48". **Sights:** Ivory front bead, metal mid-bead. **Stock:** AAA (grade III) Turkish walnut stocks, hand-cut checkering, satin finish. **Features:** Smith & Wesson-designed trigger-plate action, hand-engraved receivers, bone-charcoal case hardening, lifetime warranty. Five choke tubes. Introduced 2007. Made in Turkey, imported by Smith & Wesson.
Price: **$2,380.00**

STEVENS MODEL 512 GOLD WING SHOTGUNS
Gauge: 12, 20, 28, .410; 2-3/4" and 3" chambers. **Barrel:** 26", 28". **Weight:** 6 to 8 lbs. **Sights:** NA. **Features:** Five screw-in choke tubes with 12, 20, and 28 gauge; .410 has fixed M/IC chokes. Black chrome, sculpted receiver with a raised gold pheasant, laser engraved trigger guard and forend latch. Turkish walnut stock finished in satin lacquer and beautifully laser engraved with fleur-de-lis checkering on the side panels, wrist and Schnabel forearm.
Price: **$649.00**

STOEGER CONDOR O/U SHOTGUNS
Gauge: 12, 20, 2-3/4" 3" chambers; 16, .410. **Barrel:** 22", 24", 26", 28", 30". **Weight:** 5.5 to 7.8 lbs. **Sights:** Brass bead. **Features:** IC, M or F screw-in choke tubes with each gun. Oil finished hardwood with pistol grip and forend. Auto safety, single trigger, automatic extractors.
Price: Condor, 12, 20, 16 ga. or .410................... **$399.00**
Price: Condor Supreme (w/mid bead), 12 or 20 ga......... **$599.00**
Price: Condor Combo, 12 and 20 ga. Barrels, from **$549.00**
Price: Condor Youth, 20 ga. or .410.................... **$399.00**
Price: Condor Competition, 12 or 20 ga................. **$599.00**
Price: Condor Combo, 12/20 ga., RH or LH (2007) **$829.00**
Price: Condor Outback, 12 or 20 ga., 20" barrel........... **$369.00**

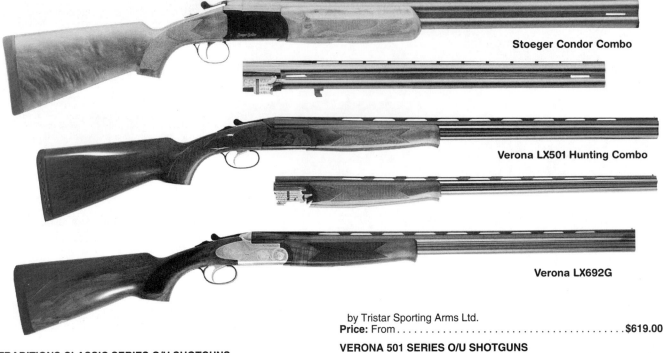

Stoeger Condor Combo

Verona LX501 Hunting Combo

Verona LX692G

TRADITIONS CLASSIC SERIES O/U SHOTGUNS

Gauge: 12, 3"; 20, 3"; 16, 2-3/4"; 28, 2-3/4"; .410, 3". **Barrel:** 26" and 28". **Weight:** 6 lbs., 5 oz. to 7 lbs., 6 oz. **Length:** 43" to 45" overall. **Stock:** Walnut. **Features:** Single-selective trigger; chrome-lined barrels with screw-in choke tubes; extractors (Field Hunter and Field I models) or automatic ejectors (Field II and Field III models); rubber butt pad; top tang safety. Imported from Fausti of Italy by Traditions.
Price: Field Hunter: Blued receiver; 12 or 20 ga.; 26" bbl. has IC and Mod. tubes, 28" has mod. and full tubes $669.00
Price: Field I: Blued receiver; 12, 20, 28 ga. or .410; fixed chokes (26" has I.C. and mod., 28" has mod. and full). . $619.00
Price: Field II: Coin-finish receiver; 12, 16, 20, 28 ga. or .410; gold trigger; choke tubes $789.00
Price: Field III: Coin-finish receiver; gold engraving and trigger; 12 ga.; 26" or 28" bbl.; choke tubes $999.00
Price: Upland II: Blued receiver; 12 or 20 ga.; English-style straight walnut stock; choke tubes $839.00
Price: Upland II: Blued receiver, gold engraving; 20 ga.; high-grade pistol grip walnut stock; choke tubes . $1,059.00
Price: Upland III: Blued, gold engraved receiver, 12 ga. Round pistol grip stock, choke tubes $1,059.00
Price: Sporting Clay II: Silver receiver; 12 ga.; ported barrels with skeet, i.c., mod. and full extended tubes $959.00
Price: Sporting Clay III: Engraved receivers, 12 and 20 ga., walnut stock, vent rib, extended choke tubes $1,189.00

TRADITIONS MAG 350 SERIES O/U SHOTGUNS

Gauge: 12, 3-1/2". **Barrel:** 24", 26" and 28". **Weight:** 7 lbs. to 7 lbs., 4 oz. **Length:** 41" to 45" overall. **Stock:** Walnut or composite with Mossy Oak Break-Up or Advantage Wetlands camouflage. **Features:** Black matte, engraved receiver; vent rib; automatic ejectors; single selective trigger; three screw-in choke tubes; rubber recoil pad; top tang safety. Imported from Fausti of Italy by Traditions.
Price: (Mag Hunter II: 28" black matte barrels, walnut stock, includes I.C., Mod. and Full tubes) $799.00
Price: (Turkey II: 24" or 26" camo barrels, Break-Up camo stock, includes Mod., Full and X-Full tubes) $889.00
Price: (Waterfowl II: 28" camo barrels, Advantage Wetlands camo stock, includes IC, Mod. and Full tubes) $899.00

TRISTAR HUNTER EX O/U SHOTGUN

Gauge: 12, 20, 28, .410. **Barrel:** 26", 28". **Weight:** 5.7 lbs. (.410); 6.0 lbs. (20, 28), 7.2-7.4 lbs. (12). Chrome-lined steel mono-block bar-rel, five Beretta-style choke tubes (SK, IC, M, IM, F). **Length:** NA. **Stock:** Walnut, cut checkering. 14.25"x1.5"x2-3/8". **Sights:** Brass front sight. **Features:** All have extractors, engraved receiver, sealed actions, self-adjusting locking bolts, single selective trigger, ventilated rib. 28 ga. and .410 built on true frames. Five-year warranty. Imported from Italy

by Tristar Sporting Arms Ltd.
Price: From $619.00

VERONA 501 SERIES O/U SHOTGUNS

Gauge: 12, 20, 28, .410 (3" chambers). **Barrel:** 28". **Weight:** 6-7 lbs. **Stock:** Enhanced walnut with Scottish net type checkering and oiled finish. **Features:** Select fire single trigger, automatic ejectors, chromed barrels with X-CONE system to reduce felt recoil, and ventilated rubber butt pad. Introduced 1999. Imported from Italy by Legacy Sports International.
Price: Combos 20/28, 28/.410 . . . . $1,599.00

Verona 702 Series O/U Shotguns

Same as 501 series model except. with deluxe nickel receiver.
Price: $1,699.00

Verona LX692 Gold Hunting O/U Shotguns

Similar to Verona 501 except engraved, silvered receiver with false sideplates showing gold inlaid bird hunting scenes on three sides; Schnabel forend tip; hand-cut checkering; black rubber butt pad. Available in 12 and 20 gauge only, five Interchoke tubes. Introduced 1999. Imported from Italy by B.C. Outdoors.
Price: $1,295.00
Price: LX692G Combo 28/.410 . . . . $2,192.40

Verona LX680 Sporting O/U Shotgun

Similar to Verona 501 except engraved, silvered receiver; ventilated middle rib; beavertail forend; hand-cut checkering; available in 12 or 20 gauge only with 2-3/4" chambers. Introduced 1999. Imported from Italy by B.C. Outdoors.
Price: $1,159.68

Verona LX680 Skeet/Sporting/Trap O/U Shotgun

Similar to Verona 501 except skeet or trap stock dimensions; beavertail forend, palm swell on pistol grip; ventilated center barrel rib. Introduced 1999. Imported from Italy by B.C. Outdoors.
Price: $1,736.96

Verona LX692 Gold Sporting O/U Shotgun

Similar to Verona LX680 except false sideplates have gold-inlaid bird hunting scenes on three sides; red high-visibility front sight. Introduced 1999. Imported from Italy by B.C. Outdoors.
Price: Skeet/sporting. $1,765.12
Price: Trap (32" barrel, 7-7/8 lbs.) $1,594.80

VERONA LX680 COMPETITION TRAP O/U SHOTGUNS

Gauge: 12. **Barrel:** 30" O/U, 32" single bbl. **Weight:** 8-3/8 lbs. combo, 7 lbs. single. **Stock:** Walnut. **Sights:** White front, mid-rib bead. **Features:** Interchangeable barrels switch from OU to single configurations. 5 Briley chokes in combo, 4 in single bbl. extended forcing cones, ported barrels 32" with raised rib. By B.C. Outdoors.
Price: Trap Single (LX680TGTSB) $1,736.96
Price: Trap Combo (LX680TC). $2,553.60

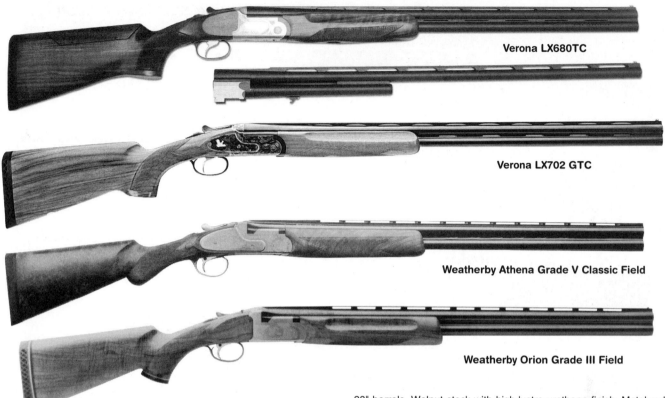

Verona LX680TC

Verona LX702 GTC

Weatherby Athena Grade V Classic Field

Weatherby Orion Grade III Field

VERONA LX702 GOLD TRAP COMBO O/U SHOTGUNS
Gauge: 20/28, 2-3/4" chamber. **Barrel:** 30". **Weight:** 7 lbs. **Stock:** Turkish walnut with beavertail forearm. **Sights:** White front bead. **Features:** 2-barrel competition gun. Color case-hardened side plates and receiver with gold inlaid pheasant. Vent rib between barrels. 5 Interchokes. Imported from Italy by B.C. Outdoors.
Price: Combo **$2,467.84**
Price: 20 ga. **$1,829.12**

Verona LX702 Skeet/Trap O/U Shotguns
Similar to Verona LX702. Both are 12 gauge and 2-3/4" chamber. Skeet has 28" barrel and weighs 7.75 lbs. Trap has 32" barrel and weighs 7-7/8 lbs. By B.C. Outdoors.
Price: Skeet **$1,829.12**
Price: Trap **$1,829.12**

WEATHERBY ATHENA GRADE V AND GRADE III CLASSIC FIELD O/U SHOTGUNS
Gauge: Grade III and Grade IV: 12, 20, 3" chambers; 28, 2-3/4" chambers. Grade V: 12, 20, 3" chambers. **Barrel:** 26", 28" monobloc, IMC multi-choke tubes. Modified Greener crossbolt action. Matte ventilated top rib with brilliant front bead. **Weight:** 12 ga., 7.25 to 8 lbs.; 20 ga. 6.5 to 7.25 lbs. **Length:** 43" to 45". **Stock:** Rounded pistol grip, slender forend, Old English recoil pad. Grade V has oil-finished AAA American Claro walnut with 20-lpi checkering. Grade III has AA Claro walnut with oil finish, fine-line checkering. **Features:** Silver nitride/gray receivers; Grade III has hunting scene engraving. Grade IV has chrome-plated false sideplates featuring single game scene gold plate overlay. Grade V has rose and scroll engraving with gold-overlay upland game scenes. Top levers engraved with gold Weatherby flying "W". Introduced 1999. Imported from Japan by Weatherby.
Price: Grade III **$2,599.00**
Price: Grade IV **$2,799.00**
Price: Grade V **$3,999.00**

WEATHERBY ORION D'ITALIA O/U SHOTGUNS
Gauge: 12, 20, 3" chambers; 28, 2-3/4" chamber. **Barrel:** 26", 28", IMC multi-choke tubes. Matte ventilated top rib with brilliant bead front sight. **Weight:** 6-1/2 to 8 lbs. **Stock:** 14.25"x1.5"x2.5". American walnut, checkered grip and forend. Old English recoil pad. **Features:** All models have a triggerguard that features Weatherby's "Flying W" engraved with gold fill. D'Italia I available in 12 and 20 gauge, 26" and

28" barrels. Walnut stock with high lustre urethane finish. Metalwork is blued to high lustre finishand has a gold-plated trigger for corrosion protection. D'Italia II available in 12, 20 and 28 gauge with 26" and 28" barrels. Fancy grade walnut stock, hard chrome receiver with sculpted frameheads, elaborate game and floral engraving pattern, and matte vent mid & top rib with brilliant front bead sight. D'Italia III available in 12 and 20 gauge with 26" and 28" barrels. Hand-selected, oil-finished walnut stock wtih 20 LPI checkering, intricate engraving and gold plate game scene overlay, and damascened monobloc barrel and sculpted frameheads. D'Italia SC available in 12 gauge only with barrel lengths of 28", 30", and 32", weighs 8 lbs. Features satin, oil-finished walnut stock that is adjustable for cheek height with target-style pistol grip and Schnaubel forend, shallow receiver aligns hands for improved balance and pointability, ported barrels reduce muzzle jump, and fiber optic front sight for quick targer acquisition. Introduced 1998. Imported from Japan by Weatherby.
Price: D'Italia I **$1,699.00**
Price: D'Italia II **$1,899.00**
Price: D'Italia III **$2,199.00**
Price: D'Italia SC **$2,599.00**

WINCHESTER SELECT MODEL 101 O/U SHOTGUNS
Gauge: 12, 2-3/4", 3" chambers. **Barrel:** 28", 30", 32", ported, Invector Plus choke system. **Weight:** 7 lbs. 6 oz. to 7 lbs. 12. oz. **Stock:** Checkered high-gloss grade II/III walnut stock, Pachmayr Decelerator sporting pad. **Features:** Chrome-plated chambers; back-bored barrels; tang barrel selec-tor/safety; Signature extended choke tubes. Model 101 Field comes with solid brass bead front sight, three tubes, engraved receiver. Model 101 Sporting has adjustable trigger, 10mm runway rib, white mid-bead, Tru-Glo front sight, 30" and 32" barrels. Camo version of Model 101 Field comes with full-coverage Mossy Oak Duck Blind pattern. Model 101 Pigeon Grade Trap has 10mm steel runway rib, mid-bead sight, interchangeable fiber-optic front sight, porting and vented side ribs, adjustable trigger shoe, fixed raised comb or adjustable comb, Grade III/IV walnut, 30" or 32" barrels, molded ABS hard case. Reintroduced 2008. From Winchester Repeating Arms. Co.
Price: Model 101 Field **$1,739.00**
Price: Model 101 Deluxe Field **$1,659.00**
Price: Model 101 Sporting **$2,139.00**
Price: Model 101 Pigeon Grade Trap, intr. 2008 . . . . **$2,299.00**
Price: Model 101 Pigeon Grade Trap w/adj. comb,
intr. 2008. . . . . **$2,429.00**
Price: Model 101 Light (2009) **$1,999.00**
Price: Model 101 Pigeon Sporting (2009) **$2,579.00**

Bill Hanus Birdgun

CZ Bobwhite

CZ Ringneck

CZ Hammer Coach

ARRIETA SIDELOCK DOUBLE SHOTGUNS

Gauge: 12, 16, 20, 28, .410. **Barrel:** Length and chokes to customer specs. **Weight:** To customer specs. **Stock:** To customer specs. Straight English with checkered butt (standard), or pistol grip. Select European walnut with oil finish. **Features:** Essentially custom gun with myriad options. H&H pattern hand-detachable sidelocks, selective automatic ejectors, double triggers (hinged front) standard. Some have selfopening action. Finish and engraving to customer specs. Imported from Spain by Quality Arms, Inc.

Price: Model 557	**$4,500.00**
Price: Model 570	**$5,350.00**
Price: Model 578	**$5,880.00**
Price: Model 600 Imperial	**$7,995.00**
Price: Model 601 Imperial Tiro	**$9,160.00**
Price: Model 801	**$14,275.00**
Price: Model 802	**$14,275.00**
Price: Model 803	**$9,550.00**
Price: Model 871	**$6,670.00**
Price: Model 872	**$17,850.00**
Price: Model 873	**$16,275.00**
Price: Model 874	**$13,125.00**
Price: Model 875	**$19,850.00**
Price: Model 931	**$20,895.00**

AYA MODEL 4/53 SHOTGUNS

Gauge: 12, 16, 20, 28, 410. **Barrel:** 26", 27", 28", 30". **Weight:** To customer specifications. **Length:** To customer specifications. **Features:** Hammerless boxlock action; double triggers; light scroll engraving; automatic safety; straight grip oil finish walnut stock; checkered butt. Made in Spain. Imported by New England Custom Gun Service, Lt.

Price:	**$2,999.00**
Price: No. 2	**$4,799.00**
Price: No. 2 Rounded Action	**$5,199.00**

BERETTA 471 SIDE-BY-SIDE SHOTGUNS

Gauge: 12, 20; 3" chamber. **Barrel:** 24", 26", 28"; 6mm rib. **Weight:** 6.5 lbs. **Stock:** English or pistol stock, straight butt for various types of recoil pads. Beavertail forend. English stock with recoil pad in red or black rubber, or in walnut and splinter forend. Select European walnut, checkered, oil finish. **Features:** Optima-Choke Extended Choke Tubes. Automatic ejection or mechanical extraction. Firing-pin block safety,

manual or automatic, open top-lever safety. Introduced 2007. Imported from Italy by Beretta U.S.A.

Price: Silver Hawk **$3,750.00**

BILL HANUS NOBILE III BY FABARM

Gauge: 20. **Barrel:** 28" Tribor® barrels with 3" chambers and extra-long 82mm (3-1/4") internal choke tubes. **Weight:** 5.75 lbs. **Stock:** Upgraded walnut 1-1/2"x2-1/4"x14-3/8", with 1/4" cast-off to a wood butt plate. Altering to 1/4" cast-on for left-handed shooters, $300 extra. **Features:** Tribor® barrels feature extra-long forcing cones along with over-boring, back-boring and extra-long (82mm vs 50mm) choke tubes which put more pellets in the target area. Paradox®-rifled choke tube for wider patterns at short-range targets. Adjustable for automatic ejectors or manual extraction. Adjustable opening tension. Fitted leather case.

Price: **$3,395.00**

CONNECTICUT SHOTGUN MANUFACTURING COMPANY RBL SIDE-BY-SIDE SHOTGUN

Gauge: 12, 16, 20, 28. **Barrel:** 26", 28", 30", 32". **Weight:** NA. **Length:** NA. **Stock:** NA. **Features:** Round-action SXS shotguns made in the USA. Scaled frames, five TruLock choke tubes. Deluxe fancy grade walnut buttstock and forend. Quick Change recoil pad in two lengths. Various dimensions and options available depending on gauge.

Price: 12 gauge	**$2,950.00**
Price: 20 gauge	**$2,799.00**
Price: 28 gauge	**$3,650.00**

CZ BOBWHITE AND RINGNECK SHOTGUNS

Gauge: 12, 20, 28, .410. (5 screw-in chokes in 12 and 20 ga. and fixed chokes in IC and Mod in .410). **Barrel:** 20". **Weight:** 6.5 lbs. **Length:** NA. **Stock:** Sculptured Turkish walnut with straight English-style grip and double triggers (Bobwhite) or conventional American pistol grip with a single trigger (Ringneck). Both are hand checkered 20 lpi. **Features:** Both color case-hardened shotguns are hand engraved.

Price: Bobwhite	**$789.00**
Price: Ringneck	**$1,036.00**

CZ HAMMER COACH SHOTGUNS

Gauge: 12, 3" chambers. **Barrel:** 20". **Weight:** 6.7 lbs. **Length:** NA. **Stock:** NA. **Features:** Following in the tradition of the guns used by the stagecoach guards of the 1880's, this cowboy gun features double triggers, 19th century color case-hardening and fully functional external hammers.

Price: **$904.00**

A.H. Fox DE Grade

Garbi Model 100

Marlin L. C. Smith 12 gauge

DAKOTA PREMIER GRADE SHOTGUN
Gauge: 12, 16, 20, 28, .410. **Barrel:** 27". **Weight:** NA. **Length:** NA. **Stock:** Exhibition-grade English walnut, hand-rubbed oil finish with straight grip and splinter forend. **Features:** French grey finish; 50 percent coverage engraving; double triggers; selective ejectors. Finished to customer specifications. Made in U.S. by Dakota Arms.
Price: From **$14,950.00**

Dakota Legend Shotgun
Similar to Premier Grade except has special selection English walnut, full-coverage scroll engraving, oak and leather case. Made in U.S. by Dakota Arms.
Price: From **$19,000.00**

EMF OLD WEST HAMMER SHOTGUN
Gauge: 12. **Barrel:** 20". **Weight:** 8 lbs. **Length:** 37" overall. **Stock:** Smooth walnut with steel butt place. **Sights:** Large brass bead. **Features:** Colt-style exposed hammers rebounding type; blued receiver and barrels; cylinder bore. Introduced 2006. Imported from China for EMF by TTN.
Price: **$474.90**

FOX, A.H., SIDE-BY-SIDE SHOTGUNS
Gauge: 16, 20, 28, .410. **Barrel:** Length and chokes to customer specifications. Rust-blued Chromox or Krupp steel. **Weight:** 5-1/2 to 6.75 lbs. **Stock:** Dimensions to customer specifications. Hand-checkered Turkish Circassian walnut with hand-rubbed oil finish. Straight, semi or full pistol grip; splinter, Schnabel or beavertail forend; traditional pad, hard rubber buttplate or skeleton butt. **Features:** Boxlock action with automatic ejectors; double or Fox single selective trigger. Scalloped, rebated and color case-hardened receiver; hand finished and handengraved. Grades differ in engraving, inlays, grade of wood, amount of hand finishing. Introduced 1993. Made in U.S. by Connecticut Shotgun Mfg.
Price: CE Grade **$14,500.00**
Price: XE Grade **$16,000.00**
Price: DE Grade **$19,000.00**
Price: FE Grade **$24,000.00**
Price: 28/.410 CE Grade **$16,500.00**
Price: 28/.410 XE Grade **$18,000.00**
Price: 28/.410 DE Grade **$21,000.00**
Price: 28/.410 FE Grade **$26,000.00**

GARBI MODEL 100 DOUBLE SHOTGUN
Gauge: 12, 16, 20, 28. **Barrel:** 26", 28", choked to customer specs. **Weight:** 5-1/2 to 7.5 lbs. **Stock:** 14.5"x2.25"x1.5". European walnut. Straight grip, checkered butt, classic forend. **Features:** Sidelock action, automatic ejectors, double triggers standard. Color case-hardened action, coin finish optional. Single trigger; beavertail forend, etc. optional. Five additional models available. Imported from Spain by Wm. Larkin Moore.
Price: From **$4,850.00**

Garbi Model 101 Side-by-Side Shotgun
Similar to the Garbi Model 100 except hand engraved with scroll engraving; select walnut stock; better overall quality than the Model 100. Imported from Spain by Wm. Larkin Moore.
Price: From **$6,250.00**

Garbi Model 103 A & B Side-by-Side Shotguns
Similar to the Garbi Model 100 except has Purdey-type fine scroll and rosette engraving. Better overall quality than the Model 101. Model 103B has nickel-chrome steel barrels, H&H-type easy opening mechanism; other mechanical details remain the same. Imported from Spain by Wm. Larkin Moore.
Price: Model 103A. From **$14,100.00**
Price: Model 103B. From **$21,600.00**

Garbi Model 200 Side-by-Side Shotgun
Similar to the Garbi Model 100 except has heavy-duty locks, magnum proofed. Very fine Continen-tal-style floral and scroll engraving, well figured walnut stock. Other mechanical features remain the same. Imported from Spain by Wm. Larkin Moore.
Price: **$17,100.00**

KIMBER VALIER SIDE-BY-SIDE SHOTGUN
Gauge: 20, 16, 3" chambers. **Barrels:** 26" or 28", IC and M. **Weight:** 6 lbs. 8 oz. **Stock:** Turkish walnut, English style. **Features:** Sidelock design, double triggers, 50-percent engraving; 24 lpi checkering; auto-ejectors (extractors only on Grade I). Color case-hardened sidelocks, rust blue barrels. Imported from Turkey by Kimber Mfg., Inc.
Price: Grade II. **$4,999.00**

LEBEAU-COURALLY BOXLOCK SIDE-BY-SIDE SHOTGUN
Gauge: 12, 16, 20, 28, .410-bore. **Barrel:** 25" to 32". **Weight:** To customer specifications. **Stock:** French walnut. **Features:** Anson & Deely-type action with automatic ejectors; single or double triggers. Custom gun built to customer specifications. Imported from Belgium by Wm. Larkin Moore.
Price: From **$25,500.00**

LEBEAU-COURALLY SIDELOCK SIDE-BY-SIDE SHOTGUN
Gauge: 12, 16, 20, 28, .410-bore. **Barrel:** 25" to 32". **Weight:** To customer specifications. **Stock:** Fancy French walnut. **Features:** Holland & Holland-type action with automatic ejectors; single or double triggers. Custom gun built to customer specifications. Imported from Belgium by Wm. Larkin Moore.
Price: From **$56,000.00**

MARLIN L. C. SMITH SIDE-BY-SIDE SHOTGUN
Gauge: 12, 20, 28, .410. **Stock:** Checkered walnut w/recoil pad. **Features:** 3" chambers, single trigger, selective automatic ejectors; 3 choke tubes (IC, Mod., Full); solid rib, bead front sight. Imported from Italy by Marlin. Introduced 2005.
Price: LC12-DB (28" barrel, 43" OAL, 6.25 lbs) **$1,962.00**
Price: LC28-DB (26" barrel, 41" OAL, 6 lbs) **$1,484.00**

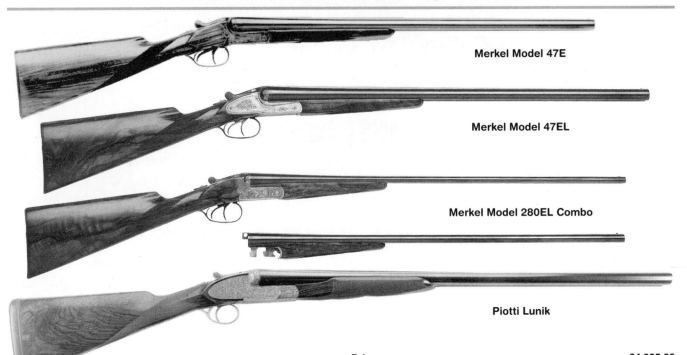

Merkel Model 47E

Merkel Model 47EL

Merkel Model 280EL Combo

Piotti Lunik

MERKEL MODEL 47E, 147E SIDE-BY-SIDE SHOTGUNS

Gauge: 12, 3" chambers, 16, 2.75" chambers, 20, 3" chambers. **Barrel:** 12, 16 ga.-28"; 20 ga.-26.75" (Imp. Cyl. & Mod., Mod. & Full). **Weight:** About 6.75 lbs. (12 ga.). **Stock:** Oil-finished walnut; straight English or pistol grip. **Features:** Anson & Deeley-type boxlock action with single selective or double triggers, automatic safety, cocking indicators. Color case-hardened receiver with standard arabesque engraving. Imported from Germany by Merkel USA.
Price: Model 47E (H&H ejectors) **$4,595.00**
Price: Model 147E (as above with ejectors) **$5,795.00**

Merkel Model 47EL, 147EL Side-by-Side Shotguns

Similar to Model 47E except H&H style sidelock action with cocking indicators, ejectors. Silver-grayed receiver and sideplates have arabesque engraving, engraved border and screws (Model 47E), or fine hunting scene engraving (Model 147E). Limited edition. Imported from Germany by Merkel USA.
Price: Model 47EL **$7,195.00**
Price: Model 147EL **$7,695.00**

Merkel Model 280EL, 360EL Shotguns

Similar to Model 47E except smaller frame. Greener cross bolt with double under-barrel locking lugs, fine engraved hunting scenes on silver-grayed receiver, luxury-grade wood, Anson and Deely boxlock action. H&H ejectors, single-selective or double triggers. Introduced 2000. Imported from Germany by Merkel USA.
Price: Model 280EL (28 gauge, 28" barrel, Imp. Cyl. and
Mod. chokes) **$7,695.00**
Price: Model 360EL (.410, 28" barrel, Mod. and
Full chokes) **$7,695.00**
Price: Model 280EL Combo **$11,195.00**

Merkel Model 280SL and 360SL Shotguns

Similar to Model 280EL and 360EL except has sidelock action, double triggers, English-style arabesque engraving. Introduced 2000. Imported from Germany by Merkel USA.
Price: Model 280SL (28 gauge, 28" barrel, Imp. Cyl.
and Mod. chokes) **$10,995.00**
Price: Model 360SL (.410, 28" barrel, Mod. and
Full chokes) **$10,995.00**

MERKEL MODEL 1620 SIDE-BY-SIDE SHOTGUN

Gauge: 16. **Features:** Greener crossbolt with double under-barrel locking lugs, scroll-engraved case-hardened receiver, Anson and Deely boxlock aciton, Holland & Holland ejectors, English-style stock, single selective or double triggers, or pistol grip stock with single selective trgger. Imported from Germany by Merkel USA.

Price: **$4,995.00**
Price: Model 1620E; silvered, engraved receiver **$5,995.00**
Price: Model 1620 Combo; 16- and 20-gauge two-barrel set **$7,695.00**
Price: Model 1620EL; upgraded wood **$7,695.00**
Price: Model 1620EL Combo; 16- and 20-gauge two-barrel
set **$11,195.00**

PIOTTI KING NO. 1 SIDE-BY-SIDE SHOTGUN

Gauge: 12, 16, 20, 28, .410. **Barrel:** 25" to 30" (12 ga.), 25" to 28" (16, 20, 28, .410). To customer specs. Chokes as specified. **Weight:** 6.5 lbs. to 8 lbs. (12 ga. to customer specs.). **Stock:** Dimensions to customer specs. Finely figured walnut; straight grip with checkered butt with classic splinter forend and hand-rubbed oil finish standard. Pistol grip, beavertail forend. **Features:** Holland & Holland pattern sidelock action, automatic ejectors. Double trigger; non-selective single trigger optional. Coin finish standard; color case-hardened optional. Top rib; level, file-cut; concave, ventilated optional. Very fine, full coverage scroll engraving with small floral bouquets. Imported from Italy by Wm. Larkin Moore.
Price: From **$38,300.00**

Piotti Lunik Side-by-Side Shotgun

Similar to the Piotti King No. 1 in overall quality. Has Renaissance-style large scroll engraving in relief. Best quality Holland & Holland-pattern sidelock ejector double with chopper lump (demi-bloc) barrels. Other mechanical specifications remain the same. Imported from Italy by Wm. Larkin Moore.
Price: From **$39,900.00**

PIOTTI PIUMA SIDE-BY-SIDE SHOTGUN

Gauge: 12, 16, 20, 28, .410. **Barrel:** 25" to 30" (12 ga.), 25" to 28" (16, 20, 28, .410). **Weight:** 5-1/2 to 6-1/4 lbs. (20 ga.). **Stock:** Dimensions to customer specs. Straight grip stock with walnut checkered butt, classic splinter forend, hand-rubbed oil finish are standard; pistol grip, beavertail forend, satin luster finish optional. **Features:** Anson & Deeley boxlock ejector double with chopper lump barrels. Level, file-cut rib, light scroll and rosette engraving, scalloped frame. Double triggers; single non-selective optional. Coin finish standard, color case-hardened optional. Imported from Italy by Wm. Larkin Moore.
Price: From **$19,200.00**

REMINGTON SPR210 SIDE-BY-SIDE SHOTGUNS

Gauge: 12, 20, 28, .410 bore, 3" chambers; 28, 2-3/4" chambers. **Barrel:** 26", 28", blued chrome-lined. **Weight:** 6.75 to 7 lbs. **Stock:** checkered walnut stock and forend, 14.5" LOP; 1.5" drop at comb; 2.5" drop at heel. **Features:** Nickel or blued receiver. Single selective mechanical trigger, selective automatic ejectors; SC-4 choke tube set on most models. Steel receiver/mono block, auto tang safety, rubber recoil pad. Introduced 2008. Imported by Remington Arms Co.
Price: SPR210, from **$479.00**

Rizzini Sidelock

Ruger Gold Label

Smith & Wesson Elite Gold

Stoeger Uplander

Stoeger Silverado Coach

REMINGTON SPR220 SIDE-BY-SIDE SHOTGUNS
Gauge: 12, 20, 2-3/4" or 3" chambers. **Barrel:** 20", 26", blued chrome-lined. **Weight:** 6.25 to 7 lbs. Otherwise similar to SPR210 except has double trigger/extractors. Introduced 2008. Imported by Remington Arms Co.
Price: SPR220, from **$342.00**

RIZZINI SIDELOCK SIDE-BY-SIDE SHOTGUN
Gauge: 12, 16, 20, 28, .410. **Barrel:** 25" to 30" (12, 16, 20 ga.), 25" to 28" (28, .410). To customer specs. Chokes as specified. **Weight:** 6.5 lbs. to 8 lbs. (12 ga. to customer specs). **Stock:** Dimensions to customer specs. Finely figured walnut; straight grip with checkered butt with classic splinter forend and hand-rubbed oil finish standard. Pistol grip, beavertail forend. **Features:** Sidelock action, auto ejectors. Double triggers or non-selective single trigger standard. Coin finish standard. Imported from Italy by Wm. Larkin Moore.
Price: 12, 20 ga. From **$106,000.00**
Price: 28, .410 bore. From **$95,000.00**

RUGER GOLD LABEL SIDE-BY-SIDE SHOTGUN
Gauge: 12, 3" chambers. **Barrel:** 28" with skeet tubes. **Weight:** 6.5 lbs. **Length:** 45". **Stock:** American walnut straight or pistol grip. **Sights:** Gold bead front, full length rib, serrated top. **Features:** Spring-assisted break-open, SS trigger, auto eject. Five interchangeable screw-in choke tubes, combination safety/barrel selector with auto safety reset.
Price: **$3,226.00**

SMITH & WESSON ELITE GOLD SHOTGUNS
Gauge: 20, 3" chambers. **Barrel:** 26", 28", 30", rust-blued chopper-lump. **Weight:** 6.5 lbs. **Length:** 43.5-45.5". **Sights:** Ivory front bead, metal mid-bead. **Stock:** AAA (grade III) Turkish walnut stocks, hand-cut checkering, satin finish. English grip or pistol grip. **Features:** Smith & Wesson-designed trigger-plate action, hand-engraved receivers, bone-charcoal case hardening, lifetime warranty. Five choke tubes.

Introduced 2007. Made in Turkey, imported by Smith & Wesson.
Price: **$2,380.00**

STOEGER UPLANDER SIDE-BY-SIDE SHOTGUNS
Gauge: 16, 28, 2-3/4 chambers. 12, 20, .410, 3" chambers. **Barrel:** 22", 24", 26", 28". **Weight:** 7.3 lbs. **Sights:** Brass bead. **Features:** Double trigger, IC & M fixed choke tubes with gun.
Price: With fixed or screw-in chokes **$369.00**
Price: Supreme, screw-in chokes, 12 or 20 ga. **$489.00**
Price: Youth, 20 ga. or .410, 22" barrel, double trigger **$369.00**
Price: Combo, 20/28 ga. or 12/20 ga. **$649.00**

STOEGER COACH GUN SIDE-BY-SIDE SHOTGUNS
Gauge: 12, 20, 2-3/4", 3" chambers. **Barrel:** 20". **Weight:** 6.5 lbs. **Stock:** Brown hardwood, classic beavertail forend. **Sights:** Brass bead. **Features:** IC & M fixed chokes, tang auto safety, auto extractors, black plastic buttplate. Imported by Benelli USA.
Price: Supreme blued finish **$469.00**
Price: Supreme blued barrel, stainless receiver **$469.00**
Price: Silverado Coach Gun with English synthetic stock. **$469.00**

TRADITIONS ELITE SERIES SIDE-BY-SIDE SHOTGUNS
Gauge: 12, 3"; 20, 3"; 28, 2-3/4"; .410, 3". **Barrel:** 26". **Weight:** 5 lbs., 12 oz. to 6.5 lbs. **Length:** 43" overall. **Stock:** Walnut. **Features:** Chrome-lined barrels; fixed chokes (Elite Field III ST, Field I DT and Field I ST) or choke tubes (Elite Hunter ST); extractors (Hunter ST and Field I models) or automatic ejectors (Field III ST); top tang safety. Imported from Fausti of Italy by Traditions.
Price: Elite Field I DT C 12, 20, 28 ga. or .410; IC and Mod. fixed chokes (F and F on .410); double triggers . .**$789.00 to $969.00**
Price: Elite Field I ST C 12, 20, 28 ga. or .410; same as DT but with single trigger . . . .**$969.00 to $1,169.00**
Price: Elite Field III ST C 28 ga. or .410; gold-engraved receiver; high-grade walnut stock **$2,099.00**
Price: Elite Hunter ST C 12 or 20 ga.; blued receiver; IC and Mod. choke tubes **$999.00**

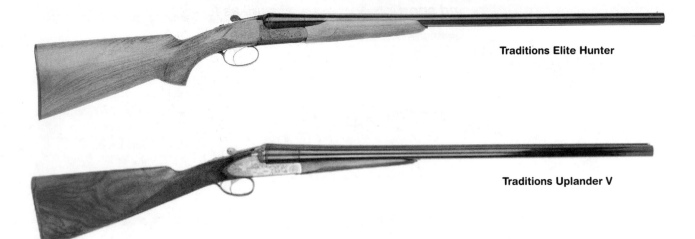

Traditions Elite Hunter

Traditions Uplander V

TRADITIONS UPLANDER SERIES SIDE-BY-SIDE SHOTGUNS
Gauge: 12, 3"; 20, 3". **Barrel:** 26", 28". **Weight:** 6-1/4 lbs. to 6.5 lbs. **Length:** 43" to 45" overall. **Stock:** Walnut. **Features:** Barrels threaded for choke tubes (Improved Cylinder, Modified and Full); top tang safety, extended trigger guard. Engraved silver receiver with side plates and lavish gold inlays. Imported from Fausti of Italy by Traditions.
Price: Uplander III Silver 12, 20 ga. **$2,699.00**
Price: Uplander V Silver 12, 20 ga. **$3,199.00**

TRISTAR BRITTANY CLASSIC SIDE-BY-SIDE SHOTGUN
Gauge: 12, 16, 20, 28, .410, 3" chambers. **Barrel:** 27", chrome lined, three Beretta-style choke tubes (IC, M, F). **Weight:** 6.3 to 6.7 lbs. **Stock:** Rounded pistol grip, satin oil finish. **Features:** Engraved case-colored one-piece frame, auto se-lective ejectors, single selective trigger, solid raised barrel rib, top tang safety. Imported from Spain by Tristar Sporting Arms Ltd.
Price: From. **$1,419.00**

WEATHERBY SBS ATHENA D'ITALIA SIDE-BY-SIDE SHOTGUNS
Gauge: D'Italia: 12, 20, 2-3/4" or 3" chambers, 28, 2-3/4" chambers. **Barrel:** 26" on 20 and 28 gauges; 28" on 12 ga. Chrome-lined, lengthened forcing cones, backbored. **Weight:** 6.75 to 7.25 lbs. **Length:** 42.5" to 44.5". **Stock:** Walnut, 20-lpi laser cut checkering, "New Scottish" pattern. **Features:** All come with foam-lined take-down case. Machined steel receiver, hardened and chromed with coin finish, engraved triggerguard with roll-formed border. D'Italia has double triggers, brass front bead. PG is identical to D'Italia, except for rounded pistol grip and semi-beavertail forearm. Deluxe features sculpted frameheads, Bolino-style engraved game scene with floral engraving. AAA Fancy Turkish walnut, straight grip, 24-lpi hand checkering, hand-rubbed oil finish. Single mechanical trigger; right barrel fires first. Imported from Italy by Weatherby.
Price: SBS Athena D'Italia SBS **$3,129.00**
Price: SBS Athena D'Italia PG SBS **$3,799.00**

Variety of designs for utility and sporting purposes, as well as for competitive shooting.

Browning BT-99 Trap

H&R Model 928 Ultra Slug Hunter Deluxe

H&R Tamer

H&R Ultra Lite Slug Hunter

H&R Topper Deluxe

BERETTA DT10 TRIDENT TRAP TOP SINGLE SHOTGUN
Gauge: 12, 3" chamber. **Barrel:** 34"; five Optima Choke tubes (Full, Full, Imp. Modified, Mod. and Imp. Cyl.). **Weight:** 8.8 lbs. **Stock:** High-grade walnut; adjustable. **Features:** Detachable, adjustable trigger group; Optima Bore for improved shot pattern and reduced recoil; slim Optima Choke tubes; raised and thickened receiver for long life. Introduced 2000. Imported from Italy by Beretta USA.
Price: **$7,400.00**

BROWNING BT-99 TRAP O/U SHOTGUNS
Gauge: 12. **Barrel:** 30", 32", 34". **Stock:** Walnut; standard or adjustable. **Weight:** 7 lbs. 11 oz. to 9 lbs. **Features:** Back-bored single barrel; interchangeable chokes; beavertail forearm; extractor only; high rib.
Price: BT-99 w/conventional comb, 32" or 34" barrels **$1,529.00**
Price: BT-99 w/adjustable comb, 32" or 34" barrels **$1,839.00**
Price: BT-99 Golden Clays w/adjustable comb, 32" or 34" barrels **$3,989.00**
Price: BT-99 Grade III, 32" or 34" barrels, intr. 2008 . . . . . **$2,369.00**

HARRINGTON & RICHARDSON ULTRA SLUG HUNTER/TAMER SHOTGUNS
Gauge: 12, 20 ga., 3" chamber, .410. **Barrel:** 20" to 24" rifled. **Weight:** 6 to 9 lbs. **Length:** 34.5" to 40". **Stock:** Hardwood, laminate, or polymer with full pistol grip; semi-beavertail forend. **Sights:** Gold bead front. **Features:** Break-open action with side-lever release, automatic ejector. Introduced 1994. From H&R 1871, LLC.

Price: Ultra Slug Hunter, blued, hardwood **$273.00**
Price: Ultra Slug Hunter Youth, blued, hardwood, 13-1/8" LOP **$273.00**
Price: Ultra Slug Hunter Deluxe, blued, laminated **$273.00**
Price: Tamer .410 bore, stainless barrel, black polymer stock . **$173.00**

HARRINGTON & RICHARDSON ULTRA LITE SLUG HUNTER
Gauge: 12, 20 ga., 3" chamber. **Barrel:** 24" rifled. **Weight:** 5.25 lbs. **Length:** 40". **Stock:** Hardwood with walnut finish, full pistol grip, recoil pad, sling swivel studs. **Sights:** None; base included. **Features:** Youth Model, available in 20 ga. has 20" rifled barrel. Deluxe Model has checkered laminated stock and forend. From H&R 1871, LLC.
Price: **$194.00**

Harrington & Richardson Ultra Slug Hunter Thumbhole Stock
Similar to the Ultra Lite Slug Hunter but with laminated thumbhole stock and weighs 8.5 lbs.
Price: . . . . **NA**

HARRINGTON & RICHARDSON TOPPER MODELS
Gauge: 12, 16, 20, .410, up to 3.5" chamber. **Barrel:** 22 to 28". **Weight:** 5-7 lbs. **Stock:** Polymer, hardwood, or black walnut. **Features:** Satin nickel frame, blued barrel. Reintroduced 1992. From H&R 1871, LLC.
Price: Deluxe Classic, 12/20 ga., 28" barrel w/vent rib **$225.00**
Price: Topper Deluxe 12 ga., 28" barrel, black hardwood **$179.00**
Price: Topper 12, 16, 20 ga., .410, 26" to 28", black hardwood **$153.00**
Price: Topper Junior 20 ga., .410, 22" barrel, hardwood **$160.00**
Price: Topper Junior Classic, 20 ga., .410, checkered hardwood **$160.00**

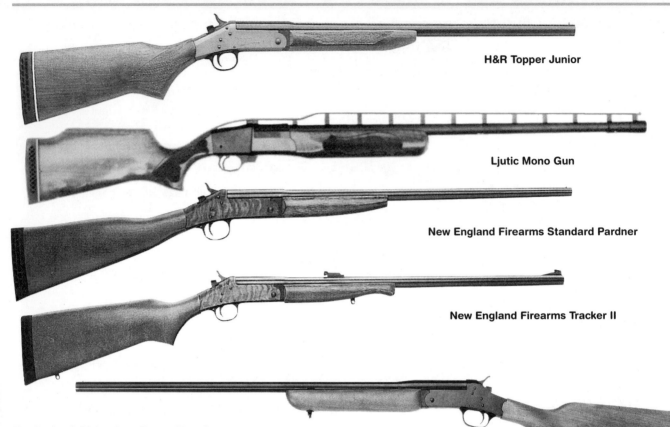

H&R Topper Junior

Ljutic Mono Gun

New England Firearms Standard Pardner

New England Firearms Tracker II

Rossi Single-Shot

Harrington & Richardson Topper Trap Gun
Similar to other Topper Models but with select checkered walnut stock and forend wtih fluted comb and full pistol grip; 30" barrel with two white beads and screw-in chokes (Improved Modified Extended included); deluxe Pachmayr trap recoil pad.
Price: **$360.00**

KRIEGHOFF K-80 SINGLE BARREL TRAP GUN
Gauge: 12, 2-3/4" chamber. **Barrel:** 32" or 34" Unsingle. Fixed Full or choke tubes. **Weight:** About 8-3/4 lbs. **Stock:** Four stock dimensions or adjustable stock available. All hand-checkered European walnut. **Features:** Satin nickel finish. Selective mechanical trigger adjustable for finger position. Tapered step vent rib. Adjustable point of impact.
Price: Standard grade Full Unsingle, from **$10,080.00**

KRIEGHOFF KX-5 TRAP GUN
Gauge: 12, 2-3/4" chamber. **Barrel:** 32", 34"; choke tubes. **Weight:** About 8.5 lbs. **Stock:** Factory adjustable stock. European walnut. **Features:** Ventilated tapered step rib. Adjustable position trigger, optional release trigger. Fully adjustable rib. Satin gray electroless nickel receiver. Fitted aluminum case. Imported from Germany by Krieghoff International, Inc.
Price: **$5,395.00**

LJUTIC MONO GUN SINGLE BARREL SHOTGUN
Gauge: 12 only. **Barrel:** 34", choked to customer specs; hollow-milled rib, 35.5" sight plane. **Weight:** Approx. 9 lbs. **Stock:** To customer specs. Oil finish, hand checkered. **Features:** Custom gun. Pull or release trigger; removable trigger guard contains trigger and hammer mechanism; Ljutic pushbutton opener on front of trigger guard. From Ljutic Industries.
Price: Std., med. or Olympic rib, custom bbls., fixed choke.. **$7,495.00**
Price: Stainless steel mono gun **$8,495.00**

Ljutic LTX Pro 3 Deluxe Mono Gun
Deluxe, lightweight version of the Mono gun with high quality wood, upgrade checkering, special rib height, screw-in chokes, ported and cased.
Price: **$8,995.00**
Price: Stainless steel model **$9,995.00**

NEW ENGLAND FIREARMS PARDNER AND TRACKER II SHOTGUNS
Gauge: 10, 12, 16, 20, 28, .410, up to 3.5" chamber for 10 and 12 ga.

16, 28, 2-3/4" chamber. **Barrel:** 24" to 30". **Weight:** Varies from 5 to 9.5 lbs. **Length:** Varies from 36" to 48". **Stock:** Walnut-finished hardwood with full pistol grip, synthetic, or camo finish. **Sights:** Bead front on most. **Features:** Transfer bar ignition; break-open action with side-lever release. Introduced 1987. From New England Firearms.
Price: Pardner, all gauges, hardwood stock, 26" to 32"
blued barrel, Mod. or Full choke.................**$140.00**
Price: Pardner Youth, hardwood stock, straight grip,
22" blued barrel **$149.00**
Price: Pardner Screw-In Choke model, intr. 2006 .... **$164.00**
Price: Turkey model, 10/12 ga., camo finish
or black............................**$192.00 to $259.00**
Price: Youth Turkey, 20 ga., camo finish or black **$192.00**
Price: Waterfowl, 10 ga., camo finish or hardwood **$227.00**
Price: Tracker II slug gun, 12/20 ga., hardwood........... **$196.00**

REMINGTON SPR100 SINGLE-SHOT SHOTGUNS
Gauge: 12, 20, .410 bore, 3" chambers. **Barrel:** 24", 26", 28", 29.5", blued chrome-lined. **Weight:** 6.25 to 6.5 lbs. **Stock:** Walnut stock and forend. **Features:** Nickel or blued receiver. Cross-bolt safety, cocking indicator, titanium-coated trigger, selectable ejector or extractor. Introduced 2008. Imported by Remington Arms Co.
Price: SPR100, from................................**$479.00**

ROSSI SINGLE-SHOT SHOTGUNS
Gauge: 12, 20, .410. **Barrel:** 22" (Youth), 28". **Weight:** 3.75-5.25 lbs. **Stocks:** Wood. **Sights:** Bead front sight, fully adjustable fiber optic sight on Slug and Turkey. **Features:** Single-shot break open, 8 models available, positive ejection, internal transfer bar mechanism, trigger block system, Taurus Security System, blued finish, Rifle Slug has ported barrel.
Price: From......................................**$117.00**

ROSSI TUFFY SHOTGUN
Gauge: .410. **Barrel:** 18-1/2". **Weight:** 3 lbs. **Length:** 29.5" overall. **Features:** Single-shot break-open model with black synthetic thumbhole stock in blued or stainless finish.
Price: .... **Appx. $150.00**

Rossi Tuffy

Rossi Matched Pair

Tar-Hunt RSG-20 Mountaineer

Thompson/Center Encore Rifled Slug

Thompson/Center Encore Turkey

ROSSI MATCHED PAIRS
Gauge/Caliber: 12, 20, .410, .22 Mag, .22LR, .17HMR, .223 Rem, .243 Win, .270 Win, .30-06, .308 Win, .50 (black powder). **Barrel:** 23", 28". **Weight:** 5-6.3 lbs. **Stocks:** Wood or black synthetic. **Sights:** Bead front on shotgun barrel, fully adjustable front and rear on rifle barrel, drilled and tapped for scope, fully adjustable fiber optic sights (black powder). **Features:** Single-shot break open, 27 models available, internal transfer bar mechanism, manual external safety, blue finish, trigger block system, Taurus Security System, youth models available.
Price: Rimfire/Shotgun, from. **$160.00**
Price: Centerfire/Shotgun **$271.95**
Price: Black Powder Matched Pair, from **$262.00**

ROSSI MATCHED SET
Gauge/Caliber: 12, 20, .22 LR, .17 HMR, .243 Win, .270 Win, .50 (black powder). **Barrel:** 33.5". **Weight:** 6.25-6.3 lbs. **Stocks:** Wood. **Sights:** Bead front on shotgun barrel, fully adjustable front and rear on rifle barrel, drilled and tapped for scope, fully adjustable fiber optic sights (black powder). **Features:** Single-shot break open, 4 models available, internal transfer bar mechanism, manual external safety, blue finish, trigger block system, Taurus Security System, youth models available.
Price: From. **$374.00**

TAR-HUNT RSG-12 PROFESSIONAL RIFLED SLUG GUN
Gauge: 12, 2-3/4" or 3" chamber, 1-shot magazine. **Barrel:** 23", fully rifled with muzzle brake. **Weight:** 7.75 lbs. **Length:** 41.5" overall. **Stock:** Matte black McMillan fiberglass with Pachmayr Decelerator pad. **Sights:** None furnished; comes with Leupold windage or Weaver bases. **Features:** Uses rifle-style action with two locking lugs; two-position safety; Shaw barrel; single-stage, trigger; muzzle brake.

Many options available. All models have area-controlled feed action. Introduced 1991. Made in U.S. by Tar-Hunt Custom Rifles, Inc.
Price: 12 ga. Professional model **$2,585.00**
Price: Left-hand model add. **$110.00**

Tar-Hunt RSG-16 Elite Shotgun
Similar to RSG-12 Professional except 16 gauge; right- or left-hand versions.
Price: **$2,585.00**

Tar-Hunt RSG-20 Mountaineer Slug Gun
Similar to the RSG-12 Professional except chambered for 20 gauge (2-3/4" and 3" shells); 23" Shaw rifled barrel, with muzzle brake; two-lug bolt; one-shot blind magazine; matte black finish; McMillan fiberglass stock with Pachmayr Decelerator pad; receiver drilled and tapped for Rem. 700 bases. Right- or left-hand versions. Weighs 6.5 lbs. Introduced 1997. Made in U.S. by Tar-Hunt Custom Rifles, Inc.
Price: **$2,585.00**

THOMPSON/CENTER ENCORE RIFLED SLUG GUN
Gauge: 20, 3" chamber. **Barrel:** 26", fully rifled. **Weight:** About 7 lbs. **Length:** 40.5" overall. **Stock:** Walnut with walnut forearm. **Sights:** Steel; click-adjustable rear and ramp-style front, both with fiber optics. **Features:** Encore system features a variety of rifle, shotgun and muzzle-loading rifle barrels interchangeable with the same frame. Break-open design operates by pulling up and back on trigger guard spur. Composite stock and forearm available. Introduced 2000.
Price: **$684.00**

THOMPSON/CENTER ENCORE TURKEY GUN
Gauge: 12 ga. **Barrel:** 24". **Features:** All-camo finish, high definition Realtree Hardwoods HD camo.
Price: **$763.00**

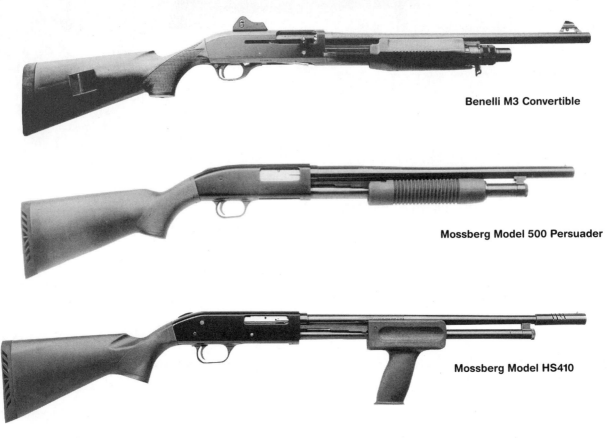

Benelli M3 Convertible

Mossberg Model 500 Persuader

Mossberg Model HS410

BENELLI M3 CONVERTIBLE SHOTGUN
Gauge: 12, 2-3/4", 3" chambers, 5-shot magazine. **Barrel:** 19.75" (Cyl.). **Weight:** 7 lbs., 4oz. **Length:** 41" overall. **Stock:** High-impact polymer with sling loop in side of butt; rubberized pistol grip on stock. **Sights:** Open rifle, fully adjustable. Ghost ring and rifle type. **Features:** Combination pump/auto action. Alloy receiver with inertia recoil rotating locking lug bolt; matte finish; automatic shell release lever. Introduced 1989. Imported by Benelli USA. Price with pistol grip, open rifle sights.
Price: With ghost ring sights, pistol grip stock **$1,489.00**

BENELLI M2 TACTICAL SHOTGUN
Gauge: 12, 2-3/4", 3" chambers, 5-shot magazine. **Barrel:** 18.5" IC, M, F choke tubes. **Weight:** 6.7 lbs. **Length:** 39.75" overall. **Stock:** Black polymer. **Sights:** Rifle type ghost ring system, tritium night sights optional. **Features:** Semi-auto intertia recoil action. Cross-bolt safety; bolt release button; matte-finish metal. Introduced 1993. Imported from Italy by Benelli USA.
Price: With rifle sights **$1,159.00**
Price: With ghost ring sights, standard stock **$1,269.00**
Price: With ghost ring sights, pistol grip stock **$1,269.00**
Price: With rifle sights, pistol grip stock **$1,159.00**
Price: ComforTech stock, rifle sights **$1,269.00**
Price: Comfortech Stock, Ghost Ring. **$1,379.00**

MOSSBERG MODEL 500 SPECIAL PURPOSE SHOTGUNS
Gauge: 12, 20, .410, 3" chamber. **Barrel:** 18.5", 20" (Cyl.). **Weight:** 7 lbs. **Stock:** Walnut-finished hardwood or black synthetic. **Sights:** Metal bead front. **Features:** Available in 6- or 8-shot models. Top-mounted safety, double action slide bars, swivel studs, rubber recoil pad. Blue, Parkerized, Marinecote finishes. Mossberg Cablelock included. From Mossberg. The HS410 Home Security model chambered for .410 with 3" chamber; has pistol grip forend, thick recoil pad, muzzle brake and has special spreader choke on the 18.5" barrel. Overall length is 37.5", weight is 6.25 lbs. Blue finish; synthetic field stock. Mossberg Cablelock and video included. Mariner model has Marinecote metal finish to resist rust and corrosion. Synthetic field stock; pistol grip kit included. 500 Tactical 6-shot has black synthetic tactical stock. Introduced 1990.

Price: Rolling Thunder, 6-shot **$471.00**
Price: Tactical Cruiser, 18.5" barrel **$434.00**
Price: Persuader/Cruiser, 6 shot, from **$394.00**
Price: Persuader/Cruiser, 8 shot, from **$394.00**
Price: HS410 Home Security **$404.00**
Price: Mariner 6 or 9 shot, from **$538.00**
Price: Tactical 6 shot, from **$509.00**

MOSSBERG MODEL 590 SPECIAL PURPOSE SHOTGUN
Gauge: 12, 3" chamber, 9 shot magazine. **Barrel:** 20" (Cyl.). **Weight:** 7.25 lbs. **Stock:** Synthetic field or Speedfeed. **Sights:** Metal bead front or Ghost Ring. **Features:** Top-mounted safety, double slide action bars. Comes with heat shield, bayonet lug, swivel studs, rubber recoil pad. Blue, Parkerized or Marinecote finish. Mossberg Cablelock included. From Mossberg.
Price: Synthetic stock, from **$471.00**
Price: Speedfeed stock, from **$552.00**

REMINGTON MODEL 870 AND MODEL 1100 TACTICAL SHOTGUNS
Gauge: 870: 12, 2-3/4 or 3" chamber; 1100: 2-3/4". **Barrel:** 18", 20", 22" (Cyl or IC). **Weight:** 7.5-7.75 lbs. **Length:** 38.5-42.5" overall. **Stock:** Black synthetic, synthetic Speedfeed IV full pistol-grip stock, or Knoxx Industries SpecOps stock w/recoil-absorbing spring-loaded cam and adjustable length of pull (12" to 16", 870 only). **Sights:** Front post w/ dot only on 870; rib and front dot on 1100. **Features:** R3 recoil pads, LimbSaver technology to reduce felt recoil, 2-, 3- or 4-shot extensions based on barrel length; matte-olive-drab barrels and receivers. Model 1100 Tactical is available with Speedfeed IV pistol grip stock or standard black synthetic stock and forend. Speedfeed IV model has an 18" barrel with two-shot extension. Standard synthetic-stocked version is equipped with 22" barrel and four-shot extension. Introduced 2006. From Remington Arms Co.
Price: 870, Speedfeed IV stock, 3" chamber,
38.5" overall, from **$587.00**
Price: 870, SpecOps stock, 3" chamber, 38.5" overall, from . . **$587.00**
Price: 1100, synthetic stock, 2-3/4" chamber, 42.5" overall . . . **$945.00**
Price: 870 TAC Desert Recon (2008), 18" barrel, 2-shot **$692.00**

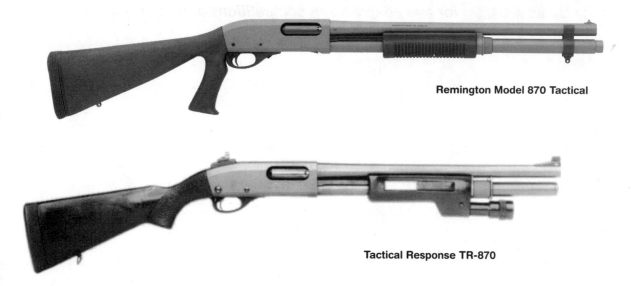

Remington Model 870 Tactical

Tactical Response TR-870

TACTICAL RESPONSE TR-870 STANDARD MODEL SHOTGUNS
Gauge: 12, 3" chamber, 7-shot magazine. **Barrel:** 18" (Cyl.). **Weight:** 9 lbs. **Length:** 38" overall. **Stock:** Fiberglass-filled polypropolene with non-snag recoil absorbing butt pad. Nylon tactical forend houses flashlight. **Sights:** Trak-Lock ghost ring sight system. Front sight has Tritium insert. **Features:** Highly modified Remington 870P with Parkerized finish. Comes with nylon three-way adjustable sling, high visibility non-binding follower, high performance magazine spring, Jumbo Head safety, and Side Saddle extended 6-shot shell carrier on left side of receiver. Introduced 1991. From Scattergun Technologies, Inc.

Price: Standard model **$1,050.00**
Price: Border Patrol model, from **$1,050.00**
Price: Professional model, from **$1,070.00**

TRISTAR COBRA PUMP
Gauge: 12, 3". **Barrel:** 28". **Weight:** 6.7 lbs. Three Beretta-style choke tubes (IC, M, F). **Length:** NA. **Stock:** Matte black synthetic stock and forearm. **Sights:** Vent rib with matted sight plane. **Features:** Five-year warranty. Cobra Tactical Pump Shotgun magazine holds 7, return spring in forearm, 20" barrel, Cylinder choke. Introduced 2008. Imported by Tristar Sporting Arms Ltd.
Price: Tactical **$349.00**

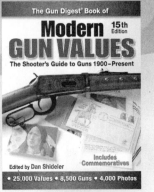

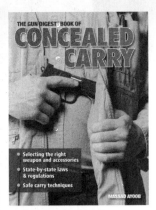
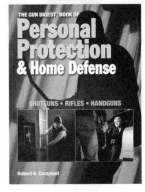